THE PAPERS OF ALEXANDER HAMILTON

Alexander Hamilton, *circa* 1790. Engraving after an oil portrait
by Alonzo Chappel.

THE PAPERS OF

Alexander Hamilton

VOLUME VI
DECEMBER 1789–AUGUST 1790

HAROLD C. SYRETT, EDITOR

JACOB E. COOKE, ASSOCIATE EDITOR

 COLUMBIA UNIVERSITY PRESS

NEW YORK AND LONDON, 1962

PREFACE

THIS EDITION of Alexander Hamilton's papers contains letters and other documents written by Hamilton, letters to Hamilton, and some documents (commissions, certificates, etc.) that directly concern Hamilton but were written neither by him nor to him. All letters and other documents have been printed in chronological order. Hamilton's legal papers will be published under the editorial direction of Professor Julius Goebel, Jr., of the School of Law, Columbia University.

Many letters and documents have been calendared. Such calendared items include routine letters and documents by Hamilton, routine letters to Hamilton, some of the letters or documents written by Hamilton for someone else, letters or documents which have not been found but which are known to have existed, letters or documents which have been erroneously attributed to Hamilton, and letters to or by Hamilton that deal exclusively with his legal practice.

Certain routine documents which Hamilton wrote and received as Secretary of the Treasury have not been printed. The documents that fall within this category are warrants or interest certificates; letters written by Hamilton acknowledging receipts from banks, endorsing margins of certificate of registry, and enclosing sea letters; letters to Hamilton transmitting weekly, monthly, and quarterly accounts, or enclosing certificates of registry and other routine Treasury forms; and drafts by Hamilton on the treasurer.

The notes in these volumes are designed to provide information concerning the nature and location of each document, to identify Hamilton's correspondents and the individuals mentioned in the text, to explain events or ideas referred to in the text, and to point out textual variations or mistakes. Occasional departures from these standards can be attributed to a variety of reasons. In many cases the desired information has been supplied in an earlier note and can be found through the use of the index. Notes were not added when in the opinion of the editors the material in the text was either self-explanatory or common knowledge. The editors, moreover, did not think it desirable or necessary to provide full annotation for Hamilton's legal correspondence. Finally, the editors on some occasions were unable to find the desired information, and on other occasions the editors were remiss.

GUIDE TO EDITORIAL APPARATUS

I. SYMBOLS USED TO DESCRIBE MANUSCRIPTS

AD	Autograph Document
ADS	Autograph Document Signed
ADf	Autograph Draft
ADfS	Autograph Draft Signed
AL	Autograph Letter
ALS	Autograph Letter Signed
D	Document
DS	Document Signed
Df	Draft
DfS	Draft Signed
LS	Letter Signed
LC	Letter Book Copy
[S]	[S] is used with other symbols (AD[S], ADf[S], AL[S], D[S], Df[S], L[S]) to indicate that the signature on the document has been cropped or clipped.

II. MONETARY SYMBOLS AND ABBREVIATIONS

bf	Banco florin
V	Ecu
f	Florin
₶	Livre Tournois
medes	Maravedis (also md and mde)
d.	Penny or denier
ps	Piece of eight

£	Pound sterling or livre
Ry	Real
rs vn	Reals de vellon
rdr	Rix daller
s	Shilling, sou or sol (also expressed as /)
sti	Stiver

III. SHORT TITLES AND ABBREVIATIONS

Annals of Congress, I, II	*The Debates and Proceedings in the Congress of the United States; with an Appendix, Containing Important State Papers and Public Documents, and All the Laws of a Public Nature* (Washington, 1834).
Arch. des Aff. Etr., Corr. Pol., Etats-Unis	Transcripts or photostats from the French Foreign Office deposited in the Library of Congress.
Archives Parlementaires, X	*Archives Parlementaires de 1787 à 1860*, First Series (Paris, 1878).
ASP	*American State Papers, Documents, Legislative and Executive, of the Congress of the United States* (Washington, 1832–1861).
Bayley, *National Loans*	Rafael A. Bayley, *The National Loans of the United States from July 4, 1776, to June 30, 1880* (Washington, 1882).
Bergh, *Writings of Thomas Jefferson*	Albert E. Bergh, ed., *The Writings of Thomas Jefferson* (Washington, 1907).
Blackstone, *Commentaries*	William Blackstone, *Commentaries on the Laws of England* (Oxford, 1776).
Boyd, *Papers of Thomas Jefferson*	Julian P. Boyd, ed., *The Papers of Thomas Jefferson* (Princeton, 1950–).
Brymner, *Canadian Archives*, 1890	Douglas Brymner, ed., *Report on Canadian Archives*, 1890 (Ottawa, 1891).
Burnett, *Letters*	Edmund C. Burnett, ed., *Letters of Members of the Continental Congress* (Washington, 1921–1938).

Davis, *Essays* — Joseph Stancliffe Davis, *Essays in the Earlier History of American Corporations* ("Harvard Economic Studies," XVI [Cambridge, 1917]).

Dorfman, *The Economic Mind* — Joseph Dorfman, *The Economic Mind in American Civilization, 1605–1865* (New York, 1946).

Executive Journal, I — *Journal of the Executive Proceedings of the Senate* (Washington, 1828).

Ferguson, *Power of the Purse* — E. James Ferguson, *The Power of the Purse* (Chapel Hill, 1961).

Fitzpatrick, *Diaries of George Washington* — John C. Fitzpatrick, ed., *The Diaries of George Washington* (Boston, 1925).

Freeman, *Washington* — Douglas Southall Freeman, *George Washington* (New York, 1948–1954).

GW — John C. Fitzpatrick, ed., *The Writings of George Washington* (1931–1944).

Hamilton, *History* — John C. Hamilton, *Life of Alexander Hamilton, a History of the Republic of the United States of America* (Boston, 1879).

Hamilton, *Intimate Life* — Allan McLane Hamilton, *The Intimate Life of Alexander Hamilton* (New York, 1910).

Hamilton, *Life* — John C. Hamilton, *The Life of Alexander Hamilton* (New York, 1840).

Hazard, *Pennsylvania Archives*, XI — Samuel Hazard, ed., *Pennsylvania Archives* (Philadelphia, 1855).

HCLW — Henry Cabot Lodge, ed., *The Works of Alexander Hamilton* (New York, 1904).

Hobbes, *Moral and Political Works* — *The Moral and Political Works of Thomas Hobbes of Malmesbury. Never before collected together. To which is prefixed, The Author's Life, Extracted from that said to be written by Himself, as also from the Supplement to the said Life by Dr. Blackbourne; and farther illustrated by the Editor, with Historical and Critical Remarks on his*

	Writings and Opinions (London, 1750).
Hume, *Political Discourses*	David Hume, *Political Discourses* (Edinburgh, printed by R. Fleming for A. Kincaid and A. Donaldson, 1752).
Hunt and Scott, *Debates*	Gaillard Hunt and James Brown Scott, eds., *The Debates in the Federal Convention of 1787 which Framed the Constitution of the United States of America. Reported by James Madison* (New York, 1920).
JCC	*Journals of the Continental Congress, 1784–1789* (Washington, 1904–1937).
JCH Transcripts	John C. Hamilton Transcripts. These transcripts are owned by Mr. William H. Swan, Hampton Bays, New York, and have been placed on loan in the Columbia University Libraries.
JCHW	John C. Hamilton, ed., *The Works of Alexander Hamilton* (New York, 1851).
Journal of the House, I	*Journal of the House of Representatives of the United States* (Washington, 1826).
Miller, *Hamilton*	John C. Miller, *Alexander Hamilton, Portrait in Paradox* (New York, 1959).
Mitchell, *Hamilton*	Broadus Mitchell, *Alexander Hamilton, Youth to Maturity, 1775–1788* (New York, 1957).
Montesquieu, *The Spirit of Laws*	Charles Louis de Secondat, Baron de La Brede et de Montesquieu, *The Spirit of Laws*, trans. Mr. Nugent (3d ed.: 2 vols.; London: Printed for J. Nourse and P. Vaillant in the Strand, 1758).
Ouverture des Etats-Généraux	*Ouverture des Etats-Généraux Faite à Versailles le 5 Mai 1789. Discours du Roi; Discours de M. Le Garde des Sceuax; Rapport de M. Le Di-*

recteur-Général des Finances, Fait par Ordre du Roi (A Dijon, de l'Imprimerie du Roi, 1789).

Postlethwayt, *Universal Dictionary*

Malachy Postlethwayt, *The Universal Dictionary of Trade and Commerce, Translated from the French of the Celebrated Monsieur Savary, Inspector-General of the Manufactures for the King, at the Custom-house of Paris; With Large Additions and Improvements, Incorporated throughout the Whole Work; Which more particularly accomodate the same to the Trade and Navigation of these Kingdoms, And The Laws, Customs, and Usages, To which all Traders are subject.* Second edition (London, Printed for John Knapton, in Ludgate-Street, 2 vols., 1757).

PRO: F.O., or PRO: C.O.

Transcripts or photostats from the Public Records Office of Great Britain deposited in the Library of Congress.

Smith, *Wealth of Nations*

Adam Smith, *An Inquiry into the Nature and Causes of the Wealth of Nations,* The Fourth Edition, with Additions in Two Volumes (Dublin, Printed for W. Colles, R. Moncrieffe, G. Burnet, W. Wilson, C. Jenkin, L. White, H. Whitestone, P. Byrne, J. Cash, W. McKenzie, 1785).

Sparks, *Diplomatic Correspondence*

Jared Sparks, ed., *The Diplomatic Correspondence of the American Revolution* (Boston and New York, 1829–1830).

Sparks, *Life of Gouverneur Morris*

Jared Sparks, *The Life of Gouverneur Morris* (Boston, 1832).

1 *Stat.*

The Public Statutes at Large of the United States of America (Boston, 1845).

6 *Stat.*

The Public Statutes at Large of the United States of America ([Private Statutes] Boston, 1856).

Webster, *Political Essays*   Pelatiah Webster, *Political Essays on the Nature and Operation of Money, Public Finances, and Other Subjects: Published during the American War, and continued up to the present year, 1791* (Philadelphia, 1791).

White, *Samuel Slater*   George S. White, *Memoir of Samuel Slater, The Father of American Manufactures. Connected with a History of the Rise and Progress of the Cotton Manufacture in England and America* (Philadelphia, 1836).

IV. INDECIPHERABLE WORDS

Words or parts of words which could not be deciphered because of the illegibility of the writing or the mutilation of the manuscript have been indicated as follows:

1. ⟨ – – – – – ⟩ indicates illegible words with the number of dashes indicating the estimated number of illegible words.
2. Words or letters in broken brackets indicate a guess as to what the words or letters in question may be. If the source of the words or letters within the broken brackets is known, it has been given in a note.

V. CROSSED-OUT MATERIAL IN MANUSCRIPTS

Words or sentences crossed out by a writer in a manuscript have been handled in one of the three following ways:

1. They have been ignored, and the document or letter has been printed in its final version.
2. Crossed-out words and insertions for the crossed-out words have been described in the notes.
3. When the significance of a manuscript seems to warrant it, the crossed-out words have been retained, and the document has been printed as it was written.

VI. TEXTUAL CHANGES AND INSERTIONS

The following changes or insertions have been made in the letters and documents printed in these volumes:

1. Words or letters written above the line of print (for example, 9th) have been made even with the line of print (9th).

2. Punctuation and capitalization have been changed in those instances where it seemed necessary to make clear the sense of the writer. A special effort has been made to eliminate the dash, which was such a popular eighteenth-century device.

3. When the place or date, or both, of a letter or document does not appear at the head of that letter or document, it has been inserted in the text in brackets. If either the place or date at the head of a letter or document is incomplete, the necessary additional material has been added in the text in brackets. For all but the best known localities or places, the name of the colony, state, or territory has been added in brackets at the head of a document or letter.

4. In calendared documents, place and date have been uniformly written out in full without the use of brackets. Thus "N. York, Octr. 8, '99" becomes "New York, October 8, 1799." If, however, substantive material is added to the place or date in a calendared document, such material is placed in brackets. Thus "Oxford, Jan. 6" becomes "Oxford [Massachusetts] January 6 [1788]."

5. When a writer made an unintentional slip comparable to a typographical error, one of the four following devices has been used:
   a. It has been allowed to stand as written.
   b. It has been corrected by inserting either one or more letters in brackets.
   c. It has been corrected without indicating the change.
   d. It has been explained in a note.

6. Because the symbol for the thorn was archaic even in Hamilton's day, the editors have used the letter "y" to represent it. In doing this they are conforming to eighteenth-century manuscript usage.

THE PAPERS OF ALEXANDER HAMILTON

1 7 8 9

To Henry Lee

[New York, December 1, 1789]

My Dear Friend

I have just received your letter of the 16th instant.[1]

I am sure you are sincere when you say, you would not subject me to an impropriety. Nor do I know that there would be any in my answering your queries. But you remember the saying with regard to Caesar's Wife. I think the spirit of it applicable to every man concerned in the administration of the finances of a Country. With respect to the Conduct of such men—*Suspicion* is ever eagle eyed, And the most innocent things are apt to be misinterpreted.

Be assured of the affection & friendship of Yr.   A Hamilton

New York December 1st 1789
H Lee Esqr

ALS, Hamilton Papers, Library of Congress; copy, Hamilton Papers, Library of Congress.
1. H inadvertently wrote "instant" rather than "ultimo." See Lee to H, November 16, 1789.

From Benjamin Lincoln

Boston, December 1, 1789. "I have been honoured with the receipt of your favor of the 20th Ulto. . . . The plan which you have adopted of receiving the bills of the Bank aforesaid, is, in my opinion judicious & important as it relates to all the ports saving those in the county of Lincoln as it will accomodate the people, and have a tendency to leave the circulating cash so dispursed as best to secure the approbation of the merchant & promote the common good. The reasons to be assigned why the system should not embrace the whole State are that attempts have been made to counterfit our bank bills by some of the people of Novia Scotia or New Brunswick, on which the said county borders and though badly done yet they gained some ⟨success⟩ evin in this town. The people in that county are little acquainted with the bank bills therefore they might with more ease be imposed upon besides no real good will arise from receiving them in those out posts as they do not circulate much if any in that quarter. I have thought it necessary to give you these hints, early, that the measure if wrong may be soon corrected. . . ."

ADfS, RG 36, Letters from the Treasury and Others, 1789–1818, Vol. 11, National Archives.

From Thomas Randall and William Heyer [1]

New York, December 1, 1789. "We have been informed by the Pilots that the Beacon on Sandy Hook has been blown down, and entirely destroyed by the late Storm. . . ."

LS, in writing of William Heyer, RG 26, Lighthouse Letters Received, Vol. "C," Connecticut and New York, National Archives.
   1. Randall and Heyer were New York City port wardens.

Treasury Department Circular
to the Collectors of the Customs

Treasury Department Decr. 1st. 1789.

Sir

The Comptroller of the Treasury will forward to you by this or the ensuing post the whole of the forms [1] necessary for making your Returns to this Office, and rendering your Accounts at the Treasury.

You will observe that in these general forms it is not required that you should make a Monthly Return of the Duties on Imports, and that in the Weekly return the Cash receipts and Disbursements (and not the Bonds) are only included. It is necessary however to observe that I have special Reasons for directing you to make out, monthly returns of the Merchandize imported to the 31st. of

Decemr. instant, in the mode pointed out by my former Circular letters,[2] after which they may be discontinued.

The public Service requires the strictest Care & punctuality in adhering to the forms now established, and in forwarding them regularly to this office: I therefore rely on your attention to these points, and if from any Circumstances you should be prevented from forwarding them in course after they are made out, you will not omit to embrace the first occasion of transmitting them as soon after as possible; so that the whole of the Returns required, may be certain of reaching me, with as little delay as possible. It is particularly desiriable that the Returns to the end of the present month may be forwarded as soon after the expiration of it as possible: unless this is done, I shall not be able to lay before the Legislature at the early part of their Sessions, that Information, relative to the Revenue, which they will necessarily require.

I am Sir   Your obedt Servt.   A Hamilton
                                                  Secy of the Treasury

P S. It is not expected that in making up your Accounts to the time the Comptrollers instructions reach you, you will be able to adhere exactly to the forms of the Receipts transmitted you either for the payment of the orders drawn on you heretofore, or other disbursements. Such as you have taken for disbursements, must accompany your accounts, as well as the orders &c with the Receipts on them—in other respects I presume you will be able to follow the forms.

LS, to Jedediah Huntington, MS Division, New York Public Library; LS, to Charles Lee, Charles Lee Papers, Library of Congress; LS, to Benjamin Lincoln, RG 36, Letters from the Treasury, 1789–1818, Vol. 5, National Archives; LS, MS Division, New York Public Library; LS, Office of the Secretary, United States Treasury Department; copy, RG 56, Circulars of the Office of the Secretary, "Set T," National Archives; LS, Essex Institute, Salem, Massachusetts; copy, Circulars of the Treasury Department, 1789–1814, Library of Congress.

1. See Nicholas Eveleigh to the Collectors of the Customs, December 1, 1789 (Circulars of the Treasury Department, 1789–1814, Library of Congress).

2. See "Treasury Department Circular to the Collectors of the Customs," October 2, 20, 1789.

From Otho H. Williams

Baltimore, December 2, 1789. "Your private letter of the 25 Ulto. by the post, came safe to hand. The Words in my Letter,[1] which you have taken Notice of, were intended merely as a reason for the appology which a deviation from the mode of remittance prescribed required; I regret that they escaped me, because they conveyed an allusion which was not designed as a reference to 'any expression of yours,' and were, therefore, improper to be addressed to you. . . . I beg you to accept of my appology. . . ."

ALS, Hamilton Papers, Library of Congress; copy, RG 53, "Old Correspondence," Baltimore Collector, National Archives.
1. Williams to H, November 14, 1789.

From Otho H. Williams [1]

Baltimore, December 3, 1789. Sends abstracts of all Maryland laws "related to *Imposts,* and *Tonnage.*" Promises to send all "Acts which relate to other branches of the revenue."

ALS, RG 53, "Old Correspondence," Baltimore Collector, National Archives.
1. This letter is in reply to "Treasury Department Circular to the Collectors of the Customs," November 25, 1789.

From Otho H. Williams

Baltimore, December 3, 1789. ". . . not knowing whether it may not be expedient for you to draw for the *Specie* reported in my last weekly return, I have omitted, to remit the *Bank Notes.* If no Warrant from you should be presented in two days; I will remit the bank Notes by the next post. . . ."

ALS, RG 53, "Old Correspondence," Baltimore Collector, National Archives.

To Thomas Willing

[*New York, December 3, 1789.* On December 9, 1789, Willing wrote to Hamilton: "We Reced your favor of the 3 Inst." *Letter not found.*]

To Stephen Smith

Treasury Department Decr. 4 1789

Sir

Your letter of the 30th of October[1] came to hand a few days since. Your transmission of the money in your hands to Boston, was influenced by prudent considerations, and corresponds in its general object with my instructions of the 20th ultimo of which I enclose a Copy.[2] Yet, without meaning to censure, what was evidently dictated by proper motives, it is necessary I should remark that every unauthorised disposition of the Public money ought to be avoided.

It is impossible for me to authorise, or for the officers of the Customs to allow, the indulgence concerning which you desire my opinion; it would be a direct contravention of the last section of the Collection law,[3] with which there is no discretion to dispense. The inconveniencies which may attend a prohibition, are proper only for the consideration of the Legislature.

That part of your letter which relates to your Bond has been communicated to the Comptroller, who I presume will forward a form by this Post.

I am, Sir   Your obedt Servt   A Hamilton

Stephen Smith Esqr
Collector for Machias

Copy, RG 56, Letters to the Collectors at Gloucester, Machias, and French-man's Bay, National Archives; copy, RG 56, Letters to Collectors at Small Ports, "Set G," National Archives.
  1. Letter not found.
  2. "Treasury Department Circular to the Collectors of the Customs in Massachusetts," November 20, 1789.
  3. "An Act to regulate the Collection of the Duties imposed by law on the tonnage of ships or vessels, and on goods, wares and merchandises imported into the United States" (1 *Stat.* 29–49 [July 31, 1789]).

From Joseph Whipple [1]

Portsmouth, New Hampshire, December 4, 1789. Transmits the New Hampshire revenue laws.

LC, RG 36, Collector of Customs at Portsmouth, Letters Sent, 1789–1790, Vol. 1, National Archives.
  1. This letter is in reply to "Treasury Department Circular to the Collectors of the Customs," November 25, 1789.

To Peter Anspach [1]

Treasury Department.
Decr 5. 1789

Sir:

Enclosed you will receive a Letter from Colo. Pickering [2] late Quarter Master General of the Army: in which he desires you to make out a Statement of the Debts intended to have been provided for by the Anticipation made for the use of his Department, by the late Super Intendant of the Finances; and of the Claims remaining Unsatisfied under it. I have to desire that you would furnish me with a Copy of this Statement as soon as possible; and transmit the Original to Colo. Pickering in order that the same, if approved of and Countersigned by him, may be transmitted to me in his late official Capacity. It is of Importance to ascertain with as much Precision as possible, what, if any Part of these Debts have been taken up by the Respective State Commissioners, or settled as [3] the Treasury by the Issue of Certificates. For which Purpose, you may (should you find it Necessary) have access to any papers in the Office of the Treasury, which may be proper for this Investigation. As the next Sessions of the Legislature (when this Paper will be Necessary) approaches fast, I wish to have it as soon as possible.

  I am Sir, Your obedt. Hble.   Servt.   A. Hamilton
                                              Secy of the Treasury
To. Mr. Peter Anspatch.
late an Assistant to
Colo Pickering Dep: Quar: Master General &a. &c.

LS, Essex Institute, Salem, Massachusetts; copy, Massachusetts Historical Society, Boston.

1. Anspach, who had been assistant quartermaster general, was engaged in settling the accounts of the department of the quartermaster general.

2. Timothy Pickering to H, November 25, 1789.

3. In the copy this word is "by."

To Jedediah Huntington

[*New York, December 5, 1789.* Letter listed in dealer's catalogue. *Letter not found.*]

LS, sold at Chicago Book and Art Auction, April 27, 1932, Lot 84.

From Beverley Randolph

Richmond December 5th. 1789.

Sir,

I did myself the Honour on the 28th. of last Month to transmit to you an abstract of the Public Debt of Virginia. Lest by any Accident, that Letter should miscarry I now forward a Duplicate of it as well as of the Abstract.

I beg leave to observe in addition to my former letter that there is a debt due from this state which is not included in the Estimate because it cannot be accurately stated.

This Debt arises from Warrants issued for militia and other services and for provisions &c. impressed for the use of the Army. These Warrants did not carry Interest but certain Taxes were specially levied for their redemption, which have not as yet taken up the whole of them nor can we say certainly whether the balances due from public Debtors on this score will be adequate to the purpose, although I believe the sum which may remain in the Hands of our Citizens after the Completion of the Collection will not be of great amount.

I have &c.   Beverley Randolph

LC, Archives Division, Virginia State Library, Richmond.

From Charles Lee

[*Alexandria, Virginia, December 6, 1789.* On December 18, 1789, Hamilton wrote to Lee: "I have received your Letter of the 6th instant." *Letter not found.*]

To John Davidson

Treasury Department, December 8, 1789. "I have duly received your letter of the 24th of November [1] and thank you for the information it contains. . . ."

Copy, RG 56, Letters to and from the Collectors at Bridgetown and Annapolis, National Archives; copy, RG 56, Letters to Collectors at Small Ports, "Set G," National Archives.
    1. Letter not found.

To Nathaniel Gorham

[New York, December 8, 1789]

I am favored with your Letter of the 24th of last Month [1] Enclosing Proposals from yourself and Mr. Oliver Phelps,[2] for the Supply of the Garrisons of West Point, and Springfield for the Ensuing Year; and agreably to your request have to inform you that the Supply has been Undertaken by the former Contractor [3] at Eight Cents, and four tenths of a Cent per Ration.

I am, with Sentiments of Esteem,   your Obedt. Humble Servt.
                                        Alexander Hamilton.[4]

ALS, sold at American Art Association-Anderson Galleries, May 2–3, 1934, Lot 114.
    1. Letter not found.
    2. Phelps, a Massachusetts merchant, combined with Gorham in land speculations as well as contracting. Their largest undertaking was the so-called Phelps-Gorham Purchase in upstate New York.
    3. Melancton Smith and Hendrick Wykoff.
    4. Text taken from catalogue of American Art Association-Anderson Galleries.

From Benjamin Lincoln

Boston, December 9, 1789. "Some of the merchants are in opinion that some allowance, in weighing should be made in weighing sugars as they are daily lightning, we have not made any. Ought we to do it? We had a few days since a quantity of wine entered from some port in France it is now represented as being bad & not worth the duties. There are other wines represented as similar. What, if any thing, is to be done in those and such like cases. Agreeably to your directions I have sent on the volume of laws of this State. . . ." [1]

ADf, RG 36, Letters from the Treasury and Others, 1789–1818, Vol. 11, National Archives; Df, RG 36, Letters from the Treasury and Others, 1789–1818, Vol. 11, National Archives.
   1. H had requested the revenue laws of each state in "Treasury Department Circular to the Collectors of the Customs," November 25, 1789.

From Thomas Willing

Bank of No America [Philadelphia] Dec 9.1789

Sir,

We Reced your favor of the 3 Ins [1] with its inclosures. One of the 15th [2] being your Official Article of Agreement Respecting the third Loan being for twenty thousand Dollars [3] the Recet of which you now acknowledge and say that the Treasr [4] would by the same post send us a warrant for the Amot. We have only this moment Reced the Warrant from the Treasurer which has prevented our Returning [it] till this time; One of the Articles of Agreement confirmd under our Signature and Seal you now have it enclosed herewith.

Our Cashier [5] writes to Mr Meredith on a Subject not only very disagreeable but very injurious to the Circulation of Treasury dfts on the Collectors. The Drafts on Norfolk are Returnd this day under protest, to the very great detriment of the Gentlemen who bot them of us—as you will be advised we beleive by Mr Sims [6] himself.

I have the honor to be Sir for the Prest Directors & Co of the Bank of No America   Your Obedt Servt

Alexr Hamilton Esqr
Secrety of the Treasury

LC, Historical Society of Pennsylvania, Philadelphia.
  1. Letter not found.
  2. Letter not found.
  3. See Willing to H, November 30, 1789.
  4. Samuel Meredith, United States treasurer from September, 1789 to December 1807.
  5. Tench Francis.
  6. Presumably Charles Simms, merchant and land speculator from Alexandria, Virginia.

From William Allibone

Philadelphia, December 14, 1789. "I have the Honor to enclose an account of monies we are now actualy in advance, on acct. of the united states, for support of the several establishments in the Bay and River Deleware, amounting to six hundred and Ten pounds Seven shillings and seven pence. . . . I need only add that being thus much in advance on account of the united states, we are left without means of complying with our other engagments now due, or of supporting the contingent expences of our office. . . ."

ALS, RG 26, Lighthouse Letters Received, Vol. "A," Pennsylvania and Southern States, National Archives.

From John Jay

New York 15th. December 1789.

Dr. Sir

The bearer will herewith deliver to you a Book[1] of accounts transmitted to me by Mr. Jefferson, and which in my opinion should be deposited in your office.

With great esteem and regard &c.   John Jay

LC, Papers of the Continental Congress, National Archives.
  1. An asterisk was placed at this point and the words "of Silas Deane" inserted as a footnote. Deane was one of the congressional agents sent to France at the outset of the Revolution to procure supplies for the American army. In 1778 he was recalled because some members of Congress believed Arthur

Lee's charge that Deane had dishonestly profited from his dealings with the French. Two years later he returned to Europe, and in 1781 he urged reconciliation between the United States and Great Britain. He was accused of being a Tory, and until his death on September 23, 1789, he lived in Europe in exile.

From Tench Coxe

Philadelphia, December 16th, 1789.

Dear Sir,

A few days ago I forwarded to you,[1] per post, a "state of our navigation,"[2] which I presume you have received. I have the honour to transmit you in this inclosure some notes upon two subjects, one of them of great importance, that may be useful when arranging our affairs with France and Spain. The rough draughts of these papers were made a few weeks before I received your letter, and I then intended to have given them to Mr. Madison in his way to New York, for the purpose of submitting them to Mr. Jefferson, in whose department I thought they might be of use. The general request at the conclusion of your letter justifies me, I hope, in troubling you with them, and in requesting that you will dispose of them as you see fit.

On No. 7, I beg leave to suggest, it may be useful to converse with Col. J. Wadsworth,[3] whose opportunities in the branch it concerns are greater than those of any other person among us.

Of the subject of No. 8 it may be truly said, that it is one of the most important objects of business in all our affairs. The calculations you will find are all within the truth, and of course the result on paper might have been rendered much greater.

I congratulate you most sincerely on the adoption of the constitution by North Carolina,[4] which almost completes this wonderful revolution. The law of New Jersey[5] abolishing the tender of their paper money, in cases wherein gold and silver have been specified in the contract, occasions a further subtraction from the objects, and of course a new inducement to the acquiescence of the opposition. The federal cause has received a fresh confirmation by our convention,[6] for I think it may be justly said, that every recognition of the principles of the general constitution, and every step towards an efficient and well balanced government by any member of the Union, is a furtherance of the object. It has been determined,

1. That the legislative power ought not to be in a single house.

2. That the judges, in addition to their former independence from fixed salaries, should be appointed during good behaviour—with some provisions for removal in case of a decay of talents, or of private virtue. This important and difficult clause is not yet digested.

3. That the executive power should be in a single person.

4. That the chief executive officer should have a qualified negative upon the proceedings of the legislature.

Messrs. Finlay,[7] Smiley,[8] and M'Lene,[9] who led the opposition to the federal constitution, have been in the majority which passed these resolutions. It is, therefore, almost certain that the constitution of Pennsylvania, which was *the great cause of our opposition* to the proceedings of the general convention, will be altered in these important particulars.[10] How near to the standard of propriety, which the gentlemen have formed for themselves, they will be able to arrive, is uncertain, for so very democratic have been our former ideas, and so much does a jealousy of the city prevail in the counties, that it must be expected they will influence in some particulars.

I beg your pardon for this digression from the original design of my letter, but the proceedings of each state even in its own arrangements are of so much importance to the order of the whole, that I thought the information I have given would not appear impertinent to the business of your office.

I have the honour to be, very respectfully, sir, your most obedient humble servant,   Tench Coxe

The Hon. A. Hamilton, Esq.

White, *Samuel Slater*, 179–80.
1. Coxe to H, November 30, 1789.
2. Although this enclosure has not been found, Coxe on another occasion described it as "the present state of the Navigation of Pennsylvania with a comparison of the same with that of the principal Nations of Europe" (Coxe to Madison, March 21, 1790, James Madison Papers, Library of Congress).
3. Jeremiah Wadsworth.
4. North Carolina ratified the Constitution on November 21, 1789.
5. This law was passed November 30, 1789 (*Acts of the fourteenth General Assembly of the State of New Jersey at a Session begun at Perth-Amboy on the 27th Day of October 1789, and continued by Adjournments, Being the First Sitting* (New Brunswick, 1789).

6. The Pennsylvania convention which drafted the state constitution of 1790 sat from November, 1789, to February, 1790, when it published a draft for public discussion and adjourned until August. Reconvening in August, the convention approved the constitution on September 2, 1790.

7. William Findley was a western Pennsylvania political leader and Anti-federalist. Although the Antifederalists opposed rewriting the state constitution, Findley, a convention delegate in 1789, adopted a conciliatory attitude and facilitated the constitutional convention's labors.

8. John Smilie was an Antifederalist leader from Fayette, Westmoreland County, Pennsylvania, who took a moderate position in the state constitutional convention, 1789–1790.

9. James McLene of Cumberland County, an important Pennsylvania radical, cooperated with Findley and Smilie to draft the new state constitution.

10. The convention substantially adopted the four points Coxe listed.

To Benjamin Lincoln

Treasury Department, December 16, 1789. "The Register of the Treasury [1] transmitted to you lately in pursuance of my Directions . . . Registers for Vessels. . . . You will oblige me in distributing them with as much dispatch as possible. . . ."

LS, RG 36, Collector of Customs at Boston, Letters from the Treasury, 1790–1817, Vol. 4, National Archives; copy, RG 56, Letters to the Collector at Boston, National Archives; copy, RG 56, Letters to Collectors at Small Ports, "Set G," National Archives.

1. Joseph Nourse.

From Benjamin Lincoln

[*Boston, December 16, 1789.* On January 19, 1790, Hamilton wrote to Lincoln: "I am favored with your letter of the 16th. of last month." *Letter not found.*]

To Sharp Delany

Treasury Department Decr. 17th. 1789.

Sir

You will use your best Exertions to pay into the Bank of north America all the Monies you can collect to the 27th. day of this month inclusive, & transmit to my office, a Certificate from the Cashier purporting the whole Sum which the Bank has received of you as Collector of the Customs of the Port of Philadelphia, to that day: after which you will defer your next payments to Bank till the first day of January next, when you will govern yourself by my former Instructions on that subject.[1] My reason for this arrangement is, to enable the Treasurer to render his accounts of the third day of the Session, according to law up to the thirty first of this month, for which purpose it is necessary I should be advised in time of the Sum paid in this month: and I shall then issue a Warrant on the Treasurer in favor of the Bank for the whole money you shall pay to the last day of this month in payment of which he will transmit to the President of the Bank a warrant on you for the amount, which will serve as a voucher for the payments made by you to the end of the present quarter. You will explain to the Bank my reasons for this direction and transmit on the 27th. of the month the Certificate of the Cashier.

I am, Sir,   Your obedt. Servt.

A Hamilton
Secy of the Treasy

Sharp Delany Esq.
Collector for the port of Philadelphia

LS, Bureau of Customs, Philadelphia; copy, RG 56, Letters to Collectors at Small Ports, "Set G," National Archives.
    1. H is presumably referring to "Treasury Department Circular to the Collectors of the Customs," September 22 and October 14, 1789.

From Benjamin Grymes

Virga. Chatham [1] Decr. 17th. 89

My Dear Sir

I wrote to you some weeks past upon some interesting business to my self and desired an immediate answer, I fear my letter [2] has miscarried as I have had no answer, therefore I must trouble you again on the subject. Mr. Robt. Morris has informed me that he expected, that the insurance of a Ship called the Aurora would be paid this winter in Certificates, (I suppose by you), which I wish to know the value of as soon as possible, as I have an offer made me for my proportion of sd. Ship. I would wish also to be informed what she was insured at, and what the present value of her is; including the interest. She was Chartered of J. Richards.[3] Josiah Watson[4] & J. Hall & J. Horner all of Virga. by Benjn. Harrison[5] agent to Mr. Morris for the secret Committee of Congress and principally insured by the Publick I am told. I must beg your frienly aid in this affair, as I have been obliged to pay a large sum of money for one of the partners viz. John Horner, who has given me full power to dispose of his one sixth part to reimburse me but fear it will not be nearly sufficient. Pray write me fully on the subject and by the first Stage. Direct to me near Fredk. to the care of Wm Fitzhugh of Chatham who joins me in Compts and best wishes   to you from yr. sincr &c.   Benjamin Grymes

ALS, Hamilton Papers, Library of Congress.
    1. "Chatham" was the Fitzhugh family estate in Fairfax County, Virginia. William Fitzhugh, who had been a member of the Continental Congress, was Grymes's uncle.
    2. Grymes to H, November 24, 1789.
    3. John Richards was Robert Morris's clerk.
    4. Josiah Watson and Company, a Virginia mercantile firm.
    5. Benjamin Harrison, son of Benjamin Harrison, a signer of the Constitution, was commission agent for Robert Morris during the American Revolution. He acted through Morris for the Second Committee of Correspondence of the Continental Congress.

From Jeremiah Wadsworth

Hartford Decr 17th 1789

Dear Sir

Last night a Man returned from Ruport in the State of Vermont with information that the two Cranes[1] were their & had counterfeited the Bank Notes of New York. One of them had been taken & let go on his securing the party he had cheated, but the true reason for leting him go was that he was the Second in the business & a plan is laid to catch the principal but I shall delay sending after them till I see you when I will state to you all the facts I knew.

The Author of the Observer[2] has in veiw to procure the good will of the Cittizens of this State to the National Government & to have the state debts adopted. He will go on if none of his projects oppose yours. Have you read him? The next week will produce an observer which proposes a Land tax & reprobates on [the] mode of Collection. I wish you would read them & if you find nothing which you disapprove say so.

The time draws near when Congress meet. I shall be called on for a Militia Bill—you know who I expect it from. Hithertoo the Merchants of this State have been nearly unanimous in their support of the impost—but they are greatly agitated at the prospect of being oblidged to pay the duties which arose before the Office was opened. Their will be so many Actions brot & such disgust given that I fear the evil will be greater than ye good. I am dear sir sincerly   Your freind   Jere Wadsworth

ALS, Hamilton Papers, Library of Congress.
   1. See H to Wadsworth, November 8, 1789.
   2. "The Observer" was the author of a series of eighteen pieces on public credit and taxes which appeared in *The* [Hartford] *American Mercury*, and were reprinted in the [New York] *Gazette of the United States*, October 28, 1789–February 17, 1790.

From George Washington

United States Decr. 17th. 1789.

Sir

As I am uncertain of the condition & even the Office in which the papers containing accounts of our disbursments for subsistence of British prisoners remain; and as it is not improbable that some negotiations may (whenever our Union under the General Government shall be completed) take place between the United States & Great Britain, in which an accurate understanding of those Accots. will become necessary—I have therefore thot, proper to suggest the expediency of having some immediate attention paid to them.

Notwithstanding, on as fair a statement of Expenditures as could now be made, much property must undoubtedly be lost by the United States for want of Vouchers and by reason of the negligence with which the business was conducted on our part; yet I was always impressed with an idea, that, under all these disadvantageous circumstances, a very considerable balance would still be found in our favor. My present wish is, to have the subject so far investigated, as that we might not commit ourselves, by bringing forward Accounts, which had better continue dormant. Shou'd there be no danger of that Kind, it would then be desirable to have the business placed in a state, which might enable us to speak from a general knowledge of facts, and in a proper tone; in case a demand of the American posts held by the King of Great Britain should draw pecuniary subjects into discussion. I believe Lists of property carried away by the British, at the time when they evacuated the posts they had occupied during the late War, are lodged in the office of Foreign Affairs.

I am sir with great esteem Your most obt. Servant

G. Washington

The Honble
The Secretary of the Treasury of the US.

LC, George Washington Papers, Library of Congress.

To Thomas Willing

[*New York, December 17, 1789.* On December 24, 1789, Willing wrote to Hamilton: "I reced by the last post yours of the 17th Inst." *Letter not found.*]

From Tobias Lear

United States Decr. 18th. 1789.

Sir

I am directed by the President of the United States to send you the enclosed letter from General Hazen [1] dated Decr. 16th. and likewise a Memorial from the same person of the 12th. inst. together with the Copy of a letter written by the Presidents command in answer to the enclosed Memorial.

I have the honor to be with perfect consideration Sir Your most Obedt. Servt.

Tobias Lear.

Secy. to the President U S.

The Honble The Secretary of the Treasury of the Ud. States.

LC, George Washington Papers, Library of Congress.
1. Moses Hazen had been in command of the Second Canadian Regiment during the Revolution. At this time he was asking for a settlement of his charges against the United States as an officer in the Continental Army.

To Charles Lee

Treasury Department, December 18, 1789. "I have received your Letter of the 6th instant,[1] with the laws of Virginia accompanying it. . . ."[2]

LS, RG 36, Collector of Customs at Alexandria, Letters Received from the Secretary, 1789–1795, National Archives.
  1. Letter not found.
  2. H had requested the revenue laws of each state in "Treasury Department Circular to the Collectors of the Customs," November 25, 1789.

Treasury Department Circular to the Collectors of the Customs

Treasury Department 18 Decr. 1789

Sir

As one of the periods for the payment of Bonds taken for Duties is arrived, it is proper that the respective Collectors should be apprised of my expectation with regard to the conduct to be observed by them. It is, that if the Bonds are not paid, *as they fall due* they be immediately put in Suit. On this point, the *most exact punctuality* will be considered as *indispensable.* And accordingly it will be expected that every bond, which shall appear in a Monthly return, after the period at which it was payable, be accompanied with a note at foot of the Return, signifying that it *is in suit* & expressing *time* of the commencement of the Suit. I am not unaware that the relaxations in this respect, which obtained in many instances un⟨der⟩[1] the State Laws, may give an Air of rigor to this Ins⟨truct⟩ion; but I consider its *strict observance* as *essenti⟨al⟩*, not only to the order of the finances, but even to the ⟨pro⟩priety of the indulgence, which the Law allows ⟨of⟩ procrastinated terms of payment of the Duties, an⟨d⟩ hence I regard this Strictness, as eventually mos⟨t⟩ convenient to Individuals, as well as necessary ⟨to⟩ the Public.

I am, Sir,   Your obedt. Servt.   A Hamilton
                                        Secy of the Treasury

LS, to Benjamin Lincoln, RG 36, Collector of Customs at Boston, Letters from the Treasury, 1789–1818, National Archives; LS, MS Division, New York

Public Library; LS, Columbia University Libraries; LS, Lincoln Memorial University, Harrogate, Tennessee; LS, Office of the Secretary, United States Treasury Department; copy, United States Finance Miscellany, Treasury Circulars, Library of Congress; copy, RG 56, Circulars of the Office of the Secretary, "Set T," National Archives.

1. Material in broken brackets has been taken from the copy in the New York Public Library.

From Otho H. Williams

Baltimore, December 18, 1789. Acknowledges receipt of Hamilton's circular letter of November 30. Discusses difficulty of reconciling exemption of tonnage charges and fees for vessels of less than twenty tons with Section 23 of "An Act for Registering and Clearing Vessels, Regulating the Coasting Trade, and for other purposes." [1] Again asks *"Whether two thirds of a Dollar* be payable to the Surveyor on small vessels." [2]

ALS, RG 53, "Old Correspondence," Baltimore Collector, National Archives.
1. 1 *Stat.* 61 (September 1, 1789).
2. See Williams to H, November 14, 1789.

From Joseph Whipple

Portsh. New Hampr. 19 Dec. 1789

Sir

Your letter of the 15th October [1] inclosing queries Concerning the Navigation of the several States remains to be answered In hopes of obtaining other information than what had fallen under my own observation prevented an earlier Answer. The enquiries that I have had opportunity of making have furnished but little addition. I now inclose answers to those queries—on Some of which I shall here enlarge presuming that it will not be unacceptable to you— Should I not confine my self precisely to the queries in extending the answers in this letter.

The Timber & plank are the only materials which are products of the State of which our vessels are at present constructed. The

LC, RG 36, Collector of Customs at Portsmouth, Letters Sent, 1789–1790, Vol. 1, National Archives; copy, RG 56, Letters from the Collector at Portsmouth, National Archives.
1. "Treasury Department Circular to the Collectors of the Customs," October 15, 1789.

Hemp Cordage & saiil Clothe are imported from Europe cheifly via
Boston or other ports out of the State. Iron from Philadelphia Pitch
Terpentine and Tar from Carolina Hemp & Flax may be raised in
N H in great quantities & Iron Oar is found in great plenty & some
Iron works are erected but for want of due encouragement for
raising & manufacturing those articles we are still importers of
them. Every article of which a Ship is constructed might be produced in the State & a Manufacture of Sail Cloth is now attempting. Our Vessels have had the Character of induring but a few years.
This was truely experienced before the late war. Contracts were
made for many Vessels which were generally Sold in Europe after
the first voyage. These contracts were for short terms and the vessels
hurried off the Stocks in three or four Months from the felling of
the timber in the forrest of which they were constructed, experience
hath evinced the ill consequence of this practice and greater attention is now paid to Seasoning the Timber as well as constructing
the Vessels—but our Ship builders are not possess'd of Capitals
Sufficient to lay in a Stock of Timber so as to have it properly
Seasoned, though they appear fully Sensible of the importance of
it. The practice of Some builders of keeping their timber in Wet
Docks (of Salt Water) facilitates its seasoning is of great advantage
to it, was it to be continued one year in this Water & have a proper
time for seasoning afterwards it would add many years to the duration of our Ships—by this means the Sap or liquid part of the Wood
is extracted while the timber is green. The Timber thus freed of its
natural juices imbibes the Waters of the Sea or is exchanged for
them Which in this River is highly charged with the salts of that
element. The timber and plank being then drawn upon the land and
seasoned or dryed in the Air to effect which another year should
be employed the Water is discharged by evaporation & the Salts remain which must tend greatly to the preservation of the Wood. In
England great attention is paid to the Season of the year for felling
their timber which generally lays several years in the timber dealers
hands before it is employed in Ship building to which may be
ascribed the great durability of their Ships. The want of any regular
establishment of trade or employ for Ships has discouraged Ship
building in this State, formerly 30 to 40 Sail of Vessels of 200 to
300 tons were built in a year they found freights of Sugar and other

produce among the west Indian Islands for England and also Tobaco Rice and Naval Stores from Carolina and Virginia—these freights were profitable—the latter Voyages might still be performed to the mutual advantage of the States connected as well as the U States N H Could furnish 20 to 30 Sail of Vessels which might be gradually encreased to a great Number. Seven eights of the produce of New Hampre. that is exported Viz Pot ashes Flaxseed & Provisions, pass by Land to ports in Masechusetts where it is Sold to Mercht. and traders who export such produce and full that proportion of the foreign goods consumed in this State are purchased in Massa. or imported through it—this is owing to the great losses sustained by our Merchants in the late War (almost the total of there personal property) which has rendered them unable to avail themselves of the Avantages that the produce of their Own State & the Consumtion of foreign Articles in it ofter them for trade—their ability therefore to force any trade is prevented & their spirit of enterprize check'd—but they are now gradually emerging from this depressed State of their Mercantile concerns which will undoubtly have the aid of Legislative Wisdom which the Constitution provides for. Our harbour is as well calculated for Navigation & our River for ship building as any perhaps in the United States which the genius of our people also favours.

It will give me great pleasure Sir to obtain and communicate when in my power every information that shall promote the establishment of any Sytem beneficial to the pulic or that shall contribute to the permanency of a constitution of goverment in which the happiness of this extensive country depends.

Questions concerning the Navigation of the Several States and Foreign Nations to which answers are requested.

Answer'd from New Hampshire.

1. What is the construction of the Vessels built in your State, and in those foreign Countries that trade with you (particularly great Britain, the United Netherlands, Denmark, and Sweden) as it respects their capacity for carrying and sailing?

Answer

Vessels of New Hampshire performing foreign Voyages are of the burthen of 70 to 300 tons—are rigged Ships, Brigs, Snows,

Sloops & Schooners cheifly the two former, they are commonly fast
Sailing Vessels for merchantmen but are not so Sharp as french nor
so burthensome as British Vessels. The little trade to this State with
foreigners is cheifly confined to British Vessels of 150 to 300 tons
burthen who arrive in Ballast & Load with Lumber * for their Sugar
Islands of these we have not more than 8 or 10 Sail in a year & a few
Small Vessels from Nova Scocia for Provisions.

2. What is the original cost where they are built including Hull
Rigging, and Apparel?

Answer—Two deck'd Vessels of about 200 tons burthen cost
here about 25 Dollars pr ton—a larger ship would cost more and a
smaller Vessel rather less. English Vessels constructed in the same
manner cost in various parts of England 8 to £ 14 Sterling pr ton.
(A vessel in Hamp. will cost say 200 tons @ 12 d   2400
    Iron and Smiths work   800
    Cordage, Canvas, Rigging, Sailmaker ⎫
    and blockmakers bill   ⎬   1200
    Joyner, Carver, extra Colking, Pitch, ⎫
    Tar, and Sundry Continginins   ⎬   600
                                                        ————
                        200 tons at 25   5000
This calculation tho' not minutely divided is in the main nearly the
Cost—which may vary according to the equipments 2 to 4 Dollars
pr Ton)

3. What is the quality of the materials of which they are made;
and their usuil duration?

Answer. The Timber and out side plank of New Hamp. Vessels
are of white oak. Sometimes the Sailing Plank is of oak of an inferior
quality. The deck plank and masts are of white pine. The yards and
top masts of Spruce. A Vessel well constricted of seasoned white
Oak will last 20 to 25 years—or more. But through want of attention
to the due Seasoning of the Timber they frequently fail in 10 or 12
years. British Vessels trading here are also constructed of white Oak
with a mixture of Elm for their Bottom timber and plank from
some parts of England. They are more durable than American Ves-

─────────

* a general term given here to all our products of Wood when in a raw or
unmanufactured State, Vizt. Pine & Oak Boards, plank & timber, Staves, Hoops,
Shingles &c

sels which is principally owing to their materials being well seasoned —and the Ships well husbanded after they are built.

4. What number of Voyages do they commonly perform in a year; to and from your State, either directly or circuitously; and what is the nature of those Voyages?

Answer. N Hampshire Vessels trade 1st to the West India Islands and other Settlements of the Dutch & French Nations with Lumber, Some Fish and Beef—whence they return with the produce of those Settlements, cheifly Mollases and Rum which they carry frequently to Carolina, Phila., or Boston for a market. 2 to 3 of these Voyages are performed in the year. 2dly. They Proceed from the west Indies with the proceeds of their Lumber Cargo for Virginia or Carolina where they take freights for Europe and return in Ballast or with Salt on which Voyages they are employed 8 to 10 months. 3dly. They perform Voyages to England, Scotland, Ireland, and France with Lumber Cargoes, Some Flax-Seed, and pot Ash and return in Ballast or with Salt. 4thly. Some have gone in Ballast for Carolina and Virginia and Load with Rice or Tobaco for Europe, but the preference given to British Vessels or the power of British Factors to engross Tobaco and other produce of those States renders these Voyages uncertain and they are Seldom attempted at present.

5. By what number of Seamen, in proportion to their burthen are they comonly Navigated?

Answer. About 5 hands to every hundred tons or twenty tons to a Man Officers included. British vessels require 2 hands more and French 2 to 3 for every hundred Tons.

6th. What is the customary pay, and subsistence of the Masters and Marriners employed in them?

Answer. A Masters pay is 10 to 12 Dollars pr month, a mates 10 Dollars an able Seaman 7 Dollars. When a Vessel is consigned to a Factor abroad or has a Super Cargo the Masters pay is greater according to the Nature of the Voyages 12 to 16 Dollars. A Masters Subsistance abroad when the Vessel is consigned to a Factor is 2/ to 4/ Stg pr day—and ships Provisions which is Beef and Bread, quantity unlimited the Value of which is about 4 Dolls pr Man pr month. Cabin Stores, as the Master and seamen fancy are furnished by themselves respectively. Sometimes the Master is furnished with some kinds of Cabin Stores as liquors &c. by the owner gratuitiously —and of late it has been practised to allow Sailors Coffee Tea. and Sugar which is growing into a Custom.

7th. What priviledge or Emoluments do those Masters and Marriners enjoy besides their Pay and subsistance?

Answer. A Masters commission on Sales of Cargo when consigned to him is 5 pr Cent—priviledges according to the burthen of the Vessel and the disposition of Owner—the liberty of carrying on outward bound Voyage 2 to 4 m feet Boards and 20 to 100 quentels Fish in the Cabbin or the Cabbin Wholly—the Mate a fourth part of that priviledge. A Sailer may carry 4 to 8 quentels Fish. Their priviledge on homward passage is unlimited as the Vessels return not one fourth part loaded or in ballast.

To William Allibone

[*New York, December 21, 1789.* On January 7, 1790, Allibone wrote to Hamilton: "I had the Honor of receiving your letter of the 21st. of December last." *Letter not found.*]

To Sharp Delany

Treasury Department, December 21, 1789. "An application has been lately made to me by the Board of wardens of the Port of Philadelphia [1] for the reimbursement of a Sum of money by them expended for the maintenance and Support of the Light house, Beacons &ca in the Bay and River Delaware. . . . As it is necessary that these Establishments Should be properly Supported, you will advance to Wm Allibone Esqr, Master Warden of the Port of Philadelphia, the Sum of 1600 Dollars. . . ."

LS, Bureau of Customs, Philadelphia; copy, RG 56, Letters to Collectors at Small Ports, "Set G," National Archives.
  1. See William Allibone to H, December 14, 1789.

From Sharp Delany

[*Philadelphia*] *December 21, 1789.* ". . . I have recd the different forms from the Comptroller and shall proceed immediately as therein directed, I would remark on two of them, that of the Tonnage Abstract directed to be countersigned by the N officer which I imagine was intended to be the Surveyor, for the N: O: has no documents to warrant him. In the weekly returns of Cash it is directed to specify in what the balle. on hand consists, such as Bank notes &c &c. on this I would observe, the 30th Secto¹ restricts the Collector from receiving anything but specie."

LC, Bureau of Customs, Philadelphia.
 1. For Section 30 of "An Act to regulate the Collection of the Duties imposed by law on the tonnage of ships or vessels, and on goods, wares and merchandises imported into the United States," see 1 *Stat.* 45 (July 31, 1789).

From Sharp Delany

[Philadelphia] Decr 21st 1789

Sir

By the 1st Secto. of the Tonnage Act¹ certain priveleges are granted to Vessells American built & owned, by the fifth Secto. of the Impost Act,² by the 1 & 2nd of the Registering Act,³ certain Qualifications are directed to entitle Vessells to the benefts granted by any Law of the UStates, I have met with no small trouble & difficulty to put a proper construction on this business and indeed am yet in want of your directions, for vessels evidently & bona fide the property of Citizens, arriving here from ports where they could not be legally registerd, and some from foreign Ports, leaves me in doubt whether they are intitled to the Priveleges of Discounts & of Tonnage. Another instance happend this afternoon, a schooner enterd about three Weeks ago under spanish papers, and I recd. accordingly foreign tonnage. The Owner Mr Leamy⁴ being then at N York, on his Arrival he claimed as an American, & demanded a Register, proving Property, & producing a Bill of Sale according to Law. I informed him, I should submit to your directions, and could not without your participation refund, as the Entries had passed through my books.

Another case—An English Vessel entered in N Jersey prior to the Tonnage Act[5] taking place, after which, she enterd here & under the 3rd Secto of that Act they claim an exemption from the Tonn[ag]e. This is not my opinion, but to avoid a Law-suit, took bond to be determind by your opinion, on these heads I request your directions and am   &c   S D

Secretary of the Treasury

LC, Bureau of Customs, Philadelphia.
   1. "An Act imposing Duties on Tonnage" (1 *Stat.* 27–28 [July 20, 1789]).
   2. "An Act for laying a Duty on Goods, Wares, and Merchandises imported into the United States" (1 *Stat.* 24–27 [July 4, 1789]).
   3. "An Act for Registering and Clearing Vessels, Regulating the Coasting Trade, and for other purposes" (1 *Stat.* 55–65 [September 1, 1789]).
   4. John Leamy, a Philadelphia merchant.
   5. See note 1.

From Joseph Whipple

Portsmouth, New Hampshire, December 21, 1789. ". . . I now inclose my Weekly Return to the 19th instant agreeably to the new Form leaving out Bonds &c. In the Forms recd. I do not observe any mention of Goods deposited for the security of the duties which the Law admits of. I shall therefore place them till otherways directed in Accots. with Bonds which I conceive will be the proper place for them. It has been contended by some importers that their Bonds given for Duties should bear date when the Amount of Duties could be ascertain'd 5 to 15 days after the entry of the Vessel which in some instances when the goods could not be landed sooner I have complied with—I should be glad of your directions on this point. . . ."

LC, RG 36, Collector of Customs at Portsmouth, Letters Sent, 1789–1790, Vol. 1, National Archives; copy, RG 56, Letters from the Collector at Portsmouth, National Archives.

From Benjamin Lincoln

Boston Decr. 22 1789

Sir

On my return from Georgia I met on file in our office your questions [1] concerning the navigations of the several States and foreign nations. An answer to those questions has been delayed from various causes. No one however has contributed more to produce it than a want of information in me, respecting some of them at the time I first saw them. I have since had an opportunity of knowing many facts relative to them, to which I was formerly a stranger; a knowledge of which was necessary prior to my attempting such an answer as I know you have a right to expect.

On your first question I would observe that the Ships built in the Massachusetts are so constructed as to combine the great objects of burthen, fast sailing & safe transportation. There is a point in which these unite. To fix it is the great art of building. Whether it has been fully investigated, or not, is quite uncertain. Although two vessels of equal tonage may not carry an equal burthen; yet the Ship carrying the least may be preferred, as the most valuable. The advantages arising from having a fast sailing Ship that will beat well to the windward and is what the mariners term a good sea boat are great. Such a Ship will have the preference to one which shall carry more if destitute of those advantages; for they will make a voyage in less time & with greater safety, therefore with more ease will they obtain freight; & the insurance will be much lower. We have here very few vessels from the Netherlands, Rusia, Denmark & Sweden; in consequence of which I am quite unable to determine their construction. Those from Great Britain & France do not differ very materially from those built in this State, which carry about as many tons in wight, as the Number of tons they measure.

2d. Question

Answer The original cost of vessels built here varies according

ADf, RG 36, Collector of Customs at Boston, Letters from the Treasury and Others, 1789–1818, Vol. 11, National Archives.

1. "Treasury Department Circular to the Collectors of the Customs," October 15, 1789.

to the size of them. Those which are employed in the Cod fishery &
coasting, from 45 to 100 tons, cost from five pounds ten, to six
pounds ℔ ton. Those of one hundred and fifty tons will cost about
seven pounds a ton. Those from one hundred and fifty, to two hundred and fifty, ten pounds ℔ ton, including sails rigging and all
appurtenances.

Answer to the 3d Question

The vessels in this part of the State are built of white oak timber
and planks, saving in some instances, timber of an inferior oak is
put into the bottom of a vessel and some times used for Cieling
planks. The decks are always of white pine. The standing masts are
of white pine & the smaller sparrs generally of spruce. If our timber
has been previously prepared by seasoning, or what is to be preferred soaked in sea water, for eight months, or a year, those parti-
cles of sap which soon become corrupt and produce early rotten-
ness in the timber, are destroyed. Vessels built with materials thus
prepared will last from twelve to fifteen years & with little repairs
twenty years. The above observations refer to ships built in this
State, at the westward of Penobscot river. The timber & planks of
vessels built at the eastward of that, is generally black birch; the
knees are spruce and the planks of the deck are white pine. The
birch is a very handsome wood and, when the sap is taken off, as it
should be in all cases, when used for timber, it very much resembles
the mahogany. It is said that vessels built with this timber will in-
dure as long as if built of the best white oak; but of this fact I have
not all that proof which gives me full satisfaction. The British,
however, seem much in favor of these vessels. A large number of
them are annually built, in the Provinces of Nova Scotia and New
Brunswick, by the Carpenters hired from this State; upon the building of some of which, a very handsome bounty is given. I think
these vessels would be better, if the builders would substitute some
spruce planks in the place of the birch, which is very brittle and
very liable to injury, in working; while the spruce is very tough
and being a lighter wood a four inch plank of this might be used in
the place of a three inch of birch. These planks will bear caulking
exceedingly well and are not so liable to shrink and swell as the
birch and oak.

Answer to the 4th. The larger vessels from one hundred and fifty tons and upward have been differently employed. Some between this State, great Britain & Ireland, Which make two voyages in a year. For three years past many have made voyages directly to the cape of Good-Hope, the Isle of France, Bourbon and the several parts of the heither India. There cargoes have consisted chiefly of lumber & provisions, such as beef butter, chiese, a few fish &c. For some of these vessels a market has been found, at the different ports. The greatest part of them return with coffe, cotten & other articles of produce; and some with manufactures, especially of the cotton. In a few instances vessels have proceeded to Canton, from whence they have returned with Bohea Teas & others of a better quality &c. The adventurers to the Isle of France, the theither Indies &c succeeded well the first year; but in the two last many have been unfortunate, owing principally to the markets being overstocked. Many vessels of the kind, above mentioned, are employed in the west India trade, (together with a number of Sloops & Schooners from seventy five, to one hundred & fifty tons). Some in exporting our prime fish to the European Markets. In these employments two voyages are made in a Year. A large number of our vessels from one hundred and Eighty tons & upward are employed in circuitous Voyages, first to the southern States, where they generally obtain freight for Europe. Many of those Vessels from the want of stock to procure cargoes more valuable return with salt, while some pass up the Baltic & thence return with Cargoes of Iron, duck, hemp &c. These make one voyage only in a year.

Answer to the 5th. Question

Vessels of one hundred and fifty tons are navigated by one seaman to eighteen tons and vessels above, one man to twenty tons. A large proportion of these should be good sea men; some may be taken from the plows.

Answer to the 6th & 7th Questions—The pay of the master varies from twenty to fifty dollars ₱ month, being governed by circumstances, where he is not the assignee.

Masters are some times allowed 3 £ ₱ month and a priviledge in the Ship of 5 ₱ Cent with other small perquisites. In voyages to the West Indies & Africa they are commonly the assignee, and receive a commission from 5 to 7½ ₱ Cent upon sales and returns: and, when this doth not happen, they are sometimes allowed: primage on owners goods & those taken on freight: masters in European employments have six pounds ⅌ month and a privilege in the vessel of 5 ⅌ Cent and an allowance of two shillings & six pence ⅌ day while in port abroad.

The pay of the mariners if from five to eight dollars pr. month. They are allowed, for subsistence, beef, pork, bread, and pulse; and, occasionally, sugar tea, coffe and rum.

Treasury Department Circular to the Collectors of the Customs

Treasury Department 23 Decr. 1789.

Sir

My opinion having been several times asked on the following points, I think it proper in order to produce uniformity of practice to convey it in a Circular Instruction.

First—Whether the tonnage of foreign vessels ought to be taken from the Registers, or ascertained by admeasurement according to the principles of the third Section of the act for registering &c.[1]

I am of opinion that the latter ought to be the case, not only because it is agreable to the letter of that Section which is general, but because it cannot be presumed that the Legislature intended to favor foreign vessels in this respect, which would be the case, if the Tonnage expressed in their registers should govern; as the mode of admeasurement prescribed by our law makes the Tonnage greater than that which prevails in other Countries.

Secondly. Whether a vessel *not licensed as a Coaster, or for the fishing trade*, going from one district to another shall enter & pay tonnage at the last? And at what rate?

I am of opinion that there must be an *entry* in each district and that *the entry* will draw with it the payment of Tonnage in each. But the rate will depend on the circumstances. If there be nothing to constitute a trading *between the districts* within the meaning of the last clause of the twenty third Section of the Coasting Act,[2] the rate of tonnage in each district will be the same & will be determined by the particular description of the Tonnage Act,[3] under which the Vessel may fall.

But if there be such a *trading between* the districts the rate of tonnage will be fifty Cents.

The question then is—What is to be deemed a trading between the districts? Without attempting a precise definition of the thing, I will state, as a guide, some cases which in my opinion are, or are not so.

First—If a vessel arriving from *abroad* at one district with a Cargo proceeds with the whole or a part of that *identical Cargo* to another district, I do not conceive this to be a trading between the districts.

Secondly—If a vessel bound to a foreign port takes in part of her outward Cargo at one district and proceeds to another to take in another part of her outward Cargo, this also is not in my opinion, a trading between the districts.

But Thirdly—If in any case a vessel not licensed as aforesaid take in a *freight* at one district to be *delivered* at another, this is to be deemed a trading between the districts and subjects her to the rate of foreign Tonnage.

I am, Sir,   Your obedt. Servt.   A Hamilton
                                            Secy of the Treasy

LS, to Sharp Delany, Bureau of Customs, Philadelphia; L[S], to Benjamin Lincoln, RG 36, Collectors of Customs at Boston, 1789–1807, Vol. 4, National Archives; LS, Hamilton Papers, Library of Congress; LS, Office of the Secretary, United States Treasury Department; copy, United States Finance Miscellany, Treasury Circulars, Library of Congress; copy, RG 56, Circulars of the Office of the Secretary, "Set T," National Archives.

1. "An Act for Registering and Clearing Vessels, Regulating the Coasting Trade, and for other purposes" (1 *Stat.* 55–65 [September 1, 1789]). For Section 3, see pp. 55–56.

2. 1 *Stat.* 55–65 (September 1, 1789). For Section 23, see p. 61.

3. "An Act imposing Duties on Tonnage" (1 *Stat.* 27–28 [July 20, 1789]).

To Tench Coxe

New York, December 24th, 1789.

Dear Sir,

Your obliging favours of the 30th of November, and 16th instant, with the communications accompanying them, have been duly received.

Accept my best acknowledgments for the attention you have paid to my request; and believe that I mean not a mere compliment, when I say that your compliance with it has procured me much useful information, and many valuable observations.

I have not leisure to add more, than that I am, with sincere esteem and regard, dear sir, your obedient servant,   A. Hamilton.

Tench Coxe, Esq.

White, *Samuel Slater*, 180.

From Sharp Delany

[Philadelphia] Decr 24th 1789

Sir

Your three letters of 17th 18th [1] & 21st I recd. I called on the President & Directors of the Bank, who at once agreed to your propositions. I shall forward the Cashiers Receipts & Pay to the Wardens agreeably to your directions.

Before I recd Yours I was under the disagreeable necessity of putting a Bond in suit, my firm determination, being without express directions from You to the contrary to return all Bonds due & unpaid to the Atty of the District [2] for suit, and that such conduct meets your approbation & opinion gives me no small satisfaction.

I am well aware of the precedents many would wish to draw from the state payments and no one has experiend them oftner than I have, & much to my uneasiness & danger.

I enclose You a notice such a[s] I give to every person indebted, five days before the bond is due, which though troublesome & chargeable to me Yet that no excuse should be made I have thought best to submit to it. I am now to turn self Accuser, being determined to make You acquainted with every transaction of the Office. In my illness and when confined to my bed, my deputy granted two Registers which on filling up the Returns for You I find done not conformably to the Law. I cannot blame my deputy for I believe from what he says he asked my advice but my situation was such that I was unable to give an opinion. The case is Two Vessells one belonging to Maryland the other to Virginia, the owners here in person & known to the Office as Citizens, and the best security joined with them, demanded Registers which as above was granted. Without a Qualification taken before the Collector where they resided, & duly transmitted no Register could legally be granted. I have wrote to the Officers of their Ports—informing them of this matter—requesting them to issue New Registers at my Charge, or if they think proper to forward me the Oath &c at their option— indeed one of the parties promised to have it sent. I shall collect answers to the Queries by next post. & am &c.   S D

Secretary of the Treasury

I made a seizure of a sloop from Halifax &c.

LC, Bureau of Customs, Philadelphia.
    1. "Treasury Department Circular to the Collectors of the Customs," December 18, 1789.
    2. William Lewis was United States attorney for the district of Pennsylvania.

From Meletiah Jordan

Frenchman's Bay [District of Maine] December 24, 1789. ". . . I wrote you the 20th. & the 25th.[1] of November last. . . . In my last I gave you some particular information of the situation of this District. There is but one Vessel in this District at present that consists of more than 30 tons burden or thereabouts, our vessels are small and follow what we call shore fishing & as it is the law of the wise Congress that no foreign ship or vessel shall unload any foreign goods in this Dist. in consequence of which all vessels of that kind trade in other districts which makes the business of a Collector exceedingly small. . . ."

LC, RG 56, Letters to Collectors at Gloucester, Machias, and Frenchman's Bay, National Archives.
    1. Letter not found.

To Beverley Randolph

Treasury Department 24 Decr. 1789

Sir

    I have been duly honored with your favors of the 28th. of November & 5th. of December, with their inclosures. And I beg leave to make my acknowledgments for the attention which has been paid to their early transmission.

I presume in the account transmitted the arrears of Interest have been added to the principal. Should the contrary be the case, permit me to request, that a statement of those arrears if any exist may be forwarded as speedily as possible.

I have the honor to be with great respect, Sir, Your obedt. & hble Servt.   A Hamilton
                                                        S of the Treasy

His Excellency
Beverly Randolph Esqr.
Govr. of the State of Virginia

LS, Archives Division, Virginia State Library, Richmond.

From Thomas Willing

[Philadelphia] Dec 24th. 1789

Sir

I reced by the last post yours of the 17th. Inst [1] with all its en-closures respecting the protest of the Treasury Drafts on Norfolk & this day they have been laid before the Directors.[2] I thank you for the trouble you have taken in your free and full explanation of this disagreeable transaction. The mistake made in the Office consider-ing the early State of the business, was a natural One, & I think with you that Mr Lindsey [3] should have paid the drafts & coverd himself under the directions, to *the Collector of Norfolk* especially with the additional circumstance, that he could not doubt the Signatures of either The Treasurer or Cashier. Its plain that he had the Money and therefore the conclusion must be, either that he was overcau-tious, being young in his Office, or else, that he meant it as a reproof to the Treasury for their mistake. However, I think you have Stated the whole transaction to him in such Strong & pointed terms, that his feelings must be roused and he will be more Cautious in future. Your resolution of calling on him for an explanation before any formal complaint was made to the president, was certainly proper, and I hope he may give you such satisfaction as to render Such complaint

quite unnecessary. I now Send you Mr Hunters[4] Letter of the 1st.
of October with both the Original returns from Norfolk & *Portsmouth* & thank you for the having so confidentially troubled them
for our Inspection. The duplicate letter for Mr Lindsey has been
Sent forward with Some of the drafts which have been Sold to Mr
Taylor—but here too, perhaps Mr Lindsey may plead a misdirec-
tion, for you have not in these latter drafts, given the full description of him as Collector, which he takes when he Signs his Official
returns, to which he adds—Collectors Office *Norfolk & Portsmouth.* The Treasurer has only directed his drafts to him as Collector of Norfolk you'l excuse me for mentioning this very trifeling
Circumstance, it argues a Suspecion perhaps, which nothing could
warrant, except Mr Lindsays past conduct—which certainly marks
him as a man of nice puntillio.

I am Sir   Most respectfully   Yr Obdt Servt.

LC, Historical Society of Pennsylvania, Philadelphia.
 1. Letter not found.
 2. See Willing to H, December 9, 1789.
 3. William Lindsay, collector at Norfolk.
 4. Presumably James Hunter of Richmond.

From Meletiah Jordan

[*Frenchman's Bay, District of Maine, December 25, 1789.* On
March 15, 1790, Jordan wrote to Hamilton: "I did myself the pleasure to write you the 24th. 25th. & 29th. December." *Letter of December 25 not found.*]

From Sharp Delany

[Philadelphia] December 26th 1789

Sir

The Cashier of the Banks receipts for   [1] dollars is inclosed,
with the opinion of some of our Merchants & Ship Carpenters on
the Queries I had the honour of receiving from You.[2] I expect further opinions from others which shall forward next post. In my return of Exports, You will have a thorough view of our Trade, as I

shall give each place separate. Mr Bingham says he wrote You [3] largely on the above subjects. I must once more Sir mention the pain I feel in being deprived making succh communications as I could wish being yet very unwell, & incapable of doing it in the manner I could wish. I am however much better, and hope soon to have sufficient strength to comply with every duty of my Office in Person.

I have the honor to be &c   S D

The Secretary of the Treasury

LC, Bureau of Customs, Philadelphia.
    1. Space left blank in MS.
    2. See "Treasury Department Circular to the Collectors of the Customs," October 15, 1789.
    3. See William Bingham to H, November 25, 1789.

From Benjamin Lincoln [1]

Boston, December 26, 1789. ". . . your Circular letter of the 18th. just came to hand and I am happy to inform you that I have anticipated your orders and early adopted that line of conduct which I thought would secure that punctuality in the payment of bonds. . . . I have the pleasure now to inform you that we have not . . . had any person a delinquent for a moment. . . ."

ADf, Collector of Customs at Boston, Letters from the Treasury and Others, 1789–1818, Vol. 11, National Archives.

From John Scott [1]

[*Chester, Maryland, December 26, 1789.* "I beg the favor of you to give me your advice & direction in the following matter. A Ship arrives at Baltimore District, lands her Cargo and then comes into this District to load, brings a permit for that purpose from the office of Baltimore, the Ship's papers are stop't there, & the officers there oblige the Capt. of the Ship to return to their office for his clearance, and a refusal is made to clear or pay fees here. Is this agreeable to the Law?" *Letter not found.*]

Extract, Columbia University Libraries. This extract was enclosed in H to Otho H. Williams, February 8, 1790.
    1. Scott was collector of customs at Chester, Maryland.

From Tobias Lear

[*New York*] *December 28, 1789.* "By the direction of the President of the United States, I have the honor to transmit to you all the letters & certificates which have come to his hands from, or relating to, Mr. Samuel Caldwell [1] of Philadelphia upon the subject of his application for an Office under the United States."

LC, George Washington Papers, Library of Congress.
    1. See Lear to H, October, 1789.

From Thomas Mifflin

[*New York, December 28, 1789.* On December 31, 1789, Hamilton wrote to Mifflin: "I have the honor of your letter of the 28th instant." *Letter not found.*]

From Meletiah Jordan

Frenchman's Bay [*District of Maine*] *December 29, 1789.* Repeats information contained in his letter of December 24, 1789.

LC, RG 56, Letters to Collectors at Gloucester, Machias, and Frenchman's Bay, National Archives.

From John Lee [1]

Penobscot [*District of Maine*] *December 29, 1789.* Describes in detail the Penobscot customs district and the problems peculiar to it.

LS, Connecticut Historical Society, Hartford.
    1. Lee was collector of customs at Penobscot.

From Wilhem and Jan Willink, Nicholaas and Jacob Van Staphorst, and Nicholas Hubbard

[*Amsterdam, December 29, 1789.* On January 25, 1790, Willink, Van Staphorst, and Hubbard wrote to Hamilton: "We had the Honor to address you the 29 Ulto." *Letter not found.*]

From Peter Anspach [1]

New York, December 30, 1789. Transmits an account of the debt owed by the United States to the creditors of the quartermaster general's department.

ALS, Essex Institute, Salem, Massachusetts; ALS, Massachusetts Historical Society, Boston; ADfS, RG 93, Miscellaneous Records, National Archives.
  1. For background to this letter, see H to Anspach, December 5, 1789; Timothy Pickering to H, November 19, 25, 1789; H to Pickering, November 19, 1789.

From Joseph Clay [1]

Savannah, December 30, 1789. "I received your very obliging favour of the 2d. Octr last [2] respecting a claim of the United States on me for a sum of money of the new emission & tho' under the peculiar circumstances of this business I can't think myself responsible yet 'tis my wish to see the United States secured in the same as soon as possible & shall do every thing in my power for that purpose. The person who received the money and appropriated it to his own use [3] (as he says prompted by penury & want) is I am told at this time in very good circumstances & writes that he only waits to know what money will be received in payment & at what rate. . . ."

LC, Georgia Historical Society, Savannah.
  1. Clay was a Savannah merchant and planter who had served as paymaster general of the Continental Army in the Southern Department.
  2. Letter not found.
  3. A detailed account of this affair may be found in Clay to _____, August 9, 1789 ("Letters of Joseph Clay, Merchant of Savannah, 1776–1793," *Collections of the Georgia Historical Society* [Savannah, 1913], VIII, 216–22).

From Nathaniel Fosdick [1]

[*Portland, District of Maine, December 30, 1789.* On February 8, 1790, Hamilton wrote to Fosdick: "Your letter of the thirtieth of December, 1789." *Letter not found.*]

1. Fosdick was collector of customs at Portland and Falmouth.

Treasury Department Circular to the Collectors of the Customs

Treasury Department Decr. 30. 1789.

Sir

In my Circular letter of the 31st. of October last I directed you to claim the duties which had arisen on Imports since the first day of August last, and prior to the organisation of the Customhouses in the respective districts, and if the same was controverted by the parties liable thereto to prosecute this claim to a legal determination.

As the decision in one case will probably form a rule in the others, it is my desire that no more than one action should be brought on this account (if any should be found necessary) and that in conducting it, you will not fail to observe (as I before recommended) all the moderation which is compatible with the end in view.

It is not necessary that the progress of the suit should be hastened at present, as it is highly probable that the subject will come under the consideration of the Legislature of their approaching meeting.

I am, Sir   Your Obedt. servant   A Hamilton
                                          Secy of the Treasy

LS, to Sharp Delany, Bureau of Customs, Philadelphia; LS, to Eli Elmer, Historical Society of Pennsylvania, Philadelphia; LS, to Jedediah Huntington, MS Division, New York Public Library; LS, to Benjamin Lincoln, RG 36, Letters from the Treasury, 1789–1807, Vol. 4, National Archives; LS, United States Finance Miscellany, Treasury Circulars, Library of Congress; LS, Columbia University Libraries; L[S], Office of the Secretary, United States Treasury Department; copy, United States Finance Miscellany, Treasury Circulars, Library of Congress; copy, RG 56, Circulars of the Office of the Secretary, "Set T," National Archives.

From Charles Lee

[*Alexandria, Virginia, December 31, 1789.* On February 12, 1790, Hamilton wrote to Lee: "Your letter of the 31st. of December came duly to hand." *Letter not found.*]

To Thomas Mifflin

Treasury Department, 31st Dec'r, 1789.

Sir,

I have the honor of your letter of the 28th instant,[1] inclosing one to you from the Comptroller General of your State.[2] I can only regret, that my delay has accrued, and take it for granted, that the business will receive all the dispatch which may be practicable.

I shall be sorry if any inconvenience results to the public Creditors of your state from the cessation of the payment of Indents within the State; but I considered myself as going very far when I determined to continue such a number of officers at the public expence, perhaps in strictness, without authority, for the sole purpose of paying indents, even to the end of the present year, especially, as so much time had elapsed, during which the Creditors might have availed themselves of the provision. I will only add, that the exchanging of old certificates for new ones, and paying of Indents at the Treasury will go on as heretofore.

I have the honor to be, With great respect, Sir, your obedt. hble. Servt.,   A. Hamilton,
                                                    Sec'y of the Trea.

His Excellency, Thos. Mifflin, Esq.

Hazard, *Pennsylvania Archives*, XI, 654–55.
  1. Letter not found.
  2. John Nicholson.

From Otho H. Williams

Baltimore, December 31, 1789. Plans to send to Hamilton copies of Maryland's revenue laws,[1] information "respecting the Commerce and Shipping of this state," [2] and the answers to Hamilton's "demands upon the subject of the Impost Laws." [3]

ADfS, RG 53, "Old Correspondence," Baltimore Collector, National Archives.
1. H had requested these laws in "Treasury Department Circular to the Collectors of the Customs," November 25, 1789.
2. H had requested this information in "Treasury Department Circular to the Collectors of the Customs," October 15, 1789.
3. H had requested this information in "Treasury Department Circular to the Collectors of the Customs," October 2, 1789.

To ─────

[*1789–1795.*] [1] Encloses the decision of the Federal District Court of Connecticut on the petition of Captain Timothy Savage. Suspects Savage of intent to defraud.

LS, Yale University Library.
1. The MS is a fragment without date or place.

From Benjamin Lincoln

[*Boston, 1789.*] Discusses the difficulty of distinguishing between goods on which duties have been paid and those on which they have not been paid. Proposes a system of branding casks, chests, and boxes, and marking bales to prevent smuggling.

LC, RG 36, Letters from the Treasury and Others, 1789–1818, Vol. 11, National Archives.

To George Washington [1]

[1789–1795]

Mr. Hamilton will with pleasure execute the command of the President by the time appointed and have the honor of waiting upon him.

AL, Photostat, George Washington Papers, Library of Congress.

I 7 9 O

From Michael Dawson [1]

Philadelphia, January 1, 1790. Applies for the contract for the maintenance of the buoys and beacons in Delaware River and Bay.

LS, RG 26, Early Lighthouse Letters, National Archives.
   1. Dawson was a Delaware River pilot who had been employed by Pennsylvania to maintain the aids to navigation in the Delaware River.

From John Davidson

[*Annapolis, January 2, 1790.* On January 22, 1790, Hamilton wrote to Davidson: "I am favored with your letter of the 2d Instant." *Letter not found.*]

From John Jay

New York 2d January 1790.

Sir

I have now the honor of transmitting to you herewith enclosed the extracts [1] requested in your letter to me of the 2d. November last, and am with great respect and esteem &c.   John Jay

LC, Papers of the Continental Congress, National Archives.
   1. At the bottom of this letter is the following:
"List of papers mentioned in, and transmitted with the aforegoing letter.
No. 1. Abstracts and Extracts from the Secret Journals of Congress.
   2. Extracts of letters from the Secret Committee, and Committee of foreign Affairs.
   3. Extracts of letters from Mr. Silas Deane.
   4. Extracts of letters from Mr. Arthur Lee.
   5. Extracts of letters from Dr. Franklin.
   6. Extracts of letters from the Joint Commissioners at the Court of France.
   7. Letter from Mr. Thomas Barclay to the Secretary for foreign affairs of 29th. June 1782, his account current with the United States dated 16th August 1782, and a recapitulation of goods purchased by Messrs. John de Neufville and Son, and disposed of by Mr. Barclay dated 14th. December 1782. . . ."

To George Washington

[New York, January 3, 1790] [1]

The Secretary of the Treasury having, in consequence of the Act for the Establishment and support of Light houses,[2] directed his Enquiries[3] to that object begs leave most respectfully to submit the result to

The President of the United States of America

New Hampshire.

In this State is only one Light house situated on a point of land on the Island of New-Castle, three miles from Portsmouth, without the walls of the Fort which commands the entrance of Piscatqua river. It is under the Superintendance of a Commissary[4] who is Captain of the Fort; and is at present in good repair.

The annual expence of maintaining it, is estimated at . . .

Dollars 217.20.

Massachusetts.

In this State are six Light-houses at the following places vizt.

    Boston
    Cape-Ann
    Plymouth
    Plumb Island
    Nantucket
    Portland.

The whole expence attending the support of these Establishments including the Officers Salaries, is estimated at . . .   Dollars 5736.

LC, George Washington Papers, Library of Congress.
    1. The MS is undated. It is found in the George Washington letter book between letters dated December 28, 1789, and January 3, 1790. In the letter of January 4 Washington wrote: "I feel myself very much obliged by what you sent me yesterday." In *JCHW*, IV, 23, this letter is dated June 18, 1790.
    2. "An Act for the establishment and support of Lighthouses, Beacons, Buoys, and Public Piers" (1 *Stat.* 53–54 [August 7, 1789]).
    3. See "Treasury Department Circular to the Collectors of the Customs," October 1, 1789.
    4. Supply Clap.

The Officers appointed for their management are,

At Boston, Captain Thomas Knox with an annual Salary of Dollars	400
At Cape Ann. Mr. Samuel Houston with Ditto	400
At Plymouth the widow of the late General Thomas [5] with Ditto	233.50
At Plumb Island Mr. Lowell [6] with Ditto	220.
At Nantucket, Mr. Paul Pinkham with Ditto	250.

At Portland, the building not being perfectly completed no person is yet appointed to superintend it.

Exclusive of the above there is an officer stiled a commissary who has the charge of supplying the whole.

This Office is now filled by Mr.   Devens,[7] but what allowance he has for executing it, the Secretary has not yet ascertained. When the building at Portland is completed, the expence of maintaining it, and the allowance of the commissary superintending the whole, will probably make the total amount of the Light house Establishment in the State of Massachusetts about . . . .

Dollars 6000
℔ annum.

Connecticut.

In this State there is only one Light house which is situated at the port of New London; it is built of stone, and has lately been repaired: In the month of May last the General Assembly ordered some Buoys to be fixed in the harbour for the safety of the navigation, but nothing has been yet done in consequence of the Act.

The annual expence of this Establishment is estimated at . . .

Dollars. 450

At New Haven there is a pier in the harbor which is private property, & a Buoy at the entrance, two other buoys are judged necessary for the safety of the navigation.

New York.

At New York there is a Light house and was lately a Beacon at Sandy hook, the annual expence of which (exclusive of an allow-

5. Mrs. John Thomas.
6. Abner Lowell.
7. Richard Devens.

ance to the Wardens of the port) is about . . .   Dollars 1500
The number of the Wardens is four, who have (besides other Duties incident to their Office) the charge of supplying and superintending this Establishment. They have each an allowance of one Dollar and an half ℔ day, when employed in visiting the works, exclusive of their provisions &c. The Master Warden is Mr. Thomas Randall. The Beacon has been recently blown down and will require to be replaced; which can be done at an inconsiderable expence.

In New Jersey.
There is no Light house, nor any establishment of that nature.

In Pennsylvania.
There is a Light house at Cape Henlopen, and several Buoys, Beacons and Piers for the security of the navigation on the Bay & river Delaware. The annual expence of these establishments which have been under the care of a Board of Wardens of the port of Philadelphia, is estimated by the present Master Warden at,

Dollars 4133.

This Office is now filled by Capt. William Allibone.

In Delaware.
There is no Light-house nor other establishment of this nature, those on the Bay & river-Delaware answering for that state.

In Maryland & Virginia
There are at present no Light houses, nor any Beacons, Buoys &ca. for the security of Vessels navigating the Bay of Chesapeak. I[n] consequence of certain Acts of the Legislatures of these States, stiled the compact Laws, considerable Sums have been collected heretofore, by a Tax upon Tonage, for raising a fund for the purpose of building Light-houses &c. at cape Henry. The commissioners appointed by the two States for superintending this work, expended on it previous to the War, in collecting materials &c, at between 7 and £8000 Virginia currency but it is presumed that no considerable Benefit can be now derived from this Expenditure. The present expence for erecting this Light-house &c. (as estimated by one of the commissioners appointed on the part of the State of Virginia) is computed at . . .   Dollars 34.076.66

The annual Expence of maintaining it would probably not exceed . . .   Dollars 2.000

In South Carolina.

There is one Light-house and the necessary Buoys and Beacons, for the security of the navigation into that harbour. The Light-house is in good condition, but the Buoys and Beacons want repair. The annual expence attending this establishment is computed at . . .   Dollars. 1.457.

The Officer having charge of them at present is Mr. Thomas Hollingsby, who is recommended by the Commissioners of Pilotage for that harbour as a person perfectly qualified for the business; his present Salary is . . .   Dollars. 257.14.

Georgia.

No information has been received from that State on this subject, although the same enquiries have been made there, as in other States.

To this statement of the substance of the information, which he has received respecting the several Establishments in question, The Secretary begs leave to add that most of the persons who have been singly charged with the care of any of them, have been recommended as proper to be continued, & that no objection has been made to any; and that in the two instances in which that care has been commited to Boards (as in the cases of Pennsylvania and New York) the principals of those Boards are well recommended.

It appears to the Secretary, that it will be expedient to conform to the plan, which exists in Massachusetts, and to substitute Individuals to Boards, where the business has been committed to them; and he thinks it probable that a reappointment of the persons who have been heretofore employed, will be most likely to produce an eligible choice, and to give satisfaction; and also that the allowances heretofore made (as far as they apply) will be a good standard for those to be established. As however it is the intention of the Legislature, that the expenditures for these establishments, should be made by Contract, which from the nature of the objects must generally be conducted on the spot, it seems advisable for this and other reasons, which will occur, that in the distant States, there should be some other persons than the immediate Superintendants of the Light house connected with them in the business.

As a temporary arrangement for this purpose, the Secretary wou'd propose that the particular Superintendents in the several States, except Pennsylvania and New York, should be put under the direction of the Collectors of the principal ports.

In New Hampshire of the Collector of Portsmouth
In Massachusetts of the Collector of Boston
In Connecticut of the Collector of New London
In South Carolina of the Collector of Charleston.
Georgia is omitted from the want of information.

Pennsylvania & New York are excepted, because their contiguity to the Seat of Government will place the particular Superintendants sufficiently under the Eye of the Secretary of the Treasury.

Pursuant to the foregoing Ideas the Secretary sub[mits] the following nomination.

At Boston Capt. Thomas Knox with a Salary of . Dollars 400 ℔ an.
At Cape Ann Mr. Samuel Houston with do. of .   .   . 400
At Plymouth, the widow of the late Genl. Thomas with
   do. of .   .   .   . 240.
At Plumb Island Mr. _____ Lowell with Do of .   .   . 220
At Nantucket Mr. Paul Pinkham with Do of 250
At New London (a person to be nominated by Genl.
   Huntington)[8] with Do. of 100
At New York Mr. Thos. Randall with ditto of   400
At Philadelphia Mr. William Allibone with do. of   500.
At Charleston, South Carolina, Mr. Thomas Hollingsby
   with Ditto of   260

No account having been received at the Treasury of the completion of the Light-house erecting at Portland in Massachusetts, the Secretary has not included it in the present nomination; he has also omitted the Port of New Haven in Connecticut, as the piers & Buoys in that harbor, appear to be private property, not that of the State.

In the States of Virginia & Maryland it appears from what is above stated in this report, that there are no establishments in those states, altho'. materials have formerly been collected for building a Light-House at Cape Henry. As the act of the seventh of August

8. Jedediah Huntington.

last relative to the support of Light houses &c. renders it necessary to obtain a cession of a proper place near the entrance of the chesapeak previous to the erection of a Light house in that Quarter, the Secretary submits it to the consideration of the President, whether it would not be advisable to determine on the place best adapted for such an Establishment, in order that an application may be made to the supreme Executive of the State, under whose jurisdiction the same may be, for a cession of the same.

It will be observed, that the secretary has not mentioned a person for taking charge of the Light-house at New Hampshire. The present Commissary (as before stated) is Capt. of the Fort, near to whose Walls the Light-house is situated. The Collector of the port of Portsmouth [9] is of opinion that the care of it should be intrusted to the captain of the Fort, but has said nothing as to the qualifications of Mr. Clap for this office; or of the Allowance made to him on this account by the State: the Secretary therefore submits the propriety of deferring any appointment for this place, 'till further enquiry is made on these points, to which immediate attention will be paid.

With respect to the Duties of the General Superintendants, as the act contemplates the maintaining, supporting and erecting the Establishments to be by Contract, the Secretary is of opinion, that in all Cases where the nature of the service or supply will possibly admit of the same being so done, with advantage to the public, the superintendants should be authorised to enter into Contract for the same, subject to the ratification of the Secretary of the Treasury, with the approbation of the President; and where the same cannot be so done, that the General Superintendants shall direct the execution of the necessary business at as low a rate as possible.

This line the Secretary is induced to suggest, as he finds on an Investigation of the different Objects of Expenditure accruing under these establishments, that cases will sometimes occur (especially in the repair of works and replacing Buoys &c.) where it will not be possible to Establish any principles of calculation for doing the same by Contract, in which case the party contracting (should such be found) would either demand an extravagant allowance for se-

9. Joseph Whipple.

curing him against the possibility of risque, or endeavour to avoid the same by exectuting his Contract in an inefficient manner.

All which is humbly submitted   Alexander Hamilton
                                        Secretary of the Treasury

From George Washington

[New York, January 4, 1790]

Dear Sir,

I feel myself very much obliged by what you sent me yesterday. The letter from Governor Johnston [1] I return—much pleased to find so authentic an acct. of the adoption by No Carolina of the Constitution. [2]

Yrs. sincerely & affectly   Go: Washington
Monday Morng ⎱
4th. Jany.   ⎰ 1789 [3]

ALS, Hamilton Papers, Library of Congress.
  1. Samuel Johnston, governor of North Carolina.
  2. North Carolina ratified the Constitution on November 21, 1789.
  3. Washington incorrectly dated this letter 1789.

From Tobias Lear

United States, January 5th, 1790.

Sir,

By direction of the President of the United States, I have the honor herewith to transmit to you a letter from the Governor of Virginia,[1] dated December 18th, 1789, enclosing an Act (which is likewise sent you) of the general Assembly of that Commonwealth, passed Novr. 13th. 1789, to convey to the United States in Congress assembled certain Land for the purpose of building a Light House on Cape Henry.

I have the honor to be, with perfect respect, Sir, Your most Obedt. & Hum. Servt.   Tobias Lear.

                                        Secretary to the President
                                        of the United States
The Honorable The Secretary of the Treasury of the United States.

LS, RG 26, "Segregated" Lighthouse Records, National Archives; LC, George Washington Papers, Library of Congress.
    1. Beverley Randolph.

From William Allibone

Philadelphia, January 7, 1790. Has received Hamilton's letter of December 21, 1789,[1] and the necessary funds to maintain the aids to navigation in the Delaware River.

LS, RG 26, Lighthouse Letters Received, Vol. "A," Pennsylvania and Southern States, National Archives.
    1. Letter not found.

To Angelica Church [1]

[New York, January 7, 1790]

Inclosed My Dear friend is a letter from your sister; which she has written to supply my deficiency. Tomorrow I open the budget[2] & you may imagine that today I am very busy and not a little anxious. I could not however let the Packet sail without giving you a proof, that no degree of occupation can make me forget you.

We hope to hear shortly that you are safe arrived & that every thing is to your wish. That Mr. Church is well, young, and sprightly. And that your sons promise all to be great men, and your daughters to be like yourself.[3]

Adieu Love to Mr Church & believe me always Yr. Affectionate friend & brother   A Hamilton

New York January 7. 1789 [4]
Mrs. A Church

ALS, Judge Peter B. Olney, Deep River, Connecticut.
    1. Angelica Schuyler Church was H's sister-in-law and the wife of John B. Church.
    2. H is referring to "Report Relative to a Provision for the Support of Public Credit," January 9, 1790.
    3. There were at this time four children in the Church family: Philip, John B., Catherine, and Elizabeth.
    4. H incorrectly dated this letter 1789.

From Sharp Delany

[*Philadelphia*] *January 9, 1790.* "By this post I forward my Cash Acct for the last week. . . . A Vessell enters—and pays tonnage or does not pay—she is sold, or intends for another Port in the United States, and demands a License. Quere, should another Tonnage for the Year be demanded & paid?"

LC, Bureau of Customs, Philadelphia.

From Jeremiah Hill [1]

Biddeford [*District of Maine*] *January 9, 1790.* Forwards "a Copy of the Certificates of Registry granted in this Office to the 31st. Ultimo." Complains that the Boston collector of customs has not answered repeated requests for registry blanks.

Copy, RG 36, Collector of Customs at Boston, Letters from the Treasury and Others, 1789–1809, Vol. 1, National Archives.
1. Hill was collector of customs at Biddeford and Pepperellborough.

From Jedediah Huntington

[*New London, Connecticut, January 9, 1790.* On January 25, 1790, Hamilton wrote to Huntington: "I am favored with your letter of the 9th. instant." *Letter not found.*]

Report Relative to a Provision for the Support of Public Credit

[New York, January 9, 1790]

Introductory Note

Sources for the ideas expressed by Hamilton in his Report Relative to a Provision for the Support of Public Credit are both varied and difficult to assess. Public credit, or the terms on which a state may borrow, had been discussed in Europe by philosophers, government officials, and political pamphleteers for almost a century before Hamilton drew up his famous Report. Many Americans had also given considerable thought to the problems involved in establishing a system of public credit. From the period of the Revolution to the presentation of the Report to Congress, public credit and finance had been the topic of numerous articles in American newspapers and periodicals. There was, moreover, substantial agreement among most of the correspondents from whom Hamilton elicited opinions on public finance; and the Secretary of the Treasury was not alone in his admiration of the credit institutions that had been established in England.

Of the many Europeans who have been said to influence Hamilton's thinking on public finance, special mention should be made of Charles Montague (later Lord Halifax). A Whig member of Parliament under William III and Chancellor of the Exchequer, he used his influence to support the institution of a public debt, the Bank of England, the excise on malt and liquors, and the first tontine in England. It has been suggested that Hamilton's use of the pseudonym James Montague in an early letter on financial policy [1] was an indication that he was aware of—and even in sympathy with—the ideas of the English statesman. This inference may or may not be farfetched, but it is supported by Hamilton's praise of policies instituted by Montague, and there can be no doubt that several of Hamilton's American contemporaries were aware of Montague's views. The author of a short note in *The American Museum* in 1789, after pointing out the similarity between the current situation in the United States and that faced by Montague, stated: "In his alarming crisis [in England], the eloquence and abilities of Mr. Montague . . . saved the nation." [2] A year later a memorial from the General Assembly of Virginia introduced its criticism of Hamilton's funding program by pointing out "a striking resemblance between this system and that which was introduced at the Revolution [in England]." [3]

Precedents for some of the ideas expressed in the Report can also be found in the various plans that had been put forward in the decade preceding 1790 by French and British finance ministers to solve problems concerning their respective national debts. Such proposals were well known to most Americans interested in public finance. Hamilton's suggestion of a tontine to be divided into six classes was probably a modified version of William Pitt's plan. An article in the *Gazette of the United States* mentioned Pitt's tontine,[4] and William Bingham presumably gave Hamilton further information on the subject.[5] Several passages in Jacques Necker's speech at the opening of the States General in 1789 are similar to parts of Hamilton's Report.[6] Hamilton had referred to Necker on an earlier occasion,[7] and copies of a pamphlet which

Report of the Secretary of the Treasury to the House of Representatives, Relative to a Provision for the Support of the Public Credit of the United States, in Conformity to a Resolution of the Twenty-First Day of September, 1789. Presented to the House on Thursday the 14th Day of January, 1790. Published by Order of the House of Representatives (New-York: Printed by Francis Childs and John Swaine, 1790).

1. H to _____, December, 1779–March, 1780.
2. *The American Museum*, VI (October, 1789), 294–95.
3. *ASP, Finance*, I, 90.
4. [New York] *Gazette of the United States*, December 2, 1789.
5. James O. Wettereau, "Letters from Two Business Men to Alexander Hamilton on Federal Fiscal Policy, November, 1789," *Journal of Economic and Business History*, III (August, 1931), 667–72; Miller, *Hamilton*, 237, note.
6. *Ouverture des Etats-Généraux*.
7. See "The Federalist No. 12," November 27, 1787, note 13; and H to the Marquis de Lafayette, October 6, 1789.

included Necker's speech were available in the United States before the close of 1789. Although on April 30, 1781, in a letter to Robert Morris, Hamilton had praised French finance in contrast to the "abuse of credit" practiced in England, he believed that the abuse had been possible only because of the strength of the credit institutions developed in England during the decade of the sixteen-nineties, and his criticism antedated the financial measures proposed by Pitt. Descriptions of British financial experience were available in most of the printed works on finance and in *Parliamentary Debates*.

David Hume and Thomas Hobbes have been frequently cited as the authors to whom Hamilton was most indebted.[8] Before Hamilton served in the Continental Congress, he had studied Hume's *Political Discourses*.[9] The essay "On Public Credit" contained in this work expresses Hume's fears concerning the growth and extent of the British debt and the impending bankruptcy to which he believed it would lead, but the section of the essay that was most often quoted during the seventeen-eighties states: "More men, therefore, with large stocks and incomes may naturally be suppos'd to continue in trade, where there are public debts: And this, it must be own'd, is of some advantage to commerce, by diminishing its profits, promoting circulation, and encouraging industry."[10]

Hobbs made fulfillment of contract the third law of nature and "the Fountain and Original of *Justice*."[11] Although Hamilton was critical of Hobbs in a reference made before the Revolution,[12] Hobbes's discussion of largesse and contract bear a resemblance to Hamilton's discussion of discrimination. In this connection, Hobbes wrote: "Whensoever a Man transfereth his Right or renounceth it, it is either in Consideration of some Right reciprocally transferred to himself, or for some other Good he hopeth for thereby. For it is a voluntary Act; and of the voluntary Acts of every Man, the Object is some *Good to himself*. . . . The mutual transferring of Right, is that which men call *Contract* . . . when a Covenant is made, then to break it is *unjust*. And the Definition of *Injustice* is no other than *the not performance of Covenant*. And whatsoever is not unjust, is *just*."[13]

Montesquieu, who influenced the thinking of many of the Founding Fathers, shared Hume's aversion to large public debts, but he also emphasized the importance of support for public credit. Security holders, according to Montesquieu, should not be taxed "as a breach in the public faith cannot be made on a certain number of subjects, without seeming to be made on all; . . . the state is obliged to give them a singular protection, that the part which is indebted may never have the least advantage over that which is the creditor."[14]

One historian has called Malachy Postlethwayt's *Universal Dictionary* "the most important document yet discovered showing background and immediate sources of some of Hamilton's principal writings, especially his Reports."[15] During the Revolution Hamilton had used the *Dictionary* as an introduction to economic theory and practice. Under various headings in the *Dictionary* some of the major points in the Report are discussed. Postlethwayt's emphasis on the importance of transfer of public securities is especially close to the view

8. Vernon L. Parrington, *Main Currents in American Thought* (New York, 1930), I, 298, 300; Mitchell, *Hamilton*, 385.
9. H to Robert Morris, April 30, 1781.
10. David Hume, *Political Discourses* (Edinburgh, 1752), 128.
11. Hobbes, *Moral and Political Works*, 157.
12. "The Farmer Refuted, &c.," February 23, 1775.
13. Hobbes, *Moral and Political Works*, 153, 158.
14. Montesquieu, *The Spirit of Laws*, II, 100.
15. E. P. Panagopoulos, *Alexander Hamilton's Pay Book* (Detroit, 1961), 6.

expressed in the Report. In an article in the *Dictionary* entitled "Action," Postlethwayt wrote: "Such is the nature of public credit, that no body would lend their money to the support of the state, under the most pressing emergencies, unless they could have the privilege of buying and selling their property in the public funds, when their occasions required. 'Tis certain, therefore, that the greatest delicacy and tenderness is to be observed, in laying any restraints upon these transactions, lest the public credit should be thereby irrecoverably prejudiced." [16] Part of Postlethwayt's article on "Bubbles" gives a similar emphasis. "The other species of bubbling," Postlethwayt wrote, "arises from the nature of our national debts; for, if between eighty and ninety millions of money are so tied up, as to remain untransferrable, unnegotiable, and not to change hands, who could ever be induced to lend the government money upon the most pressing emergency, even in consideration of the largest interest? Though parliamentary security gives the real value to the national debt, or the public funds, they would be, like the miser's treasure, useless to the possessor; or like the undiscovered riches of the earth, did not circulation and credit set a market price upon them." [17]

Precedents for some of Hamilton's ideas can also be found in Blackstone and Vatel. Blackstone's *Commentaries,* which Hamilton studied when he was preparing for admission to the bar, states: "The only advantage, that can result to a nation from public debts, is the encrease of circulation by multiplying the cash of the Kingdom . . . always ready to be employed in any beneficial undertaking, by means of it's transferrable quality. . . ." [18] Vattel, one of the writers on natural law with whom Hamilton probably became familiar during the same period, states: "What [the sovereign] . . . borrows for the service of the state, the debts contracted in the administration of public affairs, are contracts of strict right, obligatory with respect to the state and the whole nation. Nothing can dispense with the discharging of these debts." [19]

In addition to the influence which European writers may have had on Hamilton's views, it has been suggested that he obtained some of the ideas contained in the Report from contemporaries in the United States. For example, Hamilton has been called "a product of the Robert and Gouverneur Morris school," [20] and to substantiate this assertion reference can be made to Robert Morris's two letters to Congress in 1781 and 1782 [21] and to Gouverneur Morris's plan of American finances in 1789. [22] But Hamilton earlier had expressed some of the views that he shared with these two men, and the differences between the proposals of the two Morrises and the contents of Hamilton's Report are as striking as the similarities. At least three scholars have also pointed out the parallel between William Bingham's letter of November 25, 1789, to Hamilton and some of the proposals in the Report. [23] Although there are some points in

16. Postlethwayt, *Universal Dictionary,* I, 15.

17. Postlethwayt, *Universal Dictionary,* I, 385.

18. Blackstone, *Commentaries,* I, 327.

19. Emeric de Vattel, *The Law of Nations; or Principles of the Law of Nature: applied to the conduct and affairs of Nations and Sovereigns. by M. de Vattel. A Work tending to Display the True Interest of Powers. Translated from the French* (London, Printed for J. Coote, at the King's Arms in Pater-Noster Row, 1759), Vol. II, Book II, Ch. XIV, Section 216, p. 200.

20. Dorfman, *The Economic Mind,* I, 289.

21. Sparks, *Diplomatic Correspondence,* XI, 442–59; XII, 211–38.

22. Sparks, *Life of Gouverneur Morris,* III, 469–78.

23. Dorfman, *The Economic Mind,* I, 287–89; James O. Wettereau, "Letters from Two Business Men to Alexander Hamilton on Federal Fiscal Policy, November, 1789," *Journal of Economic and Business History,* III (August, 1931), 667–72; Miller, *Hamilton,* 237, note.

Bingham's letter which are similar to those in the Report, many of these points had been suggested by Hamilton before 1789, and the method for scaling down the debt proposed by Hamilton had been explicitly rejected by Bingham as "opposed to every principle of a sound and magnanimous Policy." [24]

The fact that many of the views on finance included in the Report were put forward by Hamilton before they were stated by his contemporaries suggests that his intellectual debt to his associates in and out of Congress and to current periodical literature was not as large as has sometimes been supposed. Between 1779 and 1781 in correspondence with James Duane, Robert Morris, and others, as well as in published articles signed "The Continentalist," Hamilton had discussed measures necessary for the support of public credit. [25] During his service in Congress he further elaborated his views in his "Defense of Congress" and in an answer to Rhode Island's objections to the impost. [26]

Although the experience under the Confederation was probably not a formative influence, the policies and failures of Congress served as a background of specific precedents. Funding, a national bank, and the establishment of a sinking fund had all been included among the various schemes proposed by Congress for the support of public credit. These institutions were to be financed by the sale of western lands, quotas from the states, foreign loans, and the impost. But either political or economic considerations rendered each of these devices ineffectual. The sale of western lands was impeded by the unequal effect of land cessions on various states, by the costs of surveying and protecting the land, and by the fear with which some states viewed the settlement of these lands. Quotas failed partly because of the strain which the costs of the Revolution had imposed on state finances and partly because many states believed that they had contributed more than their share to the cost of the war. Foreign loans were obtained with increasing difficulty after the Revolution because of the changes in the foreign and domestic situation of the lending nations, because of the uncertainty concerning repayment, and because of the growing tendency of foreign lenders to invest in the domestic debt of the United States. Although repeated attempts were made between 1783 and 1788 to gain the acquiescence of the states to a general impost, the different situations of various states respecting both foreign trade and domestic revenue prevented its general adoption.

During the three years preceding the presentation of the Report on Public Credit, many articles on public finance appeared in *The American Museum* and the *Gazette of the United States*. Hamilton was a charter subscriber to the former and undoubtedly read the latter. During this period an essay on some aspect of government finance and public credit was reprinted in almost every issue of *The American Museum*. Discussion was less frequent immediately after the ratification of the Constitution, but the topic regained importance during the second half of 1789. In the February, 1787, issue, "Tom Thoughtfull" described past contracts as "sacred things." [27] A reprint of Thomas Paine's *Common Sense*, Part IV, [28] was published in the March issue stating that a national debt would be a national bond and urging that public lands be used for discharge of the debt. In the same issue "an honest chearful citizen" discussed the resources which the United States could use to establish public credit

24. Bingham to H, November 25, 1789.
25. H to _____, December, 1779–March, 1780; H to James Duane, September 3, 1780; H to Robert Morris, April 30, 1781; "The Continentalist No. IV," August 30, 1781.
26. "Defense of Congress," July, 1783; "Continental Congress. Report on a Letter from the Speaker of the Rhode Island Assembly," December 16, 1782.
27. *The American Museum*, I (February, 1787), 114.
28. *The American Museum*, I (March, 1787), 180, 182.

and emphasized the increase in commerce and the decrease in taxes which would result.[29] The April issue included the report of February 15, 1786, of the Committee of Finance of Congress; in May, Washington's circular letter of 1783 was reprinted.[30] The May issue also contained a discussion of discrimination between original and current holders of government obligations. One of the articles opposing discrimination, after discussing the benefits which would accrue to the nation if justice were done to public creditors, concluded that "instead of being considered as a curse, the Public Debt will become a Public Blessing."[31] More material appeared in June, including a reference to the law of Pennsylvania which had attempted to discriminate between original and current holders of army certificates.[32] Between June, 1787, and July, 1789, few articles on finance were printed in *The American Museum*, but the August, 1789, issue revealed a renewed interest in public finance as a result of the failure of the Committee on Ways and Means to take up the question of debt service in connection with the revenues necessary for the current year.[33]

During the fall of 1789, Hamilton asked several people for information and opinions on various aspects of public finance.[34] The replies to these requests undoubtedly were used by Hamilton in drawing up the Report. For example, in the course of the Report he mentions Samuel Osgood's letter concerning postal revenues. He also refers to the ideas which "have been suggested to him" concerning the settlement of accounts between the states. Among such suggestions, which bear a close resemblance to the proposals contained in the Report, were those supplied by Oliver Wolcott, Jr. Some of the sources of revenue mentioned by James Madison and Stephen Higginson are the same as those discussed in the Report, and Hamilton's opinions on discrimination in the Report closely resemble the ideas advanced by John Witherspoon in his letter to the Secretary of the Treasury. Finally, there are many similarities of expression between the Report and the letter which Hamilton received from William Bingham.

The attempt to assess the influence of the opinions of Hamilton's contemporaries on the Report is made even more difficult by the fact that ideas were exchanged in conversations as well as in letters. Witherspoon and Bingham, for example, both closed their letters to Hamilton with the statement that they hoped that they would be able to converse with him more fully in person.[35] William Duer, who according to John Adams had a very important influence on Hamilton's Report,[36] probably expressed his views in conversation; and members of the old Board of Treasury (also mentioned by Adams) may

29. *The American Museum*, I (March, 1787), 187–90.
30. *The American Museum*, I (April, 1787), 318; I (May, 1787), 387–97.
31. *The American Museum*, I (May, 1787), 417.
32. *The American Museum*, I (June, 1787), 488; *Laws Enacted in the Second Sitting of the Ninth General Assembly of the Commonwealth of Pennsylvania, Which Commenced at Philadelphia, on the First day of February in the year of our Lord, one Thousand Seven Hundred and Eighty-Five* (n.p., n.d.) Ch. CLXXXIII, Section xiv, 465.
33. *The American Museum*, VI (August, 1789), 93.
34. The letters which H received in reply to his request for information include: William Bingham to H, November 25, 1789; Stephen Higginson to H, November 11, 1789; James Madison to H, November 19, 1789; Samuel Osgood to H, November 28, 1789, and January 20, 1790; Benjamin Walker to H, September 15, 1789; John Witherspoon to H, October 26, 1789; Oliver Wolcott, Jr., to H, November 29, 1789.
35. Witherspoon to H, October 26, 1789; Bingham to H, November 25, 1789.
36. Adams to Benjamin Rush, August 23, 1805 (cited in Manning J. Dauer, *The Adams Federalists* [Baltimore, 1953] 64, note 44).

have spoken to Hamilton. William Constable wrote in December, 1789, that he had "tried" Hamilton on various aspects of debt provision.[37] Despite the possibility of such conversations, the fact remains that before 1787 Hamilton had expressed in letters and articles many of the arguments used in the Report. Later opinions with which he came in contact may have been more valuable to him as corroboration for his own views or as an indication of opinions to which the Report should be addressed than as a source of ideas for the plan proposed.

When one turns to specific proposals made by the Report, it is possible to demonstrate that few of Hamilton's ideas were altogether original. The assumption of state debts provides a case in point. This question had been considered by several Americans in the years immediately preceding Hamilton's presentation of his Report, and it had been mentioned during the Constitutional Convention.[38] On February 27, 1788, Samuel A. Otis[39] had written to the Speaker of the Massachusetts House of Representatives: "I find it in contemplation to assume the State debts, and fund state and federal at 3%. What think you of such a project? Would it be just? And how would it affect Massachusetts? This or a Sponge I apprehend will be attempted at some period not far distant."[40] An amendment to the Constitution proposed by the North Carolina Ratifying Convention prohibited the Federal assumption of state debts or intervention in state provision for them.[41] In the August, 1789, issue of *The American Museum*, an article proposed Federal provision for the state debts on the grounds that an unequal portion of the public debt was held by citizens of various states and ". . . such attachment to local interests might distress the tranquillity of the states by creating discontents and dissentions."[42] Another argument used in the same article was that under the Constitution the states had been deprived of those tariff revenues that had been used to support state securities, ". . . under the persuasion that they would be fully recompensed under the federal government."[43] An article in the November 21, 1789, issue of the *Gazette of the United States* also used the argument of the impost to support the necessity of assumption.[44] Four days later an article in the *Gazette* proposed the assumption of state debts by the United States because these debts had been "incurred for them and in equity they ought to see . . . [them] funded."[45] On November 29, 1789, Oliver Wolcott, Jr., wrote to his father,[46] "It will probably be also proposed to consolidate the debts of the Union, in the settlement of the state accounts. This measure though difficult, is I believe necessary, as the states will by excises or otherwise, defeat any general system of revenue which can be proposed, unless this shall be effected."[47] On the same day Wolcott wrote to Hamilton outlining a plan for

37. Ferguson, *Power of the Purse*, 271.
38. Hunt and Scott, *Debates*, 421.
39. Otis was a member of the Continental Congress in 1787 and 1788.
40. Otis to James Warren, February 27, 1788 (Burnett, *Letters*, VIII, 703).
41. Louise Irby Trenholme, *The Ratification of the Federal Constitution in North Carolina* (New York, 1932), 238.
42. *The American Museum*, VI (August, 1789), 94.
43. *The American Museum*, VI (August, 1789), 97.
44. [New York] *Gazette of the United States*, November 21, 1789.
45. [New York] *Gazette of the United States*, November 25, 1789.
46. When this letter was written Oliver Wolcott, Sr., was lieutenant-governor of Connecticut.
47. George Gibbs, *Memoirs of the Administrations of Washington and John Adams, edited from the Papers of Oliver Wolcott, Secretary of the Treasury* (New York, 1846), I, 24–25.

the settlement of accounts and assumption that was similar in almost every respect to the plan suggested in the Report.[48]

Assumption could not be considered without reference to its effect on the settlement of accounts with the states. This problem hung like a cloud over every discussion of finances and current quotas from the period of the Revolution to the debate over Hamilton's Report. During the Revolution Robert Morris had expressed his fear of the effect of the unsettled balances among the states.[49] In 1783, Hamilton and Madison had taken part in the debate over settlement of accounts between the states.[50] In April of the following year a Grand Committee on the National Debt gave a report which is in Thomas Jefferson's writing. In answer to complaints of inequitable quotas, the Report notes that "almost every state thinks itself in advance" on its quota to the United States and that: "it has been the constant wish of Congress that these accounts should be settled, and the contributions of each be known and credited."[51]

Under the Confederation various plans had been proposed for the settlement of accounts between the states and the Union. They differed in the extent to which credits would be allowed to the states for expenditures in their own defense and in the proof of expenditure which was required. They disagreed upon whether the unpaid quotas, apportioned expenses of the war, and state debts assumed should be debited in the final settlement. If the expenses of the war were to be charged as debits, what ratio of apportionment should be used? Land values, population estimates, and the basis for quotas of the requisitions of Congress were suggested. But land values, population estimates, and quotas had been different at different periods during the war and postwar era, and, whatever the basis chosen, the states which had been occupied or fought over for the longest period during the Revolution favored "abatements" to make allowance for the greater difficulties which they had experienced in supporting the war.[52] Another suggestion emphasized the current financial capability of the states rather than the ability of the various states to contribute at the time the expenses were incurred.[53]

In 1787, an ordinance adopted by Congress gave wider latitude to claims for credits against the Union. This ordinance specified that "advances or disbursements . . . not sanctioned by the resolves of Congress or supported by regular vouchers" should be allowed, and it gave the Board of Commissioners power to "make such allowance for the same as they shall think consistent with the principles of general equity."[54] The states south of Maryland favored this ordinance, for their accounts had for the most part not been approved by Congress and they did not have adequate records of their appropriations.[55]

48. Oliver Wolcott, Jr., to H, November 29, 1789.
49. Sparks, *Diplomatic Correspondence*, XI, 442–59; XII, 9.
50. *JCC*, XXV, 879–922.
51. Papers of the Continental Congress, National Archives.
52. See for example H's motion: "Continental Congress. Motion on Abatements for States in Possession of the Enemy," February 17, 1783.
53. This attitude prevailed in the final settlement through the use of the ratio for direct taxes under the Constitution. See "An Act to provide more effectually for the settlement of the Accounts between the United States and the individual States (1 *Stat.* [August 5, 1790], 178–82).
54. *JCC*, XXXII, 262–66.
55. Ferguson, *Power of the Purse*, 207; and "Notes of Debates in the Continental Congress," James Madison Papers, Library of Congress. In a note to the debates, Madison lists the attitudes of each state toward measures pending before Congress.

After this ordinance had been proposed to Congress, Madison wrote: "The settlement of the public accounts has long been pursued in various shapes, and with little prospect of success. The idea which has long been urged by some of us, seems now to be seriously embraced, of establishing a plenipotentiary tribunal for the final adjustment of the mutual claims on the great and simple principle of equity." [56] The North Carolina delegates wrote to their state's General Assembly that the ordinance "will wind up the whole expenses of the War on principles perfectly equitable." [57] In more specific terms the Virginia delegates warned William Heth that Virginia should accede to the new plan "conceiving that a greater degree of Justice is attainable in an adjustment of the Accounts of Virginia against the United States in the present State of the business, than is to be expected in any later period, or by an agreement of other Commissioners than those now employed." [58] But to Massachusetts the ordinance appeared somewhat less than perfectly equitable. Samuel A. Otis wrote, ". . . I have a hint that the ordinance for appointing the three Commissioners is somehow so cooked that the Penobscott business although consolidated at £116,000, will be thrown out by the Board. . . . So true is it, in public and private concerns, that the free horse is ridden to death. The expenditures of the Board of War, the great disproportion of men we had in the field, the astonishing loss by old money, and want of alertness in bringing forward accounts, with regularity and in season will hang like a mill stone about the neck of Massachusetts for ages." [59]

The ordinance adopted by Congress in 1787 and the plans of both Robert Morris in 1783 and Gouverneur Morris in 1789 would all have increased the total Federal debt by $80,000,000 to $90,000,000. These proposals avoided the problem of settling the ratio of apportionment of the costs of the war by expressing the state credits as a debt due from the Union to the states at six percent and debiting only payments from the Union or quotas remaining unpaid. Gouverneur Morris also suggested that the sinking fund be used to purchase the state securities on the market and that the states should then be debited with their nominal amount. Capitalization of the cost of the war as a debt due from the Union to the states would have increased the power of the states and thus would have strengthened the hydra which Hamilton believed had to be beheaded. [60]

Hamilton approached with caution the question of reversing part of the policy of the ordinance passed by Congress in 1787, for he knew that the principle of settlement of the accounts between the states would require "all the moderation and wisdom of the government." The Report, nevertheless,

56. Madison to Jefferson, April 23, 1787 (Burnett, *Letters*, VIII, 589).

57. North Carolina Delegates to the North Carolina General Assembly, December 15, 1787 (Burnett, *Letters*, VIII, 689).

58. The Virginia Delegates to William Heth, April 20, 1788 (Burnett, *Letters*, VIII, 723). At this time Heth was serving as commissioner on the part of Virginia for the Illinois claim.

59. Otis to Nathan Dane, October 29, 1788 (Burnett, *Letters*, VIII, 811).

60. In 1787, Hamilton had said that if the new government were instituted, "It may then triumph altogether over the state governments and reduce them to an entire subordination, dividing the large states into smaller districts. . . . If this should not be the case, in the course of a few years, it is probable that the contests about the boundaries of power between the particular governments and the general government and the *momentum* of the larger states in such contests will produce a dissolution of the Union. This after all seems to be the most likely result" ("Conjectures About the New Constitution," September 17-30, 1787).

differed in three major respects from the ordinance of 1787: The Federal Government rather than the states would disburse payment to state creditors; the remainder of quotas still due from the states would not be charged against the states; and the cost of the war would be apportioned as a debit against the states.

But the debts outstanding from a state to her own citizens could not be so easily written off. Although the amount of these debts was considered a credit for the state in the accounts between the states, several states had already encountered difficulty in servicing their debts. Under the Confederation the attempt to service the Massachusetts state debt and her assumed Federal debts on hard money principles had precipitated Shays' Rebellion. The weight of a similar debt in South Carolina and recent crop failures in that state had left it unable to cover its current expenses without recourse to additional loans. Other states which had hoped to gain by the final settlement of accounts preferred to wait for that settlement before assumption was discussed.

As vexing as the questions of assumption and the settlement of the state accounts were the problems raised by the various proposals for discrimination between the original and subsequent holders of securities. In 1783, a circular to the states,[61] an extract from which was used by Hamilton in his Report, opposed discrimination between original creditors and transferees. But the context of the argument over discrimination soon began to change, for between 1783 and 1789 a large part of the domestic debt was either absorbed into the state debts or serviced by the states,[62] and public creditors turned increasingly to the state governments for payment of both state and Federal securities. While Pennsylvania was considering a funding act in 1785, Pelatiah Webster suggested a scheme of discrimination between original creditors and their assignees. "It is very certain," Webster wrote, "and undoubtedly confessed an all sides, that our *soldiers,* when their *services were over,* and their accounts fairly adjusted, were entitled to the liquidating balances in their favor, *in genuine money:* this was in *justice* due them for their services, and if they were paid, *no more than justice* was done them; but if, instead of this they were paid nominally *twenty shillings* in a certificate . . . which was . . . *no more than* 2s. 6d. . . . it is plain they were paid but 2s. 6d. in the pound, and the *remaining 17s. 6d. is still due to them."[63] Under Webster's plan current holders were to receive the current market price, and the difference between the nominal value and the market value of the securities when issued was to be paid to the original creditors. The securities of current holders were to be purchased on the market by commissioners in charge of a sinking fund.

As the seventeen-eighties progressed, increasing numbers of Americans began to express their opinions on discrimination. For example, the May, 1787, issue of *The American Museum* includes articles both by those favoring discrimination and by those opposing it. One critic of discrimination in this issue was quoted as saying that discrimination ". . . if given the sanction of law would forever destroy all confidence in the faith and integrity of the public."[64] The June, 1787, issue of the same periodical mentioned the Pennsylvania law which contained provision for discrimination.[65] According to Pelatiah Webster this provision applied only to final settlement certificates issued to the Army, and, in any case, it had been evaded to a considerable

61. *JCC,* XXIV, 277–83.

62. Ferguson, *Power of the Purse,* 228.

63. Webster, *Political Essays,* 271–72. In this collection this essay is marked, "First published in Philadelphia, Jan. 10, 1785."

64. *The American Museum,* I (May, 1787), 412.

65. *The American Museum,* I (June, 1787), 488.

extent in practice by the method of proof required.[66] John Witherspoon wrote to Hamilton in October, 1789: "We still have an idea meeting us in conversation and publication that a discrimination must be made between original Creditors and Speculators as they call them. . . . Discrimination is totally subversive of public credit." [67]

Some opponents of discrimination used the analogy of a lottery to illustrate their criticism. Thus, William Bingham wrote: "The purchaser [of securities] . . . may be resembled to a Dealer in a Lottery, where there are Many Blanks to a Prize. Would it be just to contest the payment due to the fortunate Ticket because it had comparatively cost a Trifle." [68] Although Hamilton in his Report does not use the analogy suggested by Bingham, he does state that the chance which the certificate holder took was "a hazard which was far from inconsiderable, and which perhaps, turned, on little less than a revolution in the Government." This problem was also considered by Hobbes when he wrote: "Also when a Prize is propounded to many, which is to be given to him only that winneth; or Money is thrown amongst many, to be enjoyed by them that catch it; though this be a Free-gift; yet so to win, or so to catch, is to merit, and to have it as due. . . . I merit not that the Giver should part with his Right; but that when he has parted with it, it should be mine, rather than anothers." [69]

Discrimination was not the only device proposed by those wishing to mitigate the effects of depreciation and speculative transfer of securities, for it was also suggested that much the same results could be achieved by scaling down the debt's principal or by reducing the interest on it. Because of past depreciation, transfer at reduced prices, and speculation, it was generally believed that the debt would not be paid at its nominal value. It had been proposed that three percent be paid on the Federal debts and the assumed debts of the states. Some believed that repudiation was a clear possibility. Even after the new government had been instituted, there were indications that creditors would willingly accept a scaled-down specie payment in lieu of an "ever widening circle of paper promises."

The idea of scaling down the debt came from many quarters. Precedents were available in the financial history of Great Britain and France; and the matter was discussed in the Continental Congress, American periodicals, and letters addressed to Hamilton in October and November of 1789. As early as February, 1783, a delegate to Congress from Virginia "said that . . . no Civil Creditor would dare to put his claims on a level with those of the army, and insinuated that the speculations which had taken place in loan office certificates might lead to a revision of that subject on principles of equity. . . ." [70] Stephen Higginson in his letter to Hamilton on November 11, 1789, warned against the payment of full interest in specie: "They cannot think it right for those, who have bought them up a 2/ to 3/ in the pound, to derive so great an income from them; and eventually to receive the full Sum of the principal in Specie. . . ." [71] Higginson also wrote: "Though it were true that by imposts and excises, when exerted as far as our case will admit, and duly and exclusively collected by the Union, a sufficient Revenue may be raised to pay the interest on the public Debts including those of the several states, and to support the

66. Webster, *Political Essays*, 269–70, note.
67. Witherspoon to H, October 26, 1789.
68. Bingham to H, November 25, 1789.
69. Hobbes, *Moral and Political Works*, 154.
70. "Notes of Debates in the Continental Congress," James Madison Papers, Library of Congress.
71. Higginson to H, November 11, 1789.

federal government; it is a very important question how far it should be applied to the first of those uses. There is nothing that would so much alarm, and rouse the feelings of the State governments and of their constituents, as a proposition, with an ability, to pay the full interest on public Securities in Specie." [72]

In contrast to the ideas expressed by Higginson were those of William Bingham, Gouverneur Morris, and Robert Morris.[73] All three were opposed in varying degrees to changes in the debt. Bingham, for example, believed that neither the principal nor interest of the debt should be reduced until the market rate of interest had been lowered; then, as in Britain, the offer to return the principal, available elsewhere at cheaper rates, would induce the creditors to make a reduction in their claims. In considering the opposing views expressed by such men as Higginson and Bingham, Hamilton faced a problem similar to that posed by assumption of state debts. He had, in short, to make sure that the reduction which was made necessary by revenue limitations and political considerations did not shake the belief of creditors—especially foreign lenders— in the ability of the new government to meet its obligations.

In his Report Hamilton proposed that the debt be scaled down by a reduction of the annual interest payments, and he advanced seven different plans for achieving that objective. Although the decision to scale down the debt apparently grew out of his belief that a reduction of the interest was necessary to bring service on the debt within the range of probable revenues, it should also be pointed out that there were precedents for some of the various plans which he suggested. Both France and England had attained the same ends by somewhat different methods. In France, refunding had been accompanied by an enforced change in the legal rate of interest for all public and private loans, while in England those holding public securities had been offered the alternative of a lower rate of interest or repayment of the principal. The problem had also been considered by various Americans. For example, an undated fragment in the Hamilton Papers, Library of Congress, of a computation in Philip Schuyler's handwriting appears to give a calculation that is based on the same principle that Hamilton used in his third plan. As early as 1781, Hamilton himself had proposed that a schedule of annuities be incorporated in a plan for a national bank in the same fashion that annuities were used by the Bank of England.[74] And the annuity plans, which Hamilton proposed in 1790, along with the added suggestion of a tontine of six classes, were probably adaptations of British precedents. In discussing the advantages of a tontine, the *Gazette of the United States* stated that William Pitt's plan for a tontine was so favorable to the public that there was some doubt that the loan would be filled.[75] The British plan set a limit upon the amount of the annuity which any survivor could receive; Hamilton's plan provided for even greater security for the public by making the limit on additions to annuities the reversion of four-fifths of the annuities.

No claim of originality can be made for Hamilton's proposals for a sinking fund. Although early in the eighteenth century a sinking fund had been established in England, it had been used not only to support public credit but as

72. Higginson to H, November 11, 1789.
73. See Charles A. Beard, ed., *The Journal of William Maclay, United States Senator from Pennsylvania, 1789–1791* (New York, 1927), 280; William Patterson's notes on Senate debates, Bancroft Transcripts, MS Division, New York Public Library; Sparks, *Life of Gouverneur Morris,* III, 10–15, 17–19; Bingham to H, November 25, 1789.
74. H to _____, December, 1779–March, 1780.
75. [New York] *Gazette of the United States,* December 2, 1789.

a source of emergency funds for current expenses. For almost a century European politicians and political theorists had considered the merits of a sinking fund as a method either for reducing a nation's indebtedness or for supporting its public credit. Blackstone spoke of sinking funds as the "last resort of the nation" for reversing the trend toward increasing debt and eventual bankruptcy; [76] and Montesquieu wrote: "When the Credit of the state is not entire, there is new reason for endeavoring to form a sinking fund, because this fund being once established, will soon procure the public confidence." [77] Richard Price, who had strongly advocated the establishment of an inviolable sinking fund in England, stated that a sinking fund of one million dollars per annum would pay off the entire debt of the United States in slightly more than twenty years.[78] Necker had advocated the institution of a *caisse d'amortissement* in his address to the States General as a means of supporting public credit.[79]

In the years preceding the presentation of Hamilton's Report to Congress, several Americans had discussed the desirability of a sinking fund. In 1778, Gouverneur Morris had proposed to Congress a sinking fund financed in part by postal revenues; [80] and in 1781, Hamilton himself had estimated that a fund of approximately $1,200,000 per annum appropriated to the payment of the debt would be a "sufficient fund for the redemption of the debt within a period of thirty-five years.[81] A report to Congress in 1786 stated: "The whole product [from sales of western lands] . . . is appropriated for the payment of the principal and interest of the national debt, and no part thereof can be diverted to other purposes." [82] Tench Coxe in a pamphlet circulated at the Constitutional Convention wrote: "The general impost . . . the sale of the lands and every other unnecessary article of public property . . . would put the sinking and funding of our debts within the power of all the states." [83] Between November, 1787, and October, 1789, several articles in *The American Museum* had discussed the theory and practice of sinking funds on both sides of the Atlantic.[84]

In any discussion of the origins of the Report's proposals for a sinking fund, special mention should be made of the system established by William Pitt in 1786, which, it has been suggested, was a model for Hamilton's plan [85] and which was recommended to Hamilton in a letter from William Bingham.[86] But other precedents and suggestions were available to Hamilton. His earlier advocacy of sinking funds antedates the system established by Pitt, and the employment of officials of cabinet rank as commissioners for a sinking fund was made more specific in Gouverneur Morris's plan of 1789 than in Bingham's letter.[87]

76. Blackstone, *Commentaries*, I, 329.
77. Montesquieu, *The Spirit of Laws*, II, 100.
78. *The American Museum*, VI (October, 1789), 387.
79. *Ouverture des Etats-Généraux*, 54–57.
80. *JCC*, XII, 929.
81. H to Robert Morris, April 30, 1781.
82. *JCC*, XXX, 73.
83. Tench Coxe, *An Enquiry into the Principles on which a Commercial System for the United States of America Should be Founded* (Philadelphia, May 12, 1787), 49.
84. See, for example, *The American Museum*, II (November, 1787), 245; IV (November, 1788), 411.
85. Charles Franklin Dunbar, *Economic Essays* (New York, 1904), 82–89.
86. Bingham to H, November 25, 1789.
87. Sparks, *Life of Gouverneur Morris*, III, 476.

Hamilton's proposals for scaled-down payments in specie rather than full payments in "paper promises" apparently satisfied the demands of most domestic creditors.[88] But there still remained the question of the policy that should be pursued toward European creditors. In his Report, Hamilton noted that there was general agreement on the fact that the foreign debt already incurred would be paid according to contract. Madison presumably accepted this view, for in November, 1789, he wrote to Hamilton: "I take it to be the general expectation that the foreign part of the debt is to be put on the most satisfactory footing. . . ."[89] An article in 1787 in *The American Museum* warned: "But in case of war who would lend us, if our neglecting seven years to pay the sum borrowed will justify our not paying at all."[90] In a similar vein an article in a 1789 issue stated: "It is problematical whether the United States could negotiate a loan at all on the present financial arrangement."[91]

Although many Americans agreed that the United States should honor its obligations to foreigners, they did not necessarily endorse Hamilton's proposals for new European loans. But Hamilton was insistent on this point, and he began his Report by emphasizing—as he had since 1780—that on occasion even the wealthiest nations of Europe had to resort to borrowing.[92] Under the Confederation the difficulty in floating foreign loans had been due almost as much to the exorbitant rates of interest that could be obtained by speculation in the domestic debt as to the fear among Europeans that such loans would not be serviced or repaid. Jefferson had recognized the effect on foreign borrowing of foreign speculation in the domestic debt when he attempted to float a European loan in 1788.[93] At that time purchase of the foreign loan would have yielded only slightly more than the stipulated five percent on the capital invested, while speculation in the domestic debt could have yielded almost twelve percent. In this connection it should be noted that Hamilton concluded his Report with a warning concerning the probable effects of foreign speculation in the domestic debt if measures were not taken to raise the value of domestic securities.

Those who were opposed to foreign loans emphasized the drain of specie that would be produced by payments to Europe and the possibility of foreign influence or intervention in domestic politics in case of default. Although Hamilton shared the fear of foreign intervention, he believed that the use of foreign specie would help to promote the economic independence of the United States. In his opinion profits derived from the investment of European funds in domestic manufacturing, commerce, and agriculture would more than compensate for the money paid out in interest to foreigners. This was a point to which he, of course, devoted considerable attention in his Report on Manufactures. These views were shared by other Americans, and in an article in *The American Museum* in August, 1789, the writer stated that after provision had been made for the payment of interest, "money will be attracted from abroad on terms of the usual interest, employed in commerce agriculture and manufacturing, will yield a profit far superior to the rate of interest, will aid in support of additional taxes, make friends and draw immigrants."[94] For his own part, Hamilton left no doubt concerning his opinion of the importance of foreign capital to the United States, for his proposals included requests for

88. For statements of opposition to reduction, see Ferguson, *Power of the Purse*, 303.

89. Madison to H, November 19, 1789.

90. *The American Museum*, I (May, 1787), 420.

91. *The American Museum*, VI (August, 1789), 97.

92. H to _____, December, 1779–March, 1780; "The Continentalist No. IV," August 30, 1781; "The Federalist No. 30," December 28, 1787.

93. Boyd, *Papers of Thomas Jefferson*, XII, 699–700.

94. *The American Museum*, VI (August, 1789), 94.

European loans amounting to $17,000,000, a sum larger than the total foreign debt outstanding in 1789 including principal and accrued interest.

The fact that Hamilton was not necessarily an innovator is illustrated by his revenue proposals, for he explicitly denied the originality of the plan proposed for raising the money needed to service the foreign and domestic debt. The writings and precedents on which he relied for formulating his views on assumption, discrimination, refunding, and the sinking fund also provided him with ideas for obtaining the funds that would be required to finance such programs. There were, of course, ample precedents in European history for a tariff, and the impost had been a subject of debate and controversy throughout most of the Confederation period. The excise, however, was a more controversial matter. Excise taxes first assumed importance in England under William III. Sir Robert Walpole had subsequently proposed a combination of impost and excise to prevent smuggling. In discussing the controversy raised by Walpole's excise bill, Adam Smith wrote: "Faction, combined with the interest of smuggling merchants, raised so violent, though so unjust, a clamour against that bill, that the minister thought proper to drop it; and from a dread of exciting a clamour of the same kind, none of his successors have dared to resume the project." [95] Several Americans had also maintained that some method in addition to an impost was needed for raising sufficient amounts of revenue. In 1782, Robert Morris had suggested an excise, and at the end of the decade an article in The American Museum criticized the sole reliance on the impost as provided by the Revenue Act of 1789.[96] In 1789 both Madison and Higginson in letters to Hamilton [97] suggested that taxes other than the impost should be imposed before the states acquired a de facto right to levy such taxes.

If the controversies raised by Hamilton's Report have at times tended to obscure the fact that he was not the first to propose many of the ideas which he advanced, the originality of his synthesis cannot be overemphasized. There are few state papers which carry implications for so many aspects of public policy and which at the same time contain such detailed provisions for the implementation of policy. The institutions suggested in the Report, the ideas upon which they were based, and even many of the phrases by which they were described were not always original. But phrases were sometimes put in a context with which their original authors would have found scant sympathy; ideas were sometimes taken from writers whose main emphasis was quite different from Hamilton's; and the institutions that the Report proposed were integrated to form parts of a political and economic system that can only be described as uniquely Hamiltonian.

Treasury Department, January 9, 1790.

[Communicated on January 14, 1790] [98]

[To the Speaker of the House of Representatives]

The Secretary of the Treasury, in obedience to the resolution of the House of Representatives, of the twenty-first day of Septem-

95. Smith, Wealth of Nations, II, 418.

96. See Robert Morris to the President of Congress, July 29, 1782 (Sparks, Diplomatic Correspondence, XII, 230); The American Museum, VI (August, 1789), 96; "An Act for laying a Duty on Goods, Wares, and Merchandises imported into the United States," (1 Stat. 24–27 [July 4, 1789]).

97. Madison to H, November 19, 1789; Higginson to H, November 11, 1789.

98. Journal of the House, I, 141. The footnotes to this document are not intended to be exhaustive. They merely indicate some of the sources of information which were available to H and are discussed in the "Introductory Note."

ber last,[99] has, during the recess of Congress, applied himself to the consideration of a proper plan for the support of the Public Credit, with all the attention which was due to the authority of the House, and to the magnitude of the object.

In the discharge of this duty, he has felt, in no small degree, the anxieties which naturally flow from a just estimate of the difficulty of the task, from a well-founded diffidence of his own qualifications for executing it with success, and from a deep and solemn conviction of the momentous nature of the truth contained in the resolution under which his investigations have been conducted, "That an *adequate* provision for the support of the Public Credit, is a matter of high importance to the honor and prosperity of the United States."

With an ardent desire that his well-meant endeavors may be conducive to the real advantage of the nation, and with the utmost deference to the superior judgment of the House, he now respectfully submits the result of his enquiries and reflections, to their indulgent construction.[100]

99. The House resolved,
"That this House consider an adequate provision for the support of the public credit, as a matter of high importance to the national honor and prosperity.

"*Resolved,* That the Secretary of the Treasury be directed to prepare a plan for that purpose, and to report the same to this House at its next meeting.

"On motion,

"*Ordered,* That the Secretary of the Treasury be directed to apply to the Supreme Executives of the several States, for statements of their public debts; of the funds provided for the payment, in whole or in part, of the principal and interest thereof; and of the amount of the loan-office certificates, or other public securities of the United States, in the State Treasuries respectively; and that he report to the House such of the said documents as he may obtain, at the next session of Congress." (*Journal of the House,* I, 117.)

For H's directive to the governors, see "Treasury Department Circular to the Governors of the States," September 26, 1789.

100. It may or may not be significant that Necker began his speech before the States General in 1789 as follows:

"Lorsqu'on est appellé à se présenter & à se faire entendre au milieu d'une assemblée si auguste & si imposante, une timide émotion, une juste défiance de ses forces sont les premiers sentimens qu'on éprouve, & l'on ne peut être rassuré qu'en se livrant à l'espoir d'obtenir un peu d'indulgence, & de mériter au moins l'intérêt que l'on ne sauroit refuser à des intentions sans reproches: peut-être encore a-t-on besoin d'être soutenu par la grandeur de la circonstance & par l'ascendant d'un sujet qui, en attirant toutes nos pensées, en s'emparant de nous en entier, ne nous laisse pas le temps de nous replier sur nous-mêmes, & ne nous permet pas d'examiner s'il y a quelque proportion entre notre tâche & nos facultés." (*Ouverture des Etats-Généraux,* 21.)

In the opinion of the Secretary, the wisdom of the House, in giving their explicit sanction to the proposition which has been stated, cannot but be applauded by all, who will seriously consider, and trace through their obvious consequences, these plain and undeniable truths.

That exigencies are to be expected to occur, in the affairs of nations, in which there will be a necessity for borrowing.

That loans in times of public danger, especially from foreign war, are found an indispensable resource, even to the wealthiest of them.

And that in a country, which, like this, is possessed of little active wealth, or in other words, little monied capital, the necessity for that resource, must, in such emergencies, be proportionably urgent.[101]

And as on the one hand, the necessity for borrowing in particular emergencies cannot be doubted, so on the other, it is equally evident, that to be able to borrow upon *good terms*, it is essential that the credit of a nation should be well established.

For when the credit of a country is in any degree questionable, it never fails to give an extravagant premium, in one shape or another, upon all the loans it has occasion to make. Nor does the evil end here; the same disadvantage must be sustained upon whatever is to be bought on terms of future payment.

From this constant necessity of *borrowing* and *buying dear*, it is easy to conceive how immensely the expences of a nation, in a course of time, will be augmented by an unsound state of the public credit.

To attempt to enumerate the complicated variety of mischiefs in the whole system of the social œconomy, which proceed from a neglect of the maxims that uphold public credit, and justify the solicitude manifested by the House on this point, would be an improper intrusion on their time and patience.

In so strong a light nevertheless do they appear to the Secretary, that on their due observance at the present critical juncture, materially depends, in his judgment, the individual and aggregate

---

101. H had used a similar expression of the need for loans in H to _____, December, 1779–March, 1780; "The Continentalist No. IV," August 30, 1781; "The Federalist No. 30," December 28, 1787.

prosperity of the citizens of the United States; their relief from the embarrassments they now experience; their character as a People; the cause of good government.

If the maintenance of public credit, then, be truly so important, the next enquiry which suggests itself is, by what means it is to be effected? The ready answer to which question is, by good faith, by a punctual performance of contracts. States, like individuals, who observe their engagements, are respected and trusted: while the reverse is the fate of those, who pursue an opposite conduct.

Every breach of the public engagements, whether from choice or necessity, is in different degrees hurtful to public credit. When such a necessity does truly exist, the evils of it are only to be palliated by a scrupulous attention, on the part of the government, to carry the violation no farther than the necessity absolutely requires, and to manifest, if the nature of the case admits of it, a sincere disposition to make reparation, whenever circumstances shall permit. But with every possible mitigation, credit must suffer, and numerous mischiefs ensue. It is therefore highly important, when an appearance of necessity seems to press upon the public councils, that they should examine well its reality, and be perfectly assured, that there is no method of escaping from it, before they yield to its suggestions. For though it cannot safely be affirmed, that occasions have never existed, or may not exist, in which violations of the public faith, in this respect, are inevitable; yet there is great reason to believe, that they exist far less frequently than precedents indicate; and are oftenest either pretended through levity, or want of firmness, or supposed through want of knowledge.[102] Expedients might often have been devised to effect, consistently with good faith, what has been done in contravention of it. Those who are most commonly creditors of a nation, are, generally speaking, enlightened men; and there are signal examples to warrant a conclusion, that when a candid and fair appeal is made to them, they will understand their true interest too well to refuse their concurrence in such modifications of their claims, as any real necessity may demand.[103]

102. This statement is similar to H's discussion in "Defense of Congress," July, 1783; H to Robert Morris, April 30, 1781.
103. See Higginson to H, November 11, 1789.

While the observance of that good faith, which is the basis of public credit, is recommended by the strongest inducements of political expediency, it is enforced by considerations of still greater authority. There are arguments for it, which rest on the immutable principles of moral obligation. And in proportion as the mind is disposed to contemplate, in the order of Providence, an intimate connection between public virtue and public happiness, will be its repugnancy to a violation of those principles.[104]

This reflection derives additional strength from the nature of the debt of the United States. It was the price of liberty. The faith of America has been repeatedly pledged for it, and with solemnities, that give peculiar force to the obligation. There is indeed reason to regret that it has not hitherto been kept; that the necessities of the war, conspiring with inexperience in the subjects of finance, produced direct infractions; and that the subsequent period has been a continued scene of negative violation, or non-compliance. But a diminution of this regret arises from the reflection, that the last seven years have exhibited an earnest and uniform effort, on the part of the government of the union, to retrieve the national credit, by doing justice to the creditors of the nation; [105] and that the embarrassments of a defective constitution, which defeated this laudable effort, have ceased.

From this evidence of a favorable disposition, given by the former government, the institution of a new one, cloathed with powers competent to calling forth the resources of the community, has excited correspondent expectations. A general belief, accordingly, prevails, that the credit of the United States will quickly be established on the firm foundation of an effectual provision for the existing debt. The influence, which this has had at home, is witnessed by the rapid increase, that has taken place in the market value of the public securities. From January to November, they rose thirty-

104. On July 29, 1782, Robert Morris had written to the President of Congress: "I need no inspiration to show that justice establishes a nation. Neither are the principles of religion necessary to evince that political injustice will receive political chastisement. Religious men will cherish these maxims in proportion to the additional force they derive from divine revelation" (Sparks, *Diplomatic Correspondence*, XII, 220).

105. See "Defense of Congress," July, 1783, in which H uses the same distinction between direct infractions and negative violation and in which he states the solicitude of Congress for the support of public credit.

three and a third per cent, and from that period to this time, they have risen fifty per cent more. And the intelligence from abroad announces effects proportionably favourable to our national credit and consequence.

It cannot but merit particular attention, that among ourselves the most enlightened friends of good government are those, whose expectations are the highest.

To justify and preserve their confidence; to promote the encreasing respectability of the American name; to answer the calls of justice; to restore landed property to its due value; to furnish new resources both to agriculture and commerce; to cement more closely the union of the states; to add to their security against foreign attack; to establish public order on the basis of an upright and liberal policy. These are the great and invaluable ends to be secured, by a proper and adequate provision, at the present period, for the support of public credit.

To this provision we are invited, not only by the general considerations, which have been noticed, but by others of a more particular nature. It will procure to every class of the community some important advantages, and remove some no less important disadvantages.

The advantage to the public creditors from the increased value of that part of their property which constitutes the public debt, needs no explanation.

But there is a consequence of this, less obvious, though not less true, in which every other citizen is interested. It is a well known fact, that in countries in which the national debt is properly funded, and an object of established confidence, it answers most of the purposes of money. Transfers of stock or public debt are there equivalent to payments in specie; or in other words, stock, in the principal transactions of business, passes current as specie. The same thing would, in all probability happen here, under the like circumstances.

The benefits of this are various and obvious.

First. Trade is extended by it; because there is a larger capital to carry it on, and the merchant can at the same time, afford to trade for smaller profits; as his stock, which, when unemployed, brings him in an interest from the government, serves him also as money, when he has a call for it in his commercial operations.

Secondly. Agriculture and manufactures are also promoted by it: For the like reason, that more capital can be commanded to be employed in both; and because the merchant, whose enterprize in foreign trade, gives to them activity and extension, has greater means for enterprize.

Thirdly. The interest of money will be lowered by it; for this is always in a ratio, to the quantity of money, and to the quickness of circulation. This circumstance will enable both the public and individuals to borrow on easier and cheaper terms.

And from the combination of these effects, additional aids will be furnished to labour, to industry, and to arts of every kind.

But these good effects of a public debt are only to be looked for, when, by being well funded, it has acquired an *adequate* and *stable* value. Till then, it has rather a contrary tendency. The fluctuation and insecurity incident to it in an unfunded state, render it a mere commodity, and a precarious one. As such, being only an object of occasional and particular speculation, all the money applied to it is so much diverted from the more useful channels of circulation, for which the thing itself affords no substitute: So that, in fact, one serious inconvenience of an unfunded debt is, that it contributes to the scarcity of money.[106]

This distinction which has been little if at all attended to, is of the greatest moment. It involves a question immediately interesting to every part of the community; which is no other than this— Whether the public debt, by a provision for it on true principles, shall be rendered a *substitute* for money; or whether, by being left as it is, or by being provided for in such a manner as will wound those principles, and destroy confidence, it shall be suffered to continue, as it is, a pernicious drain of our cash from the channels of productive industry.

The effect, which the funding of the public debt, on right principles, would have upon landed property, is one of the circumstances attending such an arrangement, which has been least

106. Compare with *Ouverture des Etats-Généraux*, 43; Postlethwayt, *Universal Dictionary*, I, 15; Sparks, *Life of Gouverneur Morris*, III, 472.

adverted to, though it deserves the most particular attention. The present depreciated state of that species of property is a serious calamity. The value of cultivated lands, in most of the states, has fallen since the revolution from 25 to 50 per cent. In those farthest south, the decrease is still more considerable. Indeed, if the representations, continually received from that quarter, may be credited, lands there will command no price, which may not be deemed an almost total sacrifice.

This decrease, in the value of lands, ought, in a great measure, to be attributed to the scarcity of money. Consequently whatever produces an augmentation of the monied capital of the country, must have a proportional effect in raising that value. The beneficial tendency of a funded debt, in this respect, has been manifested by the most decisive experience in Great-Britain.

The proprietors of lands would not only feel the benefit of this increase in the value of their property, and of a more prompt and better sale, when they had occasion to sell; but the necessity of selling would be, itself, greatly diminished. As the same cause would contribute to the facility of loans, there is reason to believe, that such of them as are indebted, would be able through that resource, to satisfy their more urgent creditors.

It ought not however to be expected, that the advantages, described as likely to result from funding the public debt, would be instantaneous. It might require some time to bring the value of stock to its natural level, and to attach to it that fixed confidence, which is necessary to its quality as money. Yet the late rapid rise of the public securities encourages an expectation, that the progress of stock to the desireable point, will be much more expeditious than could have been foreseen. And as in the mean time it will be increasing in value, there is room to conclude, that it will, from the outset, answer many of the purposes in contemplation. Particularly it seems to be probable, that from creditors, who are not themselves necessitous, it will early meet with a ready reception in payment of debts, at its current price.

Having now taken a concise view of the inducements to a proper provision for the public debt, the next enquiry which presents itself is, what ought to be the nature of such a provision? This requires some preliminary discussions.

It is agreed on all hands, that that part of the debt which has been contracted abroad, and is denominated the foreign debt, ought to be provided for, according to the precise terms of the contracts relating to it. The discussions, which can arise, therefore, will have reference essentially to the domestic part of it, or to that which has been contracted at home. It is to be regretted, that there is not the same unanimity of sentiment on this part, as on the other.

The Secretary has too much deference for the opinions of every part of the community, not to have observed one, which has, more than once, made its appearance in the public prints, and which is occasionally to be met with in conversation. It involves this question, whether a discrimination ought not to be made between original holders of the public securities, and present possessors, by purchase. Those who advocate a discrimination are for making a full provision for the securities of the former, at their nominal value; but contend, that the latter ought to receive no more than the cost to them, and the interest: And the idea is sometimes suggested of making good the difference to the primitive possessor.[107]

In favor of this scheme, it is alledged, that it would be unreasonable to pay twenty shillings in the pound, to one who had not given more for it than three or four. And it is added, that it would be hard to aggravate the misfortune of the first owner, who, probably through necessity, parted with his property at so great a loss, by obliging him to contribute to the profit of the person, who had speculated on his distresses.

The Secretary, after the most mature reflection on the force of this argument, is induced to reject the doctrine it contains, as equally unjust and impolitic, as highly injurious, even to the original holders of public securities; as ruinous to public credit.

It is inconsistent with justice, because in the first place, it is a breach of contract; in violation of the rights of a fair purchaser.

The nature of the contract in its origin, is, that the public will pay the sum expressed in the security, to the first holder, or his

107. Speculation in loan office certificates had led some observers to propose the scaling down of the debt. As early as July 29, 1782, Robert Morris had opposed this view in a report to Congress (Sparks, *Diplomatic Correspondence*, XII, 234). Later the idea of reimbursing the original creditor was suggested by Pelatiah Webster in "A Seventh Essay on Free Trade and Finance" published in Philadelphia, January 10, 1785 (Webster, *Political Essays*, 269–305).

assignee. The *intent*, in making the security assignable, is, that the proprietor may be able to make use of his property, by selling it for as much as it *may be worth in the market*, and that the buyer may be *safe* in the purchase.

Every buyer therefore stands exactly in the place of the seller, has the same right with him to the identical sum expressed in the security, and having acquired that right, by fair purchase, and in conformity to the original *agreement* and *intention* of the government, his claim cannot be disputed, without manifest injustice.

That he is to be considered as a fair purchaser, results from this: Whatever necessity the seller may have been under, was occasioned by the government, in not making a proper provision for its debts. The buyer had no agency in it, and therefore ought not to suffer. He is not even chargeable with having taken an undue advantage. He paid what the commodity was worth in the market, and took the risks of reimbursement upon himself. He of course gave a fair equivalent, and ought to reap the benefit of his hazard; a hazard which was far from inconsiderable, and which, perhaps, turned on little less than a revolution in government.

That the case of those, who parted with their securities from necessity, is a hard one, cannot be denied. But whatever complaint of injury, or claim of redress, they may have, respects the government solely. They have not only nothing to object to the persons who relieved their necessities, by giving them the current price of their property, but they are even under an implied condition to contribute to the reimbursement of those persons.[108] They knew, that by the terms of the contract with themselves, the public were bound to pay to those, to whom they should convey their title, the sums stipulated to be paid to them; and, that as citizens of the United States, they were to bear their proportion of the contribution for that purpose. This, by the act of assignment, they tacitly engage to do; and if they had an option, they could not, with integrity or good faith, refuse to do it, without the consent of those to whom they sold.

But though many of the original holders sold from necessity, it

108. Robert Morris in his letter of July 29, 1782, to the President of Congress had written that the purchaser: "in giving the creditor money for his debt [has] at least afforded him some relief, which he could not obtain elsewhere" (Sparks, *Diplomatic Correspondence*, XII, 234–35).

does not follow, that this was the case with all of them. It may well be supposed, that some of them did it either through want of confidence in an eventual provision, or from the allurements of some profitable speculation. How shall these different classes be discriminated from each other? How shall it be ascertained, in any case, that the money, which the original holder obtained for his security, was not more beneficial to him, than if he had held it to the pressent time, to avail himself of the provision which shall be made? How shall it be known, whether if the purchaser had employed his money in some other way, he would not be in a better situation, than by having applied it in the purchase of securities, though he should now receive their full amount? And if neither of these things can be known, how shall it be determined whether a discrimination, independent of the breach of contract, would not do a real injury to purchasers; and if it included a compensation to the primitive proprietors, would not give them an advantage, to which they had no equitable pretension.

It may well be imagined, also, that there are not wanting instances, in which individuals, urged by a present necessity, parted with the securities received by them from the public, and shortly after replaced them with others, as an indemnity for their first loss. Shall they be deprived of the indemnity which they have endeavoured to secure by so provident an arrangement?

Questions of this sort, on a close inspection, multiply themselves without end, and demonstrate the injustice of a discrimination, even on the most subtile calculations of equity, abstracted from the obligation of contract.

The difficulties too of regulating the details of a plan for that purpose, which would have even the semblance of equity, would be found immense. It may well be doubted whether they would not be insurmountable, and replete with such absurd, as well as inequitable consequences, as to disgust even the proposers of the measure.

As a specimen of its capricious operation, it will be sufficient to notice the effect it would have upon two persons, who may be supposed two years ago to have purchased, each, securities at three shillings in the pound, and one of them to retain those bought by him, till the discrimination should take place; the other to have parted with those bought by him, within a month past, at nine shillings. The former, who had had most confidence in the government, would in this case only receive at the rate of three shillings and the interest; while the latter, who had had less confidence would receive *for what cost him the same money* at the rate of nine shillings, and his representative, *standing in his place*, would be entitled to a like rate.

The impolicy of a discrimination results from two considerations; one, that it proceeds upon a principle destructive of that *quality* of the public debt, or the stock of the nation, which is essential to its capacity for answering the purposes of money—that is the *security* of *transfer;* the other, that as well on this account, as because it includes a breach of faith, it renders property in the funds less valuable; consequently induces lenders to demand a higher premium for what they lend, and produces every other inconvenience of a bad state of public credit.

It will be perceived at first sight, that the transferable quality of stock is essential to its operation as money, and that this depends on the idea of complete security to the transferree, and a firm persuasion, that no distinction can in any circumstances be made between him and the original proprietor.

The precedent of an invasion of this fundamental principle, would of course tend to deprive the community of an advantage, with which no temporary saving could bear the least comparison.[109]

And it will as readily be perceived, that the same cause would operate a diminution of the value of stock in the hands of the first, as well as of every other holder. The price, which any man, who should incline to purchase, would be willing to give for it, would be in a compound ratio to the immediate profit it afforded, and to the chance of the continuance of his profit. If there was supposed to be any hazard of the latter, the risk would be taken into the calculation, and either there would be no purchase at all, or it would be at a proportionably less price.[110]

109. On similar grounds Necker had criticized the proposal to reduce the interest on debts incurred under circumstances unfavorable to the state. In this connection he said: "Vous verrez, . . . que l'utilité de cette opération n'auroit aucune proportion avec les inconvéniens qui résulteroient d'une atteinte donnée aux principes universels de bonne foi nationale . . . & l'Etat racheteroit long-temps le bénéfice d'un jour" (*Ouverture des Etats-Généraux*, 41–42).

110. Necker had said, "& comme tout ce qui est soumis à une opinion arbitraire ne présente à l'esprit aucune circonscription positive, on forceroit les

For this diminution of the value of stock, every person, who should be about to lend to the government, would demand a compensation; and would add to the actual difference, between the nominal and the market value, and equivalent for the chance of greater decrease; which, in a precarious state of public credit, is always to be taken into the account.

Every compensation of this sort, it is evident, would be an absolute loss to the government.

In the preceding discussion of the impolicy of a discrimination, the injurious tendency of it to those, who continue to be the holders of the securities, they received from the government, has been explained. Nothing need be added, on this head, except that this is an additional and interesting light, in which the injustice of the measure may be seen. It would not only divest present proprietors by purchase, of the rights they had acquired under the sanction of public faith, but it would depreciate the property of the remaining original holders.

It is equally unnecessary to add any thing to what has been already said to demonstrate the fatal influence, which the principle of discrimination would have on the public credit.

But there is still a point in view in which it will appear perhaps even more exceptionable, than in either of the former. It would be repugnant to an express provision of the Constitution of the United States. This provision is, that "all debts contracted and engagements entered into before the adoption of that Constitution shall be as valid against the United States under it, as under the confederation." [111] which amounts to a constitutional ratification of the contracts respecting the debt, in the state in which they existed under the confederation. And resorting to that standard, there can be no doubt, that the rights of assignees and original holders, must be considered as equal.

In exploding thus fully the principle of discrimination, the Secretary is happy in reflecting, that he is the only advocate of what has been already sanctioned by the formal and express authority of the government of the Union, in these emphatic terms—"The re-

prêteurs à nettre à l'avenir au rang de leurs calculs le risque d'une pareille inquisition" (*Ouverture des Etats-Généraux*, 42).

111. Article VI. H's quotation differs slightly from the text of the Constitution.

maining class of creditors (say Congress in their circular address to the states, of the 26th of April 1783) is composed, partly of such of our fellow-citizens as originally lent to the public the use of their funds, or have since manifested *most confidence* in their country, by receiving transfers from the lenders; and partly of those, whose property has been either advanced or assumed for the public service. To *discriminate* the merits of these several descriptions of creditors, would be a task equally unnecessary and invidious. If the voice of humanity plead more loudly in favor of some than of others, the voice of policy, no less than of justice, pleads in favor of all. A WISE NATION will never permit those who relieve the wants of their country, or who *rely most* on its *faith,* its *firmness,* and its *resources,* when either of them is distrusted, to suffer by the event." [112]

The Secretary concluding, that a discrimination, between the different classes of creditors of the United States, cannot with propriety be *made,* proceeds to examine whether a difference ought to be permitted to *remain* between them, and another description of public creditors—Those of the states individually.

The Secretary, after mature reflection on this point, entertains a full conviction, that an assumption of the debts of the particular states by the union, and a like provision for them, as for those of the union, will be a measure of sound policy and substantial justice.

It would, in the opinion of the Secretary, contribute, in an eminent degree, to an orderly, stable and satisfactory arrangement of the national finances.

Admitting, as ought to be the case, that a provision must be made in some way or other, for the entire debt; it will follow, that no greater revenues will be required, whether that provision be made wholly by the United States, or partly by them, and partly by the states separately.

The principal question then must be, whether such a provision cannot be more conveniently and effectually made, by one general plan issuing from one authority, than by different plans originating in different authorities.

In the first case there can be no competition for resources; in the

112. *JCC,* XXIV, 282–83.

last, there must be such a competition.[113] The consequences of this, without the greatest caution on both sides, might be interfering regulations, and thence collision and confusion. Particular branches of industry might also be oppressed by it. The most productive objects of revenue are not numerous. Either these must be wholly engrossed by one side, which might lessen the efficacy of the provisions by the other; or both must have recourse to the same objects in different modes, which might occasion an accumulation upon them, beyond what they could properly bear. If this should not happen, the caution requisite to avoiding it, would prevent the revenue's deriving the full benefit of each object. The danger of interference and of excess would be apt to impose restraints very unfriendly to the complete command of those resources, which are the most convenient; and to compel the having recourse to others, less eligible in themselves, and less agreeable to the community.

The difficulty of an effectual command of the public resources, in case of separate provisions for the debt, may be seen in another, and perhaps more striking light. It would naturally happen that different states, from local considerations, would in some instances have recourse to different objects, in others, to the same objects, in different degrees, for procuring the funds of which they stood in need. It is easy to conceive how this diversity would affect the aggregate revenue of the country. By the supposition, articles which yielded a full supply in some states, would yield nothing, or an insufficient product, in others. And hence the public revenue would not derive the full benefit of those articles, from state regulations. Neither could the deficiencies be made good by those of the union. It is a provision of the national constitution, that "all duties, imposts and excises, shall be uniform throughout the United

113. Earlier H had used this argument in support of exclusive Federal taxation of foreign trade. During the Constitutional Convention H had proposed exclusive Federal jurisdiction over both branches of revenue. In essay 36 of *The Federalist* he had stated that Federal excises would be collected on articles not previously taxed by the state or by state officers. Higginson, on the other hand, supported a Federal excise and Federal excise officers as a means of securing the impost against fraud (Higginson to H, November 11, 1789). Gouverneur Morris discussed similar problems of taxation but arrived at different conclusions (Sparks, *Life of Gouverneur Morris*, III, 470–71).

States." [114] And as the general government would be under a necessity from motives of policy, of paying regard to the duty, which
may have been previously imposed upon any article, though but in
a single state, it would be constrained, either to refrain wholly from
any further imposition, upon such article, where it had been already rated as high as was proper, or to confine itself to the difference between the existing rate, and what the article would
reasonably bear. Thus the pre-occupancy of an article by a single
state, would tend to arrest or abridge the impositions of the union
on that article. And as it is supposeable, that a great variety of
articles might be placed in this situation, by dissimilar arrangements
of the particular states, it is evident, that the aggregate revenue of
the country would be likely to be very materially contracted by
the plan of separate provisions.

If all the public creditors receive their dues from one source,
distributed with an equal hand, their interest will be the same. And
having the same interests, they will unite in the support of the fiscal
arrangements of the government: As these, too, can be made with
more convenience, where there is no competition: These circumstances combined will insure to the revenue laws a more ready and
more satisfactory execution.

If on the contrary there are distinct provisions, there will be
distinct interests, drawing different ways. That union and concert
of views, among the creditors, which in every government is of
great importance to their security, and to that of public credit, will
not only not exist, but will be likely to give place to mutual jealousy
and opposition. [115] And from this cause, the operation of the systems
which may be adopted, both by the particular states, and by the
union, with relation to their respective debts, will be in danger of
being counteracted.

There are several reasons, which render it probable, that the
situation of the state creditors would be worse, than that of the
creditors of the union, if there be not a national assumption of the
state debts. Of these it will be sufficient to mention two; one, that
a principal branch of revenue is exclusively vested in the union; [116]

114. Article I, Section 8.
115. Robert Morris to the President of Congress, August 28, 1781 (Sparks,
Diplomatic Correspondence, XI, 443).
116. Although the extent to which the impost had been used to service state

the other, that a state must always be checked in the imposition of taxes on articles of consumption, from the want of power to extend the same regulation to the other states, and from the tendency of partial duties to injure its industry and commerce. Should the state creditors stand upon a less eligible footing than the others, it is unnatural to expect they would see with pleasure a provision for them. The influence which their dissatisfaction might have, could not but operate injuriously, both for the creditors, and the credit, of the United States.

Hence it is even the interest of the creditors of the union, that those of the individual states should be comprehended in a general provision. Any attempt to secure to the former either exclusive or peculiar advantages, would materially hazard their interests.

Neither would it be just, that one class of the public creditors should be more favoured than the other. The objects for which both descriptions of the debt were contracted, are in the main the same. Indeed a great part of the particular debts of the States has arisen from assumptions by them on account of the union. And it is most equitable, that there should be the same measure of retribution for all.[117]

There is an objection, however, to an assumption of the state debts, which deserves particular notice. It may be supposed, that it would increase the difficulty of an equitable settlement between them and the United States.

The principles of that settlement, whenever they shall be discussed, will require all the moderation and wisdom of the government. In the opinion of the Secretary, that discussion, till further lights are obtained, would be premature.

All therefore which he would now think adviseable on the point in question, would be, that the amount of the debts assumed and provided for, should be charged to the respective states, to abide an eventual arrangement. This, the United States, as assignees to the creditors, would have an indisputable right to do.

---

debts may have been exaggerated, several writers used this argument for assumption.

117. An article in the [New York] *Gazette of the United States*, November 25, 1789, cited the injustice of unequal treatment of various types of creditors and said: "There is but one remedy for this evil let the United States assume the whole public debt, it was incurred for them and in equity they ought to see it funded."

But as it might be a satisfaction to the House to have before them some plan for the liquidation of accounts between the union and its members, which, including the assumption of the state debts, would consist with equity: The Secretary will submit in this place such thoughts on the subject, as have occurred to his own mind, or been suggested to him,[118] most compatible, in his judgment, with the end proposed.

Let each state be charged with all the money advanced to it out of the treasury of the United States, liquidated according to the specie value, at the time of each advance, with interest at six per cent.

Let it also be charged with the amount, in specie value, of all its securities which shall be assumed, with the interest upon them to the time, when interest shall become payable by the United States.

Let it be credited for all monies paid and articles furnished to the United States, and for all other expenditures during the war, either towards general or particular defence, whether authorized or unauthorized by the United States; the whole liquidated to specie value, and bearing an interest of six per cent. from the several times at which the several payments, advances and expenditures accrued.

And let all sums of continental money now in the treasuries of the respective states, which shall be paid into the treasury of the United States, be credited at specie value.

Upon a statement of the accounts according to these principles, there can be little doubt, that balances would appear in favor of all the states, against the United States.

To equalize the contributions of the states, let each be then charged with its proportion of the aggregate of those balances, according to some equitable ratio, to be devised for that purpose.

If the contributions should be found disproportionate, the result of this adjustment would be, that some states would be creditors, some debtors to the union.

Should this be the case, as it will be attended with less inconvenience for the United States, to have to pay balances to, than to receive them from the particular states, it may perhaps, be practicable to effect the former by a second process, in the nature of a

118. See Oliver Wolcott, Jr., to H, November 29, 1789.

transfer of the amount of the debts of debtor states, to the credit of creditor states, observing the ratio by which the first apportionment shall have been made. This, whilst it would destroy the balances due from the former, would increase those due to the latter. These to be provided for by the United States, at a reasonable interest, but not to be transferable.

The expediency of this second process must depend on a knowledge of the result of the first. If the inequalities should be too great, the arrangement may be impracticable, without unduly increasing the debt of the United States. But it is not likely, that this would be the case. It is also to be remarked, that though this second process might not, upon the principle of apportionment, bring the thing to the point aimed at, yet it may approach so nearly to it, as to avoid essentially the embarrassment, of having considerable balances to collect from any of the states.

The whole of this arrangment to be under the superintendence of commissioners, vested with equitable discretion, and final authority.

The operation of the plan is exemplified in the schedule A.

The general principle of it seems to be equitable, for it appears difficult to conceive a good reason, why the expences for the particular defence of a part in a common war, should not be a common charge, as well as those incurred professedly for the general defence. The defence of each part is that of the whole; and unless all the expenditures are brought into a common mass, the tendency must be, to add, to the calamities suffered, by being the most exposed to the ravages of war, an increase of burthens.

This plan seems to be susceptible of no objection, which does not belong to every other, that proceeds on the idea of a final adjustment of accounts. The difficulty of settling a ratio, is common to all. This must, probably, either be sought for in the proportions of the requisitions, during the war, or in the decision of commissioners appointed with plenary power. The rule prescribed in the Constitution, with regard to representation and direct taxes, would evidently not be applicable to the situation of parties, during the period in question.

The existing debt of the United States is excluded from the

computation, as it ought to be, because it will be provided for out of a general fund.

The only discussion of a preliminary kind, which remains, relates to the distinctions of the debt into principal and interest. It is well known, that the arrears of the latter bear a large proportion to the amount of the former. The immediate payment of these arrears is evidently impracticable, and a question arises, what ought to be done with them?

There is good reason to conclude, that the impressions of many are more favorable to the claim of the principal than to that of the interest; at least so far, as to produce an opinion, that an inferior provision might suffice for the latter.

But to the Secretary, this opinion does not appear to be well founded. His investigations of the subject, have led him to a conclusion, that the arrears of interest have pretensions, at least equal to the principal.

The liquidated debt, traced to its origin, falls under two principal discriminations. One, relating to loans; the other to services performed and articles supplied.

The part arising from loans, was at first made payable at fixed periods, which have long since elapsed, with an early option to lenders, either to receive back their money at the expiration of those periods, or to continue it at interest, 'till the whole amount of continental bills circulating should not exceed the sum in circulation at the time of each loan. This contingency, in the sense of the contract, never happened; and the presumption is, that the creditors preferred continuing their money indefinitely at interest, to receiving it in a depreciated and depreciating state.

The other parts of it were chiefly for objects, which ought to have been paid for at the time, that is, when the services were performed or the supplies furnished; and were not accompanied with any contract for interest.

But by different acts of government and administration, concurred in by the creditors, these parts of the debt have been converted into a capital, bearing an interest of six per cent. per annum, but without any definite period of redemption. A portion of the loan-office debt has been exchanged for new securities of that import. And the whole of it seems to have acquired that character, after the expiration of the periods prefixed for re-payment.

If this view of the subject be a just one, the capital of the debt of the United States, may be considered in the light of an annuity at the rate of six per cent. per annum, redeemable at the pleasure of the government, by payment of the principal. For it seems to be a clear position, that when a public contracts a debt payable with interest, without any precise time being stipulated or understood for payment of the capital, that time is a matter of pure discretion with the government, which is at liberty to consult its own convenience respecting it, taking care to pay the interest with punctuality.

Wherefore, as long as the United States should pay the interest of their debt, as it accrued, their creditors would have no right to demand the principal.

But with regard to the arrears of interest, the case is different. These are now due, and those to whom they are due, have a right to claim immediate payment. To say, that it would be impracticable to comply, would not vary the nature of the right. Nor can this idea of impracticability be honorably carried further, than to justify the proposition of a new contract upon the basis of a commutation of that right for an equivalent. This equivalent too ought to be a real and fair one. And what other fair equivalent can be imagined for the detention of money, but a reasonable interest? Or what can be the standard of that interest, but the market rate, or the rate which the government pays in ordinary cases?

From this view of the matter, which appears to be the accurate and true one, it will follow, that the arrears of interest are entitled to an equal provision with the principal of the debt.

The result of the foregoing discussions is this—That there ought to be no discrimination between the original holders of the debt, and present possessors by purchase—That it is expedient, there should be an assumption of the state debts by the Union, and that the arrears of interest should be provided for on an equal footing with the principal.

The next enquiry, in order, towards determining the nature of a proper provision, respects the quantum of the debt, and the present rates of interest.

The debt of the union is distinguishable into foreign and domestic.

	Dollars.	Cents.

The foreign debt as stated in the schedule
B, amounts to principal   10,070,307
bearing an interest of four, and partly an
interest of five per cent.

Arrears of interest to the last of December,
1789, ...   1,640,071 62

     Making together, dollars   11,710,378 62

The domestic debt may be sub-divided into
liquidated and unliquidated; principal and interest.

The principal of the liquidated part, as stated
in schedule C, amounts to 27,383,917 74
bearing an interest of six per cent.

The arrears of interest as stated in the sched-
ule D. to the end of 1790, amount to . . .   13,030,168 20

    Making together, dollars   40,414,085 94

This includes all that has been paid in indents (except what has
come into the treasury of the United States) which, in the opinion
of the Secretary, can be considered in no other light, than as interest due.

The unliquidated part of the domestic debt, which consists
chiefly of the continental bills of credit, is not ascertained, but may
be estimated at 2,000,000 dollars.

These several sums constitute the whole of the debt of the
United States, amounting together to 54,124,464 dollars, and 56
cents.

That of the individual states is not equally well ascertained. The
schedule E. shews the extent to which it has been ascertained by
returns pursuant to the order of the House of the 21st September
last; [119] but this not comprehending all the states, the residue must
be estimated from less authentic information. The Secretary, however, presumes, that the total amount may be safely stated at 25
millions of dollars, principal and interest. The present rate of interest of the state debts is in general, the same with that of the
domestic debt of the union.

On the supposition, that the arrears of interest ought to be pro-

119. For the House order, see "Treasury Department Circular to the Governors of the States," September 26, 1789, note 2.

vided for, on the same terms with the principal, the annual amount of the interest, which, at the existing rates, would be payable on the entire mass of the public debt, would be,

	Dollars.	Cents.
On the foreign debt, computing the interest on the principal, as it stands, and allowing four per cent on the arrears of interest, ...	542,599	66
On the domestic debt, including that of the states, ...	4,044,845	15
Making together, dollars	4,587,444	81

The interesting problem now occurs. Is it in the power of the United States, consistently with those prudential considerations, which ought not to be overlooked, to make a provision equal to the purpose of funding the whole debt, at the rates of interest which it now bears, in addition to the sum which will be necessary for the current service of the government? [120]

The Secretary will not say that such provision would exceed the abilities of the country; but he is clearly of opinion, that to make it, would require the extension of taxation to a degree, and to objects, which the true interest of the public creditors forbids. It is therefore to be hoped, and even to be expected, that they will chearfully concur in such modifications of their claims, on fair and equitable principles, as will facilitate to the government an arrangement substantial, durable and satisfactory to the community. The importance of the last characteristic will strike every discerning mind. No plan, however flattering in appearance, to which it did not belong, could be truly entitled to confidence.

It will not be forgotten, that exigencies may, ere long, arise, which would call for resources greatly beyond what is now deemed sufficient for the current service; and that, should the faculties of the country be exhausted or even *strained* to provide for the public debt, there could be less reliance on the sacredness of the provision.[121]

120. For example, on November 11, 1789, Higginson wrote to H: "Though it were true, that by Imposts & excises, when extended as far as Our case will admit, & duly & exclusively collected by the Union, a sufficient Revenue may be raised to pay the interest on the public Debts, including those of the several States, & to support the federal government; it is a very important Question how far it should be applied to the first of those uses."

121. See H to Robert Morris, April 30, 1781.

But while the Secretary yields to the force of these considerations, he does not lose sight of those fundamental principles of good faith, which dictate, that every practicable exertion ought to be made, scrupulously to fulfil the engagements of the government; that no change in the rights of its creditors ought to be attempted without their voluntary consent; and that this consent ought to be voluntary in fact, as well as in name. Consequently, that every proposal of a change ought to be in the shape of an appeal to their reason and to their interest; not to their necessities.[122] To this end it is requisite, that a fair equivalent should be offered for what may be asked to be given up, and unquestionable security for the remainder. Without this, an alteration, consistently with the credit and honor of the nation, would be impracticable.

It remains to see, what can be proposed in conformity to these views.

It has been remarked, that the capital of the debt of the union is to be viewed in the light of an annuity at the rate of six per cent. per annum, redeemable at the pleasure of the government, by payment of the principal. And it will not be required, that the arrears of interest should be considered in a more favourable light. The same character, in general, may be applied to the debts of the individual states.

This view of the subject admits, that the United States would have it in their power to avail themselves of any fall in the market rate of interest, for reducing that of the debt.[123]

This property of the debt is favourable to the public; unfavourable to the creditor. And may facilitate an arrangement for the reduction of interest, upon the basis of a fair equivalent.

Probabilities are always a rational ground of contract. The Sec-

122. In his letter of November 25, 1789, to H Bingham used the same argument in a different context: "Great attention should be paid to give Satisfaction to the public Creditors by making Such Proposals to them, as are consistent with the Principles of Justice of Equity especially, as they will constitute an essential part of the monied Interest of the Country to whom Government will often be compelled to have recourse; To take Advantage of their Necessities, would be to lose their confidence."

123. In his letter to H of November 25, 1789, Bingham had said: "By conditioning that the Annuities should be redeemable, Government will have it in its power to take Advantage of the Fall of Interest below 6⅞%." Bingham had considered the debts as convertible into annuities of this type rather than as equivalent to such annuities.

retary conceives, that there is good reason to believe, if effectual measures are taken to establish public credit, that the government rate of interest in the United States, will, in a very short time, fall at least as low as five per cent. and that in a period not exceeding twenty years, it will sink still lower, probably to four.

There are two principal causes which will be likely to produce this effect; one, the low rate of interest in Europe; the other, the increase of the monied capital of the nation, by the funding of the public debt.

From three to four per cent. is deemed good interest in several parts of Europe. Even less is deemed so, in some places. And it is on the decline; the increasing plenty of money continually tending to lower it. It is presumable, that no country will be able to borrow of foreigners upon better terms, than the United States, because none can, perhaps, afford so good security. Our situation exposes us less, than that of any other nation, to those casualties, which are the chief causes of expence; our incumbrances, in proportion to our real means, are less, though these cannot immediately be brought so readily into action, and our progress in resources from the early state of the country, and the immense tracts of unsettled territory, must necessarily exceed that of any other. The advantages of this situation have already engaged the attention of the European money-lenders, particularly among the Dutch. And as they become better understood, they will have the greater influence. Hence as large a proportion of the cash of Europe as may be wanted, will be, in a certain sense, in our market, for the use of government. And this will naturally have the effect of a reduction of the rate of interest, not indeed to the level of the places, which send their money to market, but to something much nearer to it, than our present rate.

The influence which the funding of the debt is calculated to have, in lowering interest, has been already remarked and explained. It is hardly possible, that it should not be materially affected by such an increase of the monied capital of the nation, as would result from the proper funding of seventy millions of dollars. But the probability of a decrease in the rate of interest, acquires confirmation from facts, which existed prior to the revolution. It is well known, that in some of the states, money might with facility be borrowed, on good security, at five per cent. and, not unfrequently, even at less.

The most enlightened of the public creditors will be most sensible of the justness of this view of the subject, and of the propriety of the use which will be made of it.

The Secretary, in pursuance of it, will assume, as a probability, sufficiently great to be a ground of calculation, both on the part of the government and of its creditors—That the interest of money in the United States will, in five years, fall to five per cent. and, in twenty, to four. The probability, in the mind of the Secretary, is rather that the fall may be more rapid and more considerable; but he prefers a mean, as most likely to engage the assent of the creditors, and more equitable in itself; because it is predicated on probabilities, which may err on one side, as well as on the other.

Premising these things, the Secretary submits to the House, the expediency of proposing a loan to the full amount of the debt, as well of the particular states, as of the union, upon the following terms.[124]

First—That for every hundred dollars subscribed, payable in the debt (as well interest as principal) the subscribed be entitled, at his option, either

To have two thirds funded at an annuity, or yearly interest of six per cent, redeemable at the pleasure of the government, by payment of the principal; and to receive the other third in lands in the Western Territory, at the rate of twenty cents per acre. Or,

To have the whole sum funded at an annuity or yearly interest of four per cent. irredeemable by any payment exceeding five dollars per annum on account both of principal and interest; and to receive, as a compensation for the reduction of interest, fifteen dollars and eighty cents, payable in lands, as in the preceding case. Or

To have sixty-six dollars and two thirds of a dollar funded immediately at an annuity or yearly interest of six per cent. irredeemable by any payment exceeding four dollars and two thirds of a dollar per annum, on account both of principal and interest; and to have, at the end of ten years, twenty-six dollars and eighty-eight cents, funded at the like interest and rate of redemption. Or

To have an annuity for the remainder of life, upon the contingency of living to a given age, not less distant than ten years, computing interest at four per cent. Or

124. See the "Introductory Note" to this document.

To have an annuity for the remainder of life, upon the contingency of the survivorship of the youngest of two persons, computing interest, in this case also, at four per cent.

In addition to the foregoing loan, payable wholly in the debt, the Secretary would propose, that one should be opened for ten millions of dollars, on the following plan.

That for every hundred dollars subscribed, payable one half in specie, and the other half in debt (as well principal as interest) the subscriber be entitled to an annuity or yearly interest of five per cent. irredeemable by any payment exceeding six dollars per annum, on account both of principal and interest.

The principles and operation of these different plans may now require explanation.

The first is simply a proposition for paying one third of the debt in land, and funding the other two thirds, at the existing rate of interest, and upon the same terms of redemption, to which it is at present subject.

Here is no conjecture, no calculation of probabilities. The creditor is offered the advantage of making his interest principal, and he is asked to facilitate to the government an effectual provision for his demands, by accepting a third part of them in land, at a fair valuation.

The general price, at which the western lands have been, heretofore, sold, has been a dollar per acre in public securities; but at the time the principal purchases were made, these securities were worth, in the market, less than three shillings in the pound. The nominal price, therefore, would not be the proper standard, under present circumstances, nor would the precise specie value then given, be a just rule. Because, as the payments were to be made by instalments, and the securities were, at the times of the purchases, extremely low, the probability of a moderate rise must be presumed to have been taken into the account. Twenty cents, therefore, seem to bear an equitable proportion to the two considerations of value at the time, and likelihood of increase.

It will be understood, that upon this plan, the public retains the advantage of availing itself of any fall in the market rate of interest, for reducing that upon the debt, which is perfectly just, as no present sacrifice, either in the quantum of the principal, or in the rate of interest, is required from the creditor.

The inductment to the measure is, the payment of one third of the debt in land.[125]

The second plan is grounded upon the supposition, that interest, in five years, will fall to five per cent. in fifteen more, to four. As the capital remains entire, but bearing an interest of four per cent. only, compensation is to be made to the creditor, for the interest of two per cent. per annum for five years, and of one per cent, per annum, for fifteen years, to commence at the distance of five years. The present value of these two sums or annuities, computed according to the terms of the supposition, is, by strict calculation, fifteen dollars and seven hundred and ninety-two thousandth parts of a dollar; a fraction less than the sum proposed.

The inducement to the measure here is, the reduction of interest to a rate, more within the compass of a convenient provision; and the payment of the compensation in lands.

The inducements to the individual are—the accommodation afforded to the public, the high probability of a complete equivalent —the chance even of gain, should the rate of interest fall, either more speedily or in a greater degree, than the calculation supposes. Should it fall to five per cent. sooner than five years; should it fall lower than five before the additional fifteen were expired; or should it fall below four, previous to the payment of the debt, there would be, in each case, an absolute profit to the creditor. As his capital will remain entire, the value of it will increase, with every decrease of the rate of interest.

The third plan proceeds upon the like supposition of a successive fall in the rate of interest. And upon that supposition offers an equivalent to the creditor. One hundred dollars, bearing an interest of six per cent. for five years; of five per cent. for fifteen years, and thenceforth of four per cent. (these being the successive rates of interest in the market) is

equal to a capital of . . . . . . 122 dollars, 510725 parts,

125. The use of western lands in extinguishing the debt had been suggested not only by H (H to Nathaniel Chipman, July 22, 1788), but also by precedents under the Confederation, Thomas Paine in *Common Sense,* and Madison in his letter to H of November 19, 1789.

bearing an interest of four per cent. which, converted into a capital, bearing a fixed rate of interest

of six per cent, is equal to .   .   .   . 81 dollars, 6738166 parts.

The difference between sixty-six dollars and two thirds of a dollar (the sum to be funded immediately) and this last sum is

. . . . 15 dollars, 0172 parts, which at six per cent per annum, amounts at the end of ten years, to . . . . 26 dollars, 8755 parts, the sum to be funded at the expiration of that period.

It ought, however, to be acknowledged, that this calculation does not make allowance for the principle of redemption, which the plan itself includes; upon which principle the equivalent in a capital of six per cent. would be by strict calculation,

. . . . 87 dollars, 50766 parts.

But there are two considerations which induce the Secretary to think, that the one proposed would operate more equitably than this: One is, that it may not be very early in the power of the United States to avail themselves of the right of redemption reserved in the plan: The other is, that with regard to the part to be funded at the end of ten years, the principal of redemption is suspended during that time, and the full interest at six per cent. goes on *improving* at the *same rate;* which for the *last five years* will exceed the market rate of interest, according to the supposition.

The equivalent is regulated in this plan, by the circumstance of fixing the rate of interest higher, than it is supposed it will continue to be in the market; permitting only a gradual discharge of the debt, in an established proportion, and consequently preventing advantage being taken of any decrease of interest below the stipulated rate.

Thus the true value of eighty-one dollars and sixty-seven cents, the capital proposed, considered as a perpetuity, and bearing six per cent. interest, when the market rate of interest was five per cent. would be a small fraction more than ninety-eight dollars, when it was four per cent. would be one hundred and twenty-two dollars and fifty-one cents. But the proposed capital being subject to gradual redemption, it is evident, that its value, in each case, would be somewhat less. Yet from this may be perceived, the manner in which a less capital at a fixed rate of interest, becomes an equivalent for a greater capital, at a rate liable to variation and diminution.

It is presumable, that those creditors, who do not entertain a favorable opinion of property in western lands, will give a preference to this last mode of modelling the debt. The Secretary is sincere in affirming, that, in his opinion, it will be likely to prove, *to the full* as beneficial to the creditors, as a provision for his debt upon its present terms.

It is not intended, in either case to oblige the government to redeem, in the proportion specified, but to secure to it, the right of doing so, to avoid the inconvenience of a perpetuity.

The fourth and fifth plans abandon the supposition which is the basis of the two preceding ones, and offer only four per cent. throughout.

The reason of this is, that the payment being deferred, there will be an accumulation of compound interest, in the intermediate period against the public, which, without a very provident administration, would turn to its detriment. And the suspension of the burthen would be too apt to beget a relaxation of efforts in the mean time. The measure therefore, its object being temporary accommodation, could only be adviseable upon a moderate rate of interest.

With regard to individuals, the inducement will be sufficient at four per cent. There is no disposition of money, in private loans, making allowance for the usual delays and casualties, which would be equally beneficial as a future provision.

A hundred dollars advanced upon the life of a person of eleven years old, would produce an annuity *

	Dollars.	Parts.
If commencing at twenty-one, of	10	346
If commencing at thirty-one, of	18	803
If commencing at forty-one, of	37	286
If commencing at fifty-one, of	78	580

The same sum advanced upon the chance of the survivorship of the youngest of two lives, one of the persons being twenty-five, the other, thirty years old, would produce, if the youngest of the two, should survive, an annuity † for the remainder of life of

23 dollars, 556 parts.

From these instances may readily be discerned, the advantages,

* See Schedule F.
† Table Schedule G.

which these deferred annuities afford, for securing a comfortable provision for the evening of life, or for wives, who survive their husbands.

The sixth plan also relinquishes the supposition, which is the foundation of the second, and third, and offers a higher rate of interest upon similar terms of redemption, for the consideration of the payment of one half of the loan in specie. This is a plan highly advantageous to the creditors, who may be able to make that payment; while the specie itself could be applied in purchases of the debt, upon terms, which would fully indemnify the public for the increased interest.

It is not improbable, that foreign holders of the domestic debt, may embrace this as a desireable arrangement.

As an auxiliary expedient, and by way of experiment, the Secretary would propose a loan upon the principles of a tontine.‡

To consist of six classes, composed respectively of persons of the following ages:

First class, of those 20 years and under.

Second class, of those above 20, and not exceeding 30.

Third class, of those above 30, and not exceeding 40.

Fourth class, of those above 40 and not exceeding 50.

Fifth class, of those above 50, and not exceeding 60.

Sixth class, of those above 60.

Each share to be two hundred dollars. The number of shares in each class, to be indefinite. Persons to be at liberty to subscribe on their own lives, or on those of others, nominated by them.

	Dollars.	Cents.
The annuity upon a share in the first class to be	8.	40
upon a share in the second	8.	65
upon a share in the third	9.	0
upon a share in the fourth	9.	65
upon a share in the fifth	10.	70
upon a share in the sixth	12.	80

The annuities of those who die, to be equally divided among the survivors, until four-fifths shall be dead, when the principle of survivorship shall cease, and each annuitant thenceforth enjoy his dividend as a several annuity during the life, upon which it shall depend.

These annuities are calculated upon the best life in each class,

‡ See Table Schedule H.

and at a rate of interest of four per cent. with some deductions in favor of the public. To the advantages which these circumstances present, the cessation of the right of survivorship on the death of four-fifths of the annuitants, will be no inconsiderable addition.

The inducements to individuals are, a competent interest for their money from the outset, secured for life, and the prospect of continual encrease, and even of large profit to those, whose fortune it is, to survive their associates.

It will have appeared, that in all the proposed loans, the Secretary has contemplated the putting the interest upon the same footing with the principal: *That* on the debt of the United States, he would have computed to the last of the present year: *That* on the debt of the particular states, to the last of the year 1791; the reason for which distinction will be seen hereafter.

In order to keep up a due circulation of money, it will be expedient, that the interest of the debt should be paid quarter-yearly.[126] This regulation will, at the same time, conduce to the advantage of the public creditors, giving them, in fact, by the anticipation of payment, a higher rate of interest; which may, with propriety, be taken into the estimate of the compensation to be made to them. Six per cent. per annum, paid in this mode, will truly be worth six dollars, and one hundred and thirty-five thousandth parts of a dollar, computing the market interest at the same rate.

The Secretary thinks it advisable, to hold out various propositions, all of them compatible with the public interest, because it is, in his opinion, of the greatest consequence, that the debt should, with the consent of the creditors, be remoulded into such a shape, as will bring the expenditure of the nation to a level with its income. 'Till this shall be accomplished, the finances of the United States will never wear a proper countenance. Arrears of interest, continually accruing, will be as continual a monument, either of inability, or of ill faith; and will not cease to have an evil influence

126. In Robert Morris to the President of Congress, July 29, 1782, Morris had said: "The interest should be paid half yearly, which would be convenient to the creditors and to the government, as well as useful to the people at large; because by this means, if four different loans were opened at different times, the interest would be payable eight times in the year; and thus the money would be paid out of the treasury as fast as it came in; . . . and return speedily the wealth obtained by taxes into the common stock" (Sparks, *Diplomatic Correspondence*, XII, 233–34). Also see Clarence L. Ver Steeg, *Robert Morris, Revolutionary Financier* (Philadelphia, 1954), 120.

on public credit. In nothing are appearances of greater moment, than in whatever regards credit. Opinion is the soul of it, and this is affected by appearances, as well as realities. By offering an option to the creditors, between a number of plans, the change meditated will be more likely to be accomplished. Different tempers will be governed by different views of the subject.

But while the Secretary would endeavour to effect a change in the form of the debt, by new loans, in order to render it more susceptible of an adequate provision; he would not think it proper to aim at procuring the concurrence of the creditors by operating upon their necessities.

Hence whatever surplus of revenue might remain, after satisfying the interest of the new loans, and the demand for the current service, ought to be divided among those creditors, if any, who may not think fit to subscribe to them. But for this purpose, under the circumstance of depending propositions, a temporary appropriation will be most adviseable, and the sum must be limited to four per cent. as the revenues will only be calculated to produce, in that proportion, to the entire debt.

The Secretary confides for the success of the propositions, to be made, on the goodness of the reasons upon which they rest; on the fairness of the equivalent to be offered in each case; on the discernment of the creditors of their true interest; and on their disposition to facilitate the arrangements of the government, and to render them satisfactory to the community.

The remaining part of the task to be performed is, to take a view of the means of providing for the debt, according to the modification of it, which is proposed.

On this point the Secretary premises, that, in his opinion, the funds to be established, ought, for the present, to be confined to the existing debt of the United States; as well, because a progressive augmentation of the revenue will be most convenient, as because the consent of the state creditors is necessary, to the assumption contemplated; and though the obtaining of that consent may be inferred with great assurance, from their obvious interest to give it; yet 'till it shall be obtained, an actual provision for the debt, would be premature. Taxes could not, with propriety, be laid for an object, which depended on such a contingency.

All that ought now to be done, respecting it, is, to put the matter in an effectual train for a future provision. For which purpose, the Secretary will, in the course of this report, submit such propositions, as appear to him adviseable.

The Secretary now proceeds to a consideration of the necessary funds.

It has been stated that the debt of the United States consists of

	Dollars.	Cents.
The foreign debt, amounting, with arrears of interest, to	11,710,378	62
And the domestic debt amounting, with like arrears, computed to the end of the year 1790, to	42,414,085	94
Making together, Dollars	54,124,464	56

The interest on the domestic debt is computed to the end of this year, because the details of carrying any plan into execution, will exhaust the year.

	Dollars.	Cents.
The annual interest of the foreign debt has been stated at	542,599	66
And the interest on the domestic debt at four percent. would amount to	1,696,563	43
Making together, dollars,	2,239,163	09

Thus to pay the interest of the foreign debt, and to pay four per cent on the whole of the domestic debt, principal and interest, forming a new capital,

will require a yearly income of   2,239,163 dollars, 9 cents.

The sum which, in the opinion of the Secretary, ought now to be provided in addition to what the current service will require.

For, though the rate of interest, proposed by the third plan, exceeds four per cent. on the whole debt, and the annuities on the tontine will also exceed four per cent. on the sums which may be subscribed; yet, as the actual provision for a part is, in the former case, suspended; as measures for reducing the debt, by purchases, may be advantageously pursued, and as the payment of the deferred annuities will of course be postponed, four per cent. on the whole, will be a sufficient provision.

With regard to the instalments of the foreign debt, these, in the opinion of the Secretary, ought to be paid by new loans abroad. Could funds be conveniently spared, from other exigencies, for paying them, the United States could ill bear the drain of cash, at the present juncture, which the measure would be likely to occasion.

But to the sum which has been stated for payment of the interest, must be added a provision for the current service. This the Secretary estimates at six hundred thousand dollars; * making, with the amount of the interest, two millions, eight hundred and thirty-nine thousand, one hundred and sixty-three dollars, and nine cents.

This sum may, in the opinion of the Secretary, be obtained from the present duties on imports and tonnage, with the additions, which, without any possible disadvantage either to trade, or agriculture, may be made on wines, spirits, including those distilled within the United States, teas and coffee.

The Secretary conceives, that it will be sound policy, to carry the duties upon articles of this kind, as high as will be consistent with the practicability of a safe collection. This will lessen the necessity, both of having recourse to direct taxation, and of accumulating duties where they would be more inconvenient to trade, and upon objects, which are more to be regarded as necessaries of life.

That the articles which have been enumerated, will, better than most others, bear high duties, can hardly be a question. They are all of them, in reality—luxuries—the greatest part of them foreign luxuries; some of them, in the excess in which they are used, pernicious luxuries. And there is, perhaps, none of them, which is not consumed in so great abundance, as may, justly, denominate it, a source of national extravagance and impoverishment. The consumption of ardent spirits particularly, no doubt very much on account of their cheapness, is carried to an extreme, which is truly to be regretted, as well in regard to the health and the morals, as to the œconomy of the community.[127]

* See Schedule I.

127. Robert Morris in a letter to the President of Congress on July 29, 1782, had said: "It may be boldly affirmed, that no inconvenience can arise from laying a heavy tax on the use of ardent spirits. These have always been equally prejudicial to the constitutions and morals of the people" (Sparks, *Diplomatic Correspondence*, XII, 231).

Should the increase of duties tend to a decrease of the consumption of those articles, the effect would be, in every respect desirable. The saving which it would occasion, would leave individuals more at their ease, and promote a more favourable balance of trade. As far as this decrease might be applicable to distilled spirits, it would encourage the substitution of cyder and malt liquors, benefit agriculture, and open a new and productive source of revenue.

It is not however, probable, that this decrease would be in a degree, which would frustrate the expected benefit to the revenue from raising the duties. Experience has shewn, that luxuries of every kind, lay the strongest hold on the attachments of mankind, which, especially when confirmed by habit, are not easily alienated from them.

The same fact affords a security to the merchant, that he is not likely to be prejudiced by considerable duties on such articles. They will usually command a proportional price. The chief things in this view to be attended to, are, that the terms of payment be so regulated, as not to require inconvenient advances, and that the mode of collection be secure.

To other reasons, which plead for carrying the duties upon the articles which have been mentioned, to as great an extent as they will bear, may be added these; that they are of a nature, from their extensive consumption, to be very productive, and are amongst the most difficult objects of illicit introduction.

Invited by so many motives to make the best use of the resource, which these articles afford, the essential enquiry is—in what mode can the duties upon them be most effectually collected?

With regard to such of them, as will be brought from abroad, a duty on importation recommends itself by two leading considerations; one is, that meeting the object at its first entrance into the country, the collection is drawn to a point, and so far simplified; the other is, that it avoids the possibility of interference between the regulations of the United States, and those of the particular states.

But a duty, the precautions for the collection of which should terminate with the landing of the goods, as is essentially the case in the existing system, could not, with safety, be carried to the extent, which is contemplated.

In that system, the evasion of the duties, depends as it were, on a single risk. To land the goods in defiance of the vigilance of the officers of the customs, is almost, the sole difficulty. No future pursuit, is materially, to be apprehended. And where the inducement is equivalent to the risk, there will be found too many, who are willing to run it. Consequently there will be extensive frauds of the revenue, against which the utmost rigor of the penal laws, has proved, as often as it has been tried, an ineffectual guard.[128]

The only expedient which has been discovered, for conciliating high duties with a safe collection, is, the establishment of a *second*, or interior scrutiny.[129]

By pursuing the article, from its importation, into the hands of the dealers in it, the risk of detection is so greatly inhanced, that few, in comparison, will venture to incur it. Indeed every dealer, who is not himself the fraudulent importer, then becomes, in some sort, a centinel upon him.

The introduction of a system, founded on this principle, in some shape or other, is, in the opinion of the Secretary, essential to the efficacy of every attempt, to render the revenues of the United States equal to their exigencies, their safety, their prosperity, their honor.

Nor is it less essential to the interest of the honest and fair trader. It might even be added, that every individual citizen, besides his share in the general weal, has a particular interest in it. The practice of smuggling never fails to have one of two effects, and sometimes unites them both. Either the smuggler undersells the fair trader, as, by saving the *duty*, he can afford to do, and makes *it* a charge upon him; or he sells at the increased price occasioned by the duty, and defrauds every man, who buys of him, of his share of what the public ought to receive. For it is evident, that the loss falls ultimately upon the citizens, who must be charged with other taxes to make good the deficiency, and supply the wants of the state.

The Secretary will not presume, that the plan, which he shall submit to the consideration of the house, is the best that could be devised. But it is the one, which has appeared to him freest from objections of any, that has occurred of equal efficacy. He acknowl-

128. See Higginson to H, November 11, 1789.
129. Compare with Smith, *Wealth of Nations*, II, 415–16.

edges too, that it is susceptible of improvement, by other precautions in favor of the revenue, which he did not think it expedient to add. The chief outlines of the plan are not original, but
it is no ill recommendation of it, that it has been tried [130] with success.

The Secretary accordingly proposes,

That the duties heretofore laid upon wines, distilled spirits, teas
and coffee, should, after the last day of May next, cease, and that
instead of them, the following duties be laid.

Upon every gallon of Madeira Wine, of the quality of London
particular, thirty-five cents.

Upon every gallon of other Madeira Wine, thirty cents.

Upon every gallon of Sherry, twenty-five cents.

Upon every gallon of other Wine, twenty cents.

Upon every gallon of distilled Spirits, more than ten per cent.
below proof, according to Dicas's hydrometer, twenty cents.

Upon every gallon of those Spirits under five, and not more than
ten per cent. below proof, according to the same hydrometer,
twenty-one cents.

Upon every gallon of those Spirits of proof, and not more than
five per cent. below proof, according to the same hydrometer,
twenty-two cents.

Upon every gallon of those Spirits above proof, but not exceeding twenty per cent. according to the same hydrometer, twenty-
five cents.

Upon every gallon of those spirits more than twenty, and not
more than forty per cent. above proof, according to the same
hydrometer, thirty cents.

Upon every gallon of those spirits more than forty per cent. above
proof, according to the same hydrometer, forty cents.

Upon every pound of Hyson Tea, forty cents.

Upon every pound of other Green Tea, twenty-four cents.

Upon every pound of Souchong and other black Teas, except
Bohea, twenty cents.

Upon every pound of Bohea Tea, twelve cents.

Upon every pound of Coffee, five cents.

130. See 7 & 8 W. III, C. 30 (1695); 10 Geo. I, C. 10 (1724); 2 Geo. III, C.
5 (1762); 28 Geo. III, C. 46 (1788).

That upon Spirits distilled within the United States, from Molasses, Sugar, or other foreign materials, there be paid—

Upon every gallon of those Spirits, more than ten per cent below
proof, according to Dicas's hydrometer, eleven cents.

Upon every gallon of those spirits under five, and not more than
ten per cent. below proof, according to the same hydrometer,
twelve cents.

Upon every gallon of those Spirits of proof, and not more than
five per cent. below proof, according to the same hydrometer,
thirteen cents.

Upon every gallon of those Spirits, above proof, but not exceeding twenty per cent. according to the same hydrometer, fifteen
cents.

Upon every gallon of those Spirits, more than twenty, and not
more than forty per cent. above proof, according to the same
hydrometer, twenty cents.

Upon every gallon of those Spirits more than forty per cent.
above proof, according to the same hydrometer, thirty cents.

That upon Spirits distilled within the United States, in any city,
town or village, from materials of the growth or production of the
United States, there be paid—

Upon every gallon of those Spirits more than ten per cent. below
proof, according to Dicas's hydrometer, nine cents.

Upon every gallon of those Spirits under five, and not more
than ten per cent. below proof, according to the same hydrometer,
ten cents.

Upon every gallon of those Spirits of proof, and not more than
five per cent. below proof, according to the same hydrometer,
eleven cents.

Upon every gallon of those Spirits above proof, but not exceeding twenty per cent. according to the same hydrometer, thirteen
cents.

Upon every gallon of those Spirits more than twenty, and not
more than forty per cent. above proof, according to the same
hydrometer, seventeen cents.

Upon every gallon of those Spirits, more than forty per cent.
above proof, according to the same hydrometer, twenty-five cents.

That upon all Stills employed in distilling Spirits from materials of the growth or production of the United States, in any other place, than a city, town or village, there be paid the yearly sum of sixty cents, for every gallon, English wine measure, of the capacity of each Still, including its head.

The Secretary does not distribute the duties on Teas into different classes, as has been done in the impost act of the last session; because this distribution depends on considerations of commercial policy, not of revenue. It is sufficient, therefore, for him to remark, that the rates, above specified, are proposed with reference to the lowest class.

The Secretary conceiving, that he could not convey an accurate idea of the plan contemplated by him, for the collection of these duties, in any mode so effectual as by the draft of a bill for the purpose, begs leave respectfully to refer the House to that, which will be found annexed to this report, relatively to the article of distilled spirits; and which, for the better explanation of some of its parts, is accompanied with marginal remarks.

It would be the intention of the Secretary, that the duty on wines should be collected upon precisely the same plan with that on imported spirits.

But with regard to teas and coffee, the Secretary is inclined to think, that it will be expedient, till experience shall evince the propriety of going further, to exclude the *ordinary* right of the officers to visit and inspect the places in which those articles may be kept. The other precautions, without this, will afford, though not complete, considerable security.

It will not escape the observation of the House, that the Secretary, in the plan submitted, has taken the most scrupulous care, that those citizens upon whom it is immediately to operate, be secured from every species of injury by the misconduct of the officers to be employed. There are not only strong guards against their being guilty of abuses of authority; they are not only punishable, criminally, for any they may commit, and made answerable in damages, to individuals, for whatever prejudice these may sustain by their acts or neglects: But even where seizures are made with probable cause, if there be an acquittal of the article seized, a compensation to the proprietors for the injury their property may suffer, and even for its detention, is to be made out of the public treasury.

So solicitous indeed has the Secretary been, to obviate every appearance of hardship, that he has even included a compensation to the dealers, for their agency in aid of the revenue.

With all these precautions to manifest a spirit of moderation and justice on the part of government: And when it is considered, that the object of the proposed system is the firm establishment of public credit; that on this depends the character, security and prosperity of the nation; that advantages in every light important, may be expected to result from it; that the immediate operation of it will be upon an enlightened class of citizens, zealously devoted to good government, and to a liberal and enlarged policy, and that it is peculiarly the interest of the virtuous part of them to co-operate in whatever will restrain the spirit of illicit traffic; there will be perceived to exist, the justest ground of confidence, that the plan, if eligible in itself, will experience the chearful and prompt acquiescence of the community.

The Secretary computes the nett product of the duties proposed in this report at about one million seven hundred and three thousand four hundred dollars, according to the estimate in schedule K, which if near the truth, will, together with the probable product of the duties on imports and tonnage, complete the sum required. But it will readily occur, that in so unexplored a field there must be a considerable degree of uncertainty in the data. And that, on this account, it will be prudent to have an auxiliary resource for the first year, in which the interest will become payable, that there may be no possibility of disappointment to the public creditors, ere there may be an opportunity of providing for any deficiency, which the experiment may discover. This will accordingly be attended to.

The proper appropriation of the funds provided, and to be provided, seems next to offer itself to consideration.

On this head, the Secretary would propose, that the duties on distilled spirits, should be applied in the first instance, to the payment of the interest of the foreign debt.

That reserving out of the residue of those duties an annual sum of six hundred thousand dollars, for the current service of the United States; the surplus, together with the product of the other duties, be applied to the payment of the interest on the new loan, by an appropriation, co-extensive with the duration of the debt.

And that if any part of the debt should remain unsubscribed, the excess of the revenue be divided among the creditors of the unsubscribed part, by a temporary disposition; with a limitation, however, to four per cent.

It will hardly have been unnoticed, that the Secretary had been thus far silent on the subject of the post-office. The reason is, that he has had in view the application of the revenue arising from that source, to the purposes of a sinking fund. The post-master-general gives it as his opinion, that the immediate product of it, upon a proper arrangement, would probably be, not less than one hundred thousand dollars.[131] And from its nature, with good management, it must be a growing, and will be likely to become a considerable fund. The post-master-general is now engaged in preparing a plan,* which will be the foundation of a proposition for a new arrangement of the establishment. This, and some other points relative to the subject referred to the Secretary, he begs leave to reserve for a future report.

Persuaded as the Secretary is, that the proper funding of the present debt, will render it a national blessing: Yet he is so far from acceding to the position, in the latitude in which it is sometimes laid down, that "public debts are public benefits," a position inviting to prodigality, and liable to dangerous abuse,—that he ardently wishes to see it incorporated, as a fundamental maxim, in the system of public credit of the United States, that the creation of debt should always be accompanied with the means of extinguishment. This he regards as the true secret for rendering public credit immortal. And he presumes, that it is difficult to conceive a situation, in which there may not be an adherence to the maxim. At least he feels an unfeigned solicitude, that this may be attempted by the United States, and that they may commence their measures for the establishment of credit, with the observance of it.

Under this impression, the Secretary proposes, that the nett product of the post-office, to a sum not exceeding one million of

* This plan, since the framing of this report, has been received, and will be, shortly, submitted.[132]

131. Samuel Osgood to H, November 28, 1789; January 20, 1790.
132. Osgood to H, January 20, 1790. This letter was received after presentation of the Report and before printing.

dollars, be vested in commissioners,[133] to consist of the Vice-President of the United States or President of the Senate, the Speaker of the House of Representatives, the Chief Justice, Secretary of the Treasury and Attorney-General of the United States, for the time being, in trust, to be applied, by them, or any three of them, to the discharge of the existing public debt, either by purchases of stock in the market, or by payments on account of the principal, as shall appear to them most adviseable, in conformity to the public engagements; to continue so vested, until the whole of the debt shall be discharged.

As an additional expedient for effecting a reduction of the debt, and for other purposes which will be mentioned, the Secretary would further propose that the same commissioners be authorised, with the approbation of the President of the United States, to borrow, on their credit, a sum, not exceeding twelve millions of dollars,[134] to be applied,

First. To the payment of the interest and instalments of the foreign debt, to the end of the present year, which will require 3,491,923 dollars, and 46 cents.

Secondly. To the payment of any deficiency which may happen in the product of the funds provided for paying the interest of the domestic debt.

Thirdly. To the effecting a change in the form of such part of the foreign debt, as bears an interest of five per cent. It is conceived, that, for this purpose, a new loan, at a lower interest, may be combined with other expedients. The remainder of this part of the debt, after paying the instalments, which will accrue in the course of 1790, will be 3,888,888 dollars, and 81 cents.

Fourthly. To the purchase of the public debt at the price it shall bear in the market, while it continues below its true value. This measure, which would be, in the opinion of the Secretary, highly dishonorable to the government, if it were to precede a provision for funding the debt, would become altogether unexceptionable, after that had been made.[135] Its effect would be in favor of the public creditors, as it would tend to raise the value of stock. And

133. Sparks, *Life of Gouverneur Morris,* III, 476.
134. Sparks, *Life of Gouverneur Morris,* III, 473.
135. Sparks, *Life of Gouverneur Morris,* III, 477. Morris's sinking fund plan differed from that of Hamilton.

all the difference, between its true value, and the actual price, would be so much clear gain to the public. The payment of foreign interest on the capital to be borrowed for this purpose, should that be a necessary consequence, would not, in the judgment of the Secretary, be a good objection to the measure. The saving by the operation would be itself, a sufficient indemnity; and the employment of that capital, in a country situated like this, would much more than compensate for it. Besides, if the government does not undertake this operation, the same inconvenience, which the objection in question supposes, would happen in another way, with a circumstance of aggravation. As long, at least, as the debt shall continue below its proper value, it will be an object of speculation to foreigners, who will not only receive the interest, upon what they purchase, and remit it abroad, as in the case of the loan, but will reap the additional profit of the difference in value. By the government's entering into competition with them, it will not only reap a part of this profit itself, but will contract the extent, and lessen the extra profit of foreign purchases. That competition will accelerate the rise of stock; and whatever greater rate this obliges foreigners to pay, for what they purchase, is so much clear saving to the nation. In the opinion of the Secretary, and contrary to an idea which is not without patrons, it ought to be the policy of the government, to raise the value of stock to its true standard as fast as possible. When it arrives to that point, foreign speculations (which, till then, must be deemed pernicious, further than as they serve to bring it to that point) will become beneficial. Their money laid out in this country, upon our agriculture, commerce and manufactures, will produce much more to us, than the income they will receive from it.

The Secretary contemplates the application of this money, through the medium of a national bank, for which, with the permission of the House, he will submit a plan in the course of the session.[136]

The Secretary now proceeds, in the last place, to offer to the consideration of the House, his ideas, of the steps, which ought at

136. See "Report on the Further Provision Necessary for Establishing the Public Credit (Report on a National Bank)," December 13, 1790.

the present session, to be taken, towards the assumption of the state debts.

These are briefly, that concurrent resolutions of the two Houses, with the approbation of the President, be entered into, declaring in substance,

That the United States do assume, and will at the first session in the year 1791, provide, on the same terms with the present debt of the United States, for all such part of the debts of the respective states, or any of them, as shall, prior to the first day of January in the said year 1791, be subscribed towards a loan to the United States, upon the principles of either of the plans, which shall have been adopted by them, for obtaining a re-loan of their present debt.

Provided that the provision to be made as aforesaid, shall be suspended, with respect to the debt, of any state, which may have exchanged the securities of the United States for others issued by itself, until the whole of the said securities shall, either be re-exchanged, or surrendered to the United States.

And provided also, that the interest upon the debt assumed, be computed to the end of the year 1791; and that the interest to be paid by the United States, commence on the first day of January, 1792.

That the amount of the debt of each state so assumed and provided for, be charged to such state in account with the United States, upon the same principles, upon which it shall be lent to the United States.

That subscriptions be opened for receiving loans of the said debts at the same times and places, and under the like regulations, as shall have been prescribed in relation to the debt of the United States.

The Secretary has now completed the objects, which he proposed to himself, to comprise in the present report. He has, for the most part, omitted details, as well to avoid fatiguing the attention of the House, as because more time would have been desirable even to digest the general principles of the plan. If these should be found right, the particular modifications will readily suggest themselves in the progress of the work.

The Secretary, in the views which have directed his pursuit of the subject, has been influenced, in the first place, by the consideration, that his duty from the very terms of the resolution of the House, obliged him to propose what appeared to him an adequate provision for the support of the public credit, adapted at the same time to the real circumstances of the United States; and in the next, by the reflection, that measures which will not bear the test of future un-biassed examination, can neither be productive of individual reputa-tion, nor (which is of much greater consequence) public honor, or advantage.

Deeply impressed, as the Secretary is, with a full and deliberate conviction, that the establishment of public credit, upon the basis of a satisfactory provision, for the public debt, is, under the present circumstances of this country, the true desideratum towards relief from individual and national embarrassments; that without it, these embarrassments will be likely to press still more severely upon the community—He cannot but indulge an anxious wish, that an ef-fectual plan for that purpose may, during the present session, be the result of the united wisdom of the legislature.

He is fully convinced, that it is of the greatest importance, that no further delay should attend the making of the requisite pro-vision; not only, because it will give a better impression of the good faith of the country, and will bring earlier relief to the creditors; both which circumstances are of great moment to public credit: but, because the advantages to the community, from raising stock, as speedily as possible, to its natural value, will be incomparably greater, than any that can result from its continuance below that standard. No profit, which could be derived from purchases in the market, on account of the government, to any practicable extent, would be an equivalent for the loss, which would be sustained by the purchases of foreigners, at a low value. Not to repeat, that governmental purchases, to be honorable, ought to be preceded by a provision. Delay, by disseminating doubt, would sink the price of stock; and as the temptation to foreign speculations, from the low-ness of the price, would be too great to be neglected, millions would probably be lost to the United States.

All which is humbly submitted.

Alexander Hamilton, *Secretary of the Treasury.*

SUPPOSITITIOUS STATEMENT OF ACCOUNTS BETWEEN THE UNITED STATES AND INDIVIDUAL STATES.

States.	Ratio.	Balances due to the states respectively.	Proportion of each state of the aggregate of those balances according to the ratio.	Balances against certain states.	Balances in favor of certain states.	Proportion of each state in the aggregate of the balances against certain states.	Ultimate balances in favour of certain states upon the principle of an extinguishment of the balances owing by the debtor states, and a proportional allowance to the other states, adjusted according to the ratio given, and to be paid by the United States.
New-Hampshire	3	57,500	60,000	2,500		3,000	500
Massachusetts	8	180,000	160,000		20,000	8,000	28,000
Rhode-Island	1	20,000	20,000			1,000	1,000
Connecticut	5	110,000	100,000		10,000	5,000	15,000
New-York	6	135,000	120,000		15,000	6,000	21,000
New-Jersey	4	72,500	80,000	7,500		4,000	
Pennsylvania	8	170,000	160,000		10,000	8,000	18,000
Delaware	1	30,000	20,000		10,000	1,000	11,000
Maryland	6	110,000	120,000	10,000		6,000	
Virginia	10	187,500	200,000	12,500		10,000	
North-Carolina	5	90,000	100,000	10,000		5,000	
South-Carolina	5	87,500	100,000	12,500		5,000	
Georgia	3	50,000	60,000	10,000		3,000	
	65	1,300,000	1,300,000	65,000	65,000	65,000	94,500

EXPLANATION

The first column supposes a Ratio according to the present rule of representation.

The second column exhibits the balances which, on the principles of the statement suggested are supposed to be due to the several States.

The third column shews the apportionment of the aggregate of those balances according to the ratio given among the States.

The fourth column shews the balances against some States in consequence of this apportionment.

The fifth column shews the balances in favor of some States, in consequence of the same apportionment.

This completes the first Process proposed.

The second Process is illustrated by the sixth and seventh columns.

The sixth column shews the share of each State, according to the ratio given in the amount of the balances against the Debtor States.

The seventh shews the ultimate balances in favor of certain States, crediting them for their proportions of the balance due from the Debtor States.

137. There are numerous arithmetical errors in this Report which have not been noted or corrected.

SCHEDULE B

A GENERAL STATEMENT OF THE FOREIGN LOANS, SHEWING IN ABSTRACT, THE CAPITAL SUMS BORROWED, AND THE ARREARAGES OF INTEREST TO THE 31ST DECEMBER, 1789.

CAPITAL SUMS BORROWED

	Livres.	*Dollars.*	*Cts.*
Of the Royal French Treasury, on Interest at 5 per cent.	24,000,000		
In Holland, guaranteed by the French Court, at 4 per cent.	10,000,000		
Livres,	4,000,000	6,296,296	
		174,011	

Of the Royal Spanish Treasury, at 5 per cent.

Lenders in Holland,

	Florins.		
First Loan, 5 per cent.	5,000,000		
Second ditto, 4 per cent.	2,000,000		
Third ditto, 5 per cent.	1,000,000		
Fourth ditto, 5 per cent.	1,000,000		
Florins,	9,000,000	3,600,000	
Capital,	– –	10,070,307	

ARREARAGES OF INTEREST TO 31ST DECEMBER, 1789.

On the *French Loan.*

	Livres,		*Dollars.*	*Cts.*
1789, Jan. 1, Five Years Interest on the	6,000,000	at 5 per cent.	277,777.	77
Sept. 3, Six do. on the	18,000,000	do.	999,999.	96
Nov. 5, Four do. on the	10,000,000	at 4 per cent.	296,296.	

On the *Spanish Loan.*

Arrearages on the *Spanish Loan* of 174,011 Dollars,

to 21st March, 1782, at 5 per cent.	5,093.	27
March 21, Seven Years Interest on do.	60,904.	62

	Dollars.	*Cts.*
	1,640,071.	62
Total dollars,	11,710,378.	62

Note. There were certain parts of the Capital of the Dutch guaranteed Loan of 10,000,000 Florins, and of the French Loan of 18,000,000 Livres, which became due at the following periods, and remain unpaid, viz.

				Dollars.	Cts.
1787.	Sept. 3, First Payment of the 18,000,000.	1,500,000.		277,777.	77
	Nov. 5, First do. of the 10,000,000.	1,000,000.		185,185.	19
1788.	Sept. 3, Second do. of the 18,000,000.	the same.		462,962.	96
	Nov. 5, Second do. of the 10,000,000.				
1789.	Sept. 3, Third do. of the 18,000,000.	the same.		462,962.	96
	Nov. 5, Third do. of the 10,000,000.				
		Dollars,		1,388,888.	88

Treasury Department, *Register's Office*, 31st Dec. 1789.

Joseph Nourse, Register.

To the Arrearage of Interest to 31st December, 1789, above stated, Amounting to 1,640,071. 62
Add one year's Interest from 1st January, to 31 December, 1789, on 186,427, dollars, and 69 cents, being the Amount Principal Sum due to foreign officers, employed in the service of the United States, which Interest is annually payable at the House of Mons. Grand[138] Banker at Paris, at 6 per cent. 11,185. 66
Arrearages of Interest to 31st December, 1789, Dollars, 1,651,257. 28

The above Addition was adverted to, after the conclusion of the Report; but as it makes no material difference, an alteration in consequence of it, is deemed unnecessary.

Alexander Hamilton, Secretary of the Treasury.

138. Ferdinand Le Grand.

SCHEDULE C

ABSTRACT OF THE LIQUIDATED AND LOAN-OFFICE DEBT OF THE UNITED STATES, ON THE 3D MARCH, 1789.

Dollars. 90ths.

Registered Debt,

Credits given to sundries on the treasury books, by virtue of special acts of Congress, which are not yet put on the Funded Debt, — 4,598,462. 78

Certificates issued by the commissioner of army accounts, deducting those which have been cancelled and registered, — 187,578. 65

Certificates issued by the commissioners of the five departments, deducting those which have been cancelled and registered, — 7,967,109. 73

Certificates issued by the late state commissioners, deducting those which have been cancelled and registered, — 903,574. 59

Loan-office certificates issued in 1781, and expressed as specie value, deducting those which have been cancelled and registered, — 3,291,156. 37

Loan-office certificates, old emissions, reduced to specie value, agreeably to the scale made by Congress, by taking the medium of the loans made in each month, viz. 3,787,900 loaned to 1st September 1777, equal to — 112,704. 15

Dollars. 90ths.
3,787,900
2,538,572
5,146,330
11,463,802
365,983

* 3,459,000 ditto between 1st Sept. 1777 and 1st March 1778,
59,830,212 ditto between 1st March 1778, and the closure of the Loan-offices,

Deduct specie amount cancelled and registered,

11,097,818. 75

Foreign officers, amount to their credit, the interest whereof is payable at the House of Mons. Grand Banker at Paris, and included in the estimate of foreign interest,

186,427. 69

From which deduct this sum received into the Treasury on account of lands and other property, and cancelled,

28,344,833. 21

960,915. 44

Leaves the amount of the domestic debt, Dollars,

27,383,917. 67

*On the certificates issued between the 1st September 1777 and 1st March 1778, interest is payable on the nominal sum (being 3,459,000 dollars) although the specie value of the principal is only 2,538,572 dollars.

Register's-office, March 3, 1789,

Joseph Nourse, Register.

Treasury Department, *Register's-office,* January 1, 1790.

The above estimate was formed to the expiration of the late government. Some variation hath since taken place in the several parts, without making any material alteration in the aggregate amount of the domestic debt: This arises from a daily exchange at the Treasury of Loan-office and Final Settlement Certificates, for Treasury Certificates given as evidences of the registered debt, whereby the increase of the latter is carried on in proportion to the cancelment of the former.

Joseph Nourse, Register.

SCHEDULE D

AN ESTIMATE OF ALL THE INTEREST WHICH WILL ACCRUE ON THE DOMESTIC DEBT OF THE UNITED STATES, FROM ITS FORMATION TO THE 31ST DECEMBER 1790, OF SUCH PARTIAL PAYMENTS AS HAVE BEEN MADE ON ACCOUNT THEREOF, AND OF THE BALANCE WHICH WILL REMAIN TO BE PROVIDED FOR, TO PAY UP THE INTEREST FULLY TO THAT PERIOD.

	Dollars.	Cts.
The total amount of interest arising on the loan-office debt, from the opening of the several offices in 1776, to the 31st of December, 1790,	9,534,478	
The total amount of interest arising on the army debt, from the several periods of its drawing interest, to the 31st December, 1790,	5,105,099	
The total amount of interest arising on certificates issued by the thirteen state commissioners, estimated at	2,146,799	
The total amount of interest arising on certificates issued by the commissioners for the commissaries, quarter-masters, marine, cloathing and hospital departments, estimated at	737,338	
The total amount of interest arising on the debt registered at the treasury, estimated at	366,646	
The total amount of interest on debts entered in the treasury books, but for which certificates have not been issued by the Register, so as to become a part of the registered debt, estimated at	83,936	
Total	17,974,296	

	Dollars.	Cts.

From this total amount of interest, the following deductions are to be made, viz

So much paid on the loan-office debt, in old emission, equal to — 372,368. 30

In new emissions, as specie, — 39,433. 49

In bills of exchange, as ditto, — 1,663,992

So much paid by the several states in indents, paid into the treasury on account of their quotas on the existing requisitions of the late Congress, — 2,244,231. 31

So much paid by the state of New-Jersey to their own citizens, on the domestic debt, not included in the schedule of taxes, — 424,442. 22

So much paid by the state of South-Carolina, being two years interest on 222,465 dollars, and 9-90ths, the amount of certificates issued to the line of that state, at 6 per cent. is — 26,695. 73

Total amount of Interest paid, — 4,771,163. 5

Deduct three years interest, estimated in the foregoing, on 960,915 dollars, and 42-100ths, being so much of the capital of the domestic debt received in payment for lands and other public property, — 172,964. 75

Total amount of deductions, — 4,944,127. 80

13,030,168. 20

Leaves a balance of thirteen million and thirty thousand one hundred sixty-eight dollars, and 20 cents, which will accrue on the domestic debt, and for which provision is to be made to pay the interest fully up to the 31st December, 1790,

' It is to be observed, that as the certificates which have been issued for the principal of a debt of more than twenty-seven millions of dollars, are in themselves exceedingly numerous; and that as those several certificates bear an interest from different periods, it has not been practicable to form a statement of arrearages, but by ascertaining in the most accurate manner, the different periods of time from which the several parts of the domestic debt bear interest, and therefrom calculating the interest to 31st December, 1790.

Treasury Department, *Register's Office*, 31st December, 1789.

Joseph Nourse, Register.

SCHEDULE E

ABSTRACT OF THE PUBLIC DEBT OF THE STATES UNDERMENTIONED,
AGREEABLY TO STATEMENTS TRANSMITTED IN PURSUANCE OF THE
RESOLUTION OF THE HOUSE OF REPRESENTATIVES OF THE 21ST OF
SEPTEMBER, 1789.

MASSACHUSETTS   *Dollars. Cents.*

Principal with interest to the
1st day of Nov. 1789.   £. 1,548,040 7 9 Lawful.
Due to sundries for which
no certificates have yet
been issued,   20,000
                     Total,   £. 1,568,040 7 9 at 6s. per Dol.   5,226,801. 29

CONNECTICUT

Principal bearing interest
from the 1st of Feb. 1789,   560,404
To which ought to be added
for balance of state bills
emitted in the year 1780,
bearing interest at 5 per
cent. to the 1st March
1785, estimated at   24,948
                     Total,   £.   585,352 0 0 at 6s. per Dol.   1,951,173. 33⅓

NEW-YORK

Principal and interest computed to the 1st day of
January 1790,   1,032,616 2 0
From which ought to be de-
ducted for amount of principle and interest of continental securities loaned to
the state in pursuance of
their act of the 18th day
April 1786, estimated at   565,586
Leaves for state debt *proper*, £.   467,030 2 0 at 8s. per Dol.   1,167,575. 25

NEW-JERSEY

Principal unredeemed,   295,755 4 11 at 7/6 per Dol.   788,680. 65⁵⁄₉

VIRGINIA

Principal of domestic debt,   1,063,396 17 1
Ditto of foreign debt with
interest to the 1st January
1790,   40,826 1 1
                     Total,   £. 1,104,222 18 2 at 6s. per Dol.   3,680,743. 2⅞

SOUTH-CAROLINA

Principal on domestic debt,	1,069,652	2	4
Indents of interest on ditto in circulation,	71,325	7	2
Foreign debt, principal and interest, due to the 1st of January 1789,	115,810	0	1

Total, £. 1,256,787 9 7 at 4/8 per Dol. 5,386,232. 5

Total dollars, 18,201,205. 60%

It will be observed, that the period to which interest is calculated on the debts abovementioned is only specified with accuracy on the statements which have been transmitted from Massachusetts, Connecticut and New-York. From the best information which the Secretary can obtain, he presumes—That in the statement made of the debt of New-Jersey, interest has been calculated to the 31st day of December 1788. That on the debt of Virginia, interest has been calculated to the 31st day of December 1788. On that of South-Carolina, to the 1st day of April 1790.

From the states of New-Hampshire, Pennsylvania, Delaware, Maryland, North-Carolina and Georgia, no accounts of their respective state debts have been forwarded.

The Secretary is however of opinion from the result of enquiries made by him—That the state debt of New-Hampshire may be estimated at about

Dollars 300,000

That the state debt *proper* of Pennsylvania (that is exclusive of their assumption of the continental debt) at about   Dollars 2,200,000

And that of Maryland, at   Ditto   800,000

From the above statement and estimates, the amount of principal and interest of the state debts (exclusive of Delaware, North-Carolina, Georgia and Rhode-Island) appears to be about twenty-one millions and a half; but as the debts of the four last states are not included in the above sum; and it is possible that a greater arrearage of interest may be due on the state debts than is at present ascertained, the aggregate of the principal and interest may be computed at twenty-five millions of dollars.

Alexander Hamilton, *Secretary of the Treasury.*

COMMONWEALTH OF MASSACHUSETTS.

A Statement of the Debt of the Commonwealth of Massachusetts, as it respects the notes issued by the several Treasurers, to the first of November, 1789.

November 1, 1789, exclusive of half pay notes,	£. 1,403,459	16	11
Notes issued to widows and orphan children of the deceased officers of the late continental army, for the seven years half pay, agreeable to the resolves of Congress,	8,246	11	10

Interest on the foregoing notes since

October, 1781   £. 579,660 6 4

Of which has been paid   443,326 7 4

Interest remaining due, November 1, 1789,   136,333 19 0

£. 1,548,040 7 9

Remains due on the books of the committee for settling with the late continental army, to the widows and orphan children of deceased officers of said army, and to officers and soldiers for their services, about

20,000

N.B. By an act of the legislature, one third part of the revenue of Excise is appropriated to pay the exigencies of government, and the other two third parts for the payment of interest of the notes, which pays about one quarter part of the interest; the other three quarters are unprovided for.

Treasury-Office, Boston, October 31, 1789.   Alexander Hodgdon, Treasurer.

Compared with the original, in the office of the Secretary of the Treasury.

William Duer.

STATE OF CONNECTICUT

A Statement of the Public Debt of the State of Connecticut, as it stood November 1, 1789.

Notes issued to the Connecticut line, payable June 1, 1782,			£.	2,334	13	11½
Ditto	ditto	1783,		2,339	13	4
Ditto	ditto	1784,		3,252	12	1
Ditto	ditto	1785,		42,309	6	1¾
Ditto	ditto	1786,		28,189	6	3¾
Ditto	ditto	1787,		28,448	5	6¾
Ditto	ditto	1788,		21,593		4¼
Ditto	ditto	1789,		20,097	5	7¼
Ditto dated February 1, 1781, issued per act of Assembly, Nov., 1780,				153,229	8	6¼
Ditto of various dates, ditto per act of ditto, May, 1781,				33,947	11	8½
Ditto dated June 1, 1781, ditto ditto, for remounting dragoons,				1,932	8	0
Ditto of various dates, ditto ditto May, 1783,				41,841	6	1¾
Ditto issued per act of May, 1789, for old notes re-loaned,				180,890	1	0
				560,404	18	9¼

Notes issued per particular acts of Assembly, payable out of the civil List funds,   2,856 11 4

Certificates for interest, &c. issued on the state debt, up to February 1, 1789, and remaining unpaid November 1, 1789,   19,140 3 9¾

Balance of orders unpaid, drawn by Oliver Wolcott, Esq. payable out of the 1s tax, granted in January, 1783,   692 8 10.

Balance of state bills, which were emitted in March, June & July, 1780, with the interest at 5 per cent. to 1st of March, 1785, estimated at   24,948 9 1

There are a number of pay table orders drawn on former taxes, the amount, supposed not great, cannot be ascertained.

There is also out-standing, a sum of old emissions of paper, issued before the war—the amount unknown.

Account of Loan-Office and Final Settlement Certificates in the treasury of the State of Connecticut.

Loan-office certificates,	£.	442	19	7
Final settlement certificates,		2,151	17	1
	£.	2,594	16	8

Amount of interest certificates that were issued upon the evidence of the United States debt, received by the treasurer of the state of Connecticut for taxes and impost duties, and delivered to William Imlay, Esq. continental loan-officer, from January 9, 1786, to November 1, 1789,   £. 33,996 15 3

Compared with the original in the office of the Secretary of the Treasury.

A Statement of the Funds provided for the payment of the principal and interest of the public debt of the state of Connecticut.

Balances of taxes laid for the payment of interest on the state debt, and the first three classes of army notes, as appears from the treasury books, November 1, 1789, being the balance of fifteen taxes, including abatements, collecting fees &c.	£. 40,489 14 10
Balance of excise and impost bonds payable, including collecting fees, &c.	9,070 15 2
A tax of four pence on the pound, laid on the list, 1788, amounting to £. 1,462,860 10 11 for the payment of interest on the state debt, and the balance of three first classes of the state notes; the nett avails estimated at	20,266 14 4
A tax of eight pence on the pound, on the same list, laid for the payment of the balance of state bills, orders on 2s. 6d. and 1s. taxes, and part of the principal of the state debt; the nett avails estimated at	40,533 8 8
Excise for the payment of interest on the state debt, &c. estimated at	5,000 0 0

The first article in the above statement of funds will probably, upon settlement of those old taxes, fall greatly short of the sum set down; to say how
much, is merely conjectural. There will also be a loss upon the excise and
impost bonds. The amount of the excise for the current year is very uncertain.
    Comptroller's-Office. 1st December, 1789.   Ralph Pomeroy, Comptroller.

STATE OF NEW-YORK

A Statement of the debt of the State of New-York.
The following species of Certificates, &c. have been issued by the State, and
are still unredeemed, viz.

	Principal Sum, Spec. val.	Interest to Jan. 1, 1790.
Certificates for Money loaned, pursuant to resolutions of the 4th day of April, 1778,	£. 111 13 3	£. 78 14 5
for do. pursuant to a law of the 30th of June, 1780,	741 6 0	422 10 9
for horses purchased in the year 1780,	904 5 0	515 8 5
for depreciation of pay to the army date 31st July, 1780,	54,520 1 7	25,669 17 4
for pay of the year 1781, to do. dated the 1st January, 1782,	17,972 6 9	8,626 14 0
for pensions to widows of military officers,	8,104 18 2	3,647 4 2
for pay of levies, militia, &c. &c.	42,871 4 3	18,220 5 3
for other certificates received on loan, pursuant to a law passed the 18th April, 1786,	523,848 5 1	144,058 5 4
for four-fifths of the interest due on those received on loan,	105,669 9 8	
for claims on forfeited estates	25,897 8 10	3,884 12 3

Bills of credit, called New Emission, emitted pursuant to a law passed the 30th of June, 1780, bearing interest,   3,612 16 0   1,174 3 1

Ditto, emitted pursuant to resolutions of Congress, and Convention of this State, reduced to specie value,   1,047 0 0

£. 785,300 14 7   £. 206,297 15 0

There are large demands against forfeited estates, unliquidated, and other liquidated, for which no certificates have yet issued, to the amount of   41,017 12 5

There are no funds specially provided for redeeming the aforesaid Certificates, except the following, viz.

The arrears of old taxes may probably produce about   £. 10,000 0 0
Quit rents, about   20,000 0 0
Fifteen townships of new lands, or 375,000 acres, ordered to be sold (by a law passed the 25th February, 1789,) and are now surveying.

Gerard Bancker, *Treasurer of the State of New-York.*
New-York, November 30, 1789.

An Account of Continental Securities now in the Treasury of the State of New-York, viz.

	Principal.	Int. 1st. Jan. 1790.
Certificates issued by William Barber,	£. 352,471 13 1	£ 105,741 9 11
Ditto " by loan-officers in this State,	277,448 16 4	83,234 12 11
Ditto " by John Pierce, Burrall, Denning, Bindon, and Fox,	299,614 4 5	89,884 5 4
Interest facilities,	2,502 14 8	
	£. 932,037 8 6	£ 278,860 8 2

Of the above-mentioned Loan-Office and Barber's Certificates, the sum of £. 470,649 17 6 was received in on loan by the State in 1786, and one fifth of the interest that was due thereon, to the 31st December, 1784, then paid, and certificates for the remaining four fifths issued, payable in one year, of which certificates three fourths remain unredeemed, as represented in the former part of this statement.

Gerard Bancker. *Treasurer of the State of New-York.*
New-York, November 30, 1789.
Compared with the Original in the office of the Secretary of the Treasury.

An Account of Certificates due from the United States to the Inhabitants of the State of New-Jersey, which draw interest at the Treasury.

	Principal.	Annual Interest.
1st. Continental loan-office certificates,	£. 420,511 0 10	25,230 13 3
2nd. Certificates issued by John Pierce, Commissioner, for arrears of pay, &c.	147,118 15 2¼	8,827 2 6
3d. Certificates by Benjamin Thompson, Commissioner,	344,237 11 2	20,654 5 0
	£. 911,867 7 2¼	£. 54,712 0 9

Commutation

4th. Certificates issued by John Pierce, Commissioner, and given to the officers of the late Jersey line, for their commutation.   66,899 2 6

State Debt

1st. Certificates given to the officers and soldiers of the late Jersey line, for the depreciation of their pay, of which there was outstanding October 1, 1786,   99,526 11 4

2nd. Ditto given by the Commissioners in the several counties for militia pay, of which there was outstanding, October 1, 1786,   55,365 17 7½

3d. Certificates given by Silas Condict, Commissioner,   121,521 8 7

4th. Ditto given by the Treasurer and Auditor for demands against confiscated estates,   32,020 2 9

5th. Ditto issued by the Auditor for militia pay,   821 4 7½

£. 309,255 4 11

Paid into the Treasury since October 1786,   13,500 0 0

£. 295,755 4 11

Annual interest of state debt,   £, 17,745 6 3½

Compared with the Original in the Office of the Secretary of the Treasury.

Abstract of the Public Debts due from the State of Virginia.

On Interest at 6 per cent	Army debt for pay and depreciation of the officers and soldiers,	£. 936,830 7 6
	Loan-office debt,	119,382 7 4
	Certificates issued for the paper money funded,	7,183 2 3

Balance due to Foreign creditors, including the interest (at 6 per cent) to the 1st of January, 1790, on £. 9,415 0 2 part of the said balance, for which warrants have not been drawn by the creditors,   40,826 1 1

John Pendleton, Auditor of Public Accounts.

Virginia, Auditor's-Office, November 20, 1789.

Compared with the original in the office of the Secretary of the Treasury.

The Auditor-General reports the following Statement of the Debt due by the State of South-Carolina, viz

Principal Indents.

Balance issued from the treasury of the state aforesaid, and yet remaining to be issued on the 1st of October, 1789,   £. 1,069,652 2 4½

To be cancelled by

Balance of bonds for confiscated property	£. 79,985	10	0¼
Purchases of ditto, unsettled for,	12,910	0	0
Balance of amercements,	7,713	4	6
Ditto for bonds for public property,	35,065	10	6
Ditto of lands granted to 1st November, 1789,	42,568	1	7¾

Balance still to be cancelled,   Sterling,   £. 178,242 6 8

£. 891,409 15 8½

Special Indents.

Amount issued, and to be issued,	£. 440,368	0	0
Deduct, for so much received into the treasury,	369,042	12	9¾

Balance in circulation, and yet to be issued,   £. 71,325 7 2¼

Agreeably to a report of the committee of ways and means, the debts due to the State for the arrears of taxes, &c. are sufficient to cancel the above balance.

Foreign Debt.

Amount due to sundry persons, £. 93,244 17 4

Balance of interest due 1st January, 1789, £. 4,949 5 4¼
Deduct, for so much paid J. S. Cripps, agent, 2,043 16 10
Balance paid to such creditors as were here or their attorneys, £. 29,558 4 11¼

Principal and balance due 1st January, 1789, 22,565 2 9

6,993 2 2¼

£. 115,810 0 1

Funds appropriated by the Legislature.

Out of the taxes payable the 1st April, 1790, £. 10,000
Interest on the paper medium, to 1st May, 1791, 12,750
Balance of bonds given for confiscated property, payable in specie, 1,610 17 3¼
The sums due, and that shall become due, for amercements, in specie, 8,371 16 6
Balance of bonds given for duties, payable by instalments, 6,240 14 3
Bonds for duties due prior to 1st Jan. 1788, not installed, 233 3 4½
A tax of ¼th of a dollar per head, per annum, on all negroes and mus-
tizoes, and mulattoes, for ten years, from February, 1791, the num-
ber computed to be about 100,000, which will amount to 58,333 6 8

Sterling, £. 97,539 18 0¾

Auditor's-Office, Charleston, 30th November, 1789.

Compared with the original in the office of the Secretary of the Treasury.

J. McCall, Auditor.

SCHEDULE F

TABLE SHEWING THE ANNUITY WHICH A PERSON OF A GIVEN AGE, WOULD BE ENTITLED TO DURING LIFE, FROM THE TIME HE SHOULD ARRIVE AT A GIVEN AGE, UPON THE PRESENT PAYMENT OF A HUNDRED DOLLARS, COMPUTING INTEREST AT FOUR PER CENT.

Age at the time of payment.	Age when entitled.	Annuity.	Age when entitled.	Annuity.	Age when entitled.	Annuity.	Age when entitled.	Annuity.
1	21	23.453	31	42.625	41	84.522	50	174.11
2	22	20.376	32	37.365	42	74.936	50	143.14
3	23	19.415	33	35.775	43	72.440	50	128.46
4	24	18.826	34	34.970	44	71.697	50	117.64
5	25	18.457	35	34.660	45	71.840	50	108.95
6	26	18.280	36	34.619	46	72.584	50	101.60
7	27	18.188	37	34.767	47	73.752	50	95.210
8	28	18.258	38	35.235	48	75.720	50	89.971
9	29	18.383	39	35.830	49	78.025	50	85.238
10	30	18.617	40	37.006	50	81.960		
11	21	10.346	31	18.803	41	37.286	50	75.500
12	22	10.414	32	19.072	42	38.162	50	73.058
13	23	10.519	33	19.382	43	39.249	50	70.246
14	24	10.608	34	19.704	44	40.493	50	66.279
15	25	10.727	35	20.088	45	41.638	50	63.151
16	26	10.818	36	20.489	46	42.957	50	60.129
17	27	10.939	37	20.911	47	44.358	50	57.258
18	28	11.065	38	21.354	48	45.888	50	54.520
19	29	11.195	39	21.821	49	47.519	50	51.907
20	30	11.352	40	22.313	50	49.415		
21	31	11.515	41	22.836	50	47.038		
22	32	11.687	42	23.386	50	44.770		
23	33	11.846	43	23.987	50	42.534		
24	34	12.028	44	24.719	50	40.460		
25	35	12.253	45	25.396	50	38.510		
26	36	12.462	46	26.128	50	36.572		
27	37	12.682	47	26.902	50	34.726		
28	38	12.913	48	27.749	50	32.967		
29	39	13.155	49	28.647	50	31.329		
30	40	13.385			50	29.643		
31	41	13.629			50	28.073		
32	42	13.884			50	26.580		
33	43	14.190			50	25.161		
34	44	14.547			50	23.812		
35	45	14.827			50	22.483		
36	46	15.157			50	21.217		
37	47	15.512			50	20.023		
38	48	15.896			50	18.886		
39	49	16.301			50	17.806		
40	50	16.783						

SCHEDULE G

TABLE SHEWING WHAT ANNUITY WOULD BE ENJOYED BY THE SURVIVOR OF ANY TWO PERSONS OF CERTAIN AGES, FOR THE REMAINDER OF LIFE, AFTER THE DETERMINATION OF THE LIFE IN EXPECTATION, UPON THE PRESENT PAYMENT OF ONE HUNDRED DOLLARS, COMPUTING INTEREST AT FOUR PER CENT. PER ANNUM, AND THE DURATION OF LIFE ACCORDING TO DOCTOR HALLEY'S TABLES.

Age of the youngest.	Age of the eldest.	Annuity of survivor.
10	10	28.248
	15	26.392
	20	24.545
	25	22.716
	30	20.920
	35	19.168
	40	17.464
	45	15.847
	50	14.263
	55	12.782
	60	11.237
	65	10.099
	70	8.905
15	15	28.169
	20	26.198
	25	24.219
	30	22.276
	35	20.376
	40	18.528
	45	16.750
	50	15.053
	55	12.968
	60	11.948
	65	10.553
	70	9.270
20	20	28.169
	25	26.041
	30	23.923
	35	21.753
	40	19.825
	45	17.876
	50	16.018
	55	14.261
	60	12.620
	65	11.100
	70	9.707
25	25	27.816
	30	25.556
	35	23.331
	40	21.159
	45	19.047
	50	17.030
	55	15.117
	60	13.331
	65	11.689
	70	10.173
30	30	28.555
	35	26.001
	40	23.496
	45	21.061
	50	18.730
	55	16.529
	60	14.484
	65	12.600
	70	10.894
35	35	28.993
	40	26.164
	45	23.381
	50	20.702
	55	18.172
	60	15.820
	65	13.666
	70	11.724
40	40	29.673
	45	26.469
	50	23.337
	55	20.354
	60	17.604
	65	15.060
	70	12.799
45	45	30.620
	50	27.005
	55	23.375
	60	20.040
	65	16.957
	70	14.240
50	50	32.164
	55	27.731
	60	23.513
	65	19.662
	70	16.257
55	55	34.286
	60	28.843
	65	23.742
	70	19.175
60	60	37.509
	65	30.423
	70	24.044
65	65	42.481
	70	32.679
70	70	50.994

To find the Annuity upon the Survivorship of the youngest of any two lives, expressed in this table, look for the respective ages under their respective heads, and opposite the number, which corresponds with the age of the eldest will be seen the Annuity required.

SCHEDULE H

TABLE FOR A TONTINE OF SIX CLASSES, THE NUMBER OF LIVES IN EACH CLASS BEING INDEFINITE, CALCULATED ON A PAYMENT OF TWO HUNDRED DOLLARS BY EACH SUBSCRIBER, AND AT A RATE OF INTEREST OF FOUR PER CENT. THE COMPUTATION ON THE BEST LIFE IN EACH CLASS, AND ON THE SUPPOSITION THAT THE SUBSCRIBERS TO EACH CLASS WILL NOT BE LESS THAN THE RESPECTIVE NUMBERS SPECIFIED IN THE FIRST COLUMN.

Number of lives in each class.	Ages.	Annuity whilst all are in life.	Dividends at successive periods during the probable continuance of life.						
			At the expiration of 10 years.	At the expiration of 20 years.	At the expiration of 30 years.	At the expiration of 40 years.	At the expiration of 50 years.	At the expiration of 60 years.	At the expiration of 70 years.
75	1 to 20	8,426	9,722	11,490	14,042	18,054	25,278	42,130	126,390
64	21 to 30	8,676	10,272	12,666	16,314	23,110	39,618	138,666	
54	31 to 40	9,046	11,102	14,366	20,354	34,890	122,282		
44	41 to 50	9,650	12,488	17,608	30,328	106,150			
34	51 to 60	10,714	15,178	26,020	91,068				
24	61 to 70	12,802	20,518	71,802					

This Table, which is calculated on so small a number of persons, will serve to shew the greatness of the advantage to fortunate survivors, in case of a numerous subscription.

SCHEDULE I

GENERAL ESTIMATE FOR THE SERVICES OF THE CURRENT YEAR.

Civil List, as per No. 1,	254,892.73
War department, No. 2,	155,537.72
Military Pensions, No. 3,	96,979.72
Dollars,	507,410.17

With an eye to the necessary provisions for the foreign department, and to other arrangements which may be found requisite, it appeared advisable to state in the report, to which this is annexed, a sum of six hundred thousand dollars for the current service.

Treasury Department, January 5, 1790.

NO. I

ESTIMATE OF THE EXPENDITURE FOR THE CIVIL LIST OF THE UNITED STATES, ON THE PRESENT ESTABLISHMENT FOR THE YEAR 1790.

Dollars.

For the compensation to the President of the United States,	25,000	
That of the Vice-President,	5,000	
Compensation to the Chief Justice,	4,000	
Ditto to each of the five Associate Judges, 3500 dollars each,	17,500	
To the Judges of the following Districts, viz.		
District of Maine,	1,000	
New-Hampshire,	1,000	
Massachusetts,	1,200	
Connecticut,	1,000	
New-York,	1,500	
New-Jersey,	1,000	
Pennsylvania,	1,600	
Delaware,	800	
Maryland,	1,500	
Virginia,	1,800	
Kentuckey,	1,000	
South-Carolina,	1,800	
Georgia,	1,500	
Attorney-General,	1,500	69,700

Dols. Cts. Dols. Cts.

Compensation to the members of Congress, estimating the attendance of the whole number for six months, viz.		
Speaker of the House of Representatives, at twelve dollars per day,	2,190	
Eighty members, at six dollars per day,	87,600	
Travelling expences computed,	15,000	
	104,790	

Dols. Cts. Dols. Cts.

To the Secretary of the Senate, one
year's salary,   1,500
Additional allowance estimated for six
months, at two dollars per day,   365   1,865
Principal Clerk to the Secretary of the Senate,
for the same time, at three dollars per day,   547.50
Engrossing Clerk to the Secretary of the Senate,
estimated for same time, at two dollars per day,   365
Chaplain to the Senate, estimated for six months,
at five hundred dollars per annum,   250
Compensation to the door-keeper of the Senate,
for the same time, at three dollars per day,   547.50
Messenger to the Senate, for the same time, at
two dollars per day.   365
Clerk of the House of Representatives,
for one year's salary,   1,500.
Additional allowance calculated for six
months, at two dollars per day,   365.   1,865
Principal Clerk in the office of do. estimated for
same time, at three dollars per day,   547.50
Engrossing Clerk for some time, estimated at
two dollars per day,   365
Chaplain to the House of Representatives, esti-
mated for same time, at five hundred dollars per
annum,   250
Serjeant at arms, estimated for same time at 4
dols. per day,   730
Door-keeper, for same time, at 3 dollars per day,   547.50
Assistant door-keeper for do. at 2 dollars per day,   365   183,100

TREASURY DEPARTMENT

Secretary of the Treasury,   3,500
Assistant of the Secretary of the Treasury,   1,500
Five Clerks, at 500 dollars per annum each,   2,500
Messenger and office keeper,   150
Comptroller of the Treasury,   2,000
Principal Clerk to do.   800
Four clerks, at 500 dollars each,   2,000
Treasurer,   2,000
Principal Clerk to do.   600
Auditor of the Treasury,   1,500
Principal Clerk to do.   600
Twelve Clerks to do. who, besides the current
business under the New Government, has the set-
tlement of the accounts which arose under the
Confederation, in the quarter-master, commissary,
clothing, hospital, and marine departments, and
ordnance stores; and also the accounts of the secret and commercial committees of Congress, at
500 dollars each,   6,000

	Dols.	Cts.	Dols.	Cts.
Register of the Treasury,	1,250			
One Clerk on the books of the public creditors, called Funded Debt at the Treasury, transfers, &c.	500			
One Clerk in the office of the Register, employed in keeping the accounts of interest arising on the domestic debt,	500			
One do. on the principal books of the treasury, in journalizing and posting into the ledger,	500		25,850	
One Clerk in copying fair statements of the public accounts, and other transcripts as required from the treasury books,	500			
One do, in keeping the accounts of the registers, signed and sealed, &c. for ships transmitted to the collectors of the customs at the several ports; filing duplicates of registers issued by the collectors; keeping the accounts of the transfers of vessels, and other business of record, arising from Act for registering of vessels, regulating the coasting trade, and other purposes therein mentioned,	500			
Two do. on the old accounts of the treasury, and books and accounts of the thirteen late state commissioners, at five hundred dollars each,	1,000			
Messenger and office keeper to the comptroller, auditor and register's office,	150		2,150	

DEPARTMENT OF STATE

	Dols.	Cts.	Dols.	Cts.
Secretary of that department,	3,500			
Chief Clerk,	800			
Three Clerks, at 500 dollars each,	1,500			
Messenger and office keeper,	150		5,950.	

DEPARTMENT OF WAR

	Dols.	Cts.	Dols.	Cts.
Secretary of that department,	3,000			
Chief Clerk,	600			
Two Clerks at five hundred dollars each,	1,000			
Messenger and office keeper	150		4,750.	

GOVERNMENT OF THE WESTERN TERRITORY

	Dols.	Cts.	Dols.	Cts.
The Governor for his salary as such, and for discharging the duties of Superintendant of Indian affairs in the northern department,	2,000			
The Secretary of the Western Territory,	750			
The Three Judges, at eight hundred dollars each,	2,400		5,150	
Officers employed to settle the accounts between the United States and individual States.				
Three Commissioners of the General Board, at two thousand two hundred and fifty dollars per annum,	6,750			
Chief Clerk,	600			
Four Clerks, at four hundred dollars each,	1,600			
Messenger and office keeper,	150			

	Dols.	Cts.	Dols.	Cts.

Paymaster-General, and Commissioner of Army Accounts, — 1,250

Eight Clerks, at five hundred dollars each, — 4,000

One do. at four hundred dollars, — 400

One do. at four hundred and fifty dollars, — 450 — 15,200

PENSIONS GRANTED BY THE LATE GOVERNMENT

Isaac Van Vert, John Paulding, David Williams, } a pension of two hundred dollars per annum to each, pursuant to an act of Congress of 3d November 1780, — 600

Dominique L'Eglise, per act of 8th of August, 1782, — 120

Joseph Traversie, per do. — 120

Youngest children of the late Major-General Warren, per Act of 1st July, 1780, — 450

Eldest son of do. per act of 8th April, 1777, estimated at, — 600

Youngest son of General Mercer, per act of 8th April, 1777, estimated at, — 700

James M'Kenzie, Joseph Brussells, John Jordan, } per act of 10th September, 1783, entitled to a pension of forty dollars each per annum, — 120

Elizabeth Bergen, per act of 21st August, 1781, — 53.33

Joseph De Beauleau, per act 5th August, 1782, — 100

Richard Gridley, per acts of 17th November, 1775, and 26th February, 1781, — 444.40

Lieutenant-Colonel Touzard, per act of 27th October, 1778, — 360. — 3,667.73

FOR INCIDENTAL AND CONTINGENT EXPENCES RELATIVE TO THE CIVIL LIST ESTABLISHMENT

Under this head are comprehended fire wood, stationary, together with printing work, and all other contingent expences for the two Houses of Congress; rent and office expences of the three several departments, viz. Treasury, State, War, and of the General Board of Commissioners, and Paymaster-General.

Congress, estimated at, — 5,000

Treasury Department, viz.

Rent, — 500

Contingencies of the Secretary's office, — 500

Comptroller's — 400

Auditor's — 200

Register's — 200

Treasurer's — 200 — 2,000

Ditto   War Department, — 600

Department of State, — 500

Board of Commissioners, — 500

Paymaster, and Commissioner of Army Accounts, — 425 — 9,025

Dollars, — 254,892.73

This estimate corresponds with the existing provisions; but it will probably receive additions from others in the course of the session: In particular it will be observed, that there is no article respecting the salaries of Foreign Ministers, their allowances not having been regulated by law. Neither does the estimate include those objects which remain to be provided for in consequence of some deficiency in the estimate for the services of last year, and also from certain demands on the Treasury, founded on acts of the late Government, which require an appropriation by Congress, previous to their being discharged. These will form an estimate by themselves under the head of Contingencies.

Register's-Office, 5th January, 1790.   Joseph Nourse, Register.

NO. II

ESTIMATE OF MONIES REQUISITE FOR THE DEPARTMENT OF WAR, FOR THE YEAR 1790.

INFANTRY

		Dollars.	
1 Brigadier General with the pay of Lieutenant Colonel Commandant for 12 months at 50 Dollars,		600	
2 Majors,	45	1,080	
7 Captains,	35	2,940	
7 Lieutenants,	30	2,520	
8 Ensigns,	20	1,920	
1 Pay master,	10	120	
1 Adjutant,	10	120	
1 Quarter Master,	10	120	
1 Surgeon,	45	540	
4 Surgeon's Mates,	30	1,440	
28 Sergeants,	6	2,016	
28 Corporals,	5	1,680	
14 Musicians,	5	840	
490 Privates,	4	23,520	39,456.

ARTILLERY

1 Major 12 Months,	at 45 Dol.	540	
4 Captains,	35	1,680	
8 Lieutenants,	30	2,880	
1 Surgeon's Mate,	30	360	
16 Serjeants,	6	1,152	
16 Corporals,	5	960	
8 Musicians,	5	480	
240 Matrosses,	4	11,520	19,572

SUBSISTENCE

1 Brigadier General 12 Months at	48 Dol.	576	
3 Majors,	20	720	
11 Captains,	12	1,584	
23 Subalterns,	8	2,208	
1 Surgeon,	16	192	
5 Surgeon Mates,	8	480	5,760

Dols.   Cts.   Dols.   Cts.

RATIONS

For 840 Non Commissioned Officers and Privates, one ration pr. day each for 365 days, is 306,600 rations at 12 cents pr. ditto,   36,792   101,580

Clothing,   840, ⎱ 940 suits at 26
Contingencies, 100, ⎰ dollars each,   24,440

QUARTER MASTER'S DEPARTMENT

Transportation. Including the transportation of the recruits to the frontiers, the removal of troops from one station to another, the transportation of clothing, ordnance, and military stores for the troops on the frontiers—the necessary removal of ordnance military stores —the hire of teams and pack horses—the purchase of tents, boats, axes, camp-kettles, boards, fire-wood, company books, stationary for the troops, and all other expences in the quarter-master's department,   15,000

HOSPITAL DEPARTMENT

For medicines, instruments, furniture and stores for an hospital for the frontiers, also for attendance when necessary at West-Point,   1,000

ORDNANCE DEPARTMENT

For salaries for the store keepers at the several deposits, viz.

West-Point, ⎤
Virginia,   ⎬ 3 at 40 dollars pr. month,   1,400
Springfield ⎦

Charleston, 1 Store keeper at 100 dols.
              pr. annum,   100
         2 Assistants, at 15 do. pr. month,   360
1 Store keeper at Philadelphia,   500
1 ditto,   —   Rhode-Island,   96
1 ditto,   —   Lancaster,   96
1 ditto,   —   Fort Harkemer,[139] 120
His subsistence, 1 dollar pr.
   week,   52   172

RENTS OF BUILDINGS FOR DEPOSITS

Philadelphia,   752.66
Virginia,   350
West-Point,   400   1,502.66
Labourers at the several Deposits,   400
8 Artificers at the posts on the frontiers, including armourers, at 5 dollars pr. month,   480
Coopers, armourers, and carpenters employed occasionally at the several arsenals,   500

139. Fort Herkimer (formerly Fort Dayton), on the Mohawk River near Herkimer, New York.

	Dols. Cts.	Dols. Cts.
The expence of materials and constructing twenty new carriages for cannon and howitzers,	2,000.	7,646.66

Buildings for arsenals and magazines are highly requisite in the southern and middle departments, for which particularly estimates will be formed.

CONTINGENCIES OF THE WAR DEPARTMENT, VIZ.

For maps, hiring expresses, allowance to officers for extra expences, printing, loss of stores of all kinds, advertising and apprehending deserters,		3,000

CONTINGENCIES FOR THE WAR OFFICE, VIZ.

Office rent, wood, stationary, desks, book cases, sweeping, &c.		600
Subsistence due the officers of Colonel Marinus Willet's regiment in 1782,	786.6	
Pay due Lieutenant Joseph Wilcox, pay master to the regiment lately commanded by Col. David Humphreys,	315	
Pay subsistence and forage due the officers appointed by the State of Rhode-Island, under the act of Congress of the 20th October, 1786,	1,770	2,871. 6
Total Amount as above,	156,137.72	156,137.72
Deduct contingencies of the War Office, office rent, wood, stationary, desks, &c. as above, the same being included with the salaries in the civil list estimate,	600	
Dollars	155,537.72	

SUMMARY OF THE FOREGOING

Pay of the troops,	59,028
Subsistence of ditto,	42,552
Clothing of ditto,	24,440
Quarter masters department,	15,000
Hospital department,	1,000
Contingencies of the war department,	3,000
Contingencies of the war office,	600
Arrears of pay and subsistence unprovided for,	2,871. 6
Ordnance department,	7,646.66
Dollars,	156,137.72

War-Office, December 29th, 1789.

Henry Knox, Secretary for the Department of War.

NO. III

ESTIMATE OF THE ANNUAL PENSIONS OF THE INVALIDS OF THE UNITED
STATES, VIZ. TAKEN FROM RETURNS IN THE WAR-OFFICE, DATED AS
FOLLOWS:

				Dols. Cts.	Dols. Cts.
November 28, 1789,	—	New-Hampshire,	—	3,024	
December 14,	—	Massachusetts,	—	11,166	
December 1,	—	Connecticut,	—	7,296	
December 31,	—	New-York,	—	15,588	
February 2,	—	New-Jersey,	—	4,357. 6	
December 10,	—	Pennsylvania,	—	16,506	
For 1787,	—	Virginia,	—	9,276.66	
					67,213.72

Conjectural—No returns having been received.
Suppose Rhode-Island and Delaware nearly equal to
New-Hampshire, ...   3,170
   Maryland nearly equal to Connecticut, ...   7,000
   North-Carolina, South-Carolina and Georgia, nearly
equal to New-Hampshire, Connecticut and Virginia, .   19,596

                                                        29,766

                                        Dollars,   96,979.72

War-Office, 31st *December,* 1789.

H. Knox, Secretary for the Department of War.

SCHEDULE K

ESTIMATE OF THE PROBABLE PRODUCT OF THE FUNDS PROPOSED FOR FUNDING THE DEBT AND PROVIDING FOR THE CURRENT SERVICE OF THE UNITED STATES, INCLUDING THE PRESENT DUTIES ON IMPORTS AND TONNAGE.

Dollars,

Probable product of the duties on imports and tonnage, according to the acts of the last session,
Including the State of North-Carolina, this estimate may be said to correspond with the statement made by the committee of ways and means during the last session; which statement the Secretary is inclined to think is as near the truth as can be now obtained.

In the preceding estimate are comprehended wines, distilled spirits, teas, and coffee, amounting to about   600,000

Which being deducted, leaves   1,200,000

From which deducting 5 per cent for expence of collection,   60,000

                    Leaves nett product,   1,140,000

PROBABLE PRODUCT OF DUTIES PROPOSED

Imported.[140]

1,000,000 gallons wine, at	20 cents,	200,000
4,000,000 gallons distilled spirits, at	20	800,000
700,000 pounds bohea tea, at	12	84,000
800,000 pounds souchong and other black teas, at	20	160,000
100,000 pounds green tea, average at	25	25,000
1,600,000 pounds coffee, at	5	80,000

Made in the United States.

3,500,000 gallons distilled spirits from foreign materials, at 11 cents,
3,000,000 ditto, distilled from materials of the United States, at 9 cents,   270,000

             2,004,000

Deduct for drawbacks, and expence of collection, 15 per cent.   300,600   1,703,400

               Dollars,   2,843,400

140. H may have taken some of this data from a letter from William Constable to Gouverneur Morris, December 6, 1788, a copy of which is in the Hamilton Papers, Library of Congress. Constable compiled estimates of imports which were higher than those drawn up by a Continental Congress committee in 1783. This committee, of which H was a member, calculated on the basis of pre-war importations the yield of a five percent impost, but Constable asserted that the committee understated the actual quantities (see *JCC*, XXIV, 287). Constable computed the imports as follows:

Wine	1,000,000	gallons
Distilled Spirits	4,000,000	"
Bohea Tea	1,000,000	lbs.
Hyson Tea	125,000	"
Coffee and Cocoa	1,500,000	"
Molasses	3,000,000	gallons

An ACT repealing, after the last day of   [141] next, the Duties
heretofore laid upon distilled Spirits imported from abroad, and
laying others in their stead, and also upon Spirits distilled within
the United States, as well to discourage the excessive use of those
Spirits, and promote Agriculture, as to provide for the support
of the Public Credit, and for the Common Defence and General
Welfare.[142]

I. Be it enacted by the Senate and House of Representatives of
the United States of America in Congress assembled,* that after
the last day of   next, the duties laid on distilled spirits by
the act entitled "An act for laying a duty on goods, wares and merchandizes imported into the United States," shall cease; and that
upon all distilled spirits which shall be imported into the United
States, after that day, from any foreign port or place, there shall
be paid for their use the duties following, that is to say,

1st. For every gallon of those spirits more than ten per cent.
below proof, according to Dicas's hydrometer, twenty cents.

2d. For every gallon of those spirits under five, and not more
than ten per cent. below proof, according to the same hydrometer,
twenty-one cents.

3d. For every gallon of those spirits of proof, and not more than
five per. cent below proof, according to the same hydrometer,
twenty-two cents.

4th. For every gallon of those spirits above proof, but not exceeding twenty per cent. according to the same hydrometer, twenty-
five cents.

5th. For every gallon of those spirits more than twenty, and not

---

* The four first of these classes of proof correspond with the different kinds
of spirits now usually imported: The first with gin; the second with St. Croix
rum; the third with Antigua rum; the fourth with Jamaica spirits; the fifth corresponds with the usual proof of high wines; the last with that of Alcohol.
These distinctions are necessary, not only to proportion the duty, but to prevent evasions of it. According to the present act, high wines, or even Alcohol,
which is from 30 to 40 per cent. above Jamaica proof, might be imported liable
only to the duty of Jamaica proof.

141. Spaces in this document were left blank in MS.

142. This proposed act was the basis of "An Act repealing, after the last
day of June next, the duties heretofore laid upon Distilled Spirits imported
from abroad, and laying others in their stead; and also upon Spirits distilled
within the United States, and for appropriating the same" (1 *Stat.* 199–214
[March 3, 1791]).

more than forty per cent. above proof, according to the same hydrometer, thirty cents.

6th. For every gallon of those spirits, more than forty per cent. above proof, according to the same hydrometer, forty cents.

II. And be it further enacted, that the said duties shall be collected in the same manner, by the same persons, under the same regulations, and subject to the same forfeitures and other penalties, as those heretofore laid; the act concerning which shall be deemed to be in full force for the collection of the duties herein before imposed, except as to the alterations contained in this act.

III. And be it further enacted,† that the said duties, at the option of the proprietor, importer or consignee, may either be paid immediately, or secured by bond, with one or more sureties, to the satisfaction of the collector, or person acting as such, with condition for the payment of one moiety in four months, and the other moiety in eight months: Provided that where the said duties shall not exceed fifty dollars, the same shall be immediately paid; and that where the same shall exceed fifty dollars, if the said proprietor, importer or consignee shall think fit to make present payment thereof, there shall be an abatement to him or her, at the rate of seven per cent per annum, only for such present payment, the allowance of ten per cent. in the said former act notwithstanding.

And as not only a due regard to the exigencies of the public, and to the interest and ease of the community, but justice to those virtuous citizens, who, content with the emoluments of fair and honorable trade, disdain to violate the laws of their country, and the principles of probity, requires that every possible impediment should be opposed to the fraudulent views of those who wish to profit at the expence both of the fair trader and of the community.

IV. Be it further enacted,‡ that the President of the United States of America, be authorised to appoint, with the advice and consent of the Senate, such number of officers as shall appear to him neces-

† The extension of the time is for the accommodation of the merchants in consideration of the encreased rate. It is proposed to reduce the discount, because ten per cent. is more than either the interest of money, or the risk of non-payment seems to warrant. Generally speaking, transient persons are those who avail themselves of the advantage; and they, without it, would commonly pay down, from the inconvenience of procuring and leaving sureties.

‡ This appears to be the only practicable method of compassing the details of so complicated a business.

sary, to be denominated Inspectors of the revenue; and to assign to them respectively such districts or limits for the exercise of their respective offices, as he shall judge best adapted to the due execution thereof; dividing the districts, if he shall think it adviseable, into general and particular, and placing the Inspectors of the latter under the superintendance of the former, within the limits whereof they shall be respectively comprehended; and also to make such allowances to the said Inspectors, and to the Deputies and officers by them appointed and employed for their respective services in the execution of this act, to be paid out of the product of the said duties, as shall be reasonable and proper: Provided always, that the whole amount of the said allowances shall not exceed   per cent. of the said product, computed throughout the United States; and that, being once regulated by the said President, they shall be alterable in such manner only as shall from time to time be prescribed by law.

V. And be it further enacted, that the Inspector or Inspectors of the revenue for each district, shall establish one or more offices within the same, and that there shall be one at least at each port of delivery; and in order that the said offices may be publicly known, there shall be painted or written, in large legible characters, upon some conspicuous part outside and in front of each house building or place in which any such office shall be kept, these words "Office of Inspection;" and if any person shall paint or write, or cause to be painted or written, the said words, upon any other than such house or building, he or she shall forfeit and pay for so doing, one hundred dollars.

VI. And be it further enacted, that within forty-eight hours after any ship or vessel, having on board any distilled Spirits brought in such ship or vessel from any foreign port or place, shall arrive within any port of the United States, whether the same be the first port of arrival of such ship or vessel or not; the master or person having the command or charge thereof, shall report to the Inspector or other chief officer of Inspection of the port at which she shall so arrive, the place from which she last sailed with her name and burthen and the quantity and kinds of the said spirits on board of her, and the casks or cases containing them, with their marks and numbers on pain of forfeiting five hundred dollars.

VII. And be it further enacted, that the Collector or other officer, or person acting as Collector of any port, with whom entry shall have been made of any of the said spirits, pursuant to the said act laying a duty on goods, wares and merchandizes imported into the United States, shall forthwith after such entry certify and transmit the same, as particularly as it shall have been made with him, to the Inspector of the revenue, or other proper officer of inspection, of the port where it shall be intended to commence the delivery of the spirits so entered, or any part thereof; for which purpose, every proprietor, importer or consignee, making such entry, shall deliver two manifests or contents (upon one of which the said certificate shall be given) and shall at the time thereof declare the port at which the said delivery shall be so intended to be commenced, to the Collector or officer with whom the same shall be made. And every permit granted by such Collector for the landing of any of the said spirits, shall previous to such landing be produced to the said officer of inspection, who shall make a minute in some proper book, of the contents thereof, and shall indorse thereupon the word "Inspected," the time when, and his own name, after which he shall return it to the person by whom it shall have been produced; and then, and not otherwise, it shall be lawful to land the spirits therein specified; and if the said spirits shall be landed without such indorsement upon the permit for that purpose granted, the master or person having charge of the ship or vessel, from which the same shall have been so landed, shall for every such offence forfeit the sum of five hundred dollars.

VIII. And be it further enacted, That whenever it shall be intended that any ship or vessel shall proceed with the whole or any part of the Spirits which shall have been brought in such ship or vessel from any foreign port or place, from one port in the United States to another port in the said United States, whether in the same or in different districts, the master or person having the command or charge of such ship or vessel, shall previous to her departure, apply to the proper officer of inspection for the port from which she is about to depart, for a certificate of the quantity and particulars of such of the said spirits as shall have been certified to him to have been entered as imported in such ship or vessel, and of so much thereof as shall appear to him to have been landed out of her at such port, which certificate the said officer shall forthwith grant without fee or charge. And the master or person having the command or charge of such ship or vessel, shall, within twenty-four hours after her arrival at the port to which she shall be bound, deliver the said certificate to the proper officer of inspection of such last mentioned port. And if such ship or vessel shall proceed from one port to another within the United States, with the whole or any part of the spirits brought in her as aforesaid, without having first obtained such certificate; or if within twenty-four hours after her arrival at such other port, the said certificate shall not be delivered to the proper officer of inspection there, the master or person having the command or charge of the said ship or vessel, shall in either case forfeit five hundred dollars; and the spirits on board of her at her said arrival, shall be forfeited, and may be seized by any officer of inspection.

IX. And be it further enacted, That all spirits which shall be imported as aforesaid, shall be landed under the inspection of the officer or officers of inspection for the place where the same shall be landed, and not otherwise, on pain of forfeiture thereof, for which purpose the said officer or officers shall at all reasonable times attend: Provided that this shall not be construed to exclude the inspection of the officers of the customs as now established and practised.

X. And be it further enacted, That the officers of inspection, under whose survey any of the said spirits shall be landed, shall, upon landing thereof, and as soon as the casks and cases containing the same shall be gauged or measured, brand or otherwise mark in durable characters, the several casks or cases containing the same, with progressive numbers, and also with the name of the ship or vessel wherein the same was or were imported, and of the port of entry, and with the proof and quantity thereof, together with such other marks, if any other shall be deemed needful, as the respective inspectors of the revenue may direct. And the said officer shall keep a book, wherein he shall enter the name of each vessel in which any of the said spirits shall be so imported, and of the port of entry and of delivery, and of the master of such vessel, and of each importer, and the several casks and cases containing the same, and the marks of each, and if not an inspector or the chief officer of inspection for the place, shall as soon as may be thereafter, make an exact transcript of each entry, and deliver the same to such inspector or chief officer, who shall keep a like book for recording the said transcripts.

XI. And be it further enacted, That the inspector of the revenue or other chief officer of inspection within whose survey any of the said spirits shall be landed shall give to the proprietor, importer, or consignee thereof, or his or her agent, a certificate to remain with him or her of the whole quantity of the said spirits which shall have been so landed, which certificate besides the said quantity shall specify the name of such proprietor, importer, or consignee, and of the vessel from on board which the said spirits shall have been landed, and of the marks of each cask or case containing the same. And the said inspector or other chief officer of inspection shall deliver to the said proprietor, importer or consignee, or to his or her agent, a like certificate for each cask or case which shall accompany the same wheresoever it shall be sent as evidence of its being lawfully imported. And the officer of inspection granting the said certificates, shall make regular and exact entries in the book to be by him kept as aforesaid, of all spirits for which the same shall be granted as particularly as therein described. And the said proprietor, importer, or consignee, or his or her agent upon the sale and delivery of any of the said spirits, shall deliver to the purchaser or purchasers thereof, the certificate or certificates which ought to accompany the same, on pain of forfeiting the sum of fifty dollars for each cask or case with which such certificate shall not be delivered.

XII. And be it further enacted,* That upon all spirits which after the said last day of   next, shall be distilled within the United States, wholly or in part from molasses, sugar, or other foreign materials, there shall be paid for their use the duties following, that is to say—

1st. For every gallon of those spirits more than 10 per cent. below proof, according to Dica's hydrometer, eleven cents.

---

* The first class of proof here corresponds with what is understood by common proof at our distilleries and answers to that of gin. Hence our common rum, compared with the lowest kind of imported rum, and including the duty on molasses, stands charged in the proportion of 14 to 21, which difference it is presumed will afford due encouragement. The remaining classes also correspond with those above.

2d. For every gallon of those spirits under five and not more than ten per cent. below proof, according to the same hydrometer, twelve cents.

3d. For every gallon of those spirits of proof, and not more than five per cent. below proof, according to the same hydrometer, thirteen cents.

4th. For every gallon of those spirits above proof, and not exceeding twenty per cent. according to the same hydrometer, fifteen cents.

5th. For every gallon of those spirits more than twenty and not more than forty per cent. above proof, according to the said hydrometer, twenty cents.

6th. For every gallon of those spirits more than forty per cent. above proof, according to the same hydrometer, thirty cents.

XIII. And be it further enacted,† That upon all spirits which after the said last day of   next, shall be distilled within the United States, from any article of the growth or production of the United States, in any city, town or village, there shall be paid for their use the duties following, that is to say:

1st. For every gallon of those spirits more than ten per cent. below proof, according to Dicas's hydrometer, nine cents.

2d. For every gallon of those spirits under five and not more than ten per cent. below proof, according to the same hydrometer, ten cents.

3d. For every gallon of those spirits of proof, and not more than five per cent. below proof, according to the same hydrometer, eleven cents.

4th. For every gallon of those spirits above proof, but not exceeding twenty per cent. according to the same hydrometer, thirteen cents.

5th. For every gallon of those spirits more than twenty and not more than forty per cent. above proof, according to the same hydrometer, seventeen cents.

† The several classes of proof here agree with those in the preceding section, but it will be observed that the rates are lower. This will operate as an encouragement to distillation from our own materials. It is evident that a higher duty being laid on spirits distilled from foreign materials, than on those made from our own, the difference is a bounty on the latter, and places it in a better situation than if there were no duty on either; in general it may be remarked, that the rates proposed on these different kinds of spirits, though considerably higher than heretofore, are much less than they bear in most other countries.

6. For every gallon of those spirits more than forty per cent. above proof, according to the same hydrometer, twenty-five cents.

XIV. And be it further enacted, That the said duties on spirits distilled within the United States, shall be collected under the management of the inspectors of the revenue.

XV. And be it further enacted, That the said duties on spirits distilled within the United States, shall be paid or secured previous to the removal thereof from the distilleries at which they are respectively made. And it shall be at the option of the proprietor or proprietors of each distillery, or of his, her or their agent having the superintendence thereof, either to pay the said duties previous to such removal, with an abatement at the rate of two cents for every ten gallons, or to secure the payment of the same, by giving bond quarter yearly, with one or more sureties, to the satisfaction of the officer of inspection within whose survey such distillery shall be, and in such sum as the said officer shall direct, with condition for the observance of the regulations in this act contained, on his, her, or their part, and also for the payment of the duties upon all such of the said spirits as shall be removed from such distillery, within three months next ensuing the date of the bond, at the expiration of six months from the said date.

XVI. And be it further enacted,* That the inspector or inspectors of each district, shall appoint a proper officer to have the charge and survey of each distillery within his or their district, who shall attend such distillery at all reasonable times, for the execution of the duties by this act enjoined upon him.

XVII. And be it further enacted, That previous to the removal of any of the said spirits from any distillery, the officer of inspection within whose survey the same may be, shall brand or otherwise mark each cask containing the same in durable characters, and with progressive numbers, and with the name of the acting owner or other manager of such distillery, and of the place where the same was situate, and with the quantity therein, to be ascertained by actual guaging, and with the proof thereof. And the duties thereupon having been first paid, or secured, as above provided, the said

---

* This inspection is essential to a secure collection. Experience has shewn that proper dependence cannot be placed on any plan which relies on the exactness of the accounts to be rendered by the individuals interested, and such a reliance not only defeats the revenue, but throws an undue proportion of the burthen on the upright and consciencious.

officer shall grant a certificate for each cask of the said spirits, to accompany the same wheresoever it shall be sent, purporting that the duty thereupon hath been paid or secured, as the case may be, and describing each cask by its marks; and shall enter in a book for that purpose to be kept, all the spirits distilled at such distillery, and removed from the same; and the marks of each cask, and the persons for whose use, and the places to which removed, and the time of each removal, and the amount of the duties on the spirits so removed. And if any of the said spirits shall be removed from any such distillery without having been branded or marked as aforesaid, or without such certificate as aforesaid, the same, together with the cask or casks containing them, and the horses and waggons, with their harness and tackling, employed in removing them, shall be forfeited, and may be seized by any officer of inspection. And the superintendant or manager of such distillery shall also forfeit the full value of the spirits so removed, to be computed at the highest price of the like spirits in the market.

XVIII. And be it further enacted, That no spirits shall be removed from any such distillery except by a person or persons licensed in the manner herein after directed, nor at any other times than between the hour of   and the hour of   and between the hour of   and the hour of   of each day, from the   day of   to the   day of   in each year; and between the hour of   and the hour of   and between the hour of   and the hour of   of each day, from the   day of   to the   day of   in each year.

XIX. And be it further enacted,† That licenses to convey or carry spirits from the said distilleries, shall, in each district, be granted by the inspector or inspectors of the revenue thereof, to such discreet person or persons as shall appear to him or them proper for the trust, who shall respectively give bonds, with one or more sureties to the satisfaction of the said inspector or inspectors of the revenue, in a sum not exceeding   dollars, nor less than   dollars, with condition faithfully and diligently, to carry and deliver all such of the said spirits as shall be committed to their care respectively, and

† This regulation would certainly add much to the safety of the collection: But it is doubtful whether it would not be exceptionable in some parts of the country. Perhaps it may be limited to the principal cities; or it may be general, and a discretion vested somewhere, to make the necessary exceptions.

in so doing to observe the directions of this act: Provided always, That nothing herein contained shall in any wise infringe or interfere with any exclusive privilege which any individuals or bodies politic may have or be entitled to, by virtue of any charter, grant or act of incorporation touching the right of carrying or of licensing persons to carry goods and commodities within particular limits. But where any such privilege shall exist, the persons to be licensed pursuant to this act, shall execute the trust thereby reposed in them, through and by means of the person or persons who by virtue of such privilege shall be authorised to carry within such limits; and in such manner as shall be perfectly consistent with such privilege and not otherwise.

XX. And be it further enacted,‡ That upon stills which after the last day of   next, shall be employed in distilling spirits from materials of the growth or production of the United States, in any other place than a city, town or village, there shall be paid for the use of the United States, the yearly duty of sixty cents for every gallon, English wine measure, of the capacity or content of each and every such still, including the head thereof: Provided that the said duty shall not extend to any still of less than except where such still shall be worked at the same distillery, together with another of dimensions exceeding   gallons.

XXI. And be it further enacted, That the evidence of the employment of the said stills shall be, their being erected in stone, brick or some other manner whereby they shall be in a condition to be worked.

XXII. And be it further enacted, That the said duties on stills shall be collected under the management of the inspectors of the revenue, who in each district shall appoint and assign proper officers for the surveys of the said stills and the admeasurement thereof, and the collection of the duties thereupon; and the said duties shall

‡ The duty is here laid upon the stills because it would be inconvenient, to extend the inspection of the officers in its full extent throughout the country. The rates is adjusted according to an estimate of what a still of any given dimensions, worked for the usual time is capable of producing, but lest this rule should in any instance operate injuriously, it is by a subsequent provision put in the power of the proprietor to redress himself. This provision certainly opens a door to fraud, but it is presumed to be adviseable to submit to this inconvenience rather than to those which would be apt to attend the supposition of inequality.

be paid half yearly, within the first fifteen days of the months of
          and   upon demand made of the proprietor or proprie-
tors of each still at his, her or their dwelling, by the proper officer
charged with the survey thereof: And in case of refusal or neglect
to pay, the amount of the duties so refused or neglected to be paid,
may either be recovered with costs of suit in an action of debt in
the name of the inspector or inspectors of the district, within which
such refusal shall happen, or may be levied by distress and sale
of goods of the person or persons refusing or neglecting to pay,
rendering the overplus (if any there be after payment of the said
amount and the charges of distress and sale) to the said person or
persons.

And whereas the duties hereby charged upon stills, have been
estimated upon a computation that a still of each of the dimensions
herein before enumerated, worked for the usual time would produce
in the course of a year a quantity of spirits, which at the rate of
          cents per gallon, would amount to the duty charged thereon:
And as from different causes it may in some instances happen, that
the said computation may subject the said stills to greater duties
than are intended;

XXIII. Be it therefore enacted, That if the proprietor of any such
still finding himself or herself aggrieved by the said rates, shall enter
or cause to be entered in a book or on a paper to be kept for that
purpose, from day to day when such still shall be employed the
quantity of spirits distilled therefrom, and the quantity from time
to time sold or otherwise disposed of, and to whom and when, and
shall produce the said book or paper to the proper officer of inspection within whose survey such still shall be, and shall make oath,
or if a known Quaker, affirmation, that the same doth contain to
the best of his or her knowledge and belief, true entries made at
their respective dates of all the spirits distilled within the time to
which such entries shall relate, from such still, and of the disposition thereof; and shall also declare upon such oath or affirmation
the quantity of such spirits then remaining on hand, it shall be
lawful in every such case for the said officer to whom the said
book or paper shall be produced, and he is hereby required to
estimate the duties upon such still, according to the quantity so
stated to have been actually made therefrom at the rate of nine

cents per gallon, which, and no more, shall be paid for the same: Provided, That if the said entries shall be made by any person other than the said proprietor, a like oath or affirmation shall be made by such person.

And the more effectually to prevent the evasion of the duties hereby imposed to the no less injury of the fair trader than of the revenue;

XXIV. Be it further enacted,* That every person who shall be a dealer or trader in distilled spirits (except as a maker or distiller thereof) in the original casks or cases in which they shall be imported, or in quantities of twenty five gallons at one sale, shall be deemed a wholesale dealer in spirits, and shall write or paint or cause to be written or painted, in large, legible and durable characters, upon some conspicuous part outside and in front of each house or other building or place, and upon the door or usual entrance of each vault, cellar or apartment within the same in which any of the said spirits shall be at any time by him or her deposited or kept or intended so to be, the words "wholesale dealer in spirits;" and shall also, within three days at least before he or she shall begin to keep or sell any of the said spirits therein, make a particular entry in writing at the nearest office of inspection of the district in which the same shall be situate, if within ten miles thereof of every such house or other building or place, and of each cellar, vault or apartment within the same in which he or she shall intend to put or keep any

---

* The provisions in this section form an essential part of the plan. They serve to bring all those who deal in the sale of spirits in considerable quantities, and the places in which they are kept, under the immediate eye of the law. It must always be very difficult to conceal any quantity of spirits in a place which is not announced and entered in the manner prescribed. Whoever sees them in any such place, or in going from it, will know that they are liable to forfeiture, and will have inducements enough to give intelligence of the fact. And when every man can, from so simple a circumstance, discern that a fraud has been committed, it will be hardly possible for it to escape detection. Besides this, the article, whenever it leaves its concealment, is liable to discovery from the want of those indications which are necessary to shew that it was lawfully imported or made. And it is not supposeable that it can continue concealed, and pass safe through all its stages, from the importation or making, to the consumption. The consumer himself, if not interested in the fraud, will detect and disclose it. The necessity of entry is limited to a distance of ten miles, to prevent inconvenience. In remote places, where little business is done, the precaution may be relaxed, and offices of inspection will be found less necessary. Articles must be carried, for sale, to places where there is considerable demand; and if at such places the requisite guards are kept up with strictness, the end will be substantially answered.

of the said spirits; and if any such dealer shall omit to write or paint or cause to be written or painted the words aforesaid, and in manner aforesaid, upon any such house or other building or place, or vault, cellar or apartment thereof, in which he or she shall so have or keep any of the said spirits, or shall in case the same be situated within the said distance of ten miles of any office of inspection omit to make entry thereof as aforesaid, such dealer shall for every such omission or neglect forfeit the sum of five hundred dollars, and all the spirits which he or she shall have or keep therein, or the value thereof to be computed at the highest price of such spirits in the market.

XXV. And be it further enacted, That every person who shall be a maker or distiller of spirits shall write or paint or cause to be written or painted upon some conspicuous part outside and in front of each house or other building or place made use of or intended to be made use of by him or her for the distillation or keeping of spirituous liquors, and upon the door or usual entrance of each vault, cellar or apartment within the same in which any of the said liquors shall be at any time by him or her distilled, deposited or kept, or intended so to be, the words "Distiller of spirits;" and shall also, three days at least before he or she shall begin to distil therein, make a particular entry in writing, at the nearest office of inspection, if within ten miles thereof, of every such house, building or place, and of each vault, cellar and apartment within the same, in which he or she shall intend to carry on the business of distilling, or to keep any spirits by him or her distilled. And if any such distiller shall omit to paint or write, or cause to be painted or written the words aforesaid, in manner aforesaid, upon any such house or other building or place, or vault, cellar or apartment thereof, or shall, in case the same be situate within the said distance of ten miles of any office of inspection, omit to make entry thereof as aforesaid, such distiller shall for every such omission or neglect, forfeit the sum of five hundred dollars, and all the spirits which he or she shall have or keep therein, or the value thereof, to be computed at the highest price of such spirits in the market: Provided also, and be it further enacted, that the said entry, to be made by persons who shall be dealers in or distillers of spirits, on the last day of   next, shall be made on that day, or within three days thereafter, accompanied (except where the duties hereby imposed are charged on the still) with a true and particular account or inventory of the spirits, on that day and at the time, in every or any house, building or place by him or her entered, and of the casks, cases and vessels containing the same, with their marks and numbers, and the quantities and qualities of the spirits therein contained, on pain of forfeiting, for neglecting to make such entry, or to deliver such account, the sum of five hundred dollars, and all the spirits by him or her had or kept in any such house, building or place: And provided further, that nothing herein contained shall be construed to exempt any such distiller, who shall be, besides his dealing as a distiller, a dealer or trader in distilled spirits as described in the twenty-fourth section of this act, from the regulations therein prescribed; but every such distiller, so being also a dealer or trader in distilled spirits, shall observe and shall be subject to all the rules, regulations and penalties therein specified.

XXVI. And be it further enacted, that where any entry shall be made by any such dealer, of any such house, building or other place for keeping of any of the said spirits, no other such dealer, not being in partnership with the dealer aforesaid, making such entry, shall on any pretence make entry of the same house or building, or of any apartment, vault, cellar or place within the same house, building or tenement in which such first entry shall then be existing; but every such other dealer, making such further entry of the same house, building or place, or of any apartment, vault, cellar or place within the same, shall, notwithstanding such further entry, be deemed a dealer without entry, and shall be subject to the like penalties and forfeitures as any dealers without entry are subject to by this act.

XXVII. And be it further enacted, that the Inspector or Inspectors of the revenue for the district wherein any house, building or place shall be situate, whereof entry shall be made as last aforesaid, shall as soon as may be thereafter, visit and inspect, or cause to be visited and inspected by some proper officer or officers of inspection, every such house or other building or place within his or their district, and shall take or cause to be taken an exact account of the spirits therein respectively contained, and shall mark or cause to be marked in durable characters, the several casks, cases or vessels containing the same, with progressive numbers, and also with the name of each dealer or distiller to whom the same may belong, or in whose custody the same may be, and the quantities, kinds and proofs of spirits therein contained, and these words, "Old Stock." And the said inspector or inspectors shall keep a book wherein he or they shall enter the name of every such dealer or distiller within his or their district, and the particulars of such old stock in the possession of each, designating the several casks and cases containing the same, and their respective quantities, kinds, proofs and marks. And he or they shall also give a certificate to every such dealer or distiller, of the quantity and particulars of such old stock in his or her possession, and a separate certificate for each cask, case or vessel, describing the same, according to its marks, which certificate shall accompany the same wheresoever it shall be sent. And in case there shall be no officer of inspection within the said distance of ten miles of any such house or other building or place, then it shall be the duty of such dealer to whom the same may belong, to mark with the like durable characters the several casks containing the spirits therein, and in like manner as above directed to be done by the said Inspector or Inspectors. And the said dealer shall make entry thereof in some proper book or in some proper paper to be by him or her kept for that purpose, specifying particularly each cask, case or vessel, and its marks, and the quantity and quality of the spirits therein contained (of which entry he or she shall, upon request, deliver an exact copy to the Inspector or Inspectors of the revenue for the district) and if required by him or them, shall attest the same by oath, or, being a known Quaker, by affirmation. And the said dealer, with every such cask, case or vessel which shall be delivered out of his or her house or other building or place, shall give a certificate or permit, signed by himself or herself, of the like import of that above directed to be given by the said Inspector or Inspectors, which certificate shall in like manner accompany the same wheresoever it may be sent. And if any such dealer shall in the said case omit to mark the said several casks, cases or vessels containing the said spirits, or to make entry thereof in some proper book, or on some proper paper as aforesaid, he or she shall forfeit and pay for every such neglect two hundred dollars. And if in the same case he or she shall deliver out or send away any of the said spirits without such certificate by him or her directed to be furnished as aforesaid, the said spirits so delivered out or sent away, shall be forfeited, and may be seized by any officer of inspection, and the said dealer shall also forfeit the full value thereof.

XXVIII. And be it further enacted, that every proprietor of any still on which a duty shall be charged according to the twentieth section of this act, shall brand or otherwise mark in durable characters, every cask, barrel or keg containing any spirits distilled by him or her, previous to the sale thereof, with his or her name, and with progressive numbers, and shall grant a certificate with each cask, barrel or keg by him or her sold, describing the same by its marks, and purporting that the same was made by him or her, to accompany such cask, barrel or keg, wheresoever it shall be sent.

XXIX. And be it further enacted, that when any such wholesale dealer in spirits, shall bring in his or her entered house, building or place, any of the said spirits, if such house, building or place be within two miles of any office of inspection, he or she shall within twenty-four hours after the said spirits shall be brought into such house, building or place, send notice thereof in writing to the said office, specifying therein the quantity and kinds of the spirits so brought in, and the marks of the cask or casks, case or cases containing the same, on pain of forfeiting, for every neglect to give such notice, fifty dollars. And it shall be the duty of the officer to whom such notice shall be given, forthwith thereafter to inspect and take an account of such spirits.

XXX. And be it further enacted, that if any distilled spirits shall be found in the possession of any such dealer, without the proper certificates which ought to accompany the same, it shall be presumptive evidence that the same are liable to forfeiture, and it shall be lawful for any officer of inspection to seize them as forfeited; and if, upon the trial in consequence of such seizure, the owner or claimant of the spirits seized, shall not prove that the same were imported into the United States according to law, or were distilled as mentioned in the twelfth and thirteenth sections of this act, and the duties thereupon paid, or were distilled at one of the stills mentioned in the twentieth section of this act, they shall be adjudged to be forfeited.

XXXI. And be it further enacted, that it shall be lawful for the officers of inspection of each district, at all times in the day time, upon request, to enter into all and every the houses, storehouses, ware-houses, buildings and places, which shall have been entered by the said wholesale dealers in manner aforesaid, and by tasting, guaging or otherwise to take an account of the quantity, kinds and proofs of the said spirits therein contained, and also to take samples thereof, paying for the same the usual price.

XXXII. And be it further enacted, that every such dealer shall keep the several kinds of spirits in his or her entered warehouse, building or place, separate and apart from each other, on pain of forfeiting upon every conviction of neglect one hundred dollars; and shall also, upon request, shew to the officers of inspection of the district wherein he or she is so a dealer, or to any of them, each and every cask, vessel and case in which he or she shall keep any distilled spirits, and the certificates which ought to accompany the same, upon pain of forfeiting every such cask, vessel or case, as shall be shewn, together with the spirits therein contained.

XXXIII. And be it further enacted, that if any person or persons shall rub out or deface any of the marks set upon any cask or case pursuant to the directions of this act, such person or persons shall, for every such offence, forfeit and pay the sum of one hundred dollars.

XXXIV. And be it further enacted, that no cask, barrel, keg, vessel or case, marked as "Old stock," shall be made use of by any dealer or distiller of spirits, for putting or keeping therein any spirits other than those which were contained therein when so marked, on pain of forfeiting five hundred dollars for every cask, barrel, keg, vessel or case wherein any such other spirits shall be so put or kept: Neither shall any such dealer have or keep any distilled spirits in any such cask, barrel, keg, vessel or case, longer than for the space of one year from the said last day of   next, on pain of forfeiting the said spirits.

XXXV. And be it further enacted, that in case any of the said spirits shall be fraudulently deposited, hid or concealed in any place whatsoever, with intent to evade the duties hereby imposed upon them, they shall be forfeited. And for the better discovery of any such spirits so fraudulently deposited, hid, or concealed, it shall be lawful for any Inspector of the revenue, or of any Judge of any

Court of the United States, or either of them, or for any Justice of the peace, upon reasonable cause of suspicion, to be made out to the satisfaction of such Inspector, Judge or Justice, by the oath, or, in the case of a known Quaker, by the affirmation, of any person or persons, by special warrant or warrants under their respective hands and seals, to authorise any of the officers of inspection, by day or night, but if in the night time, in the presence of a constable or other officer of the peace, to enter into all and every such place and places, in which any of the said spirits shall be suspected to be so fraudulently deposited, hid or concealed, and to seize and carry away any of the said spirits which shall be there found, so fraudulently deposited, hid or concealed, as forfeited.

XXXVI. And be it further enacted, That no person shall carry on the business of distilling, rectifying or compounding of spirituous liquors in any cellar, vault, or other place below the surface of the ground; or have or use any pipes, stop cocks, or other communications under ground, for the purpose of conveying spiritous liquors from one back or vessel to another, or from any such back or vessel to its still, or to any other place, on pain of forfeiting for every such place, below the surface of the ground in which the said business shall be carried on the sum of five hundred dollars, and for every such pipe, stop-cock, or other communication under ground, the sum of two hundred and fifty dollars. And in case the said person shall carry on the said business in any such place below the surface of the ground, or shall have or use any such communication under ground, it shall be lawful for any inspector of the revenue, or Judge of any court of the United States, or Judge of any court of a particular State, or Justice of the Peace, upon reasonable cause of suspicion to be made out to the satisfaction of such inspector, judge or justice, by oath or affirmation of any person or persons, by special warrant under his or either of their respective hands and seals, to authorise any of the officers of inspection, by day or night; but if in the night, in the presence of a constable or other officer of the peace, to enter into all and every such place or places after request first made, and the cause declared, therein to search and examine for the same, and for that purpose to break the ground, wall, partition or other place; and upon finding such cellar, vault, or other building, or place below the surface of the ground, or such pipe, stop-cock, or other communication under ground, to destroy the same, and to seize such spirituous liquors as may be found below the surface of the ground, or which shall have been conveyed through such pipe, stop-cock, or other communication, which warrant or warrants may be lawfully executed by such officer accordingly. Provided that nothing herein contained shall be construed to authorise any inspector of the revenue to issue any warrant to himself, or upon his own oath, to any other officer. And provided further, That if upon such search, no place below the surface of the ground, nor any such pipe, stop-cock, or other communication be found, the said officer shall make good the ground, wall, partition, or other place so broken up as aforesaid, together with such reasonable damages as shall be adjudged by two neighboring justices of the peace, or the party or parties injured may bring his, her or their action against such officer of inspection, for the damages so sustained, which damages in either case, shall be paid out of the revenue arising from this act.

XXXVII. And be it further enacted,* That after the last day of   next, no spirituous liquors, except gin in cases, shall be brought from any foreign port or place in any other way than in casks capable each of containing one hundred gallons at the least, on pain of forfeiture of the said spirits, and of the ship or vessel in which they shall be brought. Provided always, That nothing in this act contained, shall be construed to forfeit any spirits for being imported or brought into the United States, in other casks or vessels than as aforesaid, or the ship or vessel in which they shall be brought, if such spirits shall be for the use of the seamen on board such ship or vessel, and shall not exceed the quantity of   gallons for each such seaman.

XXXVIII. And be it further enacted, That in every case in which any of the said spirits shall be forfeited by virtue of this act, the casks, vessels and cases, containing the same, shall also be forfeited.

* The first part of this section seems to be free from any solid objection. It will be constantly the interest of importers (except with a view to smuggling) to bring spirits in large casks. But the object of the latter part will not be without difficulty. It is however, submitted. Perhaps, if the restriction to casks of one hundred gallons, should appear improper, it may be limited to a less size, yet such an one as will be less apt to elude the vigilance of the officers, than the smaller dimensions now in use. The restriction would certainly add materially to the security of the revenue.

XXXIX. And be it further enacted, That every dealer by wholesale, or distiller of spirits, on which the duty is hereby charged by the gallon, shall keep or cause to be kept, an exact account of all the said spirits which he or she shall sell, send out or distill, distinguishing their several kinds and proofs; and shall every day make a just and true entry in a book or on a paper, to be kept for that purpose, of the quantities and particulars of the said spirits by him or her sold, sent out or distilled, on the preceding day, specifying the marks of the several casks in which they shall be so sold or sent out; and the person to whom, and for whose use they shall be so sold or sent out: which said books and papers shall be prepared for the making such entries and shall be delivered upon demand to the said dealers and distillers, by the inspectors of the revenue of the several districts, or by such person or persons as they shall respectively for that purpose appoint, and shall be severally returned or delivered at the end of each year, or when the same shall be respectively filled up, which shall first happen to the proper officers of inspection; and the truth of the entries made therein shall be verified upon the oath, or in the case of a known quaker, the affirmation of the person by whom those entries shall have been made; and as often as the said books and papers shall be so returned, other books and papers shall be furnished upon like demand by the proper officers of inspection, to the said dealers and distillers respectively. And the said books and papers shall from time to time while in the possession of the said dealers and distillers, lie open for the inspection of, and upon request shall be shewn to the proper officers of inspection, under whose survey the said dealers and distillers shall respectively be, who may take such minutes, memorandums, or transcripts therefrom as they may think fit. And if any such dealer or distiller shall neglect or refuse to keep such book or books, paper or papers, or to make such entries therein, or to shew the same upon request to the proper officer of inspection, or not return the same according to the directions of this act, he or she shall forfeit for every such refusal or neglect, the sum of one hundred dollars.

And as a compensation to the said dealers for their aid in the execution of this act:

XL. Be it further enacted, That for every quantity of the said spirits not exceeding one hundred and twenty gallons, which shall

be sold by any such dealer, in one day, to one person or copartnership, in the casks or cases in which the same shall have been imported, after the said last day of   next, or delivered out of
any distillery (in respect to which the duty hereby imposed is
rated by the gallon) and distilled after the said day, and of the bringing of which into his or her entered store-house, building or other
place, he or she shall give due notice according to the directions
of this act, to the proper officer of inspection, and for which he or
she shall have produced to the said officer the proper certificates
corresponding therewith, the said dealer shall be entitled to an allowance of one per cent per gallon, which allowance shall be estimated by the inspector of the revenue of each district, according
to the evidence of the entries in the books and papers kept and
returned according to the next preceding section of this act, confirmed as to the production of the proper certificates, by the certificate of the officer to whom they shall have been produced, and shall
also be paid by such inspector, according to such rules as shall be pre-
cribed in that behalf, by the Secretary of the Treasury, which
said inspector shall be furnished with money for such payment out
of the product of the duties imposed by this act. Provided always,
That if more than one delivery shall be entered as made to one person or copartnership in one day, the same shall be deemed but one
delivery and one quantity.

XLI. And be it further enacted, That the several kinds of proof
herein before specified, shall in marking the casks, vessels and cases
containing any distilled spirits be designated, corresponding with
the order in which they are mentioned by the words—First Proof
—Second Proof—Third Proof—Fourth Proof—Fifth Proof—Sixth
Proof: which words may be expressed by their respective initials.
And that it be the duty of the Secretary of the Treasury, to provide and furnish to the officers of Inspection and of the Customs,
proper instruments for ascertaining the said several proofs.

And to the end that wanton and oppressive seizures may be
effectually restrained, and that the owners and importers of spirits,
may suffer no improper damage or burthen;

XLII. Be it further enacted, That in any prosecution or action
which may be brought against any Inspector or other officer of
Inspection for any seizure by him made, it shall be necessary for

such Inspector or Officer to justify himself by making it appear, that there was probable cause for making the said seizure, upon which, and not otherwise, a verdict shall pass in his favor. And in every such action or prosecution, or in any action or prosecution which may be brought against such inspector or other officer, for irregular or improper conduct in the execution of his duty, the trial shall be by jury. And in any action for a seizure, in which a verdict shall pass for such inspector, the jury shall nevertheless assess reasonable damages for any prejudice or waste (according to the true amount in value thereof) which shall be shewn by good proof to have happened to the spirits seized, in consequence of such seizure, and also for the detention of the same, at the rate of six per cent. per annum, on the true value of the said spirits, at the time of such seizure, from that time to the time of restoration thereof, which shall be paid out of the treasury of the United States; provided that no damages shall be assessed when the seizure was made for want of the proper certificate or certificates or by reason of a *refusal* to shew any officer of inspection upon his request the spirits in any entered house, or other building or place.

XLIII. And be it further enacted, That if any inspector or other officer of inspection in any criminal prosecution against him shall be convicted of oppression or extortion in the execution of his office, he shall be fined or imprisoned or both at the discretion of the court, and shall also forfeit his office, unless the judge who shall try the cause shall certify that he was dissatisfied with the verdict.

XLIV. And be it further enacted, That no fee shall be taken for any certificate to be issued or granted pursuant to this act.

XLV. And be it further enacted, That if any of the said inspectors or other officers of inspection, shall neglect to perform any of the duties hereby enjoined upon them respectively according to the true intent and meaning of this act, whereby any person or persons shall be injured or suffer damage, such person or persons shall, and may have an action founded upon this act against such inspector or other officers, and shall recover full damages for the same, together with costs of suit.

To the intent nevertheless, that the officers to be appointed by virtue of this act who may have undesignedly erred in the execution of their respective offices, may be enabled by offering timely

and sufficient amends to the party aggrieved, thereby to avoid unnecessary expence and trouble;

XLVI. Be it further enacted, That it shall be lawful for any
inspector or officer of inspection or other person acting in aid of
the one or the other, at any time before an action shall be commenced against him or them to tender amends to the person or persons aggrieved, or to his her or their agent or attorney, and in case
such amends are not accepted, to plead such tender in bar to any
action which may be brought against him or them, together with
the plea of *not guilty,* and any other plea or pleas with leave of the
court in which such action shall be depending. And if upon issue
joined thereon the jury shall find the amends so tendered to have
been sufficient, then they shall give a verdict for the defendant or
defendants. And in such case, or in case the plaintiff or plaintiffs
shall become nonsuited, or shall discontinue such action, or in case
judgment shall be given for the defendant or defendants upon
demurrer, then the defendant or defendants shall be intitled to, and
shall recover costs of suit: But if upon issue so joined, the jury shall
find that no, or insufficient amends were tendered, then they shall
find a verdict for the plaintiff or plaintiffs and such damages as shall
be reasonable.

XLVII. And be it further enacted, That any action or suit to be
brought against any person or persons for any thing by him or
them done, as in pursuance of this act, shall be commenced within
three months next after the matter or thing done, *and shall be laid
in the proper county* in which the cause of action shall have arisen,
and the defendant or defendants in any such action or suit may
plead the general issue, and on the trial thereof give this act, and
the special matter in evidence. And if a verdict shall pass for the
defendant or defendants, or the plaintiff or plaintiffs become nonsuited, or discontinue his, her or their action or prosecution, or
judgment shall be given against such plaintiff or plaintiffs upon
demurrer or otherwise, then such defendant or defendants shall
have costs awarded to him, her or them, against such plaintiff or
plaintiffs.

And in order that persons who may have incurred any of the
penalties of this act without wilful negligence or intention of fraud,
may be relieved from such penalties;

XLVIII. Be it further enacted,* That it shall be lawful for the judge of the district court, of the district within which such penalty or forfeiture shall have been incurred, upon petition of the party who shall have incurred the same to inquire in a summary manner into the circumstances of the case, first causing reasonable notice to be given to the person or persons claiming such penalty or forfeiture, and to the Attorney-General of such district, to the end that each may have an opportunity of shewing cause against the mitigation or remission thereof; and if upon such enquiry it shall appear to the said judge that such penalty or forfeiture was incurred without wilful negligence, or any design or intention of fraud, it shall be lawful for him to remit the same, and to cause any spirits which may have been seized, to be restored to the proprietor or proprietors upon such terms and conditions as shall appear to him reasonable. And the decision of the judge, if the terms and conditions prescribed by him be complied with, shall be conclusive to the parties. Provided, That such penalty, or the value of the spirits forfeited, does not exceed five hundred dollars: But if the amount of such penalty or forfeiture exceed five hundred dollars, the person or persons claiming the same, may, within three days after such decision shall be pronounced, appeal from the same to the supreme court of the United States, which court shall summarily hear the parties, and either confirm or reverse the decision of the district judge, as shall appear to them proper. Provided always, That after the last day of May, in the year one thousand seven hundred and ninety one, such remission shall in no case exceed one half the penalty, or one half the spirits forfeited, or the value thereof.

XLIX. And be it further enacted, That all penalties and forfeitures incurred by virtue of this act, shall be for the benefit of the person or persons who shall make a seizure, or who shall first discover the matter or thing, whereby the same shall have been incurred, and if other than the inspector of the revenue shall give information thereof to such inspector or inspectors, reserving thereout for the

* A discretionary power to remit or mitigate penalties in laws of this nature is indispensable. It is peculiarly so in the commencement. Heavy penalties are frequently incurred through inadvertence, misconstruction or want of information. Instances of this kind have happened under the existing system. The discretion however which is proposed to be given in the outset, is to be abridged at the expiration of a period which will allow sufficient time for persons to become acquainted with the law.

United States the amount of the duties payable on the spirits, in respect to which, such penalty or forfeiture may have been incurred. And such penalty and forfeiture shall be recoverable with costs of suit by action of debt, in the name of the person or persons intitled thereto, or by information in the name of the United States of America. And it shall be the duty of the Attorney-General of the district, wherein any such penalty or forfeiture may have been incurred upon application to him, to institute or bring such information accordingly. Provided always that no officer of inspection, other than chief officer or officers of a district shall be entitled to the benefit of any forfeiture unless notice of the seizure by him made, shall be by him given within twelve hours next after such seizure to the said chief officer or officers. But in such case the United States shall have the entire benefit of such seizure.

L. And be it further enacted, That if any person or persons shall counterfeit, or forge, or cause to be counterfeited or forged any of the certificates herein before directed to be given, or shall knowingly or willingly accept or receive any false or untrue certificate with any of the said spirits, or shall fraudulently alter or erase any such certificate after the same shall be given, or knowingly or willingly publish or make use of such certificate so counterfeited, forged, false, untrue, altered or erased, every person or persons so offending, shall for each and every offence, severally forfeit and pay the sum of one thousand dollars.

LI. And be it further enacted, That any person or persons that shall be convicted, of wilfully taking a false oath or affirmation, in any of the cases in which oaths or affirmations are required to be taken by virtue of this act, shall be liable to the pains and penalties to which persons are liable for wilful and corrupt perjury.

LII. And be it further enacted, that if any person or persons shall give or offer to give any bribe, recompence or reward whatsoever, to any inspector or inspectors of the revenue, in order to corrupt, persuade or prevail upon such officer, either to do any act or acts contrary to his duty in the execution of this act, or to neglect or omit to do any act or thing which he ought to do in execution of this act, or to connive at, or to conceal any fraud or frauds relating to the duties hereby imposed on any of the said spirits, or not to

discover the same, every such person or persons shall for such offence, whether the same offer or proposal be accepted or not, forfeit and pay the sum of one thousand dollars.

LIII. And be it further enacted, That if any person or persons
shall assault, resist, oppose, molest, obstruct or hinder any inspector
in the execution of this act, or of any of the powers or authorities
hereby vested in him, or shall forcibly rescue or cause to be rescued
any of the said spirits, after the same shall have been seized by any
such inspector or officer, or shall attempt or endeavor so to do, all
and every person and persons so offending, shall for every such
offence, for which no other penalty is particularly provided by this
act, forfeit and pay the sum of five hundred dollars.

LIV. And be it further enacted, That if any such inspector or
officer, shall enter into any collusion with any person or persons
for violating or evading any of the provisions of this act, or the
duties hereby imposed, or shall fraudulently concur in the delivery
of any of the said spirits, out of any house, building or place,
wherein the same are deposited without payment, or security for
the payment of the duties thereupon, or shall falsely or fraudulently mark any cask, case or vessel, contrary to any of the said
provisions, such inspector or officer shall for every such offence
forfeit the sum of one thousand dollars, and upon conviction of
any of the said offences, shall forfeit his office and shall be dis-
qualified for holding any other office under the United States.

LV. And be it further enacted, that it shall be lawful for the
Inspectors of the revenue, and when requested by any such dealer,
they are hereby required to provide blank certificates, in such form
as shall be directed by the Secretary of the Treasury, and in the
cases in which certificates are hereby directed to be issued or
granted by the said dealers, to furnish them therewith the blanks
in which certificates shall be filled up by such dealers, according to
the nature and truth of each particular case, subject to the penalty
heretofore declared for granting or using false or untrue certificates.
And every such dealer shall from time to time, when thereunto
requested, account with such Inspectors respectively, for the number of certificates received by him, and for the disposition of such
of them as may have been disposed of, and shall produce and shew

the residue thereof to the said Inspector, and shall pay for every certificate for which he cannot satisfactorily account, the sum of fifty cents.

LVI. And be it further enacted, that in every case in which an oath or affirmation is required by virtue of this act, it shall be lawful for the Inspectors of the revenue, or any of them, or their lawful deputy, or the lawful deputy of one of them where not more than one in a district, to administer and take such oath or affirmation. And that wherever there are more than one Inspector for one district, a majority of them may execute all and any of the powers and authorities hereby vested in the Inspectors of the revenue: Provided, that this shall not be construed to make a majority necessary in any case in which, according to the nature of the appointment or service, and the true intent of this act, the authority is or ought to be several.

And for the encouragement of the export trade of the United States:

LVII. Be it further enacted, that if any of the said spirits (whereupon any of the duties imposed by this act shall have been paid or secured to be paid) shall after the last day of   next, be exported from the United States to any foreign port or place, there shall be an allowance to the exporter or exporters thereof, by way of drawback, equal to the duties thereupon, according to the rates in each case by this act imposed, deducting therefrom one cent per gallon, and adding to the allowance upon spirits distilled within the United States from molasses, which shall be so exported, two cents and an half cent per gallon, as an equivalent for the duty laid upon molasses by the said act for laying a duty on goods, wares and merchandizes imported into the United States: Provided always, that the said allowance shall not be made unless the said exporter or exporters shall observe the regulations hereinafter prescribed: And provided further, that nothing herein contained shall be construed to alter the provisions in the said former act, concerning drawbacks or allowances, in nature thereof, upon spirits imported prior to the said last day of   last.

LVIII. And be it further enacted, that in order to entitle the said exporter or exporters to the benefit of the said allowance, he, she or they, shall previous to putting or lading any of the said spirits on board of any ship or vessel for exportation, give twenty-four hours notice at the least, to the proper officer of inspection of the port from which the said spirits shall be intended to be exported, of his, her or their intention to export the same, and of the number of casks and cases, or either of them, containing the said spirits so intended to be exported, and of the respective marks thereof, and of the place or places where the said spirits shall be then deposited, and of the place to which, and ship or vessel in which they shall be so intended to be exported. Whereupon it shall be the duty of the said officer to inspect, by himself or deputy, the casks and cases so noticed for exportation, and the quantities, kinds and proofs of the spirits therein, together with the certificates which ought to accompany the same according to the directions of this act, which shall be produced to him for that purpose; and if he shall find that the said casks and cases have the proper marks according to the directions of this act; and that the spirits therein correspond with the said certificates, he shall thereupon brand each cask or case with the word "Exportation;" and the said spirits shall, after such inspection, be laden on board the same ship or vessel of which notice shall have been given, and in the presence of the same officer who shall have examined the same, and whose duty it shall be to attend for that purpose. And after the said spirits shall be laden on board such ship or vessel, the certificates aforesaid shall be delivered to the said officer, who shall certify to the Collector of the said port the amount and particulars of the spirits so exported, and shall also deliver the said certificates which shall have been by him received to the said collector, which shall be a voucher to him, for payment of the said allowance.

Provided nevertheless, and be it further enacted, That the said allowance shall not be made, unless the said exporter or exporters shall make oath, or if a known Quaker, affirmation, that the said spirits so noticed for exportation, and laden on board such ship or vessel, are truly intended to be exported to the place whereof notice shall have been given, and are not intended to be relanded within the United States; and that he or she doth verily believe that the duties thereupon charged by this act, have been duly paid; and shall also give bond to the collector, with two sureties, one of whom shall be the master, or other person having the command or charge of the ship or vessel in which the said spirits shall be intended to be exported; the other, such sufficient person as shall be approved by the said collector, in the full value in the judgment of such collector, of the said spirits so intended to be exported, with condition that the said spirits (the dangers of the seas and enemies excepted) shall be really and truly exported to, and landed in such ports and places without the limits of the United States, according to the late treaty of peace with Great-Britain, as shall be specified in such bond; and that the said spirits shall not be unshipped from on board of the said ship or vessel, whereupon the same shall have been laden for exportation, within the said limits, or any ports or harbors of the United States, or relanded in any other part of the same (shipwreck or other unavoidable accident excepted.)

Provided also, and be it further enacted, that the said allowance shall not be paid until six months after the said spirits shall have been so exported.

LIX. And be it further enacted, That if any of the said spirits, after the same shall have been shipped for exportation, shall be unshipped for any purpose whatever, either within the limits of any part of the United States, or within four leagues of the coast thereof, or shall be relanded within the United States, from on board the ship or vessel wherein the same shall have been laden for exportation, (unless in case of necessity or distress to save the ship and goods from perishing, which shall be immediately made known to the principal officer of the customs, residing at the port nearest to which such ship or vessel shall be at the time such necessity or distress shall arise) then not only the spirits so unshipped, together with the casks and cases containing the same, but also the ship or vessel in or on board which the same shall have been so shipped or laden, together with her guns, furniture, ammunition, tackle and apparel; and also the ship, vessel or boat into which the said spirits shall be unshipped or put, after the unshipping thereof, together with her guns, furniture, ammunition, tackle and apparel, shall be forfeited, and may be seized by any officer of the customs, or of inspection.

LX. And be it further enacted, That the said allowance shall not be made when the said spirits shall be exported in any other than a ship or vessel of the burthen of   tons and upwards, to be ascertained to the satisfaction of the collector of the port from which the same shall be intended to be exported.

LXI. And be it further enacted, That the bonds to be given as aforesaid, shall and may be discharged by producing within one year from the respective dates thereof (if the delivery of the spirits in respect to which the same shall have been given, be at any place where a consul or other agent of the United States resides) a certificate of such consul or agent, and if there be no such consul or agent, then a certificate of any two known and reputable American merchants residing at the said place, and if there be not two such merchants residing at the said place, then a certificate of any other two reputable merchants, testifying the delivery of the said spirits, at the said place, which certificate shall in each case be confirmed by the oath or affirmation of the master and mate or other like officer of the vessel in which the said spirits shall have been exported; and when such certificate shall be from any other than a consul or agent, or merchants of the United States, it shall be a part of the said oath or affirmation, that there were not upon diligent enquiry to be found two merchants of the United States at the said place. Provided always, that in the case of death, the oath or affirmation of the party dying, shall not be deemed necessary: And provided further, that the said oath or affirmation, taken before the chief civil magistrate of the place of the said delivery, and certified under his hand and seal, shall be of the same validity as if taken before a person qualified to administer oaths within the United States: or such bonds shall and may be discharged upon proof that the spirits so exported, were taken by enemies or perished in the sea, or destroyed by fire; the examination and proof of the same being left to the judgment of the collector of the customs, naval officer, and chief officer of inspection, or any two of them, of the place from which such spirits shall have been exported.

LXII. And be it further enacted, That the prosecution for all fines, penalties and forfeitures incurred by force of this act, and for all duties payable in virtue thereof, and which shall not be duly paid, shall and may be had before any justice of the peace or court of any state of competent jurisdiction, or court of the United States, of or within the state or district, in which the cause of action shall arise, with an appeal as in other cases: Provided, that where the cause of action shall exceed in value fifty dollars, the same shall not be cognisable before a justice of the peace only.

LXIII. And be it further enacted, That this act shall commence and take effect as to all matters therein contained, in respect to which no special commencement is hereby provided (except as to the appointment of officers and regulation of the districts) from and immediately after the last day of   next.

Draft of an Act Imposing Certain Inland Duties on Foreign Wines

[New York City, January 9, 1790]

An act imposing certain Inland duties on foreign Wines.[1]

A²   A   Be it enacted by the Senate and House of Representatives of the United States of America in Congress assembled That in addition to the duties heretofore laid—on Wines imported into the United States from any foreign Port or Place there shall be paid for the use of the U States upon all Wines which shall be so imported after the last day of   ³ next at the respective times of the sale thereof the following inland duties to Wit

For every gallon of Madeira Wine of the quality of London particular	Cents
For every gallon of other Madeira Wine	Cents
For every gallon of Sherry	cents

ADf, Hamilton Papers, Library of Congress.

1. This draft raises several problems. Although it is undated, it was presumably written in connection with H's "Report Relative to a Provision for the Support of Public Credit," January 9, 1790. On the one hand, it can be argued that the draft was written to implement his statement in the Report that "It would be the intention of the Secretary, that the duty on wines should be collected upon precisely the same plan with that on imported spirits." On the other hand, internal evidence in the draft gives some indication that H may also have used this document as a draft for the bill on distilled spirits, which he submitted on January 9, 1790, with his "Report Relative to a Provision for the Support of Public Credit."

2. At this point in the draft H wrote "Clauses A B & C as marked nearest the margin to be inserted." H is referring to a manuscript in the Hamilton Papers which is either a partial earlier draft or a section of this draft which consists of clauses which were to be incorporated in the final copy. These clauses have been incorporated in the draft as printed here.

3. This and subsequent spaces left blank in the draft by H.

For every gallon of Lisbon or port   cents

For every gallon of other wine   cents [4]

B   B1   And be it further enacted that the said duties shall be collected under the management of Commissioners to be denominated Commissioners of Inland Duties: And that the President of the United States of America be authorised to appoint, with the advice and consent of the Senate, so many of the said Commissioners as shall appear to him necessary; and to assign to them respectively such districts or limits for the exercise of their respective offices as he shall judge best adapted to the due execution thereof: dividing the districts if he shall think it adviseable into general and particular; and placing the commissioners of the particular districts under the superintendence of the Commissioners of the General districts within the limits of which they shall be respectively comprehended: and also to make such allowances to the said Commissioners and to the deputies and officers by them appaid for their respective services in the execution of this act as shall be reasonable and proper to be paid out of the product of the said duties: Provided that the whole amount of the said allowances shall not exceed   per Cent of the said product, computed throughout the United States.

C   B2   And be it further enacted that the Commissioner or Commissioners of inland duties for each district shall establish one or more offices within the same and that there shall be one at least at each port of delivery: and, in order that the said offices may be publicly known, there shall be painted or written in large legible characters upon some conspicuous part outside and in front of each house building or place in which any such office shall be kept, these words "Office of Inland Duties." And if any person, shall paint or write or cause to be painted or written the said words upon any other than such house or building, he or she shall forfeit and pay for so doing 100 Dollars.[5]

4. In the margin opposite this paragraph are the words "1 Lisbon 2 Port 3 Teneriffe 4 Other Wines."

5. At this point in the manuscript H first wrote and later crossed out the following:

"And be it further enacted that every importer of any of the said wines or, in his or her absence, his or her representative or Agent shall, previous to the unlading thereof, at any port of entry or delivery make report of the same in writing at the Office of inland Duties for such place; which report shall contain a true and particular account of the number and kinds of the casks

D   And be it further enacted that the Collector of any Port with
whom entry shall have been made of any of the said spirits pursuant
to the Act intitled An act laying a duty   [6] shall forthwith
after such entry certify the same as particularly as it shall have been
made with him to the proper officer of Inland duties for such port:
And every permit granted by such collector for the landing of any
of the said spirits shall previous to such landing be produced to the
said officer for his inspection; who shall make a minute in some
proper book of the contents thereof and shall indorse thereupon
the word "Inspected" and his own name; after which he shall return it to the person by whom it shall have been produced. And
then and not otherwise it shall be lawful to land the spirits therein
specified. And if the said spirits shall be landed without such indorsement upon the permit for that purpose granted the Master or
person having the charge of the ship or vessel from which the same
shall have been so landed shall for every such offence forfiet the
sum of one hundred dollars.

     And be it further enacted that whenever it shall be intended, that
any Ship or vessel shall proceed with the whole or any part of the
spirits which shall have been brought in such ship or vessel from
any foreign port or place, from one port in the United States to
another port in the said United States, the Master or person having
the command or charge of such ship or vessel, shall previous to her
departure apply to the proper officer of Inland duties for the port
from which she is about to depart for a certificate of the quantity
and particulars of such of the said spirits as shall have been certified
to him to have been entered as imported in such ship or vessel and
of so much the⟨reof as shall⟩ [7] appear to him to have been landed
⟨out of⟩ her at such port, which certificate the said officer shall
⟨forthwith⟩ grant without fee or charge: And the Master or per⟨son

---

vessels and packages containing the same, and when known, of their marks
and numbers quantities and qualities. And the Collector of the Port of Entry
at which any of the said Wines shall first arrive shall forthwith after entry
made with him certify such entry."

     6. H is probably referring to "An Act for laying a Duty on Goods, Wares,
and Merchandises imported into the United States" (1 *Stat.* 24–27 [July 4,
1789]).

     7. The material in broken brackets in this paragraph has been taken from
Article VIII of the final copy of the act which was enclosed in H's "Report
Relative to a Provision for the Support of Public Credit," January 9, 1790.

having⟩ the command or charge of such ship or vessel shall within twenty four hours after her arrival at the port to which she shall be bound deliver the said certificate to the proper officer of inland duties for such lastmentioned port. And if such ship or vessel shall proceed from one port to another within the United States with the whole or any part of the Spirits brought in her as aforesaid without having first obtained such certificate; or if within twenty four hours after her arrival at such other port the said certificate shall not be delivered to the proper officer of Inland Duties there, the Master or person having the command or charge of the said Ship or Vessel shall in either case forfiet five hundred dollars; and the spirits on board of her for which such certificate shall not have been obtained, or so delivered, shall be forfieted and may be seized by any officer of Inland Duties.[8]

And be it further enacted that all distilled spirits which shall be imported as aforesaid shall be landed under the inspection of the officer or officers of Inland duties for the place where the same shall be landed, and not otherwise, on pain of forfieture thereof; for which purpose the said officer or officers shall at all reasonable times attend. And the said spirits after they shall have been landed shall be lodged in warehouses to be provided at the charge of the respective importers thereof with the approbation of the said officer or officers. And upon each door of every such warehouse it shall be lawful for the importer or importers of the said spirits therein to affix one lock the key whereof shall be kept by him her or them, and for the officer of Inland duties, having the care of such ware house, to affix another lock, the key whereof shall be kept by him. And it shall also be lawful for the said importer or importers freely to visit examine and provide for the safekeeping of the spirits so deposited. But no part of the same shall be taken out of the Cask vessel or package wherein they were so deposited or removed from any such ware house, in any other manner than as hereinafter directed.

And be it further enacted that the officer [of] inland duties, under whose inspection any of the said Spirits shall be landed, shall previous to the same being lodged in any such warehouse brand or

8. For the material in the previous two paragraphs there is a comparable section marked "D" in the manuscript referred to in note 2. Because of the section's similarity to these two paragraphs it has not been printed.

mark in some durable manner the several Casks vessels or packages containing the same with progressive numbers, and also with the name of the Ship or Vessel, wherein the same was or were imported and of the Port of *Entry* [9] and with the quality and quantity thereof together with such other marks if any other shall be deemed needful as the respective Commissioners of Inland Duties may direct. And the said officer shall keep a book wherein he shall enter the name of each vessel in which any of the said wines shall be so imported and of the Port of Entry and Delivery and of the Master of such vessel and of each importer and the several casks and packages containing the same and the marks of each; and, if not a commissioner or the Chief officer of Inland Duties for the place, shall as soon as may be thereafter make an exact transcript of each entry and deliver the same to such Commissioner or chief Officer; who shall keep a like book for recording the said transcripts.

And be it further enacted that none of the said wines while remaining in any such warehouse shall be taken out of the Cask vessel or package wherein the same was first deposited except for the preservation thereof or to fill some deficient cask or casks therein, and in the presence of the Officer of Inland Duties under whose care such warehouses shall be; which officer shall mark each new cask vessel or package in which any of the said wines shall be pack⟨aged⟩ with the marks of that from which the same shall have been taken together with the word *exchanged* and shall immediately report the particulars of every such exchange or alterat⟨ion⟩ to the Chief Officer of Inland Duties for the place when the same shall be made; who shall note the same in the book to be by him kept.[10]

And be it further enacted that none of the said wines shall be removed out of any such warehou⟨se⟩ otherwise than in the cask vessel or package wherein the sa⟨me⟩ was first deposited or to which the same shall have been exchanged as aforesaid, nor till the duties hereby charged upon the same shall have been paid to and a certificate obtained, from the proper officer of Inland duties for the place where such warehouse shall be, of the payment thereof, which certificate shall also specify the names of the seller and buyer or person for whose use to be delivered, and the marks of each cask

9. Above the word "Entry" was written the alternate word "Delivery."
10. For the material in this paragraph there is a comparable section in the manuscript mentioned in note 2.

vessel or package to be delivered and the quality and the then quantity of the Wine therein contained according to the actual guage thereof at the time. And the said officer, together with such certificate to remain with the importer of the said wines or his or her representative, shall grant a separate permit for each cask Vessel or package to accompany the same, wheresoever it may be sent, as evidence of the payment of the duty thereupon. And the said certificates and permits shall be granted by the Chief officer of Inland duties for the place upon request notes signed by the said Importer or his or her representative and directed to the said officer specifying the names of the said buyer and seller or person for whose use any of the said wines is or are to be delivered and the particular cask vessel or package or casks vessels or packages containing the same and the quantity and quality and marks thereof. And the officer of Inland duties granting the said certificates & permits shall make regular and exact entries in the book by him to be kept as aforesaid of all wines for which the same shall be granted as particularly as therein discribed. And each delivery of any of the said wines out of any such warehouse shall be made in the presence of the officer of inland duties having charge thereof, who shall attend at all reasonable times for that purpose. And if any of the said Wines shall be delivered or removed out of any such warehouse in any other manner than as herein before directed the same shall be forfieted and may be seized by any officer of Inland Duties. And the Importer thereof or his or her representative by whom or with whose privity or by whose agent the same may have been removed or delivered contrary to the true intent of the provisions aforesaid shall also forfeit the full value of the wines so delivered or removed to be computed at the highest price of such wines in the market at the time of such delivery.

Provided nevertheless that nothing herein contained shall be construed to prevent the sale of any of the said wines on the public wharves or quays whereon the same shall have been landed. But every such sale shall be lawful and valid, if delivery of the said wines shall be made in the presence of some proper officer of inland duties, and if the duties hereby charged thereupon shall be first paid and certificates and permits obtained in like manner as if they were to be delivered out of some of the warehouses aforesaid, and not otherwise. And the officer of Inland duties in whose presence any such delivery shall be made shall mark each cask vessel or package before its removal from any of the said wharves or quays in like manner as hereinbefore directed when the said wines are to be deposited in Warehouses, and the like books shall be kept by the respective officers of Inland duties and the like entries made therein as in the cases of deliveries out of the said warehouses. And if any of the said Wines shall be designedly removed from any of the said wharves or Quays (except to be deposited in the warehouses aforesaid) otherwise than as herein directed with the privity or connivance of the Importer his or her representative the same shall be forfieted and may be seized by any officer of Inland Duties. And such Importer his or her representative shall also forfiet the full value of any of the said wines so unlawfully removed to be computed at the highest price of such wines in the market.

XI   Provided also and be it further enacted that it shall be at the option of every importer either to have the wines by him or her imported deposited in the warehouses aforesaid subject to the regulations aforesaid or to prevent the same by giving bond with one or more sureties to the satisfaction of the Chief Officer of Inland Duties for the place where the said wines shall be landed in double the amount of the duties payable thereupon by virtue of this act with condition for the payment of the said amount of three months. And if any importer shall elect to give and shall accordingly give such bond as aforesaid the wines in respect to which the same shall be given need not be deposited in any of the said warehouses. But the same shall nevertheless be landed under the inspection of the proper officer of inland duties and the same marks shall be set upon each cask vessel or package containing the same as if the said wines were to be deposited in Warehouses in manner aforesaid; and the like certificates and permits shall be obtained and for the like purposes as are hereinbefore required in respect to deliveries out of the said warehouses. And the said Chief officer of Inland duties shall make the like entries in the book to be by him kept as when the said wines shall be to be deposited in and delivered out of the said Warehouses. And if the said wines shall in such case be landed without such inspection or if the said certificates and permits shall not be obtained therefore the same shall be forfieted and may be seized by any officer of Inland duties.[11]

I   And provided further that if the importer of any of the said wines, or in his or her absence or his or her Agent, after they shall be deposited in any of the said warehouses, but previous to a sale thereof, shall be desirous of sending them on his or her own account for sale from one district of inland duties to another district of inland duties, it shall be lawful for him or her or, if absent, his or her Agent so to do, upon giving bond with one or more sureties to the satisfaction of the Chief Officer of Inland duties for the place from which they are to be sent, in double the amount of the duties thereupon, with condition for the payment of the said duties in one month; and the like certificates and permits and for the like purposes shall in this case be granted therefore as if the said duties were actually paid.

And in order to prevent the evasion of the duties hereby imposed to the no less injury of the fair Trader than of the Revenue.

II   Be it further enacted that every person who is or shall be a dealer or trader in wines in the original casks vessels and packages in which they shall be imported or in quantities of twenty gallons at one sale shall be deemed a Wholesale Dealer in Wines and shall write or paint or cause to be written or painted in large legible and durable characters upon some conspicuous part outside and in front of each house or other building or place and upon the door or usual entrance of each vault cellar or apartment within the same in which any of the said wines shall be, at any time, by him or her deposited or kept the words Wholesale Dealer in Wines and shall also make a particular entry in writing at the nearest office of Inland Duties of the district in which the same shall be situate, if within twenty miles thereof, of every such house or other building or place and of each vault cellar or apartment within the same in which he or she shall have or keep any of the said Wines. And if any such dealer shall omit to write or paint, or cause to be written or painted the words aforesaid in manner aforesaid upon any such house or other building or place or vault cellar or apartment thereof, in which he

11. In the manuscript mentioned in note 2 there is a shorter version of this paragraph marked "H."

or she shall so have or keep any of the said Wines, or shall, in case
the same be situated within the said distance of twenty miles of any
office of Inland duties, omit to make entry thereof as aforesaid, such
dealer shall for every such omission or neglect forfiet the sum of
          dollars and all the wines which he or she shall have keep or
distill therein, or the value thereof to be computed at the highest
price of such wines on the market.

XIV   And be it further enacted that every person who shall be so a
dealer in or distiller of Spirits prior to the said last day of
next shall make such entry as aforesaid on that day or within three
days thereafter and shall accompany the same with a true and
particular account or inventory of the spirits on that day and at the
time of such entry in every or any house building or place by him
or her entered and of the casks vessels and packages containing the
same with their respective marks and numbers and the quantities
and kinds of the spirits therein contained distinguishing foreign
spirits from those made within the United States and their several
denominations or names and distinguishing of those made within the
U.S. such as are of foreign materials from such as are of the growth
or production of the U States and the denomination or name of each
on pain of forfieting for neglectg to make such entry or to deliver
such account the sum of   dollars and all the spirits contained in any such house building or place.

XV   And be it further enacted, that the Commissioner or Commissioners of the District within which any house building or place
shall be situate, whereof entry shall be made as last aforesaid, shall
as soon as may be thereafter visit and inspect or cause to be visited
and inspected by his or their deputy or deputies or by some other
proper officer or officers of inland Duties every such house or other
building or place within his or their district and shall take or cause
to be taken an exact account of the spirits therein respectively contained, and shall mark or cause to be marked in durable characters
the several casks vessels or packages containing the same with
progressive numbers, and also with the name of each dealer or
distiller to whom the same may belong, or in whose custody the
same may be and the quantities and kinds of the spirits therein
contained and these words *Old Stock*. And the said commissioner

or commissioners shall keep a book wherein he or they shall enter the name of every such dealer or Distiller within his or their district and the particulars of such old Stock in the possession of each, designating the several casks vessels and packages containing the same, and their respective quantities kinds and marks. And he or they shall also give a certificate to every such dealer or Distiller of the quantity and particulars of such old stock in his or her possession and a seperate certificate or permit for each cask vessel or package describing the same according to its marks, which certificate or permit shall accompany the same wheresoever it may be sent. And in case there shall be no office of inland duties within the said distance of twenty miles of any such house or other building or place, then it shall be the duty of such Dealer or Distiller to whom the same may belong to mark with the like durable characters the several casks vessels and packages containing the spirits therein, and in like manner as is above directed to be done by the said Commissioner or Commissioners. And the said Dealer or Distiller shall make entry thereof in some proper book to be by him kept for that purpose specifying particularly each Cask vessel or package and its marks and the quantity and species of the spirits therein contained distinguished as aforesaid (of which entry he or she shall upon request deliver an exact copy to the commissioner or Commissioners of Inland Duties for the District) and if required by him or them shall verify the same by oath, or being a known quaker by affirmation. And the said Dealer with every such Cask vessel or package which shall be delivered out of his or her house or other building or place shall give a certificate or permit signed by himself or herself of the like import with that above directed to be given by the said Commissioner or Commissioners, which certificate or permit shall in like manner accompany the same wheresoever it may be sent. And if any such Dealer shall in the said case omit to mark the said several casks vessels and packages containing the said wines or to make entry thereof in some proper book as aforesaid, he or she shall forfiet and pay for every such neglect Two hundred Dollars. And if in the same case he or she shall deliver out or send away any of the said wines without such certificate or permit by him to be furnished as aforesaid, the said wines so delivered out or sent away shall be forfieted and may be seized by any officer of Inland Duties. And the said Dealer shall also forfiet the full value thereof.[12]

XVII   And be it further enacted that before any such Dealer or Distiller shall begin to draw off or remove any of the Spirits to him or her belonging from out of any Vat Cask or Vessel in his or her entered house or other building or place he or she shall send to or leave at the office of inland duties nearest to such entered house or other building or place if within two miles thereof [13] six hours notice in writing of his or her intention so to draw off or remove such wine and of the time when and of the particular house building or place where such wine is intended to be so drawn off or removed and the quantity thereof and into how many casks or other vessels the same is intended to be so drawn off or removed and of the species and proof of such spirits and of the particular cask or casks or other vessel or vessels from which such wine is so intended to be drawn off or removed; and the officer of Inland Duties within whose survey such house building or place may be if he shall deem it expedient shall attend to see such wine so drawn off or removed, and the same shall be so drawn off or removed in presence of such officer if he shall attend pursuant to such notice and shall also be packed and piled in his presence; or if such officer shall not attend pursuant to such notice then the said Dealer shall proceed to draw off remove pack and pile such wine without such presence but shall at the next visit of such officer make report to him of the quantity of such wine so drawn off packed & piled and of the particular Casks or Vessels from which the same shall have been so drawn off and removed and of the particular place where the same shall have been deposited; and no wine shall be so drawn off or removed without such notice as aforesaid. And if any such Dealer or Distiller shall so draw off or remove any of the said Wine from any such vat Cask or vessel without giving such notice as aforesaid or when so drawn off or removed without the presence of such officer shall neglect to make such report as aforesaid at the next visit of the said officer he or she shall for every such offence forfiet & lose the sum of 100 Dollars. Provided also that if any such Dealer or Distiller shall

12. In the margin opposite this sentence are the letters "Qr."
Following this paragraph H wrote "Insert L No. 1." This section, taken from the manuscript described in note 2, has been inserted here.
13. "if within the district" is written in the margin opposite this statement.

not begin so to draw off or remove the said Wine at, or within one hour after, the time mentioned in the notice for that purpose then such notice shall be void and it shall be necessary under the penalty last mentioned, to give the like notice before it shall be lawful so to draw off or remove the said Wine. Provided further That nothing in this act contained shall be construed to make it unlawful for any such dealer only so to draw off or remove any such wine at his or her pleasure for the purpose of immediately sending out the same without giving such notice as aforesaid; but such drawing off or removal for that purpose shall be lawful any thing herein contained notwithstanding.

I   And be it further enacted that in every case of removal of any spirits in the possession of any such dealer or Distiller from one cask or vessel to another or to several other casks or vessels which shall be made in the presence of any officer of Inland Duties or which shall come to his Knowlege it shall be the duty of such officer to mark every such new Cask or vessel with the quantity contained therein and with the marks of the former cask vessel or package together with the word *exchanged* and to give a certificate or permit corresponding therewith to accompany each such exchanged cask vessel or package wheresoever the same may be sent. And in cases in which any wines shall be removed from one Cask vessel or package to another in any house or other building or place further distant than two miles from any office of Inland Duties, or otherwise without the presence of an officer of inland Duties, it shall be duty of every Dealer or Distiller by whom or whose Agents the same shall be done to cause each new cask or package to be marked in the same manner as is above directed to be done by the said officer of Inland Duties; and to enter in a book to be by him or her kept for that purpose the time and particulars of every such exchange, which book may be freely inspected by any Commissioner or Commissioners of Inland Duties who shall require the same or by any officer of inland duties by him or them authorised to make such inspection. And every such Dealer or Distiller shall give a certificate or permit to accompany every such exchanged cask vessel or package of the like kind with that which is to be given by the said Officer of Inland Duties. And if in the said cases any such dealer shall omit to mark any such exchanged Cask vessel or package as aforesaid or to enter the same in manner aforesaid or to grant the said certificate or permit to accompany the same he or she shall for every such offence forfiet and pay the sum of fifty Dollars and the wine contained in any such exchanged Cask vessel or package in respect to which such omission shall happen shall also be forfieted and may be seized by any officer of Inland Duties.[14]

XIX   And be it further enacted that whenever any Wine shall be brought into any such entered house or other building or place, notice thereof within twenty four hours thereafter shall be given at the nearest office of inland duties, which notice shall express the place from whence brought, the person of whom had the quantity quality and marks of each cask vessel or package. And the officer at whose Office such notice shall be given shall enter the contents thereof in a book to be by him kept for that purpose. And if any such dealer or Distiller shall neglect to give such notice he or she shall for each such neglect forfiet the sum of fifty dollars and the wines which shall be so neglected to be noticed or the value thereof.[15]

XX   And be it further enacted that when any such entered house or other building or place of any Dealer only shall be at the distance of twenty miles from the nearest port of Delivery the dealer to whom the same shall belong shall be intitled to a draw back or allowance of one Cent on each gallon of wine whereof he or she shall give such notice as last aforesaid and for which he or she shall produce the proper permit or permits corresponding therewith and shewing that the duties hereby charged thereupon have been paid. Provided that such allowance shall not be made more than once upon the same parcel of Wine; wherefore the proper Officer to whom any permit shall be produced for obtaining such allowance shall compare the same with the cask vessel or package to which it shall relate and if it shall correspond therewith shall indorse thereupon these words "Draw back allowed" the time when and his own name: And shall certify to the officer of Inland Duties by whom such permit shall have been granted the amount of such drawback expressing in such certificate the names of the buyer and seller and the marks of the Cask vessel or package specified in such

14. In the manuscript referred to in note 2 there is a briefer version of this paragraph.
15. At this point H wrote "Insert N." The section marked "N" in the manuscript referred to in note 2 has been inserted here.

permit and the then quantity of the Wine therein; and thereupon the said Officer last mentioned, if no fraud shall appear shall pay the amount of such drawback.

And be it further enacted that if any [-----] [16] in the original cask vessel or package or other wise in a quantity of twenty gallons and upwards on its way from one place to another or in any place belonging to or in the possession of any such dealer except in the Ware houses first aforesaid without the proper permits therewith, it shall be lawful to seize the same as forfieted; and if upon the trial of such forfieture the owner or claimant of such wine shall not prove that the same was imported into the United States according to law and if imported subsequent to the said last day of that the duties hereby charged thereupon had been paid, the said wines shall be adjudged to be forfieted.

Insert O [17]

Insert P [18]

Insert Q [19]

And be it further enacted that no Cask vessel or package marked as Old Stock shall be made use of by any such Dealer or Distiller for putting or keeping therein any wine other [than] that which was contained therein when so marked on pain of forfieting Five hundred dollars for every Cask vessel or package wherein any such *other* wine shall be so put or kept. Provided always that this shall not be construed to prevent the filling up any such Cask vessel or package for sale when not more than one half deficient.[20]

S Insert [21]

16. MS torn.
17. Insertion not found.
18. Insertion not found.
19. Insertion not found.
20. In the margin opposite this paragraph are the words "except D."
21. Insertion not found.

From Gaspard Joseph Amand Ducher [1]

Edenton [North Carolina] 10 janr. 1790

Monsieur

Les representants du peuple de la caroline du nord assemblés a fayetteville ont adoptée la nouvelle constitution;[2] comme vous connoissez mon attachement pour les americains, j'espere que vous me rendez la justice de croire que je vois avec plaisir tout ce qui peut concourir à leur union et à leur prosperité.

Dès que ma Santé sera rétablie je me propose de faire un précis des nouvelles loix commerciales des états unis de l'amerique. Je désire voir augmenter les rapports commerciaux entre votre paÿs et le mien.

Deux nations n'auront jamais plus de raisons de s'unir par le Commerce; quelle est la nation d'europe qui peut consommer une plus grande quantité des denrées americaines?

Quelle puissance peut fournir aux americains a meilleur marché, le sel, le brandy, les vins, les melasses les soieries, les beaux draps, les cambricks &c &c &c?

Avec quelle nation les americains ont ils plus de profit de navigation ou l'ofres de leurs denrées qui est moitié de la valeur de plusieurs?

De quelle nation les americains ont ils plus d'émigrants a esperer en restreignant l'importation des marchandises manufacturées par cette nation?

Quelle puissance d'europe est la plus jalouse du Commerce et de la marine des autres nations?

Quelle puissance peut donner aux americains plus de réciprocité dans le Commerce et la navigation?

Quelle puissance peut influer davantage pour ouvrir aux américains des connexions commerciales avec autres puissances?

Je m'arrête ici quant à present sur les considerations de l'intéret commercial entre la france et l'amérique.

J'ai un mot a vous dire sur la révolution qui vient de s'opérer en france. Je ne crois pas, Monsieur, que vous ajoutiez aucune confiance aux mensonges importés ici de la grande bretagne. Louis 16 s'est immortalizé en rendant au peuple le droit sacré de réprésentation libre et égale, en renonçant à toute taxe non générale et non consentie par leurs representants de la nation. L'assemblée nationale a montré tant de fermeté, tant d'attachement pour la liberté et le roi qui en est le restorateur que je considère cette assemblée comme une phalange descendüe du ciel pour assurer sur la terre le triomphe de la liberté et des loix. L'assemblée nationale en france, Louis 16, Washington et Lafayette donneront la liberté à toute l'europe.

J'ai l'honneur d'être avec l'attachement le plus respectueux Monsieur Votre très humble et très obéissant serviteur   Ducher

M. Le Colonel hamilton.

ALS, Hamilton Papers, Library of Congress.
1. Ducher was French consul at Wilmington, North Carolina.
2. The North Carolina convention ratified the Constitution on November 21, 1789.

From Sharp Delany

[*Philadelphia*] *January 11, 1790.* "Inclosed is the Total amount of goods imported & the duties arising to the first Inst. . . . My Accts are ready for settlement and I intend as soon as the river shuts as business grows slack to carry them myself."

LC, Bureau of Customs, Philadelphia.

From John E. Howard [1]

[*Annapolis*] *January 11, 1790.* Encloses a statement of Maryland's public debt.

ALS, RG 56, Letters 2d Comptroller, 2d Auditor, Executive of Maryland and Georgia, 1789–1823, National Archives.
1. This letter was written in reply to "Treasury Department Circular to the Governors of the States," November 21, 1789.
Howard was governor of Maryland.

From Beverley Randolph

Richmond, January 11, 1790. Encloses a statement from Virginia's auditor which shows how the abstract of the state debt was calculated.

LC, Archives Division, Virginia State Library, Richmond.

From Nathaniel Fosdick

[*Portland, District of Maine, January 12, 1790.* On February 8, 1790, Hamilton wrote to Fosdick: "I have received your letter of the twelfth of January." *Letter not found.*]

From Aaron D. Woodruff [1]

Trenton, January 13, 1790. "In the Action of Carter agt. Kearney . . . I have repeatedly pressed the Sheriff on the Business & have recd. for Answer that you have consented to a Stay of the Execution. . . . I am inclined to doubt the Truth of the Assertion & shall be obliged to you to know how far this Indulgence has been given & whether I am at Liberty to order the Sheriff to proceed on the Execution. . . ."

ALS, Hamilton Papers, Library of Congress.
   1. Woodruff was a lawyer who practiced and lived in Trenton.

From Charles Lee

[*Alexandria, Virginia, January 15, 1790.* On February 18, 1790, Hamilton wrote to Lee: "Your Letter of the 15th of January last duly came to hand." *Letter not found.*]

From Tobias Lear

United States
January 16th. 1790.

Sir

By order of the President of the United States, I transmit you the copy of a Report from the Post Master General [1] accompanyed with the Draft of a bill respecting the establishment of the Post Office, to the end that the same may be laid before the house of representatives, with any remarks or suggestions, which may appear to you proper, in relation to the Finances.[2]

I have the honor to be with perfect respect Sir Your most Obt. Servant   Tobias Lear
               Secretary to the President of the United States

LC, George Washington Papers, Library of Congress.
1. For this report, see Samuel Osgood to H, January 20, 1790.
2. H transmitted this report to the House of Representatives on January 22, 1790.

From Sharp Delany

[*Philadelphia*] *January 18, 1790*. ". . . There is one branch of Revenue which if it did not interfere too much with some of the states would produce 100,000 Dollars ⅌ annm. I mean 2 ⅌ Ct on Sales at public Auction. This has no doubt fell under your knowledge, but if not you will give it a due decision."

LC, Bureau of Customs, Philadelphia.

From Tobias Lear

United States
January 18th. 1790.

Sir

By order of the President of the United States, I do myself the honor to transmit you a letter from His Excellency Thomas Jefferson The Secretary for Foreign Affairs to the United States, dated at Paris Augt. 27th. 1789. —and likewise the Copy of a letter from Messrs. Wilhem & Jan Willinck, N & J. Van Staphorst & Hubbard to Mr. Jefferson, dated at Amsterdam 13th. Augt. 1789. —both of which the President wishes may be returned to him, when you have duly considered those parts of them which relate to the Finances of the United States.

I have the honor to be With perfect respect Sir Your most obedient Servt.   Tobias Lear
Secretary to the President of the United States

LC, George Washington Papers, Library of Congress.

[E N C L O S U R E] [1]

Thomas Jefferson to John Jay

Paris Aug. 27. 1789.

Sir

I am honoured with your favor of June 19.[2] informing me that permission is given me to make a short visit to my native country, for which indulgence I beg leave to return my thanks to the President, and to yourself, Sir, for the expedition with which you were so good as to forward it after it was obtained. Being advised that October is the best month of the autumn for a passage to America, I shall wish to sail about the first of that month: and as I have a family with me, and their baggage is considerable, I must endeavor to find a vessel bound directly for Virginia if possible. My last letters to you have been of the 5th. and 12th instant.[3] Since these I have received information from our bankers in Holland that they

1. ALS, letterpress copy, Thomas Jefferson Papers, Library of Congress.

Julian Boyd in the *Papers of Thomas Jefferson*, XV, 360–61, annotated this letter as follows:

"TJ was in error in saying that the INFORMATION FROM OUR BANKERS had come after his letters to Jay of 5 and 12 Aug.; that information was in the letter of Willink, Van Staphorst & Hubbard of 27 July 1789, received on the 31st. The letter that TJ WROTE TO MR. [Ferdinand Le] GRAND FOR AN EXACT ESTIMATE and Grand's response (which evidently was in writing) have not been found and not recorded in SJL [Jefferson's 'Summary Journal of letters' written and received, Thomas Jefferson Papers, Library of Congress].

"The Amsterdam bankers' APPREHENSIONS THAT ANOTHER HOUSE WAS ENDEAVORING TO OBTAIN THE BUSINESS must have been communicated to TJ in person (very probably by Jacob van Staphorst), for no letter voicing these sentiments has been found. TJ may have been correct in thinking that Congress' prompt attention to a revenue bill was a PRINCIPAL factor in bringing about the remarkable change in the bankers' attitude from that exhibited in their correspondence of the preceding spring. But, as the event showed, the bankers' shrewd appraisal of the revolutionary situation in Europe, which promised to close that continent to profitable investment for some time to come and to make advisable a new estimate of the opportunities lying in America, was perhaps the decisive factor. The forming of combinations for investment in American funds, lands, canals, turnpikes, and incipient manufactures was going forward in Amsterdam even as TJ made this analysis of the change, and within a few weeks he would be asked to lend 'Civilities and Countenance' to the representative of the bankers, Théophile Cazenove, as he departed for the United States to exploit these opportunities. . . ."

2. Jay's letter to Jefferson is in the Papers of the Continental Congress, National Archives.

3. These two letters are in the Thomas Jefferson Papers, Library of Congress. Both letters discuss French domestic matters.

had money in hand sufficient to answer the demands for the Foreign officers,[4] and for the captives: [5] and that moreover the residue of the bonds of the last loan [6] were engaged. I hereupon wrote to Mr. Grand for an exact estimate of the sum necessary for the officers. He had stated it to me as being 45,653 ₶-11s-6d a year, when I was going to Holland to propose the loan to Mr. Adams, and at that sum you will see it was stated in the estimate we sent you from Amsterdam. He now informed me it was 60,393 ₶-17s-10d a year. I called on him for an explanation. He shewed me that his first information agreed with the only list of the officers and sums then in his possession, and his last with a new list lately sent from the Treasury board on which other officers were set down who had been omitted in the first. I wrote to our bankers an account of this error, and desired to know whether, after reserving the money necessary for the captives they were in condition to furnish 254,000. ₶ for the officers. They answered me by sending the money, and the additional sum of 26,000. ₶ to complete the business of the medals.[7] I delivered the bills to Messrs. Grand & co. to negociate and pay away, and the arrears to the officers to the 1st. day of the present year are now in a course of paiment. While on this subject I will ask that an order may be forwarded to the Bankers in Holland to furnish, and to Mr. Grand to pay the arrearages which may be due on the 1st. of January next. The money being in hand, it would be a pity that

4. See William Short to H, August 3, 1790, note 5.

5. On September 13, 1788, the Continental Congress "*Resolved* That out of the fund appropriated for the redemption of the American captives at Algiers or any other monies belonging to the United States in Europe, the Minister plenipotentiary of the United States at the Court of Versailles be and he is hereby authorised to make such provision for the maintenance and Comfortable subsistence of the American Captives at Algiers and to give such orders touching the same as shall to him appear right and proper.

"That Congress approve the instructions heretofore given to Mr. [John] Lamb by Mr. Jefferson their Minister at the Court of France for supplying the said Captives." (*JCC*, XXXIV, 525.)

6. Jefferson is referring to the loan opened in Holland in July, 1788. See Bayley, *National Loans*, 21–22.

7. At various times during the Revolution the Continental Congress had voted medals to be struck as rewards to officers. Robert Morris while he was Superintendent of Finance had been ordered by Congress to carry out these resolves. When David Humphreys was sent to France in 1784 as secretary to the commission for negotiating treaties of commerce with foreign powers, Morris entrusted the purchase of the medals to him. After Humphreys had left France, the duty was assumed by Jefferson.

we should fail in paiment a single day merely for want of an order. The bankers further give it as their opinion, that our credit is so much advanced on the exchange of Amsterdam that we may probably execute any money arrangements we may have occasion for on this side the water. I have the honor to send you a copy of their letter.[8] They have communicated to me apprehensions that another house was endeavoring to obtain the business of our government. Knowing of no such endeavors myself, I have assured them that I am a stranger to any applications on the subject. At the same time I cannot but suspect that this jealousy has been one of the spurs at least to the prompt completion of our loan. The spirited proceedings of the new Congress in the business of revenue has doubtless been the principal one.[9]

[ENCLOSURE] [10]

Wilhelm and Jan Willink, Nicholaas and Jacob Van Staphorst, and Nicholas Hubbard to Thomas Jefferson

Amsterdam 13th. August 1789

We had the honor to remit Your Excellency

£ 169,718.16 the 10th. Inst. in 23 Bills of Exchange and now inclose

110,281. 4 in 22 Do. ℔ inclosed List.

together £280,000 for accounts of the United States; being the Amount requisite for payment of the Arrears of Interest due to Foreign Officers and for completing the Article of Medals; The Receipt whereof We request Your Excellency's Acknowledgment to us, and to the Board of Treasury.

Your Excellency was regularly acquainted by us, that One of the Conditions which the Necessities of the United States and the then state of their Credit compelled our Submission to, to raise Monies for Payment of the last Interests, was, A Freedom to the Subscribers for 200 Bonds, to receive during all the current Year as many Bonds as they might chose at the same price, until the whole

8. See the enclosure which follows.
9. The remainder of this letter has not been printed, for it does not concern Treasury matters.
10. LS, Thomas Jefferson Papers, Library of Congress.

of the last Loan should be run off; Facility which the Subscribers availed themselves of, to keep the Price of this Effect low, more so than Circumstances and their Solidity merited. Desirous of remedying this evil and to augment the Respectability of the Claims upon the United States, We proposed to a very few of the first Dealers in Loans, to reserve for their joint account the remaining 280 Bonds of this Loan, allowing them what time they chose to receive them, as We should have no immediate need of the Money. Impressed equally with us of the propriety of our Views, and the probability of their speedy Realisation, They readily consented, and We have now publickly declared We have no more Bonds for sale; Which will We trust, so enable them to better the Price and to establish the Credit of the United States, as to render practicable at a more reasonable rate, the Negotiation of any future Loans, the United States may think it their Interest or wish to open here, The success whereof can be but little if at all doubted, after the Organisation and Operation of their New Federal Government, Which We experience to have given already great Strength and Stability to their Credit; More especially when it is considered, that under Circumstances not only less encouraging but even sometimes dismaying, We have always paid the Interests to the Day, and by this constant regularity during Seven Years, the Money Lenders are so accustomed to the punctual Receipt of their Interests at our Houses, as well as confident of its Continuance that they now rank the Americans among the most certain and solid Effects circulating here; An Advantage We deem so improveable, that an Opportunity may soon offer for transferring at least a considerable Share of the Debt due by the United States to the Court of Versailles, An Object We Know Your Excellency and believe the United States to have much at heart, as independant of doing France at this Juncture a considerable service, by Payment of the debt due to that Country, without loss at least material to the United States. Its final Reimbursement by such Shifting, would be prolonged to a Period, when it must be supposed its Discharge will be very easy to the United States. In this Situation of Things, We are of opinion Your Excellency would do well, to obtain from the United States with the least possible delay, sufficient Powers to Your Excellency or His Successor, for negotiating this Business with the Court of

Versailles, and passing the Bonds here, So that We might seize the first favorable Moment of putting the Plan into Execution. Should Your Excellency's Absence be for any length of time, and the Chargé d'Affaires not be acquainted with Business of this Nature or competent to transact it, The necessary Powers might be given to us to pass the Bonds and settle the Matter with the French Ministry; To which We would readily attend, being desirous on all occasions, to evince our Zest to promote the Interests of the United States. We are respectfully Your Excellency's Most obd & very hble Servts,   Wilhem & Jan Willink
                                    N & J. Van Staphorst & Hubbard

To Benjamin Lincoln

Treasury Department
January 19th: 1790.

Sir

I am favored with your letter of the 16th. of last month; [1] which I would have replied to sooner if my time had not been engrossed of late in preparing business for the consideration of the Legislature.

The case of Mr. Jefferies [2] (as stated by himself) appears a hard one; but I take the Construction of the law to include the Articles you mention; and there is no authority in any of the Executive Officers to dispense with it.

I am Sir,   with sentiments of esteem   Your obedt. Humble servt.

Benjn. Lincoln Esqr.
Collector of the Customs for the ports of Boston and Charleston Massachusets.

L[S], RG 36, Collector of Customs at Boston, Letters from the Treasury, 1789–1807, Vol. 4, National Archives; copy, RG 56, Letters to the Collector at Boston, National Archives; copy, Letters to Collectors at Small Ports, "Set G," National Archives.
    1. Letter not found.
    2. H is probably referring to Peter Jeffry or Jeffrey, a Boston merchant located on Tremont Street.

Report on the Petition of Christopher Saddler

Treasury Department, January 19th. 1790.
[Communicated on January 19, 1790] [1]

[To the Speaker of the House of Representatives]

In obedience to the order of the House of Representatives of the eleventh Instant.[2] referring to the Secretary of the Treasury, the petition of Christopher Sadler,

The said Secretary Most respectfully reports:

That except the letter from the Collector of the District of Boston and Charlestown accompanying the petition, there is no evidence immediately within reach, respecting the ground of the application for relief.

That though that letter is intirely satisfactory to the mind of the Secretary, that the affair is of a nature to entitle the petitioner to relief; yet he does not consider it as such a document, as, in point of precedent, would justify the interposition of the Legislature to grant it.

The Secretary will therefore take measures for a more regular authentication of the nature of the transaction, and will submit the result. To this, therefore, is the farther inducement of it's being necessary to ascertain, whether the persons, who may be interested in the forfeiture, are disposed to relinquish their right.

The Secretary, however, begs leave to avail himself of the occasion, to represent to the House, that there are other instances which have come under his notice, in which considerable forfeitures have been incurred, manifestly through inadvertence and want of information; Circumstances which cannot fail to attend the recent promulgation of laws of such a nature, and seem to indicate the necessity, in conformity to the usual policy of Commercial Nations, of vesting somewhere a discretionary power of granting relief.

That necessity, though peculiarly great in the early stages of new regulations, does not cease to operate throughout the progress of them. There occasionally occur incidents, from which heavy and ruinous forfeitures ensue, that require the constant existence of some power capable of affording relief.

The proper investment of such a power is a matter of too much delicacy and importance to be determined otherwise, than upon mature deliberation: Yet the Secretary begs leave to submit to the consideration of the House, whether a temporary Arrangement might not be made with expedition and safety, which would avoid the inconvenience of a Legislative Decision on particular Applications.[3]

All which is humbly submitted.   Alexander Hamilton,
                                      Secretary of the Treasury

Copy, RG 233, Reports of the Secretary of the Treasury, 1790–1791, Vol. I, National Archives.

1. *Journal of the House*, I, 143. The communicating letter may be found in RG 233, Reports of the Secretary of the Treasury, 1790–1791, Vol. I, National Archives.

2. On January 9, 1790, "A petition of Christopher Saddler, of Nova Scotia, in the dominion of Great Britain, mariner, was presented to the House, and read, praying to be relieved from the forfeiture of his vessel and cargo, which have been seized in the port of Boston, for a violation of the impost law of the United States; of which law the petitioner was wholly ignorant" (*Journal of the House*, I, 137).

3. The House referred the petition on January 19 to "Mr [Fisher] Ames, Mr [Jonathan] Sturges, Mr [Michael Jenifer] Stone, Mr [Samuel] Griffin, and Mr [Henry] Wynkoop" (*Journal of the House*, I, 143). On January 26, this committee reported "That, in the opinion of the committee, provision ought to be made by law for the remission or mitigation of fines, forfeitures, and penalties, in certain cases" (*Journal of the House*, I, 147). On May 26, 1790, "An Act to provide for mitigating or remitting the forfeitures and penalties accruing under the revenue laws, in certain cases therein mentioned" went into effect (1 *Stat.* 122–23).

From Peter Anspach [1]

New York, January 20, 1790. Transmits "several Estimates signed by Col. Timothy Pickering late Quarter Master General."

ALS, Essex Institute, Salem, Massachusetts.

1. For background to this letter, see Pickering to H, November 19, 25, 1789; H to Pickering, November 19, 1789; H to Anspach, December 5, 1789; Anspach to H, December 30, 1789.

From Sharp Delany

[*Philadelphia*] *January 20, 1790*. Sends accounts and abstract of duties. Encloses "opinion of two more of our Merchants on some of your Queries." [1]

LC, Bureau of Customs, Philadelphia.
1. The opinions presumably were in reply to the questions on domestic and foreign commerce which H had sent to the collectors of the customs on October 15, 1789.

To Benjamin Lincoln

Treasury Department Jany 20th 1790

Sir

A Petition from Christopher Sadler, with a Letter from you to Mr. Ames,[1] has been referred to me by the House of Representatives for examination and Opinion.[2]

The face of the thing and your Letter leave me no doubt, that the case is such an one as to require relief. Yet I could not report in favor of it on the present evidence, without making a precedent that might in other circumstances be found inconvenient.

I shall be glad therefore to have as soon as possible an official Report of the nature of the case, stating the behaviour of the Petitioner on his first arrival, and whatever circumstances there may be tending to shew that no fraud could have been intended. If these circumstances could be confirmed by affidavits it would be the more satisfactory.

It will also be necessary, that the person or persons interested in the moiety of the forfeiture should appear in the statement, and that a certificate from him or them should accompany it, expressing a willingness to relinquish the right. I presume the Officers of the Customs are the persons.

My occupations in preparing for the Legislature have caused me to delay paying attention to several of your favors; some of them will be answered by this post and the others shall be considered as soon as possible.

I remain   Sir   Your Obedt & humble servt

Alex Hamilton
Secy of the Treasury

Benjamin Lincoln Esqr
Collector for the Port of Boston

LS, RG 36, Boston Collector, Letters from the Treasury, 1789–1818, Vol. 5; fragment, RG 56, Letters to the Collector at Boston, National Archives; fragment, RG, Letters to Collectors at Small Ports, "Set G," National Archives.
    1. Fisher Ames, Federalist member of Congress from Massachusetts.
    2. See "Report on the Petition of Christopher Saddler," January 19, 1790.

To Benjamin Lincoln

Treasury Department, January 20, 1790. Instructs Lincoln to reimburse John Coffin Jones [1] "for Oil supplied the Lighthouses" in Massachusetts.

LS, RG 36, Collector of Customs at Boston, Letters and Papers re Lighthouses, Buoys, and Piers, 1789–1819, Vol. 3, National Archives.
    1. Jones was a stockholder and director of the Massachusetts Bank, 1785–1786.

From Benjamin Lincoln [1]

Boston, January 20, 1790. Discusses the type of boat that should be used to prevent smuggling. States that "As all drawbacks on goods . . . & bounties paid on articles exported too often operate as Caches on the revenue of a country the greatest barriers possible should be placed around it to prevent the practice of frauds of every kind."

ADf, RG 36, Collector of Customs at Boston, Letters from the Treasury and Others, 1789–1818, Vol. 11, National Archives.
    1. This letter is in reply to "Treasury Department Circular to the Collectors of the Customs," October 1, 1789.

From Samuel Osgood

General Post Office, New York, January 20, 1790.

In obedience to the orders of the Supreme Executive, I have the honor of laying before you such remarks and observations as have occurred to me, in attending to the Department of the Post Office;[1] many of these observations will be found to be of a general nature, and founded in opinion: for there are not documents in the office on which to found estimates that would afford satisfaction.

The existing ordinance[2] for regulating the Post Office, though very defective in many things, has not probably ever been put fully in execution; yet the smallness of the revenue arising under the same may have been the effect of various causes, some of which could not, and others might have been remedied, but not so fully as they may under the present Government.

As to the revenue of the Post Office, it may be observed—

First. That there may be so few letters written that, under the best regulations, it would not amount to any thing considerable; and the dispersed manner of settling the country may operate powerfully against the productiveness of the Post Office.

Second. The franking of letters may have been extended too far.

Third. Ship letters may not have been properly attended to.

Fourth. The rate of postage may have been too high in some instances, and too low in others.

Fifth. Stage drivers and private post riders may have been the carriers of many letters which ought to have gone in the mail.

ASP, Post Office, I, 5–7.

1. H transmitted this plan to the House of Representatives on January 22, 1790.

2. The post office was established by "An Act for the temporary establishment of the Post-Office" (1 *Stat.* 70 [September 22, 1789]), but on September 9, 1789, the House had resolved "That, until further provision be made by law, the General Post Office of the United States shall be conducted according to the rules and regulations prescribed by the ordinances and resolutions of the late Congress" (*Journal of the House*, I, 106). On July 26, 1775, the Continental Congress had established the Continental Post Office with the provision that "a line of posts" be set up "from Falmouth in New England to Savannah in Georgia" (*JCC*, II, 208). On October 18, 1782, the Continental Congress had passed "An Ordinance for Regulating the Post Office of the United States of America" (*JCC*, XXIII, 669–79), and it is this ordinance to which Osgood is referring.

Sixth. The Postmasters may have consulted their own interest in preference to that of the public.

Remedies may be applied to all these causes, except the first. With respect to that article, I have no documents on which to found an opinion that may be relied on.

The amount of revenue will undoubtedly be considerable, if the Department is well regulated. If we should form an opinion from a comparative view of the wealth, numbers, and revenue, of the Post Offices of other countries, it would be, that the Post Office of the United States ought to bring in annually nearly half a million of dollars, under similar regulations; whereas the gross receipts in any one year have not exceeded thirty-five thousand dollars; and for the two last years have been at about twenty-five thousand dollars a year.

The revenue of the Post Office, at present, arises principally from letters passing from one seaport to another, and this source will be constantly increasing.

If we average the postage paid on letters at five cents, five hundred thousand letters would produce the sum that now arises from the Post Office annually.

A revenue of five hundred thousand dollars would require ten millions, at five cents; five millions, at ten cents; and three millions and one third, at fifteen cents; which last rate is probably nearer the true average than either of the other sums.

If there be one hundred thousand persons that write in the course of a year, each of them, thirty letters, it will nearly make the number, or twenty-five thousand write severally one hundred and twenty letters.

Foreign letters should also be taken into the computation, which are very numerous, and in other countries are subjected to a heavy rate of postage.

If, however, we should place the nett revenue at one hundred thousand dollars, even this sum must be an object of great importance to the treasury of the United States. But it will require some time to get a system into operation so as to produce it.

Unless a more energetic system is established than the present one, there will be no surplus revenue that will be worth calculating upon.

The great extent of territory over which three millions of people are settled, occasions a great expense in transporting the mail; and it will be found impracticable to accommodate all that wish to be accommodated unless a great proportion of the revenue is given up for this object.

The applications for new Post Offices and new post roads are numerous; cross roads must be established, and of very considerable extent, in order to open a communication with the treasury and revenue officers.

On franked letters I have to observe, that the accounts have not been so kept in the Post Offices as that we can ascertain what the amount would be if they were charged with the usual rates of postage.

Newspapers, which have hitherto passed free of postage, circulate extensively through the Post Offices; one or two cents upon each would probably amount to as much as the expenses of transporting the mail.

The third article, if properly regulated, would be a source of great revenue. If the postage could be collected, the present rates would not produce a revenue much short of fifty thousand dollars a year. But upon the construction that has heretofore been put upon the ordinance of Congress, ship letters have operated as a clear loss to the revenue.

The clause of the ordinance is as follows: "For any distance not exceeding sixty miles, one penny-weight eight grains; upwards of sixty miles, and not exceeding one hundred miles, two penny-weights—and so on; and for all single letters to and from Europe, by the packet or despatch vessel, four penny-weights; and to the foregoing rates shall be added a sum not exceeding four-ninetieths of a dollar upon any letter, packet, or despatch, which shall come into the Post Office from beyond sea, by any other conveyance than by packet or despatch vessels."

The meaning of this clause, as it relates to ship letters, appears to be plain. Packet, or despatch vessel, can intend none other than American. All letters coming into the post office from beyond sea by other conveyance than American packets, should be charged with the four-penny weight, equal to twenty ninetieths, and the additional sum of four-ninetieths, making twenty-four-ninetieths.

And, if such letters are forwarded by land through the Post Offices, the usual rates for travelling letters should be charged over and above the twenty-four-ninetieths. The rates correspond nearly with the British rates for the like kind of letters. But whether so high a rate of postage ought to be put on letters that come by French or British packets, is a matter that is questioned by many.

The practice has been to charge two-ninetieths on ship letters delivered out of the same place where they were first received, and four-ninetieths in addition to the fixed rate of travelling letters on those forwarded to other places, if they came from beyond sea by any other conveyance than French or British packets. The two-ninetieths has been considered as a prerequisite to the Postmaster; the General Post Office has not been credited with it. And, as the Postmasters are authorized to pay one-ninetieth a letter to the captains or masters of vessels bringing the same, they take credit to themselves for the one-ninetieth in their account current with the General Post Office. In one of the Post Offices, this one-ninetieth has amounted to one hundred and sixty dollars a year, and, consequently, the twenty-four-ninetieths, if it had been charged, would have amounted to three thousand eight hundred and forty dollars a year.

The late Postmaster at this place had as perquisites over and above his commission of twenty per cent. more than all the money that arose from ship letters, and one hundred and twenty pounds a year for his trouble with respect to French and British packets.

The foregoing rates of postage were reduced twenty-five per cent. by an act of Congress, of the _____, 1787.[3]

On the fourth article, I will give my reasons for apprehending that the rates of postage are, in some instances, too high.

Wherever Congress may hold their sessions, it will be considered as the centre of the United States, and will necessarily occasion a great deal of letter writing to that place. The extremes are, in my opinion, entitled to an easy and cheap access to that place through the Post Office. Their comparative advantages derived from the General Government are smaller than those of the more central, and ought not to be diminished by the heavy rates of postage that

3. On October 20, 1787, the Continental Congress resolved to reduce the rates (*JCC*, XXXIII, 694–95).

now exist. The postage of a single letter from Georgia, or rather Savannah, to New York, is thirty-three-ninetieths of a dollar, which amounts almost to a prohibition of communication through the Post Office. If it should be reduced to about sixteen cents, the revenue would not probably be injured by it.

So far as I have been able to collect the opinions of others relative to the fifth article, the injury the general revenue has sustained in this way is greater than I had expected; perhaps no complete remedy can be devised for this evil, yet it may undoubtedly be remedied in a great measure.

In the present manner of contracting to carry the mail, especially by stage carriages, the contractors labor under disadvantages, on account of the shortness of the time. One of them has property to the amount of nearly twenty thousand dollars employed in the transportation of the mail. Whenever they undertake to carry it one or two hundred miles, it costs them several thousand dollars for horses and carriages. This property sinks considerable in his hands, if he fails to contract the next year: many of them urge this contingency as a reason for a higher charge. The advertising for proposals for carrying the mail places the Postmaster General in a disagreeable predicament: for many poor people make proposals at so low a rate that it is obvious the business cannot be done as it ought to be, and consequently there cannot be a strict adherence to the lowest proposals. Discretion must be used, and the contract must be given to him who will most probably perform the duty with punctuality. A few failures in a year injure the General Post Office more than the public can be benefited by the recovery of the penalties in the contractor's bonds.

Whether it will not be proper to give the contractors that carry the mail by stage carriages the exclusive privilege of driving stages on the post roads, is submitted for consideration.

There are, at this time, about twenty different contracts for carrying the mail, which has a greater tendency to put the business into confusion than I apprehended: every contractor consults his own interest as to the days and hours of arrival and departure of the mail, without having a due regard to the necessary connexion of the Post Office. A regular system of days and hours of departure has never been established further southward than Alexandria.

The contracts for carrying the mails to the southward of New York the ensuing year amount to . . $14,973 75
And to the eastward of the same place to . . .   6,003 15
                                                 ——————
                                                 $20,977 00

With the exclusive privilege of driving stages, and the contracts
being for a greater length of time, this sum would probably be sufficient to induce men of property to come forward, when character and reputation would be the best kind of security for the Post
Office. It is so necessary to establish regularity, in order to promote a well founded confidence in the Post Office, which I think
can hardly be effected upon the present mode of contracting, that,
if a different one should eventually cost something more, yet the
Department would be benefited by it.

It is not difficult to ascertain what ought to be given for carrying
the mail a mile; if the Legislature should fix the sum, it would then
be the duty of the Postmaster General to find out such as he could
place the most confidence in, to execute the business well. This
method has always been practised in England, so far as I understand
the regulations of the Post Office there.

On the sixth article it may be observed that very small advantages
taken by those concerned in the receipt of postage, will, in a year,
amount to a great sum. In some instances these may be justifiable:
for example, the postage of a single letter from New York to Philadelphia, is one pennyweight eight grains, or sixpence two-thirds
Pennsylvania currency. This cannot be made out in any pieces of
coin current in the United States. The letters are charged with
sevenpence, which is right: for if there must be a fraction it ought
always to be taken in favor of the Post Office.

This, however, may be remedied in two ways; the one is to make
the rates of postage to be received in each State conformable to the
currency thereof. The other is for the United States to coin pieces
that might correspond with the rates of postage.

The dead letters may afford an opportunity for defrauding the
revenue; but if the deputies' accounts are properly examined in the
General Post Office, many evils that might otherwise exist, will
naturally vanish.

With respect to the present ordinance regulating the Post Office,

I beg leave to suggest the propriety of sundry alterations and additions.

If the views of the Legislature should be to raise a revenue from the Post Office, the defects of the present system are many, and may easily be pointed out. But if there should be no such views, yet, for the purpose of establishing more security in the Department, sundry alterations will be found essentially necessary.

The two following articles operate most powerfully against the productiveness of the Post Office at present:

Any person may receive, carry, and deliver, inland letters, and is subject to no penalty, if it be done without hire or reward.

The following alterations appear to me to be necessary for greater security in the Post Office, whether revenue be or be not an object:

A more accurate description of offences and frauds that may be committed by any person employed in any way or manner whatever in the Department; and the establishment of penalties proportioned to the injuries that may happen from the committing such offences, or being guilty of such frauds.

Those that will naturally present themselves first, will be such as may be committed by the Postmaster General, and those employed in his office.

And such as may be committed by the contractors for carrying the mail, and by their agents and servants.

Many offences may probably be pointed out that have never been committed in the United States: but the opportunity to commit them is great, and when committed the injury may be irreparable, as property to a very great amount is frequently entrusted in the mail.

It therefore appears to me that it will be only exercising a due degree of caution to guard against them by defining the crimes and affixing to the commission of them such penalties as will be most likely to deter from and prevent the actual commission of them.

The duties of the Postmaster General are at present to keep an office in the place where Congress may hold their sessions. To obey such orders and instructions as he may from time to time receive from the President of the United States. To appoint Deputy Postmasters, and instruct them in their duty in conformity to the acts of Congress. To receive and examine their accounts and vouchers, and draw out of their hands, quarterly, the balances due to the United States. To render to the treasury, annually, an account of the receipts and expenditures, for examination and allowance, and to pay over the surplus moneys. To provide by contract and otherwise for carrying the mail; and to pay the necessary expenses thereof. To establish and open new Post Offices and new post roads, whenever and wherever they may be found necessary, within certain limits marked out by the acts of Congress. And in general to superintend the department, and to be accountable for it in the various duties assigned to it, except the carrying of the mail.

On any breach of oath, on due conviction, he forfeits one thousand dollars.

With respect to the accountability of the Postmaster General, I beg leave to observe that no man can, however sagacious and cautious he may be in his appointments, without subjecting himself to certain loss, be responsible for the conduct of his deputies. The calculations of loss being certain in case of responsibility, if he has not a salary sufficient to compensate such loss, he must, to save himself, transact the business, and keep the accounts in a manner that the treasury shall not be able to charge him with any more money than he chooses to be charged with; or he may endeavor to transact the business fairly, and hold the office until he finds he cannot preserve his reputation and credit, and then, if he is an honest man, he will resign.

The number of times the mail shall be carried weekly, the advertising for proposals for carrying the mail, and the establishing of new Post Offices and new post roads, appear to me to be matters that should be left in the direction of the Supreme Executive. Very great embarrassments ensue when business is pointed out in detail, and there is no power at hand that can alter the same, however necessary it may be to alter it.

The Postmaster General should be subjected to suitable penalties, in case he neglects or refuses to render true and just accounts of the receipts and expenditures, and to pay over the moneys to the treasury that may be over and above the annual expenditures, at such periods as may be required.

It may be a question whether the Postmaster General should keep an office separate from the one in which common and ordinary business is done. There may be some reasons why he should not have a separate office. Irregularities and interruptions of communications will happen, and those who have the receiving and delivering of the mail are most likely to be acquainted seasonably with them.

When the Postmaster General keeps a separate office many things that he ought to be acquainted with may entirely escape his notice.

I found the General Post Office not blended with one in which common and ordinary business was transacted, and it remains in the same situation.

The prohibition at present against receiving and carrying letters, extends to such only as do it for hire or reward; but it ought to extend to all who receive and carry letters, whether with or without reward; and penalties should be annexed to enforce an observance of it. Some few exceptions may be found necessary, where masters of vessels carry letters respecting the merchandises under their immediate care; and letters sent by a special messenger, by a friend, or by a common known carrier of goods.

Regulations may probably be found necessary respecting bye or way-letters; embezzling or destroying letters on which the postage has been paid; detaining or opening letters; secreting, embezzling, and stealing any valuable papers out of any letters; against the carriers of the mail in case they neglect or desert it; to oblige the ferrymen to set the mail across in all possible cases in a given time; to recover debts due to and from the Deputy Postmasters in a summary way.

These are some of the principal alterations that have occurred to me as being necessary to be introduced into the regulations of the Post Office, and no doubt many others may suggest themselves to the wisdom of the Legislature.

With respect to appropriating to a particular object any supposed surplus of revenue that may arise in the Department, I beg leave to observe that it will undoubtedly tend to awaken the attention of the citizens to the Department, if a certain sum should be required to be paid quarterly or semi-annually into the treasury, and be appropriated to the payment of the interest of the domestic debt, as far as it might go.

This might interest a powerful body of citizens in attending to the operations of the Department, and would probably have a greater tendency to keep the Postmasters strictly to their duty, if any should be otherwise disposed, than any authority with which the Postmaster General might be clothed.

I have enclosed the form of an act, or rather such principles as appear to me proper to be introduced into the arrangement of the Post Office, which will tend, more fully than the foregoing observations, to explain my views of the alterations that are necessary.

I am, sir, with esteem, your most obedient humble servant,

Samuel Osgood

The Honorable Alexander Hamilton, Secretary of the Treasury.

Treasury Department Circular to the Collectors of the Customs

Treasury Department
January 20. 1790.

Sir

Motives friendly to the Interests of the Officers of the Customs, as well as to the advancement of the public service, induce me to desire that I may be as soon as possible furnished with a Statement of the amount of the emoluments which have accrued to them respectively under the existing regulations, up to the first of January. As this letter will only be addressed to the Collector of each district it will be proper that a communication should be made to the Naval Officer & Surveyor.

I shall take it for granted that the information I may receive on this head, will be such as I may place absolute reliance upon.

I am, Sir,   Your Obedt. servt.   A Hamilton

LS, to Sharp Delany, Bureau of Customs, Philadelphia; LS, to Charles Lee, Charles Lee Papers, Library of Congress; LS, to Benjamin Lincoln, RG 36, Collector of Customs at Boston, Letters from the Treasury, 1789–1818, Vol. 5, National Archives; L[S] Office of the Secretary, United States Treasury Department; copy, United States Finance Miscellany, Treasury Circulars, Library of Congress; copy, RG 56, Circulars of the Office of the Secretary, "Set T," National Archives.

To Roger Alden [1]

[New York, January 21, 1790]

Sir

If you have in the Office the laws of North Carolina, I will thank you for the perusal of them. As I want them in haste, I shall be glad they may be sent by the bearer.

I am, Sir   Yr Obed serv   A Hamilton
                                              S of the Treasy

New York January 21. 1789 [2]
Roger Alden Esq

ALS, Hamilton Papers, Library of Congress.
    1. Alden, a deputy secretary of the Continental Congress from 1785 to 1789, accepted a clerkship in 1789 in the new Department of State under the temporary Secretary, John Jay. Alden headed what Jefferson called the "home office" (that is, domestic affairs) until July or August, 1790.
    2. H mistakenly dated this letter 1789.

To John Davidson

Treasury Department, January 22, 1790. "I am favored with your letter of the 2d Instant [1] Enclosing a Bank Note for Fifty Dollars; all the Remittances which you make in future must be sent . . . to the Treasurer of the United States. . . ."

Copy, RG 56, Letters to and from the Collectors at Bridgetown and Annapolis, National Archives; copy, RG 56, Letters to Collectors at Small Ports, "Set G," National Archives.
    1. Letter not found.

From Sharp Delany

[Philadelphia] January 22, 1790. "I inclose you the Exports of flour for the last year & our Inspector informs me he is confident the Quantity not returned to him would make the export not much less than 400,000 barrells. . . ."

LC, Collector of Customs, Philadelphia.

From William Livingston [1]

[*January 23, 1790*. On February 8, 1790, Hamilton wrote to Livingston: "I had the honor of receiving a few days since your Excellencys letter of the 23d. of January." *Letter not found.*]

1. Livingston was governor of New Jersey.

From Tobias Lear

United States, January 24th, 1790

Sir,

In obedience to the commands of the President of the United States, I have the honor to transmit to you a letter from His Excellency Beverley Randolph Governor of Virginia, dated January the 14th 1790, relating to the materials which were placed upon Cape Henry by the States of Virginia and Maryland for the purpose of building a Light House; and likewise the report of General Wood [1] upon the same subject, which report was enclosed in Governor Randolph's letter to the President of the United States.

I have the honor to be, with perfect respect, Sir, Your most Obedt. Servt.   Tobias Lear.

Secretary to the President
of the United States.

The Honorable The Secretary of the Treasury of the U.S.

LS, RG 26, "Segregated" Lighthouse Records, National Archives; copy, George Washington Papers, Library of Congress.
1. Lieutenant Governor James Wood of Virginia.

From Sharp Delany

[Philadelphia, January 25, 1790]

Sir

From the Journals of Congress I see You have reported [1] a Bill [2] to the consideration of the Legislature respecting Duties, which gives me much pleasure even if the Imposts you wish to take place should not carry, as the deficiencies & contrarieties in our collection & Registering Acts may be remedied. The office of Naval officer as a controuling officer is absolutely necessary—but as the collection Act now stands that officer at present is nugatory & has not any essential check. Sometime this week I intend to wait on You—as in person I think I can give more information & satisfaction to You than by Letter. I inclose the Acct. of Liquidated Bonds by this conveyance and am Sir &c   S Delany

25th Jany 1790
Alexander Hamilton Esqr
S of the T.

LC, Bureau of Customs, Philadelphia.
    1. Above this word Delany wrote the word "offerd."
    2. See "Report Relative to a Provision for the Support of Public Credit," January 9, 1790.

To Jedediah Huntington

Treasury Department, January 25, 1790. "I am favored with your letter of 9th. instant, transmitting the Accounts of the Lighthouse under your Superintendance. As the regulations for this establishment have not yet been determined on by the President I cannot at present do any thing with respect to your compensation on this Account. . . ."

LS, The Huntington Library, San Marino, California.

To Benjamin Lincoln [1]

(Duplicate) [2]

Treasury Department
January 25th. 1790

Gentlemen
    As it has become my duty to prepare a plan for the consideration of Congress, respecting the encouragement of Manufactures [3] it is of course my wish to ⟨secure in⟩formation, which can be had on the Subject.

I shall therefore be obliged to you, for such ⟨– – particular⟩s, as may assist me in forming a right judgement of the means, which may be proper to be pursued.

The several kinds of Manufactures carried on in the State—the places where they are carried on, the times of their Commencements, and the progress they have made—the situation in which they now are—the value of the raw material, and the expences of the Manufacture are all circumstances of which I should be glad to have as precise a knowledge, as can be obtained.

Manufactories of Cannon, Arms, & Gun powder are objects to which I am directed to pay particular attention.

I request an answer to these inquiries as speedily as it can be afforded with due regard to accuracy. Perhaps the information will best be conveyed successively.

I flatter myself the importance of the object in a public view, will be a sufficient apology for the trouble I give.[4]

And am   Gentlemen   Your Obedient & humble Servant

L[S], RG 36, Collector of Customs at Boston, Letters from the Treasury, 1772–1818, Vol. 6, National Archives.

1. H mistakenly addressed the envelope to Benjamin Lincoln, "Chairman of the Comm of Manufactures." On May 26, Lincoln wrote to Henry Warren, *et al.*:

"The Secretary of the treasury of the United States has requested from the academy of arts & Science in this Commonwealth, information from time to time of the Several kinds of manufactures carried on in this State, the places where the time of their commencement the progress which they have made, the situation in which they now are, the value of the raw materials the expence of manufacture and of all circumstances relative to them.

"To the manufacture of Cannon Arms & Gunpowder the Secretary wishes particular attention.

"The academy yesterday raised a committee of nine of which you are one to make the communications requested to this three are competent the Chairman always being one.

"Permit me to request that you would favour me with the state of the manufactures in the County of   as fully and as soon as may be convenient the sooner the better. I am with some Gentlemen in this neighbourhood directed by the academy to report to the Secretary agreeably to his wishes." (ADf, RG 36, Collector of Customs at Boston, Letters from the Treasury, 1772–1818, Vol. 6, National Archives.)

2. Apparently Lincoln never received the original letter. The envelope of this duplicate is postmarked New York, May 18, and Lincoln endorsed it May 20, 1790.

3. In his speech to Congress of January 8, 1790, Washington made the following remarks on the subject of manufactures:

"Among the many interesting objects, which will engage your attention, that of providing for the common defence will merit particular regard. To be prepared for War is one of the most effectual means of preserving peace.

"A free people ought not only to be armed but disciplined; to which end a uniform and well digested plan is requisite: And their safety and interest require, that they should promote such manufactories, as tend to render them independent on others for essential, particularly for military supplies." (George Washington Papers, Library of Congress.)

On January 15, 1790, the House directed H to prepare "a proper plan or plans . . . for the encouragement and promotion of such manufactories as will tend to render the United States independent of other nations for essential, particularly for military supplies" (*Journal of the House*, I, 141–42).

4. This letter indicates that H began to assemble information on manufacturing much earlier than has been supposed. As there is another copy of this letter in a closed private manuscript collection, H probably sent this letter to prominent businessmen throughout the states as well as to government officials. This is similar to the procedure he followed in enclosing questions in the "Treasury Department Circular to the Collectors of the Customs," October 15, 1789.

On May 11, 1790, Tench Coxe, who succeeded William Duer as Assistant Secretary of the Treasury, reported H's request in the following words:

"I am directed by the Secretary of the Treasury to request the early Transmission to him of such information, relative to the subject of his letter to you of the 25th of January last as you may be possessed of at this time. He also instructs me to add, that your future Communications upon the business of Manufactures, as well, in the course of the present Session of the Legislature as in future, must prove of the greatest public utility." (LS, RG 36, Collector of Customs at Boston, Letters from the Treasury, 1772–1818, Vol. 6, National Archives.)

From Richard Peters

Belmont [Philadelphia] Jan'y 25. 1790.

Dear Sir

I should sooner have acknowledged the Reciept of your kind Letter [1] respecting Mr Smith [2] but I hope not to draw you into any useless Correspondence when your Hands must be full of Matters of more general Consequence. I hoped to get Mr. S. employed here & had nearly succeeded but his Friends were culpably sure of Success & by a sudden Compromise he lost the Appointment of Treasurer to the State by one Vote tho' his Interest is far superior to that of his Opponent. These Things will happen in multitudinary Bodies & the Lord help him who depends upon them. He has need of some other Assistance than theirs. Smith has an Antipathy to an Employment in the State & a strong Inclination for one in his old Line. But how or when he can be provided for, if at all, is a Matter which must at present be doubtful at least. He goes to New York to get what we all desire & he much wants—Money. He knows you are not yet upon Velvet in this Way & wishes to avoid being importunate but hopes you may be able to afford him something towards old Scores. I know not that ever I shall have it in my Power to repay any Kindnesses shewn him in any other Way than being grateful for them. No Expectation is formed further than that of your giving him his Share in any general Arrangement which he presumes you may have thought of for all in his Circumstances.

I am with sincere Esteem   Your obedt Servt   Richard Peters

Hon: A Hamilton Esq

ALS, Hamilton Papers, Library of Congress.
  1. H to Peters, October 11, 1789.
  2. Thomas Smith, former continental loan officer.

From Otho H. Williams

Baltimore, January 25, 1790. Discusses the official value of the rix-dollars of Denmark, Sweden, and various German states.

ALS, Personal Miscellany, Otho H. Williams, Library of Congress.

From Wilhem and Jan Willink, Nicholaas and Jacob Van Staphorst, and Nicholas Hubbard [1]

[Amsterdam, January 25, 1790]

(Triplicate)
Sir!

We had the Honor to address you the 29 Ulto.[2] since when we have not received any of your respected favors.

We have now to acquaint you that the Persons employed by the Court of France here, and the principal Broker in the French funds, foreseeing that the Situation of the Finances of that Country would put it out of the Power of the Governmt. to make timely Provision for the payement of the interest and reimbursment of the instal-

LS, Connecticut Historical Society, Hartford; LC, George Washington Papers, Library of Congress.
  1. This letter was enclosed in William Short to H, January 28–31, 1790. A copy was also enclosed in H's "Report on Foreign Loans," February 13, 1793.
  2. Letter not found.

ment of Capital due the 5 Decr. last on the loan raised here by the Court of France under Guarantee of their High Mightinesses, the Monies of which were applied to the services of the united states;[3] They made ouvertures to Mr. Necker[4] the first minister of the Finances to purchase the title of Six Millions of livres, furnished by the Court of France to the united States in 1783. and the arrears of interest due thereon in order to furnish monies for the above & other pressing Objects.[5] As this transaction tended to commit the credit & reputation of the united States to the Management of Persons unconnected with their Government and without any strong Motives to induce them to uphold it, but who on the contrary would be spurred by the urging necessities to raise Monies, to effect the same on terms injurious to the rising credit of America. We on the first intelligence of any Movements here, exerted ourselves to prevent the success of the business, and Succeeded So far, that in order to remove the ground of our Objections, the

3. Rafael Bayley states:
"The king of France had, through his minister at the Hague, offered his assistance to the Americans in procuring loans in that country, but without effect. He now engaged to become, himself, responsible for the sums which might be furnished. In consequence of this and the exertions of Mr. [John] Adams, a loan of ten millions of livres was obtained in Holland.

"The money thus borrowed, although intended solely for the United States, having been obtained on the credit of France, became a debt due to that country, and was provided for in the financial contract drawn up July 16, 1782, and signed by the Comte de Vergennes and Benjamin Franklin.

"Article V of this contract says that although the loan of 5,000,000 florins of Holland, amounting on a moderate valuation to 10,000,000 livres Tournois, agreed to by the states general of the Netherlands on the terms of the obligation passed November 5, 1781, between his majesty and the states general, has been made in his majesty's name and guaranteed by him, it is nevertheless acknowledged that the said loan was made, in reality, on account and for the service of the United States of North America. By the terms of the obligation the king had agreed to pay the capital of the said loan with the interest at 4 per cent. per annum, the capital to be repaid in ten equal payments, the first to commence the sixth year after the date of the loan, and to be completed in five years thereafter, and it was therefore promised that the United States should reimburse and pay the same with interest at 4 per cent. per annum, at the royal treasury of France, in ten equal payments of 1,000,000 livres each, to commence November 5, 1787, the king 'on account of his affection for the United States, having been pleased to charge himself with the expense of commissioners and bank for the loan, of which expense his majesty has made a present to the United States.'" (Bayley, National Loans, 13–14.)

4. Jacques Necker, French Director General of the Finances.

5. For information on the French attempt to sell the debt due France from the United States and the offer made by a combine of American and French speculators to purchase it, see Short to H, November 30, 1789.

french house [6] offered to assume us in the execution of the business, as the only Certain way of Securing the Event, and hindering any depression to the Credit of the united States. We refused so long as we could imagine that by keeping aloof, we might defeat the business but when we saw that the Minister had touched upon the negotiation here, in his Memorial to the National Assembly,[7] and were informed from an Authority we would have been injustifiable in doubting, that if we did not determine to Coalesce the affair would be proposed and certainly be accepted by the french Minister, so great were his then actual wants, and thus the credit of the united States be Sported with, owing to our declining to interfere in its Support, which we were enabled to do, by the confidence the Money lenders place in us, from the care we have always taken to insure the regular Payment of their interests, we judged it our duty to Submit notwithstanding we constantly entertained the most eager wish, that the matter could have been postponed, until we should receive the directions of the united States upon what we wrote the Commissioners of the Treasury,[8] and communicated to his Excellency Thomas Jefferson,[9] respecting the transfer to the Money Lenders here, of the debt due by the united States to France. In the Interval of the negotiations upon this Subject, and the time the offer could be formally made to the Minister for his final determination a Settlement of considerable Magnitude of the french Finances by rendering the Minister more easy in Money matters, thro' the receipt of eight millions of Livres the caiste d'Escompte Supplied to the Government inclined him not to accept the proposal one [10] of us went to Paris, expressly to make him for the Purchase of six millions livres Capital and the arrears of interest, alledging that this was too Small an object to trouble the

6. The banking house of Ferdinand Le Grand and Company.

7. The memorial which Necker presented to the National Assembly on November 14, 1789, is printed in *Archives Parlementaires*, X, 56–65. See Short to H, November 30, 1789, note 4.

8. Willink, Van Staphorst, and Hubbard had written to the American Commissioners of the Treasury (Board of Treasury) on September 11, 1789, of Thomas Jefferson's "favorite wish to transfer unto Our Money-Lenders the debt due by the United States to the Court of Versailles" (copy, Thomas Jefferson Papers, Library of Congress).

9. The letter to Jefferson is dated September 24, 1789, and is printed in Boyd, *Papers of Thomas Jefferson*, XV, 471–72.

10. Nicholas Hubbard.

national assembly with, but that if we would treat for the whole debt He was ready to enter into arrangements for it. This issue to the business was highly agreeable to us, as would be the possibility of the matter laying dormant, untill we received instructions from the united States, subsequent to the arrival of our letter of 11 Sepr.[11] and of his Excellency Thomas Jefferson; but we have had the chagrin to learn that some Gentlemen have formed, and presented to the Minister a Plan for the Purchase of the whole Claim of France against the united States.[12] Half of the consideration to be paid in french Effects, and the other half in Money at the Current Prices of these Effects, which afford the Prospect of a most enormous profit to the Speculators, and we have but too much reason to apprehend there are Persons concerned in the affair, capable of influencing its acceptance by the French Ministry.[13]

The parties confident that no house could succeed to negotiate the business, or at least with any thing near the facility or advantage as the Commissioners of Congress Loans, applied to us to know if we would consent to undertake it, and to obtain our acquiesence offered us the alternative of a share in the Profits, or a Valuable Commission. Deeming ourselves the natural Guardians of the Honor and credit of the united States in their Financial Concerns here, we stood in need of no other Consideration to induce us to forego Any personal advantages, in order to ward off the depression such a Bargain would cause to the credit of the united States. These being our sentiments even if we had had the chief direction in the Business and consequently a great controul over the timely Opening of the Loans, you'll easily conceive, how much Stronger our objections are against assuming the Commission to negotiate upon the credit of the united States, for these Speculators, and the eager desire we have by every possible Means to prevent the realization of this project, to avoid that from the certain Knowledge our Money lenders would have of this Transaction, as it must pass thro' and be ratified by the National Assembly, they would learn that the credit of the united States is held in So litle repute, that the french Ministry at an enormous great Profit to the speculators, uncompensated by any

11. See note 8.
12. See Short to H, November 30, 1789.
13. Presumably Etienne Clavière and Jean Pierre Brissot de Warville.

early desirable Supply of Money to that Nation, had abandoned it
to the mercy of Speculating individuals who to fullfill their Engagements of paying off the whole in two Years, would be compelled to camish [14] upon this Market American loans to the extent
at least of twelve Millions of Guilders, to purchase the necessary
french Funds, an information that would immediately Check nay
destroy the credit of the united states, as the Money Lenders would
naturally conclude, that by waiting until the Speculators must make
good their payments they would be necessitated to vend their
American Bonds at almost any rate, exclusive of the danger, that
when the french Funds should be low they might find it their
benefit to force the sale of the american Bonds at low prices, to
profit of the fall of French Stocks. To remedy which evils our
remonstrances or opposition might provely entirely fruitless, as when
once possessed of these Claims upon our refusal to open the Loans
requisited to enable them to compleat their Views or Engagements,
they might commission any other House to do it, which not having
the same relation with the United States and consequent Interest
to support their credit would not hesitate sacrificing it to give
satisfaction to their Employers, adding to all which the impossibility
there would be for the united states during the long time it would
take, to place the nineteen Millions in Bonds that would issue from
the Exchange of debts, as the value at par of that due by the united
States to the Court of France and the Still longer Period that would
be necessary to raise the credit of the united States from the injury
it would unquestionably Sustain to negotiate any other monies they
might desire to appropriate to the Support of their credit here,
their inferior arrangements or Ameliorations, and we are persuaded
the government will fully applaud our anxious Sollicitude to avert
the Many and great Evils that would flow from the completion of
this purchase, and thankfully approve of the only Step we have
judged efficacious to overturn it immediately; which is of availing
ourselves of the present plenty of Money here to open a loan the
1st. Proximo of Three millions Florins for account of the united
States, reimbursable by yearly Instalments of ƒ600,000.—Commencing in 1801. and ending in 1805—which we communicate to

14. In the copy enclosed in H's "Report on Foreign Loans," February 13,
1793, this word reads "launch."

the French Ministry with information of our having So done, from
our knowledge of the wishes and intentions of the united states
to evince their friendship to the French Nation, by reimbursing so
soon as in their Power the debt due to France, and that we would be
ready to pay them these three Millions, on receipt of directions from
the United States to negotiate monies for this object, which we had
reason to expect Shortly and assuring them that we would Second
with all our power the wishes of our Employers, to transfer this debt
from the French nation, unto the Money lenders here in a Manner not
derogatory to the dignity & honor of the Government of the united
States or injurious to their Credit, which flattering ourselves to be
able to compleat within the Course of the next year, and at all
events with more expedition than the money could be procured in
any Other manner or thro' any other Persons, we trusted the
Ministry would refrain by any Bargain with individuals for the sale
or Transfer of the claim against the united States, from com-
promising the dignity and honor of their allies, and overturn their
well established credit here, in committing it to the direction of
Persons whose Engagements or Interests may tempt them to sacrifice it. We make not the least doubt of the Success of this Measure,
to defeat entirely all further treaty between the French Ministry
and the Persons offering to purchase the claims of France against
the united States. However to render our object the more certain,
we transmit the duplicate of this letter open to Mr. Short chargé
des affaires of the United States to be forwarded to you by him,
acquainting him of our proceedings, and urging his utmost Exertions
to engage the French Ministry to suspend the Idea of treating with
Individuals about the claim against the united States until the desire
and intentions of their Government Shall be known on the Subject,
and we are without Apprehension of this Gentleman's obtaining
the Promise we are so Sollicitous the french Ministry shall make
from our experience of his Zeal for the Service of the united States
and the Opinion he testified to us in Paris, that the Commissioners
here were unquestionably the most fit Persons to decide upon every
thing relating to the credit of the united States in Holland.

The actual state of the credit of the united states will permit us
to open the Loan upon the most favorable terms any Nation borrows Monies here, so that there will be only a deduction of 4½

pCt. for Premiums, Brokerage, Commissions and all other Charges, and we the more readily agreed to open this Loan for three Millions as we now avail the united States of the plenty of money here, which will probably have subsided or be less brisk on arrival of their orders, and because there will be no Question of obtaining a lower rate of interest than 5 pCt. now universally established here by all the Powers borrowing Money, which rise of interest is the only reason why the united States pay the same for this as for the first Loan [15] opened for their account, altho' their credit now is equal to that of any European Government accustomd to raise monies in Holland.

To Spare the united States all possible Advances of Interest while the Money shall remain unappropriated, we shall issue the recepisses at the option of the buyers to take them so late as they please, on the Expectation the three Millions will be placed in a few months. Having thus explained our motives for opening this Loan, and our attention to the Interest and credit of the United States in its price and conditions. We firmly rely upon our obtaining that approbation and Ratification from the United states which they have hitherto constantly bestowed upon all our discretionary proceedings,[16] dictated as this has been by our Sincere Zeal to cherish and promote their Credit; But if after all this our conduct shall not be honored

15. Bayley describes this loan as follows:
"The united firms [Willink, Van Staphorst, and De La Lande and Fynje] offered a loan of 5,000,000 guilders ($2,000,000), to run for ten years, at 5 per cent. interest, then to be redeemed in five years, by paying each year a fifth part. As compensation for raising this money they asked 4¼ per cent., to include all the expenses, except a charge of 1 per cent. for paying out the annual interest and a charge of ½ per cent. on the final redemption. To this last item Mr. [John] Adams refused to accede. He offered them 4½ per cent. to cover all charges except the 1 per cent. on the annual interest received and paid by them. To this they agreed, and the contract was closed, varying in no other particular from their first proposition. Five formal contracts for 1,000,000 guilders each, numbered from 1 to 5, were drawn up, "as advised by the ablest lawyers and most experienced notaries," setting forth these terms, with a great deal of verbiage, but which as Mr. Adams observes in one of his letters, "meant only that the money having been borrowed must be paid. The contract was concluded June 11, and the five formal documents were confirmed by Congress September 14, 1782." (Bayley, *National Loans*, 17.)

16. The loan was authorized by Congress on August 4, 1790, when a $12,000,-000 loan was authorized to be floated and applied to the public debt ("An Act making provision for the [payment of the] Debt of the United States" [1 *Stat.* 138-44]). See H to Willink, Van Staphorst, and Hubbard, August 28, 1790.

with their approbation, youll please to observe that we have not assumed to bind the United States to accept the Monies arising from this Loan, which the Purchasers will furnish solely upon our Personal credit, and the Confidence they place in us, and in Such case we Shall have to return back the Monies with one Years Interest to the Proprietors of the Bonds sold. A Sacrifice that with the other charges we chearfully submit to the decision of your Government If it ought to be borne by us, who expose ourselves thereto only thro' Zeal for the credit of the united States, or whether the United States will not deem it Just to assume the same.

A Speedy decision be it either way, is of to great Consequence to render it necessary for us, to press your obtaining and transmitting it to us with the least possible delay possible. If as we do not doubt the united states will accept and confirm this Loan, we will follow their directions for disposal of the Monies, on receipt of the necessary powers to enable us to pass the Bonds on their behalf and may we request your care sir, that these may be ample and Satisfactory, to prevent all reclamation of that Point.

We further submit to you, whether considering that the wants and necessities of the French Nation may render it extremely desirable, to the Ministry to raise all the Monies they can, and thus tempt them to hearken to Proposals for purchasing Parts or the whole of their claims against the united-States, it would not be proper to lodge the needfull Powers and Authority in an Agent or with us, to negotiate Monies here as Opportunities might offer, upon favorable Terms to be paid to the French Ministry against their delivring us discharged the Titles of the claims of the French Nation against the united States, until their final Extinction, which would be the sure means of defeating any other projects of individuals by rendering themSelves Possessors of such enormous claims, to become massers of the credit and in some degree of the dignity of the Government of the United States, and the only possible mode, by which the United States could in the interval of the realisation of the transfer of this Object to our money Lenders, apply any part of the Monies raised upon its Engagements to the Support of its credit here, temporary or permanent Provision for the Interests of its foreign debts or other Engagements in Europe exclusive of any Sums they may wish to appropriate for the Purposes of their domestick Finances or local improvements.

We are very respectfully Sir! Your most obedient & most Humble Servants.   Wilhem & Jan Willink

                                    N & J. Van Staphorst & Hubbard
Amsterdam 25 Jany. 1790.
To the Hble A. Hamilton Esqr. Secretary of the Treasury at Newyork

From Benjamin Lincoln

Boston, January 26, 1790. Discusses the problems involved in the re-exportation of imported wines. Suggests placing imported raisins, lemons, pepper, and pimento on the enumerated list, and states that the additional levies would produce a "handsome" sum.

ADf, RG 36, Letters from the Treasury and Others, 1789–1818, Vol. 11, National Archives.

From Thomas Mifflin [1]

Philadelphia, January 26, 1790. Encloses a statement of Pennsylvania's public debt. States that a supplementary statement of the United States securities in the state treasury will be transmitted in the near future.

Hazard, *Pennsylvania Archives*, XI, 663.
    1. This letter is in reply to "Treasury Department Circular to the Governors of the States," November 21, 1789.

To Baron von Steuben

[*New York, January 26, 1790.* "Among the documents which relate to the circumstances of your entrance into the service of the United States, are—a letter from you to Congress, dated at Portsmouth, the 6th Decr. 1777—a report of the Committee which conferred with you at York Town—and a letter from you to the President of Congress, dated in December 1782. Inclosed you will find copies of the two first, and an Extract from the last. As these may seem to militate against your claim, as founded in Contract, I think it proper, before I report to the House of Representatives upon your memorial, to afford you an opportunity of making such remarks upon those documents, as may appear to you advisable." *Letter not found.*]

Extract taken from "Report on the Memorial of Baron von Steuben," March 29, 1790 (copy, RG 233, Reports of the Secretary of the Treasury, 1790–1791, Vol. I, National Archives).

From Benjamin Lincoln [1]

[*Boston*] *January 27, 1790.* "Your faver of the 20th respecting Christopher Sadler is before us. In the morning of his arrival he came directly to the office with his papers in order to enter his vessel. His papers from Hallifax Nova Scotia were regular. He appeared to be very unhappy on his finding his mistake and applied for advice and has attended fully to the directions given him. No circumstance has taken place which leads us to believe there was any fraud committed or that he ever had any intention of fraud. . . ."

ADf, RG 36, Letters from the Treasury and Others, 1789–1818, Vol. 11, National Archives.
    1. For background to this letter, see "Report on the Petition of Christopher Saddler," January 20, 1790.

To Beverley Randolph

Treasury Department, January 27, 1790. Acknowledges receipt of a certificate from the auditor of Virginia on the manner of calculating the state's debt.[1]

LS, Archives Division, Virginia State Library, Richmond.
    1. See Randolph to H, January 11, 1790.

From Baron von Steuben [1]

New York the 27 January 1790

Sir

The Letter which you did me the honor of addressing to me Yesterday I have received,[2] and am indebted to you for affording me an opportunity to elucidate the nature of my engagement with the united states.

From the information I received of the minister of France,[3] that the preferment of foreigners to military employments had been a cause of discontent in the American Army, I foresaw the necessity of pursuing measures different from those which had been adopted by my predecessors, in order to gain admission into your Army.

Copy, with interlineations in writing of H, Connecticut Historical Society, Hartford.
    1. H incorporated this letter in his "Report on the Memorial of Baron von Steuben," March 29, 1790.
    There is an extract of a French version of this letter printed in a catalogue of the Carnegie Bookshop. The letter is described as "ALS. 7 pages," and reads as follows:

New York a de Jano.

A mon arrive a York town Le Congress me fit l'honneur de me envoyer une comitte. Pourquoi? pour connoitre les termes sous le quelles je voulois servir Les Etates Unies. Tout ce qui le pasant dans cette conference, n'a pas besoin de repetition. . . .
    Je representant a cette Comitte que je n'avois fait aucun stipulation avec les Commissionaires Americane en France, que je n'insisterai pas de faire une pour le present—que je voulois servir les Etats Unies comme volontaire, sans rang sans paye. . . .
    Je paroit que La Comittee repportat au Congres que je n'avoit point fait des Conditions, ni ne voulois rien accepte, san l'approbation generale et particuliere-ment celle du General Washington. . . .
    Voila Monsieur tout explication. . . .
    Tout ce que je vous demande, est, d'accellerez la decision aucun evenement peut rendre ma situation pire qu'elle est. . . .
    Comme je n'ai point de Secretaire . . . (sold by Carnegie Bookshop, 1958, Catalogue No. 225, Lot 424).

Presumably von Steuben sent the French version to H, who had it translated and revised and then made final corrections himself.
    2. Letter not found.
    3. Presumably Claude Louis, Comte de St. Germain, who was French Minister of War at the time that von Steuben sailed for America. St. Germain had known von Steuben in Prussia while they were both serving in the Prussian army. It was St. Germain who advised von Steuben to offer his services to Washington as a volunteer.

Being sure of Success in my entreprize, as soon as the Commander in chief & the army Should be convinced of the advantages of my military arrangements, there was but one difficulty to surmount and from the complexion of the times, that difficulty was of the greatest magnitude. It depended, upon obtaining [4] such a post in the army as would enable me to make use of the knowlege of my profession & to render it beneficial to the interest of the united States, without exciting the dissatisfaction & jealousy of the Officers of your Army. Any conditions proposed by me under these circumstances tending to ensure me a recompense proportioned [5] to my Sacrifices and my Services, would not have failed to render all negotiations abortive. But proposals to serve the united States as a volunteer without rank or pay could give no umbrage—and surely the proposition was a generous one.

Suppose however [6] I had added, that for the honor of serving the united States, I had resigned in my native Country honorable & lucrative employments; that I had come to America at my own expence for the purpose of fighting her Battles, and that after She Should have obtained her Independency, I would decline all compensation for the Sacrifices I had made, and all recompense for the Services I had rendered; I would ask sir, in what light would such a proposition have been viewed by So enlightened a Body as the Congress of the united States? To me it appears that common sense would have declared the author of Such a proposition to be either a Lunatic or a Traitor: The former, for his coming from another part of the globe to serve a Nation unknown to him, at the same time renouncing all his possessions for a cause to which he was an utter stranger, without having in view the gratification of ambition or the advancement of interest: The latter, as it might appear that his making such generous proposals to introduce himself into your army was with the most dangerous views, for which he probably received compensation from the enemy.

In either of these aspects would the Person making similar propositions have been admissible?

What measures then were necessary to be pursued to enable me

4. H substituted the words "upon obtaining" for "how to obtain a post in."
5. H substituted "proportioned" for "proportional."
6. H substituted "Suppose however" for "However, But let us Suppose."

to render those Services to the united States, which I had proposed
to myself?

Having made these observations sir, I entreat you to read my
Letter to Congress of January 1778: [7] Badly translated as it is, it will
be intelligible to you, as being one of those, who are particularly
informed of the critical situation of Congress & of the Army at that
period of the revolution.

You will easily discover sir that this Letter was dictated by no
other motive than to facilitate my reception into [8] your army: The
effect has answered my conjectures & my desires. If however I
Should be charged with having made use of illicit stratagems to
gain admission into the service of the united states, I am sure I have
obtained my pardon of the army, and I flatter myself, of the citizens
of this republic in general.

In consequence of this Letter I was directed by a Resolution of
Congress to join the army: [9] Notwithstanding which I judged it
necessary to proceed first to York town, as well to pay my respects
to that august Body who presided over a Nation whom I was going
to serve, as to learn the advantage or disadvantage which might result to me from So hazardous an entreprize.

At my arrival the Congress did me the honor of appointing a
Committee to confer with me. If my first Letter and the answer to
it had been considered by them as a Sufficient engagement, was
there any occasion for this Committee?—was there any necessity
for this conference?—all that passed in this conversation is sufficiently proved and needs no further repetition.[10]

If on [11] an impartial examination of the Subject it should appear [12]
that my propositions to this Committee were incompatible with my
first Letter to Congress, I confess that my judgement misleads me.
I represented to the Gentlemen of that Committee, that I had not
entered into any agreement with the american Commissioners in

7. A letter of "January 1778" has not been found. Von Steuben presumably
is referring to his letter of December 6, 1777, which was received in the Continental Congress in January, 1778. This letter is in the Papers of the Continental
Congress, National Archives.

8. H substituted "into" for "in."

9. See resolution of January 14, 1778, *JCC*, X, 50.

10. For the details of this committee, see von Steuben to H, September 5,
1788.

11. H substituted "on" for "by."

12. H substituted "should appear" for "appeared."

France; that I would not insist upon making any at present, but would serve the united states as a Volunteer, without rank or pay, on Condition notwithstanding [13] that my expences in the army should be defrayed. I declared to them that I had no other fortune than a Revenue of about 600 Louis d'ors, arising from posts I held in my native Country which I was going to resign [14] to serve the united states, being disposed to hazard the whole on the event. And that not until I had succeeded in my undertaking,[15] and after the united States had obtained their Liberty by a Satisfactory peace, I would ask an indemnification for my Sacrifices & disbursements, and for Such other marks of acknowledgement & generosity as in the justice of Congress Should be deemed adequate to my Services.

It appears that the Committee reported to Congress, I had made no conditions, and that I would not accept of any thing, without general approbation & particularly that of General Washington.

Although I do not allow that report to be exact in its litteral sense, yet I do not find it So extraordinary, that expectations founded upon the event of a revolution of this nature should be represented as making no [16] Stipulations. Besides it seems probable that the politicks of the times made it necessary to give Such a complexion to the report as would remove all jealousy. Permit me sir to Suggest here a question; why was not this report (like all other reports of Committees) entered upon the journals of Congress? I doubt whether it would have been contradicted by me—But at least [17] it would have afforded me an opportunity of taking precautions. I assure you sir upon my honor, that this report was never brought into view [18] previous to the year 1788,[19] and that I did not see it untill General Washington had the goodness to send me a Copy of it. But be this as it will, no Person sir is better informed than yourself [20] how difficult it was at that time to introduce a foreigner into your army, even without any Condition whatever.

13. H transposed the words "notwithstanding" and "on Condition."
14. H substituted "was going to resign" for "would relinquish."
15. H substituted "undertaking" for "pursuit."
16. H substituted "no" for "any."
17. H inserted "at least."
18. H substituted "brought into view" for "called in question."
19. The report of the committee of February, 1778, is printed as a part of a committee report of August 25, 1788, in JCC, XXXIV, 450.
20. H transposed the words "than yourself" and "is better informed."

With regard to my Second Letter of December 1782.[21] I confess I do not find in that [22] any contradiction of the [23] facts represented to have taken place in the conference at Yorktown.

In this Letter I state that my desires were to join your army as a Volunteer; that I did not ask any employ untill the approbation of the Commander in chief & the opinion of the army should assign me a place in which I could be useful: that I asked no compensation untill it was merited; provided however that my expences for my own person as well as for my suite were [24] defrayed by the united states, agreeably to the usage of European powers.

I perceive that it may be asked, why I did not at that time insist upon my Contract. I answer, that it was my wish never to mention it, as it appeared to me more honorable to the united States, and more flattering to myself to receive a recompense dictated rather by generosity than by Conditions, and that it was with reluctance & through urgent circumstances that I Saw myself obliged to rest my just pretensions upon that stipulation which was the basis of my engagement at Yorktown. But there is another reason, why this Contract was not mentioned in my Letter immediately after the conclusion of the war.

The Congress were besieged by a Crowd of foreign Officers, who were as little Satisfied as the national Troops, which was a circumstance that probably induced some respectable Persons, then members of Congress, (in whom I place the greatest confidence) to advise me to pass over in Silence all that [25] related to a former Contract & to rest my pretensions solely on the merit of my Services, & the generosity of the united States. If my memory is faithful, yourself Sir were of the number of those by whose opinion I was governed.

Once more I assure you Sir that it is with regret that I have recourse to that contract; but there remains no other resource to obtain that justice which is due to me. These sir are all the explanations [26] I can give you; if they are not Sufficient, I Submit to the consequences.

21. Von Steuben to Elias Boudinot, December 5, 1782, Papers of the Continental Congress, National Archives.
22. H inserted "in that."
23. H inserted "the."
24. H substituted "were" for "be."
25. H substituted "that" for "what."
26. H substituted "explanations" for "explications."

All that I ask of you is to accelerate the decision. No event can render my Situation more unhappy—in fact it is insupportable.

There must always remain [27] one consolation: The truth of the facts stated in my memorial [28] to Congress cannot be disputed without raising [29] a doubt of [30] the veracity of some of [31] the most worthy and respectable characters in the united States, several of whom have held, or now hold the highest places in the Government of their Country.

Having no Secretary you will please Sir to excuse my addressing you in a Language which is more familiar to me than the English.[32]

I have the honor to be with the most perfect respect   Sir   Your Very humble & obedt servt.   Steuben

To the Honorable Alexander Hamilton
Minister of Finance of the united States of America

27. H substituted "There must always remain" for "Notwithstanding, there still remains."
28. Von Steuben's memorial was presented to the House of Representatives on September 14, 1790.
29. H substituted "raising" for "placing."
30. H substituted "of" for "in."
31. H inserted "some of."
32. See note 1.

Treasury Department Circular
to the Collectors of the Customs

Treasury Department Jany 27th. 1790

Sir

The adoption of the Constitution of the United States by the state of North Carolina,[1] having raised a question concerning the operation of the 39th. Section of the Collection bill [2] and the 3d. Section of the Act for suspending part of that Act [3] and for other purposes; it is incumbent upon me to give my opinion upon the subject; which is, that they were virtually repealed by that *adoption*.

Among other reasons for this opinion, is *that article* of the Constitution which declares that all duties, imposts and excises shall be *uniform* throughout the United States.

I am Sir   Your Obedt. servant   A Hamilton
                                          Secy of the Treasy

LS, to Charles Lee, Charles Lee Papers, Library of Congress; L[S] Office of the Secretary, United States Treasury Department; copy, United States Finance Miscellany, Treasury Circulars, Library of Congress; copy, RG 56, Circulars of the Office of the Secretary, "Set T," National Archives.

    1. The North Carolina convention ratified the Constitution on November 21, 1789.

    2. "An Act to regulate the Collection of the Duties imposed by law on the tonnage of ships or vessels, and on goods, wares and merchandises imported into the United States" (1 *Stat.* 29–49 [July 31, 1789]). Section 39 reads:

    "Be it therefore further enacted, That all goods, wares and merchandise not of their own growth or manufacture, which shall be imported from either of the said two States of Rhode Island and Providence Plantations, or North Carolina, into any other port or place within the limits of the United States, as settled by the late treaty of peace, shall be subject to the like duties, seizures and forfeitures, as goods, wares or merchandise imported from any State or country without the said limits."

    3. "An Act to suspend part of an Act, intituled 'An Act to regulate the collection of the Duties imposed by Law on the Tonnage of Ships or Vessels, and on Goods, Wares, and Merchandises, imported into the United States,' and for other purposes" (1 *Stat.* 69–70 [September 16, 1789]). Section 3 reads:

    "And be it further enacted, That all rum, loaf sugar, and chocolate, manufactured or made in the states of North Carolina, or Rhode Island and Providence Plantations, and imported or brought into the United States, shall be deemed and taken to be, subject to the like duties, as goods of the like kinds, imported from any foreign state, kingdom or country, are made subject to."

From Joseph Whipple

Portsmouth, New Hampshire, January 27, 1790. Encloses the New Hampshire statutes relating to taxation and the regulation of commerce.[1]

ADf, RG 36, Collector of Customs at Portsmouth, Letters Sent, 1789–1790, Vol. 1, National Archives; copy, RG 56, Letters from the Collector at Portsmouth, National Archives.

    1. These laws had been requested by H in "Treasury Department Circular to the Collectors of the Customs," November 25, 1789.

To Benjamin Lincoln

Treasury Department, January 28, 1790. Directs Lincoln to distribute ship registers to the Massachusetts collectors.

L[S], RG 36, Collector of Customs at Boston, Letters from the Treasury and Others, 1789–1809, Vol. 1, National Archives; copy, RG 56, Letters to the Collector at Boston, National Archives; copy, RG 56, Letters to Collectors at Small Ports, "Set G," National Archives.

From William Short

Paris Jan. 28. [–31] 1790

Sir

I had the honor of addressing you a letter on the 30th. of November last in answer to yours of the 7th. of October. In it I mentioned in what manner our debt to France had become an object of ministerial consideration before the arrival of Count de Moustier,[1] who was charged with your letter,[2] & the influence which his arrival had on some of those who were negotiating with the minister.[3] Although I knew from your letter that he was not charged with the powers which he had mentioned to several, yet I did not think proper to contradict it, as he was endeavouring to operate what I thought for the advantage of the United States. Since that time the proposals made by different persons to the minister on the subject of our debt have been of two sorts. I mentioned them in my letters to Mr. Jay [4] & begged the favor of him to communicate

ALS, letterpress copy, William Short Papers, Library of Congress.

1. Eleanor François Elie, Comte de Moustier, who had been appointed Minister to the United States in 1787, returned to France in October, 1789.

2. H to Short, October 7, 1789.

3. Jacques Necker, French Director General of the Finances.

4. Since Short's letter of November 30, 1789, to H, Short had written at three different times to John Jay, Acting Secretary of State, about the purchases of the American debt. On December 15, 1789, he wrote:

"I mentioned in my letter to the Secretary of the Treasury accompanying my last to you, the nature of proposals made to the ministry here, by two different companies, for the purchase of our debt to France. They have since united & intend proposing terms more advantageous than those mentioned in my letter—from a conversation I had yesterday with M. de Montmorin, I think it certain their terms will be accepted. Should that be the case I shall lose no time in giving information of it. I will ask the favor of you Sir, to communicate this circumstance to the Secretary of the treasury." (Copy, RG 59, Despatches from United States Ministers to France, 1789–1869, September 30, 1789–December 30, 1790, National Archives.)

On January 2, 1790, Short again wrote to Jay:

"No decisive measure has yet been taken by the Minister with respect to our debt—there are before him still the two propositions mentioned in a former letter with some slight alterations. The Amsterdam bankers to which are joined those of the United States there, wish to purchase for the present only the loan of six millions. The nature of their proposal is to furnish cash for it to such an amount that it is a loan to the minister at an interest of eleven & two thirds per cent, all the charges of negotiation included. Mr. Hubbard of the house of Van Staphorst has been sent here for the purpose of concluding this affair &

it to you, not being willing to trouble you before something definitive was done. This however being deferred longer than I had supposed possible after what I had heard M. Montmorin [5] say on the proposition now before the minister, & it being not improbable that the delay may still continue I have thought it my duty to inform you of it.

The offer now before the minister is made by Mr. G. Morris & Mr. Parker [6] of Boston—it is to pay the full amount of the American debt (capital & interest) in French funds which at present produce

---

is now in negotiation on the subject. The other plan proposed first by Mr. [Daniel] Parker of Boston, & afterwards by Mr. G. Morris in conjunction with him & others was to pay the full amount of the american debt (with the interest & installments accrued) in French stocks due in Amsterdam. The first proposition made by this company was to pay only the amount of the principal of our debt—they afterwards offered to pay the full amount of the principal & interest. The profit which they count on is to arise from the present depreciation of the French funds. Mr. [Jacob] Van Staphorst one of the house of that name at Amsterdam & who resides here at present is a zealous supporter of the latter proposition. The other partners are in favor of the former. They will all however join probably in whichever of the plans the minister prefers. I have thought it proper Sir to give you this account of the present state of these negotiations, which I beg the favor of you to communicate to the Secretary of the Treasury. It has appeared to me that I ought not to interfere further than as mentioned in my letter to him of the 30th. of Novr., the more so, as the United States, not appearing at all in the negotiation, will be left at liberty respecting it. Still if a plan like that which was first proposed & which would have been injurious to the credit of the United States was again to be set on foot I should think it my duty to take the same measure which I then did." (Copy, RG 59, Despatches from United States Ministers to France, 1789–1869, September 30, 1789–December 30, 1790, National Archives.)

On January 12, 1790, Short wrote:

"I mentioned to you Sir some time ago that there were two propositions before the ministry for purchasing the American debt. One of them has been since rejected. That which is at present under consideration is made by Mr Parker of Boston & Mr Gov. Morris joined by Mr. J. Van Staphorst. The nature of it is to pay the full amount of the American debt principal & interest included, in bonds due by France to the lenders of Amsterdam. The Minister asked a security of these gentlemen for the performance of the contract. The difficulty consists in that at present. Should they be joined by houses of known credit, their offer will probably be accepted. This circumstance comes to my knowlege as a private person. I have thought it best to do nothing in the matter as Congress will by that means be perfectly at liberty respecting it. Their consent will necessarily be considered as one of the conditions of the contract." (Copy, RG 59, Despatches from United States Ministers to France, 1789–1869, September 30, 1789–December 30, 1790.)

5. Armand Marc, Comte de Montmorin Saint-Herem, French Minister for Foreign Affairs.

6. Gouverneur Morris and Daniel Parker. See note 4 above; Short to H, November 30, 1789; and Morris to H, January 31, 1790.

an annual interest equal to that of the American debt after the interest in arrear is added to the capital & also to oblige themselves, after they shall have deposited the French funds in the ministers hands to recieve them from him again & give him in their stead for a certain part of them to be agreed on, cash agreeable to their present value. This last article is to enable the minister to raise a certain sum of money on the American debt—or rather on the French funds given for the American debt, in the case of public exigencies requiring it. It is certain the Minister was determined to have accepted the offer, & has been prevented only by the want of confidence in the pecuniary abilities of those who made it. He asked security & they replied that no house could or would give security for a sum of nearly forty millions of livres—they desired that he should retain the American obligations as his security, & should deliver them only as he recieved their value in the French stocks. It seems he did not chuse to commence such a negotiation except with some house of established reputation, & this probably that his own might not be committed in the case of the contract not being carried into full execution. Mr. Morris is I believe now in correspondence with the bankers of the United States[7] in order to engage them to join him in this offer—one of them who resides at Paris[8] is much disposed to engage in it—the others I believe think differently. Thus Sir stands the affair at present—it comes to my knowledge as a private person. I have thought it best throughout the whole of these negotiations to take the least part possible in them, as it will leave the most entire liberty to the decisions of Congress, whose ratification will certainly be considered as one of the conditions of the contract.

It is useless after what I have said to add that nothing has been done by me on the subject of delaying the installments & arrears of interest agreeably to your desire. As I know Count de Moustier is desirous of doing whatever he supposes agreeable to the United States, & at the same time may prove to the Minister their confidence in him, I think this negotiation better in his hands than any other & also suppose it more conformable to your idea that the ar-

7. The bankers of the United States were the banking houses of Wilhem and Jan Willink, Nicholaas and Jacob Van Staphorst, and Nicholas Hubbard. See Morris to H, January 31, 1790.
8. Jacob Van Staphorst.

rangement should be effected by his means than mine. He has told
me that he had no doubt he should get Mr. Necker to make the offer
of delay on the conditions & in the manner you desired.[9] He
added also, what I think not so certain that he had put a stop to the
negotiation for the purchase of the American debt. Since that time
I have had a conversation with M. Montmorin which convinced me
that if any house of extensive & established credit should make the
same offer with that of Mr. Morris, that it would be accepted without hesitation. On the whole however sir I think you may consider
it as certain, either that the debt will be purchased by a company
who will subscribe to your proposals, or that the minister will make
an offer of what you desire.

I have obtained from the farmers general a return of the Vessels
& cargoes which arrived in France from the United States under
the premium of the last year. Supposing it may contribute as a
datum to the calculations which you will necessarily be induced to
make on the American commerce I do myself the honor Sir of forwarding it to you. My letters to Mr. Jay long ago, will have made
known the continuation of this premium to the first of July next—
a like return at that period will be easily obtained. A late letter from
Bordeaux informs me that several vessels have already arrived there
from the United States with flour & wheat of the last crop.

I beg leave to congratulate you Sir on the return of happiness &
unexampled prosperity to our country, & on the effect which it has
already produced in the dispositions of Europe towards us. My
ardent wishes for their long continuance are as sincere as the assurances of those sentiments of profound respect & attachment with
which I have the honor to be Sir, your most obedient & most
humble servant   W. Short

P.S. Jan. 31, 1790. In the moment of sending off my letter I recieved the inclosed from the bankers of the United States at Amsterdam [10] with a desire that I should read & forward it to you.
I think it unnecessary to mention to you Sir my astonishment at
the measure they have taken with respect to the loan, as well as
the reasons on which they ground it: they go so fully into them that

9. See H to Short, October 7, 1789.
10. Willink, Van Staphorst, and Hubbard to H, January 25, 1790.

they need no comment on my part; I cannot avoid however taking notice of the paragraph which regards me as they have given an extent to my expressions which change entirely the nature of them, & seemed disposed to make an use of them in which you will easily see they are not warranted. When Mr. Hubbard [11] was in Paris he came to explain to me the nature of the proposition he was about to make to Mr. Necker. Our only conversation was in presence of Mr Van Staphorst,[12] who recollects perfectly that what I said to him was in answer to his arguments in favor of the plan by which the Minister was to dispose of a part of our debt at a discount of $11\frac{1}{2}$ p Cent. After telling him that my determination was to remain as passive as possible in this business, I asked him whether he thought Congress would like better that their debt should be transferred with that loss to the French court—or at par in the French stocks agreeable to the latter proposal which had been made. He answered after some hesitation that he thought his plan most for the credit & honor of the United States. I added that he was the best judge of that, & that the commissioners of the United States [13] should best know what would be most agreeable to Congress in such a case. On the whole what I said must have fully convinced Mr. Hubbard that I should be far from taking on myself to advise so precipitate a measure as that which has been adopted. I suppose further that he must have been apprehensive of my objections to it, as no hint has been given me of it until it was past the season of objections on my part. My letters which will have informed you of the nature of the proposals made to the minister by other parties [14] & which are the causes of this precipitation in our bankers, together with the letter here inclosed will put you fully in possession of whatever relates to the subject on this side of the Atlantic. I have no doubt that the loan will be filled as I take it for granted that these gentlemen are too judicious to have risked such an enterprise without having before hand insured its success. In the advertisement for the loan they state that the United States having no minister in Europe authorized to direct such an operation, they have determined to open it for them. It will thus appear that it is their personal

11. Nicholas Hubbard.
12. Jacob Van Staphorst.
13. Willink, Van Staphorst, and Hubbard.
14. See note 4, and Short to H, November 30, 1789.

credit which has procured the loan, whilst it is certain that those who furnish the money have an ultimate view to Congress.

I have no doubt that this measure will prevent any thing further being done by the minister with respect to the American debt until the sentiments of Congress shall be known. He will not treat but with some house of honor & established credit, & no house of that sort will undertake such an operation against the council of the commissioners of the United States. I shall not be easy until I hear something from you Sir on these subjects. I hope the line of conduct which I have thought it proper to observe respecting them will not be disapproved by you, as by being passive I avoided risking to commit the United States when it was impossible for me to know what would be their wishes.

The Honble. Alexr. Hamilton

To Jedediah Huntington

Treasury Department 30th. Jany 1790.

Sir

By an act of the last Session,[1] provision is made for the payment of pensions to Invalids, for the space of one year from the fourth of march last, under such regulations, as the President should prescribe.

The President having signified to me his pleasure, that the business in your state may be committed to your management; it remains for me to direct the necessary provision.

I am therefore to inform you, that one *half year's* pension to each Invalid is to be paid on the fifth day of March next; which by the estimate respecting your state will require the Sum of Three thousand eight hundred Dollars. This sum you will *retain* in your hands for the purpose. I will take care, that drafts from the Treasury shall be regulated in conformity to this idea; (nevertheless you will understand that such as may be drawn, are by all means to be paid) And you will forbear Remittances, so as to be in a condition to answer the demand.

The allowance for your trouble, as established by the President, is —— —— ——[2] two per Cent, on the amount of what you pay.

Another half year's pension will be to be paid on the fifth day of June next; the payment of which is also to be committed to you, on the like terms.

The Secretary for the Department of War will write to you concerning the evidences and precautions upon and under which your payments are to be made.

I doubt not you will cheerfully execute this service, though not in the line of your office. The emolument it will bring to you, cannot be an unwelcome auxiliary; and the execution of the duty by any other person would not, under present circumstances, be equally convenient.

I am, Sir,   Your obedt. Servt.   Alex Hamilton
                                          Secy of the Treasy

Jedidiah Huntington
Collector for the port of New London Connecticut

LS, MS Division, New York Public Library.
    1. See "An Act providing for the payment of the Invalid Pensioners of the United States" (1 *Stat.* 95 [September 29, 1789]).
    2. Spaces left blank in MS.

To Benjamin Lincoln

[*New York, January 30, 1790.* On February 7, 1790, Lincoln wrote to Hamilton: "I received last night your several favors of the 27th. 28 & 30th Ulto." *Letter of January 30 not found.*]

To Joseph Whipple

[*New York, January 30, 1790.* On May 31, 1790, in a letter to Hamilton, Whipple referred to "your letters of the 30th January & 24th March last." *Letter of January 30th not found.*]

To Otho H. Williams [1]

Treasury Department, January 30, 1790. Informs Williams of regulations on payment of invalid pensions.

LS, Columbia University Libraries.
    1. This is a duplicate of the letter sent to Jedediah Huntington on the same date.

From Gouverneur Morris

Paris 31 January 1790

Dear Hamilton

I did expect that in congratulating you, which I do most sincerely, upon your Appointment, I should have communicated a Matter which would have administred much Ease and Convenience to the Affairs of your Department. I learn this morning that these Expectations are frustrated from a Quarter and in a Manner which would excite my Surprize had I not long since acquired the Habit of wondering at Nothing. I will tell you a plain story.

Mr. Necker,[1] pressed for Money, had listened to overtures for selling the Debt of the United States,[2] and mentioned the Matter to some Members of the national assembly by which Means it became known to the principal Americans and Friends of America here. I own that upon the first Mention of the Matter it appeared to me a Matter of Indifference and so I expressed myself. Our Duty is to pay to such Creditors as may possess the Demand. But further Information placed the Affair in a different Point of Light. It appeared that the Offer was for a small Part at a great Discount, and that the terms of the Bargain were to be debated in the national Assembly and consequently our Reputation sported with. Mr. Short did every thing in his Power, but having no pointed Instructions, could only express the Result of his own Judgment and Feelings. But the minister was pressed for Money and he had the Offer of Money. Under these Circumstances in Connection with a Society of Friends to America,[3] I made Mr. Necker an Offer such as in my Conception was honorable to france, to America, and to the Parties. This Proposition (after stating the Amount of the Principal and Interest which would be due on the first of January 1790

LC, Gouverneur Morris Papers, Library of Congress.
    1. Jacques Necker.
    2. See William Short to H, November 30, 1789, and January 28-31, 1790.
    3. The "Society of Friends to America" was a business association which included at various times Daniel Parker, Robert Morris, Gouverneur Morris, the Van Staphorsts, the Willinks, and Le Couteulx. The partnership existed to obtain control of the American debt to France. The story of its complicated negotiations may be followed in Gouverneur Morris, *A Diary of the French Revolution*, ed. by Beatrix Cary Davenport (Boston, 1939), 2 Vols.

and considering that as a new Capital on which the Interest was to run) contains the following Terms "On propose de l'acquerir du Gouvernement, et a cet Effet de l'acquitter en entier par des Rentes perpetuelles de la france montantes a la meme Somme." This Payment was to be made in the Year 1790 & 1791, consequently so far as france is concerned, the Offer went to a full compleat and entire Payment and that at a much earlier Period is stipulated by the Terms of the Loans themselves. To this was added a further Offer, in Case the Situation of Affairs in this Kingdom should require it, in the following terms "On rechargera de soldes en Argent la Moitie de la dite Reule au prix courant des Effets royaux." This Part of the offer has no other Merit than to secure to the Minister the Sale of the french Effects if he thought proper and is therefore a Matter rather of Convenience than advantage. I communicated this Plan before hand to Mr. Short and to the Marquis de la fayette who both considered it as an excellent Means of saving at the same time the Honor and Interest of America, while it furnished an useful Resource to france. I shewed it also to Monsieur de Montmorin, who having well weighed and considered it, assured me that he most heartily approved and would do everything in his Power to secure the Success. In the Supposition that this Plan were adopted here Application was to be made thro you to the United States to pay the Amount of this Debt in Obligations for current Guilders, calculating the Exchange at Par. Those Obligations to bear five per Cent Interest and to be paid in Installments, the first of which to commence five Years hence; consequently, as the Society was to bear all Charges of Negotiation &ca. &ca. &ca. it follows clearly that the United States would have obtained the needful Time required for their Accomodation without a farthing of Expence and without the Pain of soliciting it from this Court. It was therefore equally honorable and useful for them. It was honorable also to the Parties. First because they became eminently useful to the Societies of which they are respectively Members. And secondly because the Advantage (if any) which they were to derive, would result meerly from a careful and industrious Attention to the Variations of the Exchange and fluctuations in the Effects, and by the Use of their Funds and Credit to make Investments &ca. &ca. at the proper Times and Seasons which (as far as the Sum of forty Millions of Livres & upwards can go) must necessarily have sustained the Value of the Stocks here. And you will observe that this was clearly stated and understood.

The Proposition was delivered to Mr. Necker on the fifth of December. You will observe that in framing it, we counted upon the Aid of Money Lenders in Holland, and in Preference to others upon the Commissioners of the United States.[4] We learnt however that these Gentlemen had (notwithstanding the Remonstrances of Mr. Jacob Van Staphorst who has a real and warm Regard for America) joined with those who made the Offer to Mr. Necker. Thro the Channel that brought us this Information an Interview was brought about between Monsieur de la Chaise [5] and Mr. Van Staphorst charged with the final Proposition to Mr Necker, and me. I told those Gentlemen I was convinced that their Offer could not be accepted (by the bye Mr. Necker had told me that the Sum offered was not sufficient) and that if accepted by the Minister it could not be adopted by the Assembly and that they risqued doing great Injury to America without any Advantage to themselves. That I would communicate to them an Offer I had made and which I had great Reason to believe would be adopted. That I would offer them an Interest in it, or a Commission at their Option. That if they should not approve of holding a Concern, I would then lie still and let them make the Most of their Plans without Opposition but asked the Assurance on the Part of themselves and of their Principals (those whom they represented) that if they found their own Scheme impracticable and did not chuse to adventure with me, that they should only not oppose. This being solemnly promised, I stated the Matter to them at large, and they came so fully into my Views as to withhold the Proposition they were directed to make and send an Express on the Subject to Amsterdam. This Interview was on the eleventh of December in the Evening. Some farther Discussions were needful which we had the next Day. I avoided going to Mr. Neckers because I was to do Nothing which would defeat their Plan. On the twenty sixth Mr.

4. The Dutch bankers, Willink, Van Staphorst, and Hubbard.
5. Ferdinand Le Grand de la Chaise, a member of the French banking house of Grand and Company.

Hubbard [6] Partner of the House of Staphorst, arrived charged to make their Offer and with a Budget of Reasons in Support of it. This offer was to purchase the 6,000,000 ₶ at a Discount of about 11 ₰ Ct. It was made immediately, and on the Morning of the 28th. he called on me in Company with Mr. Van Staphorst. I had been repeatedly assured from different quarters that Mr. Necker was ready to treat with me but had not put myself in his Way. The Conversation with Mr. Hubbard was not very long. I heard what he had to say and replied with very great Precision, but so as to change entirely his Opinion. You will not wonder at this when I tell you the Purport of the Objections he had brought forward. 1st. that it was too profitable to the Parties. 2ly too burthensome to france and 3ly might injure the Credit of America by selling the Obligations too low. To the first I replied by a Smile, and the Assurance that I never expected such an Objection from Holland. This disconcerted him. To the second I answered that Mr. Necker understood his own Business and might safely be trusted in making a Bargain: but I shewed him farther that the Bargain was a good one. To the last I made the Answer which I am sure you have already made in your own Mind viz That if the Commr. of the United States could safely be trusted in making Negotiations where the Loss was to be borne by their Employers a fortiori might they be trusted where the Loss was to be borne by themselves. As all this was meerly ostensible, I pressed him hard for the real Reasons, but could get Nothing more than Assurance that there were no other than those abovementioned. As these were clearly refuted, of Course he acknowleged himself converted; but Hudibras [7] has very well observed that Who's convinced against his Will is of the same opinion still. A more effectual Change was wrought by Mr. Necker who on the 2d of this Month refused their Offer. On the Morning of the third Mr. Hubbard called and informed me of this, and in the Afternoon of the fifth he set off for Amsterdam, apparently desirous of bringing all his friends into my Views. The Business went on but slowly in Amsterdam, and Mr. Jacob Van Staphorst was amused from Time to Time and amused me with

6. Nicholas Hubbard.
7. "Hudibras" is the title and hero of a mock heroic satirical poem by Samuel Butler (1612–1680). Hudibras was a Presbyterian justice of the Commonwealth who set out to enforce the strict laws enacted by Parliament.

the Expectation that each succeeding Post would bring their definitive Answer, but this Morning he tells me with very sincere Regret what has been done. The Letter to you on this Subject [8] I have read, and will make a few Remarks on it, but shall not be very precise perhaps, as it is only from Memory of what it contained that I write. The Idea of an enormous Profit, admitting for a Moment that such were to accrue would hardly have been with them what Candid calls the sufficient Reason for Refusal, altho perhaps it might have been for Acceptance. But you can judge of the Extent of that Profit, and you will with me smile at the Absurdity of connecting with such Profit a Sacrifice in the Price of American Obligations on the vending of which at or near Par the profit must certainly depend. There is something else which perhaps is more ridiculous still viz that the United States (whose Obligations belonging to numerous Individuals are daily sold on the Change of Amsterdam) should apprehend an Injury to their Credit from trusting a farther Negotiation to Persons whose immediate Interest in supporting that Credit would be so great. They state as a great Difficulty the borrowing of twelve Millions within the Term when on the same Pledge they can borrow twenty. Their Statement of Sums is not I believe very accurate or perhaps my Memory is not accurate. However I am sure the Idea is that the greater Sum can be borrowed more easily than the lesser. There is also the further very extraordinary Idea that it is for the Interest of the United States to pay between four and five per Cent upon a Negotiation, rather than get it done for Nothing. I shall not notice many Expressions which are injurious but make, to their Affectation of Disinterestedness, the answer which Jacob Van Staphorst made to me. It is very strange that they should say all this when they must remember that in Mr. Calonne's [9] time, they offered him only fourteen millions of Livres for one Half of the thirty two and arrearages of Interest, but would not take the whole even at that Rate which is the Reason why the Bargain was broken off. I should make but a poor Excuse for so long a Story if I stopped here; but I will now proceed to give you what I conceive to be the Key of the Riddle.

8. See Willink, Van Staphorst, and Hubbard to H, January 25, 1790.
9. Charles Alexandre de Calonne, French Minister of Finance, 1783–1787.

These Gentlemen are engaged, as I suppose you knew in very extensive Speculations upon the funded Debt of America. They have lately worked this Matter to a most astonishing Benefit. Above three Millions of that Debt which cost them five Shillings in the Pound has been made the Basis of a Loan on which they receive sixty per Cent and are bound to repay it by Installments from the Interest receivable in America. The Dutch however prefer lending at five per Cent to the Congress direct. It is therefore essential to the Success of their Schemes that they should be able to suspend the one Loan always till they have compleated the other, and thus our national Interests are rendered subservient to their particular Negotiations. You will easily see that one such Operation in *which there is no Risque* is better worth pursuing than the *very great Profit* they complain of. With this Hint I think you will understand the Matter thoroughly. I must come to a Conclusion.

I did not see Mr. Necker as I expected this Afternoon, because he was gone to Council; however I must suspend (at least) the Matter with him; but you may rely on it that if the Minister at this Court, or any other Agent, be authorized fully to deal in the Business, and if the Court will not readily agree to a new arrangement respecting the Debt to contract with Individuals that the Matter can be yet managed in the Manner abovementioned; provided it be not too long delayed. As to the Loan which the Commissioners have undertaken of their own Heads, you may I think derive great Advantage from it: for in the first Place your Minister or Agent can make Terms with them to that Amount at Pleasure for the Benefit of the United States. And you may in the next Place convert the Money to very useful Purposes by sinking three or four times as much of the domestic Debt and raising the Price at the same time towards Par which will prevent the Success of Speculations by foreigners which are a Loss to America.

From Nathaniel Appleton

Boston, February 2, 1790. ". . . Agreably to your directions [1] I notifyed the Holders of public securities that no Indents of Interest would be issued at the Loan Office after the close of the year

1789. This brought so large a demand upon the Office at the close
of the Quarter that I have not been able before now to register all
the Certificates presented, & to compleat my quarterly return. . . .
I herewith transmitt an Acct Currt. of monies received & paid. . . .
If any Office should be established in this State similar to the one
I have had the honor of sustaining for many years or any other
Office you may think me competant to, for any information re-
specting my Character I can referr you most freely to any Gentle-
men from this State, or I can transmitt you the sentiments of some
Gentlemen of the first character in this Town. . . ."

LC, RG 53, Massachusetts State Loan Office, Letter Book, 1785–1791, National
Archives.
    1. See "Treasury Department Circular to the Continental Loan Officers,"
October 12, 1789.

To John Haywood [1]

Treasury Department 2nd. feby 1790,

Sir

By an act of the last Session of Congress, provision is made for
the payment of pensions to Invalids for the space of one year commencing the fourth of march last, under such regulations as the
President should prescribe.[2]

The President presuming on your readiness to perform a service
in which humanity is interested, has thought fit to name you for
the trust of making payment to the Invalids of your State.

The Secretary at War estimates the amount of the sum, payable
for one year at Eight hundred and eighty five Dollars, one half
of which is four hundred & forty two Dollars: but he states, that
there has been paid on account of this since the fourth of march,
One hundred and eighty four Dollars, which leaves two hundred
and fifty eight to be paid.

As only a moiety of the year's pensions is to be paid on the fifth
of march next, I have purchased a bill for three hundred Dollars,
which I have remitted to Mr. John Daves [3] at Newbern, with direction to receive the money & forward it to you.

The remaining moiety will be paid on the fifth of June next, for
which provision will in time be made.

The allowance for this Service will be two per Cent, on the amount of the monies paid.

The Secretary for the Department of War, will write to you concerning the evidences & precautions upon and under which the payment will be to be made.

I am, Sir,   Your obedt. Servt   A Hamilton
                                        Secy of the Treasy

John Haywood Esq.
Hillsborough No. Carolina

LS, Southern Historical Collection, University of North Carolina Library.
    1. This letter is similar to H to Jedediah Huntington, January 30, 1790. Haywood was state treasurer of North Carolina.
    2. "An Act providing for the payment of the Invalid Pensioners of the United States" (1 *Stat.* 95 [September 29, 1789]).
    3. On February 9, 1790, the Senate confirmed Daves's appointment as collector of customs at New Bern, North Carolina.

From Otho H. Williams

Baltimore 2d February 1790

Sir

I had, before the receipt of your circular letter of the 20th. Ulto, communicated to you "a statement of the amount of the emoluments which have accrued to the officers of this port respectively, under the existing regulations, up to the first of Jany."

I have communicated your letter to the Naval officer, and the Surveyor; and, that you may have the greater reliance on the statement, I will inclose herewith an Abstract account corresponding with the receipts which are filed in my office. I will also subjoin a statement, of actual expence, for Stationary, and printing, *only*. A comparison of the proportion of those expences paid, in the first instance respectively by the Collector, and by the Naval Offi⟨cer⟩ will manifest, in some measure, the proportions of services requ⟨ired⟩ of each by the existing laws.

Foreseeing the inadequacy of the compensations to the reward of the services required; and to the discharge of the necessary, and contingent, expences, I have been attentive to economy in all things.

ADfS, RG 53, "Old Correspondence," Baltimore Collector, National Archives.

The Collector's, and the Naval Officer's Office, are in my own House: and the latter gives me the use of a stable for the rent of the room. But this accomodation is not so convenient, as necessary. By Law It is requisite for the Collector to have a public store for the receipt of goods which are to be kept at the ex⟨pence⟩ and risque of the Owner. At what rate storage is to be ⟨paid⟩ or how the acct. of that business is to be kept? The law is ⟨such⟩ I presume that it was not the intention of the Legislature to ⟨make it⟩ a private business between the Collector and the Owners of Merchandize, But that the United States should have Credit By the profits if any, or be charged with the loss, which might appear upon the settlement of that account, after being audited and admitted by the secretary. As the Collector of this port is allowed one half ⅌ Cent on the monies *only* which shall be paid into the Treasury, I apprehend that he is not entitled even to one half Per Cent on the monies which he is directed to receive and pay otherwise. To save, therefore, the expence of a store keeper I made the Owners accountable for all goods (in the circumstances alluded to) where I could place confidence; and where I could not, I made use of a part of my own House or the Surveyors office for a Store without making any charge. Consequently I have not in fact, to the 31 Decr. inclusive, any Account of that sort to settle; yet in my general estimate of expences I have included a very moderate charge for the hire of a Store keeper, as I discover that under almost any arrangement that will probably exist such a provision will be proper.

It is to be regretted that the Impost system commenced with an aspect very inauspicious to the respectability of the Officers of the customs. I need not suggest to you sir that the present plan has a tendency to render them despicable, or that men who dispair of respectability will but too commonly stoop to unj⟨ust ex⟩pedients to gratifie a passion yet less patriotic than ambitio⟨us.⟩

It would not become me thus to express myself if I were resolved at all events, to preserve my present station.

I am, Sir,   Your Most obedient,   Humble Servant

O. H. Williams

⟨A. Ha⟩milton Esqr. Secretary ⟨of⟩ the Treasury.

[ENCLOSURE]¹

Abstract of fees and compensations received and paid to the Officers of the Customs in Baltimore district from 10 August to 31 Decr. 1789:

To the Collector and the Naval Officer			
	D. C		
to 12 September 1789.	233.23⅓		
17 October	364.26⅔		
3d. Decemr.	547.53⅓		
31 do.	273.26⅔	709.15 } Dols. Cents	
		709.15 } 1,418.30	

Surveyor		
to 24 August	9.66⅔	
2. Septr.	14.00.	
17. do.	21.60.	
17. October	130.55⅓	
2 Decem	259.51⅔	
31. ditto	101.13.	
		536.46⅔

Gauger	ac Sundries	114.60	
Measurer	do.	176.44	
Weigher	do.	135.02⁵⁰⁄₁₀₀	
Inspectors	do.	726.22.	
			1,152.28½
			3,107.05¹⁶⁄₁₀₀

Errors in report 14th. Jan 90.		d. c.	
Omitted in measurers Acct.		36.54½	
overchd. in Surveyor's	0.32⅓		
do. in Inspectors	2.10.	2.42⅓	
		34.12¹⁶⁄₁₀₀	
am ⅌ last report		3072.93	
		3107.05¹⁶⁄₁₀₀	

Expences of the Custom House Balte for Stationary			
& printing from 10 August to 31 December 1789 inclusive			121.31⅔
proportion paid, in the first instance by			
Collector		112.26⅓	
do . . . . by N. officer		9.05⅓	121.31⅔

[ENCLOSURE]²

Upon a presumption the propriety of which ought to be admitted, that the Importations of the 10th. of August to 31 Decmr. are equal

1. ADf, RG 53, "Old Correspondence," Baltimore Collector, National Archives.

2. ADf, RG 53, "Old Correspondence," Baltimore Collector, National Archives.

to half the business of the Year at this port, a just estimate of the emoluments of the Collectors Office will appear thus.

		in addn.	6.51
The Gross amount of duties is			56,995.62½
			57,002.13½
Deductions on UStates bottoms		3,268.98.⎫	
Ditto prompt payments		293.34 ⎬	3,562.32
			53,439.81½
Deduct also for payts. to Subaltern Officers ⎫			
1152.28½ and incidental charges &c. 490.82½ ⎬			
upon which no Commission is allowed by Law ⎭			1,643.11
			51,796.70½
Charge Com ½ ⅌ Cent on 51,796.70½. payable @ ⎫			
four, Six, and twelve, Months ⎭			258.98.
Fees ⅌ dividend with Naval Officer			709.15
From the gross amount of Commission and fees			968.13
Deduct for *actual* expences to assistants		400.00.	
Actual do. Stationary & Blanks		112.26⅓	
Allow for House rent, Office & Store keeper		200.00. very low	
do. for fuel, chandlery and a Servant,			
Subsiste, &c.		87.73.⅔	
			800.00
	residue		168.13

In forming his estimate I have no consideration of the circumstances of a *necesity* to reside in Baltimore, and the inconvenience of doing so without my family—a residence in the Country would be much cheaper and The tenement which I occupy would bring me a much higher rent than I have calculated upon in the estimate. My assistants are the same, and are employed at the same rates as those who served me under the late state laws. I cannot wish for assistants more capable, but they are insufficient for the effectual execution of the comparitively exorbitant task imposed upon the Collector. My Personal application is as constant as my health will permit and my office hours are regulated only by the hours of rising—necessary refreshment, and resting.

To Thomas Mifflin

Treasury Department, February 3, 1790. "I am honored with the Receipt of your letter of the 26th of last month, inclosing a Statement of the Public Debt of Pennsylvania. . . ."

Hazard, *Pennsylvania Archives*, XI, 664.

From Angelica Church [1]

London february the 4. 1790

You are happy my dear friend to find consolation in "words and thoughts." I cannot be so easily satisfied. I regret America, I regret the separation from my friends and I lament the loss of your society. I am so unreasonable as to prefer our charming family parties to all the gaieties of London. I cannot now relish the gay world, an irresistible apathy has taken possession of my mind, and banished those innocent sallies of a lively Imagination that once afforded pleasure to myself and friends—but do not let me pain your affectionate heart, all will be well and perhaps I may return to America.

My fathers [2] letters have releived me from the *dread* of having offended him.[3] He speaks of you with so much pride and satisfaction, that if I did not [love] you as he does, I should be a little Jealous of his attachment.

I shall send by the first ships every well written book that I can procure on the subject of finance. I cannot help being diverted at the avidity I express to whatever relates to this subject. It is a new source of amusement or rather of *interest*.

Adieu my dear Brother, remember me affectionately to Eliza. I have this moment received her letter, and have received three from you.[4] I accept this attention on your part as *I ought*, and if in return I cannot give you any agreeable information, I can at least give you the History of my Mind, which is at present very much occupied by a very great, and very amiable personage. Adieu my dear *friend*.

AL, Hamilton Papers, Library of Congress.
    1. Angelica Schuyler Church was the wife of John B. Church and H's sister-in-law.
    2. Philip Schuyler.
    3. See H to Angelica Church, November 8, 1789.
    4. One of the letters presumably was H's letter of November 8, 1789. The other two letters have not been found.

To Benjamin Lincoln

Treasury Department feby 4th. 1790.

Sir

I have received the report of the Collector, Naval Officer and Surveyor of the Port of Boston & Charlestown.[1]

As some little delay may attend the process of obtaining relief, I would advise that the Vessel and Cargo be released, upon competent Security being given to pay their value, in case the forfeiture be not remitted.[2]

I am, Sir

Benjamin Lincoln Esquire
Collector for the Port of Boston &c Massachusetts.

L[S], RG 36, Collector of Customs at Boston, Letters from the Treasury, 1789–1818, Vol. 5, National Archives; copy, RG 56, Letters to the Collector at Boston, National Archives; copy, RG 56, Letters to Collectors at Small Ports, "Set G," National Archives.
    1. Thomas Melville (or Melvill) was surveyor and James Lovell naval officer of the port of Boston and Charlestown.
    2. The endorsement reads "From Mr. Hamilton upon Saddler." See "Report on the Petition of Christopher Saddler," January 19, 1790, and H to Lincoln, January 20, 1790.

To Jeremiah Olney [1]

Treasury Department, February 4, 1790. Announces that Olney has been selected by the President to pay "pensions to Invalids for the Space of one year." [2]

LS, Rhode Island Historical Society, Providence.
    1. On June 14, 1790, the Senate confirmed Olney's appointment as collector of customs at Providence.
    2. This letter, except for the sums specified as owed to the "invalids," is the same as the one that H wrote to Jedediah Huntington on January 30, 1790.

From Benjamin Lincoln

Boston Feby 5th. 1790

Sir

Agreeably to your directions [1] I now Inclose the return of the fees of the several officers of the district of Boston and Charlestown together with an account of all the money paid to the weighers, gaugers, which was received by them respectively from the 10th. of August to the end of December last. At one view you will see what ℞ Cent the collection in this district has cost.

The emoluments of the Collector, Naval officer, and surveyor are very far short of the sum the public suppose they have received.[2] When Congress limited the collectors of the large ports to half ℞ Cent for receiving and paying out the money and that only on part of the sum they do actually receive and pay, they hardly considered how little the half ℞ Cent was compared with the trouble of receiving, paying out the money, the safe keeping of it while on hand, the high responsible light in which the collectors are held and the heavy bonds by which the public interest in their hands is covered. Nor did they I think fully attend to the circumstance that in all large ports, where our considerable sums are received, and for that reason the sum given for collecting was reduced from one to half ℞ Cent, that the officers were liable to much greater expences than in ports more private and where the manner of living is different & less costly.

Congress say that the half ℞ Cent shall be received on money paid into the treasury of the United States. No consideration therefore is made for the receiving and paying all fees, pay of inspectors wieghers, gaugers and measurers and many other small expences. Nor is anything allowed for receiving and paying out the money ordered to be paid as drawbacks and bounties. This will cause a great deduction of the half ℞ Cent.

One ℞ Cent on the whole sum received and paid out is a sum which an *interested person* thinks ought at the least to be the establishment.

I ought to remark that a very considerable proportion of the fees which have arisen from the operation of the coasting act[3] are from the necessity the people are under to take out new registers that is an advantage to the office which probably will never again arise.

Permit me farther to observe that from our return now before you, you will not be able to judge very critically of the business we shall do in this office in the term of one year. Little is transacted from the inclemency of our seasons in the months of Jany. Feby. & half March while in many other ports no check of business is experienced from the same cause.

From the fees of all the several offices some expenses are to be deducted. From those I receive as collector I have to pay an assistant, a book keeper, office room fire wood Stationary, Candles &c &c these are very heavy deductions indeed.

ADf, RG 36, Collector of Customs at Boston, Letters from the Treasury and Others, 1789–1818, Vol. 11, National Archives.
    1. "Treasury Department Circular to the Collectors of the Customs," January 20, 1790.
    2. For the rates of pay for collectors, naval officers, and surveyors, see Section 29 of "An Act to regulate the Collection of the Duties imposed by law on the tonnage of ships or vessels, and on goods, wares and merchandises imported into the United States" (1 *Stat.* 44–45 [July 31, 1789]).
    3. "An Act for Registering and Clearing Vessels, Regulating the Coasting Trade, and for other purposes" (1 *Stat.* 55–65 [September 1, 1789]).

From Otho H. Williams

Baltimore, February 6, 1790. Will "cheerfully execute the pleasure of the President respecting the payment of pensions to Invalids in this State." [1] Transmits "Account Current against the United States, with Bond account; both accompanied with Notes to explain the circumstance of their disagreeing from the Weekly returns heretofore transmitted."

ALS, RG 53, "Old Correspondence," Baltimore Collector, National Archives.
    1. The letter to Williams concerning pensions to invalids has not been found, but see H to Jedediah Huntington, January 30, 1790; H to John Haywood, February 2, 1790; and H to Jeremiah Olney, February 4, 1790.

From Benjamin Lincoln

[Boston] February 7 [1790.] Acknowledges receipt of Hamilton's "several favors of the 27th. 28 & 30th Ulto." [1] Explains why the collector at Biddeford has not received registry blanks.[2] States that the "payment of the Invalids will be undertaken with pleasure." [3]

ADf, RG 36, Collector of Customs at Boston, Letters from the Treasury and Others, 1789–1818, Vol. 11, National Archives.
    1. Letter of January 30 not found.

2. See Jeremiah Hill to H, January 9, 1790.

3. The letter to Lincoln on the payment of invalids has not been found, but see H to Jedediah Huntington, January 30, 1790; H to John Haywood, February 2, 1790; and H to Jeremiah Olney, February 4, 1790.

To Sharp Delany

Treasury Department Feby 8th 1790.

Sir

Hurry of business has prevented my answering till now your favours of the 21st of December and 9th of January.

I am of opinion that in strictness after the passing of the Registering Act,[1] nothing but the Register or Enrollment could be evidence of an American bottom, or entitle a vessel to the privileges of one.[2] Yet where from *absence* it was impossible for a vessel ("evidently and bona fide" *entitled to be registered*) to have previously obtained *one* and relaxations have taken place in her favour, I have not disapproved them.

I differ in opinion from Mr. Fisher,[3] though I am aware that there is room for that which he entertains. I conceive that at *each entry* a Tonnage of fifty cents is to be paid by all Foreign Vessels, except those built in the United States, and owned wholly or in part by subjects of foreign powers which are to pay at each entry only thirty cents, unless employed in trading between different districts when they also pay fifty cents. I reason thus:

Tonnage at different rates is to be paid on all vessels *entered* into the United States. The *entry* is then the Criterion. This entry cannot mean *one* from abroad merely, because on that construction, the second section which exempts Coasters from paying more than *once* a year would be useless,[4] as they are not to be presumed *whilst employed in the Coasters Trade* to enter from abroad.

But it may be asked, why the provision of the third section?[5] The answer is, that this will still have some effect by supposing it to operate on that description of foreign Vessels, which in other cases would pay only thirty cents. And this construction will best reconcile all the parts of the Act together.

With regard to Vessels applying for licenses[6] I incline to think, that when tonnage has been paid on entry the license ought to be granted without it; but where tonnage has not been paid, it ought to be paid previous to granting the license.

I am, sir, Your Obdt Servt   A Hamilton.

Sharp Delaney, Esquire,
Collector of the Port of *Philadelphia*.

ALS, Mr. George R. Loeb, Philadelphia; copy, RG 56, Letters to the Collector at Philadelphia, National Archives; copy, RG 56, Letters to the Collectors at Small Ports, "Set G," National Archives.
  1. "An Act for Registering and Clearing Vessels, Regulating the Coasting Trade, and for other purposes" (1 *Stat.* 55–65 [September 1, 1789]).
  2. See Delany to H, December 21, 1789.
  3. In Delany's letters of December 21, 1789, and January 9, 1790, no reference was made to a "Mr. Fisher." However, see Delany to H, August 3, 1790, in which Delany refers to James C. Fisher and Samuel W. Fisher, Philadelphia merchants.
  4. "An Act imposing Duties on Tonnage" (1 *Stat.* 27–28 [July 20, 1789]).
  5. The third section of "An Act imposing Duties on Tonnage" provided "That every ship or vessel employed in the transportation of any of the produce or manufactures of the United States, coastwise within the said States, except such ship or vessel be built within the said States, and belong to a citizen or citizens thereof, shall, on each entry, pay fifty cents per ton" (1 *Stat.* 27–28).
  6. See Delany to H, January 9, 1790.

To Nathaniel Fosdick

Treasury Department,
February 8th 1790.

Sir:

Your letter of the thirtieth of December, 1789,[1] enclosing a weekly return has been duly received. The Collector for the Port of Boston has been directed to supply you with the Registers you stand in need of; by applying you will, without doubt receive them. With respect to the Sugars imported into your District and said to be *not merchantable*. The Sixteenth Section of the Act entitled an Act to regulate the collection of Duties, &c. provides for the appraisement of *damaged goods*.[2] If the Sugars come under that description, you must be governed by the provision in this clause. I know of no other provision in the laws which the case could come under; and extra allowance, or any other principle might lead to imposition.

I am, Sir,   Your Obedient Servant.   A. Hamilton

Nathaniel F. Fosdick, Esqr.
Collector of the Customs, Portland, Massachusetts.

Copy, RG 56, Letters to and from the Collector at Portland, National Archives; copy, RG 56, Letters to Collectors at Small Ports, "Set G," National Archives.
1. Letter not found.
2. 1 *Stat.* 29–49 (July 31, 1789).

To Nathaniel Fosdick

Treasury Department
February 8th. 1790.

Sir:

I have received your letter of the twelfth of January,[1] enclosing your returns. With respect to the question you submit, I am of opinion that the true construction of the Act, is that the duties on the Cargo must be paid or secured to be paid in the first district at which a vessel arrives, except where she puts in from necessity, as provided for by the twelfth Section of the Collection Bill;[2] consequently she cannot, in any other case, proceed with her cargo, or any part thereof, without having previously paid or secured the duties on the whole, at the port of her first arrival.

I am, Sir,   Your obedient Servant.   A. Hamilton.
Secretary of the Treasury

Nathaniel F. Fosdick,
Collector for the Port of Portland Massachusetts.

Copy, RG 56, Letters to and from the Collector at Portland, National Archives; copy, RG 56, Letters to Collectors at Small Ports, "Set G," National Archives.
1. Letter not found.
2. 1 *Stat.* 29–49 (July 31, 1789).

To Richard Law

[*New York, February 8, 1790*. The dealer's catalogue description of this letter reads: "Refers to the salary of Judge Law." [1] *Letter not found.*]

ALS, sold by Stan V. Henkels, October 11, 1929, Lot 119.
    1. Law had been appointed United States judge for the District of Connecticut on September 26, 1789.

To William Livingston

Treasury Department, February 8, 1790. "I had the honor of receiving a few days since your Excellencys letter of the 23d. of January last [1] enclosing a Statement of the public debt of New Jersey. . . ." [2]

LS, Massachusetts Historical Society, Boston.
    1. Letter not found.
    2. Livingston's letter was in reply to "Treasury Department Circular to the Governors of the States," November 21, 1789.

To Otho H. Williams

Treasury Department 8th. feby 1790.

Sir

I inclose you the extract of a letter from the Collector of the District of Chester.[1]

As I recollect nothing which authorises the practice he speaks of, I conclude there must be some misapprehension; but it is proper I should communicate the matter to you, and understand from you, what can have given rise to the representation.

I remain, Sir,   Your obedt. Servt.   A Hamilton

Otho H. Williams Esqr.
Collector for the port of Baltimore

LS, Columbia University Libraries.
    1. See John Scott to H, December 26, 1789.

From James Jarvis [1]

New York February 10th. 1790.

Sir!

The ideas which I proposed to submit to your consideration some days ago, a variety of interruptions have prevented my comitting to paper, in an orderly manner until this day. They are now presented and claim, an exertion of indulgence and patience in the perusal, that I could hope for from no man but yourself in the station you fill.

In your report of the 9th. January [2] last there appear two great and predominant principles, namely the preservation of Public faith, inviolate, and the creation, to the community of the United States of America, of a powerful and active representation of their Agriculture commerce and manufactures, the most solid and desireable evidences of the industry, wealth, and power of nations!

Permit me to say, that *in general*, your plan, is so happily adapted to the genius of our country-men, and to the real interests of America as, in my opinion, leaves little to apprehend, with respect to its success, so far as is dependent on that deliberate wisdom, which has from the commencement of the rupture with Britain, to the present hour, so strongly characterized the people of these States. Indeed! I will venture to predict, that notwithstanding the delays which may rise, from the opposition of ignorant and designing men, that the good sense of our legislature, will eventually triumph; and prove to the world, by the general adoption of your plan, that justice is as well practised, as understood, in America.

After having clearly proved it both just and politic to fund the debts of the General and State governments of America, you proceed to offer to the consideration of the legislature, such proposi-

ALS, Hamilton Papers, Library of Congress.

1. Jarvis, a New York speculator, was frequently involved in business ventures with such other well-known speculators as William Duer, Andrew Craigie, Daniel Parker, and Royal Flint. His most notorious financial transaction was the abortive contract made with the Board of Treasury in 1787 to supply the United States with copper coin.

2. See "Report Relative to a Provision for the Support of Public Credit," January 9, 1790.

tions as will not only prove honorable and safe for the Public, but sufficiently tempting to induce a general acceptation by the creditors especially that portion to be denominated the enlightened & discriminating.

Tho' the success of this part of the plan, will most probably, in the event, be as compleat, as of that which depends on the decision of the legislature; yet the progress of it may be so slow, as in a great measure to defeat one of the most desireable objects in view, namely, to prevent as much as possible, foreign speculators entering the markett, but at a fair and just price, relatively to the interests of this country.

It must be granted by every reasonable and considerate mind, that each dollar in the hundred which the American funds sell for to foreigners, less than their nominal value, is that proportion of loss to this country; and therefore it will follow as the true policy of the United States that every effort be made, to excite the price up to that standard; and in order to produce this effect, in the most speedy and certain manner, it will be prudent that preparation be made by government, to enter the market, as a purchaser, with vigorous and active means. That this is a measure you contemplate as an important one, is evident from your proposals for the combined loan of ten millions of dollars, specie and debt; and that for twelve millions of specie, the possession of which, from the success of either, will furnish to government the opportunity of raising the credit of America to a level *at least,* with that of any nations of Europe.

The immediate want of that active engine, money, is the only impediment to the rapid appreciation of our funds; and this want must long be felt, from the natural and slow progress of any funding plan in a government so entirely republican as ours; and where each member of the legislature, is either authorized, or imagines himself qualified, not only to discuss the subject, but to offer measures, better adapted to the ability and honor of the country, than any which can possibly originate from others.

To remedy this evil of delay, as much as possible it would be well perhaps if proposals were ready the moment the system should be established, or as soon after as practicable, offering, to the Commissioners [3] or other authorized persons on the part of the United States, loans of specific sums in specie, and in specie and domestic debt combined, on certain terms and within the authority vested by the United States. In such case foreign speculators would be, in a manner, precluded the market, until it became good policy to admit them; which must be at the time of the market and nominal price being nearly equal; and which, necessarily would happen, at the discretion of government, they entering the market full-handed before foreigners could act, by having prepared to operate on given principles, at the moment of legislative decision.

Should it be admitted, that a plan of the sort suggested would be eligible, it now remains to point out the means of effecting it; and which will be found to be exhibited in paper No. 1 annexed hereto.[4]

The reasons why it is proposed that the limited sum of ten millions of dollars, should be extended, vested in Commissioners, and the interest made payable either in Europe or America at the dis-

3. Presumably the Amsterdam banking houses of Willink, Van Staphorst, and Hubbard.

4. "Paper Number 1," Jarvis's plan for a European loan, is in the Hamilton Papers, Library of Congress. The crux of his plan is given in the following extract from that paper:

"It is proposed that A. B. shall be authorized by the secretary of the treasury (He may receive instructions to that effect, from the legislature or the President of the United States; or he may do it in his private capacity) to go to Europe, and there agreeably to the best of his judgement, and compatible with directions given him, endeavour to obtain proposals for loans to the United States of specie, and of specie and domestic debt combined.

"It is suggested that the terms within or not exceeding, which proposals should be received may be as follows, namely—

"1st. That a sum or sums in specie, not exceeding seventeen millions of dollars, at an annual interest payable in Europe, of 4½ ꝑ Cent, be proposed.

"2nd. In addition to the annual interest, an instalment of 1½ ꝑ C. shall be paid annually, for the gradual reduction, and final extinction of the capital sum borrowed.

"3rd. The lenders as an inducement shall have the privilege of subscribing in the domestic debt of the United States, an equal amount with the sum loaned or subscribed in specie; and which sum so subscribed shall bear an equal interest, annually payable in Europe with the sum loan'd in specie; and be finally extinguished by the same annual instalments.

"4th. The lenders on their part, to pay their subscriptions at the treasury of the United States, free of all expence and charge to the United States, except five ꝑ Ct. on that moiety or part which shall be agreed to be in specie, and which said five ꝑ Ct. shall be allowed in lieu of freight, insurance, commissions, and all other charges and in consideration of the amount being paid in actual gold or silver, at the treasury as aforesaid.

"5th. The payments to be made in gold or silver. . . ."

cretion of the Commissioners, as may be found most advantageous to the interest of Ama. to form the engagements, *are* as follows.

First—If the sum is extended beyond the ten millions it will hold up an idea, *and very justly*, to the Citizens of America, that foreigners will seize the opportunity to become stock-holders, for the whole amount, and therefore that an increased demand will ensue. Of course the price will enhance from the temporary with-holding, which must follow; or from a prudential conduct in the new lenders to become possessed as soon & as certainly as possible, of the sums they may have engaged to deliver. But on the other hand if no more than ten millions of dollars, is the sum proposed, it will be understood to embrace about the amount already in the hands of foreigners, and of course that any new purchases by the Europeans, will be at limited prices, and merely on speculation, as they can be under no necessity to buy in order to fulfil engagements made with the United-States.

Second—If the power of making the negotiation is vested in commissioners, the treaty will be short, the sums agreed for, most probably large, and the supply of the money to the United States, certain and speedy. On the part of the United States, there can be no objection to this measure, because the power vested by them, will be a *limited discretion*. If I may so term it—limited as to what they may have right to do, and discretionary as to what may be proposed by the lenders *within* that power.

Third If the interest is made payable, or a power granted to agree to pay it, in Europe, it will more immediately meet the views of European lenders who are unaccustomed to look abroad for their annual interest. For if engagements are not made with them, to pay interest at their doors, still it is virtually the same thing, as long as they can, by the facility of exchange, calculate with certainty to receive their interest at stated periods, without the contingencies of winds & waves, and farther negotiation.

To this measure, there is an equal inducement to the lender and the borrower. The latter receives as an equivalent for paying interest in Europe 11⅑ ₱ Ct. difference between the 5 ₱ Ct. payable in Ama. and 4½ ₱ Ct. proposed to be paid in Europe. The former by having the interest paid at his door, has the power of selling his stock, or share of the loan, as readily as an action on any

European loan, the security between that and the American loan, with other inducements, being equal.

At the expiration of the time, for which a loan may be made, it may become inconvenient either for the borrower to pay off, or the lender to reloan—and as the money lenders of Europe, will never agree to have their money, re-imbursed or not, at given periods; or that annual instalments be paid, or not, at the option of the *borrowers;* but on the contrary will demand explicit engagements, so therefore the optional instalments of 1 ℔ Ct., held up in the proposal for borrowing ten millions of dollars, half specie and half debt, may appear exceptionable. In order to obviate this difficulty as well as to induce the United States to the measure, an annual instalment of 1½ ℔ Ct. is proposed to be paid by positive stipulation; which with 4½ ℔ Ct. interest will not require a larger annual sum, than is proposed by the ten million plan; provided the one ℔ Ct. ann: instalment, thereby proposed should be paid; and which in all events must be calculated for, in forming an adequate revenue system.

The inducement to the United States is that 6 ℔ Ct. annually from their treasury, regularly appropriated, will extinguish the amount borrowed, in about thirty two years.

If I mistake not, the most stubborn obstacles to your plan, will be found to be, *in general,* the idea of *perpetual* burthen on the country and that no positive engagements are proposed, for the final extinction of the debts; except in the self-extinguishing plans, of the life annuities and tontine, both which, however, should they prove acceptable to that certain class of stock holders to which they are peculiarly applicable can afford but very feeble assistance to the great and leading objects in view.

It is with reluctance, that I submit to doctrines teeming with mischief to the executive branch of our government; but there is no other mode of combating their most destructive effects, but by being willing to provide for that, which never will, *most probably,* and perhaps never ought to happen namely, total payment of our Public-debt, the great cement of interest between the Public and the individuals which compose it.

If the question is deliberately considered it will be found that powerful and vigorous executives are less dangerous to the liberties

of the people in limited governments, than those of a tone more
feeble; because, the line being drawn where the jealousy of the
people begins to be excited, that vigilant principle will ever prove
the best safeguard against encroachments. On the other hand, where
perfect security is imagined, and nothing to be apprehended, the
fairest opportunity of surprize and advantage presents.

If this reasoning is just, it becomes good policy to strengthen
the executive arm; and which cannot be effected by any means so
certain, and gently diffusive, as that of collecting efficient revenue.
Hence the impolicy of paying the principal of national debts, beyond that certain point, which not burthensome, becomes a stimu-
lant to industry and commerce, and a gentle compulsion to the
Citizens of a country, to pay that homage and respect to government, which is really necessary to its existence!

In a country so extensive as ours border'd by hostile tribes of
Indians on the one side; and by Jealous and ambitious powers at
each extreme it will most probably be found impracticable to avoid
Public debt. As we encrease in population and revenue, new sources
of expenditure will arise in equal proportion; as well from the necessary encouragement to Agriculture, commerce, and the Arts as
from many other national and important causes; so that what in
sound policy may be termed the evil of being out of debt, cannot
be apprehended by America.

An additional inducement to the plan now submitted to you,
will be the actual acquisition to these States of a large capital in
specie, which will not only prevent the loss and expence of negotiating bills of exchange, if found even at any rate practicable
but will restore in a great measure that equilibrium between current money, and the articles it represents in this country, which has
so long ceased to exist; & the want of which has been so injurious
to the great community of America. It will be an immediate means
in the hands of government of establishing a national coinage, and
which may be so calculated as to prevent in future the evil which
arises from exporting specie.

And here it may not be improper to observe that thro' the operation of a National bank, the capital sum obtained by the proposed
loan, will give currency to three times its amount, in bank notes,

and which, as they will in effect, be the payment from foreigners for the domestic debt they purchase of us, must prove a valuable consideration, the amount being larger, and the property more active and negotiable.

The value or rate at which the gold and silver is proposed to be received into the treasury of the United-States, may be varied and determined by some just standard, between their current prices in Europe and America; but at present it is necessary to form some data, in order to find aggregate sums, which is the reason why specific rates have been set down.

In conformity to your plan for borrowing twelve millions of dollars, in order to pay off such parts of the foreign loans as bear an interest of 5 ꝑ Ct. as well as the instalments and interest that will be due at the end of the year 1790; and to co-operate with other means for the establishment of a National bank; It is proposed that what is termed the Royal French loan, consisting of twenty four millions of livres may be considered as so much specie subscription to the new loan; the priviledge of doing which will most probably induce an equal amount in actual money in addition.

The United States will derive the benefit of hlf ꝑ Cent. ꝑ Ann., remission of interest, and the immediate relief from a heavy sum due on demand and for the payment of which they are momently liable to be called on.

The whole amount of the new loan, now proposed, is thirty four millions of Dollars at 4½ ꝑ Ct. interest and one & one hlf ꝑ Cent. annual instalment; which for thirty two years would require annually two millions and forty thousand Dollars. This Sum together with the residuary parts of the Foreign and domestic debt, stating them at ten millions of dollars at 4 ꝑ Ct. interest, and the annual current services, would demand annually three millions and forty thousand dollars.

The difference between this sum and the provision to be made by your estimate is 200.837(Dolls).81(cents)—a sum in itself trifling, and when compared to the object in view, namely the extinction of so large a portion of the debts of the United-States, not worthy the objection of any sensible man, or real friend to his country.

In paper No. 2.[5] is exhibited a statement of the aggregate debt, as ℔ your report, and the situation in which it will be when changed to what the proposed operation, will give the power of doing.

There are sufficient inducements connected with a good management of the french debt and in the purchase of the domestic debt, to incite the first houses in Europe to undertake the whole of the proposed amount, or at least so much of it, as would excite rivalship in the present European holders, of the American debt; and tend to alarm them into a compliance with your views of reloaning what they possess, combining an equal amount in specie.

There now remains an objection to combat, which will present itself with some plea of reason, namely, that by converting so large a part of the domestic debt into foreign, as is proposed, it will constitute the necessity of larger annual remittances to Europe than America can endure. But in answer, as the saving proposed is $11\frac{1}{9}$ ℔ Ct on the amount of annual interest, any rise in bills of exchange, within that amount, is provided for and when it is taken into consideration that as well from the migrations from Europe, as from the probable increase of commercial advantages in consequence of the immense increase of capital, the balance of trade in favour of this country must grow in proportion, the substance of the objection must in a great measure vanish.

Another consideration should be, that, as by this creation of wealth to America, its inhabitants will become enriched, so in any future exigence, there will be no necessity to demand on Europe for supplies of money on loan.

If what I have said should appear connected with an intention to invade your plan; or with the presumption to offer one of my own; I pray you to be assured, that no ideas of the sort, have ever suggested themselves to me; and that on the contrary, were my sentiments of your report, to be expressed corresponding with the impression it has made on my mind, you would conclude me weak enough to attempt your good opinion thro' the path of flattery!

Desiring most ardently! the happiness & aggrandizement of my country, I confess myself ambitious enough, to wish some Agency,

5. Jarvis's "Paper No. 2" is in the Hamilton Papers, Library of Congress. It contains the calculations which enabled Jarvis to arrive at the $200,837.81 that he mentions in the preceding paragraph.

in the promotion and accomplishment of these objects; but at the same time, if not blinded by self-love I would not accept of any situation, or pursue any measures, that did not combine those objects, however advantageous to myself!

I will now conclude by observing, if it should not appear to you incompatible with the interest and dignity of America, to adopt ideas similar to what are submitted, and to employ a person to procure consonant, *or more advantageous*, proposals that I should consider myself very fortunate in the appointment, whether official or from your private capacity. I am so confident of being able to succeed that if it is requested, I will go to Europe on the business by the March packett, at my own expence, and engage to return, if my life and health should continue, with[in] six months, at farthest, from this time, calculating common passages; or if it should be deemed proper for me to remain, will within that period, transmit the issue of my mission; & which I doubt not will be successful and satisfactory!

If I express myself, at any time, in too bold and aspiring a manner, I pray you to ascribe it to a desire of becoming serviceable to my country under your patronage; and to be assured, that in no event, I can feel myself other than,

Sir! Your very Respectful! & Obedient Servant.   James Jarvis

To Beverley Randolph

Treasury Department Feby. 10th. 1790

Sir

The Act for the establishment and support of Light-Houses [1] &c having made it my duty "to provide by contracts to be approved by the President of the United States for building one near the entrance of Chesapeak Bay"; The President has been pleased to refer to me your letter of the 18th. of december last, transmitting the copy of an Act of the Commonwealth of Virginia, empowering you to make, upon certain conditions, the cession necessary for that purpose.

Pursuant to the orders of the President, I beg leave to inform your Excellency, that as soon as the proper instrument shall be executed and transmitted for completing the intended Cession, arrangements will be made for carrying the object into execution.

It appears, that you are at liberty to make a cession to the extent of two Acres. There are reasons which make it desireable that the full quantity should be ceded.

With regard to the materials heretofore prepared; as it may be thought most consistent with the spirit of the Act respecting light houses, that the business, if practicable, should be executed by an intire contract, the purchase of those materials will depend on the person, with whom that contract may be made. It is however presumable, that he will find it expedient to avail himself of a supply on the spot.

I have the honor to be With perfect respect Sir   Your obedient Servt.   A Hamilton
                                                   Secy of the Treasury

His Excellency Beverly Randolph Esqr.
Governor of the Commonwealth of *Virginia*

LS, Archives Division, Virginia State Library, Richmond.
  1. 1 *Stat.* 53–54 (August 7, 1789).

From Joseph Whipple

[*Portsmouth, New Hampshire*] *February 10, 1790.* "I have inclosed herewith returns of the exports from this District. . . . In these returns will be observed the small proportion of the large quantities of Pot Ashes manufactured in this State that are exported from this District as well as of every other article of our produce."

LC, RG 36, Collector of Customs at Portsmouth, Letters Sent, 1789–1790, Vol. 1, National Archives.

From Tobias Lear

[*New York*] *February 11, 1790.* Transmits a list of the persons the President has appointed collectors, naval officers, and surveyors in North Carolina, and the names of those appointed to fill vacancies in other states.

LC, George Washington Papers, Library of Congress.

To William Seton

[*New York, February 11, 1790.* The dealer's catalogue gives the following description of this letter: "Mentions that he will soon have occasion to apply to the Bank of NY for a loan of $50,000." *Letter not found.*]

ALS, sold at Parke-Bernet Galleries, May 2, 1947, Lot 257.

To Charles Lee

Treasury Department, February 12, 1790. "Your letter of the 31st. of December came duly to hand.[1] A vessel partly the property of Citizens of Rhode Island can neither be registered as, nor admitted to the privileges of an American bottom. . . ."

Copy, RG 56, Letters to Collectors at Small Ports, "Set G," National Archives.
1. Letter not found.

From Jeremiah Olney

Providence 12th. Feby. 1790

Sir

I have Just been Honor'd with your favr. of 4th Inst. on the Subject of my being Designated by the President to pay the Invalid pensions of this State. You may be assured Sir that it affords me the most Singular pleasure to find that I am so much in the Remembrance of the President as to be Designated by him to Execute that Trust, and my Feelings Sir are no less Gratified in the Reflection that I can in any degree be Serviceable to that unfortunate Class of our Fellow Citizens.

I presume Sir, when the Secretary at War made you the Estimate of Nine Hundred Dollars for the payment of the first half years Pensions that he had not Received the last Return of Invalids paid by this State which I *as one of a Committee,* had the Honor to Transmitt him on the 1st Inst., as that Return very Considerably Excedes the above Estimate.

I have been Honor'd with Instructions from the Secretary at War, Respecting the Rule to be observed in making the payments.

I am Sorry to inform you that the Convention which is to meet in this State on the first monday in March next for the purpose of Deciding on the New Constitution, has not so Federal a Complection as I Could wish. Last monday was the Day for Electing Deligates throughout the State. We have heard from all the Towns and find on the Closest Calculation that we Can Recon only 32 Feds & 38 Antis. This makes our prospect Doubtful indeed. However the Federal Interest will Exert Every nerve to Effect if posible the Adoption of the Constitution, for without it Poverty & Distress of Every Kind will be our unavoidable lot. The antis have a plan for adjourning the Convention & posponing the Consideration of the Question to September next. Could any thing Come from Congress or Influential Characters in New York to their Friends here in time to lay before the Convention, it would have the Happiest Effect.

I have the Honor to be   Sr.   Your Most Obed. Hum. Serv.

Jereh. Olney

Honbe. Alexander Hamilton
Secretary of the Treasury

ADfS, Rhode Island Historical Society, Providence.

From William Allibone

[*Philadelphia, February 13, 1790.*] Encloses "Some observations Respecting Further Improvements in the Bay & River Delaware." Sends a copy "of the Conveyance of A Lot of Land on Cape May."

ALS, RG 26, Lighthouse Letters Received, Vol. "A," Pennsylvania and Southern States, National Archives.

From Sharp Delany

[*Philadelphia*] *February 13, 1790.* Discusses two objects "intimately connected with your present plan, and also applicable to the present revenue Laws." The first object "is that of having a Boat in our Bay which . . . is absolutely necessary to prevent smuggling." The second "is that of stores" needed for goods deposited by merchants as security.

LC, Copies of Letters to the Secretary, 1789–1790, Bureau of Customs, Philadelphia.

From Otho H. Williams

Baltimore, February 13, 1790. Discusses problems arising under Sections 7, 12, and 22 of "An Act for Registering and Clearing Vessels, Regulating the Coasting Trade, and for other purposes." [1]

ADf, RG 53, "Old Correspondence," Baltimore Collector, National Archives.
1. 1 *Stat.* 55–65 (September 1, 1789).

To Nathaniel Appleton

[*New York, February 14, 1790.* Letter listed in dealer's catalogue. *Letter not found.*]

ALS, sold by George A. Leavitt & Company, May 10, 1883, Lot 1075.

From Sharp Delany

[*Philadelphia*] *February 15, 1790.* ". . . I . . . inclose a Letter received from a very worthy Man the Weigher of this Port,[1] and formerly my Deputy—to You Sir I need not point out the necessity of having such an Officer independent from his Office—the Revenue depending so much upon it—please to bestow a small portion of your time to this subject."

LC, Copies of Letters to the Secretary, 1789–1790, Bureau of Customs, Philadelphia.
1. John Graff to Delany, no date (Copies of Letters to the Secretary, 1789–1790, Bureau of Customs, Philadelphia). In this letter Graff complains that his compensation is inadequate.

From Sharp Delany

[Philadelphia] Feby 15th 1790

Sir

On my arrival here, I frequented places where I could hear the Sentiments of our Citizens respecting Your plan of funding the Debts of the Union.[1] I found as I mentioned to you much want of information or in other words a want of real knowledge of your Plan, but I found some very loud in opposition, but to me who knew their connections I was not surprised. Harsh terms they used but on discussion unable to support them. To detail them is unnecessary as I am convinced You expected many such objections to your efforts would take place but in my communications with steady characters Your exertions meet a generous interpretation.

I am Sir with real respect   your most humble Servant

Sharp Delany

LC, Copies of Letters to the Secretary, 1789–1790, Bureau of Customs, Philadelphia.
   1. See "Report Relative to a Provision for the Support of Public Credit," January 9, 1790.

To Otho H. Williams

Treasury Department 15th. feby 1790

Sir

Your favour of the 18th. of December duly came to hand.

With regard to the difficulty of reconciling the total exemption of Vessels, under twenty tons burthen from tonnage, with the clause you quote from the 23d. Section:[1] you have yourself given the true solution. The word *such* must be understood. Vessels above Twenty tons are spoken of in the first part of the section and must be supposed to be contemplated in the clause you cite; otherwise that clause would contradict the *express* exemption granted to Vessels under Twenty Tons. The Construction which I have adopted reconciles the several laws with each other, which is always to be aimed at.

With regard to the fee of two thirds of a dollar to the Surveyor, in respect to the *vessels* and under the *circumstances* you specify, I am on the whole of opinion that he is not entitled. The general practice is against the claim, though an allowance may be proper and may require future attention.

I remain Sir   Your obedt. Servt.   A Hamilton
                                           Secy of the Treasy

Otho H: Williams Esquire
Collector
Baltimore

LS, Columbia University Libraries.
1. For Section 23 of "An Act for Registering and Clearing Vessels, Regulating the Coasting Trade, and for other purposes" see 1 *Stat.* 61 (September 1, 1789).

From Tobias Lear

United States
February 16th. 1790.

Sir

In obedience to the command of the President of the United States, I have the honor to enclose for your information, a letter from M. H. Bird [1] to the President of the United States dated at Charleston S. Ca. 23d January 1790. offering the services of the Houses of Bird, Savage & Bird, and of Mannings & Vaughan [2] to Act as Agents, if such should be wanted in Europe for the purpose of negotiating a loan, or paying of Interest to the European Creditors of the United States.

I have the honor to be with perfect respect Sir   Your most Obt. Servant   Tobias Lear.
                                           Secretary to the President of the U. States.

LC, George Washington Papers, Library of Congress.
1. Henry M. Bird, a member of the London banking firm of Bird, Savage, and Bird, had speculated extensively in the South Carolina debt.
2. Manning and Vaughan was an English banking firm. The members of this firm were William Manning, John Laurens's father-in-law, and Benjamin Vaughan, Manning's son-in-law.

From Benjamin Lincoln

Private

Boston Feby 16 1790

Dear sir.

To reduce things involved in confusion, to a state of order, in all cases requires labour and attention. The task is increased by the magnitude of the object, and is rendered perplexing indeed, where there are a deficiency of means and where different interests ably supported, and stubbornly adhearred to, must be combined for the completion of the system in view. To devise a scheme, which shall at once embrace all the great objects, necessary to the restoration of our character and importance abroad, and for the preservation of peace and happiness at home, and to bring it forward with that address and fairness which shall unite the whole, is one of the greatest burdens, the performance of which, has ever been assigned to any of the officers of the United States. Fortunate for the Union the heavy task is yours.

Permit me to say to you sir, and think it not the language of adulation, that notwithstanding the expectations of the people on your appointment, were, from a knowledge of your abilities, raised to a very extraordinary height, yet they suffered no disappointment from seeing your report,[1] saving those who are unfriendly to the great arrangements, necessary to be embraced, for the political salvation of this country. Our best citizens are very desirous of adopting your plan, and their only anxiety now arises from an apprehension lest Congress should so mutilate it, as to destroy its leading and ornimental features, and the necessary and beautiful connexion of its parts, and thereby render it, like all other of our plans of finance, unsystematical imperfect and insecure.

I have attended to the observations of various writers in the public news papers, who seem disposed to question the propriety of your report. I am pleased that neither of them have ventured fairly to represent you, or have dared fully to meet your arguments. A thousand such writers will never lose you a friend in this part of the United States, or lessen your interest here. I know you have a crowd of admirers among us, who never will forsake you, while you are permitted to act yourself.

Suffer me to hope, that if Congress, blind to the interest of the Union, should so mangle your system, as that you could be no longer responsible for the efficacy of it, that you would leave them to attempt an execution of their own plans, if they do not effect it, the blame must fall on themselves as it ought to do; and you reserved, uncensured for a pilot in a season yet more boisterous and distressing, than is the present, to which I think we shall rapedly hasten if your report should be rejected. Although I have thus expressed myself respecting your retiring from office yet God forbid that any infatuation should so possess the minds of Congress as to make the measure necessary either for your own honour or the public good.

I have the honour of being Dear sir with great esteem your most obedient servant   B. Lincoln

Alex Hamilton Esq

ALS, Hamilton Papers, Library of Congress; ADf, Collector of Customs at Boston, Letters from the Treasury and Others, 1789–1818, Vol. 11, National Archives.
1. "Report Relative to a Provision for the Support of Public Credit," January 9, 1790.

Treasury Department Circular to the Collectors of the Customs

Treasury Department
February 17th. 1790.

Sir

I find that the process marked out in my letter of the 30th. of November [1] for calculating the allowance of 10 ⅌ Cent for prompt payment has by some of the Officers been misapprehended in one particular which is with regard to the first proviso of the 19th. Section of the Collection bill confining the discount to the *excess* of the Amount of the duties above 50 Dollars. [2]

As the same misapprehension may be more extensive than has come to my knowlege I think it proper to explain myself by a Circular communication.

My intention was solely to determine the *principle* of calculation without reference to the object of that proviso.

It is clear that the abatement is only to be on the *excess*. Thus—

If the amount of the Duty were,	Dolls 150
there would be a deduction in the first place of . . .	50
Excess . .	100
10 p. Cent p. Annum for 6 Months	5.
Duty to be paid	95

That no difficulty may arise it is proper that it should be understood that any forms which shall be transmitted by the Comptroller of the Treasury for keeping and stating Accounts and making returns are to be observed of course, though no particular direction from me should accompany them; Or in other words, the transmission of such Forms by the Comptroller is to be considered as evidence of their having received my approbation.

I am Sir   Your Obedt. servant   A Hamilton
                                     Secy of the Treasy

LS, to Jedediah Huntington, MS Division, New York Public Library; LS, to Charles Lee, Charles Lee Papers, Library of Congress; L[S], to Benjamin Lincoln, RG 36, Collector of Customs at Boston, Letters from the Treasury, 1790–1810, Vol. 2, National Archives; LS, Office of the Secretary, United States Treasury Department; copy, United States Finance Miscellany, Treasury Circulars, Library of Congress; copy, RG 56, Circulars of the Office of the Secretary, "Set T," National Archives.

1. "Treasury Department Circular to the Collectors of the Customs," November 30, 1789.

2. The "first proviso" of Section 19 reads as follows:
"That all duties on goods, wares and merchandise, imported, shall be paid by the importer, before a permit shall be granted for landing the same, unless the amount of such duties shall exceed fifty dollars, in which case it shall be at the option of the party making entry, to secure the same by bond, with one or more sufficient sureties, to be approved of by the collector, and made payable as followeth, to wit. . . ." ("An Act to regulate the Collection of the Duties imposed by law on the tonnage of ships or vessels, and on goods, wares and merchandises imported into the United States," 1 *Stat.* 29–49 [July 31, 1789].)

To Charles Lee

Treasury Department Feby 18th 1790

Sir

Your letter of the 15th of January last duly came to hand.[1]

To your first & second queries you will find answers in former Letters.

To your third I reply in the negative. I do not consider the jurisdictions of Alexandria & George Town as concurent in a sense which could supercede the rule to be observed in other cases.

I remain Sir   Your Obedt servt   A Hamilton

Copy, RG 56, Letters to Collectors at Small Ports, "Set G," National Archives.
   1. Letter not found.

From Joseph Whipple

Portsmouth, New Hampshire, February 18, 1790. Encloses "a Statement of the emoluments that have accrued to the officers respectively to the 1st. of January."[1] Discusses "the effect that the late war had on the Mercantile interest to this State—that of turning the channel of business both of exports & imports thro' the State of Massts."

LC, RG 36, Collector of Customs at Portsmouth, Letters Sent 1789–1790, Vol. 1, National Archives; copy, RG 56, Letters from the Collector at Portsmouth, National Archives.
   1. In sending this statement, Whipple was complying with the request made by H in "Treasury Department Circular to the Collectors of the Customs," January 20, 1790.

From William Lindsay

Collectors's Office Norfolk &
Portsmouth [Virginia] 19th. Febry 1790.

Sir

A Captain John Brown of this Port having obtained a Register at this Office for his Sloop Polly found it to his advantage to dispose of his said Sloop in Port au Prince on his arrival there and prior to the sale he lodged his Certificate of Registry in the office of the Admiralty, agreeably to the Laws of the Port. And it appears from the French paper inclosed and copy of a letter from a respectable Gentleman of Baltimore then in Port au Prince that on application for his Register he was refused and the same unjustifiably withheld from him.[1] I therefore wish for your opinion whether from these circumstances he is not entitled to have his Bond cancelled.

I am respectfully   Sir   Your most Ob Servt.   Wm. Lindsay
                                                                    Collector

Hon'ble Alexr. Hamilton Esqr.
Secretary of the Treasury.

Copy, RG 59, Miscellaneous Letters, National Archives. This copy was enclosed in H to Thomas Jefferson, April 20, 1790.
  1. The following documents, all of which are located in RG 59, Miscellaneous Letters, National Archives, were enclosed:
Captain John Brown's Memorial to the Court of Admiralty, January 16, 1790.
Decision of the Admiralty Court, January 16, 1790.
Affidavit of the French consul in Norfolk, Virginia, February 12, 1790.
Affidavit of Captain Brown, February 16, 1790.
David Plunket to Moses Myers, January 16, 1790. Plunket, a Baltimore merchant in Port-au-Prince, states Brown's case and asks Myers to confer with the French consul about it.
John Nivison to Josiah Parker, February 16, 1790. Nivison narrates Brown's case to Virginia Congressman Josiah Parker, urging him to see H about the affair.

To Edmund Randolph [1]

Treasury Department
February 19th. 1790

Sir,

The letter herewith from the comptroller of the Treasury to me [2] and the papers accompanying it will suggest to your consideration some important questions upon which I request your opinion. There are also claims upon the public under the following circumstances respecting which I should be glad to have the benefit of your Judgement. Officers sometimes acting in boards, sometimes individually entrusted with conducting various branches of public business have obtained supplies and services from individuals for the use of the public and in many instances have settled with those individuals in an official capacity and [have settled] acknowledged balances.

The accounts of those officers with the public remain unsettled and perhaps in some cases never may be satisfactorilly adjusted. The individuals demand from the Public the sums due to them, alledging that they have nothing to do with the situation of accounts between those officers and the United States that in performing services or furnishing supplies for the use of the Government they considered those officers as mere agents and confided for payment in the ability and integrity of the Government &c. What are the principles that ought to govern in the like cases?   A. H. Secretary.

P.S. You will please to return the papers with your opinion.

To Edmund Randolph Esquire

Copy, Hamilton Papers, Library of Congress.
    1. Randolph had been appointed Attorney General on September 26, 1789.
    2. The letter from Nicholas Eveleigh has not been found.

From Meletiah Jordan

Frenchman's Bay [District of Maine] February 20, 1790. Acknowledges Treasury Department circulars of October 20, and November 20, 1789. States that the question "of receiving Bank Notes payable for Duties" does not arise "there being no vessels in this District that carry on any foreign trade."

Copy, RG 56, Letters to Collectors at Gloucester, Machias, Frenchman's Bay, National Archives.

From Otho H. Williams

Baltimore, February 20, 1790. Wishes "to know in what manner, and at what rate" the gauger is to be paid "for ascertaining the quantity of liquors, in bottles."

AL, RG 53, "Old Correspondence," Baltimore Collector, National Archives.

To Thomas Willing

[New York, February 20–23, 1790.] Asks Willing to serve as his "lawful Attorney & substitute & the lawful attorney" of John B. Church [1] "to do and perform all and singular acts matters and things as well touching the transfer and assignment of the Bank Stock and parts of Bank Stock standing in the name of the said John B. C. or otherwise to him belonging in the said capital or joint stock of the

said Bank of NA as touching the dividends issues and profits which shall or may grow due or accrue therefrom."

AL, Ontario County Historical Society, Canandaigua, New York.
1. Church was Elizabeth Hamilton's brother-in-law. His American business affairs were handled by H. In 1783 Church had been the second largest stockholder in the Bank of North America of which Willing was president. Church's stock in the bank had gradually been sold by H.

From William Heth [1]

(Private)

Richmond 21st. Feb. 1790

Dear Sir:

I have snatched up a pen to drop you a few hasty lines—not that I have any thing of real importance Just now to communicate—but to shew, that I am attentive to my promise.

The Executive of this State—[2] to whom is committed the management of the Sinking-fund—on considering your report to Congress,[3] reduced the price which the sd fund was then giving for the Military Certificates of this State, from 8/. to 6/8 in the pound. Capt Marshall [4] & Colo Carrington,[5] I am informed, sold entirely out, as well what they possess'd as original holders, as otherwise. Many other large holders—but no ways famed for political talents, or abilities have also sold out to the Sinking-fund. Very great respect is paid here, to the Judgement & opinions of Capt Marshall; and I must confess that *his* selling out, has occasioned me to doubt more of the value of the few which I possess, than ever I have before. Having been in habits of the closest intimacy & friendship with him, for many years past, I should have been able to have communicated to you, his reasons in full, for losing that confidence in his Country, which he has hitherto entertained, if he ha⟨d⟩ n⟨ot⟩ left home for Williamsburg, Just as I arrived.

The first part of your report, is highly applauded every where—but the Current of opinion appears to be strongly against all the propositions for a loan. It is said, "they are inconsistent with your *Text—Viz—That ample & complete Justice ought to be done, to every class of public Creditors—That the public faith being once solemnly pledged, ought ever to be held sacred &c.*"

An opinion prevails too, with many that, if they were to loan at 4 ℔ Ct. to be pd quarterly, instead of receiving the specie punctually, they would be obliged to take *paper;* which, like *our* present warrants for Interest, would be subject to a discount. There is not the least doubt, but numbers of the public creditors would prefer finding their demands at a *sure 4 ℔ Ct. quarterly* to that of continuing them with the State at 6 ℔ Ct. on their present uncertain tenure and I should suppose it wd. be greatly to the Interest of the creditors, to come forward in support of your plan, so as to have the public debt put on a respectable & clear footing rather than suffer it to remain longer on such fluctuating, & uncertain principles.

I am Dear Sir,   With great respect   Your Mo Ob S   Will Heth

The Hon'ble Alexr. Hamilton esqe

ALS, Hamilton Papers, Library of Congress.
    1. Heth was collector of customs at Bermuda Hundred, Virginia.
    2. Beverley Randolph.
    3. "Report Relative to a Provision for the Support of Public Credit," January 9, 1790.
    4. John Marshall had been appointed United States attorney for Virginia in September, 1789, but declined the appointment.
    5. Edward Carrington was United States marshall for Virginia.

From Joseph Whipple

Portsmouth, New Hampshire, February 22, 1790. Submits corrected statement[1] of the annual income of the Portsmouth customs officials.

LC, RG 36, Collector of Customs at Portsmouth, Letters Sent, 1789–1790, Vol. 1, National Archives; copy, RG 56, Letters from the Collector at Portsmouth, National Archives.
    1. See Whipple to H, February 18, 1790.

From Sharp Delany

Philadelphia 23rd feby 1790

Sir

In this Season when so great a Scarcity of Cash is so sensibly felt I dread to think of the Sums due on my books, within a Month they amount to better than 70,000 dollars. To prepare the parties I send notices fifteen days before the day of payment, and am in great hopes notwithstanding the times, I shall have few delinquents. My reason for mentioning this is to solicit your attention to the providing of safe & secure stores. I am confident they will be wanted, as deposits will be made on a large scale. Security therefore is absolutely necessary, I should not trouble you knowing your mind must be taken up on business of the highest nature, if the spring importations were not so near at hand. I have a plan which I shall offer you on this head, and request if you see Mr Fitzimons,[1] you may speak to him on the subject, with which I think he is well acquainted. I mean the necessity of having such secure stores. If you have had leisure to consider the business of Boats, it would give me great satisfaction to know your opinion. I have offer'd you my sentiments before on this head—[2] one reason that now induces me to trouble You is that a Vessel I seized will soon be brought to trial, and I beleive will be condemned and I am informed by intelligent people she would answer and would Cost but little, not half what one could otherwise be procured for.

I send my weekly Account of Cash and am Sir with great respect Your most humble Servant   Sharp Delany

Permit me to observe that if Mr Maddison's principles should be adopted, what a[3] field it would open for the intervention of Chancery powers throughout the Union, in publick as well as private interests.[4] I know Property sold for a trifle which afterwards brought many thousands, and again reduced—Baltimore in particular proves this—and even if a retrospect is had to Sheriffs Sales what a change and fall in the Value of Property! Can these be provided for or redressed?—though justly arising from the Revolution and the establishment of our Nation and Liberties.

LC, Copies of Letters to the Secretary, 1789–1790, Bureau of Customs, Philadelphia.

1. Thomas FitzSimons, Congressman from Pennsylvania.
2. See Delany to H, February 13, 1790.
3. In MS, "at."
4. Delany referred to James Madison's well-known proposal for discrimination between original holders and later purchasers of the public debt. Madison's motion was made on February 11, 1790 (*Annals of Congress*, I, 1237–38).

From Beverley Randolph [1]

Richmond, February 23, 1790. ". . . Whenever the particular spot, on which the light House, near the entrance of the Chesapeake Bay, is to be erected, shall be marked out, I will immediately execute, and transmit the proper Deed of cession, for the full quantity of Land granted by the act of the Assembly, of Virginia. . . ."

LS, RG 26, Lighthouse Letters Received, Vol. "A," Pennsylvania and Southern States, National Archives; LC, Archives Division, Virginia State Library, Richmond.
   1. For the background to this letter, see H to Randolph, February 10, 1790.

Report on the Petition of Francis Bailey

Treasury Department
February 23d. 1790
[Communicated on February 23, 1790] [1]

[To the President of the Senate]
Pursuant to the Order of the Senate of the United States of the
   22nd. of February instant, referring the Petition of Francis Bailey
   to The Secretary of the Treasury [2]
The said Secretary Most respectfully reports
   That he has received from the said Francis Bailey, a communication of the Invention to which he alludes in his petition.
   That it appears to him difficult to decide, to what extent that Invention will afford the Security against Counterfeiting, which is the Object of it.
   That nevertheless he is of opinion, it will be likely to add to the difficulty of that pernicious practice, in a sufficient degree, to merit the countenance of Government, by securing to the Petitioner an exclusive right to the use of his Invention.
   That with regard to the employment of the Petitioner to print such papers of a public nature, as may require precautions against Counterfeit; this, in the Judgment of the Secretary, ought to re-

main a matter of discretion, to be regulated by the success of the experiment and the convenience of the Public.

All which is humbly submitted   Alexander Hamilton
                                        Secy of the Treasury

DS, RG 46, First Congress, 1789–1791, Report from Secretary of the Treasury, National Archives.
   1. *Annals of Congress*, I, 985–86.
   2. On February 2, 1790, Robert Morris, Senator from Pennsylvania, "presented the petition of Francis Bailey, upon his new inverted method of making types, which was read." On the same date, the petition was committed to a committee consisting of Morris, Ralph Izard, and John Langdon. On February 22, "Mr. Morris, in behalf of the committee" reported, and the petition was referred to H (*Annals of Congress*, I, 979, 985). Bailey sent the same petition to the House of Representatives, and on January 29, the House acknowledged "a petition of Francis Bailey, of the city of Philadelphia, printer, praying that an exclusive privilege may be granted him, in the use of an invention which he has discovered, of forming types for printing devices to surround or make parts of printed papers for any purpose, which cannot be counterfeited." The House referred the petition to a committee which reported on February 3, "That Mr. Bailey hath communicated . . . his invention or device to prevent the counterfeiting of public papers . . ." and recommended that the petition be referred to H. H's report, received by the House on February 23, 1790, has not been found. On February 26, it was ordered "That a bill or bills be brought in for securing to the said Francis Bailey an exclusive privilege to the use of his invention . . ." (*Journal of the House*, I, 149, 151–52, 162, 164). The House bill was sent to the Senate on March 2, and the Senate, two days later, resolved that the consideration of the bill "be postponed until a 'bill to promote the progress of useful arts' shall be taken into consideration" (*Annals of Congress*, I, 987–88). No further action was taken on this bill.

Report on the Petition of Francis Bailey

[*New York, February 23, 1790.* On this date the Speaker laid before the House of Representatives "a letter and report from the Secretary of the Treasury, on the petition of Francis Bailey."[1] *Letter and report to the House of Representatives not found.*]

   1. *Journal of the House*, I, 162. See H's "Report on the Petition of Francis Bailey" to the Senate, February 23, 1790.

From Thomas Willing

Phila. feby. 24th. 1790

Sir

I have had this day the honor of your's[1] inclosing yr. power of

Substitution on behalf of Mr. Church. At present the Sale of Stock, & indeed every other Money transaction is nearly at a stand. The Produce of the State, & the Sale of Bills of Exchange will alone command it, untill we receive a Supply from Sea.

Mr. Constable [2] has inform'd me of the purchase he had made of 20 Shares, & when they appear the transfer will be compleated.

I observe what you say respectg. the sale of what remains of Mr. Church's Shares, & shall do what ever may be in my power to dispose of them whenever I receive the Certificates & your Orders to make the Sale. I am Sir with great respect

Yr. Obedt. Servt.   Thos. Willing

Alexr. Hamilton Esqr.

ALS, Hamilton Papers, Library of Congress.
   1. H to Willing, February 20–23, 1790.
   2. William Constable.

From John Daves

New Bern [North Carolina] February 25, 1790. Acknowledges receipt of two bills of exchange of three hundred dollars each.

ALS, RG 56, Letters from the Collector at New Bern, National Archives.

From Tobias Lear

[New York] February 25, 1790. Transmits papers relating to the case of Captain Hammond,[1] a shipmaster imprisoned in St. Jago.[2]

LC, George Washington Papers, Library of Congress.
   1. Thomas Hammond, master of the American sloop Brothers. A British frigate seized the Brothers and her crew for allegedly possessing coins salvaged from wrecks near Boa Vista Island, the most eastern of the Cape Verde Islands. Washington had been petitioned to seek the Americans' release. See GW, XXXI, 12, note 29; 16, note 35.
   2. Cape Verde Islands.

From Angelica Church

[February, 1790]

Many thanks to my dear Brother for having written to his friend at a moment when he had the affairs of America on his mind;[1] I am impatient to hear in what manner your Budget has been received and extremely anxious for your success.

I sometimes think you have now forgot me and that having seen me is like a dream which you can scarcely believe. Adieu I will not write this idea of being lost in the tumult of business and ambition does not enliven my spirits—*adieu soyez heureux au dessus de tout le monde.*

Hamilton, *Intimate Life*, 57.
1. See H to Angelica Church, January 7, 1790.

Report on Supplementary Appropriations for the Civil List for 1790

Treasury Department, March 1st. 1790.
[Communicated on March 2, 1790][1]

[To the Speaker of the House of Representatives]

Pursuant to the Act for establishing the Treasury Department,[2] the Secretary of the Treasury respectfully reports to the House of Representatives, that, in addition to the Estimate for the Service of the current year, which accompanied his Report of the 9th. of January,[3] there are various other objects for which an appropriation is requisite, and which are detailed in the Schedules[4] herewith submitted numbered I and II.

Among the objects specified in the Schedule No. I. the House will observe the following:

The erection of a Lighthouse on Cape Henry.

Salaries to the late Commissioners of Loans, from the 30th. of June to the 31st. of December last.

Interest on certain Loans made and necessary to be made for the current service.

Sum requisite to complete the payment of interest on the Dutch
Loans to the first of July next.

In respect to which several matters, the Secretary begs leave to
state:

First. As to the erection of a Lighthouse on Cape Henry, That the
Commonwealth of Virginia, in conformity to the act of the last
Session for the establishment and support of Lighthouses &c,[5] has
passed a Law empowering its Governor to cede to the United States,
as well the Jurisdiction over, as the right of soil in, as much land, not
exceeding two Acres, situate at a place called the Headland of Cape
Henry, as shall be sufficient to erect a lighthouse upon, which cession,
it is of course to be expected, will speedily be completed: And an
appropriation of a competent sum is, therefore necessary towards
executing the provision of the said Act for erecting a lighthouse at
the entrance of the Chesapeak, which, it is of importance to the
navigation of that part of the Union, should be accomplished as
speedily as possible.

Secondly. As to the Salaries of the late Commissioners of loans:
those officers were still in the execution of the duties they had been
appointed to perform, when the organization of the present Treasury
department took place; and it appeared to the Secretary advisable to
continue them in that situation to the end of the year, which has been
accordingly done, subject to the discretion of the Legislature in respect to compensation.

Thirdly. As to the interest on loans for the Current service: Those
which have been already made were the result of necessity. They
have been in great part satisfied, and the residue will shortly be reimbursed out of the product of the duties. But the interest, being an
extra expenditure, requires an appropriation. And as a farther anticipation of the receipts into the Treasury, to satisfy immediate demands upon it, will be unavoidable, it is necessary that this, also,
should be provided for. Obvious considerations dictate the propriety,
in future cases, of making previous provision by law for such loans
as the public exigencies may call for, defining their extent, and giving
special authority to make them.

Fourthly. As to the sum for completing the payment of interest
on the Dutch Loans to the first of July: The rate of Exchange at the
present juncture renders it peculiarly convenient to remit from this

Country the sum necessary for that purpose. And it is important to the public Credit, that immediate provision should be accordingly made.

The Secretary further begs leave to observe, that occasions occur from time to time, which fall under no stated head of expenditure, for which provision in some mode or other is necessary. A circumstance, at present existing, may serve as an example. There are persons who have been for some time associated in the practice of counterfeiting the securities of the United States in a way which renders detection difficult, and has been productive of numerous impositions on individuals.[6] The apprehension and punishment of these persons is, evidently, a matter of serious public concern, and the necessity of being able to offer rewards for that purpose, is apparent. But the want of a provision for it is an impediment. Whether the appropriation of a moderate sum, for such cases, to be disposed of under the direction of the President of the United States, would not be a proper measure, is humbly submitted to the Wisdom of the House.

                              Alexander Hamilton. Secretary of the Treasury.

Copy, RG 233, Reports of the Secretary of the Treasury, 1790–1791, Vol. I, National Archives.
    1. *Journal of the House*, I, 166.
    2. Section 2 of "An Act to establish the Treasury Department" stated that it was the duty of the Secretary of the Treasury "to prepare and report estimates of the public revenue, and the public expenditures" (I *Stat.* 65–67 [September 2, 1789]).
    3. "Report Relative to a Provision for the Support of Public Credit," January 9, 1790.
    4. The enclosures to this report are printed in *ASP, Finance*, I, 38–43.
    5. "An Act for the establishment and support of Lighthouses, Beacons, Buoys, and Public Piers" (I *Stat.* 53–54 [August 7, 1789]).
    6. See H to Jeremiah Wadsworth, November 8, 1789; Wadsworth to H, December 17, 1789; and H to Joseph Howell, Jr., March 3, 1790.

From Oliver Wolcott, Junior

                              New York March 1st. 1790

Sir

In consequence of the permission which you have given I take the liberty to suggest a plan for keeping the accounts of the *Funded Debt*

and for regulating the payment of Interest, which I now submit to
your consideration.

Let one Commissioner be appointed in each State or in convenient
districts of the union, with instructions to take up & cancell the
Certificates now in circulation & to ascertain the Interest thereon to
the day which may be fixed for commencing business under the new
system. For the sums so ascertained by the Commissioners let Credits
be passed in their books and Certificates be given transferrable at
the Offices from whence they issued.

Let the several Credits on the books of the Treasury be examined
and the Interest in like manner ascertained, & when this is done let a
Warrant issue to the Commissioner for New York to credit the sums
which may be due to individuals on the settlement of the books of
the Treasury in accounts to be opened in his office.

Let a General Account of *Funded Debt* be opened in the books of
the Treasury, to be debited with all the sums settled to the credit of
individuals by the Commissioners & to be balanced by accounts to
be opened with the books of each Commissioner. The old Certificates
taken up by the Commissioners and the accounts on which the settlements are made being returned to the Treasury will afford Vouchers
to support their accounts.

The result of this plan will be that the whole amount of the
Funded Debt will be known from one account, and the amount of
credits to individuals on the books of each Commissioner, from the
subordinate accounts—and as the interest on the whole Debt will
commence from one period, the necessary estimates may be made
with precision.

As the aggregate sum of the credits to individuals on the books of
each Commissioner will be known the Commissioners may be permitted to make transfers of any Credits on their books, under such
regulations as may be easily devised—and to facilitate the alienation
of stock, transfers from the books of one Commissioners, to those of
another, may be made by Warrants from the Secretary of the
Treasury. This mode will preserve compleat information at the
Treasury, of the state of the accounts, & will afford sufficient data
to controul the Interest accounts, of the Commissrs.

To enable the Commissioners to keep regular accounts & discharge
the Interest punctually, I would propose that the transfer books be

closed for fourteen days before the interest becomes payable and in that time let the Commissioners draw out compleat lists of the credits then existing, on which let them compute the Interest which may be due to the several Creditors and prepare the Receipts ready to be signed as the claimants shall appear.

If the accounts are properly kept, the Interest which will appear to be due, will agree with an interest for the like time computed on the gross amount of each Commissioners credit in the Books of the Treasury, to cover which interest, let one Warrant issue, to be accounted for in the following manner.

Let the Commissioners report a list of all the Credits existing on their books, when the transfers are closed in each quarter—and let them transmit monthly statements of the payments which may be made.

To prevent the inconveniencies resulting from unsettled accounts & accumulated balances, let the Interest Books remain in the Commissioners hands only one year after the Interest becomes payable—let them then be transmitted to the Treasury—the Receipts unsigned will agree with the balances of cash on hand—for which let the Commissrs. be debited as funds advanced for the payment of future Interest.

Let these Interest books remain open at the Treasury one other year, & let the balances which then remain unclaimed revert to the public.

This plan will relieve the Treasury from many minute details, to the execution of which the offices are not adequate—it will simplify all calculations of the public Debt—it will prevent forgeries— it will preserve an effectual check on the expenditure of public money—and will tend to distribute the public debts in proportion to the revenues collected in the different parts of the United States.

These being the great objects to be attended to, in a plan of this nature, I am induced to believe, that the leading Ideas now suggested, may be usefully adopted.

I have the honour to be with the most perfect respect, Sir, your Obedt sert   Oliv Wolcott

The Honble. Alexander Hamilton

ALS, Connecticut Historical Society, Hartford.

From Sharp Delany

[*Philadelphia*] *March 3, 1790.* Acknowledges receipt of $8,300 for payment of invalid pensions.

LC, Bureau of Customs, Philadelphia.

To Joseph Howell, Junior [1]

[New York, March 3, 1790]

Sir

If you have any monies in your hands for which there is not an immediate call, I request you to pay to the Honorable Jeremiah Wadsworth five hundred Dollars on account of the apprehension of certain persons engaged in counterfieting the securities of the United States; [2] for which you will please to take his Receipt expressing the object. The reason of this mode of doing the business is that there is at present no appropriation for authorizing the payment out of the Treasury. I engage to reimburse the money to you when necessary.

I am Sir   Your Obed serv   A Hamilton

New York March 3d. 1790
Joseph Howell Esqr.

ALS, Mr. Allyn Kellogg Ford, Minneapolis, Minnesota.
    1. Howell was acting paymaster general of the Army.
    2. See H to Wadsworth, November 8, 1789, and Wadsworth to H, December 17, 1789.

Treasury Department Circular to the Collectors of the Customs

Treasury Department
March 3d. 1790.

Sir

You will receive herewith an Act of Congress of the 8th. of february last entitled "An Act for giving effect to the several Acts therein mentioned in respect to the State of North Carolina and other purposes." [1] which I transmit for your government.

I am Sir   Your Obedt Servt.   A Hamilton

LS, to Charles Lee, Historical Society of Pennsylvania, Philadelphia; L[S], to Benjamin Lincoln, RG 36, Collector of Customs at Boston, Letters from the Treasury, 1789–1807, Vol. 4, National Archives; LS, Office of the Secretary, United States Treasury Department; copy, United States Finance Miscellany, Treasury Circulars, Library of Congress; copy, RG 56, Circulars of the Office of the Secretary, "Set T," National Archives.
   1. 1 *Stat.* 99–101 (February 8, 1790).

From Otho H. Williams [1]

Baltimore, March 3, 1790. States that in the Treasury circular of February 17, 1790, there is a discrepancy in the calculation of the discount for prompt payment of customs duties.

AL, RG 53, "Old Correspondence," Baltimore Collector, National Archives.
   1. The letter is incomplete.

Report on Funds for the Payment of the Interest on the States' Debts

Treasury Department, March 4th. 1790.
[Communicated on March 4, 1790] [1]

[To the Speaker of the House of Representatives]
In obedience to the Order of the House of Representatives, of the second Instant,[2]
The Secretary of the Treasury Respectfully Reports,
   That in his opinion, the funds, in the first instance requisite towards the payment of interest on the debits of the individual States, according to the modifications proposed by him in his report

Copy, RG 233, Reports of the Secretary of the Treasury, 1790–1791, Vol. I, National Archives.
   1. *Journal of the House,* I, 167.
   2. *Journal of the House,* I, 166. The House
"*Resolved,* That the Secretary of the Treasury be instructed to report to this House such funds as, in his opinion, may be raised and applied towards the payment of the interest of the debts of the individual States, should they be assumed by Congress." (*Journal of the House,* I, 166.)

of the ninth of January past, may be obtained from the following objects:

An increase of the general product of the duties on goods imported, by abolishing the discount of ten per Cent allowed by the fifth Section of the Act for laying a duty on goods, wares and merchandizes imported into the United States,[3] in respect to goods imported in American bottoms, and adding ten per Cent to the rates specified, in respect to goods imported in foreign bottoms, with certain exceptions and qualifications: This change, without impairing the commercial policy of the regulation, or making an inconvenient addition to the general rates of the duties, will occasion an augmentation of the revenue little short of two hundred thousand dollars.

An additional duty on imported Sugars. Sugars are an object of general consumption, and yet constitute a small proportion of the expense of families. A moderate addition to the present rates would not be felt. From the bulkiness of the article, such an addition may be made with due regard to the safety of Collection. The quality of brown and other inferior kinds of Sugar imported, appears to exceed twenty two millions of pounds, which, at a half cent per pound, would produce one hundred and ten thousand dollars. Proportional impositions on foreign refined sugar, and proper drawbacks on exportation, ought of course to indemnify the manufacturers of this article among ourselves.

Molasses, being in some of the States a substitute for Sugar, a small addition to the duty on that article ought to accompany an increase of the duty on Sugar. This, however, ought to be regulated with proper attention to the circumstance, that the same article will contribute largely in the shape of distilled spirits. Half a Cent per Gallon on Molasses would yield an annual sum of thirty thousand dollars. Our distillers of Spirits, from this material, may be compensated by a proportional extension of the duty on imported spirits.

Snuff, and other manufactured tobacco, made within the United States: Ten Cents per pound on the Snuff, and six Cents on other kinds of manufactured tobacco, would be likely to produce annually, from ninety to one hundred thousand dollars. From as good

3. 1 *Stat.* 24–27 (July 4, 1789).

evidence as the nature of the case will admit, the quantity of these articles, manufactured in the United States, may be computed to exceed a million and a half of pounds. The imposition of this duty would require an increase of the duty on importation, and a draw-back on exportation, in favor of the manufacture. This, being an absolute superfluity, is the fairest object of revenue that can be imagined, and may be so regulated, as, in no degree, to injure either the growth or manufacture of the Commodity.

Pepper, Pimento, Spices in general, and various other kinds of groceries. These articles will bear such additional rates, as may be estimated to yield a sum of not less than thirty thousand dollars. Computing, according to the entries in the State of New York, in 1788, the yearly quantity of pepper, and pimento brought into the United States, is not less than eight hundred thousand pounds, of which about a third is pepper. Six Cents on pepper, and four cents on pimento (with drawbacks on exportation) may, without inconvenience be laid.

Salt. An additional duty of six cents per bushel, may, in the judgment of the Secretary, with propriety be laid on this Article. It is one of those objects, which, being consumed by all, will be most productive, and yet, from the smallness of the quantity in which it is consumed by any, and of the price, will be least burthensome, if confined within reasonable limits. If a government does not avail itself, to a proper extent, of resources like these, it must of necessity overcharge others, and particularly, give greater scope to direct taxation. The quantity of this article annually imported, being at least, a million and a half of bushels, the annual product of an additional duty of six Cents may be computed at ninety thousand dollars.

Carriages, such as Coaches, Chariots &c. These articles may certainly be the subject of a considerable duty. How productive it would be, is not easy to be estimated. But it is imagined, that it would yield not less than fifty thousand dollars per annum.

Licences to practisers of the law. Certain law-writings, and various kinds of writings. The extent of this resource can only be determined upon trial; but the Secretary feels a strong assurance, that there may be drawn from it, yearly, not less than two hundred thousand dollars. The system for collecting a duty of this kind, would embrace playing-cards, and some other objects of luxury, which do not fall under the above descriptions, but which are estimated in the supposed product.

Sales at Auction (exclusive of houses or lands, or of those made in consequence of legal process, or of acknowledged insolvency). One per Cent on such Sales would, probably, produce a yearly sum of forty or fifty thousand dollars.

Wines and Spirits sold at retail. These articles are, in the opinion of the Secretary, capable of being rendered far more productive, than has been generally contemplated; and they are certainly, among the most unexceptionable objects of Revenue. It is presumed, that two hundred thousand dollars per annum may, with facility, be collected from the Retail vent of these Articles.

The foregoing objects are those, which appear to the Secretary, preferable towards a provision for the debts of the individual States. There are others, which have occurred to him as supplementary, in case the experiment should discover a deficiency in the expected product; but which, he conceives it unnecessary now to detail. He will only add, that he entertains no doubt of it's being practicable to accomplish the end, on the principles of his former report, without the necessity of taxing, either houses or lands, or the stock or the produce of farms.

The Secretary, conceiving the design of the House to have been to obtain from him a general delineation only of the funds, competent in his judgment to the provision in question, has refrained from those details, which would be indispensible, if that provision were immediately to be made; and to have furnished which, would have occasioned greater delay, than would, probably, have suited with the present state of the business, or the Convenience of the House. He, with great deference, trusts, that what is now offered will be deemed a satisfactory compliance with their Order.

The Statement required respecting the product of the duties on imports and tonnage to the last of December, as far as returns have come to hand, is contained in the Schedule herewith.

All which is humbly submitted   Alexander Hamilton
                                     Secretary of the Treasury

[SCHEDULE]

Abstract of the nett Proceeds of the Duties on Imports and Tonnage.

States	From what period	Nett Product of the Duties	Remarks
	1789.	Dollars. Cents	
New-Hampshire	11th. Aug. to 31st. Dec.	7.789.21½	The Product
Massachusetts	10th ditto, to 31st. ditto	113.439.54½	of the Duties
Connecticut	11th. ditto, to 31st. ditto	20.352.87½	of Boston are
New-York	5th. ditto, to 31st. ditto	152.198.97.	only ascer-
New-Jersey	1st. ditto, to 31st. ditto	1.971.51.	tained, up
Pennsylvania	10th. ditto, to 31st. ditto	188.497.94	to the 19th.
Delaware	1st. ditto, to 31st. ditto	6.573.98½	of December.
Maryland	10th. ditto, to 31st. ditto	87.751. 6½	
Virginia	17th. ditto, to 31st. ditto	142.028.62.	
South Carolina	31st. ditto, to 1st. ditto	55.032.61½	
Georgia	22d. ditto, to 1st. ditto	8.850.80¾	
	Dollars,	748.487.14¾	
	Deduct for Drawbacks 2 per Cent	15.689.74	
	Dollars,	768.797.40¾	

Treasury Department, March 4th. 1790   Alexander Hamilton
Secretary of the Treasury

From Tench Coxe

Phila. March 5th. [–9] 1790

Dear Sir

I observe that your report upon the public debt contains some intimations of an intention of establishing a national Bank,[1] and I learn from other gentlemen at New York that something of the kind is proposed. I do not know any of the outlines of the plan but think it may be useful to lay before you the enclosed paper which was published here during the contest concerning our Bank.[2] It was my first attempt in print, and being written at a moment of violent altercation, it was my study to render it temperate & informing. A friend of mine who happend to take a copy of it with him to England informed me that he had conversed upon it with several directors of the Bank of England and with Doctor Price[3] and some other political Arithmeticians & Oconomists, whose manner of speaking of it has induced me to think it may be worth your perusal. There are little strokes in it, which will be thought little of, when you remember it was first printed anonymously in the public papers. As those heats, which were created in Pennsylvania by the deprivation of the Bank of their Charter[4] have gone off, and as there are in office at New York gentlemen from this State who espoused the different sides I take the liberty particularly to request that the perusal of this paper may at this time be confined entirely to yourself.

I find more difficulty like to arise in the minds of the Members about the state Debts than any other part of your report, as far as I can judge from my letters. All the public creditors here are against the Assumption. Those of the Continent because it will encrease the sum among the owners of wch. the federal revenues are to be divided: & those of the state because they would rather take the chance with her than with the Union. It is unpleasing to our antis because they say we will produce the old demon, *consolidation,* wch. they raised up as a bugbear to prevent the Adoption of the constitution. Many of the fedsts. & principal country gentlemen do not like it because we owe so little as a state, & possess federal securities to a greater amount. My argument with them all is that the revolution of 1789, for as such I[5] view it, was intended to settle a great number of public difficulties—that this was among them— and that it then was & is now evident that concessions of particular advantages would be necessary to enable us to surmount those difficulties—that this is one of the very few which Pennsylvania, New Yk and other states having small separate Debts can be called upon to make—that an expensive & uncertain administration of our finances must be the Consequence of fourteen systems of revenue, and therefore that we ought to consent to the assumption.

Mr. Brown,[6] who takes this has requested me to mention him to you. I believe I may venture to say no man has shewn more spirit in support of the Constitution, or suffered more in its cause. He is certainly capable in his branch, and his paper is resorted to by several of our first literary & political Characters. With a little aid it might be rendered subservient to every honest purpose public or private, and I cannot say I think either of our other *daily* papers[7] devoted either to the cause of good government or of good men. You must make great Allowances however, Sir, for what I might say in favor of Mr. Brown for I feel gratitude towards a man that voluntarily exerted himself to stem that torrent of abuse which

my activity to carry the adoption of the f. Constitution & the re-
form of our state constitution occasioned to be poured upon me
from one of our presses.

I again notice to you the low rate of exchange here, which may
be bought in large Sums for Cash at 12 & 13 ℈ Cent discount or
145 to 147 ℈ Cent. It is an interesting fact on your department—
& I think it may also be useful to you to observe that one half the
crop of Pennsa. of wheat & nearly all the corn remain to be exported. I mention this because I observe a little address to the Prest.
of the U.S. in which a request is made that an Embargo may be
laid.[8] I believe the wheat crops of the southern & northern grain
states however, are in a much greater degree exported than ours.
Pennsa. had a very large one, but they I believe were all short in
winter grain. In the enclosed paper you will find something to this
point under the Phila. head.

I have made my report on Gunpowder & cannon to the Board
of Manufs.[9] but, having recd. an injury in my ankle, have not been
at any late meeting or able to pay any further Attention to the business—

I have the honor to be with very great respect, dear Sir   Your
most obedt. hum servt.   Tench Coxe

9th. Exche. will not command Cash today 145 ℈ Cent.

ALS, Hamilton Papers, Library of Congress.
    1. See "Report Relative to a Provision for the Support of Public Credit,"
January 9, 1790.
    2. The "contest" to which Coxe is referring was the battle over the Penn-
sylvania charter of the Bank of North America in 1785 and 1786. Coxe had
defended the bank in a pamphlet entitled *Thoughts concerning the Bank of
North America, with some facts relating to such establishments in other
countries, respectfully submitted to the honorable the General Assembly of
Pennsylvania, by one of their constituents* (December, 1786). It was this
pamphlet which Coxe enclosed.
    3. Richard Price, British nonconformist minister and writer on politics and
economics.
    4. The Pennsylvania legislature had revoked the charter of the Bank of
North America on September 13, 1785.
    5. In MS, "a."
    6. Andrew Brown, publisher of *The Federal Gazette and Philadelphia
Evening Post.*
    7. Coxe is referring to *The* [Philadelphia] *Independent Gazetteer; or, the
Chronicle of Freedom* which in January, 1790 became a weekly, and to *The*
[Philadelphia] *Pennsylvania Packet, and Daily Advertiser.*
    8. This address, dated February 16, 1790, and signed "Humanitas," appeared

originally in [Philadelphia] *Freeman's Journal*. It was reprinted in *The* [New York] *Gazette of the United States*, February 29, 1790.

9. Coxe is referring to the Pennsylvania Society for the Encouragement of Manufactures and the Useful Arts. He was a member of the board of that society.

His report on "Gunpowder & cannon" was in answer to a request made by H for that information. See H to Benjamin Lincoln, January 25, 1790.

From Josiah Parker [1]

New York, March 5, 1790. Suggests changes in the customs service in the Norfolk, Virginia, district. Believes that Norfolk is too exposed to a possible enemy assault and recommends removal of the collector's office to Portsmouth, Virginia. Advocates increasing the number of customs officials and placing them at strategic points in order to tighten customs enforcement. Discusses complaints of some officials about inadequate compensation.

ALS, Connecticut Historical Society, Hartford.

1. Parker, who had served as a colonel during the Revolution, had been a member of the Virginia House of Delegates in 1780 and 1781, and was elected to the House of Representatives from Virginia on March 4, 1789.

From Sharp Delany

[Philadelphia] March 7, 1790. Encloses "weekly Acct of Cash" and a "list of such persons as I have sued." Has "proceeded in paying the Invalids." [1]

LC, Copies of Letters to the Secretary, 1789–1790, Bureau of Customs, Philadelphia.

1. H's letter to Delany concerning the payments to invalids has not been found, but see H to Jedediah Huntington, January 30, 1790; H to John Haywood, February 2, 1790; and H to Jeremiah Olney, February 4, 1790.

To Joseph Howell, Junior

Treasury Department
8th. March 1790.

Sir

I wish you to inform me when Samuel Armstrong Paymaster

to the eighth Massachusetts regiment received the Monies upon which a balance remains due from him.[1]

I am, Sir,   Your obedt. Servt.   A Hamilton

Joseph Howell Esquire

LS, RG 93, Miscellaneous Records, National Archives.
    1. Armstrong had been regimental paymaster from 1780 to 1783. H probably wished the information in connection with Armstrong's claim against the United States. See "Report on the Petitions of William Mumford, Samuel Armstrong, and the Weighers, Measurers, and Gaugers of Portland and Falmouth, Massachusetts," March 8, 1790.

Report on the Petitions of William Mumford, Samuel Armstrong, and the Weighers, Measurers, and Gaugers of Portland and Falmouth, Massachusetts

Treasury Department, March 8th. 1790.
[Communicated on March 8, 1790] [1]

[To the Speaker of the House of Representatives]

The Secretary of the Treasury, on the petitions of William Mumford, and Samuel Armstrong, and of the Weighers, Measurers and Gaugers of the District of Portland and Falmouth in the State of Massachusetts, referred to him by an Order of the House of Representatives of the twenty sixth of February past,[2]

Respectfully Reports,

That the claim of William Mumford is of a nature not warranted by usage in like cases, and leading to inconvenient consequences. The duty he performed was that of his principal; as necessary towards his own exoneration after his service and salary had expired. It would be an inconvenient general rule, that an officer, in winding up his affairs with the Treasury,[3] is to receive a compensation for the time spent in it; and if it would not be proper one with regard to a principal, it consequently could not be so with regard to his agent. Here appear no peculiar circumstances. And the principal has been settled with.

That, as to the petition of Samuel Armstrong, the circumstance he mentions respecting his forage-account,[4] must stand on general principles. Being too late in his application for settlement, he is, of course, precluded by the existing regulations. Nor can this circumstance be a consideration (in which light it seems chiefly to have been mentioned) for the offset or discount prayed for. The propriety of this must depend on what would be proper as a general rule. And it is not admissible as a general rule, that the stock or debt of a nation should be received in discharge of balances in the hands of public Agents. There has been a provision for admitting a discount in certain cases by a resolution of Congress of the third of June 1784.[5] If the petitioner's case should fall within the intent of that provision, there will be no need of a special interposition in his favor. If it should not, such interposition would not be, in the opinion of the Secretary, advisable. The balance due from the petitioner is for monies put into his hands in the year 1783, for the pay and subsistence of the Regiment of which he was paymaster: the persons to whom it was due not having been to be found.

That the object of the petition from the Weighers, Measurers, and Gaugers of the District of Portland and Falmouth will be included in the report, which the Secretary will, as speedily as possible, lay before the House, in conformity to their Order, respecting the operation of the present Impost and Tonnage Laws.[6]

All which is humbly submitted   Alexander Hamilton,
                                       Secretary of the Treasury

Copy, RG 233, Reports of the Secretary of the Treasury, 1790–1791, Vol. I, National Archives.

1. *Journal of the House*, I, 169.
2. The House ordered "That the several petitions of William Mumford and Samuel Armstrong, and of the Weighers, Measurers, and Gaugers, of the district of Portland and Falmouth, in the State of Massachusetts, which were presented yesterday, be referred to the Secretary of the Treasury, with instruction to examine the same, and report his opinion thereupon to the House" (*Journal of the House*, I, 164).
3. Mumford had been a clerk for the commissioners for settling accounts between the United States and Pennsylvania.
4. See H to Joseph Howell, Jr., March 8, 1790.
5. *JCC*, XXVII, 541–45.
6. "Report on Defects in the Existing Laws of Revenue," April 22, 1790.

To Thomas Willing

[*New York, March 8, 1790*. On March 12, 1790, Willing wrote to Hamilton: "I have consulted the Directors on the Subject of yr. letter of the 8th Inst." *Letter not found.*]

To Richard Harison

Treasury Department
March 10th. 1790.

Sir

Inclosed is a power of Attorney from one of two persons interested in the Certificate referred to in it which is in their joint name. They are *not* general partners. You will observe the nature of the description and the manner of the execution. Is it a good power?

The question often arises in the Treasury Department how far a power executed by one *partner*, or *person* interested in stock *jointly* with others, for transferring the joint stock is valid.

I request your opinion, after mature consideration on this point, and also whether it be essential that the power should *expressly* designate the stock as joint stock, or whether other words sufficiently describing particular Certificates may serve as a substitute.[1]

I remain Sir Your Obedt. Servant

A Hamilton
Secy of the Treasy

Richard Harrison Esqr.
Attorney for the district of New York.

LS, New-York Historical Society, New York City; copy, Hamilton Papers, Library of Congress.

1. See Harison to H, March 12, 1790.

To Benjamin Lincoln

Treasury Department 10th. March 1790

Sir

Herewith you have copy of the Act for the establishment and support of Lighthouses, beacons, buoys and public piers.[1] Among other things contained in it, you will perceive that it is made the duty of the Secretary of the Treasury to provide by *contracts* to be *approved by the President of the United States,* for rebuilding when necessary and keeping in good repair the Light houses, Beacons, Buoys and public Piers in the several States, and for furnishing the same with all necessary supplies, and also to agree for the Salaries, wages, or hire of the person or persons appointed by the President for the Superintendance and Care of the same.

I am now to inform you, that the President of the United States has been pleased to commit to you, for the present, the general superintendance of the establishments of the nature mentioned in the said Act which are within the State of Massachusetts, and to appoint for the special care of each particular establishment the following persons

For Boston, Thomas Knox

For Cape-Ann, Samuel Houston

For Plumb-Island,   Lowell [2]

For Nantucket, Paul Pinkham

being the same persons who have heretofore had the charge of those establishments at the respective places.

It is understood, that the widow of the late General Warren [3] has under the State had the superintendance of the Light house at Plymouth; but whether this has been nominal or real is not known, nor how far public considerations may cooperate with personal ones to recommend a continuance of the arrangements. On this subject your opinion is requested.

LS, RG 36, Collector of Customs at Boston, Letters and Papers re Lighthouses, Buoys, and Piers, 1789–1819, Vol. 1, National Archives.

1. 1 *Stat.* 53–54 (August 7, 1789).

2. Abner Lowell. Space left blank in MS.

3. H mistakenly wrote Warren for Thomas. The reference is to General John Thomas. See Lincoln to H, March 19, 1790.

As the establishment at Portland has not been completed, it is thought adviseable to defer an appointment for that place.

The part of the business which will chiefly require your agency, is, the *providing* for keeping in good repair the Light houses, beacons, buoys and public piers in your State, and for the furnishing the same with necessary supplies. The Law contemplates the doing of this by *contracts* and makes the agency of the Secretary of the Treasury with the approbation of the President, necessary in forming those contracts. By *contracts* were probably intended agreements to repair and supply those establishments for certain fixed terms of time, at determinate rates. This, as it respects supplies will be easy and proper, but it will not, I apprehend be practicable with regard to repairs, which are too casual to admit of an estimate accurate enough to be the ground of previous contract. They must be provided for, as the occasion arises, and if possible by a contract for each particular occasion, to satisfy the Law as far as may be.

The making of the necessary contracts, is committed to you, but to satisfy the law (in respect not only to supplies, but to other matters) *where the object admits of delay* they might be sent on to me for ratification.

You will observe that the expences of the establishments in question are only to be defrayed by the United States to the fifteenth of August next, if the respective States do not in the mean time make cessions of them to the United States. I do not learn that Massachusetts has yet made such cession. Therefore your contracts for the present must not go beyond the above mentioned day. You will have, in the first place to ascertain what supplies are already provided. The expences must be paid out of the monies which come to your hand.

The compensations to be allowed to the Superintendants at the respective places are

> Boston per annum Four hundred Dollars
> Plymouth. ℔ do. Two hundred & forty ditto
> Cape Ann ℔ do. Four hundred—ditto
> Plumb Island ℔ do. Two hundred & twenty ditto
> Nantucket ℔ do. Two hundred & fifty ditto

These compensations have been regulated by those given by the

State, and appear, considering the nature of the service, and compared with what has been practised at this place, *ample*. Your opinion, how far they are sufficient, or *more* or *less* than sufficient, will be acceptable Œ*conomy* should be united with competency of reward, and by consulting it in cases of little *trouble* or *responsibility*, it will be more in the power of Government to be liberal in those of a different description.

With regard to such inferior agents as may be requisite, you will adjust the allowances according to your judgment of what is right, transmitting a statement to me.

Nothing is yet determined in respect to your own compensation for the trouble you will have in this business. A reasonable one will be a matter of course. The present Session of Congress too will decide, whether the arrangements now made, ought to be temporary, or continued.

As it is the duty of the Secretary of State to make out all civil commissions, and as there is no person at present in the execution of that office, and as a new form for this species of commissions is deemed adviseable, it is judged by the President expedient, to defer sending forward the commissions.

I am therefore to request that you will notify the parties concerned of their respective appointments; and (taking it for granted that you will afford your aid as desired) of your own; and will give such directions as you judge proper, conformably to the Law and these instructions.

I am, Sir,   Your obedient Servant   A Hamilton
                                             Secy of the Treasy

From Joseph Whipple

Portsmouth, New Hampshire, March 11, 1790. Calls attention to an omission in Hamilton's calculation of the discount permitted for prompt payment of customs duties in the Treasury Department circular of February 17, 1790.

LC, RG 36, Collector of Customs at Portsmouth, Letters Sent, 1789–1790, Vol. 1, National Archives; copy, RG 56, Letters from the Collector at Portsmouth, National Archives.

From Richard Harison

New York 12 March 1790

Sir,

In Consequence of your Letter of the 10th. Instant, I have considered the Power of Attorney Enclosed to me, and am of Opinion that it is not sufficient for the Transfer of the Certificate which it refers to. It cannot be imagined that the Securities of the United States are negotiable in a Manner less guarded than the promisory Notes or Bills of Exchange of Individuals, and it has been determined that where *they* are payable to several Persons (not in Partnership) the Right to transfer is in *all* collectively, but not in any one seperately.*

Where a general Partnership subsists, and the Securities of the Public form a Part of the Partnership Stock, I think that the Case would be different.

With Regard to the Description of the Certificates, I should think that a precise Designation of them as joint Stock the most regular was not absolutely necessary, if it appeared with sufficient Certainty & all proper Parties joined in the Power.

I am with the highest Respect &ca.   Sir,   Your obedt Servt.

* Treat. upon Bills of Exch.¹ p. 16. cites 2 Edit Dougl. 630 N. 134.²
ADf, New-York Historical Society, New York City; copy, Hamilton Papers, Library of Congress.

1. The legal citation is to John Bayley, *A Short Treatise on the Law of Bills of Exchange, Cash Bills, and Promissory Notes* (London, 1789), 16. Bayley states: "On a bill or note payable to several persons (not in partnership) the right to transfer is in all collectively—not in any individually." In a footnote Bayley cites the case of *Carrick* v. *Vickering*.

2. The case of *Carrick* v. *Vickering* was also cited by Sylvester Douglas, reporter, *Reports of Cases Argued and Determined in the Court of King's Bench in the Nineteenth, Twentieth and Twenty-first Years of the Reign of George III* (Dublin, 2nd edition, 1789), 653-54, note 134.

From Thomas Willing

[Philadelphia] March 12th 1790

Sir.

I have consulted the Directors on the Subject of yr. letter of the 8th Inst.[1] in which you say you shall shortly have Occasion for a loan of 50,000 Drs. We found it necessary to stop our Discount last Week, & I think we shall not find it convenient to open it again for three or four Weeks to come. If yr. application shou'd be postponed till the Middle of next Month, I have no doubt but we shall be able to furnish Bank paper at 30 or 60 Day's for the Sum you mention. Perhaps it may be done sooner if necessity presses you, & supplies come into the Bank in the usual manner with our Spring Trade—but the Directors must determine at the Moment of application for such large Sums as you require—they can't now say what they will, or may be able to do a Month hence. You will however be persuaded that it will give us pleasure at all times to render you every facility & accommodation in Our power.

I have the honor to be Sir, for the P. D. & Co. of &c; Yrs &c,

TW. Prest.

LC, Historical Society of Pennsylvania, Philadelphia.
    1. Letter not found.

From Oliver Wolcott, Junior [1]

Treasury Department, March 12, 1790. Has "examined the accounts of Thomas Barclay." Believes "that the final settlement thereof was delayed merely for the purpose of determining what compensation Mr. Barclay ought to receive for his services." Itemizes Barclay's charges against the United States, and states that "If the whole of these charges are admitted, the balance due to Mr. Barclay . . . will be livres 74,719 2 5."

ASP, Claims, I, 349.
    1. On October 5, 1781, Barclay was appointed United States consul in France, and on November 18, 1782, he was designated commissioner to settle

the accounts of the United States in Europe. On July 18, 1787, he was commissioned to negotiate a treaty of amity and commerce between the United States and the Emperor of Morocco.

From Oliver Wolcott, Junior

Treasury Department, Auditor's Office, March 13, 1790. "General Moses Hazen whose accounts with the United States have been the subject of a lengthy and tedious altercation is desirous of receiving a Certificate on account of the balance which has been stated to be due to him. . . ."

LS, Connecticut Historical Society, Hartford.

From Meletiah Jordan

Frenchman's Bay [District of Maine] March 15, 1790. States: "I did myself the pleasure to write you the 24th. 25th. & 29th. December." [1] Transmits "two quarterly returns of the exports from this District, two Abstracts of Duties arising on Tonnage, two Abstracts of pay to Inspectors &c with my accounts current for the two last quarters." Explains "the expense attending the seizing of the Schooner Betsey."

LC, RG 56, Letters to Collector at Gloucester, Machias and Frenchman's Bay, National Archives.
1. Letter of December 25, 1789, not found.

Report on the Memorial of John Cochran

Treasury Department, March 16th. 1790
[Communicated on March 17, 1790] [1]

[To the Speaker of the House of Representatives]
The Secretary of the Treasury, to whom it was referred to report on the Memorial of John Cochran, late Commissioner of the Loan-Office for the State of New York,[2]
Begs leave to report;
That the Salaries of the several Commissioners of the Loan Office

were, in pursuance of the Act of Congress of the 3d. of November 1785,[3] established by the late Board of Treasury, at the following rates, Viz:

	Dollars per annum
In New Hampshire . . . . at	650.
In Massachusetts . . . . . "	1500.
In Rhode Island . . . . . "	600.
In Connecticut . . . . . "	1000.
In New-York . . . . . . "	1000.
In New-Jersey . . . . . "	700.
In Pennsylvania . . . . . "	1500.
In Delaware . . . . . . "	600.
In Maryland . . . . . . "	1000.
In Virginia . . . . . . "	1500.
In North Carolina . . . "	1000.
In South Carolina . . . . "	800.
In Georgia . . . . . . "	600.

exclusive of Office-rent, Stationary and other necessary charges and the wages of such Clerks as were previously authorized by the said Board.

That on the 23rd. of March 1787,[4] a general reduction was made by Congress of the Salaries of the Officers of the Civil Department, in consequence of which the late Commissioners of the Loan Office were restricted to the Salaries above stated, without any allowance for Office-rent, Clerkship or any Contingent Expenses (except Stationary) after the 30th. of June following.

That it appears from the records of the late Board of Treasury, that many of the Commissioners remonstrated against the above reduction, as rendering the compensation inadequate to their several services; and that applications were made to Congress by the Commissioners of the Loan Office for the State of New York and Connecticut for relief.

That in the case of the former, (which was submitted to the late Board of Treasury) it was proposed by the said Board "That in such States when the transactions of the Commissioners of the Loan Office should, in the judgment of the Board, render it necessary, there should be allowed one Clerk at a Salary not exceeding four hundred dollars per annum, and one hundred dollars annually, in full for all charges for Office-rent, candles, firewood &c."

That this report was, on the 2nd. of October 1787,[5] considered by Congress and negatived; but that no determination appears to have been made on the application of the Loan Officer for the State of Connecticut.

The Secretary further states, that the official business, done by the Commissioner for the State of New York, appears to have been as extensive as suggested by the Memorialist, and that he is of opinion, that the compensation for it was not only inadequate, but, compared with that of others, in respect to service, disproportionate.

Nevertheless it does not appear to the Secretary to revise a stated or determinate allowance under the former Government, on the mere ground of inadequateness or disproportion; a precedent of which would be likely to lead to numerous applications and much embarrassment.

All which is humbly submitted,   Alexander Hamilton.
                                                          Secretary of the Treasury.

Copy, RG 233, Reports of the Secretary of the Treasury, 1790–1791, Vol. 1, National Archives.

1. *Journal of the House,* I, 176.

2. On January 15, 1790, the House received
"A memorial of John Cochran, late Receiver of Continental Taxes in the State of New York, and Commissioner of the Loan Office for the same . . . praying that a further allowance may be made for his services and expenses in the said two offices, the salary allowed by the late Congress having been very inadequate thereto." (*Journal of the House,* I, 141.)
On January 18, 1790, the House ordered that the
"Memorial of John Cochran . . . be referred to the Secretary of the Treasury, with instruction to examine the same, and report his opinion thereupon to the House." (*Journal of the House,* I, 142.)

3. *JCC,* XXIX, 870.

4. *JCC,* XXXII, 128–30.

5. *JCC,* XXIII, 589.

Report on the Memorial of the Officers of the South Carolina Regiments

Treasury Department. March 18th. 1790.
[Communicated on March 19, 1790] [1]

[To the Speaker of the House of Representatives]
The Secretary of the Treasury, on the Memorial of the late Officers
of the South Carolina line on Continental Establishment,[2]
Respectfully reports:

That it is true, as suggested in substance in the said Memorial,
that Congress, in consideration of payments in specie which had
been made to other parts of the Army, did recommend to the State
of South Carolina to pay to the Officers of it's line, a sum equal to
six months pay; which recommendation is contained in a Resolution of the 10th. of October 1786, in the words following.

"Resolved that it be, and it is hereby recommended to the State
of South Carolina, to pay to the Officers of their late line and Hospital department, the said sum of ten thousand two hundred and
seventy six dollars and twelve ninetieths, mentioned to be due to
them by the said Report, the said sum to be paid to the said Officers, agreeably to a return of the late paymaster General, and
for which the said State shall have Credit on the Specie proportion
of the last Requisition." [3]

That Warrants or Drafts on the Commissioner of Loans for the
said State, payable to Bearer, were accordingly issued by the late
Board of Treasury to the respective Officers, for the sums to them
severally due in conformity to the said Resolution; which drafts,
for want of money in the hands of the Commissioner, were not
paid.

That arrangements were afterwards taken by the said Board, towards the payment of those drafts, if returned, and consequently
no farther provision is now necessary, except with regard to the
claim of interest.

That the claim of interest may have reference to the time preceding the issuing of the drafts, and to the time subsequent to it. That
with respect to the first period, had the accounts of the said Of-

ficers been adjusted in the ordinary mode and Certificates granted, they would have borne interest from the times the pay became due: but Congress, in directing the payment of the principal only, as was the case, by the resolution recited, appear to have decided against the allowance of that which had previously accrued. That with respect to the period subsequent to the issuing of the drafts, it would be contrary to the practice of the Treasury to allow interest; which has not been usual upon warrants or drafts issued for payment of monies due.

That an innovation upon a practice, which has governed in a great extent and variety of cases, would of course be productive of much inconvenience and embarrassment; and, in many instances, would have an improper operation; as the negociations of such drafts between individuals have been without a view to interest.

That similar drafts, excluding interest, were issued to the lines of Virginia and North Carolina, and, though attended with a delay of payment, were afterwards taken up without allowance of interest; as is also daily the case in respect to Warrants issued by the late Board of Treasury, for which an appropriation was made during the last Session.

That from the foregoing facts and considerations, the Secretary is of opinion, that the claim of the Memorialists to interest ought not to be admitted. The past situation of public affairs has, unavoidably given too much occasion for complaints of individual hardship; but, in most instances, they are rather to be regretted than redressed. Confusion would ensue a departure from former decisions and established usages, where the cases are not very peculiar and very clearly distinguishable as such.

All which is humbly submitted   Alexander Hamilton,
                                     Secretary of the Treasury

Copy, RG 233, Reports of the Secretary of the Treasury, 1790–1791, Vol. I, National Archives.

1. *Journal of the House*, I, 178.
2. On March 5, 1790,
"A memorial of the late officers of the South Carolina line on Continental Establishment, was presented to the House and read, praying that provision may be made for securing to them payment of the six months' pay granted them by certain resolutions of the late Congress, and which they have never yet received." (*Journal of the House*, I, 168.)
On March 13, 1790, the House

"*Ordered*, That the memorial of the late officers of the South Carolina line on Continental Establishment . . . be referred to the Secretary of the Treasury, with instruction to examine the same, and report his opinion thereupon to the House." (*Journal of the House*, I, 174.)
  3. *JCC*, XXXI, 761.

From Otho H. Williams [1]

Baltimore, March 18, 1790. "The arrangement made in this State by the Government thereof; for the payment of Invalids was by appropriations of the County taxes which were to be reimbursed out of the state Treasury. By this arrangement the unhappy sufferers were permitted to reside among their friends, and received their subsistence at home. In consequence there has been more attention, than formerly, to their demands. I have not yet received from the Executive of this State the compleat list by which, according to instructions recd. from the Secretary of the department of War, I am to be exactly governed in this Payments, and therefore do not Certainly know what may be demanded; But I have reason to believe that there are very few invalids who have not received the first half yearly Payment from 5th March 1789. And I give you the information that you may determine whither it would not be eligible to draw out of my hands the money intended to be applied to that purpose at present. . . ."

ADfS, RG 53, "Old Correspondence," Baltimore Collector, National Archives.
  1. For background to this letter, see Williams to H, February 6, 1790, and H to Jedediah Huntington, January 30, 1790.

From Benjamin Lincoln

Boston, March 19, 1790. "I have written to the several keepers of the light-houses in this State, excepting the keeper of the light house at Plymouth, informing them that the President of the United States has been pleased to continue them in their present appointments. . . . Mrs. Thomas the widow the late General Thomas, *not Warren* has been considered as the keeper of the light house at Plymouth. . . ." [1]

ALS, RG 26, Lighthouse Letters Received, Vol. "B," New Hampshire and Massachusetts, National Archives; LC, RG 36, Collector of Customs at Boston,

Letter Book, 1790–1797, National Archives; copy, Letters to the Collector at Boston, National Archives; copy, Letters to Collectors at Small Ports, "Set G," National Archives.
1. See H to Lincoln, March 10, 1790.

From Thomas Willing [1]

Philada. March 22d. 1790

Sir

The scarcity of Money has produced a stagnation in every kind of business, beyond any thing I have known—the few who have the command of Cash here, have turn'd their Eyes to Bills of Exchange—these have got as low, as 45 nay even to 42½ ℔ Ct. & untill Exchange shall rise considerably, I dont expect to see any demand for Stock, or Public Certificates. A Single Share has been sold day by day, at 400 Drs. & none have been offered at a lower rate, that I know of—a reduction of 7½ on the price, wou'd not now command the Cash. The best way for you, is to send the Certificates & I will get the most I can, not exceeding any deduction you may fix—but having them at hand, I will retail them even by a Single Share, to accommodate you as soon as its possible. To fall the price, will avail little, when the want of purchasers, arrises from the scarcity of Money, & the great temptation from the price of Bills of Exchange.

I am most respectfully Your's   Thos. Willing

ALS, Hamilton Papers, Library of Congress.
1. This letter concerns the sale of John B. Church's stock in the Bank of North America. See Willing to H, February 24, 1790.

From Sharp Delany

[Philadelphia] March 23, 1790. "It is with no small degree of diffidence I address you again on the Subject of a Boat in our Bay. . . . I am induced to request your sentiments on the subject—for the motives for smugling being encreased—means of prevention especially at first setting out should also be taken. . . ."

LC, Bureau of Customs, Philadelphia.

To Sharp Delany

[*New York, March 24, 1790.* On April 30, 1790, Hamilton wrote to Delany "I refer you to my Letter of the 24th march." *Letter not found.*]

From Benjamin Lincoln

Boston, March 24, 1790. States that "General Warren [1] is going in the Morning to the City of New York to settle his public accounts as a Member of the Navy board, in this State." Recommends General Warren's son, Henry, for "an office in the revenue."

Copy, RG 36, Collector of Customs at Boston, Letters from the Treasury and Others, 1789–1818, Vol. 11, National Archives.
1. James Warren of Plymouth, Massachusetts, was paymaster general for the Continental Army from 1775 to 1776, and served on the Continental Navy Board from 1776 to 1781.

To Joseph Whipple

[*New York, March 24, 1790.* On May 31, 1790, in a letter to Hamilton, Whipple referred to "your letters of the 30th January & 24th March last." *Letter of March 24 not found.*]

From Matthew Parke [1]

Boston, March 27, 1790. "In consequence of being recommended to you by the Honbl. Fisher Ames, Esqr. I have had the honour of writing you Several Letters [2] respecting my Administration on the Estates of a number of Persons, late in the American Navy, no answer to either of which Letters have I yet received. . . . If the appointment you have had since my application to you *has prevented*, or may *Still prevent* you from attending to the business, I wish you to be kind enough to inform me by Post."

ALS, Hamilton Papers, Library of Congress.
1. This letter is signed M. Parke and is incorrectly endorsed A. Parke. Parke probably was the Matthew Parke who is listed in the *Boston Directory* for

1789 (*The Boston Directory. Containing, A List of the Merchants, Mechanics, Traders, and others, of the Town of Boston; in Order to enable Strangers to find the Residence of any Person* [Boston, 1789]).
2. Letters not found.

To Sharp Delany

Treasury Department March 29th 1790.

Sir:

You will please to obtain a certificate from the Cashier of the Bank of North America, expressing the sums paid in the said Bank by you in the course of the present month, upon which a warrant shall be issued for the amount.

You will not fail transmitting the said certificate by Thursday's mail, in order that it may reach me on Saturday.

I am Sir   Your Obed't Serv't   A. Hamilton.

Sharp Delany, Esq.
Collector for the Port of Philadelphia.

ALS, Mrs. Arthur Loeb, Philadelphia.

To Meletiah Jordan

[*New York, March 29, 1790.* On July 1, 1790, in a letter to Hamilton, Jordan referred to "your letter of March 29th." *Letter not found.*]

Report on the Memorial of Baron von Steuben [1]

Treasury Department. 29th. March, 1790.
[Communicated on April 6, 1790] [2]

[To the Speaker of the House of Representatives]
The Secretary of the Treasury, on the Memorial of Baron De

Copy, RG 233, Reports of the Secretary of the Treasury, 1790–1791, Vol. I, National Archives; copy, certified correct by Tench Coxe, Historical Society of Pennsylvania, Philadelphia.
1. During the seventeen-eighties, H concerned himself with Baron von Steuben's claim on the United States. The interest he took in that claim while a member of the Continental Congress in 1782 and 1783, the exchange of letters

Steuben, referred to him by an Order of the House of Representatives of the 25th. September last: [3]

Respectfully reports,

That it appears from the papers accompanying the said Memorial, that the Memorialist grounds his present claim on the United States, upon a Contract, which he alledges to have been made with Congress at York,[4] in the year 1777, previous to his joining the American Army.

That the transaction respecting this alledged Contract is stated by the Memorialist in the following words.

"At the arrival of Baron De Steuben in the year one thousand seven hundred and seventy seven, he was received by Congress with marks of distinction, and the day after his arrival, was waited on by a Committee of Congress, composed of Doctor Witherspoon, Mr. Henry,[5] of Maryland, and a third, whom at this time he cannot recollect.[6] This Committee demanded of the Baron the conditions on which he was inclined to serve the United States, and if he had made any stipulations with the Commissioners in France. He replied, that he had made no agreement with them, nor was it his intention to accept of any rank or pay; that he wished to join the army as a volunteer, and to render such services as the Commander in chief should think him capable of; adding, that he had no other fortune than a revenue of about six hundred Guineas per annum, arising from places and posts of honor in Germany, which he had relinquished to come to this country; that, in consideration of this, he expected the United States would defray his necessary expenses while in their service; that if, unhappily, this Country should not succeed in establishing their independence, or if he should not suc-

---

between H and von Steuben, and the letters he drafted for von Steuben, all attest this concern. For the background to this document, see H to Elbridge Gerry, September 6, 1788, and von Steuben to H, January 27, 1790.

2. *Journal of the House*, I, 190.

3. The House ordered that "the memorial of Baron de Steuben . . . be referred to the Secretary of the Treasury, to report thereupon . . . to the next session of Congress (*Journal of the House*, I, 123).

4. York, Pennsylvania.

5. In addition to John Henry, delegate from Maryland, and the Reverend Dr. John Witherspoon, delegate from New Jersey, the members were Francis Lightfoot Lee of Virginia and Thomas McKean of Delaware.

6. Von Steuben was mistaken, as is shown in paragraph five of this report. The members of the committee are listed in note 5.

ceed in his endeavors for their service, in either of those cases, he should consider the United States as free from any obligations towards him; but if, on the other hand, the United States should be happy enough to establish their freedom, and that he should be successful in his endeavors, in that case he should expect a full indemnification for the sacrifice he had made in coming over, and such marks of their generosity, as the justice of the United States should dictate.

"That if these terms were agreeable to Congress, he waited only their orders to join the army without delay. The Committee were pleased to applaud the generosity of his propositions in thus risking his fortune on that of the United States. The Committee then left him, in order to make their report; the next day Congress gave him an entertainment; after which the President Mr. Laurens,[7] told him, it was the desire of Congress, that he should join the army immediately, which he did."

That the evidence, adduced by him in support of it, consists principally of these documents—A Certificate from John Witherspoon, dated November 1st. 1785, another from Elbridge Gerry, dated the 23d. November 1785, and a third from William Duer, without date, (which several Certificates are annexed to the statement above recited, and refer to it) also two letters; one from Thomas McKean dated 11th. September 1788, and another from Francis Lightfoot Lee dated the 25th. September in the same year, all which Gentlemen were, at the time of the transaction, members of Congress, and three of them, towit, John Witherspoon, Francis Lightfoot Lee, and Thomas McKean, members of the Committee mentioned in the said Statement.

That the Certificate from the said John Witherspoon, is as follows.

"Princeton, Nov. 1st. 1785.

"I can recollect very distinctly, that I was one of the Committee who waited on Baron Steuben, on his arrival at York Town. He then could speak no English, and, I believe, I was the only member of the Committee who could speak French, and was therefore obliged to be his interpreter to the other members, as well as to

7. Henry Laurens of South Carolina was president of Congress from 1777 to 1778.

make the report to Congress. I am sensible, that the above is a just
and fair account of what passed on that occasion, and that we were
all sensible the Baron's proposals were honorable and generous; and
accordingly he was sent to General Washington, to receive his
directions from him.   (Signed) John Witherspoon."

That the Certificate from the said Elbridge Gerry is as follows.

"New York. 23d. Nov. 1785.
"The subscriber certifies, that, having a seat in Congress at the
time of the Baron De Steuben's arrival at York Town, he well re-
members the facts herein stated, excepting what relates to the entertainment, which, he doubts not, was provided, and to the time
of the Baron's arrival at that place, which was in the beginning of
the year 1778.

"The Subscriber further certifies, that in questions agitated in
Congress while he has been a member, respecting the allowance that
should be made in pursuance of the within stipulation, he has considered the claim of the Baron for a full indemnification and compensation, as a claim of Justice, founded in the verbal Contract of
the parties.   (Signed) E. Gerry."

That so much of the Certificate of the said William Duer, as relates to the fact is as follows.

"I was a Member of Congress and of the Board of War, when the
Baron De Steuben arrived at York Town, and though I was not
present at that place when the Baron had his first interview with
the Committee of Congress, being absent for a few days on a visit
to Manheim,[8] I perfectly remember, that the account I received on
my return to York Town, of the engagements entered into with
the Baron Steuben, by the Honorable Congress, was perfectly
similar to that which the Baron has stated."

That the material part of the letter of the said Thomas McKean
is as follows;

"My memory enables me to say, that you came to York Town
in the beginning of February 1778; that the Congress, being informed of it, proceeded to name a Committee (of which I was one)
to wait upon you, learn the objects of your visit, and to confer with
you about entering into the service of the United States. They

8. Manheim, Pennsylvania, about seventy miles west of Philadelphia.

might have received farther instructions, but I do not remember them. The Committee (of which Doctor Witherspoon was chairman) called upon you the next morning at your lodgings, when a conversation was had between the Doctor and you in French, which he interpreted to his brethren. Part of what was thus communicated was, that you came to America with a view to tender your services to Congress, that you had made no stipulations with their Commissioners in France, and was desirous to join the Army as a Volunteer, and to act there in such station as the Commander in chief should think you best qualified to fill. That you had held posts of honor and profit in the army of the King of Prussia, and afterwards (I think) of the Prince of Baden, which last you had relinquished, in order to embark in the American Cause, whose fortune you were willing to partake. That if it failed, you asked nothing but a support according to your condition while you served, and if it succeeded and your services were approved, you would expect compensation for the sacrifices you had made, and the rewards commonly bestowed by a happy and grateful people on faithful and successful servants. This, Sir, is the amount of what I recollect."

That the material part of the letter of the said Francis Lightfoot Lee, is as follows.

"I was one of the Committee appointed by Congress to wait upon you, on your arrival at York Town, and understood French sufficiently to comprehend pretty fully all that you said to the Committee.

"You informed them that you held considerable military rank in Europe, with posts and emoluments to the amount, I think, of five or six hundred Guineas. That your great desire of being serviceable to the American cause had induced you to relinquish these, and to offer your service to Congress. That you asked for neither rank nor pay: but expected your expenses in the army to be defrayed; And, if America should be successful in her Contest, you depended upon the justice and generosity of Congress, to make you amends for your losses, and reward your services: if unfortunate, you were willing to share her fortune. I do not recollect any particular stipulation for reimbursing the specific sum of money: but it was, most certainly, well understood by the Committee and Congress, that if our Contest ended happily, and your services were approved, you would have a just claim to very liberal compensation for what you had sacrificed, and for your services.

"Congress was very much pleased with your generous proposals, when reported to them: as their consequent behaviour to you sufficiently verified."

That besides the foregoing documents, there are two letters accompanying the said Memorial, one from Horatio Gates, dated the sixth of December 1785; the other from Richard Peters, dated the thirtieth of October 1785; the former of whom was President, and the latter Member of the Board of War, at the time of the said transaction.

That the letter from the said Horatio Gates contains the following passage.

"When I was President of the Board of War, I very well remember your coming to York Town, and being most honorably received by Congress. A Committee was immediately appointed to wait on you, and, after they had conferred with you, you was invited to an elegant entertainment, and every mark of distinction was shewn, that could be shewn to an officer of the first rank, into whose hands the inspection and discipline of the Army was to be intrusted. With regard to pecuniary matters, I always understood, they were to be settled upon the most liberal and generous plan; regard being to be had, not only to the high station you were to fill, but to the sacrifice you had so generously made in coming to serve this Country."

That the letter from the said Richard Peters contains the following passages:

"Belmont October 30th. 1785.
"Sir,

"In answer to your enquiries respecting my recollection of what passed at York-Town, relative to your affairs, at your arrival at that place, I will state such circumstances as I became acquainted with. They are chiefly such as I understood from members of Congress, some of whom were appointed to assist the Commissioners of the Board of War, and to explain and communicate such matters, as were necessary for our information in the business of our department.

"You were received by Congress with every mark of distinction their situation admitted, and had more particular attention paid to you, than I had known given to any foreigner. Much pleasure was expressed at the arrival of a person of your military knowledge and experience, at a time when the want of discipline in our Army, and the œconomy it produces, were severely felt and regretted. You were waited upon by a Committee appointed for that purpose, from some of whom, as well as the other members of Congress, I was informed that you had conducted yourself, as to the manner in which you agreed to enter our service, with much generosity and disinterestedness, having made no terms either as to rank or pay, leaving it to Congress, after experience of your talents and usefulness as a volunteer in our service, to fix such as your merits and exertions intitled you to. Your having made no Contract with our ministers in France, was mentioned as a circumstance which prevented embarrassments, as some terms had been made with gentlemen, which did not meet the approbation of Congress. You agreed to take the risk of our affairs. If we were unsuccessful, you would of consequence be deprived of any means of compensation for the sacrifices you had made of a handsome revenue in Europe, and must have suffered the loss of military reputation generally attendant on unsuccessful service. But I always understood and believed, that in case our cause issued happily, and your conduct was approved, Congress deemed it a matter of obligation on the United States, to indemnify you for the losses and expenses, you had sustained, as well as to compensate you for services, in common with other officers. Precedents for such indemnification having been established even antecedent to experience in service, I never looked upon this as a claim upon the generosity, but as a demand upon the justice of this Country. And although there was no written agreement to this purpose, there was clearly an implied contract. Your situation being fully stated, and your expectations explained, Congress desired you, through their President, to repair to Camp, and join the Army; and the Board of War were directed to assist you for this purpose, in such matters as were requested."

That the following documents have been supposed to militate against the admission of the Contract relied upon by the Memorialist.

First: A letter from him to Congress, dated, Portsmouth December 6th. 1777, in the following terms

"Honorable Gentlemen,

"The honor of serving a respectable nation, engaged in the noble enterprize of defending it's rights and liberty, is the only motive that brought me over to this Continent. I ask neither riches nor titles. I am come here from the remotest end of Germany at my own expense, and have given up an honorable and lucrative rank. I have made no condition with your deputies in France, nor shall I make any with you. My only ambition is, to serve you as a Volunteer, to deserve the confidence of your General in Chief, and to follow him in all his operations, as I have done during seven campaigns with the king of Prussia: two and twenty years past at such a school seem to give me a right of thinking myself in the number of experienced Officers; and if I am possessor of some talents in the art of War, they should be much dearer to me, if I could employ them in the service of a Republic, such as I hope soon to see America. I should willingly purchase, at my whole blood's expense, the honor of seeing, one day, my name, after those of the defenders of your liberty. Your gracious acceptance will be sufficient for me, and I ask no other favor than to be received among your officers. I dare hope, you will agree with this my request, and that you will be so good as to send me your orders to Boston, where I shall expect for them, and accordingly take convenient measures. I have the honor to be with respect,   Honorable Gentlemen   Your Most Obedient and very humble Servant.

(Signed) Steuben."

Secondly: A report on the files of Congress of the Committee which conferred with the Memorialist at York Town, in these words.

"The Baron Steuben, who was a Lieutenant General and Aid de Camp, to the king of Prussia, desires no Rank—is willing to attend General Washington, and be subject to his orders. Does not require or desire any command of a particular Corps or Division, but will serve occasionally, as directed by the General—expects to be of use in planning encampments, &c. and promoting the discipline of the Army. He heard, before he left France of the dissatisfaction of the Americans with the promotion of foreign Officers, therefore makes no terms, nor will accept of any thing but with general Approbation, and particularly that of General Washington." [9]

Thirdly; A letter from the Memorialist to the President of Congress, dated in December 1782, and containing this passage.

"My demands were these; to join the army as a Volunteer, that I wished to be known by the Commander in chief, and to leave it to the officers of the army if my capacity intitled me to hold a Commission in it. That the General would employ me in such a branch, where he thought my services the most useful—that I was determined not to ask a favor or reward previous of having deserved it. That however I expected from the generosity of Congress, that in imitation of all European powers, they would defray my expenses, altho' a Volunteer, according to the rank which I held in Europe, as well for myself as my Aids and servants."

That the Secretary desirous of knowing what explanation of these documents the Memorialist might have it in his power to give, did, on the 26th. of January past, write to him a letter in the words following: [10]

"Among the documents which relate to the circumstances of your entrance into the service of the United States, are—a letter from you to Congress, dated at Portsmouth, the 6th. Decr. 1777—a report of the Committee which conferred with you at York Town —and a letter from you to the President of Congress, dated in December 1782. Inclosed you will find copies of the two first, and an Extract from the last. As these may seem to militate against your claim, as founded in Contract, I think it proper, before I report to the House of Representatives upon your memorial, to afford you an opportunity of making such remarks upon those documents, as may appear to you advisable."

That to this letter, the Secretary received an answer, dated the 27th. of the same month, of which the following is a translation.

"New York. the 27th. Jany. 1790.
"Sir,

"The letter which you did me the honor of addressing to me yesterday, I have received; and am indebted to you for affording me

9. The report, dated January, 1778, is in the Papers of the Continental Congress, National Archives.
10. Letter not found.

an opportunity to elucidate the nature of my engagement with the United States.

"From the information I received of the Minister of France, that the preferment of foreigners to military employments, had been a cause of discontent in the American Army; I foresaw the necessity of pursuing measures different from those which had been adopted by my predecessors, in order to gain admission into your Army.

"Being sure of success in my enterprize, as soon as the Commander in chief and the Army should be convinced of the advantages of my military arrangements, there was but one difficulty to surmount: and from the complexion of the times, that difficulty was of the greatest magnitude. It depended upon obtaining such a post in the army, as would enable me to make use of the knowledge of my profession, and to render it beneficial to the interest of the United States, without exciting the dissatisfaction and jealousy of the officers of your Army. Any conditions proposed by me under these circumstances, tending to ensure me a recompense proportioned to my sacrifices and my services would not have failed to render all negociations abortive. But proposals to serve the United States as a Volunteer, without rank or pay, could give no umbrage —and surely the proposition was a generous one.

"Suppose, however, I had added, that for the honor of serving the United States, I had resigned in my native Country honorable and lucrative employments; that I had come to America, at my own expense, for the purpose of fighting her battles, and that after she should have obtained her independency, I would decline all compensation for the services I had rendered. I would ask, Sir, in what light would such a proposition have been received by so enlightened a Body as the Congress of the United States? To me it appears, that common sense would have declared the author of such a proposition to be either a Lunatic or a Traitor. The former, for his coming from another part of the globe to serve a nation unknown to him; at the same time renouncing all his possessions for a cause to which he was an utter stranger, without having in view the gratification of ambition, or the advancement of interest. The latter, as it might appear that his making such generous proposals to introduce himself into your army, was with the most dangerous views, for which he, probably received compensation from the enemy.

"In either of these aspects, would the person, making similar propositions, have been admissible?

"What measures then were necessary to be pursued, to enable me to render those services to the United States, which I had proposed to myself?

"Having made these observations, Sir, I entreat you to read my letter to Congress of January 1778: Badly translated as it is, it will be intelligible to you, as being one of those, who are particularly informed of the critical situation of Congress and of the Army, at that period of the Revolution.

"You will easily discover, Sir, that this letter was dictated by no other motive, than to facilitate my reception into your army. The effect has answered my conjectures and my desires. If, however, I should be charged with having made use of illicit stratagems to gain admission into the service of the United [States], I am sure, I have obtained my pardon of the Army, and, I flatter myself, of the Citizens of this Republic in general.

"In consequence of this letter, I was directed by a resolution of Congress to join the Army: notwithstanding which, I judged it necessary to proceed first to York Town, as well to pay my respects to that august body who presided over a nation whom I was going to serve, as to learn the advantage or disadvantage which might result to me from so hazardous an enterprize.

"At my arrival, the Congress did me the honor of appointing a Committee to confer with me. If my first letter and the answer to it had been considered by them as a sufficient engagement, was there any occasion for this Committee: Was there any necessity for this conference? All that passed in this conversation is sufficiently proved, and needs no farther repetition.

"If on an impartial examination of the subject, it should appear, that my propositions to this Committee were incompatible with my first letter to Congress, I confess that my judgment misleads me.

"I represented to the Gentlemen of that Committee, that I had not entered into any agreement with the American Commissioners in France; that I would not insist upon making any at present, but would serve the United States as a Volunteer without rank or pay, on condition, notwithstanding, that my expenses in the army should be defrayed. I declared to them, that I had no other fortune than a revenue of about six hundred Louis d'ors arising from posts I held in my native Country, which I was going to resign, to serve the United States being disposed to hazard the whole on the event. And that not until I had succeeded in my undertaking, and the United States had obtained their liberty by a satisfactory peace, I would ask an indemnification for my sacrifices and disbursements, and for such other marks of acknowledgment and generosity as in the justice of Congress should be deemed adequate to my services.

"It appears, that the Committee reported to Congress, I had made no conditions, and that I would not accept of any thing without general approbation and particularly that of General Washington.

"Although I do not allow that report to be exact in it's literal sense, yet I do not find it so extraordinary, that expectations founded upon the event of a revolution of this nature should be represented as making no stipulations. Besides it seems probable, that the politics of the times made it necessary to give such a complexion to the report as would remove all jealousy.

"Permit me, Sir, to suggest, here, a question: Why was not this report (like all other reports of Committees) entered upon the Journals of Congress? I doubt whether it would have been contradicted by me; but at least it would have afforded me an opportunity of taking precautions. I assure you, Sir, upon my honor, that this report was never brought into view previous to the year 1788, and that I did not see it until General Washington had the goodness to send me a copy of it. But be this, as it will; no person, Sir, is better informed than yourself, how difficult it was at that time to introduce a foreigner into your army, even without any condition whatever.

"With regard to my second letter of December 1782, I confess I do not find in that any contradiction of the facts represented to have taken place in the conference at York Town.

"In this letter I state, that my desires were to join your Army as a Volunteer; that I did not ask any employ, until the approbation of the Commander in chief, and the opinion of the Army, should assign me a place in which I could be useful: that I asked no compensation until it was merited, provided however, that my expenses for my own person, as well as my suite, were defrayed by the United States, agreeably to the usage of European Powers.

"I perceive that it may be asked, why I did not, at that time, insist upon my contract? I answer, that it was my wish never to mention it, as it appeared to me more honorable to the United States, and more flattering to myself to receive a recompense dictated rather by generosity, than by conditions, and that it was with reluctance and through urgent circumstances upon that stipulation, which was the basis of my engagement at York Town.

"But there is another reason, why this contract was not mentioned in my letter immediately after the conclusion of the War.

"The Congress were besieged by a croud of foreign officers, who were as little satisfied as the national troops, which was a circumstance, that, probably, induced some respectable persons then members of Congress, (in whom I place the greatest confidence) to advise me to pass over in silence all that related to a former contract, and to rest my pretensions solely on the merit of my services, and the generosity of the United States. If my memory is faithful, yourself Sir, were of the number of those by whose opinion I was governed.

"Once more, I assure you Sir, that it is with regret that I have recourse to that contract; but there remains no other resource to obtain that justice which is due to me.

"These, Sir, are all the explanations I can give you, if they are not sufficient, I submit to the consequences.

"All that I ask of you is, to accelerate the decision. No event can render my situation more unhappy—in fact, it is insupportable.

"There must always remain one consolation: The truth of the facts, stated in my Memorial to Congress, cannot be disputed, without raising a doubt of the veracity of some of the most worthy and respectable characters in the United States, several of whom have held, or now hold, the highest places in the government of their Country.

"Having no Secretary, you will please, Sir, to excuse my addressing you in a language, which is more familiar to me than the English. I have the honor to be &c."

The Secretary further reports.

That on the fifth of May 1778, the memorialist was appointed by Congress, Inspector General, with the rank and pay of Major General, to which was afterwards added a farther allowance for the extra service and expense incident to the office of Inspector General.

That there appears on the Journals of Congress a report of a Committee of the 30th. of December 1782, stating,

First. That the Baron de Steuben was in Europe possessed of respectable military rank, and different posts of honor and emolument, which he relinquished to come to America, and offer his services at a critical, period of the War, and without any previous stipulations.

Secondly. That on his arrival he actually engaged in the Army in a very disinterested manner, and without compensations similar to those which had been made to several other foreign officers.

Thirdly. That under singular difficulties and embarrassments in the department in which he has been employed, he has rendered very important and substantial services, by introducing into the Army a regular formation and exact discipline, and by establishing a spirit of order and œconomy in the interior administration of the regiments; which, besides other advantages, have been productive of immense savings to the United States, that in the commands in which he has been employed, he has upon all occasions conducted himself like a brave and experienced officer: The Committee are therefore of opinion, that the sacrifices and services of the Baron De Steuben justly intitle him to the distinguished notice of Congress, and to a generous compensation, whenever the situation of public affairs will admit: The Committee further report, that the Baron De Steuben has considerable arrearages of pay due to him from these States, on a liquidated account, and that having exhausted his resources, it is now indispensible that a sum of money should be paid him for his present support and to enable him to take the field another campaign, and propose that the sum of two thousand four hundred dollars be paid to him for that purpose, and charged to his account aforesaid, Whereupon, Congress resolved,

That the foregoing proposal of the Committee be referred to the Superintendant of Finance, to take order.

That on the 15th. of April 1784 Congress did also resolve,

That the thanks of the United States in Congress assembled be given to Baron Steuben, for the great zeal and abilities he has discovered in the discharge of the several duties of his office; that a gold-hilted sword be presented to him, as a mark of the high sense

Congress entertain of his character and services, and that the Super-intendant of Finance take order for procuring the same.

That the proper officers proceed to the liquidation of monies due from the United States to Major-General Baron Steuben; that the Superintendant of Finance report to Congress his opinion of the most speedy and efficacious means of procuring and paying the same, either here or in Europe.

That Baron Steuben be assured that Congress will adopt these or such others as shall appear most proper and effectual for doing him for that justice, which the peculiarity of his case authorizes.

That on the 27th. of September 1785, Congress did further re-solve,

That in full consideration of the Baron De Steuben's having re-linquished different posts of honor and emolument in Europe, and rendered most essential services to the United States, he be allowed and paid out of the Treasury of the United States, the sum of seven thousand dollars, in addition to former grants.

That the Baron De Steuben has received at different times, sums equal to the amount of the pay and emoluments annexed to his station in the American Army, to the commutation of a Major General, and to the sum expressed in the Resolution last recited.

A question arises, whether the acceptance of these appointments, emoluments and allowances did not virtually supersede the ante-cedent contract relied on by the Memorialist, admitting it to have existed.

To which he answers; "That it cannot be presumed that an in-dividual, in accepting from a government the emoluments annexed to a station, to which he is appointed, for the service of that govern-ment, unsolicited by him, could renounce a prior and more bene-ficial contract.

"That the more natural presumption is, that Congress, by con-ferring those emoluments, meant to ascertain and limit the expenses they had stipulated to bear, and to support the respectability of the office, they had thought proper to create.

"That, as a Major General, he received the pay and other emolu-ments allowed to other Major Generals of the Army; as Inspector General, he received an extra-allowance, in consideration of extra-trouble and expense.

"That the emoluments allowed to an officer in service can only be referred to the services he renders: They can have nothing to do with an indemnity for revenues relinquished, and can never be deemed, by mere inference and implication, to extinguish a Contract founded on that principle.

"That, with regard to the acceptance of the last grant, it was matter of pure necessity proceeding from a situation absolutely indigent; and that the reverse of a disposition to acquiesce in it has been uniformly manifested on his part."

Having stated the foregoing particulars, which are the most material that have come under the observation of the Secretary, relating to the Claim of the Memorialist, he proceeds to remark.

That the statement, made by the Memorialist of what passed in the conference at York Town, is authenticated by such strong, direct and collateral evidence as ought, in the opinion of the Secretary, to secure full credit to the existence of the fact. Waving the regard due to the Memorialist's own assertion, it is not supposable, that if his representation had been ill founded, it could have obtained the sanction of so many disinterested persons, Agents in, or witnesses to the transaction.

That notwithstanding this, it may be inferred as well from the written report of the Committee, as from other circumstances that the idea of a precise contract did not generally prevail. It is probable, that as the indemnity and reward for the sacrifices and services of the Baron were by him made to depend on the success of a national Revolution, the mention of them was viewed rather as a suggestion of expectations, than as a stipulation of terms. This might the more easily have happened, as it is presumable, that the situation of affairs at the time must have disposed Congress [to] an officer, who had had the opportunities of the Memorialist, as a valuable acquisition to the service, and to regard a compliance with the expectations intimated by him, in the event of success as too much a matter of course to need a stipulation.

That this view of the affair appears to the Secretary to afford a satisfactory solution of any difficulties which might result from seemingly discordant circumstances, and to place all the parts of the transaction in a simple and consistent light.

Upon the whole therefore: As it cannot with propriety be

questioned that a conversation of the kind stated by the Baron did take place at the conference at York Town. As the services rendered by him to the United States are acknowledged to have been of a very signal and very meritorious nature; As the expectations alledged to have been signified by him in the Conference are, all of them, reasonable in themselves, being nothing more than that his necessary expenses, while in the service of the United States should be defrayed by them; and that, in case they should establish their independence, and he should be successful in his endeavors to serve them, then he should receive an indemnification for the income he had relinquished in coming to this Country, and to such marks of the generosity of the government, as it's Justice should dictate. The Secretary is of opinion that whether the transaction, relied upon by the Baron, be deemed to have the force of a Contract, or not; it will be most consistent with the dignity and equity of the United States, to admit it as the basis of a final adjustment of his Claims.

Should this opinion appear well founded, it will remain to designate the rule, by which the necessary expenses of the Memorialist are to be adjusted. Taking it for granted, that his actual expenses will not be deemed a proper one, there occurs to the Secretary no better criterion, than the current allowances annexed to the Stations he filled. This excludes the half pay or commutation. It is presumed, that the current allowances to the officers of the American Army in general were regulated wholly with a view to their present support, according to their respective situations, and the half-pay granted as a future reward.

According to this principle, the Secretary has caused an account to be stated, which is hereunto annexed, in which the Memorialist is credited with his emoluments as Major-General and Inspector General (exclusive of half pay or commutation) and with an annuity of five hundred and eighty guineas, (being the amount of the income stated to have been relinquished by him) from the time he left Europe to the last of December 1789, with interest at six per cent, per annum; and is charged with all the monies, under whatsoever denomination, received by him from the United States, with interest at the like rate: upon which statement there is a balance in his favor of seven thousand, three hundred and ninety six dollars, seventy four ninetieths.

In addition to this, he would be intitled for the remainder of life to the yearly sum of five hundred and eighty guineas, as a continuation of the indemnity for the income relinquished: and to such reward as the government in it's discretion should think fit to allow: For which purpose a moderate grant of land, if deemed expedient, would suffice.

The Secretary begs leave further to state, that there is good ground to believe, that the above mentioned balance will be short of a sufficient sum to discharge the debts now owing by the Memorialist, and contracted partly to enable him to come to this Country, and partly for his subsistence here; and in the last place to observe that the situation of the memorialist, who, (being a foreigner) voluntarily came to offer his services to the United States in a critical and perilous moment; and who, from the circumstance of his having been a foreigner, is less likely to participate in the collateral rewards, which, in numerous instances await those, who have distinguished themselves in the American revolution, (while he cannot, like many other foreign officers look for rewards elsewhere) gives a peculiarity to his case, which strengthens his other pretensions. That [it] appears unequivocally, that his services have been of a nature peculiarly valuable and interesting to the American cause, and such as furnish weighty considerations, as well public as personal, for rescuing him from the indigence in which he is now involved, and from the still greater extremities with which he is threatened. A settlement on the principles suggested in this report, will terminate all the claims of the Memorialist on the United States, in a manner equally satisfactory to him and honorable to them.[11]

All which is humbly submitted   Alexander Hamilton
                                     Secretary of the Treasury.

---

11. On June 4, 1790, Congress adopted "An Act for finally adjusting and satisfying the claims of Frederick William de Steuben." This act provided: "That, in order to make full and adequate compensation to Frederick William de Steuben, for the sacrifices and eminent services made and rendered to the United States during the late war, there be paid to the said Frederick William de Steuben, an annuity of two thousand five hundred dollars, during life, to commence on the first day of January last; to be paid in quarterly payments, at the treasury of the United States; which said annuity shall be considered in full discharge of all claims and demands whatever, of the said Frederick William de Steuben against the United States." (6 Stat. 2.)

To George Washington

[Treasury Department, March 29, 1790]

The Secretary of the Treasury begs leave respectfully to inform the President of the United States of America,

That, in order to be able to furnish in the course of the ensuing month for the compensation of the members of Congress, & the Officers and Servants of the two houses, a sum of about sixty thousand dollars; for the payment of the Salaries of the Civil List to the end of the present month a sum of about forty thousand dollars; for the use of the Department of War a sum of about fifty thousand dollars; and for procuring bills to pay an arrear of interest on the Dutch Loans to the first of June next, a sum of about thirty five thousand Dollars: amounting together to about one hundred and eighty five Thousand dollars, it will be requisite to obtain a Loan of one hundred thousand dollars, There being in the Treasury now a sum not exceeding fifty thousand dollars, including thirty thousand dollars which the Bank of New York stands engaged to advance on demand to complete a Loan of fifty thousand dollars stipulated for on the seventeenth day of February last, which is considered as equivalent to a sum in the Treasury.

And in as much as the payment of former Loans and other current demands, will probably call for a considerable part of the monies which may be expected in the interim from the product of the Revenues,

Wherefore the said Secretary submits to the President of the United States the propriety of authorising a Loan to be made to the extent of the said sum of one hundred thousand Dollars.

A. Hamilton
Secy. of the Treasury

Treasury Department
March 29th. 1790.

LC, George Washington Papers, Library of Congress; LC, RG 39, Letter Book, 1789–1795, National Archives.

To Brockholst Livingston [1]

New York 30th march 1790.

Sir

I have made an agreement with Robert Morris Esquire to convey to him one hundred shares of stock in the Bank of North America upon the following terms.[2]

That he engage to pay to me or my order in London in one year from the time the transfer be made at the rate of one hundred pounds Sterling money of Great Britain for each share of the said bank stock which shall be transferred to him together with interest at five ♏ Centum ♏ annum.

That for the payment of the amount he give satisfactory security in lots & buildings in the City of Philadelphia.

I therefore request and authorise you to proceed to the City of Philadelphia on my behalf to complete the said Agreement.

By satisfactory security I understand a mortgage on lots & buildings in the City of Philadelphia of such value as would be likely to produce the amount for which they are mortgaged upon a sale for prompt payment or upon a Credit not exceeding one year; and which are wholly free from other incumbrances.

If such security shall be offered you I empower you to close the bargain causing the transfer to be made and taking the mortgage in my name.

Herewith you will receive 100 shares of Stock which if the bargain be closed you will deliver to Thomas Willing Esquire with the inclosed letter desiring him to make the transfer.[3] Mr. Willing has a sufficient power for the purpose.

Should the agreement not be completed You will please to leave with Mr. Willing 40 shares of the Stock taking his receipt & bring back the remainder to me.

As the operation is of consequence I rely on the greatest circumspection on your part.

As you may find law advice on the spot useful I authorise you to employ & pay Counsel for which you shall be reimbursed.

Wishing you a pleasant Journey   I remain   Yr Very hum st

P.S.

Should the security not appear competent for the whole sum you are at liberty to make the arrangement for a part [4]

AL[S], Columbia University Libraries.
1. Livingston practiced law in New York City.
2. In this stock transaction H was acting as agent for John B. Church. See Morris to H, November 13, 1789.
3. As president of the Bank of North America, Willing had corresponded with H concerning the sale of John B. Church's stock. See Willing to H, February 24, 1790. The enclosure has been printed separately as H to Willing, March 30, 1790.
4. Written at the end of this letter is the following receipt in the writing of H and signed by Livingston: "March 30. 1790 Received the within mentioned One hundred shares of Bank Stock of Alexander Hamilton. Brockholst Livingston"

To Robert Morris

[*New York, March 30, 1790.* On April 4, 1790, Morris wrote to Hamilton: "Mr. B. Livingston delivered me your favour of the 30th. Ulto." *Letter not found.*]

Treasury Department Circular
to the Collectors of the Customs [1]

Treasury Department
March 30th 1790.

Sir

Having observed that the several Collectors have hitherto differed in the mode of transmitting to this office, the drafts of the Treasurer of the United States which have been drawn on them and paid: I now desire that those drafts with a receipt endorsed on them, may be transmitted, as soon as they are paid, to *my Office*, when they shall be covered by a regular Warrant, and your account credited at the Treasury.

In addition to the receipt on the Bill you may for your own security take a separate receipt from the holder, which you will retain: and as a further precaution, it may be well when you forward those drafts, to do it under the eye of some disinterested person, who, in case the same should miscarry, can give evidence of their having been sent on.

I am, Sir, Your obedt. Servt.   A Hamilton

LS, to Sharp Delany, Bureau of Customs, Philadelphia; LS, to Charles Lee, Charles Lee Papers, Library of Congress; LS, to Benjamin Lincoln, RG 36, Collector of Customs at Boston, Letters from the Treasury, 1790–1810, Vol. 2, National Archives; LS, Office of the Secretary, United States Treasury Department; copy, Circulars of the Treasury Department, 1789–1814, Library of Congress; copy, RG 56, Circulars of the Office of the Secretary, "Set T," National Archives.
1. On the copy of the circular in the Library of Congress there is written "Circular except to Massachusetts." Actually this circular printed above was sent to the collector in Boston, but not to the other collectors in Massachusetts. See "Treasury Department Circular to the Collectors of the Customs in Massachusetts Except Boston," March 30, 1790.

Treasury Department Circular to the Collectors of the Customs in Massachusetts Except Boston [1]

Treasury Department
March 30th 1790

Sir

In mine of the 20th. November last [2] I directed you to take duplicate receits for all monies remitted by you to the Bank of Massachusetts on account of the United States; one of which was intended to be transmitted to the Treasurer and the other to be retained by you.

As some of the Collectors have not sent on this receit under an impression that the same should accompany their quarterly accounts; and as this mode in some instances will occasion a delay in the settlement of those Accounts, it is my wish that the receit in question be in future forwarded *to my Office* immediately upon each payment made in the said Bank in order that the same may be covered by a regular Warrant, and your account credited at the Treasury.

I am Sir Your Obedt. servant   A Hamilton

LS, First National Bank of Boston, Boston; copy, RG 56, Circulars of the Office of the Secretary, "Set T," National Archives.

1. See the "Treasury Department Circular to the Collectors of the Customs," March 30, 1790.
2. "Treasury Department Circular to the Collectors of the Customs in Massachusetts," November 20, 1789.

To Thomas Willing [1]

Treasury Department
March 30th. 1790

Sir

I have delivered to Brockholst Livingston Esquire, who will present you this, One Hundred Shares of Bank Stock, for a purpose which he will explain to you.

Should Mr. Livingston desire it, you will please to transfer the said Bank Stock or so much thereof as he may require, to Robert Morris Esqr. on his Order.

I remain with great respect   Sir   Your Obedient Servant

Thomas Willing Esquire

Copy, Hamilton Papers, Library of Congress.
1. This letter was enclosed in H to Brockholst Livingston, March 30, 1790.

To Samuel A. Otis

Treasury Department
March 31st. 1790

Sir

Upon consideration I have thought it best to issue a Warrant in your favour for two thousand three hundred dollars on account of contingent expences of the Senate &c as it would not be convenient to blend the account, with the Salary due you. For this you can receive a Certificate from the President of the Senate and leave it with the Auditor, who will pass the same in the like manner with other accounts.

I am Sir   Your obedt. Servt.   A Hamilton

Samuel A: Otis Esquire
Secy of the Senate

LS, RG 46, First Congress, 1789–1791, Letters Relating to Fiscal Matters, National Archives.

From George Washington [1]

[New York, March 31, 1790]

The Secretary of the Treasury is hereby authorised to negotiate and agree for a Loan to the United States to an amount not exceeding one hundred thousand Dollars, bearing an Interest not exceeding six ℔. Cent ℔ annum to be applied towards carrying into effect the appropriation made by the Act Entitled, "An Act making appropriations for the support of Government for the year one thousand seven hundred & ninety." [2] and according to the annexed representation. G. Washington

United States ⎫
March 31st. 1790 ⎭

LC, George Washington Papers, Library of Congress; LC, RG 39, Letter Book, 1789–1795, National Archives.
   1. This letter is in reply to H to Washington, March 29, 1790.
   2. 1 *Stat.* 104–06 (March 26, 1790).

To Ædanus Burke [1]

[New York, April 1, 1790]

Sir

I have been informed that in the house of Representatives yesterday, you made use of some very harsh expressions in relation to me.[2]

As I cannot but ascribe so unprovoked an attack to misapprehension or misrepresentation I have concluded to send you an extract from the Eulogium pronounced by me on General Greene, of the part to which alone your animadversions do relate.[3] It is in these words—

"From the heights of Monmouth I might lead you to the *plains of Springfield*, there to behold the Veteran Knyphaussen, at the head of a veteran army, baffled and almost beaten by a General without an army—aided, or rather embarrassed by small fugitive bodies of volunteer militia, *the mimicry of soldiership*."

From this, you will perceive that the epithets, to which you have taken exception, are neither applicable to the Militia *of South Carolina* in particular, nor to *Militia* in general, but merely to *"small fugitive bodies of volunteer* militia."

Having thus Sir stated the matter in its true light it remains for you to judge what conduct, in consequence of the explanation will be proper on your part.[4]

I am Sir   Your humble servt

New York April 1st 1790
Ædanus Burke Esqr

ADf, Hamilton Papers, Library of Congress; copy, Maryland Historical Society, Baltimore.

1. Burke was a Congressman from South Carolina, 1789–91.

2. The following account of Burke's speech of March 31, 1790, was printed on April 15, 1790, in *Greenleaf's New York Journal & Patriotic Register:*

"It has been asserted, said Mr. Burke, by a gentleman who now holds an eminent station under this government—'That the militia were the mere mimickry of soldiery.' This assertion was made before an immense multitude, composed of men of the first distinction, collected from various parts of the United States, and in presence of a splendid assembly of ladies; * and it was universally understood from that day to this, that the assertion referred to the southern militia, and of course to the state which he (Mr. Burke) had the honor of serving. Now, although this reflection was calculated, not only to disgrace the militia in general, but to tarnish the well earned honors and military character of the citizens of South Carolina, yet to have taken any notice of the accusation, at an earlier period than the present, might have been productive of dangerous consequences, nor could he with safety have done it. At the time I allude to, said Mr. Burke, when that gentleman made use of those expressions, prejudices, I was informed, prevailed against me on the score of federal and anti federal politics, and the then very great popularity of the gentleman in this city rendered it an unsafe proceeding of any person to bring on a serious dispute, or to have accused that gentleman of any thing that was improper or illiberal, although the facts had been indisputably ascertained. The present time he thought a more proper one.

"Mr. Burke then, in a solemn manner, declared, that the militia of the southward were not 'the *mimicks* of soldiers.' If they were not highly disciplined, said he, their bravery made more than ample amends for it. For, *long before general Green came to the southward,* they had turned the wind and tide of fortune against the British troops. This can be proved—many—too many of them sacrificed their lives at the holy altar of Liberty. Their graves are to be seen scattered over our glades and woodlands, they are now no more; but in their name, said Mr. Burke, in the presence of this honorable House of Representatives, and in the presence of that very large and respectable assemblage of free citizens (addressing himself to the gallery, which was unusually crouded) I now declare, that the assertion was false! and that the gentleman who expressed it. . . . (Here Mr. Burke was interrupted by a call of order

"* We believe Mr. Burke alluded to the audience, in St. Paul's Church, New-York, where an oration was delivered by Colonel Hamilton, on the 4th July last. The subject was general Green; and the militia were brought *into view* upon the occasion."

by sundry members, particularly Colonel [Theodorick] Bland, who, whilst he could not avoid expressing the most sincere friendship for Mr. Burke, yet he disapproved of his warmth and method of debate in the present instance. Mr. Burke then rose and proceeded nearly as follows.)

"Mr. Chairman, I do not conceive that I have been out of order; the assertion of the person who traduced the militia of South-Carolina, and the retaliation which I have made for it, are connected with the business before the committee; not only the claim on the union for the services of the militia, but the substance and reality of those services, and the national military character of the people, was not only doubted, but denied, by a gentleman, whose assertion, from his high station and talents, must have had some weight. It was from a sense of duty, Mr. Burke said, he had acted in endeavouring to remove so unmerited a reproach; he was sorry he should be supposed to be out of order, and he insisted that he had never been more guarded or cool in his life.

The portion of Burke's remarks about H which Thomas Greenleaf deleted were in a letter from Otho H. Williams to Philip Thomas, April 8, 1790:

"Secretary Hamilton in an Eulogium on Genl Greene delivered by him at the last anniversary of Independance, dropt some words which were considered derogatory to the militia of S C. Mr. Burk after recapitulating their services, and remarking on the expressions which had given offence, said he gladly took that opportunity of giving that Gentleman the lie! and doing justice. He was called to Order stopped, and sat down. After some time he rose, and told the Speaker that he was perfectly cool—*never more so in his life;* And supposing Coll. Hamilton in the gallery which was filled with Ladies, He faced about and said aloud 'I throw the lie in Colonel Hamilton's face.' He was silenced. . . ." (Maryland Historical Society, Baltimore.)

3. See "Eulogy on Nathanael Greene," July 4, 1789.

4. See Burke to H, April 1, 1790; Elbridge Gerry, Rufus King, George Mathews, Lambert Cadwalader, James Jackson, and John Henry to H, April 6, 1790; and Burke to H, April 7, 1790.

From Ædanus Burke

New York 1 April 1790.

Sir.

I was prevented, by business, from answering your letter [1] as early, this day as I wished. I shall now make a few remarks on the subject of it.

The attack which I conceived you made on the southern Militia, was, in my opinion a most unprovoked and cruel one. Whether the candour of your friends conveyed to you any intimation of it I know not: but the occasion will, I hope, excuse me if I assure you that Gentlemen from every quarter of the Union who were present deemed it a charge of a very extraordinary nature. As to myself, I have nothing to do respecting the feelings of others: I ever govern myself by my own. The insult, which I conceived was thrown at me. The too keen misery I felt from it; The recollection I had of it until yesterday: together, with the concurrent testimony of a number of public, and private men who understood you as I did must be, with me, vouchers of equal authenticity with the extract you quote from your performance, which you will recollect you did not read in the delivery of it to the public. That you proclaimed aloud in the face of, I may say, thousands that the Militia were the mere Mimicry of Soldiery: That you spoke these words when you ran into the affairs of the War to the southward, and recounted the exploits of General Greene in that quarter, is not doubted and you will find it on enquiry in this City. You may have forgot it, but some of your Friends and all your acquaintances have not forgot it. You told us besides, that there was not, to the Southward even the Embers (this was the word, I think,) of Spirit to oppose the Enemy until Genl Green arrived there, when it is notorious that the Southern Militia under General Sumpter [2] and other officers, in various desperate conflicts: the Militia of Kings Mountain, and other places, before ever Genl Greene came to s. Carolina had turned the tide of fortune against the veteran troops of Britain; and Yet in sight, and hearing of some of us, who were the representatives of a brave Gallant people, was I told publickly that these men were the mere mimicry of Soldiery.

The torture which the insult inflicted on me I had no other redress for, but to bear it; To call on you in that day would have been down right madness in me. You, on the high full tide of popularity, in your own City: I a stranger, or what little was known of me, unpopular on the score of the cry of the day, against any one suspected of not approving the new Government: Had I called you to account, and hurt a hair of your head, I knew too well the Spectre of Antifederalism would have been conjured up to hunt me down; nor have I any sort or doubt, but that, from the party heats of that period, which thank providence are now subsided I should have been dragged thro' the Kennel, or thrown into east river. And if yesterday I retorted on you rather harshly your own recollection will whisper to you, and your friends will tell you, if I mistake not, that you brought it on yourself. If I did it where you could not reply then are you exactly as I stood the day I alluded to; a situation, from which you may form some Idea, what bitterness you gave me to experience.

Thus I have very candidly, in this disagreeable business explained my feelings and motives. The conduct arising from them was such as, I trust, will stand the enquiry of all whose approbation I am fond of: Men of Sensibility and honor.

I am, Sir, Your most obedt. servt. Æ—B

The Honble A—H—Esqr.[3]

Copy, in writing of Otho H. Williams, Maryland Historical Society, Baltimore.
1. H to Burke, April 1, 1790.
2. General Thomas Sumter, leader of guerrilla troops in the Carolinas, 1780–1782, and Antifederalist Congressman from South Carolina, 1789–1793.
3. The following comment by Burke, also in Williams's writing, appears at the bottom of this letter:
"It is to be observed that this answer was written the same day with Coll. H's letter. In the order of the correspondence it was Coll H's next move. He waited, however, from the first until the fourth, when he sends his friend Mr. Rufus King to offer propositions of accomodation honorable to both of us, Thro' Mr. Gerry, my friend, this offer was accordingly accepted by me."
See Elbridge Gerry, Rufus King, George Mathews, Lambert Cadwalader, James Jackson, and John Henry to H. April 6, 1790.

From Théophile Cazenove [1]

[New York, April 1, 1790]

Les lumières et l'intégrité du Ministre des finances sont constatés par les principes qu'il établit et qu'il developpe dans le raport qu'Il a delivré le 14 Janvier dr.[2] Il y fait aux Citoyens des Etats Unis un présent digne d'Eux, en les engageant d'établir un ordre sage et immuable dans leurs finances et en les detournant de la funeste im-

AL, Hamilton Papers, Library of Congress.
1. Cazenove had been sent to the United States late in 1789 as the representative of the Dutch banking houses of Pieter Stadnitski and Son, Nicholaas and Jacob Van Staphorst, Ten Cate and Vollenhoven, and P. and C. Van Eeghen, who were interested in purchasing into the Federal liquidated debt. Between 1792 and 1794 these firms, joined by Wilhem and Jan Willink and Rutger Jan Schimmelpennick, speculated widely in lands in western New York and Pennsylvania, and in 1796 the six firms formed the Holland Land Company. Throughout this period Cazenove remained the agent and chief American representative of the group.
2. "Report Relative to a Provision for the Support of Public Credit," January 9, 1790.

politique de mepriser la foy publique. Ce raport constate les travaux et les soucis auxquels le ministre se dévoue; avec quels soins il veut écarter les désordres qui naitroient de l'infidelité, et qu'il consideroit Comme des Calamités, les resolutions qui terniroient l'honneur et les loyautés que les creanciers des Etats Unis attendent d'une nation qui s'est deja tant honorablement distinguée.

On conçoit donc que cette partie des dispositions, qui, dans le plan de la consolidation de la dette de l'Etat, rècule le payement du tiers des intérets, ne doit être attribuée qu'à des circonstances momentanées et locales, trop imperieuses et d'une nature trop délicate pour qu'un étranger s'en puisse permettre la discussion. Mais on croit ne pas s'ecarter de son devoir en soumettant à l'attention du Ministre quelques details relatifs à l'effet qu'aura necessairement en Hollande, le retard d'un tiers des intérets sur les Capitaux des Liquidated Debt. On espère que le Ministre ne croira point que ces representations sont dictées par d'ingènereux motifs. Les Hollandais savent, qu'un crèancier sage ne doit pas tout laisser faire au debiteur intègre qui cherche à s'acquiter honorablemt, et le simple mouvement d'un intérêt bien entendu, féra cò-operer aux mesures proposées dans le raport, ceux qui seront dans la position de pouvoir traitter directement de cet objet. Tels seront surtout les sentimens des maisons de Commerce, qui dans Amsterdam, dirigent les Emprunts pour les Etats Unis,[3] et les Emprunts sur les créances dont ces Etats ont reconnu la validité. Le carracterre moral et la fortune de ces Directeurs est tout à la fois la source du grand credit dont ils jouissent et le guarant de leur empressement à soutenir toutes les mesures qui s'accorderont avec l'interet permanent de ceux, qui, sur leurs avis, ont fait l'acquisition de Liquidated Debts. Le Ministre ne rendroit pas justice à ces Directeurs s'il ne les distinguoit pas de cette espéce de speculateurs qui ne s'inquietent point du sort des effets qu'ils revendent au public, et dont l'objet est simplement de saisir, de créer même, des apparences momentanément favorable pour revendre à haut prix, ce qu'ils ont acquis à bon marché.

Les Directeurs des Emprunts sur les Liquidated Debts, infidelement informés en 1786 acquirent les Certificats au taux de 60 pCt,

3. The Willinks, Van Staphorsts, and Nicholas Hubbard were the Dutch "directors" of the United States loans.

et persuadés que c'etoit le veritable taux du marché, ils ont recedé à
ce prix & au public Hollandois, Ces Capitaux de Liq: Debt, en en
subdivisant la propriété dans la forme et suivant l'usage de ces sortes
de transactions. Lorsqu'ils se sont apperçus du trop haut prix qu'ils
avoient payé, ces Directeurs se sont decidé à faire individuelemen
des sacrifices afin de prevenir le prejudice qu'une premiére erreur
pouvoit faire aux acquereurs des portions partielles qu'ils ont mis
dans la Circulation. C'est dans ce principe et dans le désir de maintenir le Credit des Etats Unis, que jusques au moment actuel, ces Directeurs ont payé, depuis 1787, & à chaque Semêstre, les Intérets sur
les Liquidated Debt, a raison des 6 pCt. qui y sont affectés. Le Ministre sait que cependant ces Directeurs n'ont rien touché pour cet
objet, & connoissant l'ètendue et l'èpoque des Capitaux de Liq: Debt
que les Holl. possèdent, le Ministre pourra connoitre l'etendue du
debours dans lequel les Directeurs se trouvent. C'est dans ce principe
encore que les Directeurs des Emprunts favoriseront toutes les mesures qui etabliront la solidité rèelle des effets qu'ils ont revendu, non
point à des speculateurs passagers, mais à cette partie du public qui
n'acquiert que pour transmettre de pere en fils, les effets qui occupent
leurs Capitaux. Ces Directeurs se consoleroit difficilement d'avoir été
les entremetteurs d'une operation onèreuse à ceux qui se seroient
confiés à leur examen: sous ce raport leur intéret est toujours à
l'unison de leur integrité, en ce que plus ils sont jaloux de maintenir
intacte la reputation de prudence que leurs bons procedés leur ont
acquise, plus ils augmentent leurs forces pour pouvoir exècuter de
plus brillantes affaires: En s'ecartant des vrais principes d'ordre et de
credit, ils detruiroient l'oiseau qui chaque jour leur donne un oeuf
précieux. Consequement l'interet de ceux qui dirigent les Emprunts
de Hollande, et l'interet des Hollandois proprietaires des crèances à
la charge des Etats Unis est absolument à l'unison de l'interet de ces
mêmes Etats Unis, puisque tout ce qui tend à l'augmentation de la
prosperité, c'est à dire de la solidité permanente des derniers, tend à
conserver les proprietés des deux premiers. C'est un ordre de choses
dont l'effet est de Confondre et de reunir en un seul intéret, les trois
interets qui au premier aspect paroissent différens; Lorsque le ministre
aura sur ce fait les informations qu'il pourra se procurer, on croit, que
toutes les fois qu'Il proposera des levées d'argent en Hollande, le
Ministre jugera utile aux Interets des Etats Unis, de laisser aux maison

chargées de ses Emprunts, la decision, de la forme et des conditions; du moment et de l'etendue de ces Emprunts, persuadé, que ces maisons ne détermineront que des conditions salutaires au Credit des Etats Unis et dans une proportion exacte entre la nature des besoins des Etats et la possibilité de les remplir.

Ce n'est donc qu'en Consideration du rapport qui subsiste entre les interets des Etats Unis et le carracterre des Capitaliste Hollandois qu'on prend la liberté d'informer le ministre des circonstances et de l'organisation des Emprunts qui ont eté faits en Hollande, et la liberté de constater combien la nature de ces Emprunts s'adapte mal aux arrangemens de finances qui reculent le payement du tiers des interets. On croit pouvoir poser pour principes

1e: que l'exploitation des vastes domaines des Etats Unis; l'etablissement des manufactures qui doivent y procurer une balance de commerce moins onereuse; les secours que l'industrieuse activité de leurs laborieux habitan reclâment de toute part; et surtout le mouvement qu'il faut donner à la circulation, exigent que l'administration suplée par des Emprunts dans l'Etranger, au manque de numeraire qui obstruie l'èlan general vers une grande puissance nationale.

2e: qu'à l'exeption de quelques sommes bornèes que les genoisons, les flamans pourront peut être fournir, c'est uniquement des Hollandois que les Etats Unis peuvent attendre les secours d'argent dont ils auront successivement le besoin.

3e: que les Capitalistes Hollandois ne laissant jamais leurs Capitaux oisifs, ce n'est que le produit de leurs épargnes ou celui de quelques remboursemens extraordinaires, qui fournit les sommes necessaires au remplissement des Emprunts Etrangers qui s'ouvrent en Hollande; qu'exiger des Hollandois une somme trop considerable à la fois, c'est exiger l'impossible: qu'en Hollande, les levées d'argent qui ne surpassent point la somme de deux ou trois millions de florins sont toujours faciles et promptes lorsque la Confiance publique porte l'argent de ce coté la. Que d'autre part, les besoins des Etats Unis ne seront jamais que graduels et bornés, qu'ainsi il existera constamment une proportion entre l'oeconomie Hollandoise et la moderation americaine: que de ces dispositions respectives il resulte des rapports, lesquels, s'ils sont sagement menagés, assureront dans tous les temps des ressources aux Etats Unis. qu'il suffira pour cela que l'administrateur des finances des E.U. plie les conditions à la mesure des prejugés et des habitudes d'un peuple sévère pour tout ce qui tient aux formes et à l'exactitude. Que le Ministre exploitera avantageusement la confiance des Hollandois, s'il maintient auprés d'eux le credit des Etats Unis dans une pureté extrême, et il ne doit pas règretter quelques sacrifices, pour conserver cette fleur de credit que les agens des E. U. ont plantée et cultiveé avec un soin, qui ne demande plus qu'un arōsement prudent pour devenir un fruit utile à tous les interessés.

4e: que les Hollandois sont habituées au respect le plus minutieux pour les engagemens qu'ils prenent, et qu'ls exigent une fidelité qui doit s'ètendre jusques à la minute dont on est convenu avec eux. Que gènèralèment les Capitalistes Hollandois ne preñent pas la peine d'examiner par eux même la Solidité des placemens d'argent qu'on leur propose, mais qu'ils s'en remettent à l'integrité & à la prudence des maisons qui protégent et presentent les Emprunts publics. Que consequemment leur confiance reposant sur un prejugé favorable plutot que sur une connoissance exacte, cette confiance se renverse au plus léger retard des remboursemens ou des interets promis. Qu'une fois inquietés sur ces sujets dans un placement ainsi fait, ils ne veulent plus s'exposer a de nouvelles apprehensions sur la solidité d'une proprieté semblable; qu'ils veulent encore moins se donner l'embarras d'examiner les circonstances qui bonifient l'espece d'effets qu'un manque d'exactitude a terni à leurs yeux; Et que toujours environnés d'occasions pour le solide employ de leurs fonds, il faut ensuite un longtemp et un concours extraordinaires de circonstances pour que les capitalistes Hollandois reviennent du prejugé qu'ils ont pris contre la solidité d'un effet qui aura une fois desapointé leur attente.

5e: que celles des Puissances qui ont veillé au maintien de leur Credit, & qui ont peut être usé à cet effet d'une sage charlatanerie, ont toujours trouvé des Secours en Hollande, et continueroient d'en trouver lors même qu'ils n'en méritent plus, si la delicatesse des Directeurs des Emprunts, n'eclairoit pas le public et n'arretoit pas le courant de sa confiance.

———————

Les maisons d'amsterdam sur le nom des quels la proprieté des grandes masses de Liquidated Debts sont inscrites sur ces Livres des E.U. ne sont point les propriètaires de ces fonds: ils ne les possedent qu'en qualité de *Trustees*.

Ceux qui dans Amsterdam ont acquis primitivement ces *Liq: Debts*
ont un commerce courrant d'effets publics: La nature de leurs affaires
est un mouvement constant d'acquisitions et de reventes. Afin de
faciliter cette revente et la circulation des fonds dont ils se chargent
en masses, ils les subdivisent en portions n'excedant pas la valeur de
f1000., et ils donnent aux titres de proprieté qu'ils font circuler une
forme que l'usage a consacré.

La premiere acquisition de Liquidated Debts qui s'est faite en
Hollande s'èlevoit à un capital de 840,000 Dollars. On les paya a
raison de 60 pCt. de leur valeur, ainsi on paya B 5,024,000 ceux ci
au change de 47 par Dollars coûterent dont f 1200,000; Cr. D'Holl.

Les Directeurs firent transferrer le capital de 840,000 B Liq. Debts
sur les noms des personnes qui jouissent de la confiance publique. Ils
subdiviserent la proprieté de ces 840,000 en Douze cens parts &
créerent douze cens titres ou obligation de f 1000; chaque portion
d'interet ayant, suivant les termes de Contrat, le droit à une douze
centieme portion des B 840,000. Ces obligations ont été débitées au
public Hollandois.
   Lorsque ces premieres 1200. portions ont eté dèbitées, les Directeurs ont acquis de nouvelles quantitées de Liquidated Debts, et toujours par masses de B 840,000, subdivisées sur les mêmes principes
que la premiere partie.

On calcule qu'actuelement il s'est consolidé *cinq* masses d'Emprunts chaqu'un de B 840,000, representés par 1200. obligations,
consequemmen une proprieté totale de 4,200,000 Dollars Capl. Liquidated Debt, representé par Six mille obligations, ou portions
d'intérêt actuellement circulant dans les Provinces Unies, et appart-
nant par petites parties de 1, 2, 3, 4, 6, ou tout au plus 10 obligations,
à un nombre eparpillé de capitalistes et de bourgeois Hollandois.

Les conditions aux quelles ces 6000. portions d'interet ont été
acquises sont détaillées et pronouncées dans le corps des 6000. titres
de proprieté qui circulent. On y promet la repartition annuelle des
interets de Six pour Cent qui se doivent payer par les Etats Unis sur
les capitaux des Liquidated Debt inscrit au nom des *Trustees*.

L'organisation de cette repartition a eté arrêtée a Convenance,
sur le principe, d'employer les ⅔ de la somme d'interets que les Etats

Unis doivent payer, pour Acquiter l'interet annuel des sommes de-boursées, et d'employer le ⅓ restant, au remboursement d'une quan-tité finie d'obligation sois portions de f 1000 qui sont dans la circula-tion.

Chaque Emprunt possedant un Capital de B 840,000 doit recevoir pour les interets de ce Capital à raison de 6 pCt. une somme annuelle de B 50,400. les quels, aprés la deduction de quelques frais produisent tous les ans f 110,000. Cr. D'hollande et doivent se partager entre les porteurs de chaque 1200. portions.
savoir f 72000. pour acquiter à chaque portion de f 1000 une somme
de f 60. Et f 38000. pour rembourser 36 portions de f 1000
avec une prime de 3 pCt pour chaque année de debours.
NB La partie chiffrée du plan imprimé[4] annexé au present me-moire expliquera plus distinctement ces details et comment par l'accumulation des interets composés, les f 1200000 Cr d'Hs. sont primitif des B 840000 se trouveront remboursés la Vingt cinquieme anneé, si les interets soit les B 50400. sont payés tous les ans par les Etats Unis; Et comment cependan a l'issue de ce terme les proprie-taires de 1200. obligations resteront chaque portion pour 1/1200 part, proprietaires du Capital de B 840,000 Liq: Debt.
Mais si au lieu de recevoir B 50400 pour interets a 6 pCt sur chaque B 840,000, les Directeurs ne recoivent que 4 pCt. soit B 33600. Ils seront dans l'impossibilité de executer les *remboursemens annuels* qui sont annoncés au public. Ils devront *publier* la *reduction* des interets et la *decomposition* des conditions primitives du Contract. Et vu le nombre de six mille portions qui sont repandues partout, cette publi-cation devra nècessairement èveiller l'attention de tout le corps des Capitalistes.

On croit qu'il est de l'interet des Etats Unis d'èviter cet eclat en Hollande et d'y prevenir une impression qui arretera la confiance que les Hollandois ont actuelement dans la bonne foi et la puissance des moyens des Etats Unis. Sans se donner la peine d'examiner la Cause de ces retards, les Hollandois ne seront frappés que de l'effet: Ils cèsseront de considerer les titres à la charge des Etats Unis comme une proprieté sur la quelle ils peuvent irrevocablement compter, Et les Etats Unis ne pourront plus lever en Hollande les sommes dont

4. The printed plan, in Dutch, may be found in the Hamilton Papers, Library of Congress.

ils auront besoin, ni si facilement, ni a aussi bon compte; Ils s'expose-
ront même à la possibilité de ne pouvoir point y trouver une somme
importante.

Sans doute le resultat des principes du Rapport et l'arreté du
Comité [5] laissent un grand espoir pour le payement subsequent des
2pCt dont le payement sera differé, mais, si le ministre n'a rien pro-
noncé de fini sur cet objet, pour laisser peut être au gros de la nation
l'espoir confus d'être debarrassé de cette charge, ce manque de *pro-
noncé* fera le même effet sur les esprits peu clairvoyan en Hollande;
ces derniers ont d'ailleur l'experience du peu de fond qu'il faut faire
sur les promesses surrogatoires et eloigneés des grandes puissances.
Enfin on croit qu'il seroit prudent de ne pas donner l'occasion au
public Hollandois de fixer son attention sur les ressources finantielles
Des Etats Unis, aussi longtemp que la perception des revenus y sera
un article de probabilités plutot qu'un point de fait.

Les Cinq Emprunts possedant un Capital de quatre millions deux
cens mille Dollars Liquidated Debt, le deficit des 2 pCt s'elevera
annuelement à B 84000. soit environs f 200,000. Cour. D'Hollande
et pour les dix années l'objet sera Deux millions de florins. Cette
somme annuelle au totale est trop considerable pour s'attendre à ce
que les Directeurs, dejà en de si grands débours, continuent à se
charger du payement exact des interets & des remboursemens promis
aux porteurs des 6000 portions. Les Directeurs devront être effi-
cassement soutenu à cet égard par les moyens que le Ministre des
finances leur fournira.

Il ne sera pas necessaire de procurer d'abord la totalité des deux
millions: Il suffira de hâter les dispositions pour subvenir aux paye-
mens des premieres années, ensuite on pourra voir quels moyens les
èvenemens dèvelopperont dans la suite.

Le ministre des finances connoit trop bien les forces et les circonstances du fisc qu'il dirige pour ne pas trouver dans ses lumieres un

5. Upon receipt of H's report the House resolved itself into a Committee
of the Whole "to take into consideration the said report and papers" (*Journal
of the House*, I, 141). Although the debates of the Committee of the Whole
were not concluded until April 26, a number of resolutions amplifying the
report were introduced on February 8, by William L. Smith of South Carolina
and Thomas FitzSimons of Pennsylvania.

moyen qui soit tout à la fois adapté aux convenances des Etats Unis et à l'objet de fournir aux Directeurs des Emprunts, les valeurs necessaires au ponctuel acquit des engagemens pris avec le public. Une nouvelle levée d'argent en Hollande pour le compte des Etats Unis Sembleroit fournir un moyen fort simple & assez sècret. Les Agens des Etats Unis pourroit être authorisés à recevoir des Directeurs des Emprunts sur le Liq. Debt les titres des 2 pCt. amènés, au lieu et place d'argent comptant pour l'acquit des sommes qu'ils prendroient dans les Emprunts nouveaux et cela pour un montant ègal au deficit sur les 4,200,000 Dollars, & au deficit d'un autre Emprunt sur 500,000 Dollars qui est organisé sur un autre plan que ceux des B 840,000. Ces 500,000 B. sont ceux qui doivent être inscrit sur les registres comme la propriété de *Est Lespinasse J.ten caten Geb: Kops et Chn. van Eeghen,* qui sont les *Trustees* de cet Emprunt là.

Il seroit bien à desirer que l'on put informer les Directeurs d'Amsterdam des intentions du Ministre relativement à cet important objet, afin qu'ils puissent régler leurs mesures sur la probabilité de *pouvoir* ou de ne *pouvoir pas* èsperer des faciltiés qui previendront le choc du discredit que l'on apprèhende. On comprend combien sur cet objet le ministre peut difficilement rien prononcer encore, mais il lui sera possible de juger de la possibilité ou de l'impossibilité d'un pareil arrangement. On attendra de sa bonté les explications qu'il jugera convenable de donner, et qu'on desireroit pouvoir faire passer en Hollande par le premier paquet Anglois destiné pour Falmouth.

New York   ce 1e Avril 1790

From Meletiah Jordan

Frenchman's Bay [*District of Maine*] *April 1, 1790.* ". . . The severity of the weather has prevented any exportations or importations (were they admissable) for this last Quarter, so that my sending blank returns of such business will I hope be dispensed with. . . . There is no possible mode of remitting from hence but in Specie to Boston, by Coasting Vessels. I must confess I would not wish to send such sums on my own risk therefore shall be glad you would point out what I must adopt for such remittance with safety to myself, & satisfaction to the United States. . . . I have in my last letters to you Sir represented the detached situation of the district, and the necessity of having a Boat to perform services. . . ."

LC, RG 56, Letters to Collectors at Gloucester, Machias, and Frenchman's Bay, National Archives.

To William Duer

[New York, April 4–7, 1790] [1]

While I truly regret, my dear friend, that the necessity of your situation compels you to relinquish a station in which public and personal considerations combine to induce me to wish your continuance, I cannot but be sensible of the force of the motives by which you are determined.[2] And I interest myself in your happiness too sincerely not to acquiesce in whatever may redound to your advantage. I confess, too, that *upon reflection* I cannot help thinking you have decided rightly.

I count with confidence on your future friendship, as you may on mine.

An engagement at the President's will not let me meet you at dinner, but I shall be happy to see you in the evening.

Adieu—God bless you, and give you the success for which you will always have the warmest wishes of   Your affectionate

A Hamilton.

JCHW, V, 444–45.
    1. J. C. Hamilton dates this letter 1789, but Lodge (*HCLW*, IX, 466) places it at the beginning of 1790. Joseph S. Davis concludes that Duer resigned as Assistant Secretary of the Treasury in late March or early April, 1790 (Davis, *Essays*, I, 176–77). Both Timothy Pickering and Tench Coxe wrote to H on April 6, 1790, asking for the position formerly held by Duer. Pickering states that "Last evening a gentleman called on me to inform me of Mr. Duer's resignation; and to urge me to apply for the vacant office." On the basis of Pickering's statement and on the assumption that H wrote immediately after Duer had resigned, this letter has been dated April 4–7, 1790.
    2. In discussing Duer's "motives," Davis has written:
    ". . . A potent reason, apparently, was the removal of the seat of government to Philadelphia and Duer's unwillingness to leave New York. Doubtless the growth of his business interests, particularly in connection with the Scioto Company and security dealings, made clear to him the unwisdom of further division of his time with official duties. Probably also he and Hamilton became conscious of at least the *political* inadvisability of his combining the office with

his business interests, in view of the outspoken criticism of "speculators" and complaints of the connection of the Treasury Department with speculation. . . . Certainly speculation in securites was not *legally* consistent with service in the Treasury Department. . . ." (Davis, *Essays,* I, 176–77.)

From Brockholst Livingston

Philadelphia 4. April 1790

D sir,

I arrived here on thursday, but Mr. Morris [1] being engaged in Court, I could not deliver him your letter [2] until the next day which prevented your hearing from me by the last post.

Mr. Morris wishes two alterations to take place in the Contract.[3] The one is that the money be not payable in London. The other is that the price on the forty shares for which he has deposited with you public securities be included in the mortgage which he is to give for the One hundred, & that his certificates be returned. As your Instructions on the first point are explicit, and totally silent on the latter I could consent to neither without your approbation.

As to the security offered, from the information I have received & a view of the property, I believe it competent to the payment of £ 10,500 sterling even on a sale for cash. Some gentlemen estimate it at £ 30,000 this currency, but Mr. Tench Coxe, who appears to have taken the greatest pains, and has favored me with an estimate in writing, values it at only £ 19,750. He thinks that by selling the estate in parcels it would produce much more. If however you consent to take a mortgage for the one hundred & forty shares it will be prudent to desire Mr. Morris to include some other property in it for if Mr. Coxes valuation is to be relied on it will not be safe to trust to the estate he now offers for the repayment of £ 14,700 sterling.

I have desired Mr. Morris to insure the buildings against fire, which is not yet done.

If you dispense with payment in London, I am advised to take a bond & mortgage in the common form, but as no proceedings can be had on the mortgage until a year after default has been made,

Mr. Morris consents to execute a warrant of Attorney to confess Judgment in any State or federal Court.

I am Sir, with respect your very obedt servant

Brockholst Livingston

The honble A. Hamilton Esqr

ALS, Hamilton Papers, Library of Congress.
  1. Robert Morris.
  2. Letter not found.
  3. See Morris to H, November 13, 1789; H to Livingston, March 30, 1790; Thomas Willing to H, February 24, 1790; and H to Willing, March 30, 1790.

From Robert Morris

Philada. April 4th. 1790

Dear Sir

Mr B. Livingston delivered your favour of the 30th. ulto.[1] on Thursday which He has made the needfull inquiries and is perfectly satisfied as to the Value & Title of my Ten Alley Estate.[2]

But your letter to me and instructions to him[3] have raised two difficulties which I did not expect. You require the payment to be made in London, nothing of this kind was mentioned that I recollect. My proposition was to pay £100 Stg for each share in twelve Months, and it was my expectation to make that payment here, because if I engage to pay in London the Credit would only be nine or Ten, instead of Twelve Months as I must so much sooner purchase bills to make the remittance. If however you prefer to have the payment made in London fix it for fifteen Months from the day the Stock is assigned & I agree. The other matter is respecting the forty Shares which having been included in our agreement, I had in Consequence of the liberation of my Certificates taken measures for obtaining some More Money in order to pay more of my debts whilst the Exchange is so favourable. If therefore I mortgage my Ten alley Estate for a part only of the purchase & leave the Certificates pledged for the redemption of the other part, you will unnecessarily do me a prejudice which I am sure you would not wish to do, I say unnecessarily, because the Estate is an Ample Security for the whole & would sell for much more at any Moment. I hope therefore that your answer will remove these two obstacles & we will perfect the business at once. Last night I had an opportunity to Speak to some of the Directors of the Bank. They promised that your wishes should be complied with and I believe Mr Fitzsimmons [4] who goes for N York in the Morning will be authorized to assure you of it. With great regard

I remain Dr Sir   Your most obedt & humble Servant

Robt Morris

The Honble Alexr Hamilton Esqr
New York

ALS, Hamilton Papers, Library of Congress.
  1. Letter not found.
  2. See Brockholst Livingston to H, April 4, 1790.
  3. See H to Livingston, March 30, 1790.
  4. Thomas FitzSimons was a director of the Bank of North America and a Congressman from Pennsylvania.

From William Short

Paris April the 4th. 1790

Sir

In my letter of the 28th. of January & the postscript of the 31st. of the same month, which I had the honor of addressing you, I made you acquainted with the then situation of the debt due by America to France & the precipitate loan negociated by the bankers [1] of the United States at Amsterdam. I informed you at the same time that I did not doubt a stop would be thus put to Mr. Neckers [2] negociation with some gentlemen here for the purchase of the American debt.[3] I find at present that the loan has produced another effect also which it was natural enough to apprehend. The Minister who was fully disposed to treat the American debt in such a manner as to give the greatest possible facility to Congress, finding now that they have three millions of florins at their disposal, & feeling every day the pressure of present exigencies, views the subject somewhat differently. He went fully into it with me some days ago.

ALS, letterpress copy, William Short Papers, Library of Congress.
  1. Willink, Van Staphorst, and Hubbard.
  2. Jacques Necker, French Director General of the Finances.
  3. For information on the plans for the purchase of the American debt, see Short to H, November 30, 1789, and January 28–31, 1790.

After complaining of the conduct of our bankers who had precipitated this loan in order to prevent his completing the negotiation which he had begun for the transfer of the American debt in a manner which would have been honorable & advantageous for all parties & that after having made him propositions themselves which were inadmissible even in the present distresses of the finances, he added that he hoped I would take on myself to give him an order on them for the three millions of florins at present in their hands. He stated the circumstances under which France had made her advances to the United States, & the embarassed situation in which she was at present—he did not doubt that Congress would regard this as the most sacred of their debts, & thought it impossible, now that they had the money at their command, they could refuse to discharge a part of that debt. I easily convinced him of the impossibility of my taking on myself to give such an order. I added my doubts whether the bankers who had undertaken this loan without consulting me,[4] would consider themselves bound by my order, & further that not knowing in what light Congress would view the loan undertaken in so unwarrantable a manner, I could not think of engaging in a business of the propriety of which I could not possibly judge without some indication from you. He was satisfied with my observations on this subject. He added that he hoped it would occasion only a small delay, as it was impossible Congress could refuse to acknowlege a loan negociated on advantageous terms, & equally impossible that having acknowleged it, they should refuse to discharge with it a part of their debt to France. He begged I would write to you fully on this subject & mention that he (Mr. Necker) had sollicited it. You will easily perceive from hence Sir the present situation of the minds of ministry relative to our debt & loan lately made in Amsterdam. The decision of Congress will certainly be taken before the arrival of this letter. Still I write it as a discharge of my promise made to Mr. Necker. I suppose it useless to repeat here the advantage which might be derived from Congress having some representative in Europe authorized to control their finances at Amsterdam. The late step of the bankers shews that they must otherwise be exposed to be embarassed by measures

4. See Short to H, January 28–31, 1790.

which may be entered into subservient rather to private speculations than public good.

I have endeavoured to find out what has been the late rate of
loans made in Amsterdam by other powers—one part of the loan
is always public, that is to say, the interest which the real lender
recieves from the borrower—the lowest rate of this for some time
past has been 5 ₱ Cent ₱ Ann.—but there is another part of the
loan called commission, which the parties are always unwilling
should be known. This commission is sometimes as high as 9 or 10
₱ Cent. The commission we pay, you know, is much lower & I
thought from some enquiries I had made that the King of Sweden
in the last loan he made had paid a commission still lower than ours.
I have since been assured that he paid a commission of about 5 ₱
Cent. From equally good authority I was assured not long ago that
the commission was really not more than 1. ₱ Cent for all charges.
I recieved this assurance twice—still as this is the banker's secret,
it is difficult to ascertain it fully. The person from whom I get the
information is a Dutchman of large fortune, & on an intimate footing with the person who procured this loan for Sweden—he is not
at all interested in business—he thinks that the United States, from
the present rate of their stocks at Amsterdam, & from their present
flourishing situation, ought to borrow money on better terms than
any power at war & particularly on better terms than Sweden—
this however is only the private opinion of a private man. I have
not yet recieved your plan of finance proposed to Congress,[5] but
I have heard that your opinion there is that Congress could borrow
in Europe at 4 ₱ Cent ₱ Ann. The bankers here think that could
not be done. Still they all agree that a good commission properly
employed would produce a considerable effect, & particularly if
Congress begin to re-imburse a part of the principal of their debt.

It may not be improper to inform you that a person left this
place a few days ago with a large sum in specie to go & purchase
the public securities in America. Although I know of this person
only with certainty, yet I have no doubt the present situation of
affairs will induce many others to adopt the same plan. As nothing

5. Short is referring to H's "Report Relative to a Provision for the Support
of Public Credit," January 9, 1790.

has been done by Congress to prevent these foreign speculations in their funds it is probable they have found it impracticable. Still the circumstance of this person's departure worthy your notice as it is for indication of a spirit which may become extensive.

Another scheme which has been set on foot here & which regards in some measure the United States has lately come to my knowlege. The Sioto Company which has been for some time selling the lands which they purchased from Congress,[6] in order to facilitate these sales, propose to recieve in payment debts due by France to individuals provided the government will recieve of them those sums & transfer to them an equal part of the debt due by the United States to France. It is certain they have been in correspondence with M. Lambert[7] the Controller general who seems disposed to adopt the plan. Yet Mr. Necker told me some days ago in speaking of the American debt that no such plan would be entered into. I suppose the reason is that under the pressure of the present moment he chuses to make use of the American debt as a means of commanding real cash rather than discharging a small part of the immense debt at present exigible. The various attempts which are thus making as well here as at Amsterdam to speculate on the American debt shew the necessity of the sentiments of Congress being made known here in order that these circumstances may be adapted to their views. I flatter myself with the hopes of hearing from you ere long on these subjects. In the mean time I beg you to recieve assurances of the sentiments of respect with which I have the honor to be Sir, your most obedient humble servant   W. Short

The Honble. Mr. Hamilton

6. In July, 1787, the Scioto Company, which was composed of a group of speculators headed by William Duer, had secured from Congress an option on approximately five million acres of land in the Ohio Valley. Joel Barlow had gone to France as the agent of the Scioto Company, and while there had organized the *Compagnie du Scioto* to sell the company's lands.
7. Charles Guillaume Lambert.

From William Allibone

Philadelphia, April 5, 1790. ". . . Agreeably to your circular letter, of the fifth of October last, the several establishments in the Bay and River Deleware have had every necessary attention paid

to them. . . . A scarcity and rise in the article of oyl is likely to
take place owing to the demand for the European Market, and the
moment any is landed here it is bot. up for that purpose, this has
Induced me to venture to engage beforehand from the Importers,
by whom we have usually been supplied, the Quantity likely to be
wanted for the ensuing year. . . ."

ALS, RG 26, Lighthouse Letters Received, Vol. "A," Pennsylvania and Southern States, National Archives.

Receipt from Benjamin Walker [1]

[New York] April 5, 1790. Has received "One hundred Pounds
New York Cury in Specie on acco of Baron Steuben."

ADS, Hamilton Papers, Library of Congress.
    1. During the Revolution Walker had been aide to Baron von Steuben, and
in 1789 he was appointed naval officer for New York.

From Tench Coxe

[Philadelphia, April 6, 1790. On May 1, 1790, Hamilton wrote
to Coxe: "Yours of the 6th of the same month also came to hand."
Letter not found.]

From Elbridge Gerry, Rufus King, George Mathews, Lambert Cadwalader, James Jackson, and John Henry [1]

New york April 6, 1790

The Subscribers appointed on the part of Mr. Hamilton and Mr.
Burke to consider whether there was an honorable Ground of accomodation between the parties in respect to certain Expressions
made use of by Mr. Burke in the house of Representatives on Wednesday last, relatively to an Eulogium pronounced by Mr. Hamilton on general Green on the 4th. of July last, having inquired into
the Circumstances, and perused the Letters which were inter-
changed by those Gentlemen on the first instant are of Opinion

that nothing more is necessary to an accomodation between them, than a right understanding of each other.²

As while on the one hand it appears from satisfactory information, that Mr. Burke did not conceive the letter from Mr. Hamilton to amount to an explicit Disavowal of an intention in any part of the Eulogium delivered by him, to cast a reflection upon militia in general, or upon the militia of South Carolina in particular; so on the other from like information it appears to us that it was Mr. Hamilton's intention in that letter to make such disavowal.

We are therefore of opinion that a proper and honorable ground of accomodation between the Parties will be, that Mr. Hamilton in another letter to Mr. Burke make an explicit declaration of his intention as above understood; and that Mr. Burke in consequence of it make to Mr. Hamilton a full and satisfactory apology for whatever on his part has taken place on the subject offensive to Mr. Hamilton.³

That as considerations resulting from the nature of the precedent in reference to the privileges of the House, render the propriety of the apology in the house questionable, we are farther of Opinion that the apology be made by Letter.

E Gerry.
R. King
Geo Mathews
Lambert Cadwalader
Jas Jackson
J. Henry

The honorable Alexander Hamilton. Esqre.

LS, Hamilton Papers, Library of Congress.

1. Gerry was a Congressman from Massachusetts; King was a Senator from New York; Mathews and Jackson were Congressmen from Georgia; Henry was a Senator from Maryland; and Cadwalader was a Congressman from Pennsylvania.

2. For information on the dispute between Ædanus Burke and H, see the exchange of letters between them on April 1, 1790.

On April 8, 1790, William Loughton Smith, Federalist Congressman from South Carolina, wrote to Otho H. Williams:

". . . the quarrell mentioned to you in my last is accommodated, by arbitration of Six Members of Congress, consisting of both houses.

"The Secy has explained, that he did not mean any reflection on the Militia in general or that of Carolina in particular. Mr. Burke, satisfied with the explanation, is sorry for having made use of any expression that should wound the feelings of the Secy or the house, whether there will be any Statement, or publication of this transaction I Know not." (Maryland Historical Society, Baltimore.)

3. See Burke to H, April 7, 1790.

From Benjamin Lincoln

Boston, April 6, 1790. "I have just now had with me Mr. Thomas,[1] son of the late General Thomas, whose Mother has the care of Light house at Plymouth.[2] When she was first appointed to that trust he was a minor otherwise he probably would have had the appointment himself. He is a Young Gentleman of a good character and I think is a fair candidate for the appointment under the United States. I have received a return from . . . the keeper of the light in Boston harbour & from . . . the keeper of the light at Cape Ann. They accept with gratitude thier appointments under the United States. . . . I am forming a contract for Oyl, to the 15th of August next . . . as soon as I can close the Matter I will lay it before you four your approbation or rejection. . . ."

ALS, RG 26, Lighthouse Letters Received, Vol. "B," New Hampshire and Massachusetts, National Archives; LC, RG 36, Collector of Customs at Boston, Letter Book, 1790–1797, National Archives; copy, RG 56, Letters from the Collector at Boston, National Archives.

1. John Thomas.
2. See H to Lincoln, March 10, 1790, and Lincoln to H, March 19, 1790.

From Timothy Pickering [1]

Philadelphia April 6. 1790.

Dr. Sir

Last evening a gentleman called on me to inform me of Mr. Duer's resignation;[2] and to urge me to apply for the vacant office. Having since reflected on a variety of circumstances which would render the office eligible, I have concluded to make known to you my willingness to take it, if you, who know me perfectly well, think I can give you the aid you would wish for and expect in an assistant.

When I went to Wyoming three years ago, vested with the office of prothonotary & the four other offices usually annexed to it in a new county, I supposed I was fixed for life. But a train of disasters & a ruinous expence have attended my removal: [3] and in the conclusion, my reward from the Legislature, for my services & sufferings in introducing the laws & Government of this State into that country, is the repeal of that law by which the disputed lands were confirmed to the Connecticut claimants, & under the faith of which I purchased a farm & erected the necessary buildings: [4] a law too which I pledged myself to those people, that the legislature would never repeal.

The education of seven sons, is a powerful motive to this application. The repeal of the confirming law will keep the Wyoming settlement in a situation which will probably for several years prevent the establishment of a tolerable school.

I intended to set out for Wyoming tomorrow: but will now wait your answer. If the office should remain vacant, & be conferred on me, it will nevertheless be absolutely necessary for me before I should go to New York, to visit my family & let my farm.

ADf, Massachusetts Historical Society, Boston.

1. See H to Pickering, May 13, 1790.
2. See H to William Duer, April 4–7, 1790.
3. After the Revolution, Pickering, a native of Massachusetts, had settled in Philadelphia. In 1787, having been designated by Pennsylvania's government to organize the new county of Luzerne, he moved to the Wyoming Valley. He soon was involved in the acrimonious controversy between the Connecticut settlers of the Wyoming Valley and the Pennsylvania authorities.
4. The law, "*An Act for ascertaining and confirming to certain persons, called* Connecticut *claimants, the lands by them claimed within the county of* Luzerne, *and for other purposes therein mentioned*," had been passed on March 28, 1787 (*Minutes of the Second Session of the Eleventh General Assembly of the Commonwealth of Pennsylvania* [Philadelphia, 1787], 190). It was repealed on April 1, 1790 (*Minutes of the Second Session of the Fourteenth General Assembly of the Commonwealth of Pennsylvania* [Philadelphia, 1790], 252).

Treasury Department Circular
to the Collectors of the Customs in Georgia Except Savannah

Treasury Department.
April 6 1790.

Sir:

I have to desire that you will remit all monies, which you may now have on hand, or hereafter receive on account of the Customs, to John Habersham, Esquire Collector for the port of Savannah, taking duplicate receipts for the same, one of which to be transmitted to my Office, and the other to be retained by you.

This mode of payment you will continue till otherwise directed by me.

I am, Sir, your obedt. Servant,   Alexr. Hamilton
                                        Secretary of the Treasury

Copy, RG 56, Circulars of the Office of the Secretary, "Set T," National Archives.

From Otho H. Williams

Baltimore, April 6, 1790. "The Brigantine Providence, Arnold Briggs, from Rhode Island, arrived at this port the 22d. February last with a large variegated Cargo, Among the rest thirtytwo Casks of New England rum—an article subject to duty, from Rhode Island, if Manufactured there; and the contrary is not pretended. . . . A deduction of ten Per Cent was allowed from the duties on the Cargo. . . . But these privileges were granted with a proviso that a Register be produced conformable to the laws of the State in which it shall have been obtained. I request to know whether the Register so produced is to be considered in lieu of all documents required of Vessels from other States: and whether the Brigantine be liable to tonage or Not? . . . I have . . . been obliged to request that there may be issued a process against William Atkinson for a trespass in unlading half a dozen Cases and boxes without a permit. . . . If I, instantly, prosecute this matter further the possible goods & the Vessel will be forfeited & in that case innocent Men must suffer and very worthy characters be exposed as Smugglers. . . . Pray advise me what I am to do to in the present case."

ADfS, RG 53, "Old Correspondence," Baltimore Collector, National Archives.

To Ædanus Burke

[*New York, April 7, 1790.* On April 7, Burke wrote to Hamilton: "Your letter of this day . . . removes all ground of dissatisfaction." *Letter not found.*]

From Ædanus Burke [1]

New York, 7th. April 1790

Sir

Your letter of this day [2] in which you explictly declare that you had no intention, in your Eulogium on General Green, to cast any reflection on Militia in general, or on any description of the Citizens of South-Carolina, removes all ground of dissatisfaction on my part.

I therefore cheerfully and explicitly retract every thing offensive which I said in the House of Representatives on Wednesday last: in relation to you, and whatever else in any stage of this disagreeable affair, may have admitted of a Construction wounding to your feelings. And I assure you of my concern that any misapprehension should have given occasion to it. Occurrences of this kind are ever to be regreted, and in an amicable issue, ought not to leave on generous minds any traces of unfriendly impressions.

I am Sir Your very hum. Servt   Æ. Burke

The Honorable Alexander Hamilton Esqr

ALS, Hamilton Papers, Library of Congress.
    1. For background to this letter, see H to Burke, April 1, 1790; Burke to H, April 1, 1790; and Elbridge Gerry, Rufus King, George Mathews, Lambert Cadwalader, James Jackson, and John Henry to H, April 6, 1790.
    2. Letter not found.

To Wilhem and Jan Willink, Nicholaas and Jacob Van Staphorst, and Nicholas Hubbard [1]

Treasury Department,
April 7th. 1790.

Gentlemen,

I have, by this opportunity, time only to acknowledge your several favors of the 11th, 12th, and 15th, of September, and 7th. of November, to the late Treasury Board, and of the 29th. of December to myself,[2] and to enclose you the first of eight setts of Bills of Exchange, as per list at foot, amounting together to one hundred thousand current Guilders, towards payment of the arrears of interest on the loans of the United States, due the first of June next.

I flatter myself, that such dispositions will shortly take place, as will secure, for the future, a punctual and regular compliance with the engagements of the United States.

I am &c.   Alexander Hamilton.

Messrs. Willink, Van Staphorst & Hubbard
Amsterdam.

Copy, RG 233, Reports of the Treasury Department, 1792–1793, Vol. III, National Archives.
    1. This letter was enclosed in H's "Report on Foreign Loans," February 13, 1793.
    2. Letter not found.

From Thomas Willing

Bank of No. America [Philadelphia] Apl. 8th. 1790.

Sir

In our last of the 12th Ulto. we had the honor to tell you, that it was probable we shou'd be in a situation by the middle of this Month to meet your application for a Loan of Fifty Thousand Dollars; but that if it became necessary for you to be accommodated sooner, & it shou'd be in our Power to do it, you might depend on our disposition to render you every facility we cou'd. We are now informed by your Letter to Mr. Morris,[1] this day communicated to us, that it will be a convenience to you to have the Loan now effected. We have therefore the Pleasure to tell you it shall be done as soon as you please, on the same terms as the former, and our Post Notes made out to whom you may direct One half payable at thirty, & the residue at 60 days after date.

I have the honor to be for the President directors & Co. of the Bank of North America.

Sir   Your Obedt. servt.   T.W.

Alexr. Hamilton Esqr.
Secretary of the Treasury of the U.S.

LC, Historical Society of Pennsylvania, Philadelphia.
    1. Letter not found.

Report on the Petition of William Finnie

Treasury-department. April 10th. 1790.
[Communicated on April 12, 1790] [1]

[To the Speaker of the House of Representatives]

The Secretary of the Treasury on the petition of William Finnie, referred to him by an order of the House of Representatives of the 25th. of September last,[2]

Respectfully Reports:

That the relief sought by the petitioner relates to the following objects:

First: An allowance for expences incident to his attendance at the seat of Government, for the settlement of his accounts.

Secondly: A compensation for a loss sustained on the sale of a Certificate issued to him for the balance which appeared due to him on that settlement.

Thirdly: Depreciation and pay in the capacity of a Commissary of Military Stores, from the first of January 1777, to the first of January 1781.

Fourthly: An allowance of land, as a Colonel of the Army, in virtue of a Commission from Congress, appointing him Deputy Quarter Master General, with the rank of Colonel.

That as to the first article; the allowance claimed would be contrary to general usage, the reverse of which would be productive of considerable expense to the public, and would often (though not in the present instance) reward delinquency, by indemnifying individuals for delays occasioned in the settlement of their accounts, by their own mismanagement.

Copy, RG 233, Reports of the Secretary of the Treasury, 1790–1791, Vol. I, National Archives.

1. *Journal of the House*, I, 192.
2. On June 29, 1789, the House received "A petition of William Finnie, Deputy Quarter-Master General in the Southern Department, during the late war . . . praying a reimbursement of moneys expended by him in the public service" (*Journal of the House*, I, 55). On September 25, 1789, the House

"*Ordered*, that the committee to whom were referred the . . . [petition] of William Finnie . . . be discharged therefrom, and that it be referred to the Secretary of the Treasury, to examine and report upon . . . to the next session of Congress." (*Journal of the House*, I, 124.)

That as to the second article: It is the common case of every person, who has received a Certificate for money owing to him from the public, and parted with it for less then it's nominal value; and cannot therefore be discriminated by particular relief.

That as to the third article, the facts are as follow.

The memorialist being Deputy Quarter Master General had frequent calls to perform services not properly appertaining to his office; in consideration of which the Board of War, in a letter to him dated the 23d of October 1779, after charging him with the care of all military and other Stores belonging to the United States, which then were, or should afterwards arrive in the State of Virginia, proceed thus: "As you have made large purchases of Cloathing and Military Stores, and taken charge of them 'til forwarded by you, the Board agree, that you shall be allowed the pay of a Commissary of military Stores, towit, fifty dollars per month from the first of January 1777, to the eleventh of February 1778, and the pay and subsistence of a Commissary of Military Stores from the eleventh of February 1778, vizt ninety dollars per month until the first day of July last, and one hundred and eighty dollars per month, from that day in compensation for your past and future services in the business before mentioned, and now committed to your direction." Payment was accordingly made to the Memorialist on this account to the first of October 1779, and on the 20th. of October 1780, an order was drawn in his favor by Samuel Hodgdon, Assistant Commissary General of Military Stores, on William Thorne, paymaster to the department, for eight hundred and ten pounds, being the amount of one year's pay at one hundred and eighty dollars per month; which sum has never been paid. It appears by a report of John D. Mercier the then Auditor, dated the 28th. of August 1786, that the petitioner had exhibited a claim for pay, rations and depreciation, as a Commissary of Military Stores, from the eighth of January 1777, to the first of January 1781, amounting to three thousand four hundred and seventy dollars, which claim was rejected by the Auditor on these grounds as stated in substance by him.

"That to support a claim on the principle of a compensation for extra service, it ought to be shewn, that such service had been performed; whereas it did not appear in the case that any extra-service had been performed after the period to which payment had been made by the Board of War; that is, the first of October 1779."

That as a claim to a stipend attached to an Office it was inadmissible; because contrary to a regulation of Congress, prohibiting the enjoyment of the emoluments of two offices by one person.

It further appears, that on a submission of the same Claim to the Board of Treasury, on the 25th. of April 1789, that Board decided against it.

From which facts the Secretary is of opinion, that a revision of the matter would be inexpedient.

That, as to the fourth article: The claim is founded upon a Commission from the President of Congress, dated the 28th. of March 1776, appointing the Memorialist Deputy Quarter Master General in the Southern Department with the rank of Colonel: But it does not appear to be warranted either by the resolutions of Congress respecting bounties of lands to officers and soldiers, or by the practice upon those resolutions. Nor does any circumstance occur, to justify the allowance to the Memorialist, without extending it to a number of other persons in a like situation.

That upon the whole matter, though the misfortunes of the petitioner, added to the zeal manifested by him in the public service, appeared to the Secretary to intitle his case to as favorable a consideration as a due attention to general principles would permit: Yet he has not been able to discover sufficient and unexceptionable ground, upon which, in his opinion, any part of the prayer of the petitioner may, with propriety, be granted.

All which is humbly submitted   Alexr. Hamilton,
                                       Secry of the Treasy.

Report on the Memorial of James Warren

Treasury-department. April 12th. 1790.
[Communicated on April 12, 1790] [1]

[To the Speaker of the House of Representatives]
The Secretary of the Treasury on the Memorial of James Warren to him referred by an Order of the House of Representatives of the third instant [2]

Respectfully reports;

That it appears, upon examination of the case of the Memorialist, that in the years 1777 and 1778, several Cargoes of Merchandize, which had been imported for the use of the United States, were consigned to his care, and that in the settlement of his accounts concerning those Cargoes by the Commercial Committee,[3] he was allowed only the nominal amount of his expenditures and commissions.

That this settlement took place on the 28th. of November 1780, (at which time there was no authority to make an allowance for depreciation) and that on the 31st. of January 1781, a Warrant was drawn by the President of Congress on the Treasurer of the State of Massachusetts for thirty two thousand five hundred and fifty three dollars, and two ninetieths of a dollar, being the liquidated balance of the Memorialist's account.

That the said Warrant was, sometime in the year 1782, discharged in specie by the State of Massachusetts, at the rate of one dollar for seventy five of the sum expressed upon the face of it.

That the Claim of the Memorialist is,

First: For an allowance of depreciation on the items of the account settled by the Commercial Committee (alledging as a peculiarity in his case, that the settlement was made by an Agent, not by himself; and that there was a demand for depreciation at the time, though not admitted for want of authority.)

Secondly: For the difference between the established rate of old emission money, when the Warrant was issued to him, and that at which it was discharged in specie; which he computes to amount to one hundred and fifteen pounds nine shillings and sixpence lawful money of Massachusetts.

In relation to which facts and circumstances, the Secretary begs leave to observe, that it is an important general rule, that regular settlements, in the established course, involving general principles, should remain untouched. That this rule, in reference to transactions during the late war, derives peculiar force from the then peculiar situation of public affairs. That in no respect is it's observance more necessary than in whatever regards questions of depreciation. That every precedent of an admission of a claim upon that ground, beyond the limits now observed at the Treasury, must be more or less dangerous. That, in particular, it seems necessary to adhere to this as a principle. That when an account has been adjusted, and a balance discharged, no claim for depreciation ought afterwards to be admitted.

That the circumstance of the settlement having been made by an Agent, is no uncommon one. Nor does the demand stated to have been made, at the time, for an allowance for depreciation, appear to the Secretary of any material weight. It is naturally to be presumed, that the interest of applicants must have rendered such demands frequent. And the completion of the settlement, without it, shews that it was not persisted in.

The Secretary, however, thinks it incumbent upon him to state to the House, that as far as regards the mode of payment, there is something distinguishable in the case. He does not find, on enquiry, that it can have had place in many instances, in the precise form: Nevertheless, the degree of force, which this circumstance may be supposed to have, is overruled, in his Judgment, by the danger of a precedent for a new species of claim for depreciation. The allowance of it too, on this ground, would seem to involve this principle. That for depreciation which may have accrued between the time an order for payment may have been given, and the time of actual payment, compensation is to be made. A principle, which, it is to be apprehended, might have extensive consequences.

All which is humbly submitted,　　　Alexr. Hamilton,
　　　　　　　　　　　　　　　　　Secretary of the Treasury.

Copy, Reports of the Secretary of the Treasury, 1790–1791, Vol. I, National Archives.
1. *Journal of the House*, I, 192.
2. On April 3, 1790,
"A Petition of James Warren was presented to the House and read, praying the settlement of an unliquidated claim against the United States.
"*Ordered*, That the said petition be referred to the Secretary of the Treasury, with instruction to examine the same, and report his opinion thereupon to the House." (*Journal of the House*, I, 188.)
3. A committee of the Continental Congress. See *JCC*, XVII, 466.

To Otho H. Williams

Treasury Department April 12th 1790.

Sir

I have considered the circumstances you state in your Letter of the 6th inst. respecting vessels owned by Citizens of Rhode Island.

I am of opinion that those vessels in the case you mention, are Subject to the Same Tonnage to which registered vessels owned by Citizens of the united States without License are liable: because if they were to enjoy all the privileges of coasting vessels, they would be placed on a more favorable footing than registered or licensed vessels, which could never have been the intention of the Legislature.

With regard to the case of Wm Atkinson,[1] if you are fully Satisfied, that there was no intention of fraud, it will be best not to hasten the prosecution of that cause, as there is now a Bill before the house to provide for the remission or mitigation of fines forfeitures and penalties in certain cases.

I am   Sir   Your Obedt Servt   A Hamilton
                                         Secy of the Treasury

O H. Williams Esqr
Collector for the Port of Baltimore

LS, Columbia University Libraries.
  1. See Williams to H, April 6, 1790.

From Benjamin Lincoln

Boston April 15. 1790.

Sir,

By the 27 Section of the Coasting act [1] it is provided that all vessels therein described & under certain circumstances shall enter within 24 hours after arrival. As no penalty is annexed to a nonperformance of the injunction in the law little attention is now paid to it, & the attention is daily decreasing, indeed it seems to decrease with the knowledge that there is no forfiture on a breach of the law. This leaves open a door through which every kind of fraud may pass without the knowledge of the officers of the customs & especially in this State where we have five or six hundred miles sea coast & almost as many harbours as leagues on our shores. From these harbours coasting vessels are constantly passing to this & the other principal towns in the State with lumber, fish, wood, &c. The harbours where they load are generally capacious & have a sufficient depth of water for any vessel & with the utmost ease they are suited in those harbours, especially in our eastern country where are but a few inhabitants. They may shift a cargo of Molasses or otherwise india produce. Our eastern vessels are mostly in that trade into those wood coasters & come to this town with the utmost safety unless they are obliged to enter before they break bulk. To appoint a sufficient number of Officers to attend to all the wharves in this town would be two heavy an expence upon the revenue. I think the fee should be small for entering these coasters then business will not have much expense but they should in all circumstances be obliged under a heavy forfeiture to enter or I am convinced the revenue will greatly suffer. I wrote some time since on the subject of employing a small vessel to inspect the coast as I have not received any answer to those suggestion I suppose you consider in measure as inadmissible. I have now to offer to your consideration one idea more to that of having a small boat which can attend to the different harbours round that bay there are many of those harbours very convenient for taking out part of the Cargo a boat of this kind may in good weather meet vessels in the offing have a man on board which will prevent their landing anythink before entery & the proper officer is on board. These are suggestions which I think it my duty to make I know your time must be so much engrossed by the many & complicated duties of your office that you cannot answer the various applications which are made to you I do not expect it silence will be a sufficient indication to me that the measure proposed cannot be adopted.

Hon Ye
Alexander Hamilton
Secy of the Treasury United States

LC, RG 36, Collector of Customs at Boston, Letter Book, 1790–1797, National Archives; copy, RG 56, Letters from the Collector at Boston, National Archives.
1. 1 *Stat.* 55–56 (September 1, 1789).

Treasury Department Circular
to the Collectors of the Customs

Treasury Department
April 16th. 1790.

Sir

I herewith enclose for your government an Act entitled "an Act to prevent the exportation of goods not duly inspected, according to the laws of the several States." [1]

I observe that the 27th. and 28th. sections of the coasting act [2] have by some of the Collecters of the Customs been so construed as to require, that all licensed vessels of the burthen of twenty tons and upwards bound to any port within their respective districts should obtain a permit to land their Cargoes previous to breaking bulk.

Upon due examination I am of opinion, that this is only required by the Law where vessels of the above description arrive at the particular *port* or *place* where the Collector or other Officer of the district *actually resides:* you will therefore govern yourself accordingly.

I am sensible that this indulgence is liable to abuses which may prove injurious to the Revenue, and must therefore recommend to you as strict an attention as possible to detect & defeat them.

I am Sir   Your Obedt. servant   A Hamilton

LS, to Charles Lee, Charles Lee Papers, Library of Congress; L[S], to Benjamin Lincoln, RG 36, Collector of Customs at Boston, Letters from the Treasury, 1789–1807, Vol. 4, National Archives; LS, The Rutherford B. Hayes Library, Fremont, Ohio; LS, MS Division, New York Public Library; LS, Mrs. Joseph Carson, Bryn Mawr, Pennsylvania; LS, Office of the Secretary, United States Treasury Department; copy, United States Finance Miscellany, Treasury Circulars, Library of Congress; copy, RG 56, Circulars of the Office of the Secretary, "Set T," National Archives.
1. 1 *Stat.* 106 (April 2, 1790).
2. 1 *Stat.* 55–65 (September 1, 1789).

From William Webb [1]

[*Bath, District of Maine, April 16, 1790.* On May 5, 1790, Hamilton wrote to Webb: "In answer to yours of the 16th. of April." *Letter not found.*]

1. Webb was collector of customs at Bath.

To Thomas Jefferson

Treasury Department April 20th. 1790.

Sir

I have the honor to enclose you copies of certain communications which have been made to me,[1] respecting the detention of the Registers of vessels of the United States in some of the Islands of his Christian Majesty, in order that such measures may be taken as shall appear adviseable towards preventing in future a practice, which has a tendency either to interfere with the policy of our Laws, or to prevent the sale of our vessels to the inhabitants of those Islands.

I have the honor to be &c.

Alexander Hamilton
Secretary of the Treasury.

LC, Papers of the Continental Congress, National Archives; copy, RG 59, Miscellaneous Letters, 1790–1799, National Archives.

1. See William Lindsay to H, February 19, 1790. The other enclosures to this letter were: David Plunket to Moses Myers, January 16, 1790; John Nivison to Josiah Parker, February 16, 1790; Affidavit of John Brown, February 16, 1790. Copies of these enclosures may be found in RG 59, Miscellaneous Letters Received, National Archives.

From Joseph Whipple

Portsmouth, New Hampshire, April 20, 1790. "I have enclosed here with my quarterly Accots. to the 31 March. There are Several Small articles of Charge in account of expences on the revenue not authorized by any particular direction, but those articles being indispensibly necessary I concieve will not be disapproved of. . . . By the 23 Section of the Act for Registering, regulating the Coasting Trade &c.,[1] Vessels found trading not licensed &c. are Subject to foreign Tonnage. An instance of this kind has occured in this district. If this punishment inflicted for a noncompliance with the Law should be considered as a fine, be pleased to direct me for my government in future. . . . I request to be informed . . . whether after the payment of 50 Cents pr. Ton under the above circumstance, Coasting Vessels shall again pay the Tonnage of 6 Cents on taking a License as required by the Said 23rd Section. . . . Your letter of the 1st Nov. last advised of a draft in me favor of John Langdon Esqr.[2] for 500 Dolls. which was paid, and the bill transmitted to The Treasurer of the United States agreeably to your direction. . . ."

LC, RG 36, Collector of Customs at Portsmouth, Letters Sent, 1789–1790, Vol. 1, National Archives; copy, RG 56, Letters from the Collector at Portsmouth, National Archives.
  1. 1 *Stat.* 55–65 (September 1, 1789).
  2. Langdon was United States Senator from New Hampshire.

To William Allibone

[*New York, April 21, 1790.* On April 29, Allibone wrote to Hamilton: "I have the Honor to acknowledge the receipt of your letter dated april 21st." *Letter not found.*]

To Jedediah Huntington

Treasury Department
April 21st. 1790.

Sir

Herewith you have Copy of the Act for the establishment and support of lighthouses beacons, bouys and public piers.[1] Amongst other things contained in it you will perceive that it is made the duty of the Secretary of the Treasury to provide by Contracts to be approved by the President of the United States for rebuilding when necessary and keeping in repair the Lighthouses, beacons, buoys & public piers in the several States; and for furnishing the same with all the necessary supplies; and also to agree for the Salaries, wages, or hire of the person or persons appointed by the President, for the Superintendance and care of the same.

I have now to inform you that the President of the United States has been pleased to commit to you for the present the general care and superintendance of the establishments of the above description within the State of Connecticut. Your Agency will peculiarly extend to the keeping in repair those establishments, and furnishing them with the necessary supplies, which you will observe the law contemplates being done by Contracts; by which were probably intended, Agreements for certain fixed periods of time at determinate rates. This with regard to supplies it is presumed will be easy and proper; but it will not I apprehend be practicable with regard to repairs which are too casual to admit of an Estimate accurate enough to be the ground of previous contract, they must be provided for as occasions arise, and wherever the thing admits of delay to send on Contracts which are made, to me for ratification.

With respect to the pier and buoys at Newhaven, as they are represented to be private property no expence must without further directions be incurred on their Account.

The accounts for your disbursements with the requisite Vouchers must be rendered at the Treasury for settlement at the expiration of every quarter; at which time it will be proper to make a report of the State of the establishment under your direction.

You will observe however that the expences of the establishments in question are only to be defrayed by the United States to the fifteenth day of August next, if the respective States do not in the mean time make cessions of them to the United States. I do not learn that Connecticut has yet made such cession. Therefore your contracts for the present must not go beyond the above mentioned day.

With regard to such inferior Agents as may be requisite, you will adjust the allowance according to your judgement of what is right having regard to former practice and consulting œconomy, and you will transmit me a Statement. Your own compensation will be regulated hereafter.

I am, Sir,   Your Obedt. servant   Alex Hamilton
                                            Secy of the Treasy

Jedediah Huntington esqr
New London.

LS, MS Division, New York Public Library.
  1. 1 *Stat.* 53–54 (August 7, 1789).

To Joseph Howell, Junior

Treasury Department
April 22d. 1790.

Sir

Inclosed you will receive a petition of John Wyley[1] late a Captain in Colonel Jacksons Regiment in the Army of the United States.[2]

You will be pleased to inform me how far the circumstances stated by the Petitioner are ascertainable at the Pay Office, and what has been the mode of payment in the like cases.

I am, Sir, Your Obedt. servant   A Hamilton
Secy of the Treasury

Joseph Howell Junr. esqr.
Pay Master General.

LS, RG 93, Miscellaneous Records, National Archives.
1. On April 21, 1790, the House referred to H "A petition of John Wiley ... praying to be reimbursed for moneys advanced in the service of the United States during the late war" (*Journal of the House*, I, 197).
2. Colonel Henry Jackson.

To Thomas Jefferson

[New York, April 22, 1790] [1]

Mr. Hamilton returns to Mr. Jefferson the draft of the letter to Mr. Grand,[2] with his thanks for the trouble Mr. J is so obliging as to take. Mr. Hamilton has used the liberty given him of indicating some alterations, less from any reserves in his own mind than from uncertainty respecting the views of others. It is proposed that the words between should be omitted and those interlined inserted.

Thursday

AL, Thomas Jefferson Papers, Library of Congress.
1. This letter is undated, but is endorsed "recd 1790. Apr. 22."
2. Jefferson's letter to Ferdinand Le Grand is dated April 23, 1790, and is printed, with a discussion of H's alterations, in Boyd, *Papers of Thomas Jefferson*, XVI, 368–69. In this letter Jefferson asked Le Grand to write to "Mr. Drost" about the terms under which Jean Pierre Droz might be willing to

come to the United States to help establish a Mint. Droz, a citizen of the Canton of Neuchâtel, Switzerland, had invented a machine that would strike the two faces and edge of a coin at a single stroke. Jefferson was not successful in his attempt to bring Droz to the United States; instead Droz was employed by the British government to set up the necessary machinery for coining copper halfpenny pieces in England.

From Robert Purviance [1]

Custom House, Baltimore
April 22d. 1790.

Sir

The Snow St. Martin from St. Ubes bound to Charleston put into this port the 10th. March in distress, upon an examination she was found insufficient to be repaired. A Sale of the vessel and Cargo has since taken place. The Collector [2] considers the Vessel and Cargo exempt from paying the Tonage & fees, in conformity with the Act providing for vessels in distress. [3] I think the provision made by that Act, to provide for Vessels in distress dont fully comprehend the present case, I consider the Act in part to guard against the payment of Tonnage and fees twice on the same Voyage. Had she arrived at her destined port, no doubt the Tonnage and Fees must been paid, Altho insufficient to undergo a repair, *Here the Voyage ends.*

Its some what remarkable this Vessel should come so far up the bay and passed so good a port as Norfolk in her situation.

I wish for your sentiments on this subject.

I am Sir with great respect   Your most Obedt. humble servant
R. Purviance N. Officer

Alexr. Hamilton esquire
Secretary of the Treasury.

Copy, RG 56, Original Letters to the Collector at Baltimore, National Archives.
   1. Purviance was naval officer at Baltimore.
   2. Otho H. Williams.
   3. Section 12 of "An Act to regulate the Collection of the Duties imposed by law on the tonnage of ships or vessels, and on goods, wares and merchandises imported into the United States" (1 *Stat.* 29–49 [July 31, 1789]).

Report on Defects in the Existing Laws of Revenue

Treasury Department April 22nd. 1790.
[Communicated on April 23,1790] [1]

[To the Speaker of the House of Representatives]
In obedience to the Order of the House of Representatives of the
19th Day of January last [2]
The Secretary of the Treasury respectfully submits the following
Report.

*First. As to the "Act imposing duties on good wares and merchan-
dizes imported into the United States." [3]*

1. Section I. The duties specified in this act, according to this
section, took effect throughout the United States *from* and *after*
the first day of August last. But as the Act for the collection of
those duties did not pass till the last of July,[4] it was of course impossible, that the officers for carrying it into execution, could be
appointed, commissioned, and ready to enter upon the execution
of their offices, at the day fixed for the commencement of the duties.
The Custom-Houses in the several States were not organised till
at different periods from the fifth of August to sometime in September; and in the intervals several importations took place. In some
instances *duties* were paid under the State Laws; in others *none*
were paid.

The Secretary conceiving it to be a clear point, that the duties
imposed by the first mentioned Act, *accrued,* as debts to the United

DS, RG 233, Original Reports of the Secretary of the Treasury, 1790–1791,
National Archives.
   1. *Journal of the House,* I, 198.
   2. The House ordered
"That the Secretary of the Treasury be directed to report to this House
such information as he may have obtained respecting any difficulties which may
have occured in the execution of the several laws for collecting duties on
goods, wares, and merchandises, and on tonnage, and for regulating the coasting trade, together with his opinion thereupon." (*Journal of the House,* I,
143.)
   3. 1 *Stat.* 24–27 (July 4, 1789).
   4. "An Act to regulate the Collection of the Duties imposed by law on the
tonnage of ships or vessels, and on goods, wares and merchandises imported
into the United States" (1 *Stat.* 29–49 [July 31, 1789]).

States, on all goods imported after the day specified for their commencement, and that the regulations prescribed by the Collection-Law were to be considered merely as auxiliary guards for securing their due payment, did not think himself at liberty, on grounds of convenience or inconvenience, to wave the claim for them. He has therefore caused it to be made, and has given directions with a view to a legal decision of the question.

But it is worthy of consideration by the legislature, whether it be adviseable to pursue, or relinquish it. The payment of the duties in this situation, has been generally unlooked for, and in most cases must be preceded by a legal determination. The enforcement of the claim would therefore be likely to be thought rigorous; and, in some instances, might be injurious. Where Merchants may have sold without reference in the *price* to the duty; where Factors or Agents may have settled accounts with, and paid over the proceeds of goods to their Principals, especially if transient persons; where duties have been paid under the State establishments; in these and other cases, there might ensue, Loss or embarassment. There must also be difficulty in ascertaining the sums which ought to be paid.

2. The distinctions between distilled spirits are conceived not to be sufficiently diversified, or accurate. This has been remarked, and a remedy proposed, in the plan submitted to the House for the support of public Credit.[5]

3. There is no general rate prescribed for estimating the draught and tare of those articles, which pay duty by weight. The consequence is, that different allowances are made at different places, according to former usage; and too much is left to discretion.

4. Unwrought Steel is rated at fifty six cents for 112 lbs; which upon an average of the cost is less than five per Cent ad valorem. As an enumerated article, it is presumed to have been the intention of the legislature, to rate it higher than five per Cent, especially as a higher rate would be in favour of the manufacture of it among ourselves, in which considerable progress has been made, particularly in the State of Pennsylvania.

5. The information received by the Secretary induces him to consider as questionable, the policy of the duty on Pickled fish, in

5. "Report Relative to a Provision for the Support of Public Credit," January 9, 1790.

its present extent. It is represented, that almost the whole of what is brought from Nova Scotia to Massachusetts, is re-exported; and this chiefly to foreign countries. And that while it forms a considerable article in an intercourse between those places, beneficial to Massachusetts, it contributes to the augmentation of her exports.

If this be true, it is difficult to discern any advantage in the duty. To the revenue, there will be rather loss than profit; as the expence incident to the collection and to the process of the drawback, will, probably, exceed the amount of the duty on the small quantity internally consumed, even taking into the calculation, the one per Cent retained as an indemnification for that expence. In a commercial light, as far as it has any operation, it seems to be rather an unfavourable one. The process of *paying* and *drawing back*, is not without inconveniencies, and the unrefunded residue, is a tax on the export-trade in that article from which, for the reason assigned, no benefit arises to the public: While the encouragement which it was the object of this regulation to give to the fisheries, loses in a great measure its effect, by reason of the drawback. And it is suggested by intelligent men, that an injurious competition in the branch of the fisheries, to which the duty is applicable, is little to be apprehended.

The Secretary, however, does not conceive himself to be possessed with sufficient accuracy of all the facts necessary to a right judgment on this point, to be willing to hazard a decisive opinion. He therefore only means to state the circumstances communicated to him; in expectation, that the Representatives from the part of the Union more immediately affected, will be able, by further lights to guide the opinion of the House to a proper conclusion.

6. A discrimination is made by this section in favour of Teas brought from China or India, in *American bottoms*. The fifth Section allows a discount of ten per Cent on *all* the duties imposed by this Act on goods, wares and merchandizes imported in *American bottoms*. A question arises, whether this discount ought to obtain in respect to the abovementioned Teas. The Secretary presumes, that the better construction is against the allowance, though within the letter of the provision; but an explanation is, perhaps, requisite to obviate controversy.

7. All goods, wares and merchandize, except Teas brought from

China or *India* otherwise than in American bottoms, are made liable to a duty of *twelve* and a *half* per Cent ad valorem. But in the clause immediately succeeding *all* China ware is rated only at *ten* per Cent ad valorem. A doubt suggests itself, whether this article be excepted out of the preceding provision; or be itself subject to an implied exception in favour of the full operation of that provision.

It is suggested, that the encouragement intended to our East-India trade by the duty of twelve and a half per Cent on India goods brought from China in foreign bottoms, will be counteracted by the want of a greater duty than is now laid on the same goods brought from Europe; as competition is more to be apprehended through that channel, than from direct importations, in foreign bottoms, from India. While the Secretary deems it proper to bring this suggestion into the view of the House, he forbears giving an opinion as to the weight it ought to have. He perceives various advantages in a direct commerce with the East Indies, and is hitherto inclined to believe it merits the patronage of the Government; but the tendency of it not yet sufficiently developed to his judgment, to leave him wholly without reserve as to the extent of the encouragement which ought to be given.

8. Commodities of our own growth or manufacture carried to a foreign port and brought back again to the United States, are, by this Act, liable to duty. This tendency of this to discourage commercial enterprise recommends the expediency of an exemption upon due proof of identity.

9. The Sea stores of Vessels, the furniture, cloathing and professional apparatus of persons arriving in this Country from abroad, seem equally liable to duties with goods brought by way of merchandize. They have been in several instances exacted; but the payment is usually accompanied with remonstrance and dis-content. If it was not the intent of the Legislature to include such articles, an explanation is necessary. Various considerations plead for exempting them under proper limitations.

10. Section II. From this section it has been doubted, whether there be at present any duty on hemp. And it has been inferred from the debates, to have been the intention of the Legislature to exempt it, till after the first of december 1790; but the construction of the Act is different. There is a duty on Cotton as well as Hemp, to take

place at a future day. But *Cotton* in the mean time is expressly excepted out of the five per Cent duty, which impliedly excludes hemp from the like exception. As the Act now stands, it will be a question, when the duty of sixty Cents per hundred weight takes place, whether it be in addition to or in lieu of the present duty.

11. Section III. Provision is here made for a drawback of the duties on goods exported within twelve months, with an exception of certain kinds of distilled spirits, and a deduction of one per Cent.

But there is no provision for entries for exportation; whence it happens, that a Vessel arriving from a foreign port, with part of her cargo destined for the United States, and other part for some other Country, is obliged to pay or secure the payment of the duties on her whole Cargo, and in strictness even to land such articles as require weighing, gauging, or measuring, in order to the ascertaining of the duties. This is complained of as a hardship, and as contrary to the prevailing usage of commercial nations. The Secretary is of opinion, that the complaint is well founded; and that it is adviseable, that entries for exportation with proper precautions and restrictions, should be authorised. The interests of the revenue can, with advantage, be consulted no further than they are consistent with the necessary freedom and facility of commercial intercourse.

The allowance of drawbacks does not obviate the subject of complaint. The necessity of advancing the money, or procuring security for the amount of the duties; the necessity of landing those articles, which require to be weighed, measured or gauged (which must in the first instance be submitted to); are material inconveniencies: And the process for obtaining drawbacks is attended with difficulty, casualty and trouble. There must be a bond given not to reland the goods; and this bond must be cancelled by certain proofs, which may not, in all cases, be obtainable, but which are, nevertheless, made a prerequisite to the payment of the drawbacks: Nor can that payment at any rate be had, till after the expiration of six months: So that even where security is given for the amount of the duties, it must often happen, that they become payable before parties can be prepared to demand the drawback; And the one per Cent retained, is, in every case, a certain loss. These circumstances, to transient persons especially, operate as a grievance.

Secondly. As to the Act imposing duties on Tonnage [6]

12. The duties mentioned in this Act are upon all ships or Vessels *entered* in the United States.

The entry therefore is the circumstance, which regulates the payment of the duty.

But a doubt has arisen, whether the duty ought to be deemed to accrue on *every* entry, or only on *entries* from *foreign* countries.

The construction which has been adopted, is, that it accrues on *every* entry, whether from abroad, or *in* one part of the United States *from* another.

One reason for this construction results from the second Section; which provides, that Vessels *built* and *owned* in the United States, whilst employed in the *Coasting* trade or fisheries, shall not pay Tonnage more than *once* a year. If the duty were confined to entries from *abroad* only, it could not arise at all on vessels employed in the coasting trade, *whilst so employed;* in which case this provision would be wholly nugatory. The last clause of the twenty third section of the "Act for registering and clearing Vessels regulating the coasting trade, and for other purposes," [7] looks also to the same construction; strongly implying the payment of tonnage generally between district and district, and enlarging the rate in a particular case.

Yet the third section of the Act now under consideration has been supposed to have a different aspect, as it subjects all vessels *except* those built *within*, and owned by citizens *of* the United States, *employed in transporting our own commodities coastwise*, to a tonnage of fifty cents at *each* entry: whence it has been inferred, that in other cases the duty is not payable at each entry; because, by the first section Vessels wholly foreign pay fifty cents, whether employed in the coasting trade or not. But this inference loses its force, when it is observed, that there are other descriptions of vessels, in respect to which it serves to *increase* the rates specified in the first section, in favour of the exclusive privilege, to transport our own commodities coastwise; intended to be secured to Vessels *built* within and *owned* by citizens of the United States. This suggests an use for the clause, which is reconcileable with the provision in the second section.

6. 1 *Stat.* 27–28 (July 20, 1789).
7. 1 *Stat.* 55–56 (September 1, 1789).

The provisions of this act however appear to be varied by the "Act for registering and clearing vessels, regulating the coasting trade, and for other purposes," in these particulars: The latter extends the privileges in the coasting trade, which by the former, seem to be confined to Vessels of the *built* of the United States, to all Vessels which are registered or enrolled; provided they obtain licenses for the purpose. It also extends the duty of fifty cents, to the transportation of foreign (as well as domestic) commodities, from district to district, by any vessel of the burthen of twenty tons and upwards, which has not a Register *or* Enrollment, *and a license* to trade.

Hence if even a registered vessel having *no license*, proceed from one district with part of an outward bound cargo to another district, in order to procure the remainder, and happen to take in a *freight* at the first place for the last, which amounts to a *"trading between the districts,"* she is subject, on her entry in the last, to foreign tonnage.

The propriety of this construction has been questioned; but a consideration of the general spirit of the coasting act; which aims at guarding the revenue against evasion, by the precautions annexed to the granting of licenses; and an accurate attention to the words of the last clause of the twenty third section of that Act, seem to leave no room for a different construction. These words are "And if any vessel of the burthen of twenty tons or upwards, not having a certificate of registry *or* enrollment, *and a license*, shall be found *trading between different districts*, or be employed in the Bank or Whale fisheries, every such ship or vessel shall be subject to the same tonnage and fees, as foreign ships or vessels."

This provision for want of having been understood in the proper sense, has, in a variety of instances, borne hard upon Individuals; who have omitted to procure licenses, and whose vessels have been on that account subjected to foreign tonnage. It is submitted to the consideration of the House, whether restitution of the sums paid, through misapprehension of a new law, would not be equitable in itself & calculated to give a favourable impression of the liberality of the government.

Perhaps indeed the expediency of the regulation itself, merits reconsideration. The necessity of paying tonnage at all, in going from one district to another, has been a subject of complaint. And it is certain, that it has in many cases, a burthensome operation. It would appear to the Secretary, upon the whole, eligible, that upon entries from district to district, tonnage should in no case be demanded, *except where a freight had been taken* in at one district for another; and that even there, in respect to vessels registered but not licensed, half tonnage only should be paid.

Thirdly. As to the "Act to regulate the collection of the duties imposed by law on the tonnage of ships or vessels and on goods wares and merchandizes imported into the United States." [8]

Sections I. II. III. & IV. The arrangement of the districts, the privileges granted to some ports, the restrictions upon others, have been represented in a few instances as requiring alteration. The Secretary is inclined to think, that some of the representations made to him will deserve attention; but as he presumes, that the course of the business will lead to the appointment of a special Committee to prepare a bill for amending the laws under consideration, there are reasons, which, with the permission of the House, would induce him to reserve a more particular communication on this part of the subject for that Committee.

14. Section V. This Section contemplates a provision of boats for securing the collection of the revenue; but no authority to provide them, is any where given. Information from several quarters, proves the necessity of having them; nor can they, in the opinion of the Secretary, fail to contribute, in a material degree, to the security of the revenue; much more than will compensate for the expence of the establishment; the utility of which will increase in proportion as the public exigencies may require an augmentation of the duties. An objection has been made to the measure as betraying an improper distrust of the Merchants; but that objection can have no weight, when it is considered, that it would be equally applicable to all the precautions comprehended in the existing system; all which proceed on a supposition too well founded to be doubted, that there are persons concerned in trade, in every country, who will, if they can, evade the public dues, for their private benefit. Justice to the body of the Merchants of the United States, demands an acknowlegment, that they have very generally manifested a disposition to

8. 1 *Stat.* 29–49 (July 31, 1789).

conform to the national laws, which does them honor, and authorises confidence in their probity. But every considerate member of that body, knows, that this confidence admits of exceptions, and that it is essentially the interest of the greater number, that every possible guard should be set on the fraudulent few; which does not in fact tend to the embarassment of trade.

The following is submitted as a proper establishment for this purpose.

That there be ten boats: two, for the coasts, bays and harbours of Massachusetts and New Hampshire; one, for the Sound between Long-Island and Connecticut; one, for the Bay of New York; one, for the Bay of Delaware; two, for the Bay of Chesapeak; (these of course to ply along the neighboring coasts); one, for the coasts, bays and harbours of North Carolina; one, for the Coasts, bays and harbours of South Carolina; and one, for the Coasts, bays & harbours of Georgia.

Boats of from thirty six to forty feet keel, will answer the purpose, each having one Captain, one Lieutenant and six mariners, and armed with swivels. The first cost of one of these boats, completely equipped, may be computed at One thousand dollars.

The following is an estimate of the annual expence

10 Captains	@ 40. dollars per month	4,800
10 Lieutenants	@ 25. ditto per ditto	3.000
60 seamen	@ 8. ditto per ditto	5.760
Provision		3.000
Wear and Tear		2.000
	Dollars	18.560

The utility of an establishment of this nature must depend on the exertion, vigilance and fidelity of those, to whom the charge of the boats shall be confided. If these are not respectable characters, they will rather serve to screen, than detect fraud. To procure such, a liberal compensation must be given, and in addition to this, it will, in the opinion of the Secretary, be adviseable, that they be commissioned as Officers of the Navy. This will not only induce fit men the more readily to engage, but will attach them to their duty by a nicer sense of honor.

15. Section VI. Collectors are here authorised, in case of necessary absence, sickness or inability, to appoint deputies. It is repre-

sented that inconveniencies have arisen from the want of the like power in the Naval officers and surveyors.

16. Section VII. Provision is here made for the case of the disability or death of the Collector; but not of the Naval Officer or Surveyor. A similar provision with respect to them appears to be not less requisite.

17. Section X. The provision of this Section seems to extend too far. It is conceived, that it ought to be confined to vessels owned wholly or in part by Citizens of the United States; as it is not supposeable, that those of other nations can be acquainted with a regulation so intirely local in its nature, or be prepared to comply with it. There is also want of a penalty to enforce its observance.

This regulation has been represented as inconvenient and useless; but the Secretary does not view it in this light. It is probable, that it will contribute to the security of the revenue, by rendering more difficult those collusions between Masters and Owners, which often take place after the arrival of Vessels upon the Coast, or within port.

18. Section XI. Masters of Vessels within forty eight hours after their arrival in any port of the United States, are to make report. It is not explained, whether they are not at liberty in the mean time, to proceed elsewhere. The construction of the officers of the Customs, in several instances, has been in favour of such liberty. But this construction does not appear to the Secretary well founded. He conceives, that the duties become payable by the act of importation, even previous to entry, and that the forty eight hours are only allowed as a reasonable time for the Master to prepare his report; after which he is to be subject to a penalty for not doing it. An explanation however may prevent disputes.

It is also submitted, whether Masters ought not to be required within twelve hours after their arrival to announce it at the Custom house, and to complete their report within twenty four, with an exception for Sundays. It is of moment, that vessels arriving, should be brought as speedily as possible, under the notice of the proper officers, and that their situation should be ascertained as early as practicable. More Time than is necessary for disclosing it with proper accuracy can be of no real use, and gives greater opportunity for concerting frauds.

In the oath here prescribed for Masters of Vessels, there is no view to those casualties, which may cause the cargo to be diminished at Sea. There ought to be room for making the proper exceptions, according to the circumstances. And it would be useful to make it a part of the oath, that any goods afterwards discovered on board shall be reported; as in the case of Importers or Consignees.

19. Section XII. It is here declared, that no goods shall be unladen, but *in open day*. It would be more safe as well as more certain to fix particular hours for the purpose according to different seasons of the year. And it is submitted, whether all lading as well as unlading of goods at other hours, unless by special license from the officers of the Customs ought not to be forbidden. If in addition to this, Masters of vessels were required to give previous notice to the Officers assigned to their respective vessels, of the times when deliveries are intended to begin, it would afford an increase of security.

This Section contains various penalties on persons concerned in unlading and removing goods, without the requisite permits. It would be a most powerful check upon fraud, if every master of a vessel concerned in one, should, on conviction, be dis-qualified under competent penalties, from having, at any time after, the command or charge of a vessel within the United States. There are however objections of weight to such a provision.

20. Section XIII. The effect of this Section is to oblige the payment, or securing of the duties, on *all* the goods brought in any Vessel, at the port at which she first arrives; though part of them be destined for another, either within the United States, or elsewhere. This regulation is a subject of complaint. Its inconvenience becomes the more apparent, when it is considered, that all the goods intended for another port, must first be landed (and certain articles measured, weighed or gauged) and afterwards reshipped. The trouble, expence and delay of such a process, are serious obstructions to trade. Balancing its commercial inconveniencies with the additional security which it may afford to the revenue, the Secretary is of opinion, that an alteration is adviseable. It should be incumbent upon the Master of the Ship, to make report at the first port, of the whole Cargo on board upon oath, distinguishing the particular goods intended for each port, and also to make oath, at every subsequent port of the particulars of the goods landed at any preceding

one, & of the persons to and for whom they were delivered; producing also certificates from the proper officers of the whole
quantity of the goods originally entered, and of so much as may
have been regularly landed. A power of securing with proper
fastenings the hatches and other communications with the holds of
ships; providing for accident and necessity, and even, if judged
requisite, to put an inspector on board, in going from one port to
another, ought to be superadded.

No person but the Owner or consignee of goods can make the
entry here required. This, from the absence of parties is sometimes
inconvenient. It is the practice of countries, whose regulations are
not deficient in strictness, to allow an agent of the party to make
entry in his absence. And though this may widen the door for
evasion; there are nevertheless strong arguments derived from convenience in its favour. Penalties proportionably severe may be inflicted upon fraud committed by any such Agent; and the permission may be confined to the case of persons absent at the time of
the arrival of the Vessel, in which the goods may have been brought.

The oath here directed to be taken by importers is not always in
their power. There may be no Invoice nor any other accurate account of the quantity, quality, or cost of articles. A qualification,
in this respect, is indispensable. Entries, without specifying particulars must, of necessity, be admitted; parties swearing, that they
have received no account of them, and that they are unknown. An
eye is had to this in the sixteenth Section, but something is wanting
to reconcile the two sections, and define a more accurate course of
proceding in the case.

21. Section XV. Inspectors are to be put on board vessels, who
are to remain on board until they are discharged. This implies
during the night as well the day; which, if practiced in every case,
would multiply the number of Inspectors to a very expensive extent. A power of securing the hatches and other communications
with the holds of vessels during the night would give greater
security, where inspectors were kept constantly on board, and
would, in many instances, obviate the necessity of doing it.

The unlading of a Vessel is here limited to fifteen working days,
after she *begins* to unload. But the commencement of the business
may be postponed as long as the parties interested think fit. If there

should be considerable delay, either an inspector must remain on board the whole time, in which case the expence may exhaust the duty, or there must be great opportunity for fraud. It seems proper, either to fix an ultimate limit for unloading, to be computed from the time of arrival, or of the Master's report, or a period, after which the expence of an inspector shall be borne by the party. The first appears to the Secretary most adviseable. And he conceives, that twenty working days, after the Master's report, would suffice.

22. Section XIX. The payment or securing of the duties, is here made a preliminary to their being landed. This, in a strict sense, is impracticable; as certain articles must first be landed, weighed, gauged or measured, before the duties can be ascertained. The object however of the provision is proper, and it must be construed to admit a gross estimate of the sum in the first instance, subject to after revision. It would, however, be desireable, that a discretion of this sort should be expressed. The Collector, together with the Naval Officer, where there is one, or alone where there is none, may be authorised to determine the amount of the duties to be paid, by an estimate of the same, according to the best of their or his judgment; and the Collector may be empowered in case of an over estimate, either to return the excess, if the money has been paid, or to endorse a credit for it on the bond.

A discount of ten per Cent is here allowed for prompt payment, on the excess of any sum of duties beyond fifty dollars. The policy of this discount is questionable. Experience shews, that in most of the States, transient persons chiefly avail themselves of it, who would in most cases pay the money without the discount, to avoid the inconvenience of suretyship.

But if even the discount ought to be continued, the rate seems to be too high. It exceeds the rate of interest, at which the Government may borrow, more than is an equivalent for the insurance of the risk of non payment. Seven per Cent would, in the judgment of the Secretary, be the extent of a proper allowance. The confining the discount to the excess beyond fifty dollars, counteracts the provision, wherever that excess is not considerable.

It is provided by the last clause of this section, that no person whose bond is unsatisfied, after it becomes due, shall have a future credit with "*the Collector*," until it shall be discharged. The words "*the* Collector" have been supposed to confine the non-allowance of Credit, to the particular Collector to whom the bond was given; in which sense a further credit might be had in another district; which would considerably lessen the utility of the regulation. The removal of this ambiguity, so as to render the exclusion general, may add to the efficacy of the provision.

23. Section XXIX. The compensations to the officers established by this section, require revision: They are in many instances inadequate; in some disproportionate. Resignations in consequence of it have taken place, and others are suspended on the expectation of a favourable alteration during the present session. It is certain, that competent allowances are essential to the idea of having the service performed by characters worthy of trust. And how much the security of the Revenue depends on this, is evident. There are many ports, where the officers receive next to nothing for their services. It were superfluous to comment on the inexpediency of such a state of things.

The Secretary, for the sake of brevity, begs leave to reserve the details on this head, for the Committee before alluded to.

24. It has been inferred from this Section, that the Collector and Naval officer are necessarily to transact their business in separate apartments. This (if it be the design of the provision from which the inference is drawn) was, probably, founded upon the idea, that the separation would lessen the danger of collusion between those officers. But it does not seem likely, that a circumstance of this sort, could have much effect in that way; while the separation leaves a good deal more in the power of the Collector, and renders the Naval Officer far less a check upon him, than if he were made an immediate witness to his transactions. The Secretary is of opinion, that it would be preferable to require them to act in conjunction and in the presence of each other; among other things jointly administering and certifying all oaths required to be taken at the Custom houses.

Section XXX. This section provides for the receipt of the duties in *gold and silver coin only*. The Secretary has considered this provision, as having for object the exclusion of payments in the paper emissions of particular states, and the securing the *immediate* or *ultimate* collection of the duties in specie; as intended to prohibit to individuals, the right of paying in any thing except Gold or Silver Coin, but not to hinder the treasury from making such arrangements, as its exigencies, the speedy command of the public resources and the convenience of the community might dictate; those arrangements being compatible with the eventual receipt of the duties in specie. For instance, The Secretary did not imagine, that the provision ought to be so understood, as to prevent, if necessary, an anticipation of the duties by treasury drafts, receivable at the several custom houses. And if it ought not to be understood in this sense, it appeared to him, that the principle of a different construction would extend to the permitting the receipt of the notes of public banks, issued on a specie fund. Unless it can be supposed that the exchanging of specie, after it has been received for bank notes to be remitted to the Treasury is also interdicted, it seems difficult to conclude, that the receipt of them, in the first instance, is forbidden.

Such were the reflections of the Secretary with regard to the authority to permit bank notes to be taken in payment of the duties. The expediency of doing it, appeared to him still less questionable. The extension of their circulation by the measure, is calculated to increase both the ability and the inclination of the banks to aid the government. It also accelerates the command of the product of the revenues for the public service, and it facilitates the payment of the duties. It has the first effect, because the course of business occasions the notes to be sent beforehand to distant places; and being ready on the spot either for payment or exchange, the first post, after the duties become payable or are received, conveys them to the treasury. The substitution of Treasury drafts, anticipating the duties, could hardly be made without some sacrifice on the part of the public. As they would be drawn upon *time*, and upon the expectation of funds to be collected and of course contingent, it is not probable, that they would obtain a ready sale, but at a discount, or upon long credit. As they would also be more or less liable to accident, from the failure of expected payments, there would be, continually, a degree of hazard to public credit. And to other considerations it may be added, that the practice of anticipations of this kind is in its nature so capable of abuse as to render it an ineligible instrument of administration, in ordinary cases, and fit only for times of necessity.

If the idea of *anticipation* should be excluded, then the relying wholly upon Treasury drafts would be productive of considerable delay. The knowlege that funds were in hand, must precede the issuing of them. Here would of course be some loss of time. And as the moment of demand, created by the course of business, would frequently elapse, there would as frequently be a further loss of time in waiting for a new demand. In such intervals, the public service would suffer, the specie would be locked up, and circulation checked.

Bank notes being a convenient species of money, whatever increases their circulation, increases the quantity of current money. Hence the payment of duties is doubly promoted by their aid; they at once add to the quantity of medium, and serve to prevent the stagnation of specie.

The tendency of the measure to lessen the necessity of drawing specie from distant places to the seat of government, results from the foregoing considerations. The slow operation of treasury drafts, would frequently involve a necessity of bringing on specie, to answer the exigencies of the government; the avoiding of which, as much as possible, in the particular situation of this country, need not be insisted upon.

But convinced as the Secretary is of the usefulness of the regulation; yet, considering the nature of the clause, upon which these remarks arise, he thought it his duty to bring the subject under the eye of the House. The measure is understood by all concerned to be temporary.

Indeed whenever a national bank shall be instituted, some new disposition of the thing will be a matter of course.

25. Sections XXXI, and XXXII. The provision in these sections respecting drawbacks, seems to require revision in several particulars.

The benefit of it is intended for any person by whom the goods may be exported, whether that person be the importer of them or another, and yet the oath to be taken by the exporter, is of such a nature as must be very difficult to any but the Importer. It declares that the goods are in *quantity, quality* and *value,* according to the *inward* entry of them, *which entry was duly* made at the time of importation: a fact, which it is evident, can rarely be *known* to any but the person who made *that* entry. This must therefore occasion, either difficulty in obtaining the drawback, or a kind of constructive swearing inconsistent with that scrupulous strictness, which ought ever to accompany an oath, and on which the security they are intended to afford must depend. To obviate both, it seems necessary to direct, that proof of the fact shall be made to the satisfaction of the Collector, by the oaths or affirmations of all the parties through whose hands the goods may have passed; in which case each can be examined, as far as his knowlege can be presumed to extend.

There is no rule prescribed for regulating the sum in which bond shall be taken; whence there is perhaps too much left to the discretion of the officers. And the cancelling of the bond is made to depend, among other things, upon the oath or affirmation of the *Master* and *Mate* of the Vessel, in which the goods are exported, attesting their delivery: a requisite which it may not always be possible to fulfil. The Master or Mate may die, or may quit the vessel, from different causes, without complying with it. These circumstances seem to require some other modifications. The Secretary has had an eye to them in the draft of the bill accompanying his report of the ninth of January last,[9] to which he begs leave respectfully to refer.

26. Section XL. This Section provides, that no goods, wares or merchandize of foreign growth or manufacture subject of the payment of duties, shall be brought into the United States otherwise than by Sea, and in ships or vessels of not less than thirty tons burthen, with an exception as to the district of Louisville, and another as to Vessels at the time of the passing of the act on their Voyage.

It is a matter which merits particular consideration, whether there ought not also to be an exception, in regard to the most easterly district of the State of Massachusetts. The situation of that district is in different views peculiar; so as, perhaps, to render it

9. "Report Relative to a Provision for the Support of Public Credit," January 9, 1790.

adviseable rather to endeavour to regulate, than to prevent the introduction of foreign articles in smaller vessels. The information received on this point will also, with the leave of the House, be reserved for the Committee before referred to.

*Fourthly. As to the "Act for registering and clearing Vessels, regu-
lating the Coasting trade, and for other purposes.*[10]

Many of the provisions of this Act are objected to; particularly
those parts, which relate to the Coasting trade and fisheries; and yet
it must be confessed, that the proper remedies or alterations are
neither obvious nor easy. The more the matter is examined, the
more difficult it appears, to reconcile the convenience of those
branches of trade, with due precautions for the security of the
Revenue.

Section II. The Idea of this section, is, that every vessel shall be
registered by the Collector of the district to which she belongs. This
regulation is a proper one, as a knowlege of the persons, on whose
oaths or affirmations the registeries are to be founded by the officer making them, is a security against imposition. But this provision seems to be contravened by that of the seventh Section; as
will be noted hereafter.

27. Section III This section directs the mode of ascertaining the
tonnage of "all ships or vessels." It is however a question whether it
means only those which are to be registered, in order to their
registry, or extends to others, in order to computing the tonnage
duty. The latter construction has been preferred for the sake of
equality and uniformity.

The mode of admeasurement prescribed has been complained of
as unfavourable to certain kinds of vessels, and as tending to enlarge the tonnage beyond the standard of other countries.

28. Section VI. Objections are made to the form of the oath
prescribed by this Section. The party is to swear, positively, to the
place where the vessel was built (which in a great number of cases
cannot, with propriety, be done); and also to the citizenship, not
only of himself, but of the other owners, and of the Master (which,
in many cases, must be equally difficult).

Inconveniencies are experienced from the want of a rule for de-

10. 1 *Stat.* 55–65 (September 1, 1789).

termining who are citizens. The consequence of it is, that every man is left to his own opinion of what constitutes one; and it is represented, that there are instances, in which persons of reputation, supposing that *residence only* conferred the character, have been ready to take the oath prescribed.

A designation of the several *descriptions* of persons entitled to the privileges of citizens under this act, requiring that the particular *one* under which each falls, should be inserted in his oath, would be the most effectual guard against error or imposition. If this should be thought to be attended with too many difficulties from our peculiar situation, it may at least be proper to annex some adequate pecuniary penalty to the obtaining of Registers by persons not citizens; and to oblige all who apply, to specify in their oaths, by what title they are citizens, that is, whether by nativity, naturalization, or otherwise, which by bringing into view the situation of each person, would serve as a useful check.

In these observations it is taken for granted, that as the Law now stands, the oath of the party is the sole guide to the officers of the Customs; that they have not any discretion in the case; and that a power in them to judge of the qualifications of individuals, in so important a respect, could not, with propriety, be established.

29. Section VII. The second section, as already remarked, directs, that Vessels be registered in the districts to which *they belong. This* admits their registry, whereever they may be, provided the oath required be taken before the Collectors of the districts to which they belong. It is conceived, that an adherence to the principle of the second section throughout, would conduce to security. And it is therefore, submitted, whether, instead of the provision in this section, it would not be adviseable to provide, that when a vessel being in a district, other than that to which she belongs, has occasion to be registered, she shall be surveyed, under the direction of the proper officer of the Port, where she may happen to be, and registered by the Collector of the district to which she may belong, upon a certificate of the officer by whom such survey shall have been made.

30. Section XI. The declaring the instrument of transfer void, unless the Register be recited in it, involves an embarassing question, as to the property of the vessel; and does not seem necessary to the

object in view; the subsequent part of the Section, which annuls the privileges of an American bottom, without such recital, answering, alone, the purpose of the provision.

31. Section XII. If in the oath on which the registry is founded it be necessary to declare, that the Master is a Citizen; it would seem equally necessary, that on a change of Master, there should be a like attestation of his citizenship, previous to the indorsement herein directed to be made: As, otherwise, a Citizen may be the Master one day; a foreigner, the next.

Section XIII. There would be less room for imposition, if, instead of allowing the Collector of the Port, where the vessel might be, to grant a new register, he were authorized merely to take the oath prescribed, in order to its transmission to the Collector of the district, where he might belong, making it the duty of the latter to issue the new Register.

32. Section XXII. This Section commences the regulations respecting vessels employed in the Coasting trade and fisheries. The proviso of it exempts all licensed Vessels under twenty tons from clearing and entering, and in its consequences removes them almost wholly from the inspection of the officers of the Customs. The tendency of this to facilitate smuggling, is obvious; as these vessels are precisely of that kind which would be most *naturally* employed in clandestinely unlading on the coast, *those* which arrive from abroad. The bond required in order to a license, is a very slender restraint; not only from the smallness of the penalty, but from the little danger of discovery: And the oath is still less effectual, because the Master who is to take it, may at any time be changed before the application for a new license. This oath too is exceptionable on other accounts. The anticipation of a *future* and *distant* oath, may be too apt to give way to the allurements of immediate interest; and if a breach of the law have been committed, when it is to be taken, it is hardly to be expected, that there will be a strict adherence to truth, at the price of incurring both disgrace and loss.

It would be perhaps more effectual and less exceptionable, if instead of this oath, one should be required previous to the granting of any license to a fishing or coasting vessel, from the owner or owners of such vessel, that she shall not, during the time for which it is to be granted, be employed with his or their permission, consent, sufferance, privity, or connivance, in any way whereby the payment of the duties imposed by Law on articles imported into the United States, may be evaded.

But it seems indispensible towards guarding against the frauds which may be committed by coasters, that they should be obliged *at every port or place where there is an officer of the customs*, to report themselves and their lading on their arrival and previous to their departure. For this purpose, the office hours ought to be so regulated and extended, as to afford the greatest possible accommodation, and avoid occasions of delay. With this precaution, and taking care that the fees are moderate, it is presumeable, that coasters may be subjected to a pretty exact inspection, without injuriously impeding their business.

While they ought, in the opinion of the Secretary, to be thus subjected to a strict supervision, at places where there are Officers, it appears to him proper, that they should be exempted from the obligation either of entering or clearing, when at places where there are none. The necessity of journeys to distant offices, frequently across rivers and bays, and at the expence of the loss of favourable winds, occasions in some parts of the Union serious obstructions to the coasting trade. As connected with this idea, it would tend to the security of the Revenue, if a disscretion were allowed to appoint inspectors at places, which are not ports of general entry or delivery, for the purpose of entering, clearing, and overseeing Coasters.

33. Section XXIII. In the remarks on the Act imposing duties on Tonnage, the construction which has obtained upon the last clause of this section has been stated together with the hardships, which have ensued to Individuals from misapprehension of it.

A different modification of the provision has also been suggested. Among other reasons to be assigned for it, is this; that, by obliging all registered Vessels to take out licenses, it unnecessarily increases the number of vessels intitled to the privileges of coasters. In the opinion of the Secretary, these ought to be confined to such as are ordinarily employed in the coasting and fishing trade; to effect which, it may be proper, that previous to the granting of any license, an oath or affirmation should be made, that the Vessel for which it is required, is bona fide intended to be employed as a coasting or fishing vessel, during the period for which it is to be granted; or the greater part of it; and even to annex a penalty to the taking out a license for any vessel, which shall not be so employed. This, in respect to fishing vessels, seems peculiarly necessary; as it is easy to see that on the pretext of that employment, licenses may be perverted from their real purpose, to that of a mere cover for illicit practices.

There is no provision for the case of a change of property within the year, for which a license may be granted, which sometimes occasions sureties to be bound for parties, they did not contemplate. This, and the repetition of the tonnage duty, which is a consequence of it, is regarded as an inconvenience, requiring to be remedied by a provision for the granting new licenses when such changes happen, upon new security, for the remainder of the year.

34. Sections XXVII and XXVIII. As there are no particular penalties annexed to a noncompliance with the requisites of these sections; it has of course been found in some instances, difficult to enforce their execution. And though it is presumed, that such noncompliance would be a good probable cause of seizure Yet if in the event of a trial it turned out in one case, that there were no foreign goods, nor ardent spirits exceeding four hundred gallons on board; and in the other, that a manifest and permit had been obtained, and that no goods were on board but such as they specified, no penalty could be inflicted. And a vexatious litigation between the Officer and the party, might be the only fruit of the seizure.

It is inferred from the last of these Sections, that a Coaster whose ultimate destination is for a place, where a Collector or Surveyor resides, having on board goods for any intermediate place, is not at liberty to land those goods at such intermediate place, till after a permit for landing shall have been obtained at the place of destination; which is complained of as a grievance, and certainly is attended in many cases with considerable inconvenience. A relaxation in this respect, may be adviseable. And to guard as much as possible against any ill effects from it, it may be expedient, that whenever a Coaster arrives at a port where a Collector or Surveyor resides, it should be incumbent upon the Master of her, to make a report in writing and upon oath, stating the goods on board at the

time of her departure from the last port left by her, at which a
Collector or Surveyor resided, and which may have been afterwards
taken in or *delivered* prior to her arrival at the place of report. In
this case, to avoid a too great multiplication of oaths, the oaths required by the 25th & 26th sections maybe dispensed with; though
it will be still useful, that the manifests should be exhibited and
certified.

35. Section XXXI. The Secretary considering it as an essential
rule, that emoluments of office should not be extended by construction or inference beyond the letter of the provision, lest a door
should be opened to improper exactions; has instructed the Officers
of the Customs to govern themselves by a *literal* interpretation of
the several clauses of this section; the consequence of which, however, is, that equal services are unequally recompensed.

This chiefly arises from that clause, which allows a fee of sixty
cents.

"For every entry of inward Cargo directed to be made in conformity with this Act, *and* for receiving of and qualifying to every
manifest of vessels licensed to trade as aforesaid."

The *entry* and the *receiving* and qualifying to a manifest being
joined together by the word *and* are understood as one service, to
which a fee of sixty cents is attached; so that when only either of
the two things is performed, and not the other, no fee is taken.

Hence there is no allowance for swearing the Master to his Manifest, and granting a certificate of its having been done, according
to the twenty fifth and twenty sixth sections of this act, because it
is not accompanied in either case, with an inward entry. Twenty
Cents for the permit to proceed to the place of destination is the
only fee understood to be demandable, for the services specified in
these sections.

The sixty cents are deemed applicable only to the services enjoined by the twenty seventh section.

A revision of this Section will, upon accurate examination be
found eligible for other reasons; which for the sake of brevity are
omitted.

The foregoing are the principal remarks which occur on the
provisions of the several acts, on which the Secretary has been
directed to report. These acts have fulfilled their objects in all

respects as well as could reasonably have been expected from the first essay on so difficult a subject. It was foreseen that experience would suggest the propriety of corrections in the system; and it is equally to be inferred, that further experiment will manifest the expediency of further correction. The work must be progressive; since it can only be by successive improvements, that it can be brought to the degree of perfection, of which it is susceptible.

As connected with the difficulties that have occurred in the execution of the Laws, which are the subject of this report, the Secretary begs leave, in the last place, to mention the *want* of an officer in each state or other considerable subdivision of the United States, having the general superintendance of all the officers of the Revenue within such state or subdivision.

Among the inconveniencies attending it, is a great difficulty in drawing from the more remote ports, the monies, which are there collected. As the course of business creates little or no demand at the seat of Government or in its vicinity for drafts upon such places, negotiations in this way are either very dilatory or impracticable; neither does the circulation of bank-paper, from the same cause, extend to them. This embarassment would be remedied by having one person in each state, or in a district of the United States, of convenient extent, charged with the receipt of all the monies arising within it, and, placed in point of residence, where there was the greatest intercourse with the seat of Government. This would greatly facilitate negociations between the Treasury, and distant parts of the Union, and would contribute to lessening the necessity for the transportation of specie.

But there are other reasons of, perhaps, still greater weight for the measure. It is, in the opinion of the Secretary, essential to a due supervision of the conduct of the particular officers engaged in the collection of the revenues, and to the purposes of exact and impartial information, as to the operation of the Laws which relate to them. It is impossible, that the first end can be answered by any attention or vigilance of an Individual or Individuals at the Head of the Treasury. Distance, and the multiplicity of avocations, are conclusive bars. And however it may appear at first sight, that the second end may be attainable from the communications of those particular Officers; yet when it is considered, how apt their representations will be to receive a tint from the personal interests of the individuals and the local interests of districts, it must be perceived, that there cannot always be sufficient reliance upon them, and that variances between them will not unfrequently serve rather to distract, than to inform the judgment. Greater impartiality, and, of course, better information may be expected from an officer, who, standing in the same relation to a larger district, composed of several smaller districts, will be more likely to be free from the influence, either of personal interests or local predilections in reference to the parts.

The Secretary begs leave, with the utmost deference, to say, that he considers an arrangement of this kind as of real importance to the public service and to the efficacious discharge of the trust reposed in him.

All which is humbly submitted   Alexander Hamilton
Secy of the Treasury

From Thomas Smith

[*Philadelphia, April 22, 1790.* On April 26, 1790, Hamilton wrote to Smith: "You mention in your Letter of the 22d. Instant." *Letter not found.*]

From Otho H. Williams

[*Baltimore, April 24, 1790.* On May 4, 1790, Hamilton wrote to Williams: "I have received yours of the 24th of April requesting my opinion with respect to the duty on the article of hemp." *Letter not found.*]

To Charles Lee

Treasury Department, April 26, 1790. "I have directed the Treasurer to draw on You for 3075 Dollars. . . ."

LS, RG 36, Collector of Customs at Alexandria, Letters Received from the Secretary, National Archives.

To Thomas Smith

Treasury Department April 26th 1790.

Sir

You mention in Your Letter of the 22d. Instant [1] that certificates have been presented to you on which there are four Years interest due.

This gives me reason to apprehend that you may have admitted the calculation of Interest on them beyond the period as fixed by Congress, which is up to the 31st December 1787—and no latter.

If this should be the case you have acted contrary to my circular instructions to the Loan Officers of the 12th Octobr last; and if any error has happened in that way, you will endeavour to rectify the same, and will discontinue the practice in future.

I am   Sir   Your obedt Servt   A Hamilton

Thos Smith Esqr
late Commissr of the Loan Office for Pennsylvania

LS, Columbia University Libraries.
  1. Letter not found.

From Tench Coxe

[*Philadelphia, April 27, 1790.* On May 1, 1790, Hamilton wrote to Coxe: "I have just received your letter of the 27th of April." *Letter not found.*]

From William Allibone

Philadelphia, April 29, 1790. "I have the Honor to acknowledge the receipt of your letter dated april 21st [1] Informing me of my appointment as Superintendant of the Light House and other establishments in the Bay and River Deleware, and containing Instructions for my Government therein, but find that no official Information had reached you, of the Legislature of Pennsylvania having made Cession of the same to the United States. . . . I did make mention of it in a letter of mine dated October 5th last. . . .[2] I am much pressed for mony to fulfill the agreements made under the

authority of your circular letter of the fifth of October last. . . .
I have been without any money of the United States to make payments since November last. . . ."

ALS, with marginal comments on H's writing, RG 26, Lighthouse Letters Received, Vol. "A," Pennsylvania and Southern States, National Archives.
1. Letter not found.
2. Letter not found.

From William Allibone

[*Philadelphia*] *April 29, 1790.* Discusses proposals for improving
navigation in Delaware River and Delaware Bay.

ALS, RG 26, Lighthouse Letters Received, Vol. "A," Pennsylvania and Southern States, National Archives.

From Thomas Jefferson

New York, April 29, 1790. Requests "two hundred and fifty dollars for the contingent expences of the Office of Secretary of State."

LC, Papers of the Continental Congress, National Archives.

To Sharp Delany

Treasury Department, April 30, 1790. "I have not yet answered
that part of your Letter of the 13th of February which relates to
the employing of Boats for the Security of the revenue. . . . I am
not empowered to authorise boats for that purpose. . . . On the
Subject of Stores for the Safe keeping of goods I refer you to my
Letter of the 24th march." [1]

LS, Yale University Library.
1. Letter not found.

To Thomas Jefferson

Treasury Department, April 30, 1790. "Agreeably to your desire,[1]
I have issued a warrant in your favour . . . for . . . two hundred
and fifty dollars. . . ."

LC, Papers of the Continental Congress, National Archives.
1. See Jefferson to H, April 29, 1790.

To Benjamin Lincoln

Treasury Department April 30th 1790

Sir

I have in a late report to the house of Representatives[1] in substance proposed, what you mention in your Letter of the 15th Inst. respecting coasters.

There is also a proposition before the house, contemplating a provision for boats to secure the revenue against fraudulent practices; it will therefore be best for the present to wait the result.

I am   Sir   Your Obedt Servt

Benj Lincoln Esqr
Collector for the port of Boston

L[S], RG 36, Collector of Customs at Boston, Letters from the Treasury and Others, 1789–1809, Vol. 1, National Archives; copy, RG 56, Letters to the Collectors at Small Ports, Set "G," National Archives; copy, RG 56, Letters to the Collector at Boston, National Archives.
  1. "Report on Defects in the Existing Laws of Revenue," April 22, 1790.

From William Allibone

Philadelphia [April, 1790]. Asks Hamilton's opinion on Allibone's recommendations[1] for improving navigation in the Delaware River and Delaware Bay.

ALS, RG 26, Lighthouse Letters Received, Vol. "A," Pennsylvania and Southern States, National Archives.
  1. See Allibone to H, April 29, 1790.

From Sharp Delany

[Philadelphia, April, 1790.] "I forward my Abstract of Duties. . . . I wish not to be troublesome to you . . . but I request your attention to my situation for without disguise my Emoluments . . . are greatly inadequate to my services."

LC, Copies of Letters to the Secretary, 1789–1790, Bureau of Customs, Philadelphia.

To Tench Coxe

New York, May 1st, 1790.

Dear Sir,

I have just received your letter of the 27th of April.[1] Yours of the 6th of the same month [2] also came to hand in due time; though peculiar reasons prevented an earlier acknowledgment of it.

The appointment of his assistant is, by the act establishing the treasury department, vested in the secretary himself. The conviction I have of your usefulness in that station, and my personal regard for you, have determined me to avail myself of the offer of service which the last mentioned letter contains.[3]

The state of the public business under my care, is such as to make me desire to see you as soon as may consist with the dispositions which your change of situation will render necessary.

I am, with great regard and esteem, dear sir, your obedient servant,

A. Hamilton

Tench Coxe, Esq.

White, *Samuel Slater*, 180–81.
   1. Letter not found.
   2. Letter not found.
   3. H selected Coxe as Assistant Secretary of the Treasury to replace William Duer who had resigned. See H to Duer, April 4–7, 1790.
   For Coxe's appointment, see "Appointment of Tench Coxe as Assistant Secretary of the Treasury," May 10, 1790.

From Otho H. Williams

[*Baltimore, May 1, 1790.*] Itemizes expenses and then adds: "I have only to hope that compensation will be made to me for my services and expences; or that I shall stand excused for retiring from a service the reward of which must depend upon indirect measures."

ADfS, RG 53, "Old Correspondence," Baltimore Collector, National Archives.

From Joseph Whipple

Portsmouth, New Hampshire, May 3, 1790. Encloses "Weekly return of receipts & payments to the 1st. instant and a monthly Schedule of Bonds given for duties in this district in the Month of April past."

LC, RG 36, Collector of Customs at Portsmouth, Letters Sent, 1789–1790, Vol. 1, National Archives.

To William Allibone

[*New York, May 4, 1790.* On the back of the letter that Allibone wrote to Hamilton on April 29, 1790, is written "Answd 4th May." *Letter not found.*] [1]

1. In the margin of Allibone's letter of April 29, H wrote the following comments which presumably are his answers to Allibone:
"The state having made a cession the limitation is of course inapplicable.
"Warrant for in his favour or the Treasurer who is directed to take measures for payt.
"Let a contract be drawn & transmitted it will be ratified of course."

From Sharp Delany

Philada. 4th May 1790

Sir

I have provided some stores and am finishing another, which I think will be sufficient for the Custom house, and as soon as completed will give you the necessary return.

I always thought the Law did not expressly give you the power of fixing Revenue boats [1] but as such was necessary and mentioned in the Collection Law.[2] The Superintendance vested in you I imagined would warrant the measure. As to me I had no other motive but the safety of the Revenue for as to the appointments given to me as Collector, it is among the least desireable parts of my Duty—at least one of the most so. Our Importations are very considerable this Spring.

I am Sir with great Respect   Your most hble Servt

Sharp Delany

LC, Copies of Letters to the Secretary, 1789–1790, Bureau of Customs, Philadelphia.
1. See H to Delany, April 30, 1790.
2. "An Act to regulate the Collection of the Duties imposed by law on the tonnage of ships or vessels, and on goods, wares and merchandises imported into the United States" (1 *Stat.* 29–49 [July 31, 1789]).

To Otho H. Williams

Treasury Department May 4th 1790

Sir

I have received yours of the 24th of April [1] requesting my opinion with respect to the Duty on the article of hemp.

There can be no doubt that this article is under the present Law Subject to a Duty of five per cent ad valorem untill the first day of December next.

I am   Sir   Your obedt Servt   A Hamilton

O H Williams Esqr
Collector for the port of Baltimore

LS, Columbia University Libraries.
1. Letter not found.

From Sharp Delany

[*Philadelphia*] *May 5, 1790.* "I take the Liberty of troubling you with the inclosed Acct of the Marshall for the purpose of shewing You the necessity of making some allterations in the mode of process. You will at once perceive there can be no inducment to any of the inferior officers of the Revenue to give information—as in the End unless the seizure should be very valuable no emoluments will come to their share. This seizure was made by me, and after all the trouble of prosecution &c I shall receive about Eight Dollars and should any seizure be made, without sufficient proof for con-

demnation, cost trouble & blame will be the seizing officers portion. . . ."

LC, Copies of Letters to the Secretary, 1789–1790, Bureau of Customs, Philadelphia.

To William Webb

Treasury Department, May 5, 1790. "In answer to yours of the
16th. of April[1] I have to observe, that the rate of foreign Tonage
may be waved in the case you state. . . . With regard to the 40th.
Section of the Collection law,[2] it is to be understood that American as well as foreign vessels are within the provisions of the Section and subject to seizure and forfeiture."

LS, United States Finance Miscellany, Treasury Circulars, Library of Congress.
    1. Letter not found.
    2. "An Act to regulate the Collection of the Duties imposed by law on the
tonnage of ships or vessels, and on goods, wares and merchandises imported
into the United States" (1 *Stat.* 29–49 [July 31, 1789]).

From William Allibone

Philadelphia, May 6, 1790. Proposes that supplies for the following year be purchased immediately to take advantage of favorable prices. Plans to inspect all navigational aids in Delaware River
and Delaware Bay at the end of May.

ALS, RG 26, Lighthouse Letters Received, Vol. "A," Pennsylvania and Southern States, National Archives.

From Stephen Higginson

Boston May 6. 1790

Sir

I have been confined several Weeks by the fashionable disorder
called the influenza, which has made sad work here. My Eyes were
so affected by it, that I have wrote but little & read less. By the
papers, & letters I have received, you must have had an unpleasant
time of it too for several Weeks. I sympathised with you, & felt the

force of various passions at different times, which must have affected you in a much higher degree. But amidst all the folly, narrowness & selfishness, that marked the discussion of your report,[1] I was pleased to observe there was a respectful impression on the minds of all, which the report had necessarily made, & which was to me a new Evidence that it would eventually obtain. The rejection of the State Debts[2] may not in the issue prove injurious—the proposition will come forward with force & advantage, after the other parts of the System are perfected; & its opposers will be compelled to adopt it with marks indicative of their own weakness, & of the sound policy & wisdom of the measure. I yet have faith that it will take place this Session; but should it be put over to the next, the effect upon the public mind may be very useful. In most of the States it will become a popular measure, I think; & the public Voice will then be strong in its favour. There has been a want of attention & arrangement with the friends to the measure. They might have compelled Georgia & some others to have been with them; & They ought not to have permitted any other Question to draw off their attention, or engage their feelings, till they had finished the Revennue business. I wish the future may in some measure compensate the past. Congress ought now to work double tides, to redeem the time They have wasted.

I have some Business at york, & have been in doubt whether to go on or not. If I thought my being there in person would tend to forward my Views before stated to you, I should at once decide. Though I do not wish to engross any part of your time, already too much occupied, either for health or enjoyment, one line expressing your Idea on that single point may be useful.

As I yet avoid writing much to save my Eyes, I shall at present forbear offering you a few Sentiments, which I thought of doing; & shall now only add, that with every Sentiment of esteem & respect I have the honour to subscribe Sir   Your very hume Servant
                                                  Stephen Higginson

ALS, Connecticut Historical Society, Hartford.
    1. "Report Relative to a Provision for the Support of Public Credit," January 9, 1790.
    2. The proposal for the assumption of state debts was defeated in the House of Representatives on April 12, 1790, by a vote of 31 to 29 (*Annals of Congress*, II, 1577).

To George Washington

Treasury Department
May 6th. 1790

The Secretary of the Treasury has the honor to inform the President of the United states of America, that he has received a letter from the Governor of Virginia [1] intimating that it is necessary an election should be made of the particular spot upon which it may be deemed proper to erect the intended Light house on Cape Henry, after which the Cession will be completed.

The said Secretary having heard the propriety of the place contemplated for that purpose by the State of Virginia, called in question, as being peculiarly exposed to accumulations of sand in its vicinity, begs leave to submit to the President the expediency of appointing a trusty and judicious person to view the ground & make the choice; with power to take with him one or two seafaring people, who may possess local information.

The said Secretary further informs the President, that by a letter received from Benjamin Lincoln Esquire,[2] it appears, that the widow Thomas, charged under the state of Massachusetts with the care of the Light-house at Plymouth has a son named   [3] Thomas, who is of good character and deserves the consideration of the President as Keeper of that Light-house.

The said Benjamin Lincoln also informs the said Secretary, that he has agreed for the supply of oil for the Light-houses in the State of Massachusetts, at the rate of one hundred & four dollars per ton, which is lower than it has of late sold for, subject to ratification by the said Secretary with the approbation of the President.

On these particulars the said Secretary requests the order of the President.[4]

LC, George Washington Papers, Library of Congress.
   1. Beverley Randolph to H, February 23, 1790.
   2. This letter is dated April 6, 1790.
   3. Space left blank in MS. Thomas's first name was John.
   4. For the reply to this letter, see William Jackson to H, May 7–10, 1790.

From James Duane

[New York, May 7, 1790]

Sir

Be so good if in your power to acquaint me of the issue of our friend the Baron's afair [1] in the house of Representatives? I know you will pardon my Sollicitude as I embark in the morning for the North.

I am affectionately your's   Jas. Duane

ALS, New-York Historical Society, New York City.
  1. Baron von Steuben had petitioned the House of Representatives for compensation for his services during the American Revolution. See H's "Report on the Memorial of Baron von Steuben," March 29, 1790.

To James Duane [1]

[New York, May 7, 1790]

The form of the bill [2] has been changed to day. He is to be paid 7000 Dollars & an annuity for life but the blank is not filled up. Nobody talks of less than 1500 Dollars. The Baron says his contract or nothing; but you & all his friends must join me in telling him that to act upon this would be to act like a boy. This must be done before you leave town.

Yr affect & Obling   A H

ALS, New-York Historical Society, New York City.
  1. For the background to this letter, see H's "Report on the Memorial of Baron von Steuben, March 29, 1790, and Duane to H, May 7, 1790.
  2. The bill to compensate von Steuben for his services in the American Revolution was passed by the House of Representatives on May 7, 1790, by a vote of 28 to 21. The bill provided for a payment of $7,000, an annuity of $2,706, and a land grant in the Northwest Territory (*Journal of the House*, I, 210–11).

From Andrew Ellicott [1]

Philadelphia, May 7, 1790. Will depart for Lake Erie at the end of May to complete the survey of the northeastern Pennsylvania lands ceded to the United States by New York.[2] Expects to be in New York next week and will furnish Hamilton with an estimate of the expenses involved.

ALS, Andrew Ellicott Papers, Library of Congress.
    1. Ellicott was a surveyor and mathematician who had worked for both Virginia and Pennsylvania. In 1789, when he moved from Baltimore to Philadelphia, he was appointed by the Federal Government to fix the southwestern boundary of New York.
    2. New York ceded these lands in February, 1780. Pennsylvania, which began negotiations for their purchase in 1789, finally obtained them from the United States in March, 1792.

From William Jackson [1]

[New York, May 7–10, 1790]

The President of the United states authorises the Secretary of the Treasury to engage Edward Carrington [2] Esquire to visit Cape Henry and to make a selection of the spot for the purpose of the Cession within mentioned (with permission to take with him one or two seafaring persons) & to make the parties a resonable allowance for expence and trouble, out of the Monies appropriated towards erecting the said Light house.

The President also thinks fit to appoint the said Thomas,[3] Keeper or Superintendant of the Light house at Plymouth, and authorises the said Secretary to ratify the provisional Contract for oil within mentioned.

By order of the President of the United states   W. Jackson

LC, George Washington Papers, Library of Congress.
    1. This letter is in reply to H to Washington, May 6, 1790.
    Jackson, who had served as a major under Benjamin Lincoln during the American Revolution, had been secretary of the Constitutional Convention in 1787. He became one of George Washington's secretaries in 1789.
    2. Carrington was the United States marshal for Virginia from 1789 to 1791.
    3. John Thomas.

To Wilhem and Jan Willink, Nicholaas and Jacob Van Staphorst, and Nicholas Hubbard

Treasury Department May 7th. 1790.

Gentlemen

Triplicates of your letter of the 25th. of January last have duly come to hand.

As the success of the negotiations for the purchase of the Debt [1] due from the United States to France would have been an unwelcome circumstance; I learn with pleasure that it had not taken place.

The distinguished zeal you have in so many instances shewn for the interests of this country, intitles you upon all occasions to a favourable interpretation of the motives by which you are actuated; and is calculated to inspire a disposition to co-operate in your arrangements, though without previous authority, as far as circumstances will justify. Nor should I be apprehensive, that a sanction to the step you have taken, would form an inconvenient precedent for the future.

But the delays naturally incident to deliberations on a matter of the first consequence, the road to which had not been made easy by the antecedent state of things, having hitherto suspended any definitive resolutions concerning the public debt, I am not now in a situation to speak explicitly in regard to the measure you have undertaken. I can only say that the United States will stand in need of the aid of Loans abroad, and that I expect the requisite provision for making them upon solid, and consequently advantageous terms, will shortly be concluded upon; in which case you will immediately hear from me.

I have the honor to remain with real esteem Gentlemen Your obt. & hble. servant

Alexr. Hamilton
Secy of the Treasury.

P.S. You have herewith triplicate of my Letter of the 7th. of April —the first & second of the bills therein mentioned have been forwarded by the british packet Antelope, Captain Curtiss, and by the

Catherine Capt. Bull bound for Amsterdam and I hope will get duly to hand.

Messrs. W. & J. Willink & N. & J. Van Staphorst & Hubbard Amsterdam.

LC, George Washington Papers, Library of Congress.
1. See William Short to H, November 30, 1789, January 28–31, 1790.

To Benjamin Lincoln

[*New York, May 8, 1790.* The endorsement on the letter which Lincoln wrote to Hamilton on April 6, 1790, reads: "Answered 8th May." *Letter not found.*]

To Beverley Randolph

Treasury Department May 8th. 1790

Sir

I have been duly honored with your letter of the 23d of february, an acknowlegement of which has been postponed by very urgent avocations connected with the Session of Congress.

I am now to inform you, that Edward Carrington Esquire has been requested to visit the Cape, and make a selection of the spot; upon whose report to you it will be satisfactory that the Cession be completed.[1]

This step has been indicated, in addition to what is mentioned in your letter, by a representation that the spot formerly in contemplation of the state is peculiarly exposed to accumulations by the drifting of the sand and that care is necessary to avoid as much as possible this inconvenience.

I have the honor to be with the greatest respect Your Excellencys most obedt. & hble Servt.   Alex Hamilton
                                        Secy of the Treasury

His Excellency Beverly Randolph Esquire
Governor of the State of Virginia

LS, Archives Division, Virginia State Library, Richmond.
1. See William Jackson to H, May 7–10, 1790.

Appointment of Tench Coxe as Assistant Secretary of the Treasury

[New York, May 10, 1790]

To Tench Coxe, greeting:

Reposing especial trust and confidence in your integrity, diligence, and abilities, I, Alexander Hamilton, secretary of the treasury of the United States, in virtue of the power to me given, by the act entitled "An act to establish the treasury department," [1] do constitute and appoint you assistant to the said secretary: To hold and exercise the said office during the pleasure of the secretary of the treasury of the United States for the time being.

In witness whereof, I have hereunto set my hand, and affixed the seal of the treasury, the tenth day of May, in the year of our Lord one thousand seven hundred and ninety.

Alexander Hamilton
Secretary of the Treasury

White, *Samuel Slater*, 182.
1. 1 *Stat.* 65–67 (September 2, 1789).

From Joseph Whipple

Portsmouth, New Hampshire, May 10, 1790. Sends an account of payments to invalid veterans. States that New Hampshire "has paid Several of those Invalids to the 31 July 1789," but that additional money "is requisite to discharge the first Moiety of the Said years Pension."

LC, RG 36, Collector of Customs at Portsmouth, Letters Sent, 1789–1790, Vol. 1, National Archives; copy, RG 56, Letters from the Collector at Portsmouth, National Archives.

From Nathaniel Appleton

Boston, May 11, 1790. "When I was in the City of N York I presented to the Auditors my account Currt. as Commissr. of the Loan Office in this State, he objected to the adjustment of part of my account for want of Vouchers to support the charge of Interest paid, & my Commissions thereon previous to the establishment of Salaries. Agreable to the Auditors direction I now transmitt to the Treasury, Three Volumes Folio . . . which contain the Vouchers alluded to. . . . I wait your orders respecting the balances of Indents, blank Loan Office Certificates, and New Emission Money on hand, as the latter was money made by this State and Loaned to the United States, but never issued; query whether it should not be returned to the State and be deducted from the original Charge. If Offices shall be opened in different parts of the Union for reloaning the Domestic Debt, I shall be ready at the shortest notice to obey your orders, if it should be thought proper to continue me in the public service."

LC, RG 53, Massachusetts State Loan Office, Letter Book, 1785–1791, Vol. "259-M," National Archives.

From Vincent Gray [1]

[*Alexandria, Virginia, May 11, 1790.* On May 21, 1790, Hamilton wrote to Charles Lee: [2] "I have this day received a letter from Mr Vincent Gray . . . dated 11th instant." *Letter not found.*]

1. Gray was deputy collector of customs at Alexandria.
2. The letter from Lee has not been printed because it pertains to routine Treasury Department matters. It may be found in RG 36, Collector of Customs at Alexandria, Letters Received from the Secretary, 1789–1795, National Archives.

Report on Money Received from, or Paid to, the States

[New York, May 11, 1790
Communicated to the House: May 11, 1790]

[To the Speaker of the House of Representatives]
The Secretary of the Treasury, in obedience to the order of the House of Representatives of the 23d of April,[1] respectfully submits the several statements, in the schedules herewith transmitted, marked A and B, and Nos. 1, 2, 3, 4, and 5.[2]
Upon these statements, the Register of the Treasury, in his re-

port to the said Secretary, makes the following remarks:

The debits and credits, in continental money, advanced from, or received out of, the treasury of the United States, as stated in the within schedule, may be relied on as the true nominal amount, stated on record in the Treasury books; but the reduction to specie value, is subject to the examination of the general board of commissioners.

The credits for specie, and also of indents paid into the treasury of the United States, on account of the existing requisitions of Congress, are accurate, and, it is presumed, conclusive. But, with respect to the extension, in specie, of the several payments into the treasury, in the emission of continental bills of credit, called old emissions, and the emissions of the 18th March, 1780, although the nominal sums specified in the subordinate statements, are as accurate as the treasury records will admit, yet, as there is no legislative guide on a question of so great importance, the treasury officers have felt themselves exceedingly embarrassed. On the one hand, they could not presume to affix a scale not warranted by any act of the Legislature, and on the other, the order of the House required a compliance as far as possible. They have, therefore, on this occasion, governed themselves by the only existing regulation of the late Congress. According to the table herewith presented, by a reduction to specie, all sums, either paid or received from the States, from the commencement of the Revolution, to 18th March, 1780, and from that period to the present date, all sums in continental money, are reduced to specie, at forty for one.

The new emissions are estimated equal to specie.

When State paper has been received by the United States from any particular State, the State making the payment has received a credit, at which, it has been accounted for, by those who have received it.

The Secretary begs leave to observe, from principles which have governed the said statements, they cannot be considered as exhibiting the actual specie value of the moneys received from the respective States.

But an impression, that it might not be advisable, on his part, to enter into considerations which are relative to the duty of the commissioners for settling accounts between the United States and the individual States, has led him to seek, in the acts of Congress and the records of the treasury, for the results by which the liquidation of the paper money should be conducted, rather than to indulge a latitude of opinion as to what might be the abstract right.

All which is humbly submitted.

ASP, Finance, I, 52.
   1. The House ordered:
   "That the Secretary of the Treasury be directed to report the sums of money, including indents and paper money of every kind, reduced to specie value, which have been received from, or paid to, the several States by Congress, from the commencement of the Revolution to the present period." (*Jour-nal of the House,* I, 199.)
   2. These schedules are printed in *ASP, Finance,* I, 53–62.

Report of Tonnage Duties Received in Each of the States

Treasury-Department, 11th. May 1790.
[Communicated on May 11, 1790] [1]

[To the Speaker of the House of Representatives]

The Secretary of the Treasury respectfully submits an Abstract of the duties which have accrued on the Tonnage of ships or vessels, from the first day of September to the thirty first day of December last, pursuant to the order of the House of Representatives of the fifth Instant.[2]

Abstract of Duties which have accrued on the Tonnage of foreign and domestic Vessels from the first of September to the thirty first of December 1789.

States.	Foreign Tonnage.	Domestic Tonnage.	Total Amount of Tonnage.
New Hampshire	469. 50	339. 30	808. 80
Massachusetts	4 829. 37½	3 855. 60	8 684. 97½
Connecticut	618. 8	722. 47½	1 340. 55½
New York	8 739. 87½	1 496. 66½	10.236. 54
New Jersey	83. 50	224. 31	307. 81
Pennsylvania	11.587. 64	1 515. 6	13.102. 70
Delaware	603. —	123. 96	726. 96
Maryland	4.994. 5½	1 728. 88½	6 722. 94
Virginia	11.210. 93½	1 423. 30½	12.634. 24
South Carolina	4 630. 59	433. 84	5 064. 43
Georgia	2 600. 17	126. 65	2 726. 82
	50.366. 72.	11.990. 5	62.356. 77

Alexr. Hamilton.
Secy. of the Treasury.

Copy, RG 233, Reports of the Secretary of the Treasury, 1790–1791, Vol. I, National Archives.
1. *Journal of the House*, I, 214.
2. The House ordered:
"That the Secretary of the Treasury report to the House the amount of tonnage duties paid in each of the States from the first of September to the first of January last, distinguishing the foreign from the domestic tonnage." (*Journal of the House*, I, 209.)

From William Heth

[*Bermuda Hundred, Virginia, May 12, 1790.*] Recommends John W. Johnston, a former clerk in Heth's office, as "a young man of great silence, of rigid truth, and on whom I placed great trust and confidence."

Copy, Papers of George Washington, Library of Congress.

To William Barton [1]

[*New York, May 13, 1790.* On August 9, 1790, Barton wrote to Hamilton: "the disposition to oblige me which you were pleased to express in Your letter of the 13th. of May." *Letter not found.*]

1. Barton, a Pennsylvania lawyer and judge, was the nephew of David Rittenhouse.

To Israel Ludlow

[New York, May 13, 1790]

Sir

Your letter of the 4th of November [1] though a considerable time on the way has some time since been received and is the only one I find among my letters on the subject.

I request that either Mr Martin [2] or yourself would as speedily as may be come on to this place and bring with you the returns of survey and Maps, which you mention to be ready. Expenditures will then be adjusted.

I am Sir   Your Obed serv

A Hamilton
Secy of the Treasury

New York. May 13. 1790 [3]

ALS, Hamilton Papers, Library of Congress.
    1. Letter not found.
    2. Presumably Absalom Martin, who operated a ferry on the Ohio River at Wheeling, Virginia.
    3. At the bottom of the letter "To Mr Israel Ludlow Fort Harmar" is written in an unidentified handwriting.

To Timothy Pickering

[New York, May 13, 1790]

Dear Sir
    The offer of your service as successor to Mr. Duer [1] reached me in due time.
    I can with truth assure you, that you were one of a very small number who held a competition in my judgment and that had personal considerations alone influenced me, I could with difficulty have preferred another. Reasons of a peculiar nature, however, have determined my choice towards Mr. Tench Coxe,[2] who to great industry and very good talents adds an extensive theoretical and practical knowlege of Trade.
    Allow me to say, that knowing, as I now do, your views to public life, I shall from conviction of your worth take pleasure in promoting them. And I hope an opportunity will not be long wanting I remain with sincere esteem and warm regard Dr Sir   Yr. Obed ser
                                                                A Hamilton

New York May 13. 1790
Timothy Pickering Esqr

ALS, Massachusetts Historical Society, Boston.
    1. Pickering to H, April 6, 1790.
    2. "Appointment of Tench Coxe as Assistant Secretary of the Treasury," May 10, 1790.

Treasury Department Circular
to the Collectors of the Customs

Treasury Department
May 13th. 1790

Sir
    The second moiety of one years pensio⟨n⟩ will be payable to the Invalids [1] on the fifth day of June next: The sum to be paid in your State is estimated to be Eight thousand two hundr⟨ed⟩ and fifty

three dollars,[2] which you will retain in your hands out of the Monies received by you for duties on Imports and Tonnage and pay the same upon such evidences as the Secretary at War shall direct, agreeably to my former instruct⟨i⟩ons of the 30th. of January last. The drafts from the Treasury shall in the mean time be regulated as to leave a sufficient sum in your hands to answer the intended purpose: such however as may be drawn are by all means to be paid.

I am Sir   Your Obedt. servant   A Hamilton
                                                  Secy of the Treasy

LS, to Sharp Delany, Collector of Customs at Philadelphia, Circulars, 1789–1809, Bureau of Customs, Philadelphia; LS, to Jedediah Huntington, MS Division, New York Public Library; LS, to Otho H. Williams, Office of the Secretary of the Treasury, Circulars, 1789–1816, Office of the Secretary, United States Treasury Department; copy, to Otho H. Williams, Circulars of the Office of the Secretary, "Set T," National Archives; copy, United States Finance Miscellany, Treasury Circulars, Library of Congress.

1. See "An Act providing for the payment of the Invalid Pensioners of the United States" (1 *Stat.* 95 [September 29, 1789]); and H to Jedediah Huntington, January 30, 1790.

2. This figure was, of course, different in each of the letters to the various collectors.

To John Haywood

Treasury Department
May 15th. 1790

Sir

Another half years pension will become due to the Invalids on the 5th. day of June next, which you will please to pay agreeably to my instructions of the 4th. of February last.[1]

In order to enable you to execute this business I have issued a Warrant on the Treasurer of the United States in your favor for 420 dollars for the payment of which the said Treasurer will forward to you a draft on John Daves esquire Collector at Newbern.

I am Sir   Your Obedt servant   A Hamilton
                                                  Secy of the Treasy

John Haywood Esqr.
Treasurer of the State of No: Carolina.

LS, Southern Historical Collection, University of North Carolina Library.
1. H is mistaken for his letter to Haywood is dated February 2, 1790.

*Treasury Department Circular
to the Collectors of the Customs*

Treasury Department
May 17th. 1790

Sir

It appears probable that the public interests would be promoted by my receiving the earliest information when breaches of the Revenue Laws take place. I therefore request; that whenever a seizure shall be made within the sphere of your duty, you will transmit me by the first opportunity an account of the transaction, containing such particulars as will enable me fully to understand the case.

I am Sir   Your Obedt Servt   A Hamilton

LS, to Charles Lee, Charles Lee Papers, Library of Congress; copy, to Sharp Delany, Office of the Secretary of the Treasury, Circulars, 1789–1816, Office of the Secretary, United States Treasury Department; LS, to Otho H. Williams, Columbia University Libraries; LS, MS Division, New York Public Library; L[S], Tioga Point Museum, Athens, Pennsylvania; copy, United States Finance Miscellany, Treasury Circulars, Library of Congress; RG 56, Circulars of the Office of the Secretary, "Set T," National Archives.

*Treasury Department Circular
to the Continental Loan Officers*

Treasury Department
May 17th 1790

Sir

There are in the possessions of the late Loan Officers of the United States,[1] several specie of public paper the holding of which must be inconvenient to them, while they ought, in propriety to be at the Seat of Government.

I therefore request that on the receipt of this letter you will be pleased to forward to me the Indents, blank Loan Office Certificates, bills of Credit, known by the name of the New Emissions, and all other public paper which may be in your hands.

I am Sir   with respect   Your Obedient Servant

A Hamilton
Secy of the Treasury [2]

Thomas Smith Esqr
Pennsylvania

LS, sold at Parke-Bernet Galleries, December 4–5, 1944, Lot 177.
   1. See "Treasury Department Circular to the Continental Loan Officers,"
October 12, 1789.
   2. Text taken from facsimile in American Art Association catalogue of
earlier sale on March 12, 1920, Lot 380.

From Joseph Whipple

Portsmouth, New Hampshire, May 17, 1790. "Inclosed is a weekly
return of monies received and paid in this district to the 15th instant. My last letter (May 10th) stated the amount of the first
Moiety of Invalid Pensioners in New Hampshire at 1661 $98/100$ Dolls.
This should have been $1660 $98/100$. . . ."

Copy, RG 56, Letters from the Collector at Portsmouth, National Archives.

Treasury Department Circular to the Collectors and Surveyors of the State of Virginia

Treasury Department May 18th 1790

Sir

   I am informed through one of the representatives of the State of
virginia, that some co-operation with the executive of that State
on the part of the Officers of the Customs is necessary to the perfect
execution of the Tobacco inspection Law. That acts directs, *that
the Tobacco inspectors Shall by every boat or other craft loaded
with Tobacco, Send a List of the marks weights &ca of every
hogshead of Tobacco there delivered, which Lists every master
of a Ship is to lodge with the naval Officer by whom his Ship is
cleared.*[1]

   It being my wish that every assistance may be afforded in the
execution of a Law at once So Salutary and important, I request that

you will continue to receive these Lists or manifests as has heretofore been practised, and that you will return them to Such persons as the Supreme executive of the State may point out to you.

I am, Sir with respect   Your obedt Servt   A Hamilton

LS, to Charles Lee, Charles Lee Papers, Library of Congress; copy, to James Gibbon, RG 56, Letters to Collectors at Small Ports, "Set G," National Archives; copy, enclosed in James Madison to Beverley Randolph, May 26, 1790, Archives Division, Virginia State Library, Richmond.
    1. "An act to amend and reduce the several acts of assembly for the inspection of tobacco, into one act," May, 1783 (William Waller Hening, *The Statutes at Large . . . Laws of Virginia* [Richmond, 1823], Vol. XI, 240–41).

From William Webb

[*Bath, District of Maine, May 18, 1790.* On May 29, 1790, Hamilton wrote to Webb: "Your letter of the 18th May has been duly received, and I learn from it, that you have purchased a Boat 'for the purpose of better securing the revenue.'" *Letter not found.*]

To Sharp Delany

Treasury Department
May 19th. 1790

Sir

The establishment of Custom house boat⟨s is⟩[1] as you are informed, under the consideration of Congress ⟨at⟩ this time. But the circumstances which led to the tem⟨porary⟩ arrangement in your district appears still to be of so ⟨much⟩ weight, as to induce to a continuance of the measure ⟨till⟩ the proposed establishment shall be completed.

I am with respect   Sir   Your obedt. Servt.

A Hamilton
Secy of the Treasury

Sharp Delany Esquire
Collector for the Port of Philadelphia.

LS, United States Coast Guard Academy, New London, Connecticut; copy, RG 56, Letters to the Collector at Philadelphia, National Archives; copy, RG 56, Letters to Collectors at Small Ports, "Set G," National Archives.
    1. Words within broken brackets have been taken from RG 56, Letters to the Collector at Philadelphia, National Archives.

To Arthur St. Clair [1]

[New York, May 19, 1790]

Dear Sir

This will be delivered to you by Mr. De Barth [2]—who is at the head of a French Colony going to make a settlement on the Scioto, within the limits of Cutler's and Serjeants purchase.[3] There is another colony under Mr. De Boullogne,[4] who have the same destination. The particulars of their situation and the circumstances which distinguish them will I presume be detailed to you from some other quarter. I write this letter at the request of the parties merely to manifest to them a friendly disposition. I am sure it cannot add to that which you will feel of your own accord towards them. The truth is, humanity and policy both demand our best efforts to countenance and protect them. There is a Western Country. It *will* be settled. It is in every view best that it should be in great measure settled from abroad rather than at the entire expence of the Atlantic population. And it is certainly wise by kind treatment to lay hold of the affections of the settlers and attach them from the beginning to the Government of the Nation.

If these emigrants render a favourable account of their situation to the country from which they come, there is no saying in what numbers they may be followed.

Among other views, I take of this subject, I think it not amiss that *various* dispositions should actuate those who people the Western Territory; which will be a consequence of emigrations from other countries.

The leaders of these emigrants and their associates are persons of considerable consequence who on that account are intitled to regard and from their misfortunes to tenderness.

Some troops for their protection will be indispensable. I know not what you can do in this respect, but I am sure you will do all you can. General Knox [5] also writes you; and sees the matter in the same light with myself. The President has been for some time too ill to be talked to; but I have no doubt of his good will to the emigrants.

They are anxious for tranquillity and of course for government. Mr. De Barth is desirous of being a justice of the peace. The other Chiefs will wish to be Militia officers. A Majority would be very pleasing to Mr. De Boullogne.

You will be ready I am sure in every thing that is proper to content them.

I remain Dr Sir   Yr. Affect & Obed ser   A Hamilton

James Livingston [6] wishes to be continued in some Indian appointment. He is really a man of merit.

New York May 19. 1790
Governor Sinclair

ALS, Columbia University Libraries.
   1. St. Clair was governor of the Northwest Territory.
   The Frenchmen mentioned by H in this letter had arrived in the United States as a result of the machinations of American land speculators. In 1787 the Ohio Company purchased one million and a half acres in the Ohio country from the United States. This was part of a joint purchase, for at the same time the Scioto Company obtained almost five million acres in the same region. The Scioto Company then sent the poet Joel Barlow to France, and he induced some Frenchmen to purchase land in what became the Gallipolis settlement.
   2. John Joseph de Barth, one of the French settlers on the Scioto lands.
   3. Manasseh Cutler and Winthrop Sargent were two of the organizers of the Ohio Company. Cutler was a clergyman, lawyer, physician, and scientist from Ipswich, Massachusetts. As lobbyist in the Continental Congress, he played a major role in negotiating the purchase from the government. Sargent, a surveyor, became secretary of the Ohio Company. In 1787 he was appointed secretary of the Northwest Territory.
   4. Charles F. Boulogne was the agent selected by Joel Barlow to accompany the first group of French migrants from France to the United States.
   5. Henry Knox.
   6. Presumably this is James Livingston of Montgomery County, New York, who was deputy superintendent of Indian affairs for the Northern Department in 1789, and a member of the New York State Assembly from 1789 to 1791.

From Stephen Higginson

Boston may 20. 1790

Sir

Since I had last the pleasure of writing to you,[1] I have learnt with uneasiness, that some gentn. in Congress have had an Idea of stop-

ALS, Connecticut Historical Society, Hartford.
   1. Higginson's last letter is dated May 6, 1790.

ping the progress of the funding System, with a view to compell an assent to the assumption of the State Debts. This Idea demands a very careful & cool attention before it be practised upon. The situation of things is to me critical & important. Shd. the question of assumption be carried over to another Session a fermentation will certainly be excited in this & other States. How great & extensive no one can now tell; but should both go over, & the whole body of public Creditors remain without any provision, an irritation much more general & violent may be apprehended. Those in Trade also will very generally receive like impressions in the latter case; &, deprived of the usual supply of Cash, by the collection of Duties & looking upon the money, may be led into combinations, & openly refuse any farther paymts. The prospect of success should be very clear, before such a measure be taken. If gentn can be assured of this, it may be well to attempt it; but very rough points may be created by it, &, from the feelings & views before discovered in the discussion of that question, will be the probable effect. It strikes me, that in the present temper of the house, the question may be brought on with much more advantage after the funding System, & the ways & means are settled. Having perfected that business, & being strongly impressed with a Sense of the necessity of such a provision for the proper Debt of the union, gentn. must feel interested in giving it a free & successful operation. They will then be much more likely to perceive the obstructions & interferences, which must arise from the provisions, which the States must make for their respective Debts, than they are now, while the whole Subject lies open, & every thing is viewed in theory only, & in a complicated state. When they come to simplify their Views, & critically attend to the means they shall have provided, they will feel the force of objections That have now no weight. They will naturally wish their own measures to have freedom & success; & upon their own principles, & by the help of their own feelings, may then be drawn into measures they had before opposed. If some member was to suggest to them, that by a mutilation of your plan,[2] they alone must respond for the success of their system, it would have much effect. These reflections having made an impression on my

2. Higginson is referring to the "Report Relative to a Provision for the Support of Public Credit," January 9, 1790.

own mind, I have suggested them to Mr Ames[3] & Mr. Strong,[4] for their consideration. The question is a nice & important one; it involves many difficulties, & good men are divided about it. I am sorry to find that Congress have taken up the subject of a navigation act at this time. It is, in my mind, premature in every View of it. That Subject must necessarily produce warmth in the discussion of it. It will strengthen impressions, already too visible, of a local & narrow kind. It will tend to keep up the Idea of seperate interests, & to prevent that union & harmony between the northern & southern members, which should be attentively cultivated; &, by such like effects, will render the house unfit to consider, as they ought, the great national Objects which yet lie before them. We have not yet got the government well settled. Important Arrangements yet remain to be made before it can have that force & dignity, which is necessary to make it stable, or to command Our confidence. Such are all those contained in your report. These are primary Objects, in their nature; & they claim the first, & chief attention of Congress.

The present is an improper time to take up the Subject, because the feelings of people this way are too highly excited. Our carrying business has this year proved much short of expectation. Many of Our Vessels have not found employ; & those which have will, many of them, scarcely be supported by it. Several causes, accidental & temporary, have united to produce a great influx of foreign Ships, which have taken the freights from American Vessels, or have reduced freights so low as to be not worth accepting. The failure of the Crops in the West Indies deprived many British Vessels of their freights; & they were compelled to come here for employ, or lay idle over the Season. The great scarcity of Ships the last year, raised the freights of produce to Europe very high in Virga. &c. Tempted by such freights, & expecting that the same rates would readily be obtained, many Vessels came from Europe to America in pursuit of them. The high prices of grain in Europe the last year, & the great gains made upon the exportations from America, engaged the attention of every one fond of speculation, & gave rise to the most extraordinary & extensive Orders. And,

3. Fisher Ames was a Federalist member of the House of Representatives from Massachusetts.
4. Caleb Strong was a Federalist Senator from Massachusetts.

lest, from the want of Vessels to take freights they should miss
their object, many ships were sent to America. But, by the amaz-
ing rise of grain & flour, many of the orders were not executed,
& the Vessels sent to take the Articles to Europe were lying at expence & without employ. They had no alternative, but were compelled to take freights on the best terms they could get. Such an
instance I do not recollect, nor will it soon again happen in all probability; but, those who have suffered, from the causes I have mentioned, will not advert to them as the true causes of their disappointment. They are not sensible of the real circumstances of the case;
& chuse to consider it, as the natural effect of the liberty to foreign
Ships to take away Our exports. It ought to be remembered, that
the foreigners who have taken such low freights, acted from necessity & not from choice, or previous design; &, that the loss, most
of them will sustain, must operate strongly to prevent so great an
influx in future. We can now afford to carry as cheap as almost
any Europeans, although We yet pay more for Our Vessels, & are
much more expensive in their outfits, than We ought to be. We
have not yet got wholly rid of the habits contracted during the
War, & do not manage Our Business with that industry & œconomy,
which must be adopted to carry with advantage. But with our
present habits & expences, the carrying will prove a living Business
at the usual rates since the peace; & in an extra case, like this year,
Our loss will prove to be less than what foreigners sustain, because,
They in general have to make a Voye. from a distant port with very
little or no freight, to seek one here. The increased number of Our
Vessels now employed in this Business, is a proof, that Those who
have heretofore pursued it derived as much benefit from it, as they
could expect in any other employment.

But although the carrying Business should be viewed, as being
sufficiently productive in general, upon its present footing, & the
ship Owners may evidence by their conduct That they so consider
it; yet, so strongly are their feelings excited by recent disappoint-
ments, They will be very importunate for farther advantages. Our
delegates in Congress will be earnestly solicitous to gratify their
Constituents; & believing the representations they may receive, will
perhaps be impelled to press the Subject with much warmth & to
an undue degree.

There has been a very unfortunate combination of circumstances

to excite uneasiness at this time. The great & unexpected dissapoint-
ments, which have happened in trade—the delays, distrusts & divisions which have appeared in Congress—the scarcity of money &
other active property, & the danger of things growing still worse
for want of the Arrangements now before Congress—These all
tend to promote an irritation, & if permitted to operate for any
length of time, may produce very serious effects. The Sentiments
& feelings of people here, with respect to Congress & the Affairs
of the Union, are very different from what they were a few months
ago. Their respect for that body, & their confidence in them is very
much lessned; & their lively hopes of enjoying peace safety & happiness exceedingly abated, & will soon give way to alarming apprehensions of a general convulsion. I do assure you there is now a
very unfavorable impression as to the affairs of the union & its
government; but I hope it may be checked.

We shall, in all apearance, have a much better legislature than
the last; & if things went on well with you, massachusetts would
soon be in very good temper.

I gave Mr. geo: Cabot a line to you.[5] He is one of our first men
in point of influence & intelligence. I knew he would be gratified
by an interview with you, & I think you will be pleased with him.
I wish you may soon be relieved from your present painful situation of suspence; & I can not yet believe, that you will long be deprived of it.

The Subject of the carrying business has led me such a jaunt,
without any previous intention, that I have not time to copy this
Letter; but, after wishing you the success and respect, which your
labours so truly merit, I must only add, that I have the honour to
be Sir with real esteem &c your very hume Servt

Stephen Higginson

5. Cabot, a well-to-do merchant of Beverly, Massachusetts, was an enthu-
siastic Federalist. He was elected a United States Senator in 1791. Letter not
found.

From Beverley Randolph

Richmond May 20th 1790

Sir,

I have had the Honour to receive your Letter of the 8th. instant.

As soon as Colonel Carrington [1] shall report to me the spot upon which the Light House is to be erected the cession to the United States shall be compleated.

I am respectfully &c.   Beverley Randolph.

LC, Archives Division, Virginia State Library, Richmond; copy, RG 26, Lighthouse Letters Received, Vol. "A," Pennsylvania and Southern States, National Archives.
1. Edward Carrington, United States marshall for Virginia.

Treasury Department Circular
to the Collectors of the Customs

Treasury Department
May 20th. 1790.

Sir

An opinion that it will conduce as well to the public convenience, as to that of your Office, has induced me to direct, that the Monies you may receive after this letter shall get to hand, be remitted from time to time, and untill further orders to the Bank of North America established in Philadelphia [1] there to be passed to the credit of the Treasurer of the United States. It will be necessary that you obtain from the Bank, duplicate receipts for all such payments and that you forward one of those receipts by the earliest opportunity to me.

I am Sir   Your Obedt Servant   Alexr Hamilton
                                       Secy of the Treasy

LS, to the Collectors of Wilmington, Delaware, Burlington and Bridgetown, New Jersey, and Philadelphia, Pennsylvania, Columbia University Libraries; copy, to the Collectors of the Ports of New York and Sag Harbor, Bank of New York, New York City; copy, to Eli Elmer, RG 56, Letters to and from the Collectors at Bridgetown and Annapolis, National Archives; copy, to Eli Elmer, RG 56, Letters to Collectors at Small Ports, "Set G," National Archives; copy, United States Finance Miscellany, Treasury Circulars, Library of Congress.
1. In the letter sent to the collectors of the ports of New York and Sag Harbor, the "Bank of New York" was substituted for the "Bank of North America established in Philadelphia."

From William Allibone

Philadelphia, May 22, 1790. "I herewith Transmit . . . five several Contracts for supplies and services for the establishments in the Bay and River Deleware. . . . There will be two others sent forward as soon as they can be effected one for Keeping the light House & one for repairs of Piers."

ALS, RG 26, Lighthouse Letters Received, Vol. "A," Pennsylvania and Southern States, National Archives.

To Benjamin Lincoln

Treasury Department, May 22, 1790. "You will be pleased to examine and settle the Account, of Mr. Devens[1] for supplying the Light Houses in your District, and for expences since the 15th of August, and so far as found right, & duly Vouched, to pay the same. The acct. & Vouchers you will then be pleased to transmit to this Office. I observe the opinion of the Attorney for the Massachusetts District[2] upon the appropriation of forfeitures under the Collection Law,[3] and I consider it as very important that the Committee of the House of Representatives now setting upon my report of amendments, to the Trade and Revenue Laws,[4] should adopt a Clause, calculated to obviate all doubts about the Construction, & policy of those Sections to which you allude. . . ."

LS, RG 36, Collector of Customs at Boston, Letters & Papers re Lighthouses, Buoys, and Piers, 1789–1819, Vol. 1, National Archives.
 1. Richard Devens, a Charlestown and Boston merchant, was commissary general of Massachusetts.
 2. Christopher Gore.
 3."An Act to regulate the Collection of the Duties imposed by law on the tonnage of ships or vessels, and on goods, wares and merchandises imported into the United States" (1 Stat. 29–49 [July 31, 1789]).
 4. "Report on Defects in the Existing Laws of Revenue," April 22, 1790.

From Sharp Delany

[Philadelphia] May 24, 1790. "I received your directions respecting the monies for the payment of the Invalids[1] and the drafts that

may be drawn by you both which shall be faithfully complied with. I also received your directions respecting seizures.[2] A due account of which shall also be forwarded. . . ."

LC, Copies of Letters to the Secretary, 1789–1790, Bureau of Customs, Philadelphia.
 1. "Treasury Department Circular to the Collectors of the Customs," May 13, 1790.
 2. "Treasury Department Circular to the Collectors of the Customs," May 17, 1790.

To Otho H. Williams

Treasury Department
May 24th 1790

Sir

I have received a letter from the Surveyor of your district [1] upon the subject of boats for the use of the officers of the Customs. I have thought it necessary to the more frugal and certain collection of the revenue to permit that boats might be purchased or built merely for harbor service, and to this, if you find it will be œconomical, or that it is necessary to ensure the faithful payment of the duties, I shall not object. Frugality in the building or purchase I shall rely on, and regularity & precision in furnishing the vouchers for their cost will be expected.

I am, Sir, with respect   Your obedient Servant

A Hamilton
Secy of the Treasury

Otho H Williams Esquire
Collector
Baltimore

LS, Columbia University Libraries.
 1. Daniel Delozier. Letter not found.

From Sharp Delany

[Philadelphia] May 25, 1790. Proposes that "the Office of the Inspector be at the Custom House." Advocates "express directions for the Collection of the duties on home spirits and stills." Proposes another "mode of prosecuting seizures . . . for as it stands at present . . . the Court receives all, and leaves no inducement to the Officers to be industriously attentive."

LS, Hamilton Papers, Library of Congress; LC, Copies of Letters to the Secretary, 1789–1790, Bureau of Customs, Philadelphia.

From Benjamin Lincoln

[*Boston, May 25, 1790.* On June 8, 1790, Hamilton wrote to Lincoln: "I have received your favor of the 25th of May." *Letter not found.*]

From John Scott [1]

[*Chester, Maryland, May 25, 1790.* On June 3, 1790, Hamilton wrote to Scott: "I have received your letter of the 25th Ulto." *Letter not found.*]

1. Scott was collector of customs at Chester.

To Sharp Delany

Treasury Department
May 26th. 1790

Sir

The preceding Circular letter of the 30th of March, having been refered to by the Comptroller of the Treasury,[1] in a letter from him, to you dated yesterday, it is now sent forward, that you may comprehend his meaning; heretofore it has been omitted, on account of the arrangement made for the Loan with the Bank, you will find by the enclosed letter of the 20th Instant[2] my intention that the money you will hereafter receive, shall be paid into the Bank of North America from time to time, and that the duplicate of the receipts with which they will furnish you, will afford here a sufficient basis for the issuing a Warrant to cover them.

I am   Sir   With respect your obedient Servant   A Hamilton

Sharp Delany Esqr
Collector
Philadelphia

LS, Collector of Customs at Philadelphia, Circulars, 1789–1809, Bureau of Customs, Philadelphia; copy, RG 56, Letters to the Collector at Philadelphia, National Archives; copy, RG 56, Letters to Collectors at Small Ports, "Set G," National Archives.
1. Nicholas Eveleigh.
2. "Treasury Department Circular to the Collectors of the Customs," May 20, 1790.

To the President and Directors of the Bank of New York[1]

Treasury Department May 26th 1790.

Gentlemen

Inclosed is a copy of a Letter lately Sent to the several Collectors of the Customs[2] therein mentioned.

I presume the object of it will be agreeable to you, as it will be serviceable to the institution under your direction. I am to request that you will direct your cashier to give duplicate receipts for Such Sum deposited, expressive of its being on account of the united States.

The monies deposited are to be carried to the account of the Treasurer of the united States, and are to be paid upon his drafts as they Shall be presented.

It will be necessary for my government that I should have *a weekly return* from the Bank of the receipts & payments on account of the united States. This I trust will not appear a matter of inconvenience.

I have the honor to be Gentlemen   Your obedt Servt

A Hamilton
Secy of the Treasy

The President, Directors & Company of the Bank of New York

LS, Bank of New York, New York City.
1. Isaac Roosevelt was president of the Bank of New York.
2. "Treasury Department Circular to the Collectors of the Customs," May 20, 1790.

To the President and Directors of the Bank of North America [1]

[*New York, May 26, 1790*. On May 29, 1790, the president and directors of the Bank of North America wrote to Hamilton: "We have reced your Letter of the 26th Inst." *Letter not found.*]

1. Thomas Willing was president of the Bank of North America.

From Benjamin Lincoln

Boston, May 27, 1790. "Your circular letter of the 17th. instant on the importance of your receiving the earliest information when breaches of the revenue law should take place came to hand by the tuesday post. . . . About five weeks since information was given that two trunks of merchandise had been in the night landed from on board the Ship Neptune Capt James Scott from London. On search the two trunks were found in a barn in the north part of the town far distant from the Ship. Immediately on possessing the good we had them appraised that we might know whether their value did or did not exceed four hundred dollars. On finding that they were worth double that money, that they had not been entered, that they were landed in the night and without a permit we felt ourselves obliged to seize the Ship also and as the mate, the Captains Son, aided in landing the good we brought a suit against him for four hundred dollars which we suppose he forfeited in aiding others in landing the goods. After the Ship was libaled She was by order of the Judge appraised and bonds given for her value, Viz About three thousand six hundred & sixty dollars. We shall be able probably to prove that the good were taken out of the Ship & in a manner contrary to law & by the knowledge of the Captain. Her trial will be had the beginning of June. . . ."

ADf, RG 36, Letters from the Treasury and Others, 1789–1818, Vol. 11, National Archives.

To George Washington [1]

Treasury Department May 28th. 1790

The Secretary of the Treasury conceives it to be his duty most respectfully to represent to the President of the United states, that there are, in his judgment, objections of a very serious & weighty nature to the resolutions of the two houses of Congress of the twenty first instant, concerning certain arrears of pay due to the Officers and soldiers of the Lines of Virginia and North Carolina.[2]

The third of those resolutions directs, that in cases where *payment* has not been made to the original Claimant in person, or to his representative, *it* shall be made to the original Claimant, or to such person or persons only, as shall produce a power of Attorney, duly attested by *two Justices* of the Peace of the County, in which such person or persons reside, authorising him or them to receive a certain specified sum.

By the Law of most, if not all the States, claims of this kind are in their nature assignable for valuable consideration; and the as-

LC, George Washington Papers, Library of Congress.

1. This document was enclosed in H to Washington, May 29, 1790.

2. These resolutions read as follows:

"*Resolved*, That the President of the United States be requested to cause to be forthwith transmitted to the Executives of the States of Virginia, North Carolina, and South Carolina, a complete list of the officers, non-commissioned officers, and privates of the lines of those States, respectively, who are entitled to receive arrears of pay, due for services in the Army, in the years one thousand seven hundred and eighty-two, and one thousand seven hundred and eighty-three, annexing the particular sum that is due to each individual, with a request to Executives of the said States, to make known to the claimants, in the most effectual manner, that the said arrears are ready to be discharged on proper application.

"*Resolved*, That the President of the United States be requested to cause the Secretary of the Treasury to take the necessary steps for paying (within the said States, respectively,) the money appropriated by Congress, on the twenty-ninth day of September, one thousand seven hundred and eighty-nine, for the discharging the arrears of pay due to the troops of the lines of the said States respectively.

"*Resolved*, That the Secretary of the Treasury, in cases where the payment has not been made to the original claimant, in person, or to his representative, be directed to take order for making the payment to the original claimant, or to such person or persons only as shall produce a power of attorney, duly attested by two justices of the peace, of the county in which such person or persons reside, authorizing him or them to receive a certain specified sum." (*Journal of the House*, I, 217–18.)

signor may constitute the assignee, his attorney or agent, to receive the amount. The import of every such assignment is a Contract, express, or implied, on the part of the assignor, that the assignee shall receive the sum assigned to his own use. In making it, no precise form is necessary, but any instrument, competent to conveying with clearness & precision the sense of the parties, suffices; There is no need of the cooperation of any Justice of the Peace, or other Magistrate whatever.

The practice of the Treasury and of the public officers in other Departments, in the adjustment and satisfaction of Claims upon the united States, has uniformly corresponded with the rules of that Law.

A regulation therefore having a retrospective operation, and prescribing, with regard to past transactions, new and unknown requisites, by which the admission of Claims is to be guided, is an infraction of the rights of Individuals, acquired under preexisting Laws, and a contravention of the public faith, pledged by the course of public proceedings. It has consequently a tendency not less unfriendly to public credit, than to the security of property.

Such is the regulation contain'd in the resolution above referred to. It defeats all previous assignments not accompanied with a *Power of Attorney* attested by *two Justices* of the peace of *the County* where the assignor resides; a formality, which for obvious reasons cannot be presumed to have attended any of them, and which does not appear to have been observed, with respect to those, upon which applications for payment have hitherto been made.

It is to be remarked, that the assignee has no method of compelling the Assignor to perfect the transfer by a new instrument, in conformity to the rule prescribed; if even the existence of such a power, the execution of which would involve a legal controversy, could be a satisfactory cause for altering by a new Law that state of things, which antecedent law and usage had established between the parties.

It is perhaps, too questionable, whether an assignee, however equitable his pretensions were, could, under the operation of the provision, which has been recited, have any remedy whatever for the recovery of the money or value which he may have paid to the assignor. It is not certain, that a Legislative act, decreeing payment to a different person, would not be a legal bar; but if the existence of such a remedy were certain, it would be but a very inconclusive consideration. The assignment may have been a security for a precarious or desperate Debt, which security will be wrested from the assignee; or it may have been a composition between an insolvent Debtor and his Creditor, & the only resource of the latter; or the assignor may be absent and incapable either of benefiting by the provision, or of being called to an account: and in every Case the assignee would be left to the casualty of the ability of the assignor to repay; to the perplexity, trouble and expence of a suit at Law. In respect to the soldiers the presumption would be, in the greater number of cases, that the pursuit of redress would be worse than acquiescence in the loss. To vary the risks of parties; to supersede the contracts between them; to turn over a creditor; without his consent, from one *Debtor* to *another;* to take away a right to a *specific thing* leaving only the chance of a remedy for retribution are not less positive violations of property, than a direct confiscation.

It appears from the debates in the house of representatives, and it may be inferred from the nature of the proceeding, that a suggestion of fraud has been the occasion of it. Fraud is certainly a good objection to any Contract, and where it is properly ascertained, invalidates it. But the power of ascertaining it, is the peculiar province of the Judiciary Department. The principles of good Government conspire with those of Justice, to place it there. 'Tis there only, that such an investigation of the fact can be had, as ought to precede a decision, 'Tis there only, the parties can be heard and evidence on both sides produced; without which, *surmise,* must be substituted to *Proof,* and *Conjecture* to *fact.*

This, then, is the dilemma incident to Legislative interference. Either the legislature must erect itself into a Court of Justice and determine each case upon its own merits, after a full hearing of the allegations and proofs of the parties; or it must proceed upon vague suggestions, loose reports, or at best upon partial & problematical testimony, to condemn in the gross and in the dark, the fairest and most unexceptionable claims, as well as those which may happen to be fraudulent and exceptionable. The first wou'd be an usurpation of the Judiciary authority, the last is at variance with the rules of property, the dictates of Equity and the maxims of good government.

All admit the truth of these positions as general rules. But when a departure from it is advocated for any particular purpose, it is usually alledged that there are exceptions to it; that there are certain extraordinary cases, in which the public good demands & justifies an extraordinary interposition of the Legislature.

This Doctrine in relation to extraordinary cases is not to be denied; but it is highly important, that the nature of those cases shou'd be carefully distinguished.

It is evident that every such interposition, deviating from the usual course of Law and Justice, and infringing the established rules of property, which ought, as far as possible to be held sacred and inviolable, is an overleaping of the ordinary and regular bounds of Legislative discretion; and is in the nature of a resort to first principles. Nothing therefore but some urgent public necessity, some impending national Calamity, something that threatens direct and general mischief to the Society, for which there is no adequate redress in the established course of things, can, it is presumed, be a sufficient cause for the employment of so extraordinary a remedy. An accommodation to the interests of a small part of the Community, in a case of inconsiderable magnitude, on a national scale, cannot, in the judgment of the Secretary, be entitled to that character.

If partial inconveniencies and hardships occasion legislative interferences in private contracts, the intercourses of business become uncertain, the security of property is lessened, the confidence in Government destroyed or weakened.

The Constitution of the United states interdicts the States individually from passing any Law impairing the obligation of contracts. This, to the more enlightened part of the community was not one of the least recommendations of that Constitution. The too frequent intermeddlings of the state Legislatures, in relation to private contracts, were extensively felt and seriously lamented; and a Constitution which promised a preventative, was, by those who felt and thought in that manner, eagerly embrac'd. Precedents of similar interferences by the Legislature of the United states, cannot fail to alarm the same class of persons, and at the same time to diminish the respect of the state legislatures for the interdiction alluded to. The *example* of the national government in a matter of this kind may be expect'd to have a far more powerful influence, that the *precepts* of its Constitution.

The present case is that of a particular class of Men, highly meritorious indeed, but inconsiderable in point of numbers, and the whole of the property in question less than fifty thousand Dollars, which when distributed among those who are principally to be benefited by the regulation, does not exceed twenty five Dollars per man. The relief of the Individuals, who may have been subjects of imposition, in so limited a case, seems a very inadequate cause for a measure which breaks in upon those great principles, that constitute the foundations of property.

The eligibility of the measure is the more doubtful, as the Courts of Justice are competent to the relief, which it is the object of the resolutions to give, as far as the fact of Fraud, or imposition, or undue advantage can be substantiated. It is true that many of the Individuals would probably not be in a condition to seek that relief, from their own resources; but the aid of government may in this respect, be afforded in a way, which will be consistent with the established order of things. The Secretary, from the information communicated to him, believing it to be probable, that undue advantages had been taken, had conceived a plan for the purpose, of the following Kind; that measures shou'd be adopted for procuring the appointment of an Agent, or Attorney by the original Claimants, or if deceased, by their legal representatives; that payment of the money should be deferred, until this had been effected; that the amount of the sums due should then be placed in the hands of the proper Officer for the purpose of payment; that a demand should be made upon him on behalf of the original Claimants by their Agent; and as a like demand would of course be made by the assignees, that the parties should be informed that a legal adjudication was necessary to ascertain the validity of their respective pretentions; and that in this state of things, the attorney general should be directed either to prosecute or defend for the original Claimants, as should appear to him most likely to ensure Justice. A step of this kind appeared to the Secretary to be warranted and dictated as well by a due regard to the defenceless situation of the parties, who may have been prejudiced, as by considerations resulting from the propriety of discouraging similar practices.

It is with reluctance and pain, that the Secretary is induced to make this representation to the President. The respect which he entertains for the decisions of the two houses of Congress; the respect which is due to those movements of humanity, towards the supposed sufferers, and of indignation against those who are presumed to have taken an undue advantage; an unwillingness to present before the mind of the President, especially at the present juncture, considerations which may occasion perplexity or anxiety, concur in rendering the task peculiarly unwelcome: Yet the principles which appear to the Secretary to have been invaded, in this instance, are, in his estimation, of such fundamental consequence to the stability, character & success of the government, and at the same time so immediately interesting to the Department entrust'd to his care, that he feels himself irresistably impelled by a sense of Duty, as well to the Chief Magistrate, as to the Community, to made a full communication of his impressions & reflections.

He is sensible, that an inflexible adherence to the principles contended for must often have an air of rigor, and will sometimes be productive of particular inconveniencies. The general rules of property, & all those general rules which form the links of Society, frequently involve in their ordinary operation particular hardships and Injuries; yet the public order, and the general happiness require a steady conformity to them. It is perhaps always better, that partial evils should be submitted to, than that principles should be violated. In the infancy of our present government, peculiar strictness and circumspection are called for by the too numerous instances of relaxations, which in other quarters & on other occasions, have discredited our Public measures.

The secretary is not unaware of the delicacy of an opposition to the resolutions in question, by the President, shou'd his view of the subject coincide with that of the Secretary: Yet he begs leave on this point to remark, that such an opposition in a Case, in which a small part of the Community only is directly concerned, would be less likely to have disagreeable consequences, than in one which shou'd affect a very considerable portion of it: and the prevention of an ill precedent, if it be truly one, may prove a decisive obstacle

to other cases of greater extent and magnitude and of a more
critical tendency. If the objections are as solid as they appear to
the Secretary, to be, he trusts, they cannot fail, with the sanction
of the President, to engage the approbation, not only of the gen-
erality of considerate men, but of the community at large. And if
momentary dissatisfaction should happen to exist in particular parts
of the union, it is to be hoped, that it will be speedily removed by
the measures which under the direction of the President, may be
pursued for obtaining the same end in an unexceptionable mode, for
the success of which the Secretary will not fail to exert his most
zealous endeavours.

It is proper, that the President should be informed, that if objections should be made by him, they will, in all probability, be effectual, as the resolutions passed in the Senate with no greater
majority than twelve to ten.

The Secretary feels an unreserved confidence in the Justice and
magnanimity of the President, that whatever may be his view of
the subject, he will at least impute the present representation to an
earnest and anxious conviction, in the mind of the Secretary, of the
truth and importance of the principles which he supports, & of the
inauspicious tendency of the measure to which he objects, co-
operating with a pure and ardent zeal for the public good, and for
the honor & prosperity of the administration of the Chief Magistrate.

All which is humbly submitted   Alexr. Hamilton
                                     Secretary of the Treasury

To George Washington

Treasury Department, May 28, 1790. Submits "five Contracts
made by the superintendant of the Light house, piers &c on the
river and Bay of Delaware" and recommends that these Contracts
be approved.

LC, George Washington Papers, Library of Congress.

From Oliver Wolcott, Junior

Treasury Department
Auditors Office May 28th. 1790.

Sir

I have examined the papers which have been transmitted to me relative to the accounts of Messrs. Joseph Gardoqui & Sons,[1] and am fully of opinion that the amount of their account being 10,057 Rs. vellon.. 22 Mars.[2] equal to five hundred and two dollars and eighty five Cents ought to be admitted to their credit. Indeed it appears that the whole of their charges except for 1920 Rials vellon have been already admitted by Thomas Barclay Esqr.[3] Commissioner of foreign accounts, and are properly credited to them in his books.

It however appears that on the 8th. of October 1789, his Excellency James Gardoqui Esqr.[4] was furnished by the late accountant of the Treasury with statements of other accounts between the public and Messrs. Gardoqui & Sons, relative to which certain explanations were judged to be necessary, and as I am informed he engaged to transmit to the Secretary of the Treasury, compleat transcripts of all their accounts with the public.

If it shall be judged proper that the settlement of this account should proceed without waiting for any explanations relative to other accounts, the business shall be compleated immediately. I have the honor to be with great respect, Sir, your obedient Servant.

Oliver Wolcott.

The Honble. Alexander Hamilton Esqr.

LC, Papers of the Continental Congress, National Archives.

1. A mercantile house of Bilbao, Spain, that furnished military supplies to the United States during the Revolution. The firm also sold prizes taken by American ships.

2. I.e., maravedis. Spanish copper coins nominally valued at one thirty-fourth of a real.

3. A Philadelphia merchant, Barclay was consul-general in France from 1781 to 1787 and negotiated the 1787 treaty with Morocco. In 1782, Congress named Barclay commissioner to settle the foreign accounts of the United States. He returned to the United States in 1788.

4. It is possible that Wolcott is referring to Diego de Gardoqui, Spanish Minister to the United States, who sailed from New York City on October 10, 1789, for Bilbao.

From Jonathan Dayton [1]

Elizabeth Town [New Jersey] May 29th. 1790

Dear sir,

In compliance with your request that I would commit to paper
and transmit to you the reasons which I conceived would justify
me in tendering military rights of land, so far as one seventh part of
each payment stipulated to be made by Judge Symmes [2] for his
purchase between the Miami rivers, should extend, at the rate of an
Acre for every Dollar to be paid, I have herein stated a few facts
which appear to me to operate conclusively in favor of such an
opinion.

Congress, in one of their resolutions of the 16th. of September
1776 pledged themselves to grant lands in the proportions therein
prescribed, to such officers & soldiers as should engage in their
service for the war and continue to the end thereof.[3] Since the
establishment of peace, the Secretary at war, in fulfilment of that
promise, and in compliance with a particular order of the late
Congress,[4] has proceeded to issue warrants to military applicants in
such proportions, as to number of Acres, as their respective ranks
entitled them. It is expressed on the face of these warrants that they

ALS, Rutgers University Library, New Brunswick, New Jersey.

1. Dayton, a New Jersey lawyer, was a member of the state Council in
1789 and speaker of the Assembly in 1790. He was an associate of John Cleves
Symmes in the Miami Purchase.

2. Symmes, a resident of Morristown, New Jersey, organized the New Jersey group that obtained the Miami Purchase in October, 1788. The grant
comprised a million acres along the Ohio River and extended northward between the Miami and Little Miami rivers in Ohio. Congress and the President later reduced this grant to 311,000 acres after extended controversy with
the Miami Associates.

When Washington appointed the governing officials of the Northwest Territory in August, 1789, he named Symmes as one of the judges.

3. JCC, V, 763.

4. On July 9, 1788, as part of "A supplement to an ordinance entitled An
Ordinance for ascertaining the mode of disposing of lands in the Western
territory" Congress ordered:

"That the Secretary at War issue warrants for bounties of land to the several
Officers and soldiers of the late continental Army who may be entitled to such
bounties, or to their respective assigns or legal representatives, certifying
therein the rank or station of each Officer, and the line, regiment corps and
company in which the Officer or soldier served." (JCC, XXXIV, 306–08.)

may be located "in any of the Districts appropriated for satisfying the bounties of land due to the late army." By the report of a Committee approved by Congress and referred to the Board of Treasury to take order on the 23rd. of July 1787,[5] the Board was authorized & empowered to contract with individuals or companies for a grant of a certain tract of land therein defined, & on certain conditions therein expressed. They were not to take less than one Dollar per Acre for the land within the tract, but were allowed in their discretion to make "a reduction by an allowance for bad land & all incidental charges and circumstances whatever" provided that such allowance did "not exceed in the whole one third of a Dollar per acre". They were to admit military rights or bounties of land in discharge of the contract, acre for acre, provided that the aggregate of such rights should not exceed one seventh part of the land to be paid for. Under these powers, the Board of Treasury made two contracts, exactly similar as they respected the point in question; the one with Messrs. Cutler & Serjeant,[6] the other with Mr. Symmes. My application to you was on behalf of Judge Symmes & his Associates, whose Agent I am, & in behalf of the Officers & soldiers of the late Jersey line who have appointed me to act for them. You will perceive by recurring to our contract with the Board, that each of our two first payments amounted to 82,198 Dollars, one seventh part or 11,742 Dollars of which were payable in military rights. The proportion of the two first payments which may be discharged by the warrants issued from the war-office, is 23,484 Dollars; for effecting which I have collected & am prepared to lodge with you the warrants so issued for 23,484 Acres. This statement brings the business to the point to be decided viz. whether warrants for 23,484 Acres of land will entitle us to a credit of 23,484 Dols. or whether in order to be entitled to that credit, we must lodge warrts. for 35,226 Acres. After making the greatest allowance in my own case, for the influence which our wishes or our interest too frequently & almost imperceptibly gain over our judgments & belief, I do not hesitate to say that, in point of right & fair construction, the former of the two positions should prevail.

5. JCC, XXXIII, 399–401.
6. Manasseh Cutler and Winthrop Sargent. See H to Arthur St. Clair, May 19, 1790.

The Board of Treasury had not power to sell the lands of the United States for less than a Dollar per Acre, but they had a discretionary power to make an allowance for bad lands, & for lakes, ponds & marshes, hardly, if at all, drainable, & for hills & mountains not tillable if accessible, by reducing the number of acres actually contained within any tract not more than one third, & thus requiring the payment for two thirds of the contents only. I appeal to your own recollection whether Congress did not mean by their resolves that the lands which were of a quality called good, or rather which were marketable, should bring a Dollar per Acre, & it would be to bring into too severe question the justice and generosity of that body, if it should be construed to have been the intention of Congress when they made the gift, or at any time since, to pay the army their bounty in either of the above descriptions, which they must have meant to have thrown in & to exempt from sale when they enabled the Board to make a deduction of one third in forming their contracts.

You will doubtless, sir, agree with me that every instrument of writing should, if possible, be so construed as to be consistent in all its parts. That When any sentence or expression contained in it admits of two constructions, the one adverse, the other favorable to the parts precedent, the favorable one should, for the sake of consistency, be adopted. In the powers under which the Board contracted there is a plain & strong injunction that "the price be not less than one Dollar per acre for the contents of the tract" [7]— it cannot be denied that the proviso immediately following might be construed to authorize the Board to receive five shillings in payment for each acre; but in this case it would be inconsistent with the first established price, & would be charging the Committee & Congress with the blunder of saying that their Commissioners shall not sell their land for less than a Dollar per acre, but for certain reasons may sell it at five shillings an acre; if, on the other hand, the construction, which I advocate, be given it, no such inconsistency will follow, but it will very properly stand thus. Congress directed the Board to dispose of lands at not less than a Dollar the acre, but knowing that in every tract of a million of Acres there would be lands which could not be occupied, or at least not without

7. JCC, XXXIII, 400. Dayton's quotation is not exact.

an expence equal to their full value, they empowered the Board
to make a reduction or allowance from the quantity contained in
any tract, provided such reduction should not exceed one third of
such quantity. Judge Symmes & his Associates contracted for a
tract of one million of acres, but of this million are only to pay for
two thirds at the rate however of a Dollar per acre, the other third
being the allowance for bad land &c.

That the sales thus made were, in your own belief, at not less than
a Dollar the Acre, appears clearly from a declaration to that effect
in your report to the house of Representatives on the subject of
public credit. "The general price, says the report, at which the
western lands have been heretofore sold, has been a Dollar per acre
in public securities." [8] And as the lands sold to the Ohio company
& to Symmes amount to seven eighths of the whole of the sales, it
is plain that those contracts were particularly alluded to. Permit me
to add that you have confirmed, as far as it was possible, the point
which I contend for, not only by the declaration just mentioned,
but by assuming that very price of a Dollar per Acre as the foundation of that calculation which makes a material part of your first
proposition for funding the debt. If the lands, heretofore disposed
of, were sold at two thirds of a Dollar, would twenty Cents estimated upon your own principles be "a fair valuation"? Would it
"seem to bear an equitable proportion to the two considerations of
value at the time & likelihood of increase"? Should the decision in
this particular be against the army, would not your determination
in the present instance seem to disagree with your assertion and
proposition in the case of your report? Having thus made the statement you requested, I now most willingly submit to you the matter
in question, &, whatever may be your decision, shall, for my own
part, very cheerfully acquiesce, for I know it will be a just one. I
should be happy in receiving a letter from you as soon as convenient on this subject, and am sir with very great respect &
esteem Yours   Jona: Dayton

The Honble Alexr. Hamilton Esqr.

8. "Report Relative to a Provision for the Support of Public Credit," January
9, 1790.

To Thomas Jefferson

[New York, May 29, 1790]

Mr. Hamilton presents his respectful compliments to Mr. Jefferson and returns him the letter from Mr. Writtenhouse on the subject of Mr. Barton.[1] As Mr. Bartons merit is well ascertained, if Mr. H_____ can be of service to him in any other way he will take pleasure in being so.

May 29

AL, Thomas Jefferson Papers, Library of Congress.
1. This letter, which is dated April 20, 1790, and is from David Rittenhouse to Jefferson, is located in the Thomas Jefferson Papers, Library of Congress. Rittenhouse recommended his nephew, William Barton, for the post of Assistant Secretary of the Treasury. Barton was a Pennsylvania lawyer and judge.

From Tobias Lear

[*New York*] *May 29, 1790.* "The President of the United States approves of the . . . Contracts . . . submitted to him by the Secretary of the Treasury. . . ."[1]

ALS, RG 26, "Segregated" Lighthouse Records, National Archives; LC, George Washington Papers, Library of Congress.
1. See H to Washington, May 28, 1790.

From the President and Directors of the Bank of North America[1]

Bank of No. America [Philadelphia] May 29. 1790

Sir,

We have reced your Letter of the 26th. Int.[2] together with a Copy of your Circular[3] to the Collectors of Wilmington & Delaware, those of Burlington & Bridgetown in New Jersey, & to the Collector of this port; Directing them to pay into this Bank from time to time, the Monies which they may receive, and that they take Duplicate recets from our Cashier for all Such payments.

As this Arangement will probably conduce to the public convenience, will be serviceable to our Institution, & it is at the Same time perfectly with the line of our business you may attend on our pointed attention to your request in every particular. Whatever Monies we may receive under this Order, shall be passed to the Credit of the Treasurers Account, & his drafts regularly paid as they may appear.

As to the Weekly return of Such receipts and payments—Our Cashier will furnish you with it, closed up to any day in each Week, which you may please to Direct.

I have the honor to be Sir. For the President Directors & Co of the Bank of No America   Your Obdt Ser

Alex Hamilton Esqr ⎫
Secy of the Treasury ⎬ NY
of the United States. ⎭

LC, Historical Society of Pennsylvania, Philadelphia.
    1. Thomas Willing was president of the Bank of North America.
    2. Letter not found, but see H to the President and Directors of Bank of New York, May 26, 1790.
    3. "Treasury Department Circular to the Collectors of the Customs," May 20, 1790.

To William Short

Treasury Department May 29th. 1790.

Sir

I am honored with your letters of the 28th & 30th,[1] which did not come to my hands 'till the 27th instant.

The conduct you have prescribed to yourself in regard to the negociations concerning the Debt of the United States, appears to be very prudent and judicious, and such as will give the United States a convenient election of the measures to be pursued in future.

Previously to the receipt of your favour, I had written to the Commissioners[2] upon the business of their letter of the 25th of January, a duplicate of which you were so good as to enclose to me. Considering their zeal, exertions and general deportment on former occasions as entitling them to the regard of Government, I wrote them in a manner corresponding with those impressions, yet so as to leave the United States at full liberty in their final determinations on the late transaction and particularly guarding against the ill consequences that would result from establishing a precedent of this nature. It is possible when our arrangements shall be completed, that the United States may find it convenient to confirm this transaction, but in the mean time it appeared most adviseable to treat it as I have mentioned.

I am to acknowlege my obligation to you for the return of the Vessels and Cargoes from the United States, that have arrived in the ports of France. It will be on many occasions a very useful document.[3]

With cordial satisfaction, Sir, I reciprocate your congratulations on the late happy change in the situation of our Country, and I feel great pleasure in receiving information so authentic, that it has influenced favourably the dispositions of the European Nations. A prosecution of the same just and salutary principles, it may be reasonably hoped, will give permanency to our present advantages and secure a larger portion of those benefits, which the United States are qualified to produce.

I have the honor to be, with great respect Sir, Your most obedt Servt. Alexander Hamilton
Secretary of the Treasury
William Short Esquire
Chargé des affaires from the United states at the Court of France

LS, William Short Papers, Library of Congress.
1. Short to H, November 30, 1789, and January 28–31, 1790.
2. H to Willink, Van Staphorst, and Hubbard, May 7, 1790.
3. See Short to H, January 28–31, 1790.

To George Washington

[New York, May 29, 1790]

The Secretary of the Treasury presents his respects of the President of the United states and submits to his consideration some remarks [1] on the Resolutions, which have passed the two Houses respecting the Lines of Virginia and North Carolina.[2]

The Secretary has taken this method of communication as the

one best calculated to place the subject under the eye of the President with least trouble to him. If any further explanation should be desired by the President, The Secretary will have the honor of waiting upon him, at any time it shall please him to appoint.

Saturday May 29th. 1790.

LC, George Washington Papers, Library of Congress.
  1. H to Washington, May 28, 1790.
  2. See H to Washington, May 28, 1790, note 2.

To William Webb

Treasury Department
May 29th. 1790

Sir

Your Letter of the 18th May [1] has been duly received, and I learn from it, that you have purchased a Boat "for the purpose of better securing the revenue". I have in some instances on previous application permitted the purchase of open Boats for Harbour service, and it is possible, that it might not have appeared improper to extend this permission to the District of Bath. But as no application has been received from you, I find myself under the necessity of suspending any allowance of the Charge, untill I receive from you an explanation of the service, for which the Boat is required & a particular Account of the Cost with regular Vouchers for the several items.

I am Sir   Your Obedient Servant.   Alex Hamilton

Wm Webb Esquire
Collector at Bath

LS, United States Coast Guard Academy, New London, Connecticut.
  1. Letter not found.

From Catharine Greene [1]

[May 30, 1790]

My Dear friend

Will you pardon one who feels like a culprit Merely because she is about to ask a favor—and that of a friend too whom she loves and admires? Surely it is not a *crime* to solicit a favor of one, Who is as Emenent for the goodness of his heart, as he is Celebrated for his abilities; and one too, who honors me by the appellation of friend. Yet if it is not? Why do I palputate—Why blush and condemn myself, and at the same time I am Justified by my reason, and prompted by my affection to commit it. Could you know my feeling upon this occasion, I am sure you would pardon me I will suppose you do, and therefore proceed.

I am, from a combination of circomstances determind to leave this on wednesday next for Bethleham [2]—tho I am daily expecting My beloved and only Brother [3]—if the constitution should be adopted by the State of Rhode Island who will be in dispair when he finds me gone and who will be one (among the Many) candidate for the collectors office in Newport. Col Wadsworths [4] absence will also be a severe disappointment to him. He is very little known among the persons who have power to serve him. What I have to ask, is therefore, that you will have the goodness to introduce him to your friends. Exclusive of all partiallity he has as honest an heart as ever Man had, his Morals are good, he is industrious and I think every way qualified to discharge his duty, and do Justice to his country. Genl Greene had the highest opinion of him and tho he had five Brothers he intrusted Captain Littlefield [5] with his Will, and all his other business in his absence. I would risque my Life and every hope of future happiness upon his integrity and I have no doubt of you having the same opinion when you know him. Your friendship to him will be received by us both, with Gratitude.

Permit me also to ask if there are any funds in france to pay The intrest of the National debt—or rather will you Permit me to beg the favor of an hours conversation with you some time betwixt this, and Wednesday?

God bless you My Dear ⟨frie⟩nd and beleive me   Most sincerly   and affectionately Yours   C Greene

Sunday May 30th 1790

ALS, Hamilton Papers, Library of Congress.
1. Catharine Greene was the widow of Nathanael Greene.
2. Bethlehem, Pennsylvania.
3. William Littlefield.

4. Jeremiah Wadsworth.
5. Littlefield had served as a captain in the Second Rhode Island Regiment from 1776 to 1780.

To Thomas Jefferson

Treasury Department May 31st. 1790.

Sir

I have the honor to transmit you a copy of a communication from the Auditor,[1] respecting the account of Messrs. Gardoqui, from which it appears that their balance of 10,057 Rials of vellon and 22 maravedies, equal to five hundred and two dollars, eighty five Cents, is admitted by him.

The promised explanations of the other accounts have not yet been transmitted to this office, but may be in the hands of Mr. Viar.[2] Should that be the case, and should they clear up the uncertainties in the accounts to which they relate, the above balance will be discharged without hesitation. If however these explanations have not yet been received by Mr. Viar, and you find him solicitous for the balance abovementioned, I will take arrangements for its discharge.

I have the honor to be &c.   Alexander Hamilton
                                         Secretary of the Treasury

LC, Papers of the Continental Congress, National Archives.
1. Oliver Wolcott, Jr., to H, May 28, 1790.
2. Josef de Viar, a Spanish agent in the United States. Although he held no diplomatic rank, he was usually referred to as a chargé in Spanish documents (Samuel Flagg Bemis, *Pinckney's Treaty, A Study of America's Advantage from Europe's Distress* [Baltimore, 1926], 182).

From Joseph Whipple

Portsmouth, New Hampshire, May 31, 1790. "I am honord with your letter of the 13th May [1] instant in which I am directed to retain in my hands One thousand eig⟨ht⟩ hundred thirty Seven Dollars for the payment of the Second Moiety of one years pension to the Invalids in this State. The amount of said Moiety pr. the list transmitted me by the Secretary at War is *Two thousand thirty seven* Dollars which corresponds with the sum appropriated . . . by your letters of the 30th January & 24th March last. . . ." [2]

LC, RG 36, Collector of Customs at Portsmouth, Letters Sent 1789–1790, Vol. 1, National Archives; copy, RG 56, Letters from the Collector at Portsmouth, National Archives.
1. "Treasury Department Circular to the Collectors of the Customs," May 13, 1790.
2. Letters not found.

From Otho H. Williams

Baltimore, May 31, 1790. "I am favored with a letter of the 18 Ulte from Messrs Bertier & Company of Philadelphia owners of a part of the goods irregularly landed from on board the Ship Vanstophorst in which they inform me 'that the kind and favorable letter they recd. last night from the honorable the Secretary of the Treasury [1] gave them the greatest hopes that I would be pleased to deliver their goods in the manner the secretary writes it may be done.' I . . . request, Sir, that you will be pleased to give me your decisive instructions in this business. . . ."

ALS, RG 53, "Old Correspondence," Baltimore Collector, National Archives.
1. Letter not found.

From Benjamin Lincoln

Boston, June 1, 1790. "A district court for the Masst district was held here this day. The case of the Ship neptune the two trunks of Merchandize & of the Molasses and liam mentioned in my last [1] have been called & are all gone by default. . . ."

LC, RG 36, Collector of Customs at Boston, Letter Book, 1790–1797, National Archives; copy, RG 56, Letters from the Collector at Boston, National Archives.
1. Lincoln to H, May 27, 1790.

To Joseph Whipple

Treasury Department
June 1st 1790

Sir

Herewith you have Copy of the Act for the establishment & support of Light houses, Beacons, Buoys and public Piers.[1] Amongst other things contained in it, you will percieve that it is made the duty of the Secretary of the Treasury to provide by Contracts to be approved, by the President of the United States, for rebuilding when necessary & keeping in repair the Light Houses, Beacons, Buoys & public Piers in the several States; and for furnishing the same with all necessary supplies; and also to agree for the Salaries, Wages, or hire of the person or persons appointed by the President for the superintendance & care of the same.

I have now to inform you that in persuance of the above Authority the President of the United States has been pleased to appoint you Superintendant of the Light House at the Mouth of Piscatqua River in your State as also of any others that may be erected in your State. It is only necessary for me to remark, that the Law contemplates the providing for keeping in repair those establishments, and furnishing the necessary supplies by Contracts; by which were probably intended agreements for Certain fixed periods of time at determinate rates.

This with regard to Supplies it is presumed will be easy & proper, but it will not I apprehend be practicable with regard to repairs which are too casual to admit of an Estimate accurate enough to be the ground of previous Contracts. They must be provided for as occasions arise; but to satisfy the Law, as far as may be, it will be desireable to endeavor to make particular Contracts.

The Officer who had the Command of the Fort being no longer continued by your State in that situation you will appoint any other person whom you may Judge proper to take immediate charge of the light House. The compensation to him you will settle, and I have no doubt you will agree upon moderate Terms. The rate formerly allowed by the State ought not I conceive, to be exceeded, but it will be well to attend to such reduction of them as may be reasonably made.

The Accounts for your disbursements with the requisite Vouchers must be rendered at the Treasury for settlement at the expiration of every Quarter; at which time it will be proper to make a Report of the State of the Establishment under your direction; And here I must observe, that as the expences of the Light house establishment are only to be defrayed by the United States to the 15th of August next; if the respective States do not in the mean while make Cessions of them to the United States, your Contracts for the present must not extend beyond the above mentioned day.

With respect to your own Compensation due regard will be had to the trouble that this duty may create.

I am Sir   Your obedient Servant   A Hamilton

P.S. You will notice the clause of the Law relative to Light Houses &c which renders necessary the transmission of the Contracts, made for their Construction, repairs, & supplies. They are to be enclosed to me, that I may lay them before the President of the United States for his approbation.

Joseph Whipple Esquire
Collector for Portsmouth New Hampshire.

LS, RG 56, Letters to the Collector at Portsmouth, National Archives; copy, RG 56, Letters to Collectors at Small Ports, "Set G," National Archives.
  1. 1 *Stat.* 53–54 (August 7, 1789).

From Jonathan Dayton

[*June 3, 1790*. On June 9, 1790, Hamilton wrote to Dayton: "I duly received your letter of the 3d. of June." *Letter not found.*]

Report on the Petition of Stephen Moore

Treasury-department. June 3d. 1790
[Communicated on June 10, 1790] [1]

[To the Speaker of the House of Representatives]
On the petition of Stephen Moore of the State of North Carolina referred to the Secretary of the Treasury, by order of the House of Representatives, of the 4th. of May 1790; [2]
The said Secretary respectfully reports:
That it is the opinion of the Secretary for the Department of War, that it is expedient and necessary that the United States should retain and occupy West-point, as a permanent Military post; the principal reasons for which opinion as stated by him in a report to Congress of the 31st. of July 1786, [3] are as follow.
"That in case of an invasion of any of the middle or Eastern States by a marine power, the possession of Hudsons river would be an object of the highest importance, as well to the invader as to the United States."

"That the reciprocal communication of the resources of the Eastern and middle States, so essential to a well-combined resistance, depends entirely on the possession of the said river by the United States."

"That West-Point is of the most decisive importance to the defence of the said river, for the following reasons."

"1st. The distance across the river is only about fourteen hundred feet, a less distance, by far, than at any other part."

"2nd. The peculiar bend or turn of the river, forming almost a re-entering angle."

"3d. The high banks on both sides of the river favorable for the construction of formidable batteries."

"4th. The demonstrated practicability of fixing across the river, a chain or chains at a spot, where vessels in turning the point, invariably lose their rapidity, and, of course, their force, by which a chain at any other part of the river, would be liable to be broken."

"These circumstances combined render the passage of hostile vessels by West-Point, impracticable."

"That the fortifications of West point, and it's dependencies, are extremely difficult to be invested and besieged. This circumstance, which greatly inhances the value of the place, arises from the broken and mountainous grounds and narrow passes, which surround the fortifications."

"A regular siege of West point, properly garrisoned and furnished, would require a large army, vast warlike apparatus, and much time. The States, therefore, in it's vicinity would have sufficient time to draw forth their utmost force for its relief."

"That, however West point may be regarded by some persons as an interior place, yet the reverse is a fact, as may be proved by a slight consideration of the facility with which it can be approached by water. It is quite practicable for vessels coming in from sea, and arriving at Sandyhook, at the close of day, to reach West point before the next morning. The navigation of the river is known to be so bold, that the passage could be easily performed during the night."

That the said Secretary of the Treasury, impressed with a persuasion that the said opinion is well founded, conceives it to be just and proper, that a purchase should be made on account of the

United States, of so much of the tract of land, called West-point, as shall be necessary for the purpose contemplated; and this for the following reasons:

First. That where the public safety requires the permanent occupancy of the property of an individual for the public use, it is just that compensation should be made for it's intire value, either by purchase with consent of parties, or by some equitable mode of appraisement. Temporary or periodical compensations, unless with the concurrence of the proprietor, are liable to this objection; that they oblige the individual to content himself with less than the full use or value of his property, by sale or otherwise, as his interest or necessities may require.

Secondly. These temporary compensations, for various obvious reasons, will be likely, in the end, to prove more expensive to the public, than an absolute purchase in the first instance.

Wherefore, the said Secretary is of opinion, that it will be advisable, that provision should be made by law, for the purchase of so much of the tract of land, called West point, as shall be judged requisite for the purpose of such fortifications and garrisons, as may be necessary for the defence of the same.[4]

All which is humbly submitted   Alexander Hamilton,
                                    Secretary of the Treasury.

Copy, RG 233, Reports of the Secretary of the Treasury, 1790–1791, Vol. I, National Archives; copy, RG 233, Reports of the Secretary of the Treasury, First Congress, National Archives.

1. *Journal of the House*, I, 236.
2. The entry in the *Journal of the House* for May 4, 1790, reads:
"A petition of Stephen Moore, of the State of North Carolina, was presented to the House and read, praying to receive compensation for the use and value of a certain tract of land at West Point, in the State of New York, on which are erected the fortifications and arsenals of the United States.
"*Ordered,* That the said petition be referred to the Secretary of the Treasury, with instructions to examine the same, and report his opinion thereupon to the House." (*Journal of the House*, I, 208.)
3. *JCC*, XXX, 447–49.
4. H's recommendations were accepted by both the House and Senate. See "An Act to authorize the purchase of a tract of land for the use of the United States" (1 *Stat.* 129 [July 5, 1790]).

To John Scott

Treasury Department
June 3d. 1790

Sir

I have received your letter of the 25th Ulto.[1] and particularly notice the information on which you found your opinion, that a Boat would be useful in the prevention of frauds on the Revenue. On such representations heretofore I have consented & on the present case, I am willing to permit that an open Boat be purchased that will enable the Officers of the Customs to go on Board Vessels in your harbor, she may be also used to ply in your River, which is not of considerable length. A great object will be to obtain, as early as possible in each case the Manifest which the Captain of every Ship is bound by Law to furnish to the first Officer of the Customs who shall demand it. The Masters of the Vessels you mention to have come into the Mouth of Chester River and to have lain there *"several days"* whether they entered afterwards or went to Sea without entering were liable to the fine imposed by the 11th Section of the Collection Law.[2] Such open violations of the Law, I trust will call forth your most particular attention & exertions.

In regard to the Waggons that come into your District tho' they are not by the law obliged to produce Certificates of the entry of their goods, yet your vigilant observation of them will be useful & when you find or have sufficient cause to believe their Loads have been illicitly imported a seizure will be Justifiable. It will however be prudent not to take any step of that nature but upon good grounds.

In regard to the entry of small Vessels, if under Twenty Tons & licensed they are not obliged to enter in one District from another, as you will find is declared by Richard Harrison & Samuel Jones Esquires in the 1st part of their opinion[3] annexed to my Circular letter of the 30th of November.

In a report[4] I had lately the honor to make the Legislature on the Revenue System, I suggested among other things the propriety of reconsidering the compensations to the Officers, and I presume they will decide upon this Business in the Course of the present Session. Information will be given of their determination.

Regular Vouchers of the Cost of the Boat will be expected & I shall rely on all possible economy in procuring her.

I am   Sir   Your Obedient Servant   Alex Hamilton

John Scott Esquire
Collector
Chester Maryland

LS, from the original in the New York State Library, Albany.
    1. Letter not found.
    2. Section 11 of this law states that a master of a ship had to report to a collector of a port within forty-eight hours after his ship had entered that port. The penalty for failing to comply with this provision was five hundred dollars (1 *Stat.* 38–39 [July 31, 1789]).
    3. Richard Harison and Samuel Jones to H, November 18, 1789.
    4. "Report on Defects in the Existing Laws of Revenue," April 22, 1790.

From Otho H. Williams

Baltimore, June 4, 1790. "By a provision in the act for Registering and clearing vessels, regulating the Coasting trade &c. See 25th Section [1]—Goods, wares, or merchandise of foreign growth, or manufacture, may be transported to and from the respective Ports of Philadelphia and Baltimore, into each other, through and across the State of Delaware, a manifest certified by the Officer of that one of the said Ports from which the said goods &c are to be transported shall be sufficient to warrant the transportation thereof to the other of the said Ports, without an intermediate entry in the State of Delaware. An inconvenience results from this arrangement, which it is impossible for any attention of the Customhouse Officers here to remedy, and which may be a cause of a clandestine communication with other places. . . ."

AL, RG 53, "Old Correspondence," Baltimore Collector, National Archives.
    1. 1 *Stat.* 61–62 (September 1, 1789).

From William Allibone

Philadelphia, June 6, 1790. Encloses "A Contract with Abraham Hargis as keeper of the light House" at Henlopen.

ALS, RG 26, Lighthouse Letters Received, Vol. "A," Pennsylvania and Southern States, National Archives.

To John Davidson [1]

Treasury Department, June 7, 1790. "The case you State [2] of the importers of Salt per the Ship Murcury, William Jessop, Master is very unfortunate. On considering the Circumstances of the Case however, & examining the Laws it does not appear that the Legislature have deposited any where the power of relieveing an importer, who has met with a disaster after securing, & ascertaining the Duty by measurement and landing the Goods. . . ."

Copy, RG 56, Letters to and from the Collectors at Bridgetown and Annapolis, National Archives; copy, RG 56, Letters to Collectors at Small Ports, "Set G," National Archives.

1. Davidson was the collector of customs at Annapolis.
2. The letter from Davidson to H in which this case was discussed has not been found.

To Jedediah Huntington

Treasury Department, June 7, 1790. Sends instructions concerning the brig *Maria.*

LS, Mr. Leland F. Leland, St. Paul, Minnesota.

From Jeremiah Olney

Providence 7th June 1790

Sir

Permitt an *old mittilary acquaintance* [1] to address you (with out apology) on a Subject particularly Interesting to himself and to request your Friendship and Influence with the President of the

United States, to promote his Interests (So far as it shall in your opinion be consistant with propriety & the public Good) in Support of an application he has made to the President to be appointed to the office of Collector for the District of Providence—this and the other Revenue appointments will probably soon be made—as Rhode Island have at last adopted the Enlightened policy to compleat the Band of Union [2]—on which happy event permitt me Sir to congratulate you! I have written my Worthy Friends Genl. Schuyler & Knox [3] on this Subject who have given me assurances of their Friendship & Influence in promoting my Wishes. I am anxious to be on the Ground myself (as probably I have Several competitors) and was I not Ingaged in the present payment of Invalids [4] (*a Service in which I feel greatly interested because it contributes to the Relief & Comfort of that meritorous Class of Citizens*) I should sett out immediately for New York. However I hope to accomplish this business in time to go on with our Senators who will probably be ready by the 20th Inst. as the Legislature is this day Specially Convened at Newport for the purpose of Choosing them. I fear we shall not be able to send Federal Characters, we shall however make every Exertion. The president of our late Convention,[5] with the advise of the Governor,[6] means to Keep back the Ratification untill about the time the Senators go forward, as they Wish to have all the *Ante* Revenue officers of the State reappointed & expect the Senators will Influence the President In the nomination of these *Bitter & Uniform* opposers of the Constitution. Having already Intruded too long on your important moments, I will hast to Conclude by saying that I am   with all possible Respect & Esteem   Sir   Your Most, Obed. Hume. Servt.

Jereh. Olney

Honble. Alexander Hamilton

ADfS, Rhode Island Historical Society, Providence.
    1. During the American Revolution Olney rose from the rank of captain to that of lieutenant colonel commandant.
    2. The Rhode Island Ratifying Convention sat from March 1–6, 1790, when it referred a bill of rights and other proposed amendments to the Constitution to the voters for their approval in an April election. The Convention then adjourned. Reconvening in May, the Convention ratified the Constitution and proposed amendments to it by a vote of 34 to 32 on May 29.
    3. Philip Schuyler and Henry Knox.
    4. See H to Olney, February 4, 1790.
    5. Daniel Owen of Glocester, Rhode Island.
    6. Arthur Fenner of Providence, an Antifederalist.

To Benjamin Lincoln

Treasury Department
June 8th. 1790

Sir

I have received your favor of the 25th of May,[1] and am much obliged to you for putting the information concerning the Manufactures of your State in a train, that promises so much authenticity & accuracy. The direction of the duplicate to you,[2] was occasioned by an opinion of some of the Members of the Legislature, that such a Committee had been appointed & that you were the Chairman.[3] I beg leave to repeat my remark that the earlier the information is transmitted, the more beneficial to the Manufacturing interest & therefore, that when one or more reports or returns shall be received, they may come forward.

I observe the several seizures made in your District & that the decrees of the Judiciary evince, that the Conduct of the Officers has been no less legal, than vigilant. There seems to be some Question from the Circumstances given in your letter whether the Captain may not have taken a false Oath. You mention that he knew of the Goods being landed. Should he appear to have known they were on board when he entered his Vessel, he lies open to prosecution.

I am Sir   very respectfully   Your Obedient Servant

A Hamilton

Benjamin Lincoln Esqr
Collector
Boston

LS, RG 36, Collector of Customs at Boston, Letters from the Treasury, 1772–1818, Vol. 6, National Archives; copy, RG 56, Letters to Collectors at Small Ports, "Set G," National Archives; copy, RG 56, Letters to the Collector at Boston, National Archives.

    1. Letter not found.
    2. H to Lincoln, January 25, 1790.
    3. For an explanation of this sentence, see H to Lincoln, January 25, 1790, note 1.

To Jonathan Dayton

Private   New York June 9. 1790

Dear Sir

I duly received your letter of the 3d. of June.[1]

I have written to Mr. Ludlow[2] directing that either Mr. Martin[3] or himself would come forward with the Map.

On the subject of a certain office[4] I can with truth assure you that no person can occur, who on the score of qualifications and merit, will appear to me better intitled than yourself; and that I shall take pleasure in mentioning you in this light to the President, if an opportunity of doing it is afforded me. Yet I will not answer how much weight the circumstance of another Gentleman[5] having been in a situation similar to the one contemplated will have in his mind or even in my own.

All I will say more is this—that I am convinced you would be an acquisition to the public service in whatever station you should be placed and that I consider you as one who ought to be embraced in some official arrangement adequate to your wishes.

I remain very truly   Yr. friend & Ser.   A Hamilton

You will perceive from the tenor of this letter that I express myself in confidence.

Jonathan Dayton Esqr

ALS, Mr. William N. Dearborn, Nashville, Tennessee.
1. Letter not found.
2. See H to Israel Ludlow, May 13, 1790.
3. Absalom Martin.
4. Dayton also wrote to George Washington asking him for an appointment as loan commissioner for New Jersey. See Dayton to Washington, June 21, 1790, Applications for Office under George Washington, Library of Congress.
5. H probably is referring to James Ewing who was appointed commissioner of loans for New Jersey in August, 1790.

To Thomas Jefferson

Treasury Department June 9th. 1790

Sir

I have the honor to inform you, that in a few days, information furnished by the several Departments and otherwise collected, will be laid before the House of Representatives,[1] for the purpose of obtaining appropriations of Money. As the expences &ca. of the Department of State will necessarily require an appropriation, I beg the favour of your directing information to be transmitted to me of the sum you may desire to be placed upon the list.

You will oblige me by directing a return to be made to this office, from time to time, of such officers connected with the Revenue, as shall be hereafter appointed.

Enclosed is a return of the persons appointed by the President of the United States to superintend certain Light houses therein mentioned, which, I presume, will be necessary to enable you to give the necessary directions about their Commissions.

I have the honor to be, very respectfully Sir, Your obedient Servt.   Alexander Hamilton
                                                Secy of the Treasury

The Honorable Thomas Jefferson Esquire
Secretary of State

LS, RG 59, Miscellaneous Letters, National Archives.
    1. "Report on Additional Sums Necessary for the Support of the Government," August 5, 1790.

To Nathaniel Fosdick

Treasury Department:
June 11th. 1790.

Sir:

It appears to be a defect in our Laws, that the Registry of a Foreign Ship, sold after condemnation is not provided for. It will be laid before a Committee of the House of Representatives now sitting upon the alterations and amendments in which the Commercial and Revenue Laws require.

I am, Sir, with respect, Your obedient Servant Alex. Hamilton.

Nathaniel F. Fosdick,
Collector, Portland

Copy, RG 56, Letters to and from the Collector at Portland, National Archives; copy, RG 56, Letters to Collectors at Small Ports, "Set G," National Archives.

From Thomas Jefferson

[New York, June 12, 1790]

Mr. Jefferson presents his compliments to the Secretary of the Treasury, and asks his perusal of the inclosed rough draught of a report[1] on the subject of measures, weights & coins, in hopes that the Secretary of the Treasury may be able to accomodate his plan of a mint[2] to the very small alteration of the money unit proposed in this report. As soon as the Secretary of the Treasury shall have read it, mr Jefferson asks the favor of him to return it,[3] as he wishes to submit it to the examination and correction of some mathematical friends.

June 12. 1790.

ADf, Thomas Jefferson Papers, Library of Congress.
 1. Jefferson's "Plan for Establishing Uniformity in the Coinage, Weights, and Measures, of the United States" July 4, 1790, was communicated to the House of Representatives, July 13, 1790 (ASP, Miscellaneous, I, 13–20).
 2. For H's final plan for a mint, see "Report on the Establishment of a Mint," January 28, 1791.
 3. For H's reply, see H to Jefferson, June 16, 1790.

From Royal Flint[1]

New York, June 14, 1790. Discusses the qualifications of various residents of Rhode Island who were candidates for positions in the Treasury Department.

ALS, Hamilton Papers, Library of Congress.
 1. Originally a resident of Connecticut, Flint became a prominent New York

businessman. In the seventeen-eighties he had been closely associated in several ventures with William Duer and Jeremiah Wadsworth.

To Jeremiah Olney

[*New York, June 14, 1790*. Letter listed in dealer's catalogue. *Letter not found.*]

ALS, sold at Merwin-Clayton, June 6, 1907, Lot 32.

From Joseph Whipple

Portsmo. New Hamp. June 14, 1790

Sir

I am favour with your letter of the 1st. Instant ⟨wh⟩ich mentions a "copy of the Act for the establishment of Light houses, Beacons, Buoys & public piers" [1] to be therewith Sent. This act was omitted to be enclosed with your letter & as I conceive a knowledge of its contents essential to my understanding perfectly the business which is required by it, I shall only observe at present that the Legislature of this State at their last Session thought proper to postpone the decision on a motion for the Cession of Fort Wm. & Mary & the Light house [2] to the United States. This matter will probably be taken up at the Session now holding at Concord as was intended at the time of postponement. I am informed that the care & support of the Fort & Lighthouse was let out by Contract for a limittd time which will not terminate till Sometime after the 15th of Augst next. The establishment of Soldiery previous to this Contract was withdrawn.

Inclosed herewith is a Weekly Return of monies recd. and paid in this district for the Week past.

I have the hon⟨our to be,⟩ &c

LC, RG 36, Collector of Customs at Portsmouth, Letters Sent, 1790–1791, Vol. 2, National Archives; copy, RG 56, Letters from the Collector at Portsmouth, National Archives.

1. 1 *Stat.* 53–54 (August 7, 1789).
2. The fort and lighthouse were in Portsmouth harbor.

To Otho H. Williams

Treasury Department
June 14th. 1790

Sir

I have received your Answer to my Enquiries,[1] relative to the case of the Snow St Martin.

The Act of Congress transmitted you from this Office on the 3d Instant will shew you the line of proceeding to obtain relief in the case of the Ship Van Staphorst.[2] Messrs. Bertier & Company have had the same information.

I am Sir   with respect   Your Obedient Servant   Alex Hamilton

Otho H. Williams Esqr
Collector
Baltimore

LS, Columbia University Libraries.
  1. Letter not found, but see Robert Purviance to H, April 22, 1790.
  2. See Williams to H, May 31, 1790.

From William Allibone

Philadelphia, June 15, 1790. Encloses a maintenance contract for the Delaware River establishment.

ALS, RG 26, Lighthouse Letters Received, Vol. "A," Pennsylvania and Southern States, National Archives.

To Thomas Jefferson

[New York, June 16, 1790] [1]

Mr. Hamilton presents his Compliments to Mr. Jefferson. He has perused with much satisfaction the draft of his report on the subject of weights and measures.[2] There is no view which Mr. H has yet taken of the matter which stands opposed to the alteration of the money-unit as at present contemplated by the regulations of Congress either in the way suggested in the report or in that mentioned in the note of yesterday. And there are certainly strong reasons to render a correspondency desireable. The idea of a general standard among nations, as in the proposal of the Bishop D Autun [3] seems full of convenience & order.

Wednesday

AL, Thomas Jefferson Papers, Library of Congress.

1. Henry Cabot Lodge (*HCL*, IV, 3) and John C. Hamilton (*JCH*, IV, 23) date this letter June 13, 1790.

2. In the JCH Transcripts, the beginning of this letter reads: "Mr. H The Secretary of the Treasury has the honor to acknowledge the reception of the Report of the Secretary of state on the subject of Measures Weights & Coins."

3. Charles-Maurice de Talleyrand-Perigord, Bishop of Autun, in March, 1790, presented a proposal to the National Assembly for standardizing the French system of weights and measures. He also suggested the creation of a joint Anglo-French commission, consisting of members of the French Academy of Sciences and the British Royal Society, to develop a common standard for both nations. Talleyrand enclosed his plan to Sir John Riggs Miller, under whose direction the British Parliament was considering the problem of standardization. At the same time the French Minister in London informed the British Ministry of the proposal. The British, however, rejected the French offer, and the National Assembly enacted a new standard that was based on Talleyrand's plan.

From Thomas Jefferson [1]

New York June 17th. 1790

Sir

I have the honor to enclose you an estimate of the probable expences of the Department of State for one year from the 1st. day of April last past, not including the diplomatic establishment abroad, for which there is a Bill before Congress to make a special appropriation.

I have given directions that a list shall always be sent to your office of all Commissions to be made out for persons connected with the revenue, and whenever you think proper, the Commissions themselves shall be sent to your office to be forwarded thence. I have the honor to be with sentiments of the most perfect esteem and respect &c.   Thomas Jefferson.

LC, Papers of the Continental Congress, National Archives.

1. This letter is in reply to H to Jefferson, June 9, 1790.

To Thomas Newton, Junior [1]

[*New York, June 17, 1790.* On June 27, 1790, Newton wrote to Hamilton: "Your favor of the 17th I received this day." *Letter not found.*]

1. Newton was a Norfolk, Virginia, lawyer.

To Jeremiah Olney [1]

Treasury Department
June 17th. 1790.

Sir,

I take an opportunity as early as the hurry of business will permit, of transmitting to you my instructions and other communications to the several Collectors of the United States.

As far as they may not be locally inapplicable to Rhode Island, I shall expect a careful observance of them.

I am, Sir, Your obedt. Sert.   Alex. Hamilton
          Secy of the Treasry.

Jeremiah Olney Esquire,
Collector
Providence, Rhode Island.

Copy, RG 56, Letters to the Collector at Providence, National Archives; copy, RG 56, Letters to Collectors at Small Ports, "Set G," National Archives.
1. Olney was not appointed collector of customs at Providence until June 14, 1790. The delay in his appointment arose from the fact that Rhode Island did not ratify the Constitution until May 29, 1790. See Olney to H, June 7, 1790.

To Thomas Harwood [1]

[*New York, June 18, 1790.* On July 2, 1790, Harwood wrote to Hamilton: "I received your Letter of the 18th. Ulto." *Letter not found.*]

1. The Senate confirmed Harwood's appointment as United States commissioner of loans for Maryland on August 7, 1790.

To George Washington

[Treasury Department, June 18, 1790]

The Secretary of the Treasury has the honor respectfully to submit to the President of the United states for his consideration, a Contract (with the letter that accompanied it) betwen William Allibone Superintendant of the Light-house, Beacons, Buoys & public Piers on the river and Bay of Delaware and Abraham Hargis, Keeper of the Light-house at Cape Henlopen.[1] The yearly Salary of £130. altho' it appeared high, is found, on Examination the same as was allowed to this person by the State of Pennsylvania. The allowance of £13. for the several supplies and services specifyed, does not appear unreasonable.

Treasury Department
June 18th. 1790

LC, George Washington Papers, Library of Congress.
  1. See Allibone to H, June 6, 1790.

From Eli Elmer [1]

[*Bridgetown, New Jersey, June 19, 1790.* On July 29, 1790, Hamilton wrote to Elmer: "Your letter of the 19th ultimo was duly received." *Letter not found.*]

  1. Elmer was collector of customs at Bridgetown.

To Beverley Randolph

Treasury Department June 19th 1790

Sir

It appearing from the representation of Col. Carrington [1] that he will be unable to execute in convenient time the business committed to him, relative to the lighthouse on Cape Henry, the President of the united States has been pleased to transfer that duty to Thomas Newton Esqr [2] of Norfolk. The necessary instructions for this Gentleman were dispatched to him by the last mail,[3] and on his report to you it will be Satisfactory to the President that the cession be completed.

I have the honor to be with the greatest respect   Sir   Your obedient Servt   Alexander Hamilton
                                         Secretary of the Treasury

His Excelly Beverly Randolph Esqr
Governor of Virginia
Richmond

LS, Archives Division, Virginia State Library, Richmond.
   1. Edward Carrington. Letter not found, but see H to Randolph, May 8, 1790.
   2. See Tobias Lear to H, November 21, 1789.
   3. Letter not found.

To George Washington

Treasury Department June 21st. 1790.

The Secretary of the Treasury has the honor respectfully to submit to the President of the United states, for his approbation, the enclosed Contract for timber, boards, Nails and Workmanship, for a Beacon to be placed near the Light-house on Sandy hook; the terms of which, he begs leave to observe are, in his opinion favourable to the U. States.

LC, George Washington Papers, Library of Congress.

From Tobias Lear [1]

[New York] June 21 [1790]. "The President . . . approves of the enclosed contract for . . . the Light House on Sandy Hook."

LS, RG 26, "Segregated" Lighthouse Records, National Archives; LC, George Washington Papers, Library of Congress.
   1. Lear erroneously dated this letter "June 21st. 1789."

To Joseph Whipple

[New York, June 21, 1790. On July 23, 1790, Whipple wrote to Hamilton: "I have delayed to answer your favor of the 21st June." Letter not found.]

To William Allibone

[*New York, June 22, 1790.* On July 3, 1790, Allibone wrote to Hamilton: "I found your letter of the 22d of last month." *Letter not found.*]

From Jeremiah Olney [1]

Providence 23rd. June 1790.

Sir

Since my Return to Providence I have made enquiry Respecting fit persons to be Surveyors for Warren, Bristol & Pawcatuck River —but I cannot find but one person for the Port of Bri[s]tol, a Mr. Samuel Bozworth [2] who is, as I am informed a very Good Character, & held the office under the State. Mr. Ellery [3] probably may inform you of Suitable persons for the other Two ports.[4] Danl. Updike as mention in my memorandom for Surveyor Should be Daniel Eldridge Updike.[5] My Commission came on with Colo. Barton.[6]

ADf, Rhode Island Historical Society, Providence.
    1. This letter is incomplete.
    2. Bozworth was appointed surveyor of the port of Bristol, Rhode Island, on July 3, 1790.
    3. William Ellery, who had been continental loan officer, had been appointed collector of customs for Newport, Rhode Island, in June, 1790.
    4. On July 3, 1790, Nathaniel Phillips was appointed surveyor at Warren and Barrington, Rhode Island, and George Stillman was appointed to this position at Pawcatuck River, Rhode Island.
    5. Updike was a merchant and justice of peace for Wickford, Rhode Island. He was appointed surveyor of North Kingstown, Rhode Island, on July 3, 1790.
    6. William Barton was a prominent Rhode Island Federalist who had been a member of the Rhode Island Ratifying Convention of 1790.

From Henry Knox

[*New York, June 24, 1790.* On August 5, 1790, in Schedule B of his "Report on Additional Sums Necessary for the Support of Government," Hamilton referred to "The Secretary at War in his Letter to the sec'y of the Treasury dated 24 June 1790." *Letter not found.*]

To Benjamin Lincoln

Treasury Department, June 24, 1790. "No official information has been yet received of the Cession of the Light House at Portland Head. . . .¹ If you could procure . . . an Account of the Cost of the Light House, so far as it is built—the height to which it is carried—the height to which it is proposed to be carried, and an estimate of the expence that will attend the Completion of it, I shall be obliged to you."

LS, RG 36, Collector of Customs at Boston, Letters and Papers re Lighthouses, Buoys, and Piers, 1789–1819, Vol. 4, National Archives; copy, RG 56, Letters to the Collector at Boston, National Archives; copy, Letters to Collectors at Small Ports, "Set G," National Archives.
    1. The lighthouse was several miles south of Portland, District of Maine, on Cape Elizabeth.

From Charles Lee

[*Alexandria, Virginia, June 25, 1790.* On July 4, 1790, Hamilton wrote to Lee acknowledging receipt of Lee's "letter of the 25th Ultimo." *Letter not found.*]

From Jeremiah Olney

Providence, June 25, 1790. "Your favor of 17th. Inst. transmitting your instructions and communications to the several Collectors of the United States came to hand this day. . . ."

Copy, RG 56, Letters from the Collector at Providence, National Archives.

From Sharp Delany

[Philadelphia, June 26, 1790]

Sir
    I am at a loss how to construe the late Act extending the Revenue Laws to R Island ¹ and request your opinion & directions as soon as

may be on the subject. The Impost Laws [2] lays a duty on all goods imported into the United States from & after the first of August 1789. R Island not being one at the time the Act passed, could not be looked on as in the Union. The Act extending the Impost & Tonnage to that State, says it is to take place in five days after passing. I have a case though I entertain doubts of the true construction which requires as above your opinion & instruction. The Owners of the India Men lately arrived in that State has heretofore sent goods here, & of course paid or secured the Duties. Since R Island was comprehended in the Union other Goods have arrivd here & the owners claim an exemption of Duty. I have prevailed on them to bond from the above motives, under a promise that in a due representation to & consideration of the matter by you, I would should your opinion be conformable abate the Duties and cancel their Bonds. I am not so uneasy about the above, but other goods may come under like circumstances, and though equity and perhaps my opinion of the Law may lead me to exact the Duties Yet there is room for a Contrary opinion, from the Letter of the Law of Impost, or its being in under the last Law a Casus omissus.

I am &c   S Delany

June 26th 1790
Alexdr Hamilton Esqr Secry of the Treasury

LC, Copies of Letters to the Secretary, 1789–1790, Bureau of Customs, Philadelphia.
    1. "An Act for giving effect to the several Acts therein mentioned, in respect to the State of Rhode Island and Providence Plantations" (1 *Stat.* 126–28 [June 14, 1790]).
    2. "An act for laying a Duty on Goods, Wares, and Merchandises imported into the United States" (1 *Stat.* 24–27 [July 4, 1789]).

To George Washington

Treasury Department
June 26th. 1790

The Secretary of the Treasury has the honor respectfully to inform the President of the United states, that he has received a letter from the Collector of Charleston [1] in South Carolina, from which he learns that some misconception has arisen as to the nature of the qualifications of Mr. Thomas Hollingsby, who on the joint recommendation of the Collector & commissioners of Pilotage for that port was appointed Superintendant of the Light-house. These Gentlemen appear to feel much concern, that they shou'd have so expressed themselves, as to promote his appointment to that Duty; and the Collector from his anxiety on the subject has ventur'd to detain the letters directed for Mr. Hollingsby 'till the pleasure of the president, after this information, shou'd be Known. Under these circumstances, the Secretary respectfully submits to the President an opinion, that the public interests will be promoted by the appointment of another person as superintendant, who may employ Mr. Hollingsby in the station of Keeper, for which the Collector and Commissioners intended to recommend him. He takes the liberty further to add, that Edward Blake Esqr.[2] has been strongly recommended as a suitable person by the Honorable Mr. Tucker[3] of the south Carolina Delegation, which is confirmed by the Collector of Charleston.

Alexander Hamilton
Secy. of the Treasury

LC, George Washington Papers, Library of Congress.
1. George A. Hall. Letter not found.
2. Blake was subsequently appointed.
3. Thomas T. Tucker represented South Carolina at the Continental Congress in 1788 and 1789. He was a Federalist member of the House of Representatives from 1789 to 1793.

To George Washington

Treasury Department
June 26th. 1790

The Secretary of the Treasury has the honor respectfully to inform the President of the United states that the Collector of Charleston in south Carolina[1] has stated to him,[2] that a proposal has been made by James Robinson[3] of Newport, Rhode Island, to the Collector, through the Commissioners of Pilotage of that Port, to supply six hundred gallons of spermaceti Oil, for the use of the Light house, at two shillings & six pence, Rhode Island Money, pr. gallon.

The Contract, which appears to the Secretary favourable to the United states, awaits the determination of the President.

Alexander Hamilton
Secy. of the Treasury

LC, George Washington Papers, Library of Congress.
    1. George A. Hall.
    2. Letter not found.
    3. Robinson was a Newport, Rhode Island, merchant.

From Thomas Newton, Junior [1]

Norfolk [*Virginia*] *June 27, 1790.* "Your favor of the 17th I received. . . ." [2] Agrees to select the site for the Cape Henry lighthouse. Proposes that a small lighthouse be constructed at "old Point Comfort."

LS, RG 26, Lighthouse Letters Received, Vol. "A," Pennsylvania and Southern States, National Archives.
    1. For the background to this letter, see H to Randolph, June 19, 1790.
    2. Letter not found.

From Tobias Lear

United States June 29. 1790

The President of the United States approves of the proposal, communicated to him on the 26th Inst. by the Secretary of the Treasury, made by James Robinson to the Collector of Charleston in South Carolina, to supply six hundred Gallons of Spermaciti Oil for the use of the Light-house, at two shillings and six pence per Gallon.

The President of the United States likewise assents to the removal of Mr. Thomas *Hollingsworth* [1] from the office of Superintendant of the Light-house of Charleston in South Carolina, and to the appointment of Edward Blake Esquire to that place, for the reasons communicated to him by the Secretary of the Treasury on the 26th Inst.

By the Command of the President of the United States.
              Tobias Lear.
              Secretary to the President of the United States.

[ENCLOSURE] [2]

Return of the persons appointed by the President of the United States, for the Superintendance of certain Light-houses, Beacons, Buoys and public Piers in the United States.

1790.	*In the State of Massachusetts.*
March 10th.	Benjamin Lincoln, Boston, Superintendt. of all the Light-houses, Beacons Buoys & public piers in the State of Massachsetts.
Do.	Thomas Knox, Supert. of the Lighthouse, Boston.
Do.	Samuel Houston Supt. of the Light house, Cape Ann.
Do.	Abner Lowell, Supt. of the Do. at Plumb-Island.
Do.	Paul Pinkham Supt. of Do. at Nantucket.
May 8th.	John Thomas Supt. of Do. at Plymouth.

In the State of Connecticut.

April 21st. Jededh. Huntington Supt. of Light Houses; Beacons, Buoys, and public piers within the State of Connecticut.

In the State of New York.

April 21st. Thomas Randall, New York, Superintendt. of the Light house; Beacons, buoys and public piers at Sandy hook and elsewhere in the state of New-York.

1790. *In the State of Pennsylvania,*

April 21st. William Allibone, Philadelphia, Supert. of the Light house, Beacons, Buoys & public piers at Cape Henlopen, & elsewhere on the Bay & river Delaware.

In the State of South Carolina.

June 29th. Edward Blake, Charleston, Supt. of the Light-Houses, Beacons, Buoys and public piers in the State of South Carolina.

LS, RG 26, "Segregated" Lighthouse Records, National Archives; copy, George Washington Papers, Library of Congress.
1. Lear mistakenly wrote "Hollingsworth" instead of "Hollingsby."
2. LC, George Washington Papers.

From Charles Lee

[*Alexandria, Virginia, June 29, 1790.* On July 17, 1790, Hamilton wrote to Lee: "Your letter of the 29th June has been duly received." *Letter not found.*]

From Jeremiah Olney

Providence, June 29, 1790. Asks Hamilton for the "forms of the several returns to be made from time to time." Thinks that the surveyor should have a boat at Pawtucket to meet incoming ships. Asks for permission to purchase a set of scales and weights. Desires instructions on the collection of a tonnage duty which the state previously levied for defraying the cost of dredging the harbor.

Copy, RG 56, Letters from the Collector at Providence, National Archives.

From Charles Lee

[*Alexandria, Virginia, June 30, 1790.* On July 9, 1790, Hamilton wrote to Lee: "These are to acknowlege the receipt of . . . your Letter of the 30th June." *Letter not found.*] [1]

1. Because it pertains to routine Treasury Department matters, H's letter to Lee has not been printed.

To Jeremiah Olney

Treasury Department,
June 30th. 1790.

Sir,

I am obliged to you for the information contained in your letter of the 23d. Instant.[1]

It will be agreeable to me, that you purchase Scales, & Weights, for the use of the Port of Providence.

I have permitted small Sail Boats fit for harbor service to be purchased or built by some of the Collectors, & will not object to one for the purpose mentioned in your letter.

These purchases will no doubt be made with due attention to œconomy, & must be supported by regular vouchers.

I am Sir   Your Obedient Servant   Alexander Hamilton.

Jerh. Olney Esquire,
Collector for Providence, R. I.

Copy, RG 56, Letters to the Collector at Providence, National Archives; copy, RG 56, Letters to Collectors at Small Ports, "Set G," National Archives.

1. The letter of June 23 as printed above presumably is incomplete as it does not contain the questions which H answered on June 30, 1790. On June 29, 1790, not having received an answer from H, Olney repeated some of those questions. These were answered by H on July 7, 1790.

From Meletiah Jordan

Frenchman's Bay [District of Maine] July 1, 1790. "Herewith I have the honour to transmit to you one Register, one Enrolment, my Account current for the last Quarter, Abstract of Duties on Tonnage, Abstract of pay to Inspectors &c with the necessary Vouchers. . . . I have concluded to remit the Ballance in my hands to the Bank of Boston agreeable to your letter of March 29th. . . .[1] The Schooner Betsey, siezed on account of the United States last fall, has been condemned at a Court of Admiralty held at Portland, the first Tuesday in June last. . . ."

LC, RG 56, Letters to Collectors at Gloucester, Machias, and Frenchman's Bay, National Archives.
1. Letter not found.

From Benjamin Lincoln

[Boston, July 1, 1790.] Recommends Barzillas Delano "as a suitable person" to be the keeper of the lighthouse at Portland Head.

ALS, RG 26, Lighthouse Letters Received, Vol. "B," New Hampshire and Massachusetts, National Archives.

From Benjamin Lincoln

Boston, July 1, 1790. States that the lighthouses on Thatcher and Plum Islands need to be repaired and that the cost of the work will be $137.83⅓.

ALS, RG 26, Lighthouse Letters Received, Vol. "B," New Hampshire and Massachusetts, National Archives; LC, RG 36, Collector of Customs at Boston, Letter Book, 1790–1797, National Archives; copy, RG 56, Letters from the Collector at Boston, National Archives.

From Peter Anspach [1]

N. York July 2nd. 1790

Sir,

In my memorial of yesterday to Congress [2] and which I am informed has been referred to you I forgot to deliver a Copy of the a/c paid by Mr. Quackenbush,[3] to his attorney for defending suits brought against him by Public creditors; I also in a letter from Col. Pickering to me, dated in March 1789 I recd one inclosed from him, addressed to the late Board of Treasury; which not reaching me until about the time or after the said board ceased transacting public business, prevented my delivering it to either of the gentlemen composing the board and the letter has therefore lain dormant until the other day when I found it put up among some of the letters to me from the quarter master general; and as it probably is on the subject of money being furnished to me, I therefore take the liberty of now of inclosing it and the abovementioned a/c's to you.

Honble. Alexr. Hamilton Esqr.

ADf, Essex Institute, Salem, Massachusetts.
    1. For background to this letter, see Timothy Pickering to H, November 19, 25, 1789; H to Pickering, November 19, 1789; H to Anspach, December 5, 1789; Anspach to H, December 30, 1789.
    2. An entry in the *Journal of the House* for July 1, 1790, reads as follows:
    "A petition of Peter Anspach, of the City of New York, in behalf of Timothy Pickering, late Quartermaster General of the Armies of the United States, was presented to the House and read, praying the liquidation and settlement of a claim of the said Timothy Pickering against the United States.
    "*Ordered,* That the said petition be referred to the Secretary of the Treasury, with instruction to examine the same, and report his opinion thereupon to the House." (*Journal of the House,* I, 254–55.)
    For H's report on this petition, see "Report on Additional Sums Necessary for the Support of the Government," August 5, 1790.
    3. Nicholas Quackenbush of Albany had been a deputy quartermaster general during the American Revolution.

From Thomas Harwood

[*Annapolis*] *July 2, 1790.* "I received your Letter of the 18th. Ulto.[1] and in obedience to your direction, I have cancelled the Indents, blank Loan Office Certificates, New Emission Money in the manner directed, the package I have forwarded to Otho H Williams at Baltimore with directions to Ship it to you. . . ."

LS, Maryland Historical Society, Baltimore.
    1. Letter not found.

From William Allibone

Philadelphia, [July] *3, 1790.*[1] "Having returned by this day from a visit of Inspection to the several establishments in the Bay & River Including the light house, it was not without Concern I found your letter of the 22d of last month.[2] Accompanied by the Contract made with abraham Hargis and communicating the disinclination of the President of the United States to approve the allowance of £130 per annum with the other benefits granted to him as keeper of the Light House, And the more so, it having always heretofore been thot. moderate and having the precedents of more than Twenty years standing before me I tho't it the part in which I was least likely to Err. And sure I am that £130 will maintain a Small family for a year but in Humble Stile. Am Induced to believe that the other Benefits must have been considered of much more value than they are, A house to live in has undoubtedly its Natural Vallue, but it is a necessary appendix to the light House, it being between three & four miles to any inhabitants and they seperated by a navigable water over which not even a ferry is kept, it is absolutely necessary that the Keeper should live upon the spot, and it could not be expected he could find himself a house being removable at pleasure: and it would not only be Improper but of dangerous Tendency to employ A man who had not some family about him, to do what might be necessary in case of Sickness &c. These are considerations making it necessary to find the keeper a house. . . . I cannot help Flattering myself with A hope that . . . the President of the United States will view the allowance intended [for Hargis] as not more than adequate to the Service & Situation & be pleased to approve thereof. . . ."

ALS, RG 26, Lighthouse Letters Received, Vol. "A," Pennsylvania and Southern States, National Archives.
    1. Allibone mistakenly dated this letter June 3. See Allibone to H, June 6, 1790; H to George Washington, June 18, 1790.
    2. Letter not found.

To Eli Elmer

[*New York, July 3, 1790*. On July 29, 1790, Hamilton wrote to Elmer: "Your letter of the 19th ultimo was duly received and I am apprehensive that an answer to it which was written on the 3d of July has been mislaid." *Letter of July 3 not found.*]

To Richard Harison

[New York, July 3, 1790]

Sir

The Collection law[1] rates the ruble of Russia at 100 Cents. The 3d. Section of the act to explain the act "for registering and clearing vessels" &c[2] declares that so much of the Collection law as rates the ruble of Russia at 100 Cents be and that the same is thereby *repealed* and made *null* and *void*.

Discounts have been allowed by some of the Collectors on bonds taken prior to the passing of the repealing Act; the ruble of Russia having been rated *too high*.

Were they warranted in so doing? Or in other words—Is there any *peculiarity* in the wording of the repealing clause, which gives it a retrospective operation?

I am Sir   Yr. Obed serv   Alexander Hamilton

New York July 3. 1790
Richard Harrison Esqr

ALS, New-York Historical Society, New York City.
    1. 1 *Stat.* 29–49 (July 31, 1789).
    2. "An Act to explain and amend an Act, intituled 'An Act for registering and clearing Vessels, regulating the Coasting Trade, and for other purposes'" (1 *Stat.* 94–95 [September 29, 1789]).

From Benjamin Lincoln

Boston, July 3, 1790. "Your favour of the 24th Ulto. came by the last post. I have seen one of the Gentlemen to whom was committed the building the light-house at Portland and find that the house is fifty eight feet in height that it must be raised Eight feet higher which will cost about one hundred dollars. The whole expence which has been incurred for the land the Light-house and for a dwilling-house for the keeper amounts to thirteen hundred dollars. . . . The expence to finish the whole will, from the best light I can obtain, amount to about seven hundred dollars. . . ."

ALS, RG 26, Lighthouse Letters Received, Vol. "B," New Hampshire and Massachusetts, National Archives; LC, RG 36, Collector of Customs at Boston, Letter Book, 1790–1797, National Archives; copy, RG 56, Letters from the Collector at Boston, National Archives.

From Tobias Lear

[New York] July 4, 1790. Asks that "the dates of the Warrants, which are to be issued for the Superintendants of the Light houses &c . . . be affixed to the names on the enclosed lists."

Copy, RG 26, "Segregated" Lighthouse Records, National Archives.

To Charles Lee

Treasury Department, July 4, 1790. "A Bill of the Treasury of the United States on you No.370 for 1000 Dollars is received at this Office with your letter of the 25th Ultimo." [1]

LS, RG 36, Collector of Customs at Alexandria, Letters Received from the Secretary, National Archives.
    1. Letter not found.

To John Adams

[New York, July 5, 1790]

Sir

I have the honor to inform the Vice President of the United States and to request him to cause an intimation to be given to the Honoble The Members of the Senate that at one oClock to day, an oration will be delivered at St Pauls Church in commemoration of the declaration of Independence by a Member of the Society of the Cincinnati [1] and that seats are provided for his and their accommo- dation. Peculiar circumstances prevented an earlier communication. The Requisite number of tickets have been sent to the Secretary of the Senate.

I have the honor to be with the most perfect respect Sir   Your Obed & hum ser   A Hamilton
                    Vice President of the NY Society of the Cin.
Monday July 5
vice President of the United States

ALS, Adams-Clement Collection, Smithsonian Institution.
    1. Because the Fourth of July fell on a Sunday in 1790, it was celebrated on Monday, July 5. The speech at St. Paul's was delivered by Brockholst Livingston.

From William Allibone

Philadelphia, July 5, 1790. Describes "a visit of Inspection to the several establishments" under Allibone's supervision. Intends to draw up contracts for the repair of buoys, piers, and beacons.

ALS, RG 26, Lighthouse Letters Received, Vol. "A," Pennsylvania and South- ern States, National Archives.

To Jeremiah Olney

                                        Treasury Department
                                        July 6. 1790
Sir;

From your letter of the 23d. June, a doubt has arisen, with respect to the name of the Person whom you recommend as Surveyor for North Kingstown.

One of the Senators of your State informs me, that he is acquainted with Daniel Updike, but knows of no person by the name of Daniel Eldridge Updike.[1] If they are not two distinct persons, it will be necessary to ascertain the true name of the Gentleman intended for the office, and to communicate it to me, as speedily as may be, in order that the appointment may suffer no delay.

I am, Sir, Your Obedt. Servt.   A. Hamilton.

Jeremiah Olney Esqr.
Collector of the Port of Providence, Rhode Island.

Copy, RG 56, Letters to the Collector at Providence, National Archives; copy, RG 56, Letters to Collectors at Small Ports, "Set G," National Archives.

1. Daniel Updike and Daniel Eldridge Updike were cousins. Daniel Updike was a lawyer in North Kingstown, Rhode Island. In March, 1790, the Rhode Island Ratifying Convention appointed him its secretary, and in May, 1790, the voters elected him attorney general. Daniel Eldridge Updike was a merchant and a justice of the peace in North Kingstown.

To Jeremiah Olney

Treasury Department,
July 7th. 1790.

Sir,

Yours of the 29th. of June has been received. The Comptroller informs me that the forms for keeping and rendering your accounts, have been forwarded under cover to the Collector of Newbury Port; I doubt not they have since come to hand.

I have generally authorised such boats as are requisite for the Surveyors & Inspectors to go on board of vessels, that is for harbour Service; for this purpose you may provide one, together with the necessary Scales, & weights, observing due œconomy in the purchase of those articles.

I here inclose copy of a circular Letter respecting Light houses, Beacons, Buoys & public piers,[1] lest it should have been omitted at the time when copies of the other instructions were transmitted: [2] You will please to furnish me with all the information therein required with regard to the establishment at your port.

By the Act entitled "An act for the establishment of Light Houses &c." [3] You will perceive that the provision does not a present so far, as to authorise machines for the clearing of harbours to facilitate the navigation: still this is a matter that may merit a future contemplation, and I shall therefore bear it in mind. The Tonnage formerly imposed by the State, for the purpose of defraying those expenses, could not now with propriety be collected by you.

I am Sir   Your Obedt. Servt.   A. Hamilton.

Jerh. Olney Esqr.
Collector for the Port of Providence.

Copy, RG 56, Letters to the Collector at Providence, National Archives; copy, RG 56, Letters to Collectors at Small Ports, "Set G," National Archives.
    1. "Treasury Department Circular to the Collectors of the Customs," October 1, 1789.
    2. See H to Olney, June 17, 1790.
    3. 1 *Stat.* 53–54 (August 7, 1789).

To George Washington [1]

[New York, July 8, 1790]

Memorandum of the substance of a Communication made on Thursday the Eighth of July 1790 to the Subscriber by Major Beckwith as by direction of Lord Dorchester.

Major Beckwith began by stating that Lord Dorchester had directed him to make his acknowlegements for the politeness which had been shewn in respect to the desire he had intimated to pass by New York in his way to England; [2] adding that the prospect of a War between Great Britain and Spain would prevent or defer the execution of his intention in that particular. He next proceeded to observe that Lord Dorchester had been informed of a negotiation commenced on the other side of the water through the Agency of Mr. Morris; [3] mentioning as the Subscriber understood principally by way of proof of Ld. Dorchesters knowlege of the transaction that Mr. Morris had not produced any regular credentials, but merely a letter from the President directed to himself, that some delays had intervened partly on account of Mr. Morris's absence on a trip to Holland as was understood and that it was not improbable those delays and some other circumstances may have impressed Mr. Morris with an idea of backwardness on the part of the British Ministry. That his Lordship however had directed him to say that an inference of this sort would not in his opinion be well founded as he had reason to believe that the Cabinet of Great Britain entertained a disposition not only towards a friendly intercourse but towards an alliance with the United States. Major Beckwith then proceeded to speak of the particular cause of the expected rupture between Spain and Britain [4] observing that it was one in which all Commercial nations must be supposed to favour the views of G. Britain. That it was therefore presumed, should a war take place, that the U States would find it to be their interest to take part with Great Britain rather than with Spain.

Major Beckwith afterwards mentioned that Lord Dorchester had heared with great concern of some depredations committed by some Indians on our Western frontier.[5] That he wished it to be believed that nothing of this kind had received the least countenance from him. That on the contrary he had taken every proper opportunity of inculcating upon the Indians a pacific disposition towards us; and that as soon as he had heared of the outrages lately committed he had sent a message to endeavour to prevent them. That his Lordship had understood that the Indians alluded to were a banditti composed chiefly or in great part of Creeks or Cherokees over whom he had no influence; intimating at the same time that these tribes were supposed to be in connection with the Spaniards.

He stated in the next place that his Lordship had been informed that a Captain Hart [6] in our service and a Mr. Wemble and indeed some persons in the Treaty at Fort Harmar [7] had thrown out menaces with regard to the Posts on the Frontier and had otherwise held very intemperate language; which however his Lordship considered rather as effusions of individual feelings than as the effects of any instruction from authority.

Major Beckwith concluded with producing a letter signed Dorchester; [8] which letter contained ideas similar to those he had expressed though in more guarded terms and without any allusion to instructions from the British Cabinet. This letter it is now recollected hints at the non execution of the treaty of peace on our part.

On the Subscriber remarking the circumstance that this letter seemed to speak only the sentiments of his Lordship Major Beckwith replied that whatever reasons there might be for that course of proceeding in the present stage of the business, it was to be presumed that his Lordship knew too well the consequence of such a step to have taken it without a previous knowlege of the intentions of the Cabinet.

ADf, George Washington Papers, Library of Congress.

1. This report was handed to Washington by H. On July 8, 1790, Washington wrote in his diary: "About noon the Secretaries of State, and of the Treasury called upon me—the last of whom reported a communication made to him by Majr. Beckwith Aid de camp to Lord Dorchester—Governor of Canada, wch. he reduced to writing." Washington then quoted this report (Fitzpatrick, *Diaries of George Washington*, IV, 137).

After his interviews in the fall of 1789 with H and several other American officials, George Beckwith left the United States (see "Conversation with George Beckwith," October, 1789). He again was sent to the United States for a few weeks in March and April, 1790. Soon after Beckwith's return to Canada in May, 1790, news of the Nootka Sound controversy reached Lord Dorchester, Governor General of Canada. On May 6, 1790, the British Secretary of State for Home Affairs, William Wyndham Grenville, had written Dorchester that the Spanish seizure of British ships in Nootka Sound off the western coast of Vancouver Island, might lead to war. Although he did not anticipate a Spanish attack on British possessions in North America, Grenville feared that a war might provide the Americans with an opportunity to seize the Northwest posts. He requested Lord Dorchester to send someone to America who would give information on any "hostile designs, if any such should be meditated against the forts or against Canada itself" (see the several letters Grenville wrote to Dorchester on May 6, 1790, in Brymner, *Canadian Archives*, 1890, 131–33). George Beckwith was chosen for the mission.

2. Before news had reached him of the Anglo-Spanish conflict in Nootka Sound, Lord Dorchester had planned to go to England on leave of absence. He had intended to stop in the United States en route.

3. Gouverneur Morris.

4. See note 1.

5. Indian raids on the American frontier had been particularly vicious in the spring of 1790. The Miami and Wabash tribes were raiding settlements in Kentucky and attacking boats on the Ohio and Wabash rivers.

6. Captain Jonathan Hart, First United States Infantry, was a member of the expedition against the Miami Indians in 1790 which was led by General Josiah Harmar. While taking part in St. Clair's expedition against the Indians in the fall of 1791 he was killed.

7. The Treaty of Fort Harmar, between the United States and the Wyandots, Delawares, and other Indians, was signed on January 9, 1789.

8. The letter from Dorchester to Beckwith, dated June 27, 1790, is printed in Brymner, *Canadian Archives*, 1890, 143. Dorchester had written Beckwith two letters on that date, one public and one secret. It was, of course, the latter which Beckwith showed to H.

From Tench Coxe [1]

Philada. July 9th. 1790

Dear Sir

I find by several letters from New York that the bill relative to the residence has hitherto stood its ground, which affords a further hope that this agitating business will be settled by the present Attempt. It has really become necessary for the Government has been exceedingly depreciated by it even here. Many who consider it as a great Object, still think it not worth the expence of time, money & character which it is like to cost.

The public creditors are to have a meeting this Evening—but it is not much liked by some of the most judicious of them. It is suspected to have our elections, as much as public credit for its object. I do not think however that it will do any harm. The Assumption, if mentioned, then will be supported I think by a considerable strength. Tis probable it will be spoken of in the course of what will fall from the Speakers. You may be satisfied that the Assumption has gained ground very considerably in this city, and that it will not lose the supporters it now has, who believe it the sine qua non of a satisfactory funding System. The hope of making better terms by a concert with the friends of Assumption has made a pretty strong impression on the minds of several influential men to whom I have suggested it, tho they think it will not be easy to make some of the strong opponents admit the Idea.

I direct this letter to be sent down to you immediately as the information on this last point will be satisfactory & may be wanted.

I am with my very respectful compliments to Mrs. Hamilton, dear Sir, yr. affectionate & obed. Servant   Tench Coxe

I expect to make my Absence ten days from my time of departure as at first proposed.

ALS, Hamilton Papers, Library of Congress.
    1. The residence and assumption measures, which are discussed in this letter, were parts of one of the most famous bargains in American political history. The proposal for the Federal Government's assumption of state debts (which was part of H's larger funding scheme) was defeated by the House of Representatives on April 12, 1790, by a vote of 31 to 29 (*Annals of Congress,* II, 1577). Then, in the latter part of June, H agreed to seek to convert northern Congressmen to the plan to have the national capital on the Potomac rather than at Philadelphia, while Madison and Jefferson agreed to use their influence to obtain the support of southern Congressmen for assumption. On July 1, the Senate by a vote of 14 to 12 passed an act for establishing the national capital on the Potomac with Philadelphia serving as the temporary capital (*Annals of Congress,* I, 1040). On July 9, this bill passed the House by a vote of 32 to 29 (*Annals of Congress,* II, 1737), and became law on July 16 ("An Act for establishing the temporary and permanent seat of the Government of the United States," 1 *Stat.* 130 [July 16, 1790]). On July 21, the Senate voted 14 to 12 in favor of the funding bill with the assumption amendment (*Annals of Congress,* I, 1054-55). On July 24, the House defeated a motion to "disagree to the proposition for the assumption of the State debts" (*Annals of Congress,* II, 1753), and on July 26, the House approved the as-

sumption plan by a vote of 34 to 28 (*Annals of Congress*, II, 1755). The fund-ing measure, of which assumption was a part, became law on August 4. See "An Act making provision for the (payment of the) Debt of the United States," 1 *Stat.* 138–44.

To John Jay

[New York, July 9, 1790]

My Dear Sir

Certain Circumstances of a delicate nature have occurred, con-cerning which The President would wish to consult you.[1] *They press.* Can you consistently with the Governor's situation [2] afford us your presence here? I cannot say the President directly asks it, lest you should be embarrassed; but he has expressed a strong wish for it.

I remain yr. Affect & Obed   A Hamilton

New York Friday 9th. 1790
The Honble C Justice Jay

ALS, Columbia University Libraries.
    1. Washington wished to confer with Jay on the subjects discussed by George Beckwith in his conversation with H on July 8, 1790 (H to Washing-ton, July 8, 1790). On July 8, Washington wrote in his diary: "I requested Mr. Jefferson and Colo. Hamilton, as I intend to do the Vice President, Chief Justice and Secretary at War, to revolve this matter in all its relations in their minds that they may be the better prepared to give me their opinions thereon in the course of 2 or three days" (Fitzpatrick, *Diaries of George Washington*, IV, 139).
    2. Governor William Livingston of New Jersey, who was Jay's father-in-law, died on July 25, 1790. A note on this letter in Jay's writing states: "Living-ston then ill."

From Thomas Jefferson

New York July 9. 1790

Dear Sir

You were so kind as to say you would write to our bankers in Holland to answer my draught for a part of the balance due me for salary etc.[1] I suppose in fact it will be necessary to clear their minds on the subject, for tho' they know that the diplomatic expences in Europe were paid on the funds in their hands, yet as I am here they will naturally expect your instructions should accompany my draught. It will be for £350 sterling, expressed in gilders, I do not know as yet how many gilders exactly, nor in whose favor I shall draw. Messrs. Leroy & Bayard [2] are to negociate the matter so that it may be finished in the morning before the packet sails and also before we set out on our party [3] which I understand is to be at 9. oclock. It will suffice I presume if you say in general terms that I shall make the draught & that it will be for about £350. sterl. expressed in gilders. I apprehend a duplicate also of your letter will be necessary. I shall accompany them with a letter of advice naming the drawer & sum in gilders exactly. I will take the liberty of sending to you at 8. oclock in the morning for the letters; and am with great & sincere esteem dear Sir your most obedt humble servt

Th: Jefferson

Colo. Hamilton.

ALS, letterpress copy, Thomas Jefferson Papers, Library of Congress.

1. This, of course, refers to Jefferson's pay when he was the United States Minister to France. For H's letter, see H to Willink, Van Staphorst, and Hubbard, July 17, 1790.

2. Le Roy and Bayard was a New York mercantile firm. The members of the firm were Herman Le Roy and William Bayard.

3. The entry in Washington's diary for July 10 reads as follows: "Having formed a Party, consisting of the Vice President, his lady, Son and Miss Smith; the Secretaries of State, Treasury, and War, and the ladies of the two latter; with all the Gentlemen of my family, Mrs. Lear and the two Children, we visited the old position of Fort Washington and afterwards dined on a dinner provided by Mr. Mariner at the House lately Colo. Roger Morris, but confiscated and in the occupation of a common Farmer." (Fitzpatrick, *Diaries of George Washington*, IV, 141–42.)

From Benjamin Lincoln

Boston July 9, 1790

Sir,

The time will soon arrive when we may expect that large quantities of pickled & dryed fish will be imported here from Nova Scotia. Upon their arrival they are charged with a duty, on the pickled fish seventy five Cents ⅌ barrel & on the dryed fish fifty cents ⅌ Quintal. These fish are not consumed in the United States and are entitled to a draw back upon their being exported to a foreign market. By this operation of the law the Union do not receive enough to pay the expences of inspection &c. The one ⅌ cent is not sufficient to discharge them.

I also find that the public will be in debt when they shall have paid the bounties on fish and salted provisions for the saving of one cent on a bushell will not pay the expence which will necessarily arise from weighing and that inspection to the loading them which is required. From the nature of this business it must be expensive and especially in cases when fish are shipped in the bulk for they cannot be received but in fine weather and frequently a whole day is expended in lading seventy or eighty Quintals. Besides the frequent removal of the scales and weights from one end of the town to the other & the pay to labourers add much to the expence. Is it understood that the weighers pay the expence of Labourers to put the casks into the scale &c or is that to be charged against the United States?

I find the practice is different respecting the time of payment of the bounties on Fish & Salted provisions. Some pay them at the time of Shipping, others mean to wait untill evidence shall be produced that articles have been landed in some foreign port. I shall be obliged by your ideas on the subject.

Hon Secy of the Treasury

ADf, RG 36, Collector of Customs at Boston, Letters from the Treasury and Others, 1789–1818, Vol. 11, National Archives; LC, RG 36, Collector of Customs at Boston, Letter Book, 1790–1797, National Archives; copy, RG 56, Letters from the Collector at Boston, National Archives.

From Tench Coxe [1]

[Sunbury, Pennsylvania, July 10, 1790]

Dear Sir

I am now at my father's on my way to Jersey to spend a day or two with my two eldest Children before I finish the time proposed for my Absence.

The public Creditors had a small meeting last Night, and appointed a new standing Committee. They appeared moderate & prudent, but solicitous for a good funding System. They did not attempt any business or resolutions, but left every thing in the Discretion of their Committee, according as events may prove. I think they well be pleased with an excise, and that the body of the people will not be averse to it. Some of the strict executive parts of the proposed law were the causes of their exceptions to it, but tho they may be unpleasant it is [to] be duly considered whether an equal collection could be effected without them. I find the principal Creditors viewed the leaders of the opposition to the excise bill with Jealousy, tho they do not approve some parts of it.

I understand here that the principal man among the opponents to the Assumption is Mr. Pettit,[2] who was to set out for New York to day. I am of opinion that his objections to it would be much weakened, if he could be convinced either that it is the sine qua non of funding, or that the terms of the new loan might by its means be meliorated.

Exchange has advanced in Philada. to 172½ or 3½ ⅌ Cent premium.

The importations of European goods are expected to be very great this Autumn.

I enclose for my little friend Philip [3] a copy of the elements of Geography, which I mentioned. With my very respectful Comps. to Mrs. Hamilton I have the honor to be, dear Sir,   Your affectionate & obedt. Servt.   Tench Coxe

Sunbury, Bucks
July 10th. 1790

ALS, Hamilton Papers, Library of Congress.
  1. For background to this letter, see Coxe to H, July 9, 1790.
  2. Charles Pettit was a Philadelphia merchant. In 1785 and 1786 he had led the successful movement in the Pennsylvania legislature to fund the Federal debt owed to Pennsylvanians. Although defeated for election to the First Congress, Pettit was a member of the state delegation which in 1790 presented the state's Revolutionary claims against the Federal Government.
  3. Philip Hamilton, H's oldest son.

From Thomas Newton, Junior

Norfolk [*Virginia*] *July 11, 1790.* "I wrote you the 27th of last month, this serves to cover a Certificate [1] of two of the most able seamen we have in these parts, of the most proper spot for erecting a Light house, the stone which was formerly intended for the purpose, will be in the two acres, as that is reserved by our act of Assembly I imagine it will make no differance. The Gentlemen are of opinion that it Woud be best to build with wood, in which opinion

I join, as it wou'd take three or four years in all probability to finish one of stone, whilst that of wood cou'd be done by October twelve months or less time, as it cou'd be framed & all the materials carried to the spot in a proper season. . . ."

ALS, RG 26, Lighthouse Letters Received, Vol. "A," Pennsylvania and Southern States, National Archvies.
 1. DS, in writing of Newton, RG 26, Lighthouse Letters Received, Vol. "A," Pennsylvania and Southern States, National Archives. This document, which is dated July 10, 1790, and which is signed by James Maxwell and Paul Loyay, states that they "do not consider the drifting of the sands as dangerous" to the proposed lighthouse.

From Richard Harison

New York 12 July 1790.

Sir

Your Letter of the 3d. Instant was left at my House during my Absence upon the Circuit, or it would have recieved an earlier Answer.

I have since my Return considered the Case therein mentioned, with the several Acts referred to; and the Result in my Mind is notwithstanding the peculiar Wording of the repealing Clause that the Conduct of the Collectors is to be considered as warranted by Law. I am apprised of the Distinction between the mere Repeal of a Statute, and the declaring it to be null & void. This Distinction I think can only take Place with Respect to *continuing Acts,* such as Leases, granted when warranted by a Statute afterwards declared to be null, & which therefore are avoided as to the Remainder of the Term. But to apply the Rule to the Case under Consideration would be to make the Officers of Government responsible for having acted according to Law, and therefore would be Subversive of every Principle of Justice. I am persuaded that it could not have been the Intention of the Legislature that the repealing Clause should operate in such a Manner, and Arguments to that Effect might be drawn even from the Words themselves.

I am with the utmost Respect, Sir, Your obedt Servt. &ca.

Hon. Alexr Hamilton Esqr.

ADf, New-York Historical Society, New York City.

From Tobias Lear

[*New York*] *July 13, 1790.* Encloses "the Warrants for the Super-intendants of the Lighthouses &c."

LS, RG 26, "Segregated" Lighthouse Records, National Archives; copy, George Washington Papers, Library of Congress.

To Benjamin Lincoln

Treasury Department, July 14, 1790. Encloses the commissions for the various lighthouse keepers in Massachusetts.

LS, RG 36, Collector of Customs at Boston, Letters and Papers re Lighthouses, Buoys, and Piers, 1789–1819, Vol. 1, National Archives.

To George Washington [1]

[New York, July 15, 1790] [2]

In my second interview with Major Beckwith which was on Thursday the 22d.[3] instant I spoke to him nearly as follows

I have made the proper use of what you said to me at our last interview.[4]

As to what regards the objects of a general nature mentioned by you, though your authority for the purpose from Lord Dorchester is out of question, and though I presume from his Lordship's station & character and the knowlege he appears to have of what is passing on the other side of the water with regard to Mr. Morris,[5] that the Step he has taken through you is conformable to the views of your Cabinet and not without its sanction; yet you are no doubt sensible that the business presents itself in a shape, which does not give the proper authenticity to that fact, and is wholly without formality. You must also be sensible that there is a material difference between your situation and that of Mr. Morris. His Credentials though not formal proceed from the proper source. Your's are neither formal nor authoritative.[6]

This state of things will of course operate in what I am going to say on the subject.

As to what relates to friendship between Great Britain and the United States, I conceive myself warranted in declaring that there is in this country a sincere disposition to concur in obviating with candor and fairness all ground of misunderstanding which may now exist, in reference to the execution of the late Treaty of Peace and in laying the foundation of future good understanding by establishing liberal terms of commercial intercourse.

As to alliance; this opens a wide field. The thing is susceptible of a vast variety of forms. 'Tis not possible to judge what would be proper or what could be done unless points were brought into view. If you are in condition to mention particulars, it may afford better ground of conversation.

I stopped here for an answer.

Major Beckwith replied that he could say nothing more particular than he had already done.

That being the case (continued I) I can only say that the thing is in too general a form to admit of a judgment of what may be eventually admissible or practicable. If the subject shall hereafter present itself to discussion in an authentic and proper shape, I have no doubt we shall be ready to converse freely upon it: And you will naturally conclude that we shall be disposed to pursue whatever shall appear under all circumstances to be our interest as far as may consist with our honor. At present I would not mean either to raise or repress expectation.

Major Beckwith seemed to admi⟨t⟩ that as things were circumstanced nothing explicit could be expected and went on to make some observations which I understood as having for object to sound whether there existed any connection between Spain and us and whether the questions with regard to the Mississippie were settled.

Perceiving this I thought it better in a matter which was no secret to avoid an appearance of Mystery and to declare without hesitation, as I did—

"That there was no particular connection between Spain and the U States within my knowlege, and that it was matter of public notoriety that the questions alluded to were still unadjusted."

The rest of our conversation consisted chiefly of assurances on my part that the menaces which had been mentioned by him as having been thrown out by some individuals with regard to the Western posts were unauthorised, proceeding probably from a degree of irritation, which the detention of the posts had produced in the minds of many—and of a repetition on his part of the assurances which he had before given of Lord Dorchesters disposition to discourage Indian Outrages.

Something was said respecting the probable course of military operations in case of war between Britain & Spain which Major Beckwith supposed would be directed towards South America alleging however that this was mere conjecture on his part. I hinted cautiously our dislike of an enterprise on New Orleans.[7]

AL, George Washington Papers, Library of Congress; ADf, Hamilton Papers, Library of Congress.
1. On the back of the last sheet of the draft, H wrote the following note:
"Note. Mr. Jefferson was privy to this transaction. The views of the Government were to discard suspision that any engagements with Spain or intentions hostile to Great Britain existed—to leave the ground in other respects vague & open, so as that in case of Rupture between G B & S—the U States might be in the best situation to turn it to account in reference to the Disputes between them & G B on the one hand & Spain on the other."
This conversation resulted from instructions given to H by Washington after H had reported to the President his conversation with Beckwith on July 8. After Washington had heard, or read, H's report of that date, he made the following comment in his diary:
"The aspect of this business in the moment of its communication to me, appeared simply, and no other than this;—We did not incline to give any satisfactory answer to Mr. Morris, who was *officially* commissioned to ascertain our intentions with respect to the evacuation of the Western Posts within the territory of the United States and other matters into which he was empowered to enquire until by this unauthenticated mode we can discover whether you will enter into an alliance with us and make Common cause against Spain. In that case we will enter into a Commercial Treaty with you and *promise perhaps* to fulfil what they already stand engaged to perform. However, I requested Mr. Jefferson and Colo. Hamilton, as I intended to do the Vice President, Chief Justice and Secretary at War, to revolve this matter in all its relations in their minds that they may be the better prepared to give me their opinions thereon in the course of 2 or three days." (Fitzpatrick, *Diaries of George Washington*, IV, 139.)
On Wednesday, July 14, Washington again took up the question of the proper treatment to be accorded Beckwith. After a conversation with H and John Jay, the Chief Justice, Washington directed that in his conversations with Beckwith H should:
"treat his communications very civilly—to intimate, delicately, that they carried no marks official or authentic, nor in speaking of Alliance, did they convey any definite meaning by which the precise object of the British Cabinet could be discovered. In a word, that the Secretary of the Treasury was to extract as much as he could from Major Beckwith and to report to me, with-

out committing, by any assurances whatever, the Government of the U. States, leaving it entirely free to pursue, unreproached, such a line of conduct in the dispute as her interest (and honour) shall dictate." (Fitzpatrick, *Diaries of George Washington*, IV, 143.)

2. In the first sentence of this letter, H stated that the interview with Beckwith was held "on Thursday the 22d instant." Beckwith, on the other hand, stated that the conversation was held on July 15. (See "Conversation with George Beckwith," August 7–12, 1790). It is, of course, not possible to determine which of the two men was correct, but as it seems unlikely that H would have waited eight days before carrying out the plan of action agreed upon with Washington (see note 1), July 15 has been accepted as the more likely date.

3. See note 2.

4. See H to Washington, July 8, 1790.

5. Gouverneur Morris.

6. The question of the extent to which Beckwith, an unofficial representative, could speak for the British Ministry and the question of Morris's credentials had been discussed by H and Beckwith on July 8, 1790 (see H to Washington, July 8, 1790).

7. The conversation reported by H also was reported by George Beckwith to Lord Dorchester. Beckwith's account reads as follows:

"I have communicated to the President, the subjects, on which we have conversed; however authoritative they may be on your part, in so far as respects Lord Dorchester, and however evident it is to me that His Lordship is apprized by Your Cabinet of Mr. Morris's Agency, yet You must be sensible, that official formality is wanting, but it is conceived that His Lordship would not have gone the lengths he has, without being acquainted with the general views of your administration, as they respect this country. Having premised this, I feel warranted to assure You, that there is the most sincere good disposition on the part of the government here to go into the consideration of all matters unsettled between us and Great Britain, in order to effect a perfect understanding between the two countries, and to lay the foundation for future amity; this, particularly as it respects commercial objects, we view as conducive to our interest.

"In the present stage of this business it is difficult to say much on the subject of a Treaty of Alliance; Your rupture with Spain, if it shall take place, opens a very wide political field; thus much I can say, we are perfectly unconnected with Spain, have even some points unadjusted with that Court, and are prepared to go into the consideration of the subject.

"The speeches or declarations of any persons whatever in the Indian Country or to the westward, suggesting hostile ideas respecting the forts, are not authorized by this government.

"Lord Dorchester's conduct with respect to the Indians is held by us to be a strong proof of His Lordship's dispositions to promote harmony and friendship.

"It appears to me that, from the nature of our Government, it would be mutually advantageous, if this negotiation could be carried on at our seat of government, as it would produce dispatch and obviate misconception." (Dorchester to William Wyndham Grenville, September 25, 1790, Public Archives of Canada, Ottawa, Ontario.)

Conversation with George Beckwith [1]

Secret

. . . supposed 7.[2] There is one thing more which I wish to mention to You; I do it altogether as from one gentleman to an other, and I trust it will be so considered. I have decided on doing it at this time from the possibility of my not having it in my power to come to such an explanation hereafter.

If it shall be judged proper to proceed in this business by the sending or appointing a proper person to come to this country to negotiate on the spot, whoever shall then be Our Secretary of State, will be the person in whose department such negotiation must originate, and he will be the channel of communication with the President; in the turn of such affairs the most minute circumstances, mere trifles, give a favorable bias or otherwise to the whole. The President's mind I can declare to be perfectly dispassionate on this subject. Mr. Jefferson our present Secretary of State is I am persuaded a gentleman of honor, and zealously desirous of promoting those objects, which the nature of his duty calls for, and the interests of his country may require, but from some opinions which he has given respecting Your government, and possible predilections elsewhere, there may be difficulties which may possibly frustrate the whole, and which might be readily explained away. I shall certainly know the progress of the negotiation from the president from day to day, but what I come to the present explanation for is this, that in any case any such difficulties should occur, I should wish to know them, in order that I may be sure they are clearly understood, and candidly examined, if none takes place the business will of course go on in the regular official channel.

——————— 3

"I cannot form any opinion upon the manner, in which our administration may proceed in the business You mention, I shall make the proper use You may depend on it of what You have said, nor shall it ever be brought by me in a way to convey an impression different from the causes which occasioned it."

——————— 4

I am persuaded it will not, it is not necessary for me to say, that in this I am steadily following up, what I have long considered to be the essential interest of this country; on this point I have already so fully explained my ideas, that a repetition is needless.

D, Public Archives of Canada, Ottawa, Ontario. This document was enclosed in Lord Dorchester to William Wyndham Grenville, September 25, 1790.
1. In addition to the remarks which H reported to George Washington (see H to Washington, July 15, 1790) he made, according to Beckwith, the comments printed above.
2. In Beckwith's code "7" was H.
3. Although Beckwith drew a line between the above remarks of "Supposed 7" and those of this unidentified informant, H probably made the latter as well as the former remarks.
4. See note 3.

From George Cabot

Beverly [Massachusetts] July 16, 1790. Recommends Colonel Joshua Orne [1] for the position of collector at Marblehead.

ALS, Applications for Office under George Washington, Library of Congress.
1. Orne had served in Lee's Additional Continental Regiment, 1777–1778. He was not appointed to the Marblehead post.

From Jeremiah Olney

Providence, July 16, 1790. "Your favours of 6 & 7 Inst have been received. The name of the person recommended for Surveyor at the port of North Kingstown is Daniel Eldridge Updike. There is also another person of the same place by the name of Daniel Updike who is the State's Attorney. . . . The forms transmitted by the Comptroller for Keeping the accots &c have been received. . . . In purchasing the boat and scales, you have permitted for this district, I shall observe due economy. . . ."

Copy, RG 56, Letters from the Collector at Providence, National Archives.

To Charles Lee

Treasury Department, July 17, 1790. "Your letter of the 29th June [1] has been duly received. I thank you for the information therein communicated."

From Benjamin Lincoln

Boston July 17 1790

Sir

I now take up my pen to give you an account of the seizure of the Schooner Bee of about 30 Tons from Nova-Scotia and to relate the circumstances which led to & have taken place in consequence thereof. On Wednesday last I had information that a Schooner of about Thirty five tons from Nova-Scotia had been for some days in the offing but had run in at night; that lighters had taken out of her a considerable quantity of fish & that the next night the remainder about 70 Quin[1] was to be unladen. I considered the detection of this fraud as a matter of importance for they were not only evading the duties but they were drawing from us a bounty of five Cents upon every quintail. We immediately made our arrangments for intercepting the vessel that night but they did not attempt to execute their design the next day (Thursday). As we had an account on what wharf the fish were landed, we discovered the purchaser and the lighter from which the fish were landed. The lighter men acknowledged the fact & that the following night they were to fall down & receive the remainder. The Surveyor[2] steped on board with an officer or two and came to anchor with the Lighter at the place where the Schooner was to meet her. The Schooner boat soon came on board with the Captain who was detained and possession was taken of the Schooner. They had landed two hundred & odd Quintals of fish which had been purchased in Boston, as American caught fish, and which were reladen for the European market. The Captain and an other Person who came in the vessel with him were owners of the fish.

We prosecuted each of them for the fine of four hundred dollars. The Captain was taken and committed. His partner was taken also but being in possession of the money he had received for his fish had it in his power to secure the officer. They, and the vessel will be tried at the next district Court which will be held in Salem in Sepr.

There is about seventy Quintals of fish remaining on board the

Schooner. Mr Gore³ the district Atty gives it as his opinion that it is not liable to seizure. Permit me to ask what shall be done with it?

ADf, RG 36, Collector of Customs at Boston, Letters from the Treasury and Others, 1789–1818, Vol. 11, National Archives.
1. I.e., quintal.
2. Thomas Melville.
3. Christopher Gore, United States attorney for Massachusetts.

To Thomas Smith

[*New York, July 17, 1790.* "Your son has delivered at this office a trunk said to contain loan office certificates for $1,436,700.00; specie loan office certificates for $74,500.00, bills of exchange for $25,170.00, bills of exchange for renewal for $4,392.00." *Letter not found.*] ¹

LS, sold at Goodspeed's Book Shop, January, 1938, Item 123.
1. Text taken from extract in dealer's catalogue.

To Wilhem and Jan Willink, Nicholaas and Jacob Van Staphorst, and Nicholas Hubbard

Treasury Department,
July 17th. 1790.

Gentlemen,

It being understood, that you have retained in your hands a sufficient sum to discharge the balance of salary, due to Mr. Jefferson, as Minister plenipotentiary at the Court of France, it has been deemed inexpedient to change the course of the thing, by paying him that balance here. He, therefore has informed me,¹ that he will draw upon you, on that account, for three hundred and fifty pounds sterling, to be expressed in Guilders; which I accordingly request you will be pleased to pay, in conformity to the tenor of his drafts, and for which a due credit will be allowed you. It is my desire, that his drafts should, at all events, be honored though you should not have retained monies for that purpose, as is understood to be the case.

I am &c.   Alexander Hamilton.

Messrs. Willink, Van Staphorst & Hubbard.
Amsterdam.

Copy, RG 233, Reports of the Treasury Department, 1792–1793, Vol. III, National Archives. This letter was enclosed in H's "Report on Foreign Loans," February 13, 1793.
1. See Thomas Jefferson to H, July 9, 1790.

From Jeremiah Olney

Providence, July 19, 1790. "The rigging, Sails cables and anchors belonging to the Brig Happy Return, lately stranded at Dublin, arrived here on the fifteenth instant; presuming those articles were, at some rate or other dutiable, I demanded a bond of the owners to secure the duties until the exact amount could be ascertained. . . . Having promised . . . to postpone the final adjustment of the matter until I obtained your opinion thereon, I ask, Sir, the favor of your particular directions. . . ."

Copy, RG 56, Letters from the Collector at Providence, National Archives.

From Timothy Pickering

Wilkesbarre [Pennsylvania] July 20. 1790.

Dear Sir

Conveyances to and from this place rarely offer, which, I suppose, prevented my receiving your favor of May 13th until a few days past.

In appointments to public employments, when I had such to make, I am not conscious that personal considerations ever influenced my choice. The same principle determines me to be satisfied, and, if you will allow the expression, to approve of your appointment of the successor to Mr. Duer.[1] The very causes of preference mentioned by you led me to expect that preference would be given; and under similar circumstances, I hope I possess sufficient independance of mind to have done the same.

I feel myself greatly obliged by your friendly assurances of promoting my views to public life, and your expressions of personal regard for me; but whether your endeavours to serve me should or should not be successful, and if I forever remain in obscurity, yet I shall never forget those qualities & talents which during an acquaintance, of twelve years with you, have commanded my affection & respect.

With the utmost sincerity I remain, Dear Sir,   your obedt. servant
Timothy Pickering

Honble. Alexander Hamilton Esqr.

ALS, Massachusetts Historical Society, Boston.
    1. Tench Coxe succeeded William Duer as Assistant Secretary of the Treasury on May 10, 1790.

Report on Vacant Lands

Treasury-department, July 20th. 1790.
[Communicated on July 22, 1790] [1]

[To the Speaker of the House of Representatives]
In obedience to the order of the House of Representatives of the
    20th. of January last,[2] The Secretary of the Treasury,
Respectfully reports;

That in the formation of a plan for the disposition of the vacant lands of the United States, there appear to be two leading objects of consideration; one, the facility of advantageous sales according to the probable course of purchases; the other, the accommodation of individuals now inhabiting the Western Country, or who may hereafter emigrate thither.

The former, as an operation of finance, claims primary attention: the latter is important, as it relates to the satisfaction of the inhabitants of the Western Country. It is desirable, and does not appear impracticable to conciliate both.

Purchasers may be contemplated in three classes. Monied individuals and companies, who will buy to sell again. Associations of persons, who intend to make settlements themselves. Single persons, or families now resident in the Western Country, or who may emigrate thither hereafter. The two first will be frequently blended, and will always want considerable tracts. The last will generally pur-

Copy, RG 233, Reports of the Secretary of the Treasury, 1790–1791, Vol. I, National Archives; LC, George Washington Papers, Library of Congress.
    1. Journal of the House, I, 276.
    2. The House ordered "that the Secretary of the Treasury be directed to report to this House on a uniform system for the disposition of lands and property of the United States" (Journal of the House, I, 143).

chase small quantities. Hence a plan for the sale of the Western lands, while it may have due regard to the last, should be calculated to obtain all the advantages which may be derived from the two first classes. For this reason, it seems requisite, that the general Land-office should be established at the seat of Government. 'Tis there, that the principal purchasers, whether citizens or foreigners, can most easily find proper agents, and that contracts for large purchases can be best adjusted.

But the accommodation of the present inhabitants of the Western Territory, and of unassociated persons and families who may emigrate thither, seems to require that one office, subordinate to that of the Seat of Congress, should be opened in the North western, and another in the South western Government.

Each of these offices, as well the general one as the subordinate ones, it is conceived, may be placed with convenience under the superintendance of three Commissioners, who may either be pre-established officers of the Government, to whom the duty may be assigned by law, or persons specially appointed for the purpose. The former is recommended by considerations of Œconomy, and, it is probable, would embrace every advantage which could be derived from a special appointment.

To obviate those inconveniences, and to facilitate and ensure the attainment of those advantages which may arise from new and casual circumstances springing up from foreign and domestic causes, appears to be an object for which adequate provision should be made, in any plan that may be adopted. For this reason, and from the intrinsic difficulty of regulating the details of a specific provision for the various objects which require to be consulted, so as neither to do too much nor too little for either, it is respectfully submitted, whether it would not be advisable to vest a considerable latitude of discretion in the Commissioners of the General Land Office, subject to some such regulations and limitations as follow. Vizt.

That no land shall be sold, except such, in respect to which the titles of the Indian tribes shall have been previously extinguished.

That a sufficient tract or tracts shall be reserved and set apart for satisfying the subscribers to the proposed loan in the public debt, but that no location shall be for less than five hundred Acres.

That convenient tracts shall from time to time be set apart for the purpose of locations by actual settlers, in quantities not exceeding to one person one hundred acres.

That other tracts shall, from time to time, be set apart for sales in townships of ten miles square, except where they shall adjoin upon a boundary of some prior grant, or of a tract so set apart, in which cases there shall be no greater departure from such form of location, than may be absolutely necessary.

That any quantities may, nevertheless, be sold by special contract, comprehended either within natural boundaries or lines, or both.

That the price shall be thirty Cents per acre to be paid, either in gold or silver, or in public securities, computing those which shall bear an immediate interest of six per cent, as at par with gold and silver, and those which shall bear a future or less interest, if any there shall be, at a proportional value.

That Certificates issued for land upon the proposed loan, shall operate as warrants within the tract or tracts which shall be specially set apart for satisfying the subscribers thereto, and shall also be receivable in all payments whatsoever for land by way of discount, Acre for Acre.

That no credit shall be given for any quantity, less than a township of ten miles square, nor more than two years credit for any greater quantity.

That in every instance of credit, at least one quarter part of the consideration shall be paid down, and security other than the land itself, shall be required for the residue. And that no title shall be given for any tract or part of a purchase, beyond the quantity for which the consideration shall be actually paid.

That the residue of the tract or tracts set apart for the subscribers to the proposed loan, which shall not have been located within two years after the same shall have been set apart, may then be sold on the same terms as any other land.

That the Commissioners of each subordinate office shall have the management of all sales, and the issuing of Warrants for all locations in the tracts to be set apart for the accommodation of individual settlers, subject to the superintendency of the Commissioners of the general Land-office, who may also commit to them the management of any other sales or locations, which it may be found expedient to place under their direction.

That there shall be a Surveyor General, who shall have power to appoint a Deputy Surveyor General, in each of the Western Governments, and a competent number of Deputy Surveyors to execute, in person, all Warrants to them directed by the Surveyor General or Deputy Surveyors General within certain districts to be assigned to them respectively. That the Surveyor General shall also have in charge, all the duties committed to the Geographer General by the several resolutions and ordinances of Congress.

That all warrants issued at the General Land Office, shall be signed by the Commissioners or such one of them as they may nominate for that purpose, and shall be directed to the Surveyor General. That all warrants issued at a subordinate office shall be signed by the Commissioners of such office, or by such one of them, as they may nominate for that purpose, and shall be directed to the Deputy Surveyor General within the government. That the priority of locations upon Warrants shall be determined by the times of the applications to the Deputy Surveyors; and in case of two applications for the same land at one time, the priority may be determined by Lot.

That the Treasurer of the United States shall be the receiver of all payments for sales made at the General Land office, and may also receive deposits of money or securities for purchases intended to be made at the subordinate offices, his receipts or certificates for which shall be received in payment at those offices.

That the Secretary of each of the Western Governments, shall be the receiver of all payments arising from sales at the office of such Government.

That controversies concerning rights to patents or grants of land shall be determined by the Commissioners of that office, under whose immediate direction or jurisdiction, the locations, in respect to which they may arise, shall have been made.

That the completion of all contracts and sales heretofore made, shall be under the direction of the Commissioners of the General Land Office.

That the Commissioners of the General Land Office, Surveyor-General, Deputy-Surveyors General, and the Commissioners of the

Land Office, in each of the Western Governments, shall not purchase, nor shall others purchase for them in trust, any public lands.

That the Secretaries of the Western Governments shall give
security for the faithful discharge of their duty, as receivers of the
Land Office.

That all patents shall be signed by the President of the United
States, or by the Vice-president or other officer of government act-
ing as President, and shall be recorded in the office, either of the
Surveyor General, or of the Clerk of the Supreme Court of the
United States.

That all officers acting under the laws establishing the Land-
Office, shall make oath faithfully to discharge their respective
duties, previously to their entering upon the execution thereof.

That all Surveys of land shall be at the expense of the purchasers
or grantees.

That the fees shall not exceed certain rates to be specified in the
law, affording equitable compensations for the services of the
Surveyors, and establishing reasonable and customary charges for
patents and other Office papers for the benefit of the United States.

That the Commissioners of the General Land Office shall, as
soon as may be, from time to time, cause all the rules and regulations
which they may establish, to be published in one gazette, at least, in
each State, and in each of the Western Governments, where there
is a Gazette, for the information of the citizens of the United States.

Regulations, like these, will define and fix the most essential particulars which can regard the disposal of the Western lands, and
where they leave any thing to discretion, will indicate the general
principles or policy intended by the Legislature to be observed; for
a conformity to which the Commissioners will, of course, be responsible. They will, at the same time, leave room for accommodating
to circumstances which cannot, beforehand, be accurately appreci-
ated, and for varying the course of proceeding, as experience shall
suggest to be proper, and will avoid the danger of those obstructions and embarrassments in the execution, which would be to be
apprehended from an endeavor at greater precision and more exact
detail.

All which is humbly submitted   Alexander Hamilton
                                     Secretary of the Treasury.

From Benjamin Lincoln

Boston July 23 1790.

Sir.

In my last I suggested my apprehensions that we should suffer by having thrown in upon us the fish from Nova Scotia.[1] I am hourly more and more confirmed in the idea and that we shall pay the bounty on much more fish than we shall like. Our vessels are permitted to fish on the coast of Nova-Scotia and make the fish on shore. Many of them are in this practice and return in the fall with the voyage. If they are disposed to take in fish on freight at the port where they shall make their own we cannot discover it for our people & the Nova Scotians not only take their fish on the same banks but make them in the same harbour & probably on the same beaches. There are great quantities of fish brought from the eastern part of our State to this market. We have no other controul over the vessel freighting the same but to prevent her unlading untill she has a permit to do it. We are called every day to inspect fish but we have no means of determining whether they were foreign caught fish or not. I confess my self at a loss how to point out a mode effectually to guard against the impositions we shall suffer in these cases.

However I think it may be Checked by removing the present duty on foreign fish for although as the law now standes, there is a draw back of the duties on the exportation of the fish, as Ninety Nine is to a hundred. Yet the importers are affraid of the duty and take every measure to avoid it. The consequence of this is that they are smuggled in & get so intermixed with the fish caught by the americans that they cannot after be discovered and seperated from them [and] therefore draw a bounty as our own. To prohibit the exportation of foreign fish might be the most effectual measure. Policy however may forbid a step of this kind.

The difficulties attending this business will be few where the fish is exported directly to a foreign market from the port in which it is cured but as very considerable proportion of the fish is exported from this port where very little indeed is cured.

If masters of vessels upon thus entering the fish, which shall be exported from one port to an other in the United States should be obliged to make oath that it is fish caught by Citizens of these States in that case we should have a check. And if the merchant prior to his being intitled to receive the bounty should be obliged to give all the proof which the nature of the case would admit of that the fish entered for exportation was fish caught by the Citizens of the United States and in vessels owned by them. Or if he should be obliged to make oath on the entery of the fish for exportation that they were according to his best knowledge & belief caught by our Citizens &c we should have an other check.

Indeed as I said before I feel my self at a loss how we shall effectually guard against the evil imposition mentioned unless we greatly embarrass the merchant and encumber trade—evils Congress wishes to avoid. Though conscious of this Yet I supposed that would not apologize for my neglect should I omit to mention them.

ADf, RG 36, Collector of Customs at Boston, Letters from the Treasury and Others, 1789–1818, Vol. 11, National Archives.
  1. Lincoln to H, July 17, 1790; see also Lincoln to H, July 9, 1790.

From Joseph Whipple

Portsmo New Hamp. July 23. 1790

Sir

I have delayed to answer your favor of the 21st. June [1] in expectation that I should be enabled to inform the moti⟨v⟩es which induced the Legislature again to Negative a motion for the Cession of the Light house.

I am informed that the house of Representatives rejected the report of a Committee for Cedeing the Light house & 3 Acres of Land which included the ground Occupied for a parade & platform to the fortress Wm. & Mary—but voted to Cede the Light house with one fourth of an Acre of Land (which takes in a point of Rocks near the Fort). This Vote of the House was in the Senate Negatived.[2] The grounds on which this branch of the Legislature Acted I could not learn, not having Seen one of the Members, nor the president of the State [3] who precided in the Senate & to whom I have written On the Subject.

As the Matter is now circumstanced be pleased to give me your further directions respecting the payment or the Offer of payment for the year directed by the Act of Congress. The present Contract made by the State for the Support of the Light house for one year (which commenced in Feb. last) was £175 or 583 Dollars. The person who Supplied the light prior to the Contract & since the 15th of August last is now in advance 90 Dolls.—which he expects from the United States—& his estimate for a years expence was only 300 Dollars including the pay of a Soldier who attended the light.

I am very respectfully Sir yr. M. Obt. sert.

Hon Alex. Hamilton Esqr.

LC, RG 36, Collector of Customs at Portsmouth, Letters Sent, 1790–1791, Vol. 2, National Archives; copy, RG 56, Letters from the Collector at Portsmouth, National Archives.

1. Letter not found.
2. The New Hampshire legislative journals do not agree with Whipple's account. According to the journals, the committee of the New Hampshire Senate to which the matter was referred never reported. In the New Hampshire House of Representatives the members approved a committee report which recommended the cession of a quarter acre, and the House directed its committee to bring in a bill for the cession. There is, however, no record that the House ever considered such a bill. See the journals in The New Hampshire State Papers (Albert Stillman Batchellor, ed., *Early State Papers of New Hampshire* [Concord, 1893], XXII, 5–31, 40–93).
3. Josiah Bartlett was elected president of New Hampshire by the legislature in June, 1790. Although he was a practicing physician, and had no legal training, Bartlett served on the superior court from 1782 to 1790 and received the post of chief justice of New Hampshire in January, 1790.

To Benjamin Lincoln

Treasury Department
July 25th 1790

Sir

I have received your favor of the 9th Instant, and duly observed the useful hints in it relative to the exportation of & re-exportation of salted provisions & Fish.

The question with regard to Weighers will probably meet the attention of the Legislature in the present Session.

I observe with great satisfaction your successful endeavors to detect the Breaches of the Revenue Laws and to secure the offenders in the case of the Schooner Bee.[1]

The Fish that remained on Board the Schooner is capable of Entry. I presume however that the Attorney for the U States [2] has advised the seizure of the 200 Quintals which were unlawfully landed if they have been found.

I am Sir   with great respect Your

Benjn Lincoln Esqr

L[S], RG 36, Collector of Customs at Boston, Letters from the Treasury, 1789–1807, Vol. 4, National Archives; copy, RG 56, Letters to the Collector at Boston, National Archives; copy, RG 56, Letters to Collectors at Small Ports, "Set G," National Archives.
   1. See Lincoln to H, July 17, 1790.
   2. Christopher Gore.

To Thomas Newton, Junior

[*New York, July 25, 1790.* On August 6, 1790, Newton wrote to Hamilton: "Your Letter of the 25th Ult. I received this day." *Letter not found.*]

To Otho H. Williams

Treasury Department
July 25th. 1790

Sir

Enclosed you will find an advertismen⟨t⟩ relative to the supply of Rations for the Troops of the United Sta⟨tes⟩ which you will be pleased to have inserted in your best Newspaper for the term of four Weeks. The account of the expenc⟨es⟩ I must also request you to procure, and discharge and I shall direct, the Receipt to be admitted, as a Voucher for the amount in your subsequent settlement.

I am Sir   with respect   Your Obedient Servant   A Hamilton

Otho H. Williams Esqr
Collector
Baltimore.

LS, Columbia University Libraries.

From Morgan Lewis [1]

Rhynbeck [2] [New York] 26th. July 1790

My Dear sir

I perceive by the public Prints that Congress have rejected the Revennue System you offered them.[3] Which Circumstance puts a period to my Expectations of being enabled to return to the City. It has not however, in my Mind, weakened my Obligations to you. I feel the weight of them as sensibly, as if your Wishes with Regard to me, had been compleatly gratified. Instances of disinterested Friendship, are Things I have so rarely met with, that I have almost been induced to doubt their Existence. Indeed, if my Memory does not fail me, I may with Truth assert the present, the only One I ever experienced. Accept Sir my sincere Acknowledgements, and be assured I shall ever retain a grateful Sense of the Value of your Friendship.

The Removal of Congress will probably carry you shortly to Phia.[4] If Mrs. L can learn the Time of your intended departure, She means if possible to see Mrs. H. before it takes place. She desires her Love & best Wishes to you both. Be assured you have mine, and tho' they cannot prove as serviceable to you as those of many Others, 'tis not that they are less sincere. Adieu. A tender of Services by One who has it not in his power to serve, would be ridiculous. But, should Accident in some future Day render it otherwise; I shall not forget the Right you have to command.

Dr Sir   Your sincere Friend & hum Servt.   Morn. Lewis

ALS, Hamilton Papers, Library of Congress.
  1. Lewis was an assemblyman from New York City.
  2. Rhinebeck, Dutchess County, New York.
  3. This is apparently a reference to the revenue system suggested by H in the "Report Relative to a Provision for the Support of Public Credit," January 9, 1790.
  4. The law of July 16, 1790, provided that "prior to the first Monday in December next, all offices attached to the seat of the government of the United States, shall be removed to . . . Philadelphia" (1 *Stat.* 130). H moved to Philadelphia in October, 1790.

To Benjamin Lincoln

Treasury Department, July 27, 1790. ". . . I request that you will be so obliging as to inform me, whether you have received and found right, a parcel of 150 Ship Registers prepared according to law & forwarded to your Office on the 9th of December last, and another parcel of 200, also forwarded to your office on the 16th of the same Month. . . ."

L[S], RG 36, Collector of Customs at Boston, Letters from the Treasury and Others, 1789–1809, Vol. 1, National Archives; copy, RG 56, Letters to the Collector at Boston, National Archives; copy, Letters to Collectors at Small Ports, "Set G," National Archives.

To Eli Elmer

Treasury Department, July 29, 1790. "Your letter of the 19th ultimo [1] was duly received and I am apprehensive that an answer to it which was written on the 3d of July [2] has been mislaid. I do not perfectly comprehend from whence arises the expectation that no owner will appear for the goods taken into your keeping from the vessel cast on shore in distress. . . . The expenses of storage must in this and all other cases be paid by the owners of the Goods."

Copy, RG 56, Letters to and from the Collectors at Bridgetown and Annapolis, National Archives; copy, RG 56, Letters to Collectors at Small Ports, "Set G," National Archives.
   1. Letter not found.
   2. Letter not found.

To Benjamin Lincoln

Treasury Department, July 30, 1790. "I have been favored with your information, respecting the light House at Portland Head some days; [1] but it has not been deemed proper to ask from the Legislature, the needful Authority to finish that Building untill the Cession by the State should be received. . . . The repairs stated in your letters relative to the Light Houses on Plumb & Thatchers Islands [2]

& Boston Harbor,³ appearing necessary you will proceed in them with all possible Economy. . . ."

LS, RG 36, Collector of Customs at Boston, Letters and Papers re Lighthouses, Buoys, and Piers, 1789–1819, Vol. I, National Archives.
  1. See Lincoln to H, July 3, 1790.
  2. See Lincoln to H, July 1, 1790.
  3. See Lincoln to H, April 6, 1790.

To Sharp Delany

[*New York, July 31, 1790.* Letter listed in dealer's catalogue. *Letter not found.*]

ALS, sold at Thomas Birch's Sons, December, 1891, Item 95.

From Oliver Wolcott, Junior

Treasury Department
Auditors office July 31st. 1790.

Sir,

By your direction I have examined the accounts of the several Loan officers, who serv'd under the late ordinance of Congress, and have now the honor to communicate my observations thereon.

The accounts of Nathaniel Gilman, of New Hampshire, Nathaniel Appleton, of Massachusetts, William Ellery of Rhode-Island, William Imlay of Connecticut, John Cochran of New York, James Ewing of New Jersey, Thomas Tilton¹ of Delaware, Thomas Harwood of Maryland, William Skinner of North Carolina, John Neufville of south Carolina, and Richard Wylley² of Georgia, have been settled in this office and are found to have been correctly stated; agreeably to the forms prescribed, and supported by the necessary Vouchers.

The accounts of Thomas Smith of Pennsylvania under the first arrangement of the Loan Offices, are very extensive, and have never been settled: he has however made regular returns to the Treasury of his transactions; the accounts which arose in his office under the last ordinance of Congress, have been settled to the present year, and have been found very accurate.

The accots. of John Hopkins of Virginia are now under examination, and are nearly completed, and are also found accurate.

I have the honor to be with great respect   sir   Your Obt servant

Oliv: Wolcott Jnr.

LC, George Washington Papers, Library of Congress.
    1. Presumably this is James Tilton, a Dover, Delaware, physician. After
serving one term in the Continental Congress, 1783–1785, Tilton served as
Continental loan officer from 1785 to 1789.
    2. Spelled either Wylie or Wylley.

From William Allibone

Philadelphia, August 1, 1790. Expresses concern over delays in
the approval of the contracts for repairs on the Cape Henlopen lighthouse and for the lighthouse keeper's salary.

ALS, RG 26, Lighthouse Letters Received, Vol. "A," Pennsylvania and Southern States, National Archives.

From Jeremiah Olney

Providence, August 2, 1790. "Enclosed are a Register and License
given at the Custom House at New York for the Sloop Charlotte
belonging to Warwick within this District; . . . in conformity to
the law for registering vessels,[1] it appeared to me to be necessary that
she should be registered anew at this office, which has this day been
done. . . ."

Copy, RG 56, Letters from the Collector at Providence, National Archives.
    1. "An act for Registering and Clearing Vessels, Regulating the Coasting
Trade, and for other purposes" (1 *Stat.* 55–65 [September 1, 1789]).

From Sharp Delany

[Philadelphia, August 3, 1790]

Sir

It is with no small degree of uneasiness that I so often trouble You,
but the solicitations of those concerned oblige & urge me to it. I

recd. Your answers [1] respecting the Ship Brigida, and Mr Ingersolls [2] Vessell, in regard to this last I made the objections you notice, but could not get answers sufficiently satisfactory for me to proceed. The Captn is now sent forward to give You information.

In regard to the other my difficulty lay in Mr Leamys [3] having only a claim or right of property under the power of Atty but no special title to the Vessell, and this it appears Mr Leamy had not. The first Secto of the Registering Act,[4] I always construed that unless the Vessell at the time that Act passed belonged to a Citizen or Citizens such Vessell could not be Registered And though American built, being foreign property when the Act operated, and afterwards becoming the property of a Citizen Yet I held she could not be intitled to a Register, and refused one in consequence to Messr Fishers [5] of this City for the Ship Birmingham under such circumstances. I beg Your further consideration and direction on this last head, as it gives me much concern from the Tenor of your last in the case of Fishers for these Gentlemen bought out the owner in England for the purpose of fixing her in the Bristol Trade but from my construction the Register could not be obtained or granted. I beg leave to mention the schooner Betsey of Mr Ingersol was duly registerd here the 15th December last.

I am &c

Sharp Delany
August 3rd 1790

To A Hamilton Esqr
Secretary of the Treasury

LC, Copies of Letters to the Secretary, 1789–1790, Bureau of Customs, Philadelphia.

1. The correspondence concerning this and other matters mentioned in this letter has not been found.

2. Jared Ingersoll, a Philadelphia lawyer and attorney general of Pennsylvania, is the only Ingersoll listed in the Philadelphia directory for this year.

3. John Leamy is listed in the Philadelphia directory as "Agent for his Catholic Majesty."

4. "An Act for Registering and Clearing Vessels, Regulating the Coasting Trade, and for other purposes" (1 Stat. 55–65 [September 1, 1789]).

5. James C. Fisher and Samuel W. Fisher were merchants whose firm was located at 13 Mulberry Street, Philadelphia.

From William Short

Paris August the 3d. 1790

Sir

I have had the honor of recieving both the original & duplicate of your letter of the 29th. of May. Mine of the 4th. of April had not then reached you. In it I mentioned the subject of a conversation I had a few days before with Mr. Necker [1]—the hopes he had founded on the unauthorized loan made at Amsterdam [2] & his impatience, occasioned by the distressing penury of French finances, to know the decision of Congress on that subject. Since that period the situation of finances here has deteriorated, & of course his impatience increased. He is persuaded of the zealous desire which Congress have always manifested to discharge that sacred debt. He knows their possession of the loan in Holland,[3] & concludes there can be no doubt that it will be immediately appropriated agreeably to his wishes. It was on this reasoning he founded his expectations, mentioned in my former letter, that I would give him an order on the Bankers [4] for its amount. There was no difficulty in shewing him the impossibility of my giving such an order; but it was evident that he counted on it from Congress.

I find from your letter that no decision will be taken relative to the loan until the arrangements of finance in general shall be completed. This would seem to involve a doubt as to its appropriation agreeably to the hopes of Mr Necker. Still as it is only a doubt I have not communicated it to him. Should it be the design of Congress to annul a part of the French debt by this loan the policy of its being done without loss of time is evident, in order to avoid the paying interest both on the loan & the part of the French debt to which it would correspond.

You will think it advisable also perhaps (in case of this loan being adopted to discharge a part of the foreign debt) to appropriate such part of it as may be necessary to the payment of the principal & interest due the foreign officers here.[5] There are two reasons in favor it. 1. that the interest on what is due them is greater than on the other debts & 2. because being dispersed in different parts of Europe their complaints of a want of punctuality, are not only more loud, but more disseminated, than those of the other creditors. Besides the sum being inconsiderable, & due for the most part to French subjects, it would not be ill regarded. And particularly if Congress were to shew a disposition to transfer the remaining part of the French debt to Holland. This I still think might be done with very little, perhaps without any pecuniary sacrifice—& the political advantages with which it would be attended, are too evident to need being mentioned.

Complaints have been made to ministry by some merchants of Havre trading to the United States, of the difficulties with which they meet there, relative to tonnage, & particularly in going from one State to another. These complaints have not come to me officially & I do not suppose the present situation of affairs here will admit of their being attended to. Still I think it proper to mention to you that such complaints do exist; because I am persuaded you are fully impressed with the propriety of fostering a commercial intercourse, which though opposed by a variety of obstacles, presents the perspective of great advantages in future to both nations. Time of itself will unquestionably ⟨secure⟩ these advantages; but from the dispositions which prevail here at present I have no doubt such arrangements might be made as would accelerate the event. Our commerce by becoming more generally diffused, would be less dependent on any particular country.

I inclose you a return of the Ships both American & foreign, together with their burthen, coming from the United States to France in 89. Also the quantity of flour &c. imported during the same term. I expect soon a return of these articles from the 1st. of January to the 1st. of July 1790. which I will do myself the honor of forwarding to you.

I have recieved your report on finance,[6] which I have communicated to several persons here. They read it as well as myself with infinite pleasure. I am happy to learn that Congress are adopting it, as I am persuaded it will be fixing the credit of the United States on the firmest basis. I know at least that the impression which the report made on those who read it here, was a full persuasion both of the abilities of the author & the competence of the United States to a fulfillment of all their engagements.

I beg you to be assured of the sentiments of respect & attachment
with which I have the honor to be   Sir,   your most obedient servant
W. Short
The Honble. Mr. Hamilton Secretary of the Treasury.

ALS, letterpress copy, William Short Papers, Library of Congress.
  1. Jacques Necker, Director General of Finances.
  2. This is a reference to the Holland loan of 1790. Although this loan was
authorized in August, 1790, by "An Act making provision for the (payment
of the) Debt of the United States" (1 *Stat.* 138–44 [August 4, 1790]) and "An
Act making Provision for the Reduction of the Public Debt" (1 *Stat.* 186–87
[August 12, 1790]), negotiations for the loan had been opened in Amsterdam
by Willink, Van Staphorst, and Hubbard early in 1790 without authorization.
Rafael A. Bayley describes the 1790 Holland loan as follows:
  "Under these acts the Secretary of the Treasury, Alexander Hamilton, authorized the houses of W. & J. Willink, N. & J. van Staphorst, and Hubbard to
open negotiations for a loan of three million florins or guilders ($1,200,000),
giving them authority to pledge the good faith of the United States for the
payment of the interest and the repayment of the principal. The contract for
the money has never been printed, but a translation of the original is to be
found among the 'Washington Papers' in the Department of State. It is dated
November 12, 1790. It provided that the loan should be reimbursable within
fourteen years, in five annual payments of 600,000 guilders each, the first payment to be made February 1, 1800, and on that day annually until paid.
  "Three thousand bonds or obligations of the United States, for one thousand
guilders each, were to be issued, and in the December preceding each annual
payment the numbers of six hundred of these were to be drawn by lot, in the
presence of a notary, the numbers so drawn to be reimbursed in the following
February. Coupons for the annual interest at 5 per cent. per annum were to
be attached to each bond. For commission and all expenses connected with the
loan the United States were to pay 4½ per cent. on the principal." (Bayley,
National Loans, 23.)
  3. See Willink, Van Staphorst, and Hubbard to H, January 25, 1790.
  4. Willink, Van Staphorst, and Hubbard.
  5. Rafael A. Bayley states:
  "The Continental Congress was unable, when the war closed, to pay the
army in full, much difficulty being found in obtaining even enough money to
send the soldiers to their places of enlistment. The foreign officers, so far as
pay was concerned, probably fared rather better than the American soldiers,
a strong effort being made to pay them as large a portion of the amount due
them as possible; but to pay them in full, could not be done. An adjustment
of their accounts was made in 1782, and a part of their demands was paid in
cash. For the balance, certificates of indebtedness were given, bearing an interest of 6 per cent. These certificates, like all paper of the Continental Congress,
depreciated rapidly in value, and in January, 1784, under a resolution of Congress, they were called in and new certificates were issued, dated 'ye 5th April,
1784,' bearing interest at 6 per cent. from January 1, payable annually at the
house of M. Grand, banker, in Paris. No time for the redemption of these
certificates was named. The total amount of certificates or bonds issued was
$186,988.78. Their redemption began in 1792 under instructions from the Secre-
tary of the Treasury, who directed that a part of the Holland loan of 2,950,000
guilders should be used for that purpose, paying the holders of the bonds in
gold or its equivalent, and not in the depreciated paper currency of France. In

vided for. Two petitions preferring claims, for the satisfaction of which among others those orders were issued, one from Peter Anspach [3] on behalf of Timothy Pickering late Quarter Master General and the other from Abraham Skinner [4] late Commissary General of Prisoners, have been presented to the House during the present Session and referred to the said Secretary: pursuant to which reference he begs leave to state—

That those orders were issued to satisfy debts which had been contracted by the said late quarter Master General for supplies furnished and services performed in relation to his department, subsequent to the first of January 1782, before which time all transactions in paper money had ceased, and contracts and dealings had begun to be wholly carried on in Specie; and to discharge demands upon the United States on account of supplies and accommodations to the officers of the American army, in captivity during the late war.

---

on the same subject. On September 17, 1789, the House directed the Secretary to report an estimate of money for the civil list and for paying outstanding warrants of the Confederation Treasury Board. H replied in a report dated September 19 which the House received September 21. On September 23 the House asked H for a detailed analysis of these unpaid warrants. This second report is the one to which H is referring as dated September 24. Actually H's letter to the House bears the date September 25, but the Register, Joseph Nourse, dated the statistical portion of the report September 24. See "Report on the Estimate of the Expenditure for the Civil List and the War Department to the End of the Present Year," September 19, 1789, and "Report on a Particular Statement of the Warrants Issued by the Late Superintendent of Finance and by the Board of Treasury," September 25, 1789.

3. For background to Anspach's petition, see Timothy Pickering to H, November 19, 25, 1789; H to Pickering, November 19, 1789; H to Anspach, December 5, 1789; Anspach to H, December 30, 1789, July 2, 1790.

On July 1, 1790,

"A petition of Peter Anspach, of the City of New York, in behalf of Timothy Pickering, late Quartermaster General of the Armies of the United States, was presented to the House and read, praying the liquidation and settlement of a claim of the said Timothy Pickering against the United States.

"Ordered, That the said petition be referred to the Secretary of the Treasury, with instruction to examine the same, and report his opinion thereupon to the House." (Journal of the House, I, 254–55.)

4. On March 2, 1790, "A petition of Abraham Skinner was presented to the House and read, praying to be reimbursed for moneys advanced, and losses sustained by the petitioner, whilst Commissary General of Prisoners of the United States, during the late war" (Journal of the House, I, 166). It was ordered that the petition lie on the table, but on July 27, the House ordered that Skinner's petition "be referred to the Secretary of the Treasury, with instruction to examine the same, and report his opinion thereupon to the House" (Journal of the House, I, 282).

The sums due on the former account were understood, when incurred, to be immediately, or in a short time payable in specie, in many instances by special contract, in others, from the course of the business. The then Quarter Master General alleges, and the allegation is supported by some evidence, that he and his assistants relying on being enabled to make due payment, have rendered themselves in a number of cases personally answerable for its being done.

The sums due on the latter account have been understood to be payable in like manner with those due on the former. Assistances to this effect have been repeatedly given; and correspondent expectations have been entertained by those to whom the money is due. The said late Commissary of Prisoners appears to have made himself personally liable in some instances and represents that he has done it in all.

Such having been the nature of both these species of claims, warrants in the usual course were issued by the Superintendant of Finance on the Receivers of the States of Rhode Island, New York & Delaware; which warrants not being satisfied, by reason of the want of means, were afterwards returned into the Treasury by the Officers to whom they were granted.

It has happened, that several persons have brought in the Certificates they received from the Quarter Master General and his deputies, to the Commissioner for settling the accounts of that department, to be cancelled and have received other certificates in lieu of them, which now constitute a part of the general debt. To what extent this has been done is not ascertained, nor can be so without going over an immense mass of cancelled papers.

It does not appear that this circumstance has attended the class of claims relating to Prisoners.

If an appropriation should be made, it can only operate for the benefit of those who have never made a different election by accepting in exchange the certificates alluded to. It is a rule necessary to be maintained in all cases that wherever such an election has been made the parties shall be concluded by it.

In respect to those claims which remain as they originally stood, The Secretary is of opinion, that they ought to be discharged in specie. And he is informed, that they have always been considered in this light at the Treasury, though the embarassments of the finances have unavoidably postponed the payment.

The expences which have been incurred in relation to the Treaties [5] contemplated by the Acts of Congress of the 22nd. of October 1787 and 2d. of July 1788 [6] appear to exceed the sums which have been actually advanced on account of them. This excess is not finally ascertained. The expediency of an appropriation equal to the sum remaining unpaid of the grant of the 2d. of July to answer such further demands as may be liquidated and admitted in the course of the Treasury is respectfully submitted.

An estimate of the probable expence of a Treaty with the Indians of the Wabash and Miami rivers is inserted, in order that a provisional reservation of a competent sum may be made, if it should be judged eligible.

The Statement respecting the warrants issued by the late Board of Treasury is intended as explanatory of the disposition of the sum of One hundred and ninety thousand dollars appropriated by the Act of the 29th day of September last,[7] towards discharging those warrants.

In regard to the debt due to foreign officers,[8] the Secretary begs leave to submit to the House of Representatives the expediency of directing the same to be paid out of the Loan of Twelve Millions of dollars, which is authorised by the Act of the fourth instant making provision for the public debt: [9] In addition to other cogent inducements for paying off this debt, is the circumstance that it bears an interest of *six per Cent*, payable in *Europe*.

It will occur to the House of Representatives that all the revenues which shall exist at the close of the present Session are appropriated

5. These were the treaties of Fort Harmar negotiated by Arthur St. Clair in January, 1789. One of them was with the Six Nations (except the Mohawks) and the other was with the Wyandots and western tribes.
6. These acts provided funds for a treaty. However, the act of 1788 restricted treaty expenses to $8,000 and stipulated that the remaining $26,000 be used to extinguish Indian claims (*JCC*, XXXIII, 696; XXXIV, 285–86).
7. "An Act making Appropriation for the Service of the present year" (1 *Stat.* 95).
8. See William Short to H, August 3, 1790, note 5.
9. "An Act making provision for the (payment of the) Debt of the United States" (1 *Stat.* 138–44 [August 4, 1790]).

to the payment of the interest of the public debt, subject to such priorities and reservations as may result from appropriations heretofore made, or those which may be made, during the present session. Hence it will be perceived to be necessary to reserve and appropriate, before the termination of the session, such proportion of the revenues which have accrued, or may be expected to accrue in the course of the present year, as may be sufficient to satisfy, not only the demands on the treasury already established, but those which are likely to be established in the progress of the adjustments of depending claims, resulting from the transactions of the former government. A reservation and appropriation of fifty thousand Dollars for this purpose will, probably be found convenient.

The Secretary begs leave further to state, that there is a probability of a surplus of about One Million of Dollars accruing from the duties now in operation to the end of the present year over and above all the sums for which appropriations have been heretofore made and are now proposed: And to submit it as his opinion, that it will be expedient to authorise the application of this surplus to purchases of the public debt in the Market.

As long as these purchases can be made at rates below the true value of the Stock, there will be an absolute gain of all the difference to the Government. And very considerable savings to the nation will result from raising the price of Stock by this operation; inasmuch as foreigners must pay a higher price for what they buy.

It may even be worthy of consideration, whether authority ought not to be given to extend the purchases beyond the limit of that surplus upon a credit not exceeding a certain *specified* and *short* term; relying for this purpose on the aid of Loans.

In the execution of an arrangement of this nature, due regard may be had to the possibility that the *collection* of the duties accruing in the ensuing year, may not keep pace with the demand for paying the early interest.

All which is humbly submitted   Alexander Hamilton
                                        Secretary of the Treasury

[SCHEDULE] A

ADDITIONAL ESTIMATE OF MONIES
REQUIRED FOR THE SERVICES OF THE PRESENT YEAR.

For the payment of the Civil and Military Establishments under the Acts passed during the present Session—for defraying the Expense of the enumeration Law—for the payment of Claims founded upon Contracts made by the late Government, and which have been adjusted at the Treasury since the former Estimate of Extraordinaries was presented under date of 1st. March 1790—to make good some deficiencies in the former Appropriation by Congress—and for other Purposes.

	Dollars. Cts.	Dollars. Cts.
For the payment of the Civil & Military Establishments provided for by Acts passed during the present Session		
Judicial Department		
For the Salary of the District Judge for the State of Rhode Island, from July 3d. 1790 the time of his appointment to 31 December 1790, at 800 Dollars pr. Annum	398. 90	
For the Salary of the District Judge, for the State of North-Carolina, from June 8th. 1790 the time of his appointment to the 31 December 1790, at 1500 Dollars pr. Annum	850. 68.	
		1,249 58
Government of the Territory of the United States South of the River Ohio		
The Governor for his Salary as such, and for discharging the Duties of Superintendant of Indian Affairs in the southern Department, from the 8th. June 1790 the time of his appointment to 31 December 1790, at the rate of 2000 Dollars pr. Annum	1,134. 24.	
Secretary for same time—at 750 Dollars pr. Annum	425. 34.	
Two Judges, at 800 Dollars each amounts to	907. 39.	
		2,466 97
Frederick William Steuben		
For the payment of his Annuity for one year, commencing on the 1 January 1790 and ending 31 December following		2,500 —
Department of War		
Additional Expense of this Department for the Year 1790 in consequence of the "Act for regulating the Military Establishment of the United States passed the 30 April 1790" as estimated by the Secretary at War.		

Dollars. Cts. | *Dollars. Cts.*

Pay, Subsistence and Forage for a Battalion of Infantry and sundry Staff Officers in addition to those now in service to commence on the 1 July 1790.

PAY

1 Major .... 6 months .. at 40 Dollars ...	240.—	
4 Captains .. " ... " ...... 30 .... " each	720.—	
4 Lieutenants " ... " ...... 22 ...." .. " ..	528.—	
4 Ensigns ... " ... " ...... 18 ...." .. " ..	432.—	
16 Serjeants .. " ... " ...... 3 50/100. " ..	336.—	
16 Corporals . " ... " ...... 2 75/100. " ..	264.—	
8 Musicians . " ... " ...... 2 .... " ..	96.—	
264 Privates .. " ... " ...... 2 .... " ..	3,168.—	
		5,784. —

STAFF

2 Inspectors 6 months at .. 30 Dolls. each	360.—	
3 Adjutants ...... " ...... 10 .... " ..	180.—	
3 Quarter Masters " ...... 5 .... " ..	90.—	
1 Pay Master .... " ...... 5 .... " ..	30.—	
4 Senior Musicians " ...... 3 50/100. " ..	84.—	
		744. —

3 Surgeons Mates more are specified in the before mentioned Act of the 30 April two of whom being only employed under the former Acts of Congress are found necessary for the service. Pay from the 1 May to 31 Decr. 1790 at 24 Dolls. pr. Month . . . .   576. —

SUBSISTENCE

For 1 Major 6 Months or 184 days at 4 Rations
Per day is	736.	
4 Captains .... " ... at 3 pr. day ..	2,208.	
4 Lieutenants .... " ..... 2 pr. " ..	1,472.	
4 Ensigns .... " ..... 2 pr. " ..	1,472.	
Rations. 6,992. at 12 Cents		839. 4

3 Surgeons Mates from 1 May 245 days at
2 Rations each per day 1470 Rations at 12 Cents   176. 40

FORAGE

1 Major .... 6 Months at 10 Dollars ..	60.—	
2 Inspectors .... " .... 10 ... "	120.—	
3 surgeons Mates 8 Months . 6 ... "	144.—	
		324. —

RATIONS

308 Non Commissioned Officers & privates—
184 days Viz from 1 July to 31 Decr. 1790
is 56.672 Rations at 12 Cents pr. 6,800. 64

CLOTHING

308 Suits at 20 Dollars pr. . . . is . . .   6,160. —

	Dollars. Cts.	Dollars. Cts.

Quarter Masters Departmt

Including the Transportation of the Recruits to the frontiers—the removal of Troops from one Station to another, the transportation of Clothing, Ordnance, & Military Stores to the respective posts, the hire of Teams and Pack horses, the purchase of Tents, boats, axes, camp-kettles boards, firewood, Company books, Stationary for the Troops and all other expences in the Quarter Masrs. Department . . . . 5,000. —

Hospital Departmt

Medicines Instruments &c. . . . . 250. —

Contingencies of the War Dept

For Maps, hiring Expresses, Printing, loss of Stores of all kinds, advertising and apprehending deserters . . . . 750. —

Dolls. 27,404. 8

The Pay of the non Commissioned Officers and Privates of the Infantry and Artillery now in service is extended at the rate of the Old Establishment until the 31 December 1790, on a supposition that the distances of their several Stations will prevent an Arrangement for replacing them on the new Establishment until that Period. But the alteration of the Pay, Subsistence & Forage of the Officers which will commence on the 1 May 1790, in consequence of the Act of the 30th. of April last, reduces the sum required for them in the Estimate of the 31 December last—2,252. 40/100 Dollars. It is however to be observed that in the said Estimate of the 31 December last the Sum of 824 Dollars required for the forage of the Officers now in Service for the present year was omitted—this Sum being allowed for that purpose will leave a Surplus in the last Estimate of 1,428 40/100 Dolls. already provided for by the last Appropriation, which being deducted from this Estimate will leave the Sum of 1,428. 40

25,975. 68

In an additional Estimate the Secretary at War states to the Secretary of the Treasury that there will be required to pay Captain Aaron Holden—Pay for January, February, March, & April 1783 . . . . 160.—
Ditto. for his Subsistence . . . . 44.25.

204. 25

There is also required to pay Stephen Moore Proprietor of West-Point, so much heretofore short estimated by the Secretary at War for

	Dollars. Cts.	Dollars. Cts.

Rent for the Year 1789 . . . . . 37.50.
And also for the Year 1790 . . . . 37.50.

	75. —	
		26,254 93

Light Houses, Beacons, Buoys &c.

In addition to the sum heretofore Granted for the Support, Maintenance and Repairs of Light Houses Beacons, Buoys & public Piers—there will be required for the State of Rhode Island. . . . . Dollars 445

 " North Carolina . . . . .

		445

☞ The Secretary of the Treasury has not yet received a full Estimate for North Carolina it is therefore left open for a future appropriation.

The former Estimate for the support of the Light House and Beacon at Sandy Hook for the Year 1790 proves less than the necessary Expenditures according to accounts settled at the Treasury by the Sum of Dollars. 539.95
To which add so much which will be required up to 31 December 1790 . . . . 387.19

	927. 14	

There are other Objects relating to the security of the Navigation which do not fall within the letter of the Act respecting Light Houses &c. but which being of a similar nature it is presumed wou'd come within the reason of a provision for the Objects expressed in that Act. An Appropriation for this purpose is therefore submitted of

	1,000. —	
		1,927 14

For defraying the Expense of the Act for the Enumeration of the Inhabitants of the U.S.

The allowance to the Marshalls under the said Act is as follow's. Vizt.

	Dollars
For the District of Maine	200.—
" . . . New Hampshire . . .	200.—
" . . . Massachusetts . . .	300.—
" . . . Rhode Island	100.—
" . . . Connecticut	200.—
" . . . New York	300.—
" . . . New-Jersey . . .	200.—
" . . . Pennsylvania . . .	300.—
" . . . Delaware	100.—
" . . . Maryland	300.—
" . . . Virginia	500.—
" . . . Kentucky	250.—
" . . . North Carolina . . .	350.—
" . . . South Carolina . . .	300.—
" . . . Georgia	250.—

	3,850. —	

	Dollars. Cts.	Dollars. Cts.

"By the said Act the Assistants to the Marshalls are allowed at the rate of One Dollar for every

One hundred and fifty persons by them returned where such persons reside in the Country: and where such persons reside in a City or town containing more than five thousand Persons, they are allowed One Doller for every three hundred persons: and where from the dispersed situation of the Inhabitants in some divisions, One Dollar for every One hundred & fifty Persons shall be insufficient, the Marshalls with the approbation of the Judges of their respective Districts may make a further allowance to Assistants in such divisions as shall be deemed an adequate Compensation provided the same does not exceed One Dollar for every fifty Persons by them returned."

If therefore three dollars are estimated for every five hundred Persons thus to be returned, and the Enumeration is calculated at three millions of Inhabitants, there will be required from the Treasury of the United States to pay the said Assistants . . . . 18,000. —

21,850 —

For the payment of Claims founded upon Contracts made by the late Government and which have been adjusted at the Treasury since the former Estimate of Extraordinaries was presented under date 1 March 1790

Indian Department

To Richard Butler late Superintendant of Indian Affairs in the Northern Department appointed by Act of Congress of the 14 August 1786 for the amount of his Account for Supplies furnished to Indians and for Pay of an Interpreter and Labourer from 10th July 1786 to 14 October 1788 . . . . 337. 67

To Richard Butler Executor to the Estate of William Butler deceased, for said Williams pay as Deputy Superintendant of Indian Affairs Northern Dept. from 17th March 1787 to 14 October 1788 pr. Act of Congress of 8th. August 1786 . . . . 788. 35

To James O Hara Attorney for George Loveless for his services under the Superintendent of Indian Affairs in the Northern Department from the 8th. February 1788 to the 14 October following 209. 77

To James O Hara attorney for Joseph Nicholson for his services under the said Superintendant as an Indian Interpreter from 11th. February 1788 to 14th October following 255. 73

	Dollars. Cts.	Dollars. Cts.

To James Rankin employed by said Superintendant, for his pay and Expences as a Messenger
to the Indian Nations from 22 January 1788
to 14 October following 878. 78

To Isaac Williams employed by the Superintendant of Indian Affairs for the Northern Department for his Pay as an Interpreter to the
Wyandott Indians from 20th. of March 1788
to 14th October following . . . .   416. —

To William Wilson employed by said Superintendant as a Messenger to the Indian Nations
being for a balance due him 958. 80

To the Secretary at War for so much advanced
by him for George Morgan White Eyes an
Indian Youth lately at Princeton College placed
under the Superintendance of Col George Morgan by Congress, Vidé their Act of 13th. October 1781. being for sundry Articles of Cloathing a Horse and Money supplied him to carry
him back to his own Country as pr. Account
settled at the Treasury Amounting to
. . . . Dollars   425.52

Deduct so much thereof remaining of the
Grant of Congress by their Act of Appropriations for the Services of the Year 1789
. . . . 244.10

                                                    181. 42

To the Secretary at War for so much advanced
by him to Governor St. Clair for Indian services out of the Sum of twenty thousand Dollars granted by Congress for the "Expences
which may attend Negotiations or Treaties
with the Indian Tribes and the appointment
of Commissioners for managing the same" by
Act dated the 20th. August 1789, but which
the Comptroller of the Treasury does not admit as a part of the Sum thus appropriated
upon the account thereof stated for Settlement
by the Secretary at War . . . .   500. —

For supplying the Troops with Rations and for Transportation Service

To James O Hara Contractor for the Year 1788
for the Amot. of sundry accounts adjusted at
the Treasury the 4th. & 8th. of June 1790 under
a Contract made with the late Board of Treasury 4,073. 83

Late Loan Office

To Richard Wylie (late Loan Officer for the
State of Georgia) for so much unprovided for
and for the full payment of his account as
settled at the Treasury the 14th. May 1790
Vizt.

For his Salary from 3 July 1786
to 31st. of December 1789. at Dollars.90
600 Dollars pr. Ann. 2,096.66
Stationary and Office expences   85.78
                    Dolls . . . 2,182.60 Cents

Deduct sundry Sums already appropriated Vizt.
By Act for the Services of the year 1789 included under the Loan Office head &c. sum of
6225 Dollars 345.86
By Act for the Services of the Year 1790 under
the Head of Loan Office & included in the Sum
of 6,725 Dollars   . . . 340.—
Also for so much stated to be the balance, but
as his Account was not at that time settled, &
was debited with a Sum of money he had not
received a variation arises therefrom of
. . . . 692.50
                    1,378.36

                                        804. 24.

To the Representatives of the Honble John Laurens Esqr. deceased, late Special Minister from
the United States to the Court of Versailles, for
his Salary from the 11th. of December 1780
(the day of his appointment) to the 5th. of
September 1781 (the day Congress permitted
him to join the Army) at the rate of £2500
Sterling pr Annum, agreeably to an Act of
Congress for that purpose dated the 1 March
1785 . . . .   8,188. 73
To LeRoy & Bayard Merchants of New York
For so much due to them on a Contract made
with the Secretary of the Treasury on the 29th.
of March 1790—
They Contracted to deliver and agreeably to
the same they have delivered Bills of Excha.
on Amerstdam to the Amount of 100,000 Current Guildres in favour of the Commissioners
of Loans for the United States, for the Payment
of the Dutch Interest becoming due in the Year
1790 at the rate of 400 Dollars for every 1140
Current Guilders and which Amounts to
                    Dollars. Cts
. . . . 35,087.71.
Deduct so much heretofore appropriated
. . . . 32,000.—
                                        3,087. 71

To Constant Freeman of the Province of Canada
To discharge a Bill of Exchange dated Quebec
5th. August 1776 drawn by William Thompson
William Irvine, Christopher Greene, John
Lamb, Timothy Bigelow and Danl. Morgan On
Meredith and Clymer

	Dollars. Cts.	Dollars. Cts.

	Dollars.		
For the sum of	1,677.70.		
" Interest on Do	1,386.85.		
Sundry Costs of Protest . . .	58.73.		
Amounting to Dollars . . .	3,123.28/100	3,123.	28.

according to the Auditors adjustment thereof
the 10 July 1790 and admitted by the Comptroller of the Treasury the 15th following.
This Claim so far as respects the advance of
money to relieve the distresses of the American
prisoners being in every respect similar to that
of John McCord, to whom Congress by their
Act this session have made payment, It is therefore submitted for an appropriation . . . .
To John Neufville late Loan Officer for the State
of South Carolina for a balance due to him on
a settlement of his Account at the Treasury
on the 30th. April last, for his Salary and Stationary from the 27 July 1786 to the 31 December 1789 is . . . . Dollars 2,796.81.
Deduct so much already provided for. Vizt.
By Act making appropriation for the
year 1789 . 6 months salary   400.—
Do. for 1790 . . ditto . .   400.—
Do. in the Estimate of Extraordinaries . . .
. . . . 1,241.23.

2,041.23

leaves to be provided for . . .   755. 58.
To Monsr. LeRay de Chaumont as Stated by the
Auditor and admitted by the Comptroller of
the Treasury the 31st May 1790 . . . . .
"For the balance of an Account admitted by
Thomas Barclay Esqr. Commissr. for adjusting
the accounts of the United States in Europe
dated 15th June 1784.

                  sols. denrs.
Amounting to Livres 4684. 16.   6
equal to 892.35
Also for the balance of an Account
settled by James Milligan Esqr. including Interest to 18th. August 1784 which
sum is Credited in the Books of the
Treasury" 8,158.98

         9,051. 33

Western Territory

To Andrew Ellicott employed to compleat the
Survey directed by a Resolve of Congress of
26 August 1789. for so much unprovided for,
and payment of the balance upon the settlement of his account at the Treasury the 26th.
March last Vizt.

	Dollars. Cts.	Dollars. Cts.

The Amount of his Account thus settled is 2,359.78
Deduct the amount Granted for this service by the Act making appropriations for the present Year . . . . 2,160.—

199. 78.

To Isaac Guion employed for the purpose of carrying into Effect the Resolve of Congress of 26th. August 1789. for the Amount of his adjusted Claim for services and Expences by direction of the President of the United States   632. 80
To Thomas Franklin employed by the late Board of Treasury as Auctioneer to sell Lands surveyed by the United States in the Western Territory. 16 Days at 3 Dollars per day . .   48. —

Bills of Exchange Drawn for the
Exigencies of the Late War
For to discharge the Claim of Shedden Patrick & Compy. Merchants of the City of New York, founded on an account adjusted at the Treasury the 17 May 1790, being for a sett of Bills of Exchange No. 39, drawn on the Honble Benjamin Franklin and which remain upaid   200. —

34,691 80

To Make Good Some Deficiencies in the Former Estimates on Which Appropriations Were Made by Congress

TREASURY DEPARTMENT
For repayment to the Treasurer of the United States Costs of Protest on a Bill of Exchange which was drawn by mistake on the Deputy instead of the Collector and was therefore returned under Protest for non payment . . .   41. 47
For the payment of two additional Clerks to be appointed by the Secretary of the Treasury employed in the Treasurers Office for the purpose of counting & examining the Old & New Emissions of Continental Money & Indents— estimate for 5 Months at 500 Dolls. pr. Annum   416. 64
To repay to the Treasurer so much which was appropriated for the use of his Office for the Year 1789 and which was applied with other Contingent monies for the use of the Office of the Secretary of the Departmt. the Comptrollers Auditors and Registers . . . . . .   100. —
For the Salary of an additional Clerk employed in the Office of the Secretary of the Treasury from the 10th. May 1790 to 31 December following both days inclusive at 500 Dollars pr. Ann 323. 28

Dollars. Cts. | Dollars. Cts.

The Incidental and Contingent Expences of the Treasury Department are found to exceed the Sum estimated and Appropriated for the Year 1790 . . . . Vizt.—
The Sum appropriated was . . .
. . . . Dollars   1,800.—
The Expenditures upon Accots. Officially settled, have been to this time . . . .   1,396.77.
leaving on hand only the Sum of
. . . . Dolls. . .   403.23/100

There will be required to pay Rent of the House occupied for the several Offices . . . . .   500.—
Ditto for the use of an additional Office for the Auditor . . . .   40.—
For new Books & Stationary for the Dept . . . .   500.—
For printing Registers and other forms under the Act for Registering Vessels . . . .   200.—
For Cases and Boxes for public accounts . . . .   250.—
For Wood—12 fire places estimate 60 Cords at 5 Dollars . . . .   300.—
And for Contingencies . . . .   150.—
                                              1,940.—
Deduct so much on hand . .   403.23

                                                        1,536.   77

DEPARTMENT OF STATE

The Secretary of State in addition to the Sum heretofore appropriated for him (previous to his arrival) estimates for his Department as follows . . . . Vizt.
The Interpreter of the French Language continued in Office under the Act of Congress of 11th. February 1781. For his Salary from 1 January to 31 December 1790 . . . .   250.—
For an additional Sum of fifty Dollars to his Office keeper and Messenger for the Year 1790 to put him on a footing with the Office keeper & Messenger in the Treasury Department . . . .   50.—
For the additional Clerk (in his Office for the Home Department) from the 1 April 1790 to the 31 December following at 800 Dollars pr. Ann. . . . .   600.—
The Extra expences of his Office

	Dollars. Cts.	Dollars. Cts.

are estimated more than was provided for . . . .   250.—

                           1,150. —

INDIAN DEPARTMENT

To Richard Winn, late Superintendant of Indian
Affairs in the Southern Department, for the
difference between the Pay of a Superintendant
of Indian Affairs at 1000 Dollars per Annum
as fixed by Congress on the 8th. of August 1786
and the Pay of a Deputy at only 500 Dollars
per Annum from the 29th. of August 1788 to
the 29th of November following as per Account adjusted at the Treasury . . . . .   125. —

To James Burnside late Clerk to the Commissioner for settling the Accounts of the Marine,
Clothing & Hospital Departments for his Salary
from 8th May 1789 to the 1st. August following; founded on a Certificate of the Auditor of
the Treasury dated in his Office the 16th. of
February 1790 and which should have been
stated in the former Estimate of Extraordinaries
and added to the Sum of 628. 26/100 Dollars
which was appropriated for a Similar Purpose.   110. 31.

To Thomas Smith late Loan Officer for the State
of Pennsylvania, for Six Months service in the
present Year at the rate of his former Salary,
as a Compensation for Executing the Business
of exchanging the Pennsylvania Loan Office
Certificates for those of the United States . .   750. —

For the Payment of an Account presented by
Richard Phillips late Steward of the Household of the President of Congress under the
former Government for sundry Expenditures
for Marketing and for sundry articles purchased between the 17th. of December 1788
and the   1789 when he delivered up the
furniture and other Articles preparatory for
the reception of the President of the United
States.

Amounting to .... Dollars ...... 138.36.
And for the discharge of sundry Accounts
brought in. ....   Vizt.
Walter Nichols ... for Groceries £ 8.17.
Cobus Mires ...... " Wood ... 11. 2.
——Bradhurst ... " Milk ..... 3.19.
Henry Arcularius " Bread .... 6.16.
Appleby & Matlock " Beer ..... 5.—.
Richard Phillips .. " Salary ... 14.12.
Palsey Phillips .... " Do 24.15. 8
           New York £75. 1. 8
          = to 187.70   326. 6.

	Dollars.	Cts.	Dollars.	Cts.

To John Halstead formerly a Commissary in Canada for the Balance which remains unpaid of a Grant made to him by Congress as per their Act of 4th. June 1788 . . . . . . $\qquad$ 39. 62

To the Estate of Hugh Smith late Post Master at the Head Quarters of the Army, for a balance due to the deceased for his Services on the settlement of the Accounts of Peter Baynton Esqr. late Comptroller of the Post Office as adjusted at the Treasury on the 12th. of November 1782 and which is now claimed by Daniel Dennison Administrator of sd. Estate . . . . . 120. 65.

5,039 80

Note This Claim is stated payable in Specie; because the several Officers of the Post Office have received their respective balances in Specie.

To Complete the Survey Directed by Act of Congress of the 26th. of August 1789.

Mr. Andrew Ellicott who proceeded with this business as far as it was practacable last year has been employed since the 1 June 1790 in carrying on the said Survey—before his departure from New-York he left with the Secretary of the Treasury an Estimate of the Expense (exclusive of his allowance) which would attend the perfecting the same Amounting to . . . . . Dollars 1,452.— 4 Months allowance for his own Services at 5 Dollars pr. day . . . 610.—

2,062 —

The House of Representatives having by their Act for settling the Accounts of the United States made a provision whereby the Clerks employed or to be employed by the General Board of Commissioners shall receive like Salaries as Clerks employed in the Treasury Department. There will be required to pay such additional Salary for Six Months . . . . . 200 —

To Matthias Ogden Assignee of Albion Cox for the amount of an Account settled at the Treasury the 4th. August 1790 being for a pair of dyes made for the purpose of striking Indian Medals; by direction of the late Board of Treasury . . . . 140 —

Loan Officers, to be appointed under "An Act making provision for the Debt of the United States."

for the state of New Hampshire . . . . . . 650.—
" . . . . Massachusetts . . . . 1,500.—
" . . . . Rhode Island &c.
    Providence Plantations . . . . 600.—

	Dollars. Cts.	Dollars. Cts.
" .... Connecticut .... 1,000.—		
" .... New York .... 1,500.—		
" .... New Jersey .... 700.—		
" .... Pennsylvania .... 1,500.—		
" .... Delaware .... 600.—		
" .... Maryland .... 1,000.—		
" .... Virginia .... 1,500.—		
" .... North Carolina .... 1,000.—		
" .... South Carolina .... 1,000.—		
" .... Georgia .... 700.—		
Dollars 13,250.—		
Per Annum, Estimate for five Months salary		5,500 —
Dollars		104,327 22

Treasury Department   Registers Office
August. 6th. 1790   Joseph Nourse Regr

To Alexander Hamilton Esqr.
Secretary of the Treasury

[SCHEDULE] B

ADDITIONAL ESTIMATE

FOR WHICH NO PROVISION HATH BEEN MADE BY CONGRESS.

	Dollars. Cts.	Dollars. Cts.
Amount of Orders drawn by the late superintendant of Finance, and stated by the Secretary of the Treasury in his Report to the House of Representatives made in Obedience to their Order of 17th. Septr. 1789		93,463 21
Indian Affairs under the late Government. For the Extinguishment of Indian Claims in pursuance of the Acts of Congress of the 22 October 1787 and 2 July 1788. The Act of 22 October 1787 appropriated fourteen thousand Dollars for defraying the expense of holding a general Treaty with the Indians	14,000. —	
The Act of 2 July 1788 grants the Sum of twenty thousand Dollars in addition to the above sum appropriated, and restricts the allowance for holding a Treaty with the Indians to Eight thousand Dollars and directs—"That the whole of the said twenty thousand dollars together with six thousand dollars of the said fourteen thousand dollars be applied solely to the purpose of Extinguishing Indian Claims to the Lands they have already ceded to the United States by obtaining regular conveyances for the same, and for extending a purchase beyond the limits hitherto fixed by Treaty" . .	20,000. —	
Total appropriated by Congress	34,000.	

	Dollars. Cts.	*Dollars. Cts.*

Of the Sum thus appropriated, there have been paid from the Treasury to the Governor of the Western Territory as follow's

Under the Act of 22 October 1787.

1787 November 6th ..... Dollars .... 300.—

1788. February. 4 .... 10,333.

" .... 5 .... 1,000.

"December. 9 .... 500.

1789. May ...... 23 .... 1,867.

Total of the appropriation of Octor. 22d. 1787...   14,000. —

Under the Act of 2 July 1788

1789. May ..... 23 ...... Dollars .... 2,000.—

"   " .... " 2,068. 7

"   " .... " 779.15

"   " .... " 1,220.75

                          6,068. 7

The balance of thirteen thousand nine hundred and thirty one Dollars 83/90 ths remains unpaid of the foregoing appropriations 13,931. 83   13,931 92

                  Dollars . . .   34,000. —

The Governor of the Western Territory in his Estimate dated June 14th. 1789, submitted to the President of the United States the 4th. January 1790, and which was laid before the Senate and House of Representatives; States as follow's

Estimate of the expense with which a Treaty with the Indians of the Wabash and Miami Rivers would probably be attended. Their Numbers are supposed to be from twelve **to** fifteen hundred Men.

                  Vizt.

Indian Goods asso[r]ted to the Value of . .   6,000. —

Stores and necessaries . . . .   650. —

Transportation . . . .   2,500. —

Messengers and Interpreters . . . .   1,000. —

Store-keepers . . . .   300. —

Commissioners Wages . . . .   500. —

Contingencies . . . .   200. —

The Provisions cannot be estimated at less than 30,000 Rations which at Contract price will amount to . . . .   5,000. —

                                   16,150 —

The Secretary at War in his Letter to the sec'y. of the Treasury dated 24 June 1790,[10] observes— That this Estimate contemplated Treaties with the Wabash Indians but which do not appear to have been authorized by the Legislature.

Warrants drawn on the late Treasurer of the United States, by the late Commissioners of the Board of Treasury. There have been presented at the Treasury **for**

10. Letter not found.

Dollars. Cts. | *Dollars. Cts.*

payment, sundry Warrants which were not included in the particular statement of Warrants drawn by the late Board of Treasury (on Michael Hillegas late Treasurer of the United States) referred to by the Secretary of the Treasury in his Report to the House of Representatives made in Obedience to their Orders of the 17th. September 1789.

This omission arose from the Accots. of the late Treasurer and Receivers of Taxes not being adjusted at the Treasury; The Register therefore had no Certain guide to ascertain the particular Warrants which formed the aggregate Amot. of the excess of Warrants drawn by the late Board beyond the actual Receipts of Monies into the Treasury, but was obliged to state them from the best materials he could collect

This aggregate amount was Stated at 189,906. 34

And the United States by their Act making appropriations for the Year 1789 have granted "a sum not exceeding One hundred & ninety thousand Dollars for discharging the Warrants issued by the late Board of Treasury and remaining unsatisfied."

The Register finds that of this sum appropriated by Congress Warrants have been taken up and paid to the Amount of 69,251. 8

That the Paymaster General and others have in their hands, Warrants which were issued for the Pay of the Army and which are included in the particular Statement aforesaid to the Amount of   80,915. 49

Leaving a sum to be applied towards taking up Warrants to Amount of 39,833. 43

Dollars   190,000. —

The Warrants since presented and which were not included in the particular statement aforesaid are as follow's—Vizt.

Warrants No. 748 drawn by the Board of Treasury the 28th. August 1787 in favour of John Pierce (late) Paymaster General for Fifty thousand Dollars being for Pay, Subsistence and Forage due to the Officers and Men in the first American Regt. under the Command of Lieut. Col Harmar to the 1 July 1787 . . .   50,000. —

The Board of Treasury when they drew the Warrant above stated on the Treasurer, drew also to a similar amount on several of the Receivers of Taxes in different States in favor of the Treasurer, in order for payment; of which it appears, there only were paid by the said Receivers to amount of . . . .   30,200. —

Leaving Warrants unpaid in the hands of the Paymaster General and others . . . . . .   19,800. —

	Dollars. Cts.	Dollars. Cts.

(as follows)
In the Hands of the present Pay Masr. General

On James Ewing No. 187 .. for 2,000—
" 189 ...... 2,000—
Thomas Smith .... 192 ...... 2,000—
" 193 ...... 2,000—
" 194 ...... 2,000—
" 196 ...... 2,000—
Dollars 12,000.—

In hands of Sundries

Dollars

On James Ewing No. 396 .. for 500—
" 455 150
" 456 150
" .... 457 ...... 150—
" .... 458 ...... 150—
" .... 459 ...... 200—
" .... 460 ...... 300—
" .... 300 ...... 300—
" .... 507 ...... 500—
" .... 506 ...... 500—
Thomas Smith .... 191 ...... 2,000—
.... 195 ...... 2,000—
.... 197 ...... 1,000—
7,150.—

The Register stated from the information of the Pay Master General that it was probable of Warrants No 1043 a 1051 both inclusive, to the amount of Fifty thousand Dollars, that there had been paid in Philadelphia by the Receiver of Taxes the sum of . . . . . . 4,086.45. but the accounts of Mr. Smith (the said receiver) shews that no part thereof had been paid by him: this sum therefore forms a part for which the sum of 190,000 Dolls. was appropriated.

August 7. 1789 Warrant No 1202 in favr. of Joseph Howell junr. Paymaster Genl. being for four months pay in 1783 due to Capt. Brackenbridge late of the Virginia Line . . . 160.00

4,246. 45.

May 19th. 1789 Warrant No. 1154 in favor of James O Hara late Contractor for supplying the Western posts with Provisions being the balance due him for provisions issued and supplies furnished in the Quarter Masters Department from the 1 July 1787 to the 1st. of July 1788 . . Amounting to Dolls. 4,223.29
May 20, 1789 Warrant No 1157 in favr, of Ditto, being for provisions issued to Indians from 1 Decr 1787. to 30th. June 1788, and for 41,789½ Rations of provisions furnished the Governor of the Western Territory for Indian Treaties

	Dollars. Cts.	Dollars. Cts.
in 1788 . . . . 2,133.57		
	6,356. 86	
July 11th. 1789 Warrant No. 1182 in favor of John Jordan for his Pension agreeably to an Act of Congress of 15 Septr. 1783	10. —	
Total Amount of Warrants presented for Payment at the Treasury	30,413. 41	

The Register from a View of the State of these Warrants conceives, that when the Treasurer's Account shall be finally settled, and the Accounts with the several receivers of Taxes (who acted as Treasurers) shall be fully closed, that some of the Warrants particularly stated and supposed not to have been paid will appear to have been paid; and on the other hand it is presumed the Warrants above mentioned to the Amot. of Thirty thousand four hundred and thirteen Dollars forty one ninetieths, will be found to form a part of the Excess of Warrants drawn by the late Board of Treasury to the Amount of 189,906.34/90 Dollars before stated. But this is only to be presumed until from actual settlement of the Treasurer's and the accounts of the Receivers of Taxes it shall be clearly ascertained. As it is probable that the appropriation above referred to will be sufficient to cover all the Warrants issued by the late Board of Treasury which remained actually unpaid; And as the words in which that Appropriation is made, seem to be general enough to Embrace Warrants not specified in the former Estimate, it is presumed not to be necessary to carry out any sum for an additional appropriation or Grant.

Debt due to Foreign Officers—the Interest whereof is payable annually at the House of Monsr. Grand Banker at Paris, by Act of Congress of the 3d. February 1784, as follows

Resolved, "That the Superintendant of Finance be, and he is hereby directed to take measures as far as may be consistent with the Finances of the United States, for remitting annually to the foreign officers of the late corps of Engineers, the Legionary Corps lately commanded by Brigr. General Armand, to Major Seconde, and Capt. Beaulieu late of General Pulaski's Corps, and to Captain Ponthiere, late Aid de Camp to Baron Steuben, the Interest of such sums as may remain due to them respectively after the payments which shall have been made to them in consequence of the resolution of the 22d. January last."

	Dollars. Cts.	Dollars. Cts.

Certificates for Debt due were issued to the following Officers. Vizt.

	Livres.	sols.	Drs.
To General Armand	57,951.	12	—
" Colonel Ternant	42,583	2	9
" Major George Schaffner	30,855	3	7
" Major De Bert de Majan	30,160	13	7
" Major De Bellecour	30,717	10	9
" Major De Bert assignee of			
Captain John Sharp	2,239	6	5
" Reede & Forde assignee of do	5,400	—	—
" Jona. B. Smith .... do .... do	7,085	16	4
" Captain Verdier	14,444	4	4
" Capt. De Fontiveux	13,103	5	7
" Lieut. Des Couteurs	14,767	4	.
" Cornet Raffaneau	9,494	11	7
" Major De Segond	30,402	6	—
" Major Du Pontiere	26,957	15	2
" Captain Beaulieu	9,640	8	9
" Captn. Peter Castaing	8,826	9	7
" Capt. Baron D-Uhtrick	22,408	5	3
" Capt. Buffault	18,814	19	1
" Lieut. Col Murnan	35,029	4	—
" Lieut. Col De Brahm	35,212	4	—
" Jona. B. Smith assignee of			
Captn. Philip Strubing	6,880	13	7
" Lt. Col. Villefranche	34,612	—	—
" Lt. Col Gimat	32,493	14	4
" Major Rochefontaine	25,556	12	9
" Lieut. Colo. Cambray	20,248	18	4
" Lieut. Col Fleury	15,875	—	—
" General Kos-ciusko	66,314	18	9
" Major Le'Enfant	19,002	13	4
" ...... Ditto	2,320	9	7
" Captain Capitaine	17,328	10	9
" Chevalier De la Colombe	22,993	10	—
" General Du Portail	86,222	14	—
" General Laumoy	55,530	3	7
" Colonel Gouvion	43,172	12	9
" The Estate of Col Malmady	13,580	18	9
" Col La Radier Balleux	14,349	4	—
" Col de Flury	25,006	—	—
" Monsieur de Pontgebeau	33,696	14	4
" Col Cambray	17,430	15	7
" Royal Flint Attorney to			
Catherine Green Assignee of			
Baron Glaubeck	3,029	15	6

Livres	1,009,740	2	8. equal to

186,988.81/90 Dollars. One Years Interest thereon ⎫
  at 6 pr. Cent. ⎭ is . . . . | 11,219 | 33

Dollars | 134,764 | 56

Treasury Department Register's Office July 28, 1790 Joseph Nourse Regr.

To Alexander Hamilton Esqre.
Secretary of the Treasury

Report on the Petition of Jacob Rash

Treasury-department, August 5th. 1790.
[Communicated on August 7, 1790] [1]

[To the Speaker of the House of Representatives]
The Secretary of the Treasury having considered the petition of
Jacob Rash, referred to him on the 29th. day of June last,[2] respect-
fully reports:

That the reasons which induced the late Congress of the United
States, to grant a renewal of Continental Loan Office Certificates,
destroyed through accident appear of equal weight in regard to other
evidences of the public debt, which have been the subjects of similar
casualty.

That justice to the petitioner, therefore, seems to require that an
opportunity of renewing his certificates be granted to him; and as
there are several applications of the same nature, it is respectfully
suggested, that it will be expedient to provide by law for administering Relief to all who shall be found similarly circumstanced, under
the following cautionary regulations, which are in most particulars,
the same as those provided in the case of Loan Office Certificates, so
far as they will apply to the different species and circumstances of
the Certificates.

1st. That the Certificates renewed be issued to those who shall
appear to have been the holders of them at the time they were destroyed, or if dead, to their legal representatives.

2nd. That the Certificates destroyed be advertized in the Newspapers of the State where the accident happened, and in the State
where they were issued: which advertizement shall be continued
six weeks, and shall contain the numbers, dates, sums, names in which
the Certificates were taken out, and the time when, the place where,
and the means by which the same were destroyed.

3d. That a copy of the advertizement be lodged in the Office of
the Commissioner of Loans within the State, in which the Certificates, alledged to have been destroyed, were issued, together with
such testimony as can be procured, ascertaining the time when, the
place where, and the means by which the destruction happened;

which copies and testimonies shall be duly certified by the said Commissioner to be laid by the party claiming the renewal, before the Comptroller of the Treasury, who shall finally decide on the sufficiency thereof.

4th. That the party, claiming the renewal, enter into bond to the United States, with two or more sufficient freeholders as sureties (their sufficiency to be judged of by the said Comptroller) in double the amount of the value of the certificates claimed to be renewed, with condition to indemnify the United States against the holders of the Certificates said to be destroyed, should any such afterwards appear.

5th. That no Certificates be renewed before the expiration of three months after the publication of the advertizement above mentioned, and that there be an endorsement on each renewed Certificate, signifying that the same was issued in lieu of one destroyed by accident, and describing the original.

In regard to Certificates which have not been destroyed by accident, but which have either been lost or captured, or otherwise taken away, it appears extremely difficult to devise any mode of relief to the sufferers, which will not subject the United States to so much hazard of imposition and injury, as to render the expediency of it questionable. If the House should, nevertheless, be of opinion that Justice requires, it may be granted under the same regulations, which are proposed in respect to Certificates destroyed.

All which is humbly submitted.   Alexr Hamilton.
                                    Secry. of the Treasury.

Copy, RG 233, Reports of the Secretary of the Treasury, 1790–1791, Vol. I, National Archives.
1. *Journal of the House,* I, 293.
2. On June 29, 1790,
"A petition of Jacob Rash, of Lenox, in the State of Massachusetts, was presented to the House and read, praying that duplicates may be granted him of certain certificates of final settlement, amounting to two hundred and sixty-five dollars, the property of the petitioner, which were destroyed by fire, in the Year one thousand seven hundred and eighty five.
"*Ordered,* that the said petition be referred to the Secretary of the Treasury, with instructions to examine the same, and report his opinion thereupon to the House." (*Journal of the House,* I, 253.)

To Walter Stewart [1]

[New York, August 5, 1790]

My Dear Sir

I thank you for the interest you are so obliging as to take in procuring for me a house. My wish has been to have it first ascertained what arrangement would be made, if any, by your Magistracy or other public Men, in regard to *offices* for the accommodation of the department. If any public buildings should be destined to that purpose, my next wish would be to have a house as near my destined office as possible. A cool situation & exposure will of course be a very material point to a New Yorker. The house must have at least six rooms. Good dining and drawing rooms are material articles. I like elbow room in a yard. As to the rent the lower the better consistently with the acquisition of a proper house. But I must leave that to what is practicable.

When Judge Wilson [2] was in Town he obligingly offered to look out for me. Without adverting to your friendly undertaking I requested him to do so. I mention this that you may have the goodness to communicate with him: For *two houses* would be more than I shall *probably* have occasion for.

The manner in which you speak of Mr Smith confirms my former impressions.

I remain   Yr Affect & Obed serv   A Hamilton

Augt. 5. 1790
General Stewart

ALS, New-York Historical Society, New York City.
　1. Stewart had been a colonel in the Second Pennsylvania Regiment during the Revolution and at this time was a merchant in Philadelphia.
　2. James Wilson was a justice of the Supreme Court.

To George Washington

Treasury Department, August 5, 1790. "The Secretary of the Treasury has the honor respectfully to submit to the President of the United states a contract . . . for shingling two houses, and building a breast-work for the foundation of the light-house at Cape-Henlo-

pen. He begs leave to offer an opinion, that the terms of this agreement appear to him advantageous to the United states."

LC, George Washington Papers, Library of Congress.

From Jonathan Elmer [1]

New York, August 6, 1790. Recommends appointment of John
Conway [2] as the captain of a revenue cutter.[3]

Copy, George Washington Papers, Library of Congress.
    1. Elmer, surrogate of Cumberland County, New Jersey, had been a member
of the United States Senate from 1789 to 1791.
    2. Conway was a former sheriff in Middlesex County, New Jersey.
    3. Similar letters of recommendation of Conway were sent to H on August
16, 1790, by Lambert Cadwalader and Thomas Sinnickson, William Paterson,
and James Shureman. All are copies, and all are located in the George Washington Papers, Library of Congress.

From Thomas Newton, Junior [1]

Norfolk [Virginia] August 6, 1790. "Your Letter of the 25th Ult.
I received this day. . . .[2] I employ'd the surveyor chain Carriers &c
& shall furnish him with an acct thereof & transmit a plat of the two
acres's survey of the Cape [3] as soon as the surveyor supplies me
therewith to you."

ALS, RG 26, Lighthouse Letters Received, Vol. "A," Pennsylvania and Southern
States, National Archives.
    1. For background to this letter, see Newton to H, June 27, July 11, 1790.
    2. Letter not found.
    3. Cape Henry.

Conversation with George Beckwith [1]

[New York, August 7–12, 1790] [2]

[Beckwith] "As our packet is to sail to morrow I wish to know,
whether any thing has occurred to occasion an addition to the communications, which you were pleased to make to me on the 15th. of
last month."

Supposed 7.³ No, nothing at all. I at the same time think myself warranted to acquaint you, that Mr. Morris's letters by your June packet mark an alteration in the disposition of your Cabinet, according more with the spirit of Lord Dorchesters communications by you, than seemed to be the case before; Mr. Morris has been asked, whether we should be disposed to send a minister, if such was your disposition; to this Mr. M. has been too shy in his reply; but I conclude your communications on that point had not then reached England.⁴

[Beckwith] "No, they were not forwarded from Quebec until late in May, and I think it right to say the matter respecting the mutual appointment of Ministers was fully explained."

[Hamilton] "I believe you will recollect, that shortly after the arrival of the Creek Indians I mentioned to you, that I took no part whatever in Colonel MacGillivray's negotiation, that I was ignorant of his intentions in coming here, and that I had no concern in Indian Affairs: ⁵ I judged it necessary to come to this explanation at that time from particular circumstances."

Supposed 7. The step You took on that occasion was very satisfactory.

[Beckwith] "The object of my present application is this, I have rigidly adhered to the same system since that time, but when your Treaty shall be completed, and every thing finally concluded, I should wish to see Mr. McGillivray. You undoubtedly have heard from public report, that some of the Southern Indians have been at Halifax, and the public prints assert, they are gone to Quebec; now I wish to ascertain who they are, and by what authority they act."

[Hamilton] I may mention in confidence to you, that we are by no means satisfied with the conduct of the Spanish Officer, who arrived lately from the foreign possessions of that Crown; ⁶ we cannot prove it positively, but have every reason to think, that he has been using endeavours to check or even to frustrate our negotiations with the Creek Indians, and with this view that he has made them large presents in this city; this we consider as perfectly unwarrantable. I am not sure whether our disapprobation of this conduct may have yet been communicated, but if not, it will immediately. Now if we take this step with respect to the servants of the Spanish Government, it occurs to me it may seem inconsistent to give You a toleration to negotiate with the same party, this I throw out for Your consideration.

[Beckwith] "I have no authority to negotiate; I wish merely to come to an explanation with Colonel Mc.Gillivray on the points I stated to You."

[Hamilton] There is a person here, who calls himself a British Officer, who has been busy with the Indians, and who drew away two or three of them one night; he is a man of low character, and has been wandering about through the West India Islands of different nations; it is therefore highly problematic, whether such a man may not be a Spanish Agent; if any thing had appeared to lead to the idea of this man's being employed by Your Government, I should have mentioned it to You in direct terms.[7]

[Beckwith] "Such a man, or such men, may have three objects; they may be pushing a personal interest, they may be employed by Spain, or (what I confess I think improbable) they may be employed by the Government here; in any of these events it would make no sort of difference, as it respected me; peace and friendship between you and the Creek Indians, is evidently not hostility with us, and I trust it will never be viewed in that light here."

[Hamilton] Certainly not. I shall think of Your application; from the forms of our Government, the Treaty although matured, must be approved by the Senate, and I shall let You know to morrow or next day, whether Your request is considered as leading to any sort of inconvenience or not; but I cannot think for many reasons, that we should employ any person or persons whatever in the manner You have described.

[Beckwith] "I am far from believing You would, I only expressed all the possible circumstances of such a case."

D, Public Archives of Canada, Ottawa, Ontario.
1. This document was enclosed in Lord Dorchester to William Wyndham Grenville, September 25, 1790.
2. This conversation, although undated in Beckwith's report, must have taken place between August 7 and August 12. During the course of the conversation H said that the treaty with the Creek Nation "although matured must be approved by the Senate." The treaty was sent to the Senate on August 7 and was approved by that body on August 12.
3. "7" was Beckwith's code number for H.
4. The most important of those letters from Gouverneur Morris was the one to George Washington dated May 29, 1790. In describing his conversation with the Duke of Leeds and William Pitt, Morris wrote that Pitt asked him "whether

we would appoint a minister if they would." "I told him," Morris reported, "I could almost promise that we should, but was not authorized to give any positive assurance" (*ASP, Foreign Relations*, I, 123–25).

5. In August, 1789, Washington had sent a commission to negotiate with the powerful Creek Indians of the Southwest. The Creeks and the State of Georgia had been unable to reach any agreement in boundary negotiations, and it was thought that the intervention of the United States might settle their differences. United States officials also hoped to persuade the Creeks to give up their alliance with the Spanish in Louisiana. In November, 1789, the members of the commission returned to New York and reported they had been unsuccessful in their negotiations with the chief of the Creek Indians, Alexander McGillivray. In the spring of 1790, McGillivray was persuaded to come to New York City. With twenty-nine other leaders of the Creeks, he arrived in New York on July 20. A treaty between the United States and McGillivray was dated August 7, 1790.

6. Probably Carlos Howard who at this time came to New York from St. Augustine, Florida, ostensibly on sick leave.

7. Probably an Englishman named Thomas Dalton. According to George Beckwith, McGillivray described Dalton as

". . . a loyalist during the war, [who] had settled in Nova Scotia with his family since the peace; about two years ago he came to the Bahamas in a small craft with some fish, where he was cast away, and shortly afterwards he came into our nation. After discovering the dispositions of this man I recommended it to him to quit the country, but he excused himself saying he was sick, which indeed he was, he remained ill in the lower Creek country for five months, during which I was absent; on my return I found him recovered, and I accompanied him to the seacoast, where I put him on board *one of our ships*, from whence he might have got a passage in some small vessel to the Bahamas; but he had other projects, he had got together some of the Chiefs of the lower Creeks during my absence, had imposed himself upon them for a person of consequence, and made them believe, that he could do great things for them in England; instead therefore of looking out for a passage for the Bahamas in a small vessel he proceeded to London in the ship, and plagued the English Ministry for some time, who I fancy discovered him to be a man of no pretensions to notice. I was very much surprized to find him here on my arrival . . . he has been plaguing me very frequently by messages and notes from day to day, and I was not able to get rid of him, until General [Henry] Knox left directions for him to be told, that if he came again he would be sent to Jail." (Quoted in Lord Dorchester to William Wyndham Grenville, September 25, 1790, Public Archives of Canada, Ottawa, Ontario.)

From Thomas Newton, Junior

Norfolk [*Virginia*] *August 7, 1790.* Forwards the plan of the Cape Henry lighthouse site. Assumes that Hamilton has received Virginia's act of cession.

ALS, RG 26, Lighthouse Letters Received, Vol. "A," Pennsylvania and Southern States, National Archives.

First Conversation of August 8–12 with George Beckwith [1]

[New York, August 8–12, 1790] [2]

. . . Supposed 7.[3] I have mentioned Your application with all the circumstances attending it; there will be no sort of difficulty in Your seeing Mr. Mc.Gillivray whenever you please; [4] General Knox,[5] at whose house he resides, is apprized of it, and will introduce You to him. I cannot think it probable, that any of the attempts to sound Your ideas or dispositions during our negotiations with the Creeks have originated with our Government; it is a mode of acting so very different from that which we should have taken, if any suspicions had existed relative to You personally or to Your government.

I have already mentioned my wish, that when matters shall be brought to a point, and a serious discussion take place between Great Britain and us, pains may be taken to guard against any jealousies in the manner of it; we are a new people, which may occasion a coyness; some of us possibly may entertain doubts of your wanting to mark a superiority, and such an idea may give a turn to the whole negotiation.

D, Public Archives of Canada, Ottawa, Ontario.
   1. This document was enclosed in Lord Dorchester to William Wyndham Grenville, September 25, 1790.
   2. This conversation took place shortly after the "Conversation with George Beckwith," August 7–12, 1790.
   3. "7" was Beckwith's code number for H.
   4. See "Conversation with George Beckwith," August 7–12, 1790.
   5. Henry Knox.

Second Conversation of August 8–12 with George Beckwith [1]

[New York, August 8–12, 1790]

[Beckwith] "Having heard that Governor St. Clair had asserted since his arrival in this place,[2] that the Indians in the Western Territory are induced to continue their hostilities by traders under the protection of Detroit purchasing their prisoners for a sum of money, who compel such prisoners into indentures of a limited servitude for the purposes of repayment and on disadvantageous terms, I judged it of importance to come to an explanation with gentlemen in authority here on such suggestions as these, although the Officers of the King's government, under Your Lordship's orders, are not directly implicated in this business. I therefore explained the matter to 7.[3] adding, that I was the more particularly desirous of doing so, as, what I then communicated, did not arise from common report merely, but had been mentioned to me, in the presence of several persons that very morning by an officer attached to the person of the President, who said, that his information proceeded from Governor St. Clair himself. I acquainted 7. that it consisted with my knowledge, that prisoners had indeed been purchased by persons in Detroit from the Indians, but that this had been done upon principles honorable to the parties, and to the general feeling of humanity; that a young man, so purchased, an inhabitant of Kentucky, had actually arrived here lately on his way home, but I had not seen him, and that a procedure of the nature suggested, was as contrary to Your Lordship's dispositions, as to the general spirit of Your Lordship's instructions to the Officers in the Upper country. 7 assured me, that he had not heard of the circumstance himself, that Governor St. Clair had communicated many things respecting the excesses committed by the Savages, to which the Government here had previously been strangers; although no considerable stroke had been struck, yet the aggregate amounted to some importance, that nothing had appeared from the conversations with the Indians, which marked any thing unfriendly in our Government; they indeed had said when proposals were made to them, that they must consult their father at Detroit, but nothing further. 7. added, that circumstances rendered it probable, measures would shortly be taken for an expedition into the Indian Country in that quarter, and he mentioned it to prevent any alarm at our posts, although he relied on my not speaking of it here; [4] but he did not say against which of the nations beyond the Ohio this expedition was intended to be directed."

D, Public Archives of Canada, Ottawa, Ontario.

1. This document was enclosed in Lord Dorchester to William Wyndham Grenville, September 25, 1790.

2. After futile negotiations with Indian tribes in the Ohio Valley, Arthur St. Clair, governor of the Northwest Territory, decided that only war could produce any "probability of an accomodation with the Indians." With the approval of the Secretary of War and the President, he organized an expedition against the Wabash Indians. St. Clair was in New York City in August to confer with Government officials (ASP, Indian Affairs, I, 92, 98).

3. "7" was Beckwith's code number for H.
4. See note 2.

To Robert Van Rensselaer [1]

[*New York, August 8, 1790.* The dealer's catalogue description of this letter reads: "introducing Count Andreani [2] who is much interested in mineral lands." *Letter not found.*]

ALS, sold at Anderson Galleries, December 6, 1915, Lot 140.
1. Colonel Robert Van Rensselaer of Claverack, New York, was the brother of Mrs. Philip Schuyler.
2. On June 20, 1790, Thomas Jefferson wrote from New York City to David Rittenhouse: "There is a Count Andriani, of Milan, here, who says there is a work on the subject of weights and measures published by Trisi of Milan" (Bergh, *Writings of Thomas Jefferson*, VIII, 41).

From William Barton

Philadelphia, August 9, 1790. "The experience I have had of your very polite attention to me, and the disposition to oblige me, which you were pleased to express in Your letter of the 13th. of May,[1] induce me to hope for a continuance of Your kind Offices in my behalf. Permit me, therefore, to acquaint You, that I have written to Mr. Jefferson, offering my services in the station lately occupied by Mr. Alden.[2] When at New York, I presented to Mr. J. a letter of introduction from Mr. Rittenhouse,[3] who is my mother's brother, and has known me from my Childhood. Wishing, however, that further information might be given to that gentleman by others, I took the liberty of using the names of several gentlemen, at New-York, to whom I have the honor of being known. Perhaps, Sir, I presumed too far on this occasion, in mentioning You, whose personal knowlege of me is, indeed, very inconsiderable. Yet, as You are not unacquainted with my *Character*, I will rely on Your indulgence, in this instance. . . ."

ALS, Hamilton Papers, Library of Congress.
1. Letter not found. Perhaps Barton had written H in April asking for Duer's post as Assistant Secretary of the Treasury. It is clear that his uncle, David Rittenhouse, did so. See H to Thomas Jefferson, May 29, 1790.
2. Roger Alden had been the principal clerk in the Department of State.
3. David Rittenhouse. See H to Jefferson, May 29, 1790, note 1.

To Samuel Russell Gerry

Treasury Department
August 9th. 1790

Sir

You will find enclosed a Commission for the Office of Collector of the Customs for the District of Marblehead to which the President of the United States, with the concurrence of the Senate, has been pleased to appoint you. On the receipt of it you will be pleased to obtain from the Office of your predecessor [1] the laws, & my several Circular letters for your government and information. The forms transmitted from this department to the late Office at Marblehead, will also receive due attention from you. The requisitions of the laws in regard to the Oath & securities will be complied with no doubt and the necessary information will be given to me.

I am Sir   with respect   Your Obedient Servant   A Hamilton

Saml. Russel Gerry Esqr
Collector of the District of Marblehead

LS, Columbia University Libraries.
   1. The former collector at Marblehead, Richard Harris, died in office.

From Morgan Lewis

Rhinebeck [New York] 9th. August 1790.

Dr sir,

I observe that by the funding Plan adopted by Congress, certain Commissioners are to be appointed for the purpose of receiving Subscriptions to the Loan &ca.[1] I do not know if I shall have your good offices for the Appointment to be made in this State. I will not ask them, because as those Officers are to be immediately under your Direction, I think you ought to be at perfect Liberty to procure appointments for whomsoever you wish. The Design of this Letter is principally to acquaint you, that I have Reason to believe Applications have been made to Mr. Morris [2] & some Other Gentlemen of supposed Influence with the President for their Interest in favor of a Connection of mine.[3]

I am with Esteem   your Friend & Servt.   M Lewis

ALS, Hamilton Papers, Library of Congress.
1. "An Act making provision for the (payment of the) Debt of the United States" (1 *Stat.* 138–44 [August 4, 1790]). On August 6, 1790, Washington submitted his nominations for commissioners of loans to the Senate.
2. Presumably Robert Morris, who at this time was a Senator from Pennsylvania.
3. This may be a reference to Peter R. Livingston. Lewis had married Gertrude Livingston, a cousin of Peter R. Livingston. When Dr. John Cochran resigned as commissioner of loans in New York in 1793, Livingston applied for the post.

From Beverley Randolph

Richmond, August 9, 1790. Sends Hamilton deed of cession and plat of the two acres for the Cape Henry lighthouse.

LS, RG 26, Lighthouse Letters Received, Vol. "A," Pennsylvania and Southern States, National Archives; LC, Archives Division, Virginia State Library, Richmond.

To Daniel Eldridge Updike

Treasury Department, August 9, 1790. Encloses Updike's commission as the surveyor of the port of North Kingstown, Rhode Island.

LS, Hamilton College Library, Clinton, New York.

To Nathaniel Gilman [1]

Treasury Department, August 10, 1790. "The Treasurer has my directions to draw upon you for the sum of One Thousand, Seven hundred and Sixty five & 63/90 Dollars, stated by you to be in the late Loan Office of the United States. You will be pleased to pay his Draughts, & a Warrant shall be issued to cover the amount of them, when transmitted hither as Vouchers for the settlement of your Accounts. . . ."

LS, Yale University Library.
1. Formerly Continental loan officer for New Hampshire, Gilman had been appointed commissioner of loans for New Hampshire on August 6, 1790, but declined the appointment. He was replaced on December 24, 1790, by William Gardner.

From Sharp Delany

[*Philadelphia*] *August 11, 1790.* "I was satisfied respecting the ship Brigada[1] by your first letter,[2] but as I had refused a Register for the Birmingham was the cause of my writing a second time,[3] & pointing out the reason for such refusal. . . . The Schooner Betsey is rated as foreign and all others without due papers as you may see by my Quartely settlements. . . ."

LC, Copies of Letters to the Secretary, 1789–1790, Bureau of Customs, Philadelphia.
1. See Delany to H, August 3, 1790.
2. Letter not found.
3. Letter not found.

From Edmund Randolph

New York August 11th. 1790

Sir

I beg leave to answer a question which you propounded to me some time ago.

Several quarter Masters and other public officers, some with salaries, others with Commissions, have received public Money to disburse for public use. Of this money they were robbed, notwithstanding reasonable care on their part. Are they entitled to an allowance for the sums lost; or must their relief depend on legislative provision?

If these public officers were in the same predicament with common Carriers, nothing but robbery by public enemies or destruction by fire and such accidents would excuse. If on the other hand they are to be considered as factors, robbery by theives, without negligence, creates a title to the allowance.

By what criteria shall the analogy be tried? The differencies between a common carrier and a factor are many. But I need only remark that the former holds himself forth as a public servant, and undertakes a single act in doing which there is scarcely any discretion. The latter has a claim for belief and confidence on his constituents, who have probably elected him from a knowledge of him.

Besides he possesses every authority of the principal as to the particular subject. Public convenience too, while it requires, that common carriers should be held by rigid rules requires that confidential agents should be dealt with more leniently. I must therefore compare these public Officers to Factors, and conclude that they are not liable for the money lost in spite of reasonable care.

But as you were pleased, Sir, to mention the interposition of the Legislature, permit me to add, that the relief solicited by those Officers, might be exposed to less exception if previously sanctified by Congress.

Edmund Randolph.

Copy, Hamilton Papers, Library of Congress.

From Edmund Randolph

New York, August 12th. 1790.

Sir,

In answer to your Official letter of the 19th. of February last I beg leave to observe: that the supplies and services therein mentioned as having been furnished and rendered by individuals for the use of the Public, were undoubtedly from the nature of Contracts, originally debits against the United States: that the Officers who granted the Certificates, debentures or other acknowledgments for those supplies and services, were merely the Agents of the United States: that it is the quality of Agents, to bind their principals and that unless some act between the Officer and creditor shall have made the debt peculiarly the debt of the Officer in his private character, it must remain the debt of the United States. I need not say to you, Sir, how various the forms have been in which business of this sort was transacted; no[r] dwell a moment on the propriety of making exceptions from these general principles, in particular cases.

Edmund Randolph.

Copy, Hamilton Papers, Library of Congress.

From George Washington

United States
August 13th. 1790

Sir

The sessions of Congress having closed, and it being my intention to go to Virginia as soon as the public business will permit, and wishing to have my mind as free from public cares during my absence from the seat of government, as circumstances will allow, I am desirous of having such matters as may, by Law, or otherwise, require the Agency or sanction of the President of the United States, brought to my view before my departure. I therefore request that you will cause such business within your Department as may be necessary to receive the aid or approbation of the President, submitted to me as soon as its nature will permit; particularly such matters as relate to the revenue System, Loans & appropriations of money.

I am sir   Yr. most obt. servt.   G. Washington

LC, George Washington Papers, Library of Congress.

To David Humphreys

Treasury Department
New York Aug 14. 1790

Sir

Inclosed is a letter to Messrs. Wilhem and Jan Willinck and Nicholas and J Van Staphorst and Hubbard [1] Merchants Amsterdam, by which, as you will perceive I have directed them to honor your drafts upon them immediately for the sum of One thousand seven hundred and fifty Spanish Milled Dollars and annually for the sum of two thousand two hundred and fifty like dollars to be computed from the fourteenth day of August next and to continue until further order. This is the most convenient arrangement I can now make and I trust will answer your purpose [2] for the present.

Send me if you please a couple of your signatures for copies of the letter to Messrs Willincks &c

I have the honor to be with great consideration & esteem Sir Your Obedient & hum serv   A Hamilton
                                             Secretary of the Treasury

P. S You will please inclose your signature as mentioned in the inclosed letter.

David Humphreys. Esquire

ALS, The Andre deCoppet Collection, Princeton University Library.
    1. Letter not found.
    2. See Thomas Jefferson to H, August 14, 1790, note 1.

From Thomas Jefferson

New York August 14th. 1790.

Dr: Sir,

Colonel Humphreys will be entitled to draw from the Treasury of the United States from about this date till further order, at the rate of two thousand two hundred and fifty dollars, a year, and in addition to this sum for postage of letters, the amount of which cannot be known beforehand, and will not be considerable. This is to be charged to the fund of the foreign department. I must ask the favour of you to let him know in what manner he can receive this money in the several situations he will be in.[1] I think he ought to receive the full sum and to have nothing to do with the loss or gain of exchange, charges of negociating &c. I have the honor to be with great respect and esteem Dear Sir &c.   Thomas Jefferson

LC, Papers of the Continental Congress, National Archives.
    1. Jefferson was sending David Humphreys to Europe on a threefold mission. His most important task was to brief William Carmichael, United States chargé d'affaires at Madrid, on the administration's Mississippi River policy. Second, Humphreys was to negotiate an exchange of diplomatic missions with Portugal. Third, he was to transmit some papers to Gouverneur Morris who was then on an informal mission to Great Britain.

To Thomas Jefferson

[New York, August 14, 1790]

Dear Sir

I inclose you a warrant for 500 Dollars for Col Humphreys use;[1] and shall for the present take arrangements for paying his salary or allowance by a Credit on our Commissioners in Holland.[2] Hereafter we will endeavour to put this matter upon some more convenient footing.

I draw in your favour to avoid introducing Col Humphreys into the books of the Treasury which would excite more conjecture than is perhaps desireable in the outset considering the nature of his mission. I hope this will be agreeable to you and remain with very great respect and esteem Dr Sir   Yr Obed ser   A Hamilton

Aug 14. 1790
The Secretary of State

ALS, Thomas Jefferson Papers, Library of Congress.
    1. D, Thomas Jefferson Papers, Library of Congress.
    2. Willink, Van Staphorst, and Hubbard. See H to David Humphreys, August 14, 1790.

From John C. Wynkoop [1]

Kinderhook [*New York*] *August 16, 1790.* "The goodness of your heart will naturally execuse the workings of filial affection and induce you to pardon me for writing you once more in behalf of my Father Mr. Cornelius Wynkoop [2] of Kingston in the County of Ulster. I find that Mr. John Cochran has been lately appointed Loan officer for this State. If therefore you can recommand my Father as a Clerk to that Gentleman, I shall ever esteem it a peculiar favor. . . ."

LS, Hamilton Papers, Library of Congress.
    1. Wynkoop was an attorney. His wife's family lived in Kinderhook.
    2. Before the American Revolution Cornelius C. Wynkoop had been a New York City shopkeeper. During the war he served as an assistant commissary of issues. Letter not found.

From Benjamin Lincoln

Boston, August 17, 1790. States that members of the lighter that unloaded fish illegally from the schooner from Nova Scotia [1] "had no idea that they were breaking the law of the United States." Asks approval for oil contract for lighthouses. States that "the Light Houses at the Gurnet [2] are nearly ready to tumble down from the want of repairs."

LC, RG 36, Collector of Customs at Boston, Letter Book, 1790–1797, National Archives; copy, RG 56, Letters from the Collector at Boston, National Archives.
  1. See Lincoln to H, July 17, 1790.
  2. Gurnet Point is at the entrance to Plymouth Bay.

To Joseph Whipple

[*New York, August 17, 1790.* In a letter of September 13, 1790, Whipple referred to Hamilton's "letter dated the 17th. August." *Letter not found.*]

To Jeremiah Olney

Treasury Department, August 18, 1790. "It appears on examination that the Sloop Sharlottes [1] license ought to have been dated in July last, as you supposed. . . . I beg your attention to that part of my Circular letters, that instructs the Collectors to make weekly returns to this office, of their receipts and payments and of the Cash in their hands. . . ." [2]

Copy, RG 56, Letters to the Collector at Providence, National Archives; copy, RG 56, Letters to Collectors at Small Ports, "Set G," National Archives.
  1. *Charlotte.* See Olney to H, August 2, 1790.
  2. See "Treasury Department Circular to the Collectors of the Customs," September 22, October 2, 14, 1789.

To Meletiah Jordan

[*New York, August 19, 1790.* On January 1, 1791, Jordan wrote to Hamilton: "Your letter of the 19th. of August . . . I have received." *Letter not found.*]

To Beverley Randolph

Treasury Department
August 19th 1790

sir

I have the honor to acknowledge the Receipt of your letter of the 9th instant, containing a Cession of two Acres of Ground on Cape

Henry to the United States, intended for the Site of the Light House. On the return of the President, who is now on a visit to Rhode Island, measures will be taken for the early completion of a Building, so necessary to the Commerce of the States on the Chessapeak.

I have the honor to be very respectfully   Your Excellencys Most Obedient Servant   Alexander Hamilton

His Excellency Beverly Randolph Esquire
Govr of Virginia Richmond.

LS, Archives Division, Virginia State Library, Richmond.

From William Allibone

Philadelphia, August 20, 1790. Complains of the difficulty of obtaining contractors for maintenance work on the aids to navigation in the Delaware River. Urges Hamilton to expedite approval of the contract for the repairs to the Cape Henlopen lighthouse.

ALS, RG 26, Lighthouse Letters Received, Vol. "A," Pennsylvania and Southern States, National Archives.

From Sharp Delany

[Philadelphia] August 20, 1790. "My last Quarters Accounts I forward for settlement by this Post—with receipts of the Bank June 26th 9,000 Dollars & July 31, for 35,000. I took the Liberty of mentioning to you before the necessity of having a similarity of Papers throughout the different Custom houses of the Union. I beg leave to lay it before you again. . . ."

LC, Copies of Letters to the Secretary, 1789-1790, Bureau of Customs, Philadelphia.

Treasury Department Circular to the Collectors of the Customs

Treasury Department
August 20. 1790.

Sir,

The act of July last, imposing duties on the tonnage of vessels,[1]

provides for the restitution of the foreign duty which has been incurred, by ships or vessels of the United States, by reason of their not having a certificate of registry or enrollment and a licence, when trading Coastwise, or engaged in the fisheries. This refund is to be made in each instance, at the custom house where the duty was paid; and in such manner, that the American tonnage duty of six Cents is to be retained for the United States; and the extra sum of forty four Cents, to which foreigners only, are liable, is to be repaid.

I am, Sir, Your Obedient Ser   Alexander Hamilton

LS, to Charles Lee, Charles Lee Papers, Library of Congress; L[S], to Benjamin Lincoln, RG 36, Collector of Customs at Boston, Letters from the Treasury, 1789–1807, Vol. 4, National Archives; L[S], Office of the Secretary, United States Treasury Department; copy, RG 56, Circulars of the Office of the Secretary, "Set T," National Archives; copy, United States Finance Miscellany, Treasury Circulars, Library of Congress.
1. "An Act imposing duties on the tonnage of ships or vessels (1 Stat. 135–36 [July 20, 1790]). H is referring to Section 4 of this measure.

From William Allibone

Philadelphia, August 21, 1790. "Enclosed herewith is a new Contract with Abraham Hargis [1] as keeper of the Light House at Cape Henlopen. . . . Mr. Hargis in agreeing to a reduction of his Sallary expresses a full confidence that when his comparative situation with respect to other Keepers of Light Houses, is fully Investigated, it will be augmented again, And alledges in support of that expectation that Exclusive of his being the largest of the Light Houses, His Situation is more disadvantageous then any other Keeper, Altho' their Sallerys and perquisites may be no more. . . ."

ALS, RG 26, Lighthouse Letters Received, Vol. "A," Pennsylvania and Southern States, National Archives.
1. For the old contract, see Allibone to H, July 3, 1790.

From Samuel Meredith [1]

[*New York, August 21, 1790.* On August 28, 1790, Hamilton wrote to Meredith: "I received your letter of the 21st Instant." *Letter not found.*]

1. Meredith was treasurer of the United States from September 11, 1789, to December 1, 1807.

To Robert Morris

[New York, August 21, 1790]

The Secretary of the Treasury has the Honor to return the enclosed letter to Mr. Morris.

August 21. 1790

Letter sent, in unidentified handwriting, New Hampshire Historical Society, Concord.

From Henry Knox

[New York] 23d August, 1790.

An estimate of the expense of employing, for three months, one thousand seven hundred militia, and four hundred continental troops, in an expedition against the Wabash Indians—two hundred of the militia to be mounted.[1]

The Militia.

The pay, ... $24,012
The subsistence and rations at 16-90ths of a dollar, . 31,302
Forage for the field and staff officers, ... 234
$55,548

The Continental Troops

Additional expense of subsistence and rations to the continental troops, during the same period. This expense arises from the contract; the price of the ration at fort Washington is stated at six and a half ninetieths of a dollar; but, from that post to the places of operation, the price will be sixteen-ninetieths, ... 4,146
The quartermaster's department, including the hire of four hundred horses, purchase of boats, and transportation, . . 30,000
Contingencies, ... 10,306
$100,000

The contractors are to execute the duties of the quartermaster's department; the extra services, therefore, which will be required of them, independent of the sum set down for contingencies, will amount to sixty-five thousand six hundred and eighty-two dollars. One half of this sum may be necessary to be advanced immediately, to enable them to perform effectually the services required.

ASP, Indian Affairs, I, 98.
    1. The expedition against the Indians took place in September and October, 1790.

From Tobias Lear

[*New York*] *August 23, 1790*. Transmits "three Commissions [of customs officials] which have received the signature of the President."

LC, George Washington Papers, Library of Congress.

From Jeremiah Olney

Providence, August 23, 1790. Suspects that "a note for one hundred Dollars, issued . . . at the Bank of New York" is a counterfeit. Asks Hamilton for instructions. Asks if the expense of appraising imported goods should be defrayed by the importer or the government.

Copy, RG 56, Letters from the Collector at Providence, National Archives.

To Samuel and John Smith [1]

[*New York, August 23, 1790*. The dealer's catalogue description of this letter reads: "On financial matters." *Letter not found.*]

ALS, sold by Anderson Galleries, May 2, 1922, Lot 642.
    1. Samuel and John Smith, Baltimore merchants, were brothers.

From Tobias Lear

[*New York*] *August 24, 1790*. States that the President has approved the contract for repairs on the Cape Henlopen lighthouse.

LS, RG 26, "Segregated" Lighthouse Records, National Archives; LC, George Washington Papers, Library of Congress.

To William Allibone

[*New York, August 25, 1790*. The endorsement on the letter that Allibone wrote to Hamilton on August 21, 1790, reads: "Answd. 25th Augt. 90." *Letter not found.*]

From Benjamin Lincoln

Boston 25 August 1790.

Sir

Sometime since, a Cargo of Sugars were imported into this Town, among them, were two or three tons of the worst kind, indeed it could hardly be called Sugar; it sold for about ⅖ths of what the remainder of the Cargo sold for, can any allowance be made on account of the duty?

The British Consul[1] arrived here a few days since, with his family, he has brought a quantity of household furniture. By a resolve of Congress,[2] Consuls are not entitled to any peculiar advantages respecting the Duties on the articles they import. Is there any Law now in being which will justify me should I deliver the Furniture, without securing the Duties? I wish you would favour me with your ideas and direction on the subject.

I have the honour of being Sir, with perfect esteem your obedient servant.

The honourable Secretary of the Treasury

Copy, RG 36, Collector of Customs at Boston, Letters from the Treasury, 1789–1807, Vol. 4, National Archives; copy, RG 56, Letters from the Collector at Boston, National Archives.
1. The British consul for Boston was Thomas MacDonough.
2. On September 28, 1787, Congress had resolved:
"Whereas doubts have in certain instances arisen whether foreign consuls residing in the United States, are entitled to an exemption from such legal imposts and duties on merchandizes by them imported for their own use, as are payable by other Subjects of their respective Nations.
"*Resolved* That no consuls of any nation are entitled to such exemptions in the United States." (*JCC*, XXXIII, 552.)

From Tobias Lear

United States.
August 26th. 1790.

sir

In obedience to the command of the President of the United states, I have the honor to inform you that he approves of the enclosed Drafts of a Power and Instructions which have been submitted to him, respecting a Loan of twelve million of Dollars; [1] but thinks an addition to the instructions given to the Agent,[2] to the following effect might be proper, for reasons which he will assign to you, Vizt. "That the Agent shall never open a loan for more than one million of Dollars at a time, nor open a new loan 'till the old one has been expressly approved of by the President of the United States."

I have the honor to be with the highest respect sir   Yr. most Obt. humble servant   Tobias Lear.

Secretary to the President of the United states.

LC, George Washington Papers, Library of Congress.
    1. Section 2 of "An Act making provision for the (payment of the) Debt of the United States," which became law on August 4, 1790, reads in part: "Be it further enacted, That the President of the United States be, and he is hereby authorized, to cause to be honored on behalf of the United States, a sum or sums, not exceeding in the whole twelve millions of dollars . . ." (1 Stat. 139).
    2. The Dutch bankers, Wilhem and Jan Willink, Nicholaas and Jacob Van Staphorst, and Nicholas Hubbard.

To Charles Lee

Treasury Department
August 26. 1790.

Sir

I had this morning the honor of a Message from the President of the United States [1] signifying his wish, that the Monies for which he may have occasion during his absence from the seat of Government may be found in your office. I have therefore to request that you will pay to the order of the President of the United States any monies he may desire.

I am Sir   Your Obedient Servant   Alexander Hamilton

Copy, RG 56, Letters to Collectors at Small Ports, "Set G," National Archives.
   1. Letter not found. Washington was about to leave for a vacation at Mount Vernon.

Meeting of the Commissioners of the Sinking Fund

[New York, August 26, 1790]

Pursuant to the act, entitled "An act making provision for the reduction of the public debt," [1] the following persons named therein, on Thursday, the 26th day of August, 1790, at the city of New York, met and proceeded to business, viz.

John Adams, Vice President of the United States and President of the Senate,

John Jay, Chief Justice,

Thomas Jefferson, Secretary of State,

Alexander Hamilton, Secretary of the Treasury.

The Secretary of the Treasury communicated for the information of the Board sundry papers,[2] as follow:

No. 1. Statement of the probable product of duties on imports and tonnage from the first of August, 1789, to the last of December next, and of the amount of the appropriations thereout; shewing what surplus will remain at the end of the present year, after satisfying those appropriations.

No. 2. Abstract of the nett amount of duties which have accrued from August, 1789, to the 31st of March, 1790.

No. 3. Statement of the moneys now in the treasury and in the hands of the several collectors of the customs, and which may be expected to be received to the end of the year 1791, together with the sums to be paid out of the same; shewing what surplus will remain to be disposed of according to the act above mentioned.

No. 4. General statement of the domestic debt.

The Board adjourned till to-morrow.

ASP, Finance, I, 234–35.
   1. 1 *Stat.* 186 (August 12, 1790). Section 2 states: "*And be it further enacted,*

That the purchases to be made of the . . . debt, shall be made under the direction of the President of the Senate, the Chief Justice, the Secretary of State, the Secretary of the Treasury, and the Attorney General for the time being; and who, or any three of whom, with the approbation of the President of the United States, shall cause the said purchases to be made in such manner, and under such regulations as shall appear to them best calculated to fulfill the intent of this act."

2. These papers are printed in *ASP, Finance*, I, 238–39.

To George Washington

[New York, August 26, 1790]

The Secretary of the Treasury respectfully begs leave to submit to the President of the United States copies of a letter from Messrs. Wilhem & Jan Willink and Nicholas and Jacob Van Staphorst & Hubbard of the 25th. day of January last, and of an answer thereto of the 7th. day of May following.

The President will perceive that the last mentioned letter was formed upon a plan not to discourage the progress of the Loan which had been set on foot, and yet to leave a final determination upon it open.

The undertaking that loan without previous authority, was irregular and in that view exceptionable; though the motives assigned for it have considerable force as they respect the credit of the United States; and, so far as they may be supposed to have really operated, afford a plausible apology for the measure.

As far however as the giving a sanction to it might serve as a precedent, it would not be free from objection; for it certainly would consist neither with the dignity nor the interest of the government to encourage its Agents in the practice of employing its credit in unauthorised loans.

But as an acceptance of the loan may be accompanied with a prohibition of similar attemps hereafter, which would doubtless have the effect of preventing them, it is submitted as the opinion of the Secretary, that the irregularity of the proceeding ought not to preclude such acceptance, if the loan itself be in other respects desirable; and the following considerations appear in his judgment to render it so. The terms are probably as advantageous as the present agitations of Europe, which must necessarily create an unusual demand for money, authorise an expectation of obtaining.

A sum of one hundred and seventy two thousand Dollars will be wanting at the commencement of the ensuing year to discharge the interest which will then fall due on the Dutch Loans, which it is essential to the credit of the United States should be paid, and the timely payment of which could with difficulty be accomplished in any other way. There was on the 21st. of March last due to Spain for principal and interest of her advances and loans, the sum of, two hundred & forty thousand and eight Dollars, and eighty nine Cents: And to France there will be due at the end of the present year for arrears of interest and certain instalments of the principal of her Loans a sum little short of three millions eight hundred thousand Dollars.

Powerful considerations of different kinds, which will readily occur to the mind of the President urge to exertions to discharge these demands. The Minister of the Finances of France has, thro' the Chargé D'affaires of the United States at that Court, *solicited* that the money arising from the Loan in question, of which he has been apprised, might be applied in part payment of the Debt due to that nation.[1] Its peculiar situation at the present juncture contains an appeal to the sensibility, as well as to the policy and honor of this Country in favor of that requisition.

If these reasons appear to the President sufficient to induce his sanction to the loan in question, it will remain to consider, under what act, it will be most expedient to authorise its being made, whether that of the 4th.[2] or that of the 12th.[3] of the present month, or whether it may not be advisable to authorise it partly under one & partly under the other.

It is conceived that the business may easily take the latter form, if deemed eligible; and this is recommended by the consideration that it will contribute in a degree to all the purposes which require to be promoted.

If two thirds of the sum should be borrowed on account of the twelve millions and the remaining third on account of the two millions, the next half years interest in Holland may be discharged, the arrears of Interest on the Debt due to Spain may be paid off, a respectable payment may be made to France as a prelude to more considerable ones, and a sum of consequence to the operation, would remain towards the reduction of our Debt and supporting our funds in conformity to the intention of the last mentioned Act.

All which is humbly submitted   Alexander Hamilton
                                        secretary of the Treasury

LC, George Washington Papers, Library of Congress.
    1. See William Short to H, April 4, 1790.
    2. "An Act making provision for the (payment of the) Debt of the United States," 1 *Stat.* 138–44. Section 2 of this act authorized a loan of $12,000,000.
    3. "An Act making Provision for the Reduction of the Public Debt," 1 *Stat.* 186–87. Section 4 of this act authorized a loan of $2,000,000.

To George Washington

Treasury Department, August 26, 1790. "The Secretary of the Treasury has the honor respectfully to submit to the President of the United States a new contract made by William Allibone,[1] Superintendant of the Light-house and other establishments on the Delaware, with Abraham Hargis as Keeper of the said ligh house. . . ."

LC, George Washington Papers, Library of Congress.
    1. See Allibone to H, August 21, 1790.

Meeting of the Commissioners of the Sinking Fund

[New York, August 27, 1790]

At a board convened at the City of New York on Friday the 27th. of August 1790. pursuant to the Act entitled, "An Act makeing provision for the reduction of the Public Debt" [1]

Present

John Adams, vice President of the United states & President of the Senate
John Jay, Chief justice
Thomas Jefferson, secretary of State
Alexander Hamilton, secretary of the Treasury

The Board came to the following resolution subject to the approbation of the President of the United States.

That the Secretary of the Treasury cause to be applied a sum not exceeding fifty thousand Dollars per month, computing from the first day of September next, towards the purchase of the present Domestic Debt of the United states; that the purchases begin at the City of New York and there continue until the end of October next, and that they be then transferred to the City of Philadelphia and there continue until the last day of December next, unless sooner otherwise ordered. That they be made by the Treasurer, under the direction of the Secretary, of the Treasury, at the market price, & in an open and public manner. And that the said Treasurer be directed to keep a regular account of his purchases, of the times when, prices at which, and of the persons from whom they are made, and to render the same for settlement, to the Auditor of the Treasury at the end of every quarter of a year, and when settled to present a Copy thereof to the Board.

The foregoing resolution is a true copy from the minutes in my possession

A. Hamilton
secy of the Treasury

Approved Augt. 28th, 1790
Go. Washington
President U. States

LC, George Washington Papers, Library of Congress.
1. 1 *Stat.* 186–87 (August 12, 1790).

From Jeremiah Olney

Providence, August 27, 1790. "Enclosed is my Return of Cash for the last week. . . . Lest the original letter of which the enclosed is a duplicate, should have miscarried, I beg leave to call your attention to its contents.[1] A small importation, besides the Sails &c was made by Messrs Jos & Wm Russell in the Brig Mary from Dublin, the duties on which remains unliquidated on account of those articles which they conceive ought to pay no duty."

Copy, RG 56, Letters from the Collector at Providence, National Archives.
1. See Olney to H, July 19, 1790.

To Walter Stewart

New York Aug 27 1790

Dear Sir

Since I wrote you last,[1] I have engaged a house for an *office*, which is at the corner of Chestnut, and, I think, third Street, or in other words, the house of Mr. Coxe,[2] formerly occupied by the President of Congress.

I give you this intimation that you may endeavour to procure one for me, as near *that* as you can, having regard to the quality and situation of the house.

One near Mrs. Allen's[3] has been mentioned to me, now occupied by Mr. Mead,[4] who, it is said is about to leave it. From the description I have had of it I am led to think it may suit me. But I leave all to you.

If a house, in a convenient situation, cannot be had in time I would wish only to take it for a few months that I may be at liberty to look out for a better. I remain   Yr friend & ser   A Hamilton

ALS, New-York Historical Society, New York City.
    1. H to Stewart, August 5, 1790.
    2. Presumably Daniel Coxe, a Philadelphia merchant whose house was at 93 Chestnut Street.
    3. An entry in the Philadelphia Directory for 1791 reads: "Allen Mrs. gentlewoman, 155 Chestnut Street."
    4. George Meade was a Philadelphia merchant, who was the brother-in-law and former partner of Thomas FitzSimons. Meade's house at this time was on Walnut Street just west of Third Street.

From George Washington

United States August 27th 1790.

(*Secret*)

Provided the dispute between Great Britain and Spain[1] should come to the decision of Arms, from a variety of circumstances (individually unimportant and inconclusive, but very much the reverse when compared and combined) there is no doubt in my mind, that New Orleans and the Spanish Posts above it on the Mississippi will be among the first attempts of the former, and that the reduction of them will be undertaken by a combined operation from Detroit.

The *Consequences* of having so formidable and enterprising a people as the British on both our flanks and rear, with their Navy in front, as they respect our Western settlements which may be seduced thereby, as they regard the Security of the Union and its commerce with the West Indies, are too obvious to need enumeration.

What then should be the answer of the Executive of the United States to Lord Dorchester,[2] in case he should apply for permission to march Troops through the Territory of said States from Detroit to the Mississippi?

What notice ought to be taken of the measure, if it should be undertaken without leave, which is the most probable proceeding of the two?

The opinion of the Secretary of the Treasury is requested in writing upon the above statement.[3]

Go: Washington

The Secretary of the Treasury.

LS, George Washington Papers, Library of Congress; Df, in writing of David Humphreys, George Washington Papers, Library of Congress.
   1. This was the Nootka Sound crisis. Nootka, on the west coast of Vancouver Island, was the center of the Northwest fur trade. Late in 1789 the Spanish, who claimed the area by the Treaty of Tordesillas in 1494, seized two British trading ships in Nootka Harbor. News of this action did not reach Britain until the spring of 1790. See H to Washington, July 8, 1790.
   2. Dorchester was Governor-General of Canada.
   3. Washington also asked John Jay, Thomas Jefferson, and Henry Knox for their opinions on these matters.

From John Wheelock [1]

Dartmouth College [Hanover, New Hampshire]
August 27th. 1790

Sir!

The Trustees of this literary Institution have desired me to express their congratulations at the prosperous state of our national finances under your wise direction. They have desired me to communicate the high sense, which they retain of your talents, and political knowledge.

Influenced by an exalted Opinion of your merit, they make a tender of the highest Honours, that any University can confer. They beg, Sir, your acceptance of the *Degree* of *Doctor* of the *Laws* of *Nature* and *Nations*. It is a testimony unequal to their respect; but it is the best within their power to give. The Diploma will be completed, and forwarded to you by some safe conveyance, so soon as may be convenient.

I have the honour to be, in behalf of the Board of Trustees,   Sir! Your most obedient, & very humble servant,   John Wheelock

The honourable Alexander Hamilton Esq: L.L.D.&c. &c.

LS, Hamilton Papers, Library of Congress.
    1. Wheelock was the son of Eleazar Wheelock, founder and first president of Dartmouth College. He succeeded his father as president upon the latter's death in 1779.

To Thomas Jefferson

[New York, August 28, 1790]

Dear Sir

I request the favour of you to furnish me with two Copies of each of the following acts certified or exemplified under the Great Seal. That intitled "An Act making provision for the debt of the United States" [1] and that intitled "An Act making provision for the reduction of the public Debt" [2] and also with two copies exemplified or certified in like manner of my Commission as Secretary of the Treasury.

As a Vessel is expected to sail this Evening for Amsterdam by which I wish to forward some of those copies [3] I shall be obliged by their being ready as soon as possible.

I have the honor to be With great respect & regard Sir

New York Aug 28. 1790
T Jefferson Esqr

AL[S], RG 59, Miscellaneous Letters, 1790–1791, National Archives.
    1. 1 *Stat.* 138–44 (August 4, 1790).
    2. 1 *Stat.* 186–87 (August 12, 1790).

3. These documents were enclosed in H to Willink, Van Staphorst, and Hubbard, August 28, 1790.

From Tobias Lear

United States.
August 28th. 1790

T. Lear has the honor respectfully to observe to the Secretary of the Treasury in reply to a request [1] from the naval officer of the District of New York [2] which was this day submitted to the President of the united States, that altho' it is contrary to the general sentiment and wish of the President that any officers under the general government and particularly one of such importance as the naval officer of New York, shou'd be long absent from their trusts; yet in the present instance if the reasons assigned by the naval officer shou'd appear sufficient to the Secy. of the Treasury, and a Deputy is appointed who shall be approved of by the Secretary; The President consents to the absence of the naval officer of New York for six months.

By the Presidents command   T: Lear

Secy to the President of the U. States.

The Secretary of the Treasury.

LC, George Washington Papers, Library of Congress.
1. See H to George Washington, August 28, 1790.
2. Benjamin Walker, a business associate of William Duer, was going to France as an agent for the Scioto Company.

From Tobias Lear [1]

[New York] August 28, 1790. States that the President has approved the Cape Henlopen lighthouse keeper's contract.

LS, RG 26, "Segregated" Lighthouse Records, National Archives; LC, George Washington Papers, Library of Congress; copy, RG 26, Lighthouse Deeds and Contracts, National Archives.
1. This letter is in reply to H to George Washington, August 26, 1790.

To Samuel Meredith

Treasury Department
August 28th. 1790

Sir

I received your letter of the 21st Instant [1] and delayed answering it untill it could be determined whether there would be occasion for your presence here. It being intended that the purchases to be made at New York under "the Act providing for the Reduction of the public Debt" [2] shall be effected by the Treasurer of the United States, and it being deemed proper to commence the operation on the first Monday in September next, (the sixth day of that Month) I find it necessary to request your return to the Seat of Government, so early as to admit of three days reflection on the mode of proceeding.

I am Sir very respectfully   Your Obedient Servant   A Hamilton

During your absence some Bills have been drawn by your Clerk Mr Samuel Anderson, with my permission on the Bank of North America. The receipts for the Cash from the Bank of New York having been first exhibited, the Cashier of the Bank of North America has been requested to pay them.

Samuel Meredith Esquire
Treasurer of the U States.

LS, Ursinus College Library, Collegeville, Pennsylvania.
    1. Letter not found.
    2. This act provided for the creation of a sinking fund for the purchase of government securities on the open market (1 *Stat.* 186–87 [August 12, 1790]). See also "Meeting of the Commissioners of the Sinking Fund," August 27, 1790.

From Timothy Pickering [1]

Philadelphia August 28. 1790.

Dear Sir,

The inclosed letter,[2] I sent at its date from Wyoming by a private hand, in a packet addressed to Mr. Hodgdon [3] to be forwarded to you: but to-day it came to hand, thro' the post office.

I find that Congress have been pleased to grant 40,000 dollars to discharge certain arrears due from my late department.[4] Mr. Anspach has written to me [5] on the subject. He states that the mode of paying the creditors, in the ordinary course thro' the treasury department will be circuitous & tedious & occasion much trouble to him & Mr. Wolfe,[6] in certifying the accounts to be discharged. To avoid this inconvenience, I have informed him That I would take the liberty to suggest to your consideration the expediency of issuing from time to time such gross sums to him as you should think proper; an account of the expenditure of which for your satisfaction he might lay before you, previous to the issuing every fresh supply; the sums so issued to be lodged for safety in the bank. He will probably wait upon you respecting this matter. My object in this intimation is to facilitate settlements with the creditors, & to do it without imposing uncompensated burthens on Mr. Anspach & Mr. Wolfe.

I am respectfully yr. most obedt. servt.   T.P.

Honble. A Hamilton Esqr.
Secy. of the Treasy.

ADfS, Massachusetts Historical Society, Boston.
    1. For background to this letter, see Pickering to H, November 19, 25, 1789; H to Pickering, November 19, 1789; H to Peter Anspach, December 5, 1789; Anspach to H, December 30, 1789, July 2, 1790. Also see "Report on Additional Sums Necessary for the Support of the Government," August 5, 1790.
    2. Presumably Pickering to H, July 20, 1790.
    3. Samuel Hodgdon was a Philadelphia merchant who was a friend and business associate of Pickering. He had served as commissary general of military stores from 1781 to 1784, and he was appointed quartermaster general of the United States Army in March, 1791.
    4. "An Act making certain appropriations therein mentioned" (1 *Stat.* 185–86 [August 12, 1790]).
    5. Anspach to Pickering, August 13, 1790, Massachusetts Historical Society, Boston.
    6. David Wolfe. See Pickering to H, November 19, 1789.

To George Washington

Treasury Department
August 28th. 1790

The Secretary of the Treasury has the honor respectfully to submit to the President of the U. States for his determination a request from the Naval officer of the District of New York.[1] The Secretary humbly remarks, that it appears desireable, as far as possible, to avoid absences of such important Officers for so long a duration, but that if the nature of the reasons should induce the President to grant the request, the naval Officer will no doubt leave his public business in the hands of a Deputy, of competent abilities, for whom he will be responsible.[2]

Alexander Hamilton
Secretary of the Treasury

LC, George Washington Papers, Library of Congress.
  1. Benjamin Walker. William Duer was sending Walker, a business associate, to France to untangle the Scioto Company's affairs.
  2. For the reply to this letter, see Tobias Lear to H, August 28, 1790.

From George Washington [1]

[New York, August 28, 1790]

By virtue of the several Acts, the one entitled, "An Act making provision for the Debt of the U. States." [2] and the other entitled, "An Act making provision for the reduction of the Public Debt." [3]

I do hereby authorise and empower you, by yourself, or any other person or persons, to borrow on behalf of the United States, within the said States or elsewhere, a sum or sums, not exceeding in the whole fourteen millions of Dollars and to make or cause to be made for that purpose such Contract or Contracts as shall be necessary, and for the interest of the said States; subject to the restrictions and limitations in the said several acts contained: And for so doing this shall be your sufficient Warrant.

In testimony whereof I have caused the seal of the United States to be hereunto affixed. Given under my hand at the City of New York this twenty eighth day of August in the year of our Lord one thousand seven hundred and ninety.

G. Washington

LC, George Washington Papers, Library of Congress.
  1. A copy of this document was enclosed in H's "Report on Foreign Loans," February 13, 1793. This document is in reply to H to Washington, August 26, 1790.

2. This act, which became law on August 4, 1790, authorized a loan of $12,000,000 (1 *Stat.* 139).

3. This act, which became law on August 12, 1790, authorized a loan of $2,000,000 (1 *Stat.* 187).

From George Washington [1]

[New York, August 28, 1790]

Having thought fit to commit to you the charge of borrowing on behalf of the United States a sum or sums not exceeding in the whole Fourteen Millions of Dollars pursuant to the several Acts, the one entitled, "An act making provision for the Debt of the United States," [2] the other entitled, "An Act making provision for the reduction of the Public Debt." [3]

I do hereby make known to you, that in the execution of the said trust, you are to observe and follow the orders and directions following Vizt. Except where otherwise specially directed by me you shall employ in the negotiation of any Loan or Loans which may be made in any foreign Country   [4]

You shall borrow or cause to be borrowed on the best terms which shall be found practicable (and within the limitations prescribed by Law as to time of repayment and rate of interest) such sum or sums as shall be sufficient to discharge, as well all installments or parts of the principal of the foreign Debt, which now are due or shall become payable to the end of the year one thousand seven hundred and ninety one, as all interest and arrears of interest, which now are, or shall become due in respect to the said Debt, to the same end of the year one thousand seven hundred and ninety one; and you shall apply or cause to be applied the monies which shall be so borrowed with all convenient dispatch to the payment of the said instalments and parts of the principal and interest and arrears of the interest of the said debt. You shall not extend the amount of the loan which you shall make or cause to be made, beyond the sum which shall be necessary for completing such payment, unless it can be done upon terms more advantageous to the United States than those upon which the residue of the said debt shall stand or be. But if the said residue or any part of the same can be paid off by new Loans upon terms of advantage to the United States you shall cause such further loans, as may be requisite to that end, to be made, and the proceeds thereof to be applied accordingly. And for carrying into effect the objects and purposes of aforesaid, I do hereby further empower you to make, or cause to be made with whomsoever it may concern such Contract or Contracts being of a nature relative thereto, as shall be found needful and conducive to the interest of the United States.

If any negotiation with any Prince or State to whom any part of the said Debt may be due, should be requisite, the same shall be carried on thro' the person who in capacity of Minister, Chargé des Affaires, or otherwise, now is, or thereafter shall be charged with transacting the affairs of the United States with such Prince or State, for which purpose I shall direct the secretary of State, with whom you are in this behalf to consult and concert, to cooperate with you.

Given under my hand at the City of New York this twenty eighth day of August in the year of our Lord one thousand seven hundred and ninety.

G: Washington [5]

LC, George Washington Papers, Library of Congress; copy, William Short Papers, Library of Congress.

1. A copy of this document was enclosed in H's "Report on Foreign Loans," February 13, 1793. For background to this document, see H to Washington, August 26, 1790; Washington to H, August 28, 1790.

2. 1 *Stat.* 138–44 (August 4, 1790).

3. 1 *Stat.* 186–87 (August 12, 1790).

4. Space left blank in MS. In the copy in the William Short Papers, the words "William Short, Esquire" were inserted.

5. In the copy in the William Short Papers there is an endorsement in H's writing at the end of this letter which reads: "A True Copy A Hamilton Secretary of the Treasy."

To Wilhem and Jan Willink, Nicholaas and Jacob Van Staphorst, and Nicholas Hubbard [1]

Treasury Department
August 28th 1790

Gentlemen

Since the date of my last letter to you,[2] the Legislature of the

LS, William Short Papers, Library of Congress.

1. A copy of this letter was enclosed in H's "Report on Foreign Loans," February 13, 1793.

2. This letter is dated July 17, 1790.

United States have passed two Acts, that is to say, on the fourth[3] and twelfth[4] of the present month; by which, among other things, they empower the President to cause to be borrowed on account of the United States Fourteen Millions of Dollars; The execution of which power has been by him committed to me: as will appear by a copy of each of those acts and of the President's commission or warrant to me[5] herewith transmitted, authenticated in due form.

In consequence of these proceedings I am now in condition to determine on the provisional Loan announced in your letter of the 25th day of January last; and after due consideration I have concluded to accept and ratify it. For this purpose I send a power,[6] which I doubt not you will find competent, executed under my hand and the seal of the Treasury.

While I pursue, by this acceptance, what appears to me to be the interest of the United States, I am pleased with the opportunity of doing a thing, which will be agreeable to you. At the same time, your own judgment will suggest to you, that in dismissing all scruple about the manner in which the business has been undertaken, I give you a proof of my confidence, that no inconvenience will result from the precedent. The qualifications annexed by you to the undertaking, shew, that you were fully sensible of its delicacy, and satisfy me, that I need not press upon you the inadmissibility of any thing of a like nature in future; however cogent the motives to it. The situation of the United States, hereafter, will not, I trust, expose their friends to such disagreeable dilemmas, as they have been accustomed to in times past.

You will perceive, that my authority to you goes as well to the making a new loan, as to the confirmation of that, which you have undertaken. The design of this is, not to *double or increase* the loan, but to enable you to give such a form to the business, as circumstances may require. Your engagements, of course, must not extend beyond the sum of three Millions of Florins.

You will observe also, that by the first act the time of reimburse-

3. "An Act making provision for the (payment of the) Debt of the United States" (1 *Stat.* 138–44 [August 4, 1790]).
4. "An Act making Provision for the Reduction of the Public Debt" (1 *Stat.* 186–87 [August 12, 1790]).
5. George Washington to H, August 28, 1790.
6. See enclosure.

ment of the loans to be made in virtue of it, is not to exceed fifteen years. That which is mentioned in your letter, will somewhat, though but little exceed this limit. I presume you can easily arrange the installments so as to come within it. I shall be glad it may be so modified, if the state of the business will permit. But as the last act has no such limitation of time, I do not mean that the difference should be an obstacle.

I should also wish for particular reasons, that the business may be so regulated as to give it the form of two loans; one, for two millions under the first Act, and the other, for one million under the second. But neither about this am I so solicitous, as to be willing that it should constitute an embarrassment. And it can only be proper, if the time of reimbursement can be made to correspond with the first act.

I destine a million and a half of this sum as a payment to France under the direction of Mr. Short [7] our Chargé des affaires at that Court, whose order for the purpose you will be pleased to follow. Of this, however, I rely on your prudence, that nothing will be said, till you receive his instructions to remit or pay.

It cannot escape your observation, not only, that the faith of our Government is fully pledged by the laws, of which I send you copies, for the performance of the conditions of the Loans which shall be made in consequence of them, but that there is an actual *appropriation* of unexceptionable funds for payment of the Interest. This, if properly considered, ought materially to influence the terms upon which the future loans shall be made. The nature of our present Government is such, that absolute reliance may be placed on its pecuniary dispositions, *once made*.

I have the honor to be with great consideration and esteem, Gentlemen, Your obedt. Servt.   Alex Hamilton
                                          Secretary of the Treasy

Messrs. Wilhem & Jan Willink and Nicholas & Jacob Van Staphorst and Hubbard
Amsterdam

7. William Short.

[ENCLOSURE]

Commission to Wilhem and Jan Willink, Nicholaas and Jacob Van Staphorst, and Nicholas Hubbard [8]

[New York, August 28, 1790]

To all to whom these Presents shall come:

Whereas by an Act passed the fourth day of August, in this present year, entitled "An Act making provision for the debt of the United States," it is, among other things, enacted, That the President of the United States be authorized to cause to be borrowed, on behalf of the United States, a sum or sums, not exceeding in the whole, twelve millions of dollars, and that so much of that sum as may be necessary to the discharge of the said arrears and instalments, and (if it can be effected upon terms advantageous to the United States) to the paying off the whole of the said foreign debt, be appropriated solely to those purposes; and that the President be moreover further authorized to cause to be made such other contracts respecting the said debt, as shall be found for the interest of the said States: Provided nevertheless, that no engagement nor contract shall be entered into, which shall preclude the United States from reimbursing any sum or sums borrowed, within fifteen years after the same shall have been lent or advanced.

And whereas, by another Act passed the twelfth day of August in the present year, entitled "An Act making provis[ion] for the reduction of the public debt," it is, also, among other things, enacted, that the President of the United States be authorised to cause to be borrowed, on behalf of the United States, a sum or sums, not exceeding in the whole, two millions of dollars, at an interest not exceeding five per cent.

And whereas, by virtue of the said several Acts, the President of the United States of America hath been pleased, by a certain Commission or Warrant under his hand, to authorize and empower the Secretary of the Treasury for the time being, by himself or any other person or persons, to borrow, on behalf of the United States, within

8. Copy, RG 233, Reports of the Treasury Department, 1792–1793, Vol. III, National Archives. This document was enclosed in H's "Report on Foreign Loans," February 13, 1793.

the said States or elsewhere, a sum or sums not exceeding, in the whole, fourteen millions of dollars, and to make or cause to be made, for that purpose, such contract or contracts as shall be necessary, and for the interest of the said States, subject to the restrictions and limitations in the said several Acts contained.

And whereas Messrs. Wilhem and Jan Willink and Nicholaas and Jacob Van Staphorst and Hubbard have, by letter bearing date the twenty fifth day of January 1790, communicated to me, that they have entered into a certain provisional agreement or arrangement, for a loan of three millions of florins, for the use of the United States of America, bearing an interest of five per centum per annum, and reimbursable by yearly instalments of six hundred thousand florins, commencing in the year one thousand eight hundred and one, and ending in the year one thousand eight hundred and five.

And whereas it appears to me, for the interest of the United States, to accept the said loan.

Now, therefore, Be it known, that I, Alexander Hamilton, Secretary of the Treasury of the United States, for the time being, by virtue of the power and authority in me vested by the President of the United States, and in his name, and in behalf of the United States of America, and to their use, do by these presents, accept, agree to, ratify and confirm the loan aforesaid, provisionally undertaken by the said Wilhem and Jan Willink, and Nicholaas and Jacob Van Staphorst and Hubbard. And I do hereby authorise and empower the said Wilhem and Jan Willink and Nicholaas and Jacob Van Staphorst and Hubbard, or, in case of the death of any of them, the survivors, to borrow on behalf of the United States, either by way of confirmation of the said provisional agreement or otherwise, as need may be, a sum or sums not exceeding, in the whole, three millions of florins, subject to the restrictions and limitations in the said several Acts contained, and above recited. And for that purpose, in the name of the said President, on behalf of the United States of America, to execute such contracts, obligations and instruments, as shall be necessary and conformable to usage in the like cases, and the faith of the United States to pledge for the performance of the terms thereof; and if the same shall be deemed requisite to stipulate for the ratification thereof by the President of the United States; hereby giving and granting to the said Wilhem and Jan Willink, and Nicholaas and Jacob Van Staphorst and Hubbard, and the survivors of them, all my power and authority in the premises, and ratifying, allowing and confirming whatsoever they shall lawfully do therein.

In Testimony whereof, I have caused the seal of the Treasury to be affixed to these presents, and have hereunto subscribed my hand, the twenty eighth day of August, in the year of our Lord 1790.

Alexander Hamilton.
Secretary of the Treasury.

To William Short [1]

Treasury Department
August 29th. 1790

Sir

You are already apprised of the loan which was commenced in the united Netherlands, by Messrs. Wilhem & Jan Willink and Nicholas & Jacob van Staphorst and Hubbard, with a view on their part to the service of the United States, and that the same has been submitted to our Government for their acceptance. On due consideration of the circumstances of that Loan and the views with which the above Gentlemen have undertaken it, I have determined, in consequence of power vested in me, to accept and ratify the same. I have accordingly authorised and empowered Messrs. Willinks, van Staphorsts and Hubbard [2] to complete and carry the said Loan into full effect.

My present object is to inform you, that I have destined a Million & a half of florins, as soon as that sum shall be received by the above Gentlemen on account of that Loan, as a payment through you to France, and I have given them directions accordingly. It is my wish, that you take the earliest opportunity to inform yourself with certainty, that they are in Cash, from the Loan, to pay your draughts, and that you then proceed to possess yourself of the Funds, and to make this payment. You will no doubt avail the United States of all proper advantages in making the negotiation for the above sum, which the course of Exchange between Paris and Amsterdam will admit. It is probable, that your bills will command a premium that will more than indemnify our Treasury for the charges of the Loan, so far as the amount of this payment to France. It may be proper, on this occasion, that you express the satisfaction which the United States feel in giving an earnest of their sincere desire and intention to discharge their pecuniary obligations to France. Referring you to the Secretary of State for instructions with regard to the timing of the intended payment,

I have the honor to be   very respectfully, Sir.   Your obedt. Servt.

Alexander Hamilton
Secretary of the Treasury

William Short Esquire
Chargé des affaires of the United States

LS, William Short Papers, Library of Congress.
   1. A copy of this letter was enclosed in H's "Report on Foreign Loans," February 13, 1793.
   2. H to Willink, Van Staphorst, and Hubbard, August 28, 1790.

To Thomas Jefferson

[New York, August 30, 1790]

Mr Hamilton presents his Compliments to the Secretary of State, and requests the favor of having two more authenticated Copies of his Commission as Secretary of the Treasury made out, and three Copies of his Commission or power for making the Loan,[1] likewise authenticated.

Mr Hamilton will probably stand in need of those Instruments before he will have an opportunity of Seeing Mr Jefferson.

30th August 1790

Letter sent, in unidentified handwriting, RG 59, Miscellaneous Letters, 1790–1799, National Archives.
   1. See George Washington to H, August 28, 1790.

From Thomas Jefferson

New York Aug. 30. 1790

Dear Sir

During my absence from the seat of government, which will be for about two months, the removal of my office and other circumstances will call for advances of money which I am absolutely unable to calculate before hand. The following heads may give some idea what they will be.

		Dollars
Sep. 30. for a quarter's salaries		1504.16
"　Arrearage account . . . . . about		325.
"　debts due here . . . . . about		25.
"　expences of removal [1]		

Thus unable to fix a precise sum, and having perfect confidence in the discretion of mr Remsen,[2] I must beg the favor of you to have his draughts for the above purposes answered at the treasury, on account, and I hereby render myself responsible for the due application of the money of which an account shall be rendered, on my return.

The collections of the acts of the last sessions are to be sent to the members of Congress by post, and ought to be franked; but I shall not be present to perform that duty. If you would be so good as to frank the packets, I shall be much obliged to you. I know of no other official papers to be dispatched in my absence. Yet if any such should occur, I would venture to ask your extending the same favor to them also, on mr Remsen's explaining to you the nature of the occasion. I have the honor to be wtih the most perfect esteem & respect   Dear Sir your most obedt. humble servt.　　　　　　　Th: Jefferson

The Secretary of the Treasy.

LS, letterpress copy, Thomas Jefferson Papers, Library of Congress.
　1. This refers to the transfer of the government from New York City to Philadelphia.
　2. Henry Remsen, Jr., was the chief clerk of the Department of State.

From Thomas Smith

[*Philadelphia, August 30, 1790.* On September 23, 1790, Hamilton wrote to Smith: "I duly received your letter of the 30th Ultimo." *Letter not found.*]

From Benjamin Lincoln

Boston Augt 31. 1790

Sir

I received by the last post a letter under the date of the 24 instant from Mr. Coxe [1] Assistant secy in which he says The Secy of the Treasury has instructed me to inform you that he has urgent occasion for the returns of bonds taken in your office which were formally requested to be made in monthly schedules. I was much surprised on finding those observations as I could not or could any in the office recollect our receiving any such request. I have since examined your letter in full but do not find any request or order which look like it. As the above paragraph conveys in very explicit terms a reproof for an ommission of duty I have thought it but justice to my self to give you the above state of facts & on a P.S. of the same letter Mr. Coxe goes on I believe to add that your quarterly account ending the 30th of June is also wanted. I do know but I have done wrong by keeping it so long in my hand my ideas were that as soon as my proceeding account was passed upon a state of it would have been forwarded for without that I cannot know what ballance to carry forward or how to sittle my own books. I was so convinced of the propriety of there forwarding a statement of the Acct as settled & that nothing on their part would be omitted that I concluded that from the hurry of business they had not passed on it & that it would be useless to croud them with a second Acct before the first was out of the way. If in your opinion it is not necessary for the comptroller to forward to me a state of my Acct as settled I will in future give no cause for a similar hint to the one above.

Not Forwarded [2]

LC, RG 36, Collector of Customs at Boston, Letter Book, 1790–1797, National Archives.

1. Tench Coxe.

2. This notation, which is in Lincoln's writing, indicates that he did not send this letter.

Treasury Department Circular to the Commissioners of Loans

Treasury Department
August 31st 1790

Sir,

The President of the United States having been pleased to appoint you to the Office of Commissioner of loans in virtue of the Act making provision for the debt of the United States, I transmit your Commission and a copy of the law [1] under which you are to act. On the receipt of this letter you will proceed to qualify yourself for the duty, by taking the oath required, before one of the Judges of the supreme Court, or of the district court of the United States, or, if they should be absent or too remote, before one of the Judges of the superior court of your State, and by providing satisfactory Bondsmen not less than two in number to enter with you into a security in the sum of Ten thousand Dollars—for your good behaviour in the said office. I have written to the Attorney of the United States for the district in which you reside, requesting his consideration of the sureties you may offer, and I trust you will present to him such persons as are unexceptionable, that I may be able to declare them satisfactory. Any deficiency in the securities submitted to me must produce delay, and would consequently be injurious to the United States, and the public Creditors. You will find enclosed the form of the Bond to be signed by yourself and your sureties. In a short time I shall give you such further instructions, and directions as the law permits and the public Interests requires. I think it necessary however to apprise you, that during the reception of subscriptions to the Loan, which is to be made in the Certificates of the State debts, it will be necessary to the public safety, that you reside at the place where the checks and documents relative to the debt of your State are deposited.

I am, Sir, with respect, Your Obedt. Servant   A Hamilton
Secy of the Treasy

P.S. I find the Secretary of State has already transmitted your commission, so that it will not be found in this enclosure.[2]

LS, to Nathaniel Appleton, The Bostonian Society, Boston; LS, to Nathaniel Gilman, The Andre deCoppet Collection, Princeton University Library; LS, to Thomas Smith, The American Swedish Historical Museum, Philadelphia; LS, to James Tillary, Delaware Historical Society, Wilmington.

1. "An Act making provision for the (payment of the) Debt of the United States" (1 *Stat.* 138–44 [August 4, 1790]).

2. At the bottom of the letter sent to Gilman there is an additional postscript which reads: "P.S. It may be of consequence to your future convenience to know, that a great probability exists, that it will be found necessary to remove your Office to the principal seat of Commerce in your State, when the Loans shall be compleated."

Treasury Department Circular
to the District Attorneys

Treasury Department
August 31. 1790

Sir

A confidence in your disposition to promote the public interests, has induced me to trouble you on a subject in which the safety of Government is concerned. The 12th. section of the Act of the Legislature of the 4th instant "making provision for the debt of the United States"[1] subjects the quantum and sufficiency of the Security to be given by the Commissioners of the New Loans to my judgment so however as that it does not exceed Ten thousand dollars. I have determined to require of Jabez Bowen[2] Esquire whom the President has been pleased to appoint for your State at least two sureties to be jointly and severally bound with him in the penalty of Eight thousand Dollars, with condition for his good behaviour. The station you fill and the knowlege which must arise from your professional practice have made me desirous to avail myself of your opinion and as it cannot in any way create a responsibility in you, I have taken the liberty to direct the Commissioner to propose his list of names to you. Your sentiments on the sufficiency of some two or more of them will be a service to the United States and a very great satisfaction to me.

I am Sir   very respectfully   Your Most Obedt. servant

Alexander Hamilton

LS, to William Channing, New York State Historic Sites (Senate House), Education Department, Albany; LS, to Pierpont Edwards, sold at Anderson Galleries, February 16, 1906, Lot 109; LS, to Richard Harison, New-York Historical Society, New York City.

1. 1 *Stat.* 138–44 (August 4, 1790). For Section 12, see p. 142.
2. In the letter to Harison, the name John Cochran is substituted; in the letter to Edwards the name William Imlay was substituted. Imlay was appointed commissioner of loans for Connecticut on August 6, 1790.

From Pierpont Edwards [1]

[*August, 1790.* "George Smith, John Caldwell & John Morgan . . . are men of good standing . . . and may be taken as sureties." [2] *Letter not found.*]

ALS, sold by Anderson Galleries, February 16, 1906, Lot 75.
1. For background to this letter, see "Treasury Department Circular to the District Attorneys," August 3, 1790. Edwards was United States attorney for the district of Connecticut.
2. Extract taken from dealer's catalogue.

INDEX

COMPILED BY JEAN G. COOKE

ing others in their stead . . . ," 138-
68; collection of duties on, 100-1,
104, 429; distinction between, 374;
and drawbacks, 377; duties on, domestic, 143, imported, 138-43, and
payment of public debt, 99-100; plan
for duties on, 102-5; proposed tax
on retail sale of, 289; and Report on
Public Credit, 374; use of pernicious, 99-100
Distilleries, see Distilled spirits
District of Maine, see Maine
Domestic debt, see Public debt
Dorchester, Guy Carleton, Lord: and
George Beckwith's conversations
with Hamilton, 485-86, 495; George
Beckwith's report to, 496; and communication with U.S. through
George Beckwith, 547; and dispute
between Great Britain and Spain,
573; and Indian depredations, 485,
495, 496; and Indian hostilities, 550-
51; letter of presented by George
Beckwith, 485; letters to Lord Grenville, 486, 496, 498, 548, 550, 551
Douglas, Sylvester, Reports of Cases
Argued and Determined in the
Court of King's Bench in the Nineteenth, Twentieth and Twenty-first
Years of the Reign of George III,
300
Dover, Del., 514
Drawbacks: on distilled spirits, 164-67,
327; Benjamin Lincoln on, 194; and
partial cargo, 377; and pickled and
dried fish, 375, 489-90, 507-8; revision of necessary, 389; on snuff and
other manufactured tobacco, 288;
on wines, 180-81
Dried fish: bounty on, 507-8; drawback on, 489-90, 507-8; duty on,
489-90
Drost, see Droz, Jean Pierre
Droz, Jean Pierre: and mint, 371-72
Duane, James, 55; letter from, 407;
letter to, 407
Dublin, 501, 571
Ducher, Gaspard Joseph Amand: letter from, 181-83
Duer, William, 253, 464; Assistant Secretary of Treasury, 120, 209, resignation, 346-47, 355-56, 401, 416, 501-
2, 552; Hamilton's indebtedness to
for Report on Public Credit, 56;
letter to, 346-47; and Scioto Co.,

352, 575, 578; and von Steuben, 312,
313
D-Uhtrick, _____ Baron (Capt.):
debt due, 542
Du Portail, Louis Le Bèque (Brig.
Gen.): debt due, 542
Dutch, see United Netherlands
Dutchess County, N.Y., 511
Dutch loans, see Loans
Duties, 55, 79-80; abstract of, from
August, 1789, to March 31, 1790,
567, from Philadelphia, 400; accrual
of before establishment of customs
houses, 16, 39, 373-74; "An Act repealing . . . the Duties heretofore
laid upon distilled Spirits . . . and
laying others in their stead . . . ,"
138-68; allowance for prompt payment, 269-70; anticipation of, 388;
on articles of stranded vessels, 501;
and bank notes, 1-2, 273, 387-88; and
bonds given for, 18, 26, 36, 377; on
cocoa, 137; on coffee, 102, 104, 137;
collection of, and North Carolina,
225-26, and Rhode Island, 226; and
Connecticut, 16; and Constitution
of U.S., 225; on cotton, 376-77; on
damaged goods, 250-51; discount for
prompt payment, 299, 385; on distilled spirits, 99-101, 102-5, 137, 138-
68, 429 (see also Distilled spirits);
enumerated list of, 25, 218, 374;
estimate of, 137; on fish, dried and
pickled, 374-75, 489-90, 499, 507-8;
and foreign consuls, 565; on goods
from China and India, 375-76; on
goods exported and re-imported,
376; on goods of persons arriving
from abroad, 376; on hemp, 376-77,
397, 403; on luxuries, 99-100; on
molasses, 137, proposed increase,
287; and partial cargo, 377; payment
of, 18, 286, 383-84, 385; and payment of interest on loans, 281; for
payment of public debt, 99-105, 524;
place of payment, 251; probable
surplus of revenue accruing from,
524; proposal to abolish discount on
goods imported in American ships,
287; proposals for branding and
marking to prevent smuggling, 41;
proposed, on law writings, 288-89,
for licenses to lawyers, 288-89; proposed increase, on carriages, 288, on
goods imported in foreign ships, 287,

Western posts, 485; and British prisoners, 17; contractor for, *see* O'Hara, James; evacuation of, 495; and Nootka Sound controversy, 486

Western territory, 55, 532-33; and bounty lands, 441-42; and dispute between Great Britain and Spain, 573; estimated expenses of, 131-32; Hamilton on, 421; and Indians, 550; and land companies, 502; lands in, Jonathan Dayton on sale of, 441-44, and funding of the public debt, 92, 444, proposed price of, 504, sale of, 502-6; and proposed land office, 503, 504, 505; and proposed loan, 504; and proposed surveyor general, 505; and public debt, 503, plan for ceding in payment of, 90, 91-92; purchasers of, 502; settlers of, 502; townships in, 504 (*see also* Northwest territory; Southwest territory)

West Indies, 29, 424, 548; commerce of, 21, 23, 573

Westmoreland County, Pa., 13

West Point, 134; necessity of, 453-55; purchase of recommended, 454-55; rent of, 527-28; supplies for, 8

Wheeling, Va., 416

Wheelock, Eleazar, 574

Wheelock, John: *letter from*, 573-74

Whipple, Joseph: *letters from*, 6, 19-24, 26, 226, 262, 271, 275, 299, 368-69, 402, 411, 419, 450-51, 464, 508-9; *letters to*, 233, 309, 451-53, 469, 560; and lighthouses of New Hampshire, 47, 48

Whisky, *see* Distilled spirits

White Eyes, George Morgan, 530

Wickford, R.I., 470

Wilcox, Joseph, 135

Wiley, *see* Wyley

Wilkesbarre, Pa., 501

Willett, Marinus, 135

William III (king of England), 52, 65

Williams, David: pension, 132

Williams, Isaac, 530

Williams, Otho H., 479; accounts of as collector of customs at Baltimore, 241-44; and Ædanus Burke, 354; *letters from*, 4, 19, 37, 40-41, 210, 241-44, 248, 265, 273, 286, 307, 357, 397, 401, 451, 457; *letters to*, 233, 252, 266-67, 365, 403, 429, 465, 510; *letter to* Philip Thomas, 335;

and the *St. Martin,* 372; Treasury Department circular to, 417, 418

Williamsburg, Va., 274

Willing, Thomas: and John B. Church's bank stock, 329; *letters from*, 9-10, 34-35, 278-79, 301, 308, 359; *letters to*, 5, 17, 273-74, 296, 332; president of Bank of North America, 14, 32

Willink, Jan: and proposed purchase of debt due France, 234

Willink, Wilhem: and proposed purchase of debt due France, 234

Willink, Wilhem and Jan, 337

Willink, Wilhem and Jan, Nicholaas and Jacob Van Staphorst, and Nicholas Hubbard, *see* Willink, Van Staphorst, and Hubbard

Willink, Van Staphorst, and Hubbard, 255, 256, 338; and accounts of U.S., 188-90; and Algerian captives, 186-88; authorized to make new loan, 581-82, 584; commission to, 582-85; and debt due to France, 189-90, 210-14, 215, 227-29, 231, 236-37, 516, 582, 585-86; debts to foreign officers, 186-88; and Dutch loan (September 14, 1782), 216; and Dutch loan (August, 1790), 210-18, 230-32, 238-39, 349-50, 358-59, 446-47, 516, 518, 568-70, 581, 584, 585-86; and David Humphreys, 557, 558-59; and interest on Dutch loans, 531; and Thomas Jefferson's salary, 488-89; *letters from*, 38, 210-18; *letters to*, 358-59, 409-10, 500-1, 580-85; *letters to* Thomas Jefferson, 188-90, 212-13; and medals for officers, 188; provisional loan of 1790, *see* Dutch loan (August, 1790); request for authority to make loans for U.S. to pay France, 217; request for power to negotiate transferal of debt due to France, 189-90

Wilmington, Del.: collector of customs at, *see* Bush, George

Wilmington, N.C.: French consul at, *see* Ducher, Gaspard Joseph Amand

Wilson, James, 545

Wilson, William, 530

Wines: "Draft of an Act Imposing Certain Inland Duties on Foreign Wines," January 9, 1790, 168-81; duties on, *see* Duties; French, 9;